THE VICTORIAN CABINET-MAKER'S ASSISTANT

417 ORIGINAL DESIGNS WITH

DESCRIPTIONS AND DETAILS OF CONSTRUCTION

•

AS ORIGINALLY PUBLISHED IN 1853 BY

BLACKIE AND SON

With a new introduction by
JOHN GLOAG, F.S.A.

DOVER PUBLICATIONS, INC.
NEW YORK

Published in Canada by General Publishing Company, Ltd.,
30 Lesmill Road, Don Mills, Toronto, Ontario.
Published in the United Kingdom by Constable and Company, Ltd.,
10 Orange Street, London WC2H 7EG.

This Dover edition, first published in 1970, is an unabridged re-
publication of the anonymous work originally published by Blackie
and Son in 1853 under the title *The Cabinet-Maker's Assistant: A
Series of Original Designs for Modern Furniture, with Descriptions
and Details of Construction*. The present volume also contains a new
introductory essay, specially prepared for this edition by John Gloag.

DOVER *Pictorial Archive* SERIES

Standard Book Number: 486-22353-1
Library of Congress Catalog Card Number: 73-103140

Manufactured in the United States of America

Dover Publications, Inc.
31 East 2nd Street
Mineola, N.Y. 11501

INTRODUCTION
TO THE DOVER EDITION

FIRST published by Blackie and Son in 1853, *The Cabinet-Maker's Assistant* is not only a well-planned technical work of reference, but also a directory to current styles, for the plates reveal the state of design in the early Victorian furniture trade two years after the Great Exhibition of 1851. The *Assistant* has three divisions, the first two containing instructions in drawing and geometry for the benefit of apprentices and those beginning their careers as cabinet-makers, and practical information about material and the techniques of veneering and carving. So far it follows the pattern of earlier books, such as *The Practical Cabinet-Maker, Upholsterer and Complete Decorator* by Peter and Michael Angelo Nicholson, and an anonymous work entitled *Practical Carpentry, Joinery and Cabinet-Making*, both issued in 1826; but the third division gives the *Assistant* the status of a copy book, and as such it would be found, well-thumbed and in constant use, on the benches of small, independent cabinet-makers and chair makers, and in the larger workshops of such manufacturing centers as High Wycombe, in Buckinghamshire. That division consists of 101 plates of designs for furniture, including some examples of work shown at the Crystal Palace (four chairs, plate LXVII, and various ornamental details, plates XCVII to XCIX). Sixty-three pages of descriptions and structural details precede the plates.

In the 1850s cabinet-makers still used the woods familiar to their Georgian predecessors, though a few decorative timbers unknown in the eighteenth century were available, such as sissoo, which came from Bengal and resembled Indian rosewood. A change in the quality of mahogany is recorded in the second division (pages 27–37); and home-grown oak had apparently been almost entirely superseded by imports from Europe, and especially from North America. From 200,000 to 300,000 cubic feet of American oak was shipped to England annually from Quebec.

For the student or collector of Victorian furniture, the plates are by far the most interesting and instructive part of the book, for they show the impact of the new and often extravagant ideas launched by the Great Exhibition—ideas that changed the vernacular Victorian style that had developed during the 1840s. The solid mahogany and buttoned leather upholstery associated with that style was later identified with philistine taste and an excessive love of comfort. Certainly the solidity of such furniture was reassuring and the gleaming, ruddy mahogany far from unpleasing to the eye; the chairs, tables, and massive sideboards continued the classical tradition in design, and were still well-proportioned, though a little thick and coarse, with many concessions to comfort unknown, and perhaps unwanted, in the previous century. Some characteristic forms of the vernacular Victorian style, such as balloon-back chairs, had appeared early in the 1830s, and slender versions of these, with some pretensions to elegance, appear on plate LXV, where six drawing-room chairs are shown. (Compare these with earlier examples from Loudon's *Encyclopaedia* and a trade card, *c.* 1840–50, shown on pages [vi] and [vii].) Two of the "National Emblem" chairs, figs. 1 and 4 on plate LXVI, are also variations of the balloon-back, as are three of the four chairs from the Great Exhibition, figs. 1, 2, and 4 on plate LXVII; but the only example that closely resembles the earlier type is the dining-room chair on plate XXIV (fig. 1). No examples are given of the elegant and highly decorative furniture of *papier-mâché* that became fashionable in the middle years of the century; chairs, occasional tables, even case furniture, cabinets and bookcases, were made from this material, japanned black and ornamented with floral sprays, painted and inlaid with mother-of-pearl; but the production and decoration of such articles represented a separate branch of manufacture, with which the cabinet-maker, who handled wood only, was not concerned.

From the mid-1820s until the Great Exhibition, copy books for the furniture trade illustrated designs that retained a tenuous loyalty to the classical tradition of the Georgian period; and previews of the Victorian vernacular style are given in the plates of *The Cabinet-Makers' and Upholsterers' Guide, Drawing Book and Repository of New and Original Designs for Household Furniture* that George Smith published in 1826; in *The Modern Style of Cabinet Work*, published by T. King early in the 1830s; and in that monumental work, *The Encyclopaedia of Cottage, Farm, and Villa Architecture and Furniture*, edited by John Claudius Loudon, issued in 1833, and many times reprinted. The influence of Scott's novels

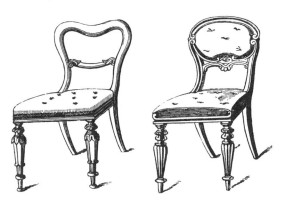

Forerunners of the balloon-back single chair, characteristic of the Victorian vernacular style. From *The Encyclopaedia of Cottage, Farm, and Villa Architecture and Furniture*, by J. C. Loudon (London: 1833). Figs. 1936 and 1937, page 1063.

had stimulated romantic interest in the Middle Ages, and this was reflected by a growing taste for pre-Georgian furniture styles: not only mediaeval, but early Tudor, Elizabethan, Jacobean and Carolean. The study of these periods was encouraged by the publication in 1836 of the first book on English antiques, entitled *Specimens of Ancient Furniture*, with drawings engraved by Henry Shaw and imaginative but unreliable descriptions by Sir Samuel Rush Meyrick. Two years later Richard Bridgens issued a volume with sixty plates, illustrating antique furniture interspersed with his own designs, which he called *Furniture with Candelabra and*

Interior Decoration. There was no text, and through some oversight the individual plates were not numbered, a defect that also occurs in *Specimens of Ancient Furniture*. The drawings were by Bridgens, many of them engraved by Shaw, and the plates were listed under three headings: "Designs in the Grecian style," "Designs in the Elizabethan style," and "Designs in the Gothic style." In both works the illustrations of antique examples were often misleading; some of those selected had been inexpertly doctored by their owners (or by the dealers who had sold them), so that richness of effect was increased by spurious carving. The "original" designs by Bridgens were odd mixtures with ornament that recalled the Flemish and German copy books of the sixteenth and early seventeenth centuries; and several examples in *The Cabinet-Maker's Assistant* may well have been inspired by Bridgens, notably the chiffonier on plate XLIV, with the strapwork panels in the cupboard doors and the fret surmounting the upper tier; the cabinet on plate XLVIII; the occasional table, fig. 1 on plate LIV; and the wardrobe on plate LXXXIX.

In the 1830s something loosely described as "the English style" had emerged; it is mentioned by King in the "Address" that prefaces his description of the plates in *The Modern Style of Cabinet Work*. "As far as possible," he wrote, "the English style is carefully blended with Parisian taste; and a chaste contour and simplicity of parts is attempted in all the objects, which, being in some degree confined in dimensions and form, present rather a difficulty in the adaption of Grecian, Roman, and Gothic Ornaments."[1] Loudon in his *Encyclopaedia* stated that "The principal Styles of Design in Furniture, as at present executed in Britain, may be reduced to four" and described them as "the Grecian or modern style, which is by far the most prevalent; the Gothic or perpendicular style, which imitates the lines and angles of the Tudor Gothic Architecture; the Elizabethan style, which combines the Gothic with the Roman or Italian manner; and the style of Louis XIV, or the florid Italian, which is characterised by curved lines and excess of curvilinear ornaments."[2]

The Grecian style, when Loudon wrote, still suggested the elegant Greek Revival furniture of the last years of the eighteenth and the opening decades

[1] *The Modern Style of Cabinet Work*. The Second Edition, Improved. London: published by T. King, 17 Gate Street, Lincoln's Inn Fields. Price £2. 1832.

[2] *Encyclopaedia of Cottage, Farm, and Villa Architecture and Furniture*, by J. C. Loudon. London: Longman, Rees, Orme, Brown, Green & Longman. 1833. Book III, Chap. VI, page 1039.

of the nineteenth centuries; Gothic was still affiliated to the urbane, Georgian interpretation of mediaeval design and ornament; but the so-called Elizabethan style was something unmellowed by the modish taste of eighteenth-century patrons or the skill of the cabinet-makers who served them. It was often called "Old English," and may well have been what King meant by "the English style," though not one of the seventy plates in *The Modern Style of Cabinet Work* resembles the type of furni-

Three variations of early Victorian balloon-back dining-room chairs, with buttoned upholstery. Reproduced from a trade card by an unknown maker, *circa* 1840–50.

ture that Loudon and Bridgens illustrated and described as Elizabethan.

Until the Great Exhibition, Loudon's loose classification of styles was valid; thereafter anarchy prevailed in furniture design, with different fashions of decoration used on the same type of structure, a consequent loss of relationship between form and ornament, and the debasement of good proportions. Nobody knew quite what to do; customers "knew what they liked" but seldom knew what they wanted; and the furniture manufacturer was committed to an unceasing pursuit of novelty for its own sake. The Preface to *The Cabinet-Maker's Assistant* admitted the paucity of imagination that had drained inspiration from the trade. "Every one connected with Cabinet-Making," said the anonymous editors, "is aware of the difficulty of obtaining good and novel Designs for Furniture." The next sentence supplied a solution that happily made no demands on imagination; a mechanistic solution, so simple that any apprentice in the earliest stages of his training could understand its advantages. "When, however, such designs are obtained, every one is equally aware how comparatively easy it is to adapt them to the kind of work required; they may, in fact, be multiplied indefinitely, by engrafting the decorations of one on the forms of another, and in many other ways that will suggest themselves to every practical man." This interchangeability of ornament was generally accepted by makers during and after the middle of the century.

The editors of the *Assistant* gave expert guidance

for applying a diversity of ornament to a range of articles; they were aware that the taste for so-called Elizabethan furniture still persisted, and had been reinforced by many ornate pieces shown at the Great Exhibition, particularly by the famous Kenilworth sideboard. This was adorned with panels depicting scenes from Sir Walter Scott's novel *Kenilworth*, executed with masterly skill by Warwickshire carvers; the sideboard, or buffet, was made by Cookes and Sons from, it was alleged, one huge oak, felled in the grounds of Warwick Castle. The ornamental details are late sixteenth-century in character, but they are subordinated to the dominating realism of the carved panels and figures. (See illustration on page [viii].) Examples of the "Elizabethan" style on a more modest scale are provided by the pedestal sideboards in the *Assistant*, on plate XI (figs. 1 and 2), also on plates XII and XIII, and the more ambitious slab sideboard on plate XV. Many of the high-backed upholstered chairs, described as "Elizabethan" by Victorian makers, were derived from late seventeenth-century prototypes, and ten of them occupy plates LXVIII through LXX. "This is a variety of chair in which great scope is given for taste and embellishment," said the editors. "In most cases they are intended for covering with embroidery and needle-work." The mixed parentage of the chair shown in fig. 1 on plate LXVIII is explained by the description, which states that the design "elements . . . are drawn from various styles—French, Flemish, and old English—each of which contributes to certain of its parts." The front legs certainly have rococo affinities; the cresting on the back, and the pierced fret that separates back from seat, are Flemish, while the spiral uprights flanking the back are variations of the "barley-sugar" twist which was introduced during the second half of the seventeenth century. Another chair, fig. 2 on the same plate, is varied by turned front legs, typically Victorian in shape, with an apron of Flemish ornament below the seat rail.

The "Elizabethan" style flourished during the late 1830s, and throughout the next two decades, but thereafter declined. The Victorians were naturally attracted to the work of a period that in many ways resembled their own; the enterprising and adventurous new rich of the late sixteenth century had rejoiced in massive ornament and elaborately carved furniture and chimneypieces; the prosperous middle class of the mid-nineteenth century also desired visible reminders of their expanding affluence, and what better evidence could they have of solid worth than lavishly ornamented furniture? Plate after plate of the *Assistant* supplied the furniture trade with the means and models for satisfying an appetite for ostentation tempered with comfort. Concurrently with the ambiguities of the "Elizabethan" style, a revival of rococo introduced C-shaped scrolls, acanthus foliations, and convoluted shapes to English and American drawing-rooms; but Victorian rococo lacked the gay fantasy and fragility of the original. That revival began twenty years before the *Assistant* was published, at a time when furniture makers and their customers tended to identify the period of Louis XIV with rococo, though the style was created by the great French ornamentalists and *ébénistes* in the reign of Louis XV. The term rococo was applied indiscriminately to any highly ornamented French furniture of the eighteenth century. In the late Victorian period the furniture trade used the all-embracing label of "Louis style" for anything that suggested French taste.

Examples of Victorian rococo include a case for a mural clock, fig. 3, plate VIII; two long-case clocks, figs. 2 and 3, plate IX; a sideboard back, fig. 6, plate XVI; two easy chairs, figs. 3 and 6, plate XXVI; two table legs, figs. 4 and 5, plate XXVII; and the details of sofas, plate XXXII. The drawing-room sofas on plates LIX and LX suggest the style, but the carved ornament lacks the fluidity and crispness that characterizes rococo. The chimneypiece mirrors, figs. 1 and 2 on plate L, have something of the spirit of the original style. (When the *Assistant* was published the traditional term *looking glass* had been replaced in the furniture trade by *mirror*, a word hitherto reserved for small hand glasses in toilet sets. Victorian ladies and gentlemen equated that word with social inferiority, a snobbish prejudice which survived far into the present century.) Two rococo window cornices with typical C-scrolls appear on plate LXXI, figs. 4 and 5; two music stools, figs. 3 and 7 on plate LXXIV; and the legs and apron of the portable bed-chair and ottoman seat on plate XCV all have traces of the style. But the "Elizabethan" style claimed the majority of the plates: it had not yet been ousted in favour of the mediaeval style, though one plate, LXXXI, illustrates a mediaeval bedstead, for execution in oak, birch, or walnut, "or any light-coloured wood . . . but not mahogany, which, to show the full beauty of its grain, requires broad and rounded surfaces." That bed was a trade interpretation of the furniture designed by Augustus Welby Northmore Pugin

The Kenilworth buffet or sideboard, made by Cookes and Sons of Warwick, and shown at the Great Exhibition of 1851. An example of the Warwickshire school of carving, depicting scenes from Sir Walter Scott's novel *Kenilworth*. Reproduced from *The Art-Journal Illustrated Catalogue*, page 123.

(1812-1852), and had no remote connection with the work of the Gothic revivalists, of whom Pugin was easily the most gifted. Apart from this solitary plate the editors of the *Assistant* ignored the current popularity of the mediaeval style, and no design in the book shows the influence of the Gothic revival. There is one exotic example of a secretaire bookcase in "the Moorish or Alhambra style," illustrated by fig. 1 on plate XXXVIII, a description presumably justified by the horse-shoe arched heads to the glazed doors of the upper part; but no pointed arches or Gothic ornament appear in any of the designs. The experiment in the "Moorish" style was almost certainly prompted by examples at the Great Exhibition; the confident use of profuse ornament in so many of the designs suggests the same source of inspiration; but nearly all the plates of the *Assistant* represent a static condition of design, with the trade playing for safety with established styles, "engrafting the decorations of one on the forms of another," as directed by the editors in their preface.

JOHN GLOAG F.S.A.

London
August, 1969

PLATE LXXXIII.

STATE BEDSTEAD.

J.H. le Keux Sc.

Inches.   6 Feet.

The Cabinet Makers' Assistant

Original Designs for Furniture

Drawn by A. Maclure.

Eng'd by J.A. le Keux.

PREFACE.

Every one connected with Cabinet-Making is aware of the difficulty of obtaining good and novel Designs for Furniture. When, however, such designs are obtained, every one is equally aware how comparatively easy it is to adapt them to the kind of work required; they may, in fact, be multiplied indefinitely, by engrafting the decorations of one on the forms of another, and in many other ways that will suggest themselves to every practical man. It is the object of the Cabinet-Maker's Assistant, to lay before the Trade a collection of such original and tasteful Designs; in which will be included examples of all the articles of superior furniture usually manufactured; those chiefly in demand being figured most copiously. When several Designs of the same article are given, they are, as far as size will permit, placed on the same Plate, thus affording easy means of comparison and selection. The Designs are all drawn to a scale, and care has been taken to render them thoroughly practical. They include an extensive range, from the most simple to the most elaborate in style; and are thus fitted to serve as models for furniture for the houses of all grades of the middle and upper classes of the community. While thus wide in range, the major part of the Designs have, at the same time, been executed with a view to combine, as far as possible, elegance and durability with moderate expense. Each Plate is accompanied with letter-press descriptions, elucidated, when requisite, by sections and other practical details, shown by Wood-cuts, explaining fully the method of constructing the articles figured.

To render the Work still further useful, and make it acceptable to workmen as well as to employers, it is accompanied by practical observations on the nature and applicability of the various kinds of woods in general use among Cabinet-Makers; in which are given directions for selecting, cutting up, and seasoning wood; and instructions as to the most economical methods of constructing and finishing the various articles of furniture most usually manufactured.

As the workman who would attain to any eminence in his trade ought to possess a competent knowledge of Drawing, a preliminary section, specially dedicated to his instruction in this department of his profession, has been introduced. This section embraces Practical Geometry; the Use of Drawing Instruments; Drawing, Perspective, and Light and Shade; together with a variety of information useful and necessary to the Mechanical Draughtsman.

CONTENTS

AND

LIST OF PLATES.

FIRST DIVISION.

SECOND DIVISION.

THIRD DIVISION.

CONTENTS AND LIST OF PLATES.

THE

CABINET-MAKER'S ASSISTANT.

INSTRUCTIONS IN DRAWING.

ON THE NATURE AND USE OF SOME OF THE INSTRUMENTS NECESSARY IN GEOMETRIC DRAWING.

PREVIOUS to entering on the subject of the following pages, treating of practical geometry, it may be neither unnecessary nor uninteresting to many of our readers, to offer a few observations upon the nature of those drawing instruments that are employed in the construction of the problems, and to point out some of the more convenient methods of using them, to those who may not already be familiar with their management.

Cases of mathematical drawing instruments are of various sorts and sizes, containing assortments of those that are more generally useful, and are of greater or less extent to suit the occasions of the draughtsman, or his fancy. The number of these instruments, however, which are absolutely necessary for drawing the problems in plane practical geometry is very limited, and may be comprehended under the plane scale, or straight-edge, the compasses, and the pen or pencil employed in drawing lines. As much of the accuracy of any geometric drawing, or construction, depends on the efficiency of the instruments employed, it becomes a matter of great importance to have these of a good quality; and it is much recommended to the young draughtsman, to provide himself with those only that are of most general application, but *of the best construction.* This will be less expensive than purchasing an assorted case, which may contain some things that are not so essential to him as the correctness of the principal drawing implements. The cabinet-maker is besides independent, since he can easily provide himself with a case to suit his own convenience, and the instruments that he may from time to time procure as he advances.

Compasses.—The compasses, from its simple construction and extensive application, occupies the most prominent place in any descriptive account of drawing instruments. The general form must be familiar to every one. It consists of two pointed legs of equal length, connected by a joint which admits of their being separated, so that they may be set to any required distance from one another. The great excellence of a pair of compasses lies in the joint which must permit of a free motion of the legs, regular and uniformly smooth, so stiff as not to be easily disturbed by the necessary manipulation in drawing, and not so much so as to be inconveniently managed in the adjustment. When the joint is so stiff that the legs have a spring on attempting to open or shut them, the instrument is of no use, as it is evident that no accuracy can be attained in its employment. It follows, that in selecting a jointed compass of any kind, this is the point to which the attention ought to be chiefly directed. There are several different kinds of joint; the best are those in which it is constructed of two different metals, generally steel and brass, which combination has the effect of making the motion more uniform, and the wear more equable. The axis consists of a steel pin with a fixed metal head at one end, and a broad flat nut screwed on to the other; this nut is turned by means of a small appropriate turn-screw, so that the joint may be made stiffer or easier at pleasure. The ordinary kind of axis is simply a screw upon which the joint works, and by turning it the stiffness may be regulated, but this is by no means so good a form as the first mentioned. The commoner instruments may be easily known by the axis being rivetted in different manners. These ought to be avoided, as they soon become loose, and generally unequally so, and any attempt to remedy the defect by the hammer generally ends in increasing the evil. The points of compasses, of all kinds, should be formed of well tempered steel, so that they may neither bend nor break in use. In those in which both the legs terminate in points, they should be of equal length, and formed so that their extremities may meet nicely together when the instrument is closed. When, from accident, this is not the case, they may easily be repaired by means of a piece of oil-stone, taking care to sharpen the points so that they may hold on the paper without piercing or injuring it. When the points have become blunted by use they must also be sharpened, as the slipping of the instrument is productive of serious inconvenience; this is particularly the case when the compasses are opened wide, as in setting off a distance approaching to the full stretch of the compasses.

Most persons at first handle a pair of compasses somewhat awkwardly, either in taking distances between the points, or in describing circles; a little care and practice will soon induce ease and facility in their management. In working the compasses in taking distances, the instrument being opened far enough to introduce the middle and third fingers between the legs, it will readily be seen that one of the legs may be held by the thumb and the third finger, while the other is moved forwards and backwards very easily by the fore and middle fingers, the fore finger pressing on the outside to shut, and the middle one acting on the inside to open the compasses to any desired extent. In this manner the compasses are managed with one hand, which is convenient when the other is holding a ruler or other instrument. In taking a distance, the compasses ought to be held upright, and one point set at one end of the distance, while the other is adjusted to the required extent. After this is done the legs ought not to be touched, particularly when the distance measured has to be transferred frequently, as in marking equal divisions upon a line; this may easily be avoided by holding the head of the compasses only, and making it step along the line by a turning motion produced by the thumb and two forefingers. Care ought to be taken to avoid working the compasses with both hands at once, and not to use them otherwise than nearly upright. Grasping the compasses in the hand ought also to be avoided. In describing circles or arcs with the compasses, one foot is set on the point designed for the centre, the head being held between the thumb and middle finger, with the fore finger resting, but not pressing on it; by then rolling the head between the finger and thumb, and, at the same time, touching the paper with the other point, a

circle may be described with great ease, either with pen or pencil. In describing circles it should be observed that the paper be not pressed at the centre with much more weight than that of the compasses; large holes may thus be avoided, which too frequently disfigure drawings, when they are made by those who are careless or awkward in the use of their instruments. When the drawing is to be coloured, these central marks become doubly obtrusive and injurious to its effect. Where great nicety is required, the central points may be protected from receiving injury from the sharp point of the compasses, by the employment of a horn centre; this consists of a little piece of transparent horn, provided with three extremely minute steel points on its under side, which effectually prevent it from slipping on the paper; this being placed over a marked point, its position is seen through the horn; the compasses are then applied, and the circle described in the usual way. The employment of these centres is extremely advantageous where it is necessary to describe a number of circles from the same point, when, without some contrivance of the kind, a mark of greater or less importance cannot be avoided.

Hair Compasses and Spring Dividers.—There are two other kinds of compasses or dividers that must be mentioned, each admitting of great accuracy of adjustment. One, called the *hair compasses*, has a spring point attached to one of the legs, which is acted upon by a screw passing through one of the shanks, so that on the instrument being opened nearly to any required distance, by the help of the screw, the points may be set with the greatest exactitude to the distance. These compasses are objectionable, as they require very great care in

their management; the spring being so much weaker than the other parts of the instrument, is apt to yield, and the point attached to it consequently alters its position in using it. This objection is obviated, or is not so much felt in the second kind, called the *spring dividers,* represented in the annexed engraving. This is a most useful form of the compasses, from its great firmness, and the ease with which any number of small equal divisions may be set out by its means, with the utmost accuracy and security. In this instrument there is no joint, being formed of a single piece of steel properly tempered—the upper part D is so arranged, as, by its elasticity, to have a tendency to keep the points extended. Any required distance between the points is readily adjusted, by means of a nut B running upon a screw with a fine thread, which, passing through an opening in one of the legs, is fastened to the other by means of a joint A, which permits of some motion, in order that the nut may always act perpendicularly upon the leg on which it presses. These spring dividers are made of many different sizes, according to the purposes to which they are applied. The draughtsman will sometimes find it very convenient to have by him more than one pair of these compasses, particularly where the same measure occurs frequently in his work, as, from the fineness of the screw, the time consumed in constantly changing the setting of the instrument may be very considerable. The instrument represented in the engraving is of the full size, and will be found exceedingly useful for any distances not exceeding three-fourths of an inch. It may here be remarked, that spring compasses of all kinds, should never be laid aside for any length of time with the screw tightened, as this has a tendency to deteriorate the spring, upon which so much depends. Also, if they are pinched up for the sake of more easily moving the nut, the legs should not be allowed to fly back suddenly.

One of the most convenient forms of the compasses is that in which one of the points can be removed, and others substituted, for the purpose of drawing lines; these are the pencil holder, the pen point, and sometimes the dotting roller; any of these can be adapted according to the work in hand, the change being easily effected. The best kind of connection in such compasses, consists of a hollow socket in one of the shanks, which is slit at one side; into this an end of each of the supplementary pieces fits with exactness, and is held in its place with sufficient firmness by the elasticity of the metal forming the socket. There is sometimes also added an extra piece, or arm, by the addition of which the compasses may be made to describe circles of a much greater size than they could do of themselves; this is simply a straight piece, one end of which receives the marking point, and the other slips into the shank of the compasses; by this means one leg becomes about double the length of the other. Another kind of fastening for these changes is the substitution of a small clamping screw for the elasticity of the socket; but this is not only an inconvenient arrangement, but the apparatus soon wears out, and is not easily repaired. The pencil holder ought not to be in the form of a port-crayon, with a ring to tighten it; this is very unhandy, independently of its want of durability. A better mode of holding the pencil is by means of a piece of brass tubing, of greater or less size, which is attached to one of the legs, and being slit

its whole length, a properly sized pencil is firmly held in it without further trouble, and may be easily pushed forward by degrees, as it is worn away by use. This is sometimes facilitated by having a second tube within the one attached to the leg of the instrument; in this the pencil is placed, and is adjusted a little more easily, and with less risk of injury to the slit tube. This is an excellent method, as is also one that will be subsequently described.

Drawing Pen.—Some of the parts of this instrument vary with the purposes to which it is applied, as, for describing circles, or drawing straight lines; but the essential portion consists of two steel blades, tapering in their form with a spring between them, and brought nicely together to a point, or nearly so. The annexed engraving exhibits one of the most useful forms of the pen for drawing straight lines.

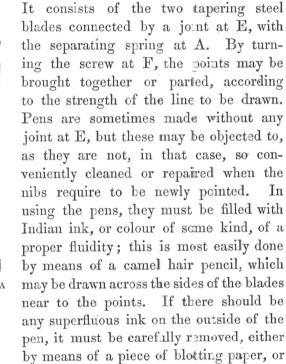

It consists of the two tapering steel blades connected by a joint at E, with the separating spring at A. By turning the screw at F, the points may be brought together or parted, according to the strength of the line to be drawn. Pens are sometimes made without any joint at E, but these may be objected to, as they are not, in that case, so conveniently cleaned or repaired when the nibs require to be newly pointed. In using the pens, they must be filled with Indian ink, or colour of some kind, of a proper fluidity; this is most easily done by means of a camel hair pencil, which may be drawn across the sides of the blades near to the points. If there should be any superfluous ink on the outside of the pen, it must be carefully removed, either by means of a piece of blotting paper, or soft cloth, such as velvet; want of attention to this, is sure to produce a blot when the instrument is applied to the ruler, and the draughtsman cannot be too particular in this respect, if he wishes to make clean ink drawings. When the pen is used, it must be drawn steadily but lightly along the edge of the ruler, taking care that it is in such a position that both the points touch the paper equally; it ought also to be inclined a little, and in drawing it along, this inclination should be kept as nearly as possible the same. The drawing of very fine lines depends in a great measure, upon the quality of the pen, and the good order in which it is kept. The sharpening or setting of these instruments requires to be done very carefully. A thin slip of oil-stone will be found very convenient for this purpose, when repair is necessary. The best method is to screw up the blades until the points are in close contact; they are then to be passed along the stone in a perpendicular position, until both the tips appear to agree exactly. The pen is then to be held steadily in the left hand, while, with the right, the oil-stone is rubbed against the backs of the blades at the point, until both are brought to an edge of equal fineness. The inner side of the blades should not be touched, further than to remove the barbs that may have arisen, and should be kept quite flat. The instrument must next be examined, and the points retouched, if they require it, until they are perfect. Cabinet-makers, from being accustomed to the setting of edge tools, will find little difficulty in keeping their pens in good order; they must, at the same time, recollect that too great care cannot be bestowed on them. When laid aside, the ink ought always to be cleaned out, and on no account should it be allowed to dry in the pens, as it is not only cleaned with greater difficulty, but the points will become corroded and destroyed.

Dotting Pen.—It is frequently convenient in drawing, to employ an interrupted or dotted line. The drawing of such a line by hand, occupies a good deal of time, but when well executed is the best method; an instrument may, however, be used which effects a considerable saving of labour. It consists of two steel blades precisely similar to the drawing pen in form, but between the points is placed a small notched wheel or roller, as seen at E in the figure. The ink is inserted between the blades, as in the pen, when the wheel, being drawn along any surface, will leave a line composed of equidistant points or short lines. There is a little uncertainty in using this kind of roller, as it will not always begin to mark when required, or always mark regularly. The best way is to get it to work upon a separate piece of paper, and then to apply it to the drawing where desired. If the line produced should fail in regularity, it is not possible to go over it again with the roller without producing blots. There are generally several sets of wheels for producing lines of different characters; these may be changed in the instrument by relaxing the screw, which allows the pivots to escape from the holes at the extremities of the blades.

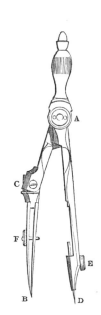

The size of compasses varies with their use; they are to be had from three or four inches in length upwards; a convenient size is from five to six inches, which, with its arm, will describe a tolerably large circle in a drawing; they are made as much as twelve inches in length in metal, and above that they are of wood, with metal points and crayon holders.

Bow Compasses.—Small circles are generally described by compasses of a suitable size, called *bow compasses*, these are very convenient from the facility with which they may be used, being provided with a short handle, by means of which they may be turned round between the finger and thumb. The instrument consists of a small pair of compasses, as represented in the engraving, the legs of which open about a centre A; one of the legs is fitted permanently with a pen, which is furnished with a joint at C, in order that it may be set as nearly perpendicular as possible to the surface on which the circle is described. The stiffness of this joint can be regulated by the screw at C, and the strength of the line by the screw F, as already described. In these small compasses, it is found very convenient to have them provided with what is called a needle point; this consists of an arrangement at the extremity of the leg, by which a fine needle may be secured by a small clamping screw E, so that when the point loses its efficiency another may be substituted.

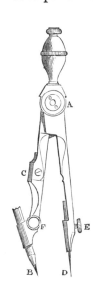

The pencil bow compasses is represented in the annexed engraving. It is similar in construction to the last described, having a joint at C, in the leg which forms the pencil holder; this may either be an arrangement of tubes fitting into one another, as previously described, or it may be as in the figure, where the pencil is clipped in a socket which is tightened by a screw F. This instrument is also provided with a needle point. Excellent bow compasses are made with the ordinary points, and without the joint at C; the advantage of the joint is, that by its means the pen point *may be brought* more nearly perpendicular in describing circles with it, which is of some importance, the line drawn being much clearer than when the pen slopes.

It is frequently necessary to describe smaller circles than even the bow compasses can well be made to do; for this purpose, a pair of very fine spring compasses is employed. They are made both with pen and pencil points; that in the engraving is provided with the latter. In these, as in the already described spring dividers, there is no joint, the instrument being made of a single piece of steel, the part D forming the spring. The opening between the points is regulated by the screw and nut B, the former, passing through an opening in one leg, is secured to the other at A. By means of such instruments, very minute circles may be described with great accuracy. The figure represents the compasses of the full size, but they are frequently made smaller.

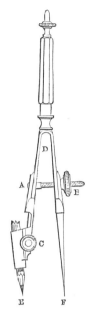

Rulers.—Having described the different kinds of compasses by which the circle is described, it remains to notice the *plane scale*, or *straight edge*, by means of which straight lines are drawn. These rulers are made of various materials, most of the hard woods being employed, as well as ivory, and different metals; they are of any length, according to the wants of the draughtsman. Those generally used in drawing are composed of wood or ivory, but more frequently the former; these materials being preferable, on account of their lightness; a metal ruler, when of any length, being inconveniently heavy in using it; the latter, however, has the very important advantage of retaining its form more truly, while wood is very apt to warp, a defect which, when it does occur, renders the ruler in a great measure useless. An excellent kind of ruler, when well made, is one with a thin slip of brass let into the edge, and against which the marking point glides; these are generally made of pear-tree, a wood that seems to answer the purpose admirably. From their liability to suffer from time and use, rulers must be frequently verified. This may be done by drawing a line carefully along the edge, and then reversing the ruler, so that it may be presented on the other side of the line as exactly as possible, and drawing a second line over the first; on examination, it will be seen whether both coincide or not; if they do not, the rule is false, and ought not to be used until the defect is remedied. Great care is necessary in drawing these proof lines, for although it may appear an easy matter to draw a line along the edge of a ruler, it requires some little practice to do so truly, that is, to copy its edge with exactitude; the hand must be held so that the pen or pencil may not deviate in the least, during its progress, from its inclination to the surface when first applied, more especially sideways. It may be remarked, that it is a much easier thing to describe a circle truly, than to draw a perfectly straight line. This is well exemplified in the ease with which the turner produces a true circle in his work, and the difficulty that the joiner experiences in making his edges accurately straight.

In selecting or proving rulers, they may be compared with one another; by placing the edges of two close together and holding them against the light, any irregularities will shew themselves by a greater or less breadth of light being allowed to pass between them. If they are quite close, the two rulers may either be curved so as to fit one another, or they may be perfectly straight; if a third is now found to agree with both, in comparing them together by this method, then they are all three correct and to be depended on. By the application of this principle, perfectly straight metal edges are easily produced. Three thin flat bars are prepared as far as possible with the file; they are perfected by grinding their edges alternately together, interposing a little fine emery and oil; by changing the bars successively and repeatedly, and at proper intervals, the straight edge is sure to be produced at last. The bars may be an eighth of an inch thick, two inches wide, and must not very much exceed two feet six inches in length. Pressure on any particular part must be avoided as much as possible in the grinding.

Pencils.—For general purposes, the pencils used for drawing lines and circles ought to be rather of a hard quality; these produce a much clearer line than the softer kinds, and, when good, the marks or lines may be easily removed by the India rubber without trouble. Pencils are to be had which are made expressly to fit into compasses; but it will be found better to use a piece of a good lead pencil, and pare it away nicely until it is of a proper size; the side of the wood in which the lead does not lie, ought to be slipped off altogether.

A convenient mode of cutting the pencil for drawing straight lines, is to bring the lead to a fine edge, taking care to keep one side of the wood as flat as possible, and parallel with the edge. By applying the flat side of the pencil to the ruler, the point is brought close to it, and is prevented by its form from turning during its progress; the line may thus be much more accurately and easily drawn than with a round point; this particular form of the lead enables it not only to draw a clearer line, but to retain its sharpness much longer than any other. The same method may be applied in cutting the points of pencils for the compasses.

China Ink.—The other material that is employed in drawing with the compasses is generally China ink. This ought to be of the best quality; the common kinds of it are all more or less filled with gritty or sandy particles, which interfere with the flowing of the ink from the pen, besides being of a dull brown colour. The quality of the ink may be easily ascertained by applying the end of the cake to the tongue, when, if there are any coarse particles or sand in its texture, they will be felt immediately. In using it, the ink ought to be rubbed down with a little clean water upon a plate or saucer, until the fluid is brought to any depth of colour required, but not so thick that it will not flow freely from the pen; a little experience will soon show how far this may be carried. In rubbing down the cake, it ought to be turned occasionally, so that the edges may be rounded off, this prevents it from splintering off in little bits which are troublesome. Common ink may also be employed, but it is not so good as the China ink, being more apt to run and blot when lines are drawn close to each other with it, or where many lines are drawn from the same point; also, if a drawing is required to be subsequently tinted, the ink runs when wetted, producing a very disagreeable effect.

In drawing a straight line, its position is usually indicated by two points; when these are marked, they ought to be made as small and distinct as possible, so as to leave no room for uncertainty in placing the ruler. It is then applied exactly to the points, leaving as much space as the thickness of the marking point requires; this is easily found by trial, if necessary, by placing the point precisely over each mark, and arranging the ruler accordingly; but practice will enable any one to judge very closely of the proper distance without this trouble. Care ought to be taken to place the marks through which a line is to be drawn, at as great a distance from one another as convenient; by this, any slight inaccuracy in placing the ruler is diminished. Serious inconvenience arises sometimes from neglect of this, as a deviation from its true direction, that may be inappreciable or immaterial in a short line, may become again very apparent when others are combined with it, or are dependent on it. The points which direct a line are most frequently indicated or found by the intersection of two lines, or two arcs of circles; certain precautions are necessary sometimes, in order that the exact place of the intersection may be clearly seen—for this purpose the lines must not be made to cross each other at a very small angle, if it can be avoided, because the less this is, the greater uncertainty is there of the exact place of the intersection; also, when the lines are not made very fine and clear, the difficulty of ascertaining it is much increased, particularly with a very small angle. The lines ought to cross each other well, so that the point of intersection may be clearly and distinctly evident. It must always be recollected that the nearer the points are to each other which give the direction of a long line, the more care must be taken to have no uncertainty, for any error that may be committed is increased in proportion to the length of the line drawn.

We have now described the nature of the few instruments that are essentially necessary for the production of circles and straight lines in drawing, and have endeavoured to point out the most convenient modes of using them for this end. Circles and straight lines, in themselves, are of small service, unless directed by intelligence to the attainment of a specific object; it is the province of practical geometry to show how they may be combined among themselves and together, for the production of results which may either add to our knowledge, or be applicable to some practical and useful purpose. In this way geometry becomes connected with all the mechanical arts, and among the rest not the least important one, with that of the cabinet-maker. This is evident if drawing alone were considered, which is indispensable in his calling: but in his work and operations he frequently carries into effect the problems of geometry. The kind of drawing, also, which he employs, is essentially geometric, and dependent on geometric principles; it is of the utmost importance to him, therefore, that he should become familiar with the principles, as well as with the different processes of drawing.

The business of the cabinet-maker is either to execute any piece of work that he may undertake in an accurate and efficient manner, in accordance with a given design, or to produce the design himself. His power of execution either way, depends on his knowledge of drawing; in the one case, it will enable him to comprehend more clearly, and with greater facility, the intentions of another, and so to work with greater certainty and precision in carrying out the design; and in the other, it will enable him to express his own ideas in an intelligible form. Nothing can more conduce to this end, and to the attainment of skill in the workman, than the acquirement of strict geometric principles. In the comparison of work, that is always the best which approaches more nearly to geometric precision in the lines and surfaces; nor is this merely conducive to external beauty, for the strength and durability of any structure, independent of the material, depends on such precision, and any inaccuracy not only frequently impairs outward beauty, but produces, in a corresponding degree, a real want of firmness and stability.

The limits of this work preclude the possibility of entering fully on the theoretical part of the sciences connected with drawing; but in the subsequent parts, we shall endeavour to impart such practical explanations of the principles of its different departments, as may enable the cabinet maker with ease to execute such drawings as he may require, or to give form to subjects of his own invention. This art, as applied to mechanical purposes, is so based upon geometric principles, that it becomes essentially necessary for the student to make himself familiar with the construction of plane geometric figures; a series of these, the most applicable to the purposes of the cabinet-maker, are offered in the following pages, and it is strongly recommended to the beginner to commence by drawing these carefully and accurately. It would be of great service to him were he to endeavour to become acquainted with so much of the elementary principles of geometry, that he may be able to prove, by demonstration, the truth or fallacy of the processes which are employed, and not merely to rest satisfied that they are correct; this would not only fix the problems more firmly in his memory, and be highly conducive to advancement in his daily pursuits, but also afford him a source of great enjoyment and rational recreation in his leisure hours.

It must not be imagined that there is any mystery attached to the acquirement of this kind of knowledge; the elementary parts of geometry, so far as will be found necessary, are exceedingly easy, and of evident application in the various constructions. All that is required, is a little attention in following out a connected train of reasoning from the simplest principles, which are in themselves self-evident. It must be borne in mind, that if they are understood with so much readiness, they are apt to escape from the recollection with equal facility, if not impressed by unwearied practice, and by being repeated and reflected upon in all their details, until they may become so familiar as to present themselves when occasion requires.

The young draughtsman, then, ought to make himself thoroughly acquainted with the terms used and with the constructions in practical geometry; these he should be able to draw with readiness, not only from a copy, but from recollection. No other instruments ought to be employed but the ruler and compasses, avoiding the use of squares and other aids that may be ordinarily useful or convenient in drawing; by this means, he will more readily attain to the mastery of his instruments. He ought to bestow all the pains he can upon the figures, endeavouring to produce them as clear and neat as he can. This attained, will be one important step in his progress as a draughtsman. He may probably experience some difficulty at first, and be apt to condemn his own awkwardness in the use of the compasses; this he must expect, and not be discouraged by it. A very little practice and experience will soon give dexterity; nothing of the kind can be acquired without some trouble at first; and it must be recollected, that the more care and attention that is bestowed at the outset, the greater will be the subsequent progress, as there will thus be less to overcome, or perhaps, to correct at an after period.

PRACTICAL GEOMETRY.

Geometry is that science which treats of the magnitude and forms of the objects by which we are surrounded, as relates to the three dimensions of *length, breadth, and thickness*, and also of portions of space considered as possessing these dimensions.

Theoretical geometry demonstrates the absolute truths of the science by abstract reasoning.

Practical geometry, by rules deduced from the demonstrations of theoretic geometry, teaches the truthful construction of figures upon given conditions.

The whole system of geometry is founded upon simple and self-evident truths, which cannot receive, and do not require, any proof or demonstration. In practical geometry it is unnecessary to enumerate these, but the definition and application of some of the terms used in the science is requisite for the right understanding of the intention of the problems and their solutions.

Definitions.—A *point* is that which has position, but no magnitude nor dimensions, neither length, breadth, nor thickness.

A *line* is length, without breadth or thickness. The extremities of lines are points, and when two lines cross each other, their intersection is a point. In practice, it is usual to consider as points and lines the smallest marks that can be formed by mechanical means; these are strictly and truly solid bodies, possessing the three dimensions of length, breadth, and thickness; but in practical geometry they are understood as occupying no space.

A *surface, or superficies,* is an extension, or a figure of two dimensions, length and breadth, but without thickness. A shadow gives a very good notion of a superficies; its length and breadth can be measured, but it has no depth or thickness. The quantity of space contained in any surface is called the *Area*.

A *body, or solid,* is a figure of three dimensions, namely, length, breadth, and depth or thickness. The term may be applied to any visible object, but in geometry it is understood to signify the space contained within the different surfaces.

Lines may be drawn in any direction, and are called accordingly either right, or curved, or mixed of these two.

A right, or straight line, lies all in the same direction between its extremities, and is the shortest distance between two points. In description, it is generally indicated by a letter placed at each end, as the line A B.

A————B

Every line which is not a straight line is a *curved line.* It continually changes its direction between its extreme points. The variety of curves is unlimited. Plane geometry includes only one, the circle; the rest are divided into different sections according to their properties.

A mixed line is composed of straight and curved lines connected in any form.

Parallel lines are always at the same perpendicular distance from one another, and they never meet though ever so far produced. Curved lines may also be parallel, when the perpendicular distance between them remains always the same.

Oblique, or converging, straight lines change their distance, and would meet or intersect each other, if produced, on the side of the least distance.

A rectilineal angle is formed at the common point of origin, or intersection of two straight lines. Thus, the straight lines B A and B C, diverging from the point B, form an angle of which B is called the *Vertex.* The lines containing an angle are called the *Sides.* In description, a letter is generally placed at the vertex, as B, and also one somewhere on each of the sides, as A and C, and the angle is called "the angle A B C," placing the letter which indicates the vertex between the other two. The angle may sometimes be called "the angle B," or, "at B," when there is no risk of mistake. The magnitude of an angle does not depend on the length of the sides, but on the greater or less divergence of the lines which contain it.

Angles are either *right* or *oblique,* and the latter either acute or obtuse, according as they are greater or less than a right angle.

A right-angle is formed when one line meeting another, or standing upon it, makes the angles on both sides of it equal to each other; and the straight line which stands on the other is said to be *perpendicular to it.*

An *acute angle* is any angle that is less than a right-angle, as *b.*

An *obtuse angle* is any angle that is greater than a right-angle, as *c.*

An angle is measured by the portion of the circumference of a circle intercepted between the sides containing it, and which is described from the vertex as a centre. All circles being similar figures, and bearing the same proportion to their diameters, similar sectors of different circles are to one another as the whole circles, and the arcs of the similar sectors are to one another as the circumferences; hence, it is not the actual length of the arc that determines the quantity of the angle, but the proportion that it bears to the whole circumference, of which it is a part. The arc of a circle being thus the measure of angular magnitude, for its expression by number, the whole circumference is divided into 360 equal parts, called *degrees;* and for those angles that do not contain whole numbers of these parts, each degree is divided into sixty equal parts, called *minutes;* and these again are subdivided into sixty *seconds,* and so on. Degrees, minutes, and seconds, are indicated by the signs °, ′, ″, placed over the numbers which represent them; thus, 51°, 25′, 52·85″, is read fifty-one degrees, twenty-five minutes, fifty-two seconds, and eighty-five hundredth part, and represent an angle which is measured by the seventh part of the circumference of a circle. It is evident that the right-angle is measured by the fourth part of a circumference, as in the diagram, where A B C is a right-angle, and the intercepted arc is a quadrant or quarter of a circle. This is divided into 90°, or one-fourth part of 360. By drawing lines from the centre B, through each point of division, the angle is divided into equal angles, in the present case, into nine equal parts, each containing 10°; and the angle which each of these lines makes with B C, the horizontal line is called an angle of 10° or 20°, &c. The right-angle thus containing 90°, the acute angle contains a less, and the obtuse angle any greater number of degrees.

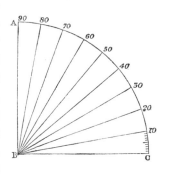

The division of the circle into 360°, is called the

sexagesimal division; among other advantages, it possesses the important property, that 360 may be divided by a great many whole numbers, without a remainder. It is proper to mention, that in some French works the circle will be found divided into 400°, for the measurement of angles, and these are subdivided by 10, &c. The quadrant, or right angle, is thus made to consist of 100°. This is called the centesimal division.

Any angle which is more than two right angles, is called a *reverse angle*.

When any angle is less than two right angles, the deficiency is called the *supplement of the angle*.

When any angle is less than a right angle, the deficiency is called the *complement of the angle*.

Superficies are either *plane* or *curved*.

A *plane*, or *plane superficies*, is that with which a straight line may every way coincide; or, if the line touch the plane in two points, it will touch it in every point. This affords one of the most accurate and ready tests by which the truth of a plane surface is determined, the workman applying a straight edge, or one as nearly straight as can be, to his work in various directions; if the edge is found to touch the surface in all its points, and in every way that it is applied, he concludes that his object has been attained.

A *curved superficies* is such as will not coincide with a straight line in every direction. There are certain curved surfaces to which the straight line may be applied; but when this is the case, it is only in one sense that it can be so, as will readily be understood; for instance, a straight line may be applied to the surface of a cylinder, as a garden roller, in the direction of its length, but in no other, leaving the ends out of the question.

Plane figures are bounded either by right lines or curves.

Plane figures bounded by right lines have names, according to the number of their sides or of their angles, for they have as many sides as angles.

Three is the least number of straight lines by which space can be circumscribed. These lines incline to each other, and meeting, form three angles. The figure is hence called a *triangle*. The straight lines which form it are called the *sides of the triangle*.

These figures receive different denominations from the relation of their sides and angles.

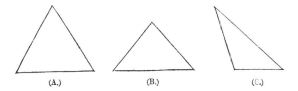

(A.) (B.) (C.)

The *equilateral triangle* is that which has all its sides equal. (A.)

The *isosceles triangle* is that which has two of its angles equal. (B.)

A triangle all of whose sides are unequal, is called a *scalene triangle*. (C.)

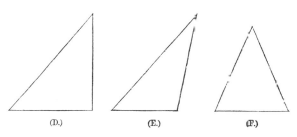

(D.) (E.) (F.)

A *right angled triangle* is that which has one of its angles a right angle. (D.)

An *obtuse angled triangle* is that which has an obtuse angle. (E.)

An *acute angled triangle* is that which has all its angles acute angles. (F.)

For the convenience of reference, different letters are marked at each of the angles of the triangle, and it is described by means of those letters; as the triangle A B C.

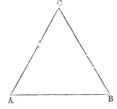

Any side of a triangle may be called its *base*, and the opposite angular point its *vertex*; thus, A B, one of the sides of the triangle A B C, may be called the base, and the angle at C the vertical angle of the triangle.

The *altitude of a triangle* is a line which is drawn from the angle opposite to the base line, perpendicular to it, or the base produced when necessary; thus, C D is the altitude of the triangle A B C, the base A B being produced so as to meet it. In the same way, C D is the altitude of the right angled triangle A D C.

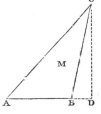

The side of a right angled triangle which is opposite to the right angle, is called the *hypotenuse* of the triangle; thus, A C is the hypotenuse of the right angled triangle A D C.

The triangle is the simplest of all the rectilineal figures, and the most important in geometry, as by its means the properties of all other figures bounded by straight lines, and which may be resolved into component triangles, are investigated and determined.

Figures of four sides and angles are called *quadrilaterals*, or *quadrangles*, and receive different denominations according to the relations of those sides and angles.

A *parallelogram* is a quadrilateral which has both its pairs of opposite sides parallel, and it takes the following particular names:—namely, rectangle, square, rhombus, and rhomboid.

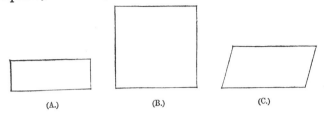

(A.)   (B.)   (C.)

A *rectangle* is a parallelogram having all its angles right angles, the term being generally applied to those figures in which the opposite pairs of sides are of unequal lengths. (A.)

A *square* is an equilateral rectangle having all its sides equal, and all its angles right angles. (B.)

When the angles of a parallelogram are oblique, and the opposite pairs of sides are unequal in length, the figure is called a *rhomboid*. (C.)

A *rhombus* is an equilateral rhomboid, having all its sides equal, but its angles oblique. The figure is also called a *lozenge*.

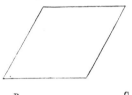

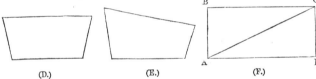

(D.)   (E.)   (F.)

A *trapezoid* has only one pair of opposite sides parallel. (D.)

A *trapezium* is a quadrilateral which has not its pairs of opposite sides parallel. (E.)

Those angles of a quadrilateral which are at each extremity of one of the sides, are called *adjacent angles*, as B A D and A D C, while those which are not so, as A B C and A D C, are called *opposite angles*. A straight line, as A C, which joins the opposite angles, is called a *diagonal*. (F.)

A quadrilateral is generally described by means of letters which are placed at each of the angles of the figure, as the quadrangle A B C D, or sometimes the letters indicating the opposite angles are alone employed, as the parallelogram A C.

Plane figures having more than four sides, are in general called *polygons*, and they receive other particular names according to the number of their sides or angles.

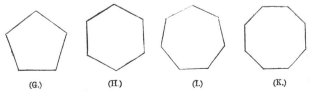

(G.)   (H.)   (I.)   (K.)

A *pentagon* is a polygon of five sides. (G.)

A *hexagon* is a polygon of six sides. (H.)

A *heptagon* is a polygon of seven sides. (I.)

An *octagon* is a polygon of eight sides. (K.)

A *nonagon* has nine, a *decagon* ten, an *undecagon* eleven, and a *dodecagon* twelve sides. Polygons that have more than twelve sides (except that of fifteen, which is called a *quindecagon*) are generally designated by the number of their sides.

A polygon is *regular* when it has all its sides equal, and all its angles equal, as in the above figure of the pentagon, hexagon, &c. It may be remarked that the equilateral triangle and the square, are both of them regular polygons of three and four sides respectively, and are sometimes called, the former a *trigon*, and the latter a *tetragon*.

An *irregular polygon* has its sides or angles unequal, or both, as in the figure which is called an *irregular pentagon*.

The *angle* of any regular polygon is that formed by the meeting of two of its sides.

The *centre* of a regular polygon is that point within it which is equidistant from similar points in each of the sides.

The *angle at the centre* is that which is formed by the meeting of two lines at the central point, which are drawn from the ends of one of the sides.

A *circle* is a plane figure bounded by one curved line, which is everywhere equally distant from a point within it called the *centre*. The space contained is the circle, the containing line is called the *circumference; b c d* is the circumference of the circle, and *a* the centre. It may not be improper to remark that the terms circle and circumference are frequently confused; thus we say, "Describe a circle from a given point," instead of saying, "Describe the circumference of a circle from a given point;" the circumference being the curved line thus described, everywhere equally distant from the centre; whereas the circle is, strictly speaking, the superficial space included within the circumference.

The *radius* of a circle is a straight line drawn from the centre to the circumference, as *b a* or *b c*. All the radii of a circle are equal.

The *diameter* of a circle is a right line drawn through the centre, and terminated both ways by the circumference, as *a b*. The diameter of a circle is equal to twice the length of the radius.

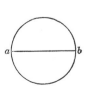

An *arc* of a circle is any part of the circumference, as *c e d* or *c f d*.

A *chord* is a straight line joining the extremities of any arc, as *c d*, which, it is to be observed, is equally that of the arc *c e d* or *c f d*, and the chord is said to subtend them. The diameter is the greatest chord of a circle, and it divides it into two equal parts called *semicircles*.

A *segment* is any part of a circle bounded by an arc and its chord, as *c e d* or *c f d*; each of these are segments into which the circle is divided by the chord *c d*.

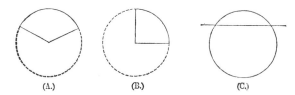

(A.)   (B.)   (C.)

A *sector* is any part of a circle bounded by an arc, and two radii drawn to its extremities. (A.)

A *quadrant*, or quarter of a circle, is a sector having a fourth part of the circumference for its arc, and its two radii are perpendicular to each other. (B.)

A *secant* is a straight line that cuts a circle, being drawn from a point without the circumference. (C.)

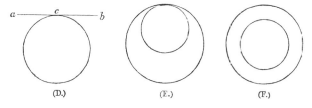

(D.)   (E.)   (F.)

A straight line which touches a circle without cutting it, is called a *tangent*, as *a b*, which touches the circle in *c*; and this point *c* is called the *point of contact*. (D.)

Circles may also be tangential, that is, when they have a single point of contact; and they may either touch each other externally or internally, as (E.)

Concentric circles are such as are described from the same centre. (F.)

Circles which are not described from the same centre, are said to be *eccentric* to one another.

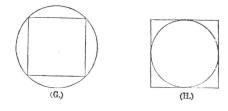

(G.)   (H.)

A right lined figure is *inscribed in a circle*, or the circle *circumscribes* it, when all the angular points of the figure are in the circumference of the circle. (G.)

A right lined figure circumscribes a circle, or the circle is inscribed in it, when all the sides of the figure touch the circumference of the circle. (H.)

" *Identical* figures, are such as have all the sides and all the angles of the one, respectively equal to all the sides and all the angles of the other, each to each; so that if the one figure were applied to, or laid upon the other, all the sides of the one would exactly fall upon and cover all the sides of the other; the two becoming as it were but one and the same figure."

Similar figures have all the angles of the one equal to all the angles of the other, each to each; and the sides about the equal angles, proportional.

PROBLEM 1.—At a given point in a straight line, to make an angle equal to a given angle.

Let E be a point in a straight line E F, at which it is required to make an angle equal to a given angle A B C. From the vertex B, with any radius B *g*, describe an arc of a circle meeting the sides B A and B C in points *g* and *h*. From the point E, with the same radius, describe an arc meeting E F in *k*, and of indefinite length towards *l*. From *k*, with a radius equal to the distance between the points *g* and *h*, describe an arc intersecting *k l* in *l*. The arc *k l* is thus made equal to *g h*. From E, draw a straight line through *l* towards D, then will the angle D E F be equal to the given angle A B C. In the solution of this problem, when the angle is very obtuse, it will be found advantageous to divide the arc which measures it into two parts, and to measure each of them successively upon the arc of construction; by this means, the true point of intersection required, will be more distinctly seen than when the arcs cut each other at a very small angle. It must be remarked of the solution of the problem here given, that the character of the given angle has not been specified in the enunciation; that is, it is not said whether it is to be considered as an acute or a reverse angle, or whether the greater or the lesser portion of the circumference of the circle that may be described from the vertex, and intercepted by the sides, is to be taken as its measure; but the construction need not differ, since the distance *d e* of the extremities of the lesser and greater arcs is the same. This is the principle of an instrument made use of by all artizans, called a *bevel*, which is very convenient for the drawing and transference of angles. In its absence, the workman may verify his operations by

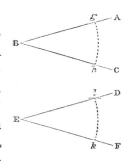

means of the above problem ; as, for instance, in the production of a many sided figure, say of six sides, all the angles being equal. Having drawn the figure on paper, or otherwise, and measured equal distances from an angle upon the sides containing it ; the same distances are measured, and marked upon the work, from the angle to be proved. The distance, then, between the two points on the drawing, may be taken by a pair of callipers, compasses, or other means at hand ; and if the corresponding distance on the work is the same, the angle is correct. If the reverse angle is greater, the marked points will be within the ends of the callipers ; and if less, beyond them.

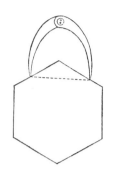

PROBLEM 2.—At a given point in a straight line, to erect a perpendicular to it.

Let C be a given point in a straight line A B, at which it is required to erect a perpendicular to it. From C, measure upon A B equal distances, C*d* and C*e*, on each side of it. From *d* and *e* as centres, with any radius greater than C*d* or C*e*, describe arcs intersecting each other, as at *f*. From C draw a straight line through *f*. This is the perpendicular required.

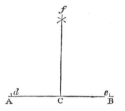

PROBLEM 3.—From a given point, to let fall a perpendicular upon a given straight line.

Let C be a given point, from which it is required to let fall a perpendicular upon a straight line A B. From C as a centre, with any radius, describe an arc of a circle which will cut A B in two points, *d* and *e*. From *d* and *e* as centres, with any radius greater than the half of *d e*, describe intersecting arcs, as at *f*, on the other side of A B. A line drawn through the two points C and *f*, will be the perpendicular required. It is evident that the second point *f*, might be marked between C and the line, or beyond it, if necessary ; but it is generally best to find it on the side of A B, on which the given point is not placed, for the more distant the points are from one another, the less risk there is of making a considerable error in the angle, when the line is drawn.

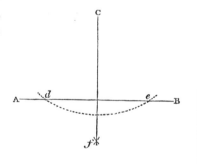

It may here be observed, that the perpendicular drawn to any line from any point, is the shortest distance between them.

PROBLEM 4.—From a given point, at, or nearly opposite to the extremity of a straight line, to let fall a perpendicular on it.

Let C be a given point, opposite to the extremity of a straight line A B, from which it is required to let fall a perpendicular on it. From any point *e*, in A B, as a centre, with a radius equal to the distance *e* C, describe an arc of a circle, extending it on both sides of A B. From *f*, any other point in A B, by preference between *e* and B, with a radius equal to *f* C, describe arcs, intersecting the first at points C and D. A straight line C D, drawn through C and D, will be the perpendicular required.

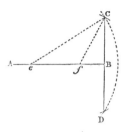

PROBLEM 5.—From the extremity of a straight line, to erect a perpendicular to it.

Let it be required to erect a perpendicular to a given straight line A B, from its extremity B. From any convenient point *c*, describe an arc of a circle greater than a semicircle, and cutting A B in *d*. Through *d* and *c* draw a straight line to meet the arc in a point *e*. Join *e* B by a straight line. This is the perpendicular required. Or,

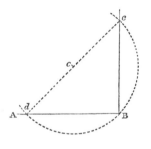

Let A B be the straight line, and A the point at which it is required to erect a perpendicular to it. From A, with any radius A E, describe an arc of a circle ; and from E, with the same radius, a second, intersecting the first in C. Through E and C draw a straight line of indefinite length ; and from C, with the radius A E, describe an arc intersecting it at the point D. Draw D A, which is the perpendicular required. Both these solutions are modifications of the same principle, namely, that the angle in a semicircle is a right angle ; that is, all the angles formed by lines drawn from the extremities of the diameter to meet in points in the circumference, are right angles. The draughtsman will do well to bear this principle in mind, as it is of such easy application in the drawing of lines perpendicular to one another. It is plain that the construction is applicable to any point in the line, whether situated at the extremity or not. The following is also a convenient method :—

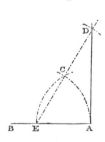

Let A B be the given line, and B the extremity at which it is required to erect a perpendicular to it. From B, with any radius B c, describe a large arc of a circle. From c, with the same radius, describe an arc intersecting it at d, and from d a second intersect-

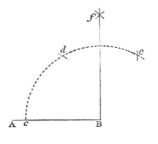

ing it at e; from e and d, with any radius, describe arcs intersecting each other at f, and draw f B, which is the perpendicular required.

PROBLEM 6.—To erect a perpendicular to a straight line by means of a scale of equal parts.

Let D be a scale of five equal parts, and let B be the extremity of a straight line A B, at which it is required to erect a per-pendicular to it. From B, upon B A, make B e equal to three of the parts upon the scale. From B, with a radius equal to four of them, describe an arc of a circle towards C, and from e, with

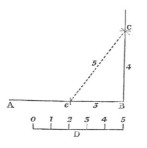

the whole five parts, describe an arc intersecting the first at a point C. A straight line drawn through C and B, is perpendicular to A B as required.

This method of drawing or proving perpendiculars will be found exceedingly convenient, either on a large scale or in the absence of the usual means; for it is plain that a temporary square may be readily constructed by the aid of the principle, and with great exactitude when the scale is good. The fol-lowing is also a method of drawing perpendiculars that may be adopted with advantage, particularly on a large scale.

PROBLEM 7.—From a given point in a straight line, to erect a perpendicular to it by rectilineal construction, that is, by employment of the ruler alone.

Let A B be the given straight line, and C, a point in it, from which it is re-quired by straight lines only to erect a perpendicular to it. In A B take any point D, and from it draw a line D E forming any angle with A B, and equal in length to the distance D C. Through E and C draw a straight line, and produce it beyond A B to G, until C G is equal to C D;

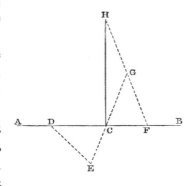

make C F equal to C E. Through F and G draw a line, and produce it beyond G to H, until G H is equal to F G or C D. A straight line drawn from C through H, will be perpendicular to A B as required.

It is generally by means of an instrument called a *square*, that lines are drawn perpendicularly, or at right angles with one another. Two of the edges or sides of this should meet each other, and make an angle of 90°. There are several forms of the instrument in use, according with the different pur-poses to which it is applied. In these it very often happens that, either from faulty construction or the effects of air and usage, the angle is not perfectly true. They ought therefore to be verified before employing them, where great exactitude is required, as without this, any error that exists is sure to become a source of serious inconvenience, frequently involving a very great amount of needless labour. In order to see whether a square is true, it is only necessary to draw a line, as A B, with a good rule or straight edge, upon a plane sur-face; the square is then

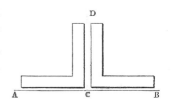

adjusted as for drawing a perpendicular, and a line C D drawn, forming an angle A C D. The square being now turned, and placed in the angle B C D, if both the angles are found to be equal, the instru-ment is true; but if they are unequal, it is false; and it is easily seen whether its angle is greater or less than it ought to be, and also how much.

PROBLEM 8.—Through a given point, to draw a line parallel to a given line.

Let C be a point through which it is required to draw a line parallel to a given line A B. From C, draw a line meeting A B in a point d. From d, with the radius d C, describe an arc C e,

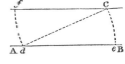

meeting A B in e. From C as a centre, with the same radius, describe an arc d f, and make it equal to the arc C e. Through C and f draw a straight line. This line is parallel to A B as required. This solution of the problem depends on a property of parallel lines, that they make equal alternate angles with a line which intersects them; that is, if C d is a line intersecting the parallel lines A B and f C, the angles f C d and C d B, are equal. Hence, if the point C were at such a distance from A B as to render it inconvenient to employ the line C d as a radius for the arcs of construction, it would be sufficient to make the alternate angles equal by the employment of a shorter radius. Otherwise—

Let A B be the given line, and C the given point through which a line parallel to it is required to be drawn. From C, describe an arc touching A B in e, from any point d in A B ; with the same radius C e, describe an arc as at f, and through C draw a straight line touching this arc at f, which will be the parallel line required. Otherwise—

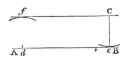

This problem may be solved by rectilineal construction, that is, by means of the ruler alone.

Let it be required to draw a line through a given point C, parallel to a line A B. From C draw a straight line to intersect A B in any point D, and produce it until D E is equal to D C. From E draw another line to intersect A B at any point F, and produce the line to G, until F G is equal to F E. Through C and G draw a straight line. This line is parallel to A B. This is an exceedingly convenient method of drawing parallel lines, especially on a large scale.

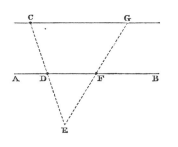

PROBLEM 9.—To draw a straight line parallel to a given line at a given distance from it.

Let it be required to draw a straight line parallel to a given straight line A B, at a distance from it equal to m n. In the given line A B, take any two points e and f as centres, and from them, with a radius equal to m n, describe the arcs g and h ; a line C D drawn to touch these arcs without cutting them, will be parallel to A B as required.

The principle here employed, is one of constant recurrence in the different methods adopted for the production of parallel lines ; namely, that the perpendicular distance between parallel lines remains constantly the same. A workman will draw, with great precision upon his work, a line parallel to one of its edges at a given distance, by means of a rule held firmly in one hand, while a pencil is kept by the other at the free end, and both are moved along and guided by the edge. From the above principle, it will be seen that every thing during the drawing of the line must occupy the same relative position, otherwise the perpendicular distance will vary, and the lines would not be parallel. This is also the principle of the carpenter's gauge, by which a much surer result is obtained, from the comparative immovability of the parts. The various kinds of planes

by which different mouldings are produced, are also examples of the production of parallel lines dependent on the same principle.

PROBLEM 10.—To find a point that shall be at two given distances from two given straight lines.

Let A B and C D be the two given lines, and let it be required to find the point that shall be at a distance from A B, equal to m n, and from C D, equal to o p. Parallel with A B, and at a distance from it equal to m n, draw a line e f (Prob. 9), and also a line g h parallel to C D, at a distance from it equal to o p. The point E, where these lines intersect each other, is that sought, being evidently at the given distances from the lines.

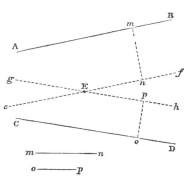

PROBLEM 11.—Through a given point to draw a line, to form an angle with a given line, which shall be equal to a given angle.

Let C be a point through which it is required to draw a line, to form an angle with a given line A B, which shall be equal to a given angle D e B. Join C and e by a straight line from e, with any convenient radius e f, describe an arc f g, between the lines e D and e C. From C, with the same radius, describe an arc F G, equal to f g, and on the other side of C e. Through C and G draw a line to meet A B in a point E ; then is the angle C E B equal to the given angle D e B, and the side E C is drawn through the point C, as required. Here D e and C E have been made parallel, they are consequently intersected by A B, so that D e B and C E B are corresponding angles, and therefore equal.

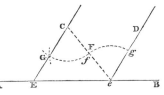

PROBLEM 12.—To find the middle point of a given straight line, or to divide it into two equal parts.

Let A B be the given straight line. From A and B, the extremities of the given line, as centres, with any convenient radius which is evidently greater than the half of it, describe arcs of circles intersecting each other at points C and D, on opposite sides of A B. Through C and D draw

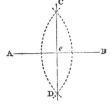

a straight line; this will intersect A B at a point *e*, which is its middle point, or the parts A *e* and B *e*, into which it is divided, are equal. The two points C and D might also be determined on the same side of A B, if convenient; but the method given is the shorter, when practicable. When A B is of a length to render the construction inconvenient, equal parts may be marked off from each end of the line, and the portion remaining between them bisected; the middle of this part is the middle of the whole line.—Many workmen are in the habit of resolving this Problem by trials with the compass, until a distance is found which may nearly be the half of the line; but this process is certainly longer than the geometric construction, and the result never so exact, since, after a few attempts to save time, he generally rests satisfied with an approach to the true measure.

PROBLEM 13.—To bisect a given angle, that is, to divide it into two equal parts.

Let it be required to divide a given angle A B C, into two equal parts.
From the vertex B, with any radius B *d*, describe an arc *d e*, meeting the sides B A and B C in points *d* and *e*, respectively.

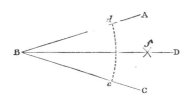

From *d* and *e* as centres, with any radius, describe arcs intersecting each other as at *f*. A straight line B D drawn through B and *f*, will divide the given angle into two equal angles ABD and CBD, as required. It is evident that by repeating the process of bisection, the angle may be divided into 4, 8, 16, &c., parts, or into any number which is the product of two, multiplied repeatedly into itself. Otherwise—

The Problem may be solved by rectilineal construction, or by the ruler alone:—

Let B A C be the given angle which it is required to divide into two equal angles. Upon A B, one of the sides, mark any two points D and E. Upon A C, make A F equal to A D, and A G to A E. Join D G and F E by straight lines; these will intersect each other at a point H. A straight line drawn through A and H, will divide the angle B A C into two equal angles, B A H and C A H.

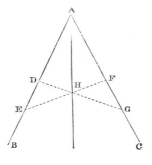

This latter method of dividing an angle will be found useful occasionally, when it is necessary to operate on a large scale; two cords of any kind, being substituted for the intersecting lines.

PROBLEM 14.—To trisect a right angle, or to divide it into three equal parts.

Let A B C be a right angle. From the vertex B, with any radius B *d*, describe an arc or quadrant, meeting the sides B A and B C in points *d* and *g*. From the point *d*, with the same radius, describe an arc intersecting *d g* in a point *f*; and from *g*, with the same radius, an

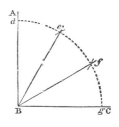

arc intersecting it at a point *e*. Straight lines drawn from B, through the points *e* and *f*, will divide the right angle A B C into three equal parts, as required.

It is evident, that, as a right angle contains 90°, and the radius of a circle is the chord of the sixth part of the circumference, equal to 60°, the difference, or 30°, is the third part of the quadrant by which a right angle is measured.

It must be observed that the solution of the general problem to divide any given angle into three equal parts, cannot be effected by a geometric construction produced by the ruler and compass alone. Instruments have, however, been invented by which this may be effected, but the workman will probably find it a more convenient method to employ careful trials with the compass for this purpose, taking care to measure the third part of the arc which measures the angle, and *not* of the chord of that arc, as is very commonly done.

PROBLEM 15.—Upon a given straight line, to construct an equilateral triangle.

Let A B be a given straight line, on which it is required to construct an equilateral triangle. From the extremities A and B of A B as centres, with a radius equal to A B, describe arcs of circles intersecting each other at a point C. Draw straight lines C A and C B. Then A B C is an equilateral triangle.

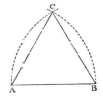

PROBLEM 16.—Upon a given base line to make an isosceles triangle, each of whose other two sides shall be equal to a given line.

Let it be required to construct an isosceles triangle upon a given base line A B, and each of the other sides to be equal to a given line *m n*. From A and B as centres, with a radius equal to *m n*, describe intersecting arcs at C. Draw straight lines C A and C B. Then is A C B the isosceles triangle required.

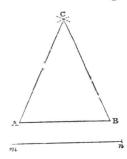

PROBLEM 17.—To construct a triangle, of which the sides shall be equal to three given straight lines, any two of which are greater than the third.

Let it be required to construct a triangle whose sides shall be equal to three given straight lines, *ab*, *ac*, and *cb*. Draw a straight line A B, and make it equal to *ab*. From A as a centre, with a radius equal to *ac*, describe an arc of a circle towards C; and from B, with a radius equal to *bc*, describe an arc intersecting the first at a point C. Draw straight lines C A and C B. Then is A B C the triangle required.

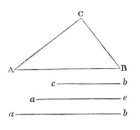

It may here be noticed with respect to triangles, that they are permanent in their figures, that is, the sides which determine it will form one figure only; and in practice, no force applied to a constructed triangle, if loosely attached at the angles, will change its form, unless one that destroys some part of the material of which it is composed.

PROBLEM 18.—To construct a triangle of which one angle and the two containing sides are given.

Let it be required to construct a triangle of which two of the sides are given equal to *ab* and *bc*, and the angle *a'b'c'* which is contained by them. Draw a straight line B C, and make it equal to *bc*, one of the given lines. At the point B in it, make an angle *a'*B C, equal to the given angle *a'b'c'* (Prob. 1), and produce the side B *a'* to A until it is equal to *ba*. Join A C by a straight line, which is the third side of the figure, and the required triangle is constructed.

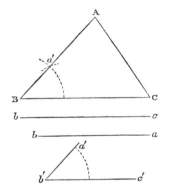

PROBLEM 19.—To construct a triangle of which one side is given, and the two adjacent angles.

Let *ab* be the given side, and *cab* and *cba* the two adjacent angles given; it is required to construct the triangle. Draw a straight line A B, equal to *ab*. At A make an angle *c'*A B, equal to *cab* (Prob. 1), and at B make an angle *c"*B A on the same side of A B, and equal to *cba*. Produce the sides A *c'* and B *c"* of these angles until they meet in a point C. Then is A B C the triangle required.

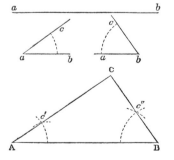

PROBLEM 20.—To construct a triangle of which a side is given, and two angles, one of which is opposite to the given side.

Let it be required to construct a triangle of which *ab* is a given side, *cab* and *acb* two angles, of which *acb* is to be placed opposite to the given side *ab* in the triangle. Draw a straight line A B, equal to *ab*, and at the extremity A make an angle *c'*A B, equal to *cab* (Prob. 1). Produce the side A *c'* indefinitely towards D, and at *e*, any point in A D, and on the side of it towards A B, make an angle A *ef*, equal to *acb* (Prob. 1). Lastly, through B draw a straight line parallel to the side *ef* (Prob. 8), meeting A D in a point C. Then is A B C the triangle required.

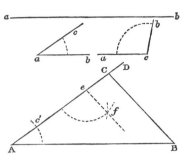

PROBLEM 21.— To construct a triangle of which two of the sides are given, and an angle opposite to one of them.

Let it be required to construct a triangle of which the two given sides are *ab* and *bc*, of which *bc* is greater than *ab*, and let *abc* be the given angle which is to be placed opposite to one or other of the given sides. This problem evidently divides itself into two cases, according as the angle is to be placed opposite to the greater or the lesser line. First, let the angle be opposite to the greater line *bc*. Draw a straight line A B, equal to *ab* the shorter line. At A, one of its extremities, make an angle *c'* A B, equal to the given angle *abc* (Prob. 1). Produce the side A *c'* indefinitely towards D, and from B as a centre, with a radius equal to *bc*, describe an arc intersecting A D in a point C. Join C B by a straight line. Then is A B C the triangle required.

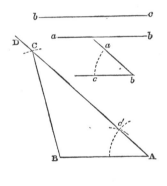

Next, let the angle be placed opposite to the lesser line *ab*. In this case, the construction affords two solutions. Draw a straight line B C, equal to *bc*, and at one extremity C, make an angle *a'* C B, equal to the given angle *abc* (Prob. 1). Produce the side C *a'* towards D indefinitely. From B as a centre, with the

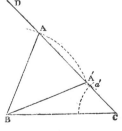

radius equal to *a b*, describe an arc of a circle, which will intersect C D in points A and A′. Join B A and B A′ by straight lines. Then each of the triangles A B C and A′ B C, have two of their sides, A B, B C of the one, and A′ B, B C of the other, respectively equal to the given lines *a b* and *b c*, and the angle at C made equal to *a b c*, opposite to a side B A or B A′, equal to the lesser line *a b*.

In the latter part of this problem, it is assumed that a triangle may be constructed with the given quantities. Sides and angles may be proposed with which no triangle could be formed on the conditions given ; when this is the case, the construction will always show it.

PROBLEM 22.—The hypothenuse, and one side of a right angled triangle being given, to find the other side.

Let A B be the hypothenuse, and C D the side. Bisect the hypothenuse, A B, in *e* (Prob. 12) ; from *e* as a centre, with a radius equal to *e* A, or *e* B, describe the arc C B. From A as a centre, with a radius equal to the length of the given line C D, describe another arc, intersecting the former at C. Join C A, and C B ; then C B will be the required side of the right angled triangle A B C.

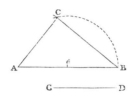

The last eight Problems contain all the methods of constructing triangles that are of any importance to the cabinet-maker ; they may be variously applied, and some of them will be found very useful in the construction of plans, &c., particularly when any of the sides are interrupted, so as to prevent a direct measure being taken. It may have been observed, that in the Problems, certain of the parts being given, the rest were derived from them ; this proceeds from the constant dependence of the parts of triangles upon one another. Of these relations, the most remarkable and important is a property of the angular magnitudes, that their sum is always equal to two right angles, or 180°, neither more nor less. This is common to all triangles, however they may vary in form. A triangle consists of six parts, namely, three sides and three angles ; but as one of the angles is always the result of the other two, the number of variable parts is only five : any three of these being ascertained, the triangle may be completely described, as seen in the Problems.

PROBLEM 23.—To make a triangle similar to a given triangle upon a given line, which is to correspond to one of the sides indicated.

Let A B C be the given triangle, and H K the given line which is to correspond to the side A B in the triangle. From the angular points A and B

of the given triangle, with any radius, describe the arcs *d e* and *f g*. From the extremity H of H K, with the same radius, describe an arc *m n*, and make it equal to *d e*. From K, with the same radius, describe an arc *o p*, and make it equal to *f g*. From H, through the point *n*, draw a straight line ; and from K, through the point *p*, draw also a straight line ; these, being produced, will meet in a point L ; then

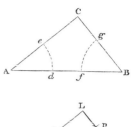

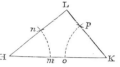

the triangle H L K will be similar to the triangle A B C, with the side H K corresponding to the side A B, as required. It is evident, that if the given line H K were equal to A B, the two triangles would be identical, and the construction would then be much simpler, being that of Problem 17, in which the triangle is constructed, the three sides being given. The following, also, is a very useful method :—

Let A B C be the given triangle, and C D the given line which is to correspond with B C in the triangle. From C draw C E parallel to B A, and from D draw D E, parallel to C A (Prob. 8), producing both the lines until they meet in the point E. Then is C D E a triangle similar to the given triangle A B C, and C D in it corresponds to the side B C, as required. Here C D has been made a continuation of the side B C of the triangle ; but not necessarily so, for it may be placed anywhere in the same plane, provided it is parallel with B C, and the construction completed as in the Problem ; this will be found of great convenience in practice. A remarkable property of the right angled triangle may here be pointed out, which is, that if a line be drawn from the right angle perpendicularly upon the hypothenuse, the triangle will be divided into two triangles, which are similar to one another, and to the whole triangle.

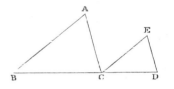

Upon the construction of similar triangles depends, in general, the solution of those Problems in which proportions are found.

PROBLEM 24.—To divide a given line into any number of equal parts.

Let B C be the given line, and let it be required to divide it into five equal parts. From one extremity B, draw a line B A, forming any angle with B C, but, by preference, acute. Upon B A, measure five equal parts from B to A ; join

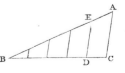

A C by a straight line; and from each of the other points draw lines, as D E, &c., parallel to A C (Prob. 8). The points where these lines meet the given line B C, will divide it into the required number of equal parts. Otherwise—

Let A B be the given line, and let it be required to divide it into four equal parts. Draw a straight line C D, of indefinite length, and upon it mark four equidistant points at 1, 2, 3, and 4. From C, and the last point 4, with a radius equal to C 4, describe arcs intersecting

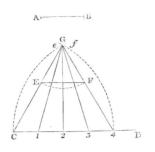

each other at G, and join G C and G 4 by straight lines. From G, with a radius equal to A B, describe an arc E F, meeting G C and G 4 in E and F; join E F by a straight line; this line is equal to A B. Join G 1, G 2, and G 3 by straight lines; these will intersect E F and divide it into four equal parts, thus indicating the fourth part of A B.

The first of these methods is, generally, to be preferred. In practice, when it may sometimes not be easy to draw the parallel lines, the following process may be employed.

Let A B be the given line, and let it be required to divide it into five equal parts. From an extremity A, of A B, draw a line A C of indefinite length, and forming any angle B A C with it. From B, draw a line B D on the other side of A B, and forming an

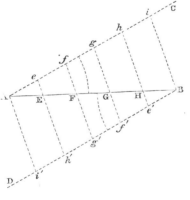

angle A B D, equal to B A C (Prob. 1); thus the two lines A C and B D are parallel. Upon A C, mark five points of equal distance at *e f g h* and *i*; and upon B D, with the same measure, mark also five equidistant points at *e' f' g' h'* and *i'*. Join B *i* by a straight line, also *h e', g f', f g', e h',* and A *i'*. These lines will intersect A B at points E, F, G, and H, and divide it into five equal parts, as required. It is evident that the intersecting lines are parallel to one another. This indicates an easy method of drawing equidistant parallel lines between parallels; as, for instance, if it were required to divide a board, with parallel sides, into a number of slips of an equal width. Let A B C D be the surface whose sides, A B and C D, are

parallel, and whose breadth A C is 9 inches. Let it be required to divide it into seven slips. No measure upon a rule will divide this exactly, and

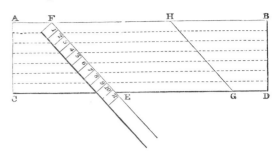

7 inches will not extend across the surface or board; but if the half of 7 be added to it, or 3½ is added to 7, then the amount, or 10½ inches, will extend in an angular manner across the board, and if points are marked, at intervals of 1½ inches, at the edge of the measure, at E F, and again at another part of the surface, as G H; lines drawn through these marks will be equidistant and parallel, and will divide the surface as required.

PROBLEM 25.—To find a fourth proportional to three given straight lines.

Let it be required to find a line proportional to *a d*, in the ratio of *a c* to *a b*. From any point A, draw two divergent lines A *m* and A *n*. Upon one of them, A *m*, measure *a c*, from A to C;

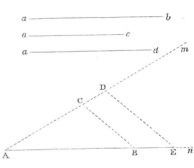

and upon A *n* measure *a b*, from A to B. Measure also *a d* upon A *m*, from A to D. Join C B by a straight line, and, from D, draw a line parallel with it (Prob. 8), meeting A *n* in a point E. Then is A E the fourth proportional sought; or A C (*a c*) is to A B (*a b*) as A D (*a d*) is to A E. If it had been required to find a line less than *a d*, in the ratio of *a b* to *a c*, then *a d* would have been measured upon A *n*, and the parallel drawn to intersect A *m*, when the distance between A and this intersecting point would be the proportional required.

By this last problem, scales or drawings may be reduced, or enlarged proportionally, so that each part of a given scale or drawing, shall bear the same proportion to similar parts of another scale or drawing, of a different size.

Let A B represent the length of one scale or drawing, divided into the given parts A *d*, *d e*, *e f*, *f g*, *g h*, *h* B; and let D E be

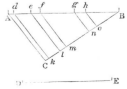

the length of another scale or drawing required to be divided into similar parts. From the extremity B, draw the line B C equal to D E, forming any angle with A B; join A C, and draw *d k*, *e l*, *f m*, *g n*, *h o*, parallel to A C, and the parts C *k*, *k l*, *l m*, &c., will be to one another, or to the whole line B C, as the parts A *d*, *d e*, *e f*, &c., are to one another, or to the given line or scale A B.

The Problem may be solved by means of numbers, which is very essential when great size precludes the possibility of drawing. It is seen that a proportion consists of four terms, the first and last of which, as A C and A E in the above case, are called the *extremes*; and A B and A D, which are between them, are called the *means*.

A fundamental property of the terms of a proportion, and one of the utmost importance, is, that the product of the extremes is equal to that of the means when they are multiplied together. This will readily be seen by the substitution of numbers for the quantities in the problem. Let A C equal 3, A B equal 6, A D equal 4, and A E equal 8. Such a proportion is usually written, 3 : 6 : : 4 : 8; and is read, three is to six as four is to eight. If, now, the extreme terms 3 and 8 are multiplied together, and also the means 6 and 4, the product of both is 24. It is evident from this, that if the proportion is incomplete, or only three of the terms are known, this affords the method of finding the fourth; for if the product of the known terms, forming the extremes or the means, is divided by the third, the quotient must be the fourth term of the proportion. Thus, in the above example, if one of the extremes and the two means are known, or 3 : 6 : : 4 is to some number unknown, then four times 6, or 24 divided by 3, will give 8, the number sought; or if the two extremes and one mean are given, or 3 is to an unknown quantity as 4 is to 8, then three times 8, or 24 divided by 4, will give 6, which is that required.

PROBLEM 26.—To find a third proportional to two given lines.

Let it be required to find a third proportional to two given lines, *a b* and *a c*, in the ratio of *a c* to *a b*; or let *a c* : *a b* : : *a b* : the line sought. From any point A, draw two divergent lines A *m* and A *n*. Upon one of them, A *m*, measure *a c*, from A to C, and upon both, measure *a b* from A to B and B'. Join C B by a straight line, and from B' draw a line parallel with it, (Prob. 8), meeting A *n* in a point D;

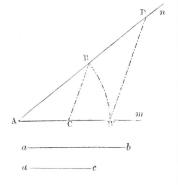

then is A D the line sought; or A C (*a c*) : A B (*a b*) : : A B (*a b*) : A D. If the ratio were *a b* : *a c*, then the line would be less than *a c*, and the construction is changed as in the last Problem.

It is plain that in speaking of a third proportional, four terms are understood; for one of the terms must be repeated to complete the two ratios of which the proportion consists. If *a c* and *a b* are represented by the numbers 2 and 4, respectively, then the proportion may be either 2 : 4 : : 4 : 8, or 4 : 2 : : 2 : 1, the product of the extreme and mean terms remaining the same.

PROBLEM 27.—To find a mean proportional between two given lines.

Let it be required to find a mean proportional between two given lines, *a b* and *b c*. Draw a straight line, and upon it make A B equal to *a b*, and B C equal to *b c*. Bisect the whole line A C in D (Prob. 12), and from D as a centre, with the radius D A or D C, describe a semicircle upon A C. From B raise a straight line perpendicular to A C (Prob. 2), and produce it to meet the circumference in a point E. Then is B E a mean proportional between the given lines *a b* and *b c*; or A B (*a b*) : B E : : B E : B C (*b c*).

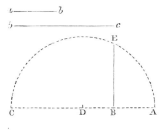

If *a b* and *b c* are given in number, the mean proportional between them is the square root of their product. Let *b c* = 8, and *a b* = 2, their product is sixteen, the square root of which is 4, and the proportion results 8 : 4 : : 4 : 2. The extraction of the square roots of numbers is an arithmetical process that requires a little practice to effect it with correctness and facility; the workman will find it more convenient to refer to any of the published tables, which will give correct results, without the trouble of calculation.

PROBLEM 28.—To divide a given line into parts proportional to those of a given divided line.

Let it be required to divide a given line A B similarly with a given line *a b*, which is divided into parts *a c*, *c d*, *d e*, and *e b*. Parallel with A B, draw a straight line *a' b'* (Prob. 8), equal to *a b*; and upon it make *a' c'* equal to *a c*, *c' d'* to *c d*, &c.; through *a'* and A

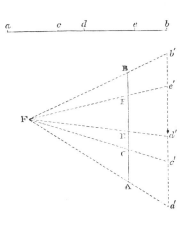

draw a line; also through b' and B; these lines, produced, will meet in a point F. Draw lines e' F, d' F, and c' F; these will intersect A B at points C, D, and E, and divide it into parts that are correspondingly proportional to those of ab; that is, A B : ab :: A C : ac :: C D : cd, &c., as required; the corresponding parts bearing the same proportion among themselves that the whole lines have.

PROBLEM 29.—To divide a given line in any given ratio.

Let it be required to divide a given line A B into parts that shall have the ratio to one another that ac has to bc. From one extremity A of A B, and at any angle, draw a line A c'' equal to ac. On the other side of A B, from B draw a line B c' parallel to A c'' (Prob. 8),

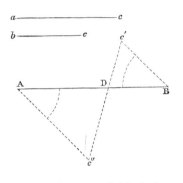

and equal to bc. Join c' c'' by a straight line; this will intersect AB at a point D, and divide it into parts A D and D B, which have the ratio to each other that ac has to bc, or A D : D B :: ac : bc.

The ratio may be given in number. Let ac : bc be as 4 : 3. The parallel lines being drawn as before, but of indefinite length, four equal parts must be measured upon A c'', and three of the same parts upon B c'; the construction is then completed by joining the extremities of the measured parts.

Should it be required to solve the problem by number, the proportion stands: As the sum of the terms of the given ratio is to the whole line in number, so is one of the terms of the ratio to the corresponding part of the divided line. Let the ratio be as 4 to 2, and let the given line or number be 9; then, as the sum of 4 and 2, or 6, is to 9, so is 4 to 6, or 2 to 3; consequently, 6 and 3 are the numbers sought. The workman will do well to exercise himself in these arithmetical solutions of the problems of proportion, as well as in their geometrical construction, for they are of great importance in the course of his operations, as no work can be correctly enlarged or diminished without their aid.

PROBLEM 30.—To find the centre of a given circle.

Let A C B D be the given circle, the centre of which it is required to find. Draw any chord A B, and at its middle point raise a perpendicular to it (Prob. 12), producing it both ways to meet the circumference of the circle in points C and D. This straight line C D is the diameter of the circle; and its middle point

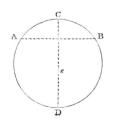

is the centre. Bisect C D therefore in e (Prob. 12), which is the centre sought.

PROBLEM 31.—To describe a circle, the circumference of which shall pass through three given points that are not in the same straight line.

Let it be required to describe a circle that shall pass through three given points, A, B, and C, which are not in the same straight line. Connect the points by two lines in any way, as A B and B C. Raise perpendiculars to the middle of each (Prob. 12), and produce these until they meet in a point D.

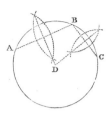

This point is the centre of the circle, which is to be described with a radius equal to the distance between it and any one of the points, as D A, D B, or D C.

PROBLEM 32.—The arc of a circle being given, to complete the circle.

Let it be required to complete the circle of which A B C is the arc given. Mark any point B in the arc, and join B A and B C by straight lines. Raise perpendiculars to the middle of each of these lines (Prob. 12), which, being produced, will intersect each other in a point D. From

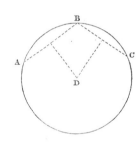

D, with the radius D A, D B, or D C, describe the remaining portion of the circle. This is evidently another form of the preceding problem.

PROBLEM 33.—To divide a given arc of a circle into two equal parts, or to bisect it.

Let it be required to divide a given arc A B C into two equal parts. Draw the chord A C, and raise a perpendicular to its middle point D (Prob. 12). This, being produced, will cut the arc at a point B, and divide it into two equal parts, B A and B C.

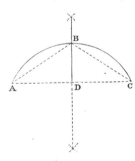

PROBLEM 34.—The arc of a circle being given, to draw perpendiculars to it from any points in it without finding the centre.

Let A B be the given arc; and first let e be a point in it, remote from the extremities, from which it is required to raise a perpendicular to the arc. On each side of e, measure equal

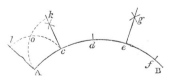

distances *e d* and *e f*. From *d* and *f* as centres, with any radius greater than *e d*, describe intersecting arcs at *g*; a straight line, drawn through *e* and *g*, will be perpendicular to the arc A B, as required.

Next, let the given point be at A, one extremity of the arc. From any point *c* in the arc, not very distant from A, raise *c k* perpendicular to it, by the first part of the problem. From *c*, with the radius *c A*, describe the arc A *k*; and from A, with the same radius, describe the arc *c l*, making the part *o l* equal to *o k*; a straight line drawn through A and *l* will be perpendicular to the arc, as required.

PROBLEM 35.—From a given point, to let fall a perpendicular upon a given arc of a circle, without having the centre.

First, let it be required to let fall a perpendicular upon the arc A B, from a given point C, which is re- mote from the extremities A and B. From C, with any

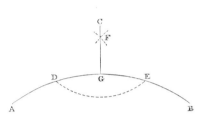

radius greater than the least distance between it and the arc, describe an arc cutting A B in points D and E. From these points, with a radius greater than the half of the distance D E, describe arcs in- tersecting each other at a point F; a straight line drawn through C and F will meet the arc A B in a point G, and be perpendicular to it, as required. It is plain, that the intersecting arcs at F might have been described on the other side of A B, with the same result; either method may be employed as circumstances may indicate, but it is generally ad- visable that the point F should be determined as far as possible from C, for the avoidance of error in drawing the line.

Next, let C be nearly opposite to the extremity A. From any point D in the arc, raise D E perpendicu- lar to it (Prob. 34), and produce it indefinite- ly. From C,

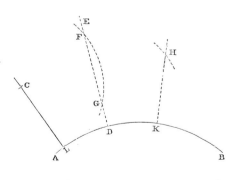

with a sufficient radius, describe an arc intersecting D E, in points F and G. From these points, with the same radius, describe arcs intersecting each other at H, and from H let fall a perpendicular H K upon A B, by the first case of this Problem; make D L, upon the arc, equal to D K; a straight

line, drawn from L through C, is the perpendicular required.

PROBLEM 36.—To construct a square, the sides of which shall be equal to a given line

Let A B be the given line. Draw C D equal to A B. From the extremities C and D, with a radius equal to C D, describe arcs C F and D E, intersecting each other in *g*. Bisect the arc C *g*, or D *g*, in *h* (Prob. 33), and make the arcs *g* E and *g* F each equal to *gh*. Draw the straight lines C E, D F, and E F; then C D E F is the square required. Otherwise—

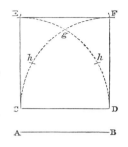

Let it be required to construct a square on a given line A B. From A and B as centres, with a radius equal to A B, de- scribe arcs of circles B D and A E, intersecting each other in C. From C, with the same radius, de- scribe an arc intersecting the first in points D and E. From these points describe the arcs at F and G. Join F A and G B by straight lines, and draw H I between their points of intersection with the arcs D B and A E; then is A H I B a square, con- structed on A B, as required. This is an applica- tion of a principle employed in the construction of perpendiculars; namely, that the angle in a semi- circle is a right angle; for F A B and A B G are evidently in semicircles; the sides are consequently perpendicular to one another.

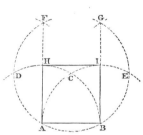

PROBLEM 37.—About a given point, to construct a square with a side equal to a given line.

Let it be required to construct a square having a side equal to a given line A B, and about a given centre C. Through C draw a straight line D C E, and F G a straight line intersecting it, at right angles, at the point C (Prob. 2). From C, with any sufficient ra- dius, describe a quadrant F D, and draw the chord D F. Upon D F

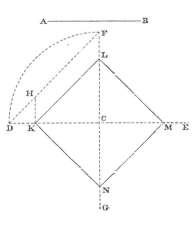

measure A B, from F to H; and from H draw a line H K, parallel to C F (Prob. 8), and meeting C D in a point K. Measure C K upon C F, C E, and C G, from C to L, M, and N, respectively. Join K L, L M, M N, and N K by straight lines; then is K L M N a square constructed about the point C, with a side equal to A B, as required.

Problem 38.—To construct a rectangle whose sides shall be equal to two given straight lines.

Let A B and C D be the given straight lines. Draw a line E F equal to A B, and at each of its extremities, E and F, raise E H and F G perpendicular to it (Prob. 5), and equal to C D. Join G H by a straight line. Then is E F G H the rectangle required.

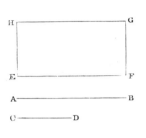

Problem 39.—To construct a rhomboid with two given straight lines, and with an angle equal to a given angle.

Let A and B be the given sides, and H C I the given angle. Draw a straight line D E equal to A, and at one extremity D, make an angle L D E equal to the given angle H C I (Prob. 1).

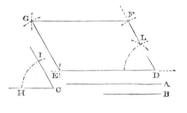

Produce the side D L indefinitely; and from D, with a radius equal to B, describe an arc intersecting it at F. From F as a centre, with the radius A or D E, describe an arc towards G; and from E, with the radius B or D F, another arc intersecting it at a point G. Join F G and G E by straight lines. Then is D E G F the rhomboid required, whose sides are respectively equal to A and B, and with an angle equal to the given angle.

Problem 40.—To construct a rhombus or lozenge, of which the diagonals are given.

Let a b and c d be the given diagonals. Draw a straight line A B equal to a b, and a straight line F G, intersecting A B at right angles at its middle point E (Prob. 12). From A draw a line A H, parallel to E F (Prob. 8) and equal to c d. Join H B by a straight line; this will intersect F G at a point C. Upon E G, make E D equal to E C. Join A C, B D, and A D; then is A C B D the rhombus required.

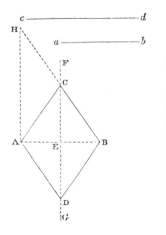

Problem 41.—To construct a trapezium, the four sides being given, and one angle.

Let a b, a c, c d, and b d be the given sides, and c a b the given angle. Draw a straight line A B equal to a b, and at one extremity A, make an angle c' A B equal to c a b (Prob. 1). Produce the side A c' to C, until A C is equal to a c. From C, with a radius equal to c d, describe an arc towards D,

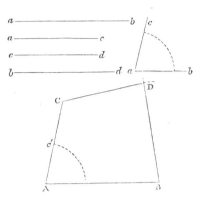

and from B, with a radius equal to b d, describe another intersecting it at a point D. Join C D and B D; then is A C D B the trapezium required. It is plain, that any pair of the sides may be made to contain the angle, and any order assumed for the succession of the sides. It may be observed, that it is a necessary condition for the possibility of constructing the figure, that any three of the sides shall be greater than the fourth.

Problem 42.—To construct a trapezoid, the four sides being given.

Let a b, c d, a c, and b d be the given sides, of which let a b and c d be parallel in the figure. Draw A B equal to a b, and upon it, from B, measure c d from B to F. From A, with a radius equal to a c, describe an arc of a circle towards C; and from F, with a radius equal to b d, describe a second arc intersecting

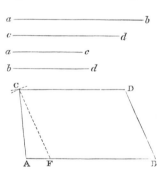

the first at a point C, and join C A; this line is equal to c a. From B draw a line parallel to C F (Prob. 8), and equal to b d. Join C D, which is thus parallel to A B and equal to c d; then is A C D B the trapezoid required. In the solution of this problem with the lines given, any two of the sides may be made parallel; but this cannot be done with all the quantities that might be proposed, the necessary condition being that, of the given lines, the difference of those that can be made parallel shall be greater than the difference between the other two sides.*

* It will easily be seen, by trial, that, as these differences approach to equality, the distance between the lines that are parallel diminishes; until, upon becoming equal, the possibility of construction ceases. It is also obvious, as in the last Problem, that any three of the lines shall be greater than the fourth.

PROBLEM 43.—An isosceles triangle being given, to draw a line parallel to the base line, so that it shall be equal to each of the equal parts of the other two sides intercepted between it and the base line.

Let A B C be the given triangle. From any point D, in A C, draw a line D E parallel to A B, and equal to D A (Prob. 8). Through A and E draw a line, and produce it to meet C B in a point F. From F draw a line F G parallel to A B. This line is equal to each of the parts G A and F B, of C A and C B,

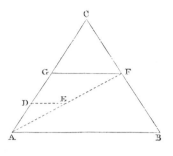

respectively, which are intercepted between it and the base. It is manifest, that a line may be drawn parallel to the base line, that shall have any given* ratio to the parts intercepted between it and the base. For this purpose, the line of construction D E must be made in the given ratio to D A, and the construction completed as in the Problem.

PROBLEM 44.—Upon a given line, to construct a trapezoid, the other three sides of which shall each be equal to a given line, which is greater than the third part of that given.

Let A B be the given straight line, and c d the given side. Bisect A B in E, and c d in e (Prob. 12). From E, on A B, make E C and E D on each side of it equal to the half of c d. From C and D raise perpendiculars to A B (Prob. 2), of

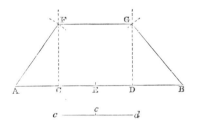

indefinite length. From A and B, with a radius equal to c d, describe arcs intersecting the perpendiculars in points F and G, respectively. Draw A F, F G, and B G; then is A B G F the trapezoid required.

All the quadrilaterals possess the remarkable property that, if the sides are bisected, and the successive middle points connected by straight lines, a parallelogram of some sort is produced. That is, let A B C D

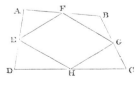

be a trapezium, each of whose sides is bisected in points E, F, G and H, respectively; these points being joined by straight lines, a parallelogram E F G H is produced. It may be observed, that the area of this parallelogram is the half of that of the trapezium.

The application of the diagonal in quadrilaterals is of great importance in most structures, since it confers stability. If any figure is constructed of four pieces of wood, or other material, connected at the angles by means of joints, it is plain that its character may be changed, the parts being movable; but if a diagonal piece is added, the figure is immediately converted into two triangles, each of which being, as before observed (Prob. 17), permanent in its form, their combination is also permanent. This is a method of rendering work firm that is familiar to every workman. The change that takes place in the form of a parallelogram by the parts being made movable, is applied in the construction of a kind of parallel rule much made use of in drawing.

The diagonal lines afford a valuable means of verifying work. In the square and the rectangle, it must be recollected that the diagonals are equal. In the parallelograms that are oblique angled, the diagonals are unequal; the greater being opposite to the greater angles. The two diagonals of any parallelogram mutually bisect each other; and in those that are equilateral, as the square and the lozenge, the diagonals intersect each other at right angles.

PROBLEM 45.—Two straight lines convergent to an inaccessible point being given, and a point between, or beyond them, to draw a line through the given point that shall, if produced, meet them at their point of convergence.

Let A B and C D be the converging lines, and E a point between them, through which it is required to draw a line to converge with them. Through E draw a straight line M E F, to meet A B and C D in points M and F. Parallel to M F (Prob. 8), at any convenient distance, draw a line M' G, meeting A B and C D at points M' and G. Find a fourth proportional to M' G in the ratio of M F to M E, that is, make M F : M E : : M' G : M' H (Prob. 25).

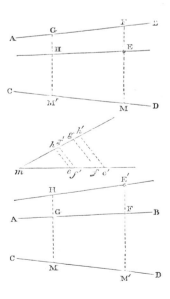

Through H and E draw a straight line; this line will converge with A B and C D towards their point of meeting. When the given point E' is beyond the lines, the construction is similar; or the proportion is M' F : M G : : M E : M H. Otherwise—

Let A B and C D be the convergent lines, and
E a point through which it is required to draw a
line that shall con-
verge with them.
In A B, take any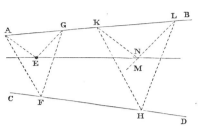
convenient' points
A and G, and F
any point in C D.
Join A F and F G
by straight lines.
Join also A E and E G. From K, or any point
in A B, at a convenient distance from G, draw
K H, parallel to A F (Prob. 8), meeting C D in H.
From H draw H L parallel to F G, meeting A B
in L. From L draw a line L M parallel to G E,
and from K a line parallel to A E, meeting L M
in a point N. Through E and N draw a straight
line ; this line converges with A B and C D toward
their inaccessible point of meeting. The construction is similar when the given point is beyond
the lines.

PROBLEM 46.—Two convergent lines being given.
which would meet, if produced, in an inaccessible
point, to find a point in each that shall be equidistant from that point.

Let A B and C D be the two convergent lines.
From E, any point in A B
raise E F perpendicular to
it (Prob. 2), and meeting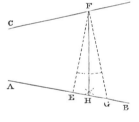
C D in F. From F raise
F G perpendicular to C D,
meeting A B in G. Bisect
the angle E F G (Prob. 13)
by the straight line F H,
meeting A B in H. Then
are F and H points equidistant from the point in
which A B and C D would meet, if produced, to
their inaccessible point of meeting.

PROBLEM 47.—Two convergent lines being given,
which would meet, if produced, in an inaccessible
point, to draw a line between them that would bisect
the angle formed by them at the point of meeting.

Let A B and C D be the convergent lines. Let
E F be drawn joining the
points E and F, which are
equidistant from the point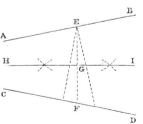
of meeting of the given
lines (Prob. 46), and draw
a line H I perpendicular
to its middle point G
(Prob. 12). This line, if
produced with the convergent lines, would bisect the
angle formed by them at their point of meeting,
as required.

The Problem may also be solved by the following
method :—

Let C H and C B be the convergent lines. From
H, any point in C H, raise H G perpendicular to it
(Prob. 2), and of any
convenient length. From
E, any point in C B, raise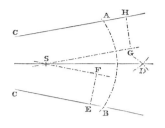
E F a perpendicular to it,
making it equal to H G.
Through G draw a line
parallel to C H (Prob. 8),
and through F a line
parallel to C B ; these lines, being produced, will
intersect each other in a point S. From S with any
sufficient radius, describe an arc A B, meeting the
given lines in points A and B. Bisect this arc
(Prob. 33), that is, from A and B, with any radius,
describe intersecting arcs at D. Through D and S
draw a straight line. This line, if produced, would
bisect the angle formed by the given lines at their
point of meeting.

There are many other methods by which lines may
be drawn to inaccessible points ; those given are the
simplest, and will be found sufficient. The cabinet-
maker will find them available in perspective drawing, in which they are of great importance.

PROBLEM 48.—Three points, not in a straight
line, being given, to find the altitude of the arc of a
circle that will pass through them, the position of
the chord being determined, but without having the
centre.

Let it be required to find the altitude of an arc of
a circle that will pass through three given points A, B,
and C, the line joining
A and C being the chord.
Draw straight lines B A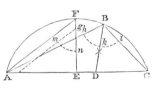
and B C between the
points, and bisect the
angle A B C thus formed,
by the straight line B D (Prob. 13). Raise E F perpendicular to the middle point E, of A C (Prob. 12).
At g, any point in E F, make an angle E g m, equal
to A B D, the half of the angle A B C (Prob. 1).
Through A, draw a line parallel to g m (Prob. 8),
which will meet E F at a point F. Then E F is
the required altitude of the arc. It is obviously
necessary to determine the position of the chord,
since any of the lines forming the triangle A B C
may be assumed as such, and thus affect the altitude. This Problem, as well as the two following,
depends on a property of segments of circles, that
they contain one angle and no other; that is, if lines
are drawn from the extremities of an arc to meet in
any points in that arc, all the angles formed by them
will be equal. In the case of the angle contained
by a semicircle, this has already been pointed out,
and that it contains a right angle; any segment
which is less than a semicircle, contains an obtuse

angle; and in any segment which is greater than a semicircle, the angle contained is acute.

PROBLEM 49.—Three points not in a straight line being given, to find a number of other points in the arc of the circle that will pass through them, without employment of the centre.

Let A, B, and C, be the three given points, and let A C be the chord line. Join A B and B C by straight lines. From A and C, with the same radius, describe arcs *d e* and *f g*, making *d h* equal to *k g*, and *k f* equal to *h e*. Divide *h e* and

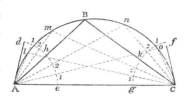

k f each into the same number of equal parts; divide also *d h* and *k g* into the same number of equal parts. From A draw a straight line through the first point of section from *d*, upon the arc *d h*; and from C draw a line through the first part of section from *g*, in the arc *g k*: these lines will intersect each other in a point *l*, which is one of the points required. Proceed in the same manner with the other points of section on the arcs, taking them successively from *d* towards *e*, in the arc *d e*, and from *g* towards *f*, in the arc *g f*; other points in the arc will thus be found, as *m*, *n*, and *o*, and means may be taken for drawing the curve. The most expeditious and accurate method is probably by means of a thin slip of wood. The points having been found, nails may be placed in them, and the slip of wood bent round these; the curve may then be traced on the side of it next to the nails. It may be observed that, if the whole arcs *d e* and *f g* are divided into equal parts, the points of the arc so found will be equidistant.

PROBLEM 50.—An arc of a circle being given, to find a number of points in the supplementary part of the circle, without having the centre.

Let A B C be the given arc. Draw the chord A C, and from A and C draw lines to meet in any point B, of the arc. At the extremities A and C of A C, make angles C A *k* and A C *m*, each equal to A B C; that is, make the arcs *h k* and *l m* each equal to *f g*. Divide the arcs *h k* and *l m*, each into the same number of equal parts. Lines drawn from A, through the points of section in the arc *h k*, in succession, from *k* to *h*; and lines drawn from C through the points of section in the arc *l m*, in succession,

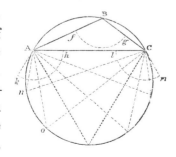

from *l* to *m*, will intersect each other at points *n*, *o*, &c., which are points in the circumference of the circle of which A B C is an arc.

PROBLEM 51.—From a given circle, to cut off a segment that shall contain an angle equal to a given angle.

Let A B D be the given circle, and *a b c* the given angle. At any point B in the circle, draw B C, a tangent to it; and at B make an angle C B *e*, equal to *a b c* (Prob. 1); produce the side B *e* to meet the circum-ference in a point A; then is A D B a segment of a circle that will contain an angle equal to that given. The reason of this is, that the angles formed by a tangent, and a chord drawn to the

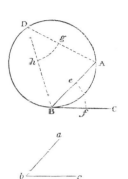

same point in a circle, are equal to those in the alternate segments, into which the circle is divided by the chord; that is, the angles A B C and A D B are equal; and if the tangent C B were produced from B, the angle which it would make with the chord B A would be equal to that which is contained by the segment A B of the circle. This principle has been applied in the last Problem.

PROBLEM 52.—To describe the arc of a circle, of which the chord and the height or versed sine are given.

Let *a b* be the given chord, and *c d* the given height of the arc. Draw A B equal to *a b*, and D C perpendicular to its middle point D, and equal to *d c* (Prob 2). Produce the line also from D in-definitely towards E. Join A C by a straight line, and bisect it (Prob. 12) by a line drawn perpendicular to it, producing it to meet D E in a point F. Then is F C or F A the radius of the circle, of which the re-quired arc is a part; and it may be described from F as a centre. Otherwise—

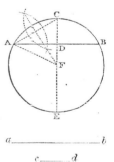

Let *a c* be the given chord, and *d b* the given height of the arc. Draw A C equal to *a c*, and bisect it by a line drawn perpendicular to it, making D B equal to *d b*, and the part D E of indefinite length. Join A and B by a straight line. At the extremity A of A B, make an angle B A *k*, equal to the angle A B E (Prob. 1),

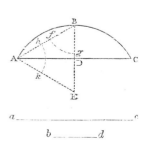

and produce the side A k to meet D E in a point E. From E, with the radius E A or E B, describe the arc A B C, which is that required.

The solution of this problem by number is easily effected, and will be found exceedingly useful. It is evident that half the chord is a mean proportional between the parts into which it divides the diameter. Hence, to find the radius, divide the square of half the given chord by the height of the arc, and to the quotient add the height of the arc; the sum will be the diameter of the circle of which the arc is a part, and the half of this will be the radius; for example, let the given chord be 16 feet, and the height of the arc 4 feet. The square of 8, or half the chord, is 64, which, divided by 4, gives 16; to which, if 4 be added, the diameter will be found to be 20 feet, the half of which, or 10 feet, is the radius sought. It is evident that the length of the chord may also be found, when the parts into which it divides the diameter are known, being the square root of their product, when multiplied together.

PROBLEM 53.—The chord of an arc of a circle being given with the length of the radius of the circle of which it is a part, to find the height of the arc.

Let A C be the chord of a given arc A B C, and A D the given radius. From A and C, with the radius A D, describe intersecting arcs at D, and from D let fall a perpendicular upon A C (Prob. 3), producing it to meet the arc in a point B; then is E B the height of the arc required; or, by number, deduct the square of half the chord from the square of the radius; the square root of the remainder, deducted from the radius, will give the height of the arc; for example, let the given chord be 16 feet, and the given radius 10 feet, the square of 8, or half the chord, is 64, which, deducted from 100, the square of the radius, leaves 36, the square root of which is 6, and represents E D in the diagram. This, deducted from 10, the radius, leaves 4 feet for the height of the arc.

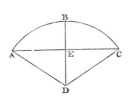

PROBLEM 54.—At a given point in the circumference of a circle, to draw a tangent to the circle.

Let A be a point in the circumference of a circle described about a centre B, at which it is required to draw a tangent to the circle. Join B A by a straight line, and from any convenient point C, with the radius C A, describe an arc of a circle,

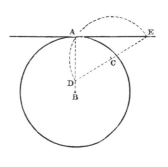

not less then a semicircle, meeting A B in a point D, and passing through A. Draw the diameter D C E; a straight line drawn through A and E is the tangent required. It is plain that the angle E A D is a right angle, being the angle in a semicircle; therefore E A is perpendicular to the radius B A, and is a tangent to the circle.

PROBLEM 55.—Through a given point beyond a circle, to draw a tangent to the circle.

Let E B F be a circle, of which C is the centre, and let A be a point from which it is required to draw a tangent to the circle. Join C A by a straight line, and bisect it in D (Prob. 12). From D as a centre, with the radius D C,

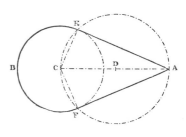

describe a circle cutting that about C at points E and F; straight lines drawn through A E and A F are both of them tangents to the circle. This solution is, likewise, dependent on the construction of a right angle by means of a semicircle.

PROBLEM 56.—A circle and a tangent to it being given, to find the point of contact of the tangent.

Let A B C be the given circle, and let the tangent be drawn from a point D, it is required to find the point of contact. From any point f in the tangent draw a line to the centre E; bisect it in g (Prob. 12), and from g as a centre, with the radius $g f$ or g E, describe a semicircle; this

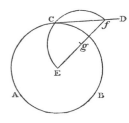

will intersect the circle A B C at a point C, which is the point of contact sought.

The Problem may also be easily solved by drawing a chord of the circle parallel to the tangent (Prob. 8), and then bisecting the arc (Prob. 33) which this chord subtends. The point of bisection is the point of contact required. This method has the advantages of easy application, and that it does not require the centre to be known.

PROBLEM 57.—To draw a tangent to a given circle, or the arc of a circle at a given point in it, without having the centre.

Let A be a point in a given circle, at which it is required to draw a tangent to it without employment of the centre. Draw any chord A B in the circle; bisect the arc A B in e (Prob. 33). From A, with the radius A e, describe an arc meeting the chord A B in f, and produced be-

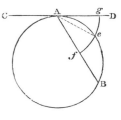

yond *e* until *eg* is equal to *ef*. A straight line C D drawn through A and *g*, will be the tangent required.

PROBLEM 58.—To draw a tangent to a given circle, that shall make an angle with a given straight line equal to a given angle.

Let it be required to draw a tangent to a circle about a centre C, that shall make an angle with a given line A B, equal to a given angle *a e f*. At any point E in A B, make an angle A E F equal to *a e f*, the given angle (Prob. 1). From the centre C, let fall a perpendicular C G upon E F (Prob. 3), cutting the circle in a point H. Through this point draw a straight line I K, either parallel with E F (Prob. 8), or perpendicular to C G (Prob. 2), producing it to meet A B in a point K. This line is a tangent to the circle, and makes an angle A K I with A B, which is equal to *a e f*, as required.

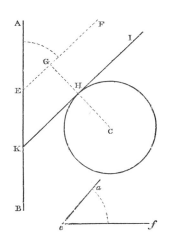

PROBLEM 59.—To describe a circle, with a given radius, that shall touch a given line in a given point.

Let C be a point in a given line A B, and *m n* the given radius. From C raise a perpendicular to A B (Prob. 2), and upon it make C D equal to *m n*. From D as a centre, with the radius D C, describe a circle. This is the required circle, touching the given line in the point C. The Problem has two solutions, since a circle may be described on each side of A B.

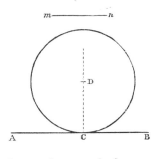

PROBLEM 60.—To describe a circle, with a given radius, that shall touch a given line and pass through a given point.

Let A B be the given line, C the given point, and *m n* the given radius. From C let fall a perpendicular C D upon A B (Prob. 3), and produce it from C until D E is equal to *m n*. Through E draw a straight line E F, parallel to A B (Prob. 8). From C, with a radius equal to *m n*, describe an arc intersecting E F in a point

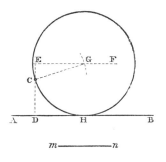

G. The point G is the centre sought; and from it, with a radius equal to G C, which was made equal to *m n*, describe a circle. This will touch the line A B in a point H, and pass through the given point C, as required.

In the case where C D is less than twice the given radius, there are two solutions to the Problem; one on each side of the perpendicular. When C D is equal to twice the given radius, there is only one, and there can evidently be none when it is greater.

PROBLEM 61.—To describe a circle that shall touch a straight line in a given point, and pass through another given point which is not in the line.

Let C be the given point in a straight line A B, and D the given point which is not in the line. From C raise C E, a perpendicular to A B (Prob. 2), and of indefinite length. Join C D by a straight line, and, from its middle point F, raise a perpendicular to it (Prob. 2), which, being produced, will meet C E in a point G. From G as a centre, with the radius G C or G D, which is equal to it, describe a circle. This will touch A B at the point C, and also pass through the given point D, as required.

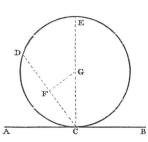

It is plain that if D were a point in the perpendicular to A B at the point C, the straight line joining them is the diameter of the required circle, and the centre sought would be its middle point.

PROBLEM 62.—To describe a circle that shall touch a given straight line, and pass through two given points which are in a line parallel with it.

Let A B be the given straight line, C and D the given points. Join C and D by a straight line, and from its middle point E let fall a perpendicular upon A B (Prob. 2), meeting it in a point F. Join D F by a straight line, and from its middle point G raise a perpendicular to it (Prob. 2), which being produced will meet E F in a point H, which is the centre sought. From H, with a radius equal to H F, H C, or H D, describe a circle; this will touch A B in the point F, and also pass through the given points C and D, as required.

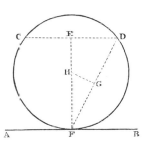

The position of the centre will vary with the distance of the points C and D from each other, and the given line. When the perpendicular distance between them and the line is equal to half their intervening space, then the middle point of the line which joins them is the centre sought. When that distance is greater or less than the half of the distance of the points from each other, the centre will be either between the line which joins the points and the given line, or beyond them.

PROBLEM 63.—To describe two circles, with given radii, that shall touch each other, and also a given straight line.

Let it be required to describe circles with radii respectively equal to C D and E F, which shall touch each other, and also a given line A B. From any point *g* in AB, raise *g k* a perpendicular to it (Prob. 2), and equal to C D, the greater of the two given radii. Upon *g h* measure E F from *g* to *k*, and through *k* draw *k m* parallel to A B

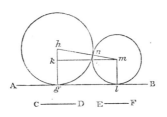

(Prob. 8). From *h*, with a radius equal to the sum of C D and E F, describe an arc of a circle intersecting *k m* in a point *m*. From *h*, with a radius equal to C D, describe a circle; and from *m*, with the radius E F, also describe a circle. These two circles will touch each other, and also the given line A B, as required.

PROBLEM 64.—Two circles being given, one of which is not contained by the other, to draw straight lines that shall be tangents to both.

Let the given circles be described about centres A and B, of which that about A is the greater. Draw any radius A H of the greater circle, and

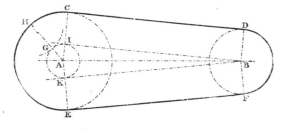

upon it from H, make H G equal to B D, the radius of the lesser. From centre A, with the radius A G, describe a circle. From B, draw tangents B I and B K to this circle (Prob. 55), and from A, draw radii through the points I and K, to meet the greater circle in points C and E. Through C and E draw lines parallel to I B and K B, respectively (Prob. 8). These lines will touch the circle about B, in points D and F, and they will be tangents to both the circles as required. Otherwise—

Let the given circles be described about centres A and B, of which that about A is the greater. Through A and B draw a straight line, producing it indefinitely beyond the lesser circle. From the

centre A, draw any radius A D, and from B, draw a radius B E, parallel to A D (Prob. 8), and on the same side of the line A B. Through D and E

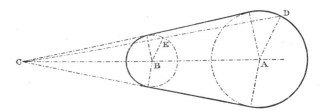

draw a line extending it to meet the production of A B in a point C. From C draw tangents to the circle about B (Prob. 55), which, being extended, will also be tangents to that about A, as required.

PROBLEM 65.—Two diverging lines being given, to describe a circle that shall touch them both, and one of them at a given point.

Let B E and B F be two given lines divergent from a point B, and let A be a given point in one of them, B E. Upon B F make B C equal to B A. From A, raise a perpendicular to B E (Prob. 2), and from C a perpendicular to B F; these, being produced,

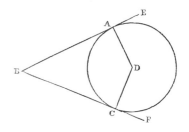

will intersect each other at a point D. From D as a centre, with the radius D A or D C, describe a circle. This will touch each of the lines and B E at the given point A. When the point B is not accessible, points of equal distance from it may be determined by Prob. 46, and the construction completed as above; or the line which bisects the angle drawn, and the point where it intersects the perpendicular is the centre sought.

PROBLEM 66.—To describe a circle with a given radius that shall touch two given straight lines which are not parallel.

Let *m n* be a given radius, with which it is required to describe a circle that shall touch two given lines A B and C D which are not parallel. At any point E in C D, raise E F perpendicular to it (Prob. 2), and equal to *m n*; through F draw G H parallel to C D (Prob. 8). At any point I in A B raise I K perpendicular to it, and also equal to *m n*; and through K draw L M parallel to A B. The two lines G H and L M will intersect each other in

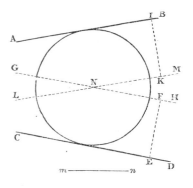

a point N. From this point, with the radius mn, describe a circle; this will touch the given lines, as required.

PROBLEM 67.—To describe a circle that shall touch three given straight lines, one of which is not parallel with the other two.

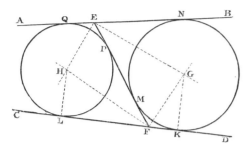

Let AB, CD, and EF, be the three given lines. Bisect each of the angles DFE and BEF by straight lines (Prob. 13), which, being produced, will intersect each other in a point G. From G let fall a perpendicular GK upon CD (Prob. 3), and from G, with the radius GK, describe a circle; this will touch each of the given lines at points K, M, and N, respectively. A second circle may be described which also fulfils the given conditions. Bisect each of the angles CFE and AEF (Prob. 13), by lines which, produced, will intersect each other at a point H; let fall HL perpendicular to CD (Prob. 3), and from H, with the radius HL, describe a circle; this will also touch each of the lines at points L, P, and Q, respectively.

PROBLEM 68.—To describe a circle, with a given radius, that shall touch a given circle at a given point.

Let ab be the given radius, and, first, let it be required to touch a given circle, described about a centre C internally, at a point A. Draw the radius C A, and from A make A B equal to ab. From B, with the radius ab, describe a circle; this will touch that about C internally at the point A as required. Next, let it be required to touch a given circle described about a centre C externally, at a point B. Draw the radius C B, and produce it beyond the circle, until B A is equal to ab. From A, with the radius A B, describe a circle; this will touch that about C externally, at the point B, as required. Should it be required to find the point of contact of two circles that touch each other, it must be recollected that the straight line which passes through their centres will also pass through the point of contact, or will do so when produced, if necessary.

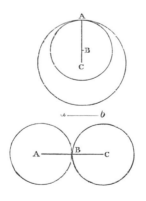

PROBLEM 69.—To describe a circle with a given radius, to be touched externally by two given circles.

Let ab be the given radius, and let the given circles be described about centres C and D, with radii C E and D F, respectively. Produce ab from b, until bf is equal to D F. From D as a centre, with a radius equal to af, describe an arc of a circle towards G. From b, upon bf, make bc equal to C E; and from C, with a radius equal to ac, describe an arc intersecting the first at a point G. From G as a centre, with the radius ab, describe a circle; this will be touched externally by the given circles, as required.

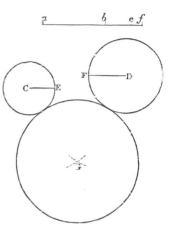

If it is required that the circle to be described should be touched internally by the circles, the difference between each of the radii of the given circles and the radius given, must be employed for finding the centre. By combining these means, the circle may be described so as to be touched externally by one, and internally by the other, given circle. The construction will show when the Problem becomes impossible, that is, when the conditions cannot be fulfilled with the things given.

PROBLEM 70.—To describe a circle about a given triangle.

Let A B C be the given triangle. Draw straight lines E G and F H perpendicular to the middle points E and F of any two of the sides, as A B and A C of the triangle (Prob. 12). These, being produced, will intersect each other at a point K. From K as a centre, with a radius K A, K B, or K C, equal to the distance between it and any

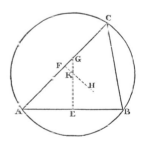

of the angles of the triangle, describe a circle. This will circumscribe the triangle, as required. This problem evidently reduces itself into describing a circle through three points which are not in a straight line. It must be observed, that the centre will be either within or without the figure, according as the triangle is acute, or obtuse angled. When it is right angled, the centre is the middle point of the hypothenuse, or that side which is opposite to the right angle.

PROBLEM 71.—To inscribe a circle in a given triangle.

Let A B C be the given triangle. Bisect any two of the angles, as B A C, and B C A, by straight lines (Prob. 13), which, being produced, will intersect each other in a point D. From D let fall a perpendicular (Prob. 3), upon any one of the sides, as A C, meeting it in a point E. From D as a centre, with the radius D E, describe a circle. This will touch each of the sides of the triangle, and they will be tangents to it.

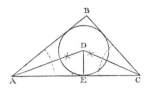

PROBLEM 72.—To describe a circle within three given lines, which would form a triangle, if produced to inaccessible points.

Let A B, D C, and E F, be the given lines, and let the vertical angle of the triangle which they would form, be contained by C D and F E. Draw the straight line *m n*, which would bisect the angle formed by the production of D C and B A (Prob. 47); also *r n*, to bisect that formed by A B and E F. These will intersect each other at a point *n*. From *n* let fall a perpendicular *n s* on one of the sides, as A B (Prob. 3), and from *n*, with the radius *n s*, describe a circle. This will touch each of the given lines, and be inscribed within them, as required.

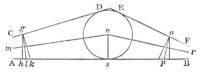

PROBLEM 73.—To divide the circumference of a circle into five and ten equal parts, and to inscribe a regular pentagon or decagon.

Let the given circle be described about a centre *o*. Draw the diameters A C and B D at right angles to one another (Prob. 2). Bisect the radius A *o* in E (Prob. 12), and from E, with the radius E B, describe an arc, to meet A C in F. The distance B F is the chord of the fifth part of the circumference. It is to be measured, therefore, from B to G, and H, &c., and the points of section being connected successively by straight lines, the inscribed pentagon will be produced. Bisect the arc H B in *k* (Prob. 33), then is B *k*, or H *k*, the tenth part of the circumference, and it may be measured upon it for the production of the inscribed decagon, if required. The distance *o* F, is also the chord of the tenth part of the circumference, and may be employed in the construction.

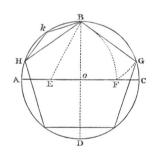

PROBLEM 74.—Upon a given straight line, to construct a regular decagon.

Let A B be the given line. Bisect it in C (Prob. 12), and from B raise B D perpendicular to it (Prob. 5), and equal to A B. Produce A B from B, until C E is equal to C D. From A and B as centres, with the radius A E, describe intersecting arcs at F; and from F, with the same radius, describe a circle. This circle will circumscribe a regular decagon, of which the side is equal to A B. Upon its circumference, therefore, measure A B from B to G, G to H, &c.; connect the successive points of section by straight lines, and the figure required will be produced.

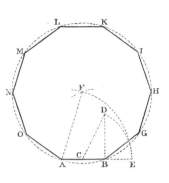

PROBLEM 75.—Upon a given straight line, to construct a regular pentagon.

Let A B be the given line. From B, one of its extremities, raise B *c* perpendicular to it (Prob. 5), and equal to the half of A B. Through A and *c* draw a straight line, and produce it beyond *c*, until *c d* is equal to *c* B. From A and B as centres, with a radius equal to the distance B *d*, describe arcs intersecting each other at *e*. From *e*, with the radius *e* A or *e* B, describe a circle. This will circumscribe a pentagon whose side is equal to A B. Upon its circumference measure A B, from B to F, F to G, G to H. Connect the successive points of section by straight lines, and the figure A B F G H will be the pentagon required.

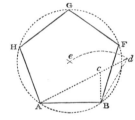

PROBLEM 76.—To divide the circumference of a given circle into six and twelve equal parts, and to inscribe an equilateral triangle, a regular hexagon or six-sided figure, and a dodecagon or regular twelve-sided figure.

Let the given circle be described about a centre B. Draw any radius B A, and from A, with the same radius, describe an arc, meeting the circumference in points C and D. Join C D by a straight line; and from C, with the radius C D, describe an arc intersecting the circumference in E; join C E and D E by

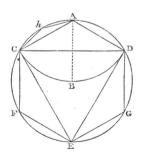

straight lines; then is C D E the inscribed equilateral triangle required. From C and D, with a radius equal to A B, describe arcs intersecting the circumference in points F and G; it will thus be divided into six equal parts at the points A, D, G, E, F, and C. Straight lines drawn between these points will form the inscribed hexagon. Bisect each of the arcs as A C in *h*, and join the points A *h*, *h* C, &c.; each of these is the twelfth part of the circumference, and may be measured upon it for the completion of the dodecagon if required.

PROBLEM 77.—To divide the circumference of a given circle into twelve equal parts, and to inscribe within it a regular dodecagon or twelve-sided figure.

Let the given circle be described about a centre C. Draw two diameters, A B and C D, at right angles to one another (Prob. 2). From A, with the radius A C of the circle, describe arcs intersecting the circumference in points F and G; from D, at I and H; from B, at K and L; and from E, at

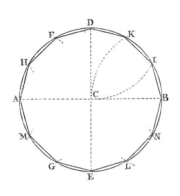

M and N. These, with the points A, B, E, and D, divide the circumference into twelve equal parts. To form the inscribed dodecagon, join the successive points of section, as D K, K I, I B, &c., by straight lines, and it will be produced, as required.

In Problem 14, the same process was employed for the bisection of a right angle, and the principle was then explained. It is plain, that as the circumference of a circle measures four right angles, or all the angles about any point, if each of these is divided into three equal parts, the whole circumference will be divided into twelve parts, all of which are equal.

PROBLEM 78.—Upon a given straight line to construct a regular hexagon.

Let A B be the given line. From A and B as centres, with the radius A B, describe arcs intersecting each other in C. From C, with the radius C A, describe a circle. This is the circle that may be circumscribed about a hexagon, whose side is equal to A B. Upon its circumference measure A B from B to D, D to E, E to F, F to G, and G to A. Join the successive points of section thus found by straight lines. Then is A B D E F G the hexagon required.

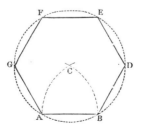

PROBLEM 79.—Upon a given line to construct a regular dodecagon.

Let A B be the given line. Raise C D perpendicular to the middle point C of A B, and of indefinite length (Prob. 12). From B, with the radius B A, describe an arc intersecting C D in a point E. From E, upon E D, make E F equal to E A or E B or A B. From F, with the radius F B or F A, describe a circle. This circle will circumscribe a dodecagon, whose side is equal to A B. Upon its circumference measure A B from B to G, G to H, H to I, &c. The successive points of section being joined by straight lines, the required dodecagon is completed.

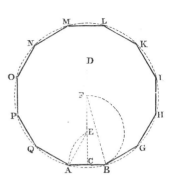

PROBLEM 80.—Within a given square, to inscribe the greatest possible regular octagon.

Let A B C D be the given square. Draw the diagonals A C and B D, intersecting each other at the point *e*. From each of the angles A, B, C, and D, with a radius equal to *e* D, the half of one of the diagonals, describe arcs of circles, meeting each of the sides of the square in points *g n*, *f k*, *h m*, *l o*. Join the points *f o*, *g h*, *k l*, *m n* by straight lines, and the required octagon will be produced.

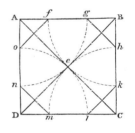

PROBLEM 81.—Upon a given straight line, to construct a regular octagon.

Let A B be the given straight line. Produce A B both ways, towards *k* and *l*. From the extremities A and B of the given line, raise A E and B F perpendicular to it (Prob. 5), and of indefinite length. Bisect each of the angles E A *k* and F B *l* (Prob. 13) by straight lines, A H and B C, which are to be produced until each of them is equal to A B. From H and C draw lines H G and C D, parallel to A F and B E (Prob. 8), and equal to A B. From G and D, with a radius equal to A B, describe arcs intersecting A E and B F in points E and F, respectively. Join G E, E F, and F D, by straight lines; then is A B C D E F G H a regular octagon constructed upon A B, as required.

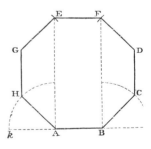

PROBLEM 82.—To divide the circumference of a circle into four and eight equal parts, and to inscribe within it a square, and regular octagon.

Let the given circle be described about the centre M. Draw any diameter A C, and perpendicular to it draw the diameter B D (Prob. 2); the circumference is thus divided into four equal parts, at the points A, B, C, and D. Join A B, B C, C D, and D A by straight lines; Then is A B C D a square inscribed within the circle. Bisect each of the quadrants A B, B C, &c., in points e, f, g, and h, respectively (Prob. 33); these points, with the former, will divide the circumference into eight equal parts. Join A e, e B, B f, &c., by straight lines; then A e B f C g D h is a regular octagon, and it is inscribed within the circle, as required.

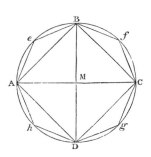

PROBLEM 83.—About a given circle, to describe a square, and a regular octagon.

Let A C B D be the given circle. Draw two diameters, A B and C D, at right angles to one another (Prob. 2). At the points A, B, C, and D, draw tangents to the circle (Prob. 54), and produce them both ways to meet two and two in points E, F, G, and H. Then E F G H is a square circumscribing the circle. Draw the diagonals E G and F H, and, at the points where these intersect the circumference of the circle, draw tangents to it, as h k, &c. (Prob. 54), to meet the sides of the square. These, with the intercepted portions of the sides of the square, will form a regular octagon circumscribing the circle, as required.

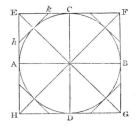

PROBLEM 84.—About any given regular polygon, to circumscribe a circle.

Let A B C D E be the given regular polygon. Bisect any two of the angles, as E A B and C B A, by straight lines (Prob. 13); these, if produced, will intersect each other at a point F. From F, with the radius F A, or the distance to any of the angular points, describe a circle. This will circumscribe the figure, as required. When the number of the sides of the polygon is even, the line

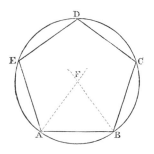

which joins two opposite angles is the diameter of the circle which will circumscribe it, and its middle point will be the centre required.

PROBLEM 85.—Within a given regular polygon, to inscribe a circle.

Let e f g h k be a given regular pentagon, within which it is required to inscribe a circle. Draw straight lines perpendicular (Prob. 12) to the middle points C and D of two of the sides, as k h and k e, respectively. These, being produced, will intersect each other at a point B. From B as a centre, with a radius B C or B D, describe a circle; this will be inscribed within the figure, or will touch each of its sides, as required.

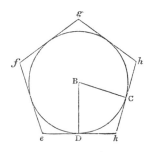

In this Problem, when the number of sides of the polygon is even, the line which joins the middle points of two parallel sides is the diameter of the circle, which may be inscribed in the figure; and its middle point is the centre sought.

The construction of the regular polygons is generally effected by the division of the circumference of the circle into equal parts, and connecting the successive points of section by straight lines. The division of the circle into *all* numbers of equal parts, however, is not possible by geometric methods; but certain numbers are derived from its primary geometric divisions, which are two, five, or ten, and six equal parts: and from these others are derived.

From the foregoing geometric divisions of the circumference of the circle, may be derived its partition into greater numbers of parts by the continued bisection of the arcs so found, and their differences, and so to construct the inscribed polygon. Hence, from the hexagon, by continued bisection, will arise regular polygons of 12, 24, 48, 96, &c. sides; from the square, those of 8, 16, 32, 64, &c. sides; from the pentagon and decagon, those of 20, 40, 80, 160, &c. sides. The differences of these systems also afford arcs which divide the circumference equally—that between the hexagon and decagon giving rise to its division into 15 parts; and hence, polygons of 30, 60, 120, &c. sides, may be constructed, and so on.

The division of the circumference of the circle into seven, nine, eleven, and other parts, cannot be effected geometrically, and the corresponding figures inscribed; approximations must, therefore, be had recourse to, and some of these afford results which do not differ much from the truth.

PROBLEM 86.—To divide the circumference of a circle approximately into seven equal parts, and to inscribe within it a heptagon.

Let the given circle be described about a centre A, with a radius A B. Draw the chord B C equal to A B, the radius of the circle. From A let fall A K perpendicular to B C, meeting it in K (Prob. 3). This line, A K, is nearly equal to the chord of the seventh part of the circumference of the circle. Measure it, therefore, upon the circumference from any point B to D, D to E, &c. Join the successive points of section by straight lines. Then is B D E F G H I a heptagon inscribed within the circle.

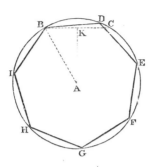

PROBLEM 87.—To divide the circumference of a given circle approximately into nine equal parts, and to inscribe within it a nonagon.

Let the given circle be described about a centre A. Draw a diameter B C, and from A a radius A D, perpendicular to it (Prob. 2). Bisect A D in E (Prob. 12). From any convenient point F in the diameter, and on the same side with A D, raise F G perpendicular to it, of indefinite length (Prob. 2). Upon F G measure five equal parts F 1, 2, 3, &c. Divide their sum F 5, into three equal parts (Prob. 24) F a, a b, b 5. Next, bisect the space b 3 in H (Prob. 12). Draw a straight line through 5, and the point E in A D, to meet the diameter B C, or its production, if necessary, in a point K; and between K and H draw a straight line. This will intersect A D at a point L. Then is D L very nearly the chord of the ninth part of the circumference of the circle. Measure D L, therefore, upon it from any point D to M, M to N, &c.; connect the successive points of section by straight lines, and D M N O P Q R S T will be a nonagon inscribed in the given circle. This is a very close approximation.

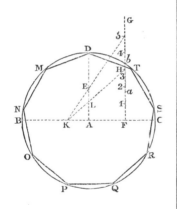

PROBLEM 88.—To divide the circumference of a given circle approximately into eleven equal parts, and to inscribe within it an undecagon.

Let the given circle be described about a centre A. Draw a radius A B of the circle. Bisect it in C (Prob. 12); bisect C B in D, C D in E, and

CE in F. Then is AF the chord of the eleventh part of the circumference of the circle very nearly. From any point B in it, measure A F, from B to G, G to H, &c., connect the successive points of section by straight lines, and B G H I K L M N O P Q will be the inscribed undecagon.

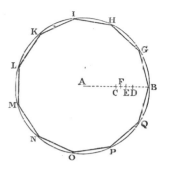

PROBLEM 89.—A regular polygon being given, to construct another having the same perimeter, but double the number of sides.

Let the given polygon be a regular pentagon, of which the side is A B. Bisect two of the adjacent angles of the figure, as those at A and B (Prob. 13), by straight lines, which, being produced, will meet in a point C, and form a triangle A B C. Upon a line D E, equal in length to the half of A B, construct (Prob. 23) a triangle D F E, similar to the triangle A B C. Erect a perpendicular from the middle of D E, and produce it beyond F to G, until F G is equal to F D or F E. From G, with a radius G D or G E, describe a circle.

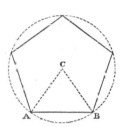

This is the circle which will circumscribe a decagon whose side is equal to D E. Upon its circumference measure D E as often as it will contain it, and construct the decagon, which will be that required.

PROBLEM 90.—A regular polygon being given, to construct another having the same perimeter, but any different number of sides.

Let the given polygon be a regular hexagon whose side is A B, and let it be required to construct a regular octagon having an equal perimeter. Divide A B into eight equal parts (Prob. 24). Draw a line D E equal to A C, which contains six of these parts, and upon it construct (Prob. 81) an octagon, which will be that required. In this case the polygon required has a greater number of sides than that given. Let it be reversed, or let the octagon be given whose side is D E. Divide D E into six equal

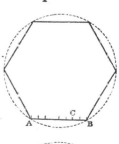

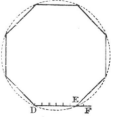

parts, and produce it from E to F, until E F is equal to two of them. Draw A B equal to D F, and upon it construct a hexagon (Prob. 78), which will be that required. In the same manner, whatever difference there may be in the number of sides, always divide the side of the given polygon into the same number of equal parts as there are sides required in the new figure, adding to, or deducting from it, according to the difference.

PROBLEM 91.—On a given straight line, to construct a polygon of any number of sides.

Let A B be the given line, and let it be required to construct a regular heptagon upon it. Produce A B from B indefinitely, and from B as a centre, with any radius as B A, describe a semicircle. Divide the semicircle into seven equal parts (Prob. 86), and draw B D 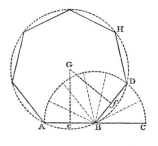 through the second division from C, making it equal to B A. B A and B D are two sides of the required figure. Bisect each of them respectively in e and f, and raise perpendiculars at these points, which, being produced, will meet in a point G. From G, with the radius G A, describe a circle, upon the circumference of which measure A B from D to H, &c.; join the points of section by straight lines, and the required heptagon will be produced. In this manner, a polygon of any number of sides may be produced, always dividing the semicircle into the required number of sides, and drawing a line to the second division, in order to find the position of a second side. Otherwise—

Let A B be a given line, on which it is required to construct a pentagon. Produce A B indefinitely from B, and from B as a centre, with any radius as B A, describe a semicircle upon A C. Divide the semicircle into five equal parts (Prob. 73). From 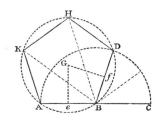 B draw a straight line B D, through the second of these divisions from C, which will be equal to B A. Through the remaining points of section draw lines B H and B K of indefinite length; and from D and A, with the radius A B, describe arcs intersecting them at points H and K. Join D H, H K, and K A, by straight lines, and the required pentagon will be produced.

The principle of the construction is, that the exterior angle, as D B C of the polygon, is equal to the angle at the centre. The methods are very convenient occasionally, as the exterior angle may be marked by any of the instruments usually employed in the measurement of angles; and the particular angle for each polygon is easily ascertained by calculation, being four right angles, or 360° divided by the number of sides. For convenience, the following table exhibits the angles of the first ten polygons :—

No. of Sides.	Name of Polygon.	Angle at Centre.	Angle of Polygon.	Angle at base of elem. triangle.
3	Trigon or triangle ...	120°	60°	30°
4	Tetragon or square ...	90	90	45
5	Pentagon..............	72	108	54
6	Hexagon	60	120	60
7	Heptagon..............	$51\frac{3}{7}$	$128\frac{4}{7}$	$64\frac{2}{7}$
8	Octagon	45	135	$67\frac{1}{2}$
9	Nonagon	40	140	70
10	Decagon	36	144	72
11	Undecagon	$32\frac{8}{11}$	$147\frac{3}{11}$	$73\frac{7}{11}$
12	Dodecagon	30	150	75

The angle of the polygon, or that formed by the meeting of two of its sides, is equal to the difference between 180° and the angle at the centre; for example, the angle at the centre of the regular octagon is 45°, which, subtracted from 180°, leaves 135° for the angle of the polygon.

The triangle B C D, in the following problem, is called the elementary triangle of the polygon; that is, any regular polygon may be decomposed into as many identical elementary triangles as the figure has sides. The angle at B is that at the centre of the polygon; those at the base are equal each to the half of the angle of the polygon; for example, in the octagon, the angles at the base of the elementary triangle corresponding with C and D, are each of them the half of 135° or $67\frac{1}{2}$°. It is plain that polygons may be constructed by means of their elementary triangles, a method that will be very serviceable to the cabinet-maker.

The following Problem shows a convenient method of employing the above table :—

PROBLEM 92.—To inscribe any regular polygon in a given circle, by means of the angle at the centre.

Let A be a given circle, within which let it be required to inscribe a regular hexagon. At B, the centre of the circle, by means of any instrument employed in the measurement of angles, mark an angle of 60°, which is that of the hexagon. Pro- 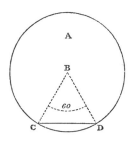 duce the sides containing it, until they meet the circumference of the circle in points C and D. The chord of the arc C D is that of the sixth part of the circumference of the circle, and may be measured upon it for the construction of the polygon.

PROBLEM 93.—Within a given circle, to inscribe a regular polygon of any number of sides.

Let A D B F be the given circle, within which let it be required to inscribe a regular pentagon. Draw the diameter A B, and divide it into five equal parts (Prob. 24). From the middle point *e* of A B, raise a perpendicular (Prob. 2), and produce it beyond the circumference of the circle, until F C is equal to three-fourths of the radius *e* F.

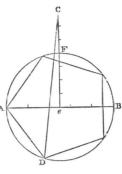

Draw a straight line C D through the second division from the extremity A, and meeting the circle in D. The chord of the arc A D will be nearly the length of the side of the inscribed pentagon, and may be employed accordingly. Otherwise—

Let A E F B *g* be the given circle, within which it is required to inscribe a hexagon. Draw the diameter A B. From the middle point C of A B, raise a perpendicular to it (Prob. 2), producing it beyond the circle, until *g* D is equal to three-fourths of the radius C *g* of the circle. Divide the radius C A, into six equal parts (Prob. 24), and from D draw a line D E,

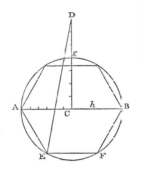

through the second division from C, producing it to meet the circumference in a point E. Draw E F parallel to the diameter A B, meeting the circle in F. E F is the length of one of the sides, and being applied successively to the circumference of the circle, the required polygon will be produced.

In a like manner, polygons of any numbers of sides may be inscribed within given circles, always dividing the diameter or the radius into a number of equal parts, corresponding with the number of sides of the required polygon. It must be recollected that these methods are only approximations.

The solution of this general problem for the inscription of polygons has given rise to many very beautiful and ingenious constructions, but these are all liable to the same objection, namely, that they are not strictly correct, or are not so in all cases, although they may approach sufficiently near the truth to be very useful general rules. Those given will be found to be very available in practice, and have the advantage of being exceedingly simple; but, where possible, it is always better to employ the true geometrical construction, as given in the previous problems, for each of the polygons up to twelve sides.

The following table exhibits the relations of the side of any of the first ten polygons, with the radius of the circumscribing circle, each in its turn being taken as unity:—

No. of Sides.	Length of Radius when the Side is 1.	Length of the Side when the Radius is 1.
3	·57735	1·73205
4	·70710	1·41421
5	·85065	1·17557
6	1·00000	1·00000
7	1·15237	·86777
8	1·30657	·76536
9	1·46190	·68404
10	1·61804	·61803
11	1·77470	·56347
12	1·93188	·51763

By the above table, it is easy to find either the length of the radius of the circumscribing circle, the side of the polygon being given, or, the side of the polygon, the radius of the circumscribing circle being given; the question being simply one of finding a fourth proportional to three given terms. In the first case, let the given side of a pentagon be 3, then 1 : ·85065 :: 3 : 2·55195 the length of the radius required. In the second case, let the given radius of a circle circumscribing a pentagon be 2·55195, then 1 : 1·17557 :: 2·55195 : 3, the side of the pentagon required.

Three of the polygons, only, are so constituted, that by the adaptation of their sides and angles to each other, the repetition of the same figure about a point in a plain surface will completely fill the space about it. These are the equilateral triangle, the square, and the hexagon. The interior triangle of an equilateral triangle is one-third of two right angles; consequently, six such triangles have their vertices in the same point. The angle of a square is a right angle, and four squares may be arranged about a point; and that of the hexagon being two-thirds of two right angles, three hexagons will thus meet in the same point. But although these are the only three regular polygons that will alone fill up the space about a point, they may be combined among themselves, and with others, so as to do so; the necessary condition being, that the sum of the angles of the different figures so meeting shall be equal to four right angles. The following is a list of all the various combinations that fulfil this condition:—

1. When three polygons are combined, there are ten arrangements, and the number of sides must be 3,7,42; 3,8,24; 3,9,18; 3,10,15; 3,12,12; 4,5,20; 4,6,12; 4,8,8; 5,5,10; and 6,6,6.

2. When four polygons are combined, there are four arrangements, and the number of sides must be 3,3,4,12; 3,3,6,6; 3,4,4,6; and 4,4,4,4.

3. When five polygons are combined, there are two arrangements, and the number of sides must be 3,3,3,4,4; and 3,3,3,3,6.

4. And when six polygons are combined, there is only one arrangement, and they must be all equilateral triangles. All these may be placed without regard to order, but their regular combination gives rise to many beautiful arrangements, which are of great importance in ornamentation.

PROBLEM 94.—To cover a surface with equilateral triangles.

Construct an equilateral triangle A B C (Prob. 15), in order to have two lines A C and B C divergent at an angle of 60°.

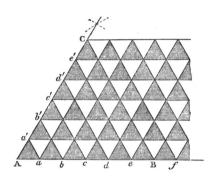

Upon these lines measure equal parts A a, a b, &c., upon A B; and A a', a' b' &c., upon A C; each equal to the side of the equilateral triangle that is to be employed. From the points a, b, &c., upon A B, draw lines parallel to A C (Prob. 8), and from the points a', b', &c., in A C, draw lines parallel to A B. Join a' a, b' b, &c., by straight lines, and the surface will be divided into a number of equilateral triangles, as A a a', &c., which completely cover it.

PROBLEM 95.—To cover a surface with regular hexagons.

Draw two straight lines, A B and A C, divergent from A, and making an angle C A B, with one another, equal to 60° (Prob. 15).

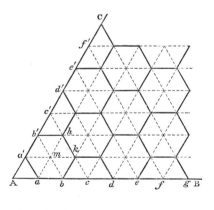

Upon each of these, measure the side of the hexagon from A to a, a to b, &c., upon A B, and from A to a', a' to b', &c., upon A C; divide the surface into equilateral triangles as in the last problem. It will easily be seen, that about each point, as m, there are six equilateral triangles, which together form a hexagon, as a b k h b' a', of which the diagonals a h, b b', and a' k, may be obliterated. By proceeding in the same manner with the several groups of triangles, the surface will be left covered with regular hexagons, as required.

PROBLEM 96.—To cover a surface with regular hexagons and equilateral triangles.

Let the lines of construction be drawn as in Prob. 15, and the surface divided into equilateral

triangles, whose sides are equal to the sides of the required figures. Three groups of the triangles which form hexagons, connected two and two, as at d, e, and f, are to be employed for the hexagonal figures, and the remaining triangle will fill up the intervening space. In this case, the

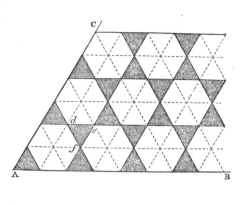

space about a point is filled up by two hexagons and two equilateral triangles.

PROBLEM 97.—To cover a space with lozenges, arranged in groups of three.

Draw two straight lines A B and A C, forming an angle C A B, equal to 60°. divide the space, as in Prob. 94, into equilateral triangles, and arrange them into hexagonal groups, divide each hexagon, as a b c d e f, into lozenges, by means of the radii g b, g d, and g f, drawing the radii

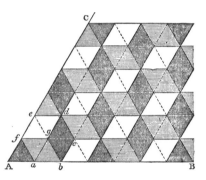

in each polygon parallel with those in the others. The surface will thus be divided as required.

A kind of polygon that is much used in ornament, is a figure in which the angles are alternately salient, and re-entrant; this produces a very beautiful star-formed figure. The character of such polygons varies with the number of the angles; they are generally derived from the regular polygons, and are constructed by the same means, that is, by the division of the circumference of a circle. For this purpose, instead of connecting the successive points of section on the circumference, the alternate points are joined, or lines are drawn between those that are at any equal interval; always passing over two, or three, or more points, according to the number in the polygon, and the character of the star that it is desired to produce.

PROBLEM 98.—To cover a surface with regular octagons and squares.

Draw two straight lines A B and A C at right angles to one another (Prob. 5). Upon each, measure the breadth of the octagon to be employed, from A to d, d to e, &c., upon A B; and from A to d', d' to e, &c., upon A C. From d', e', and f' draw lines parallel to A B (Prob. 8), and from d, e, f, and g, draw lines parallel to A C. The surface is thus divided into squares. Draw A F diagonally through the squares. Take Ah, the half of the diagonal of

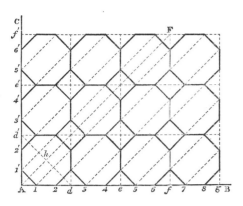

one of the squares, and from d, e, f, and g upon A B, and d', e', and f' upon A C, measure the distance on each side of them, upon the respective lines A B and A C, the points, 1.1′, 2.2′, 3.3′, &c., will thus be found; from each of these points draw lines parallel to A F (Prob. 8) the diagonal of a series of the squares; these will intersect the lines forming the squares, and indicate the angles of the octagonal figures, which must be connected by straight lines where necessary, and it will be found, that the surface is covered with squares and octagons, as required.

PROBLEM 99.—To construct regular star-formed polygons.

Let it be required to construct all the regular star-formed polygons of nine points. Let the circumference of a circle be divided into nine equal parts, at points 1, 2, 3, &c. (Prob. 87.) First, join the alternate points of section, as 1 3, 3 5, &c., until all the points are connected, and the line has returned again to the first point. This

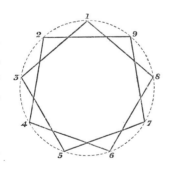

will produce the figure whose points contain the greatest angle.

Next, in joining the points, draw lines between the first and fourth points, thus passing over two, 4 and 7, 7 and 1. In this way an equilateral triangle is produced. By commencing again with 2, and afterwards with 3, and proceeding in the same manner, two other triangles will result, which combined, will produce the figure.

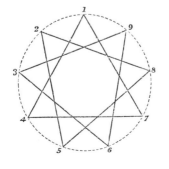

Lastly, join the first and the fifth points; the

fifth and the ninth, the ninth and the fourth, and so on, passing three points; when the line has returned again to the first point, the figure will be completed. There are thus three star-formed polygons derived from the nonagon, and these are all that it is possible to construct from it.

The number of these figures that can be constructed from any regular polygon, is the half of the number of its sides diminished by three, when the number is odd; and when the number is even, it is half of the number of sides diminished by four. In the above case, the nonagon was used. If nine is diminished by three, there remains six, the half of which is three, the number produced. It is to be observed that it is not necessary that the star should be inscribed within the circle, or the polygon of construction; the same forms will be produced by drawing the lines beyond the points, until they meet, the only difference being, that the figures which result will be much larger than in the former case. These star-formed polygons are of great service in the construction of inlaid work of all kinds, as floors, &c., affording appropriate forms for the purpose. In the general application of the principle to ornament, it may also be observed, that the connection of the points may be effected by curved lines, as circles, or by regularly and systematically mixed lines; by this means an infinite variety of forms may be produced, which are well adapted for frets, and so forth. Many of the beautiful, and apparently complicated figures, so frequently employed in Moorish ornament, are constructed upon this simple principle, which affords unlimited scope for ingenuity in the designer, and the display of his art in the tasteful division and filling up of spaces that may be appropriately occupied by such ornament.

The construction of similar figures is probably one of the most familiar forms under which geometry presents itself, being the principle upon which all objects are repeated or imitated, as in models, drawings, plans, &c.; or where any object is represented, these being merely similar figures constructed upon a certain scale or proportion.

In the case of similar triangles (Prob. 23), it has been explained, that certain of the parts being equal, the whole figures were similar, whether they were equal or not. It is plain that, as any polygonal figure may be divided into a number of triangles, according to the number of its sides, and each of these may be repeated, with their corresponding sides proportionally greater or less, that by dividing such a figure into its component triangles, and reconstructing these, commencing with a side either equal or proportional, and placing them in the same relation with one another, the group of triangles will present a form which is either equal to, or greater or less than the original figure, according as the corresponding sides have been made equal or proportional. To this principle of similar triangles is reducible the system of construction, adopted in making one figure similar to another.

PROBLEM 100.—To make a figure identical with a given rectilineal figure.

Let *a b c d e f* be the given rectilineal figure. Divide the figure into its component triangles, that is, draw the diagonals *d f*, *c f*, and *a c*. Draw a straight line AF equal to *a f* for the corresponding side, and upon it construct a triangle A C F, equal to *a c f* (Prob. 23). Upon A C construct a triangle A B C, equal to *a b c*; upon C F a triangle

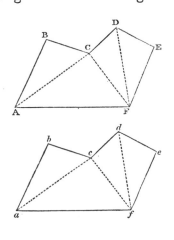

C D F, equal to *c d f*; and upon D F a triangle D E F, equal to *d e f*. Then is the whole figure A B C D E F identical with *a b c d e f*, as required. This is evident; for each of the triangles successively constructed being identical with those of the given figure, and with corresponding sides and angles, the whole, collectively, must be so also.

PROBLEM 101.—To make a figure similar to a given rectilineal figure, upon a straight line which is to correspond to a side indicated.

Let *a b c d e* be the given figure, and let A E be the given line which is to correspond to *a e* in the figure. Divide the given figure into its component triangles, by drawing the diagonals *b e* and *b d*. Upon A E construct a triangle A E B, similar to *a e b* (Prob. 23); upon E B a triangle E D B, similar to *e d b*; and upon B D a triangle B C D, similar to *b c d*. Then is the whole figure A B C D E similar to the given figure *a b c d e*.

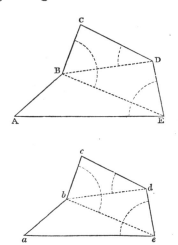

PROBLEM 102.—To make a figure similar to a given rectilineal figure, upon a given line which is parallel to one of the sides, and is to correspond with that side in the figure.

Let *a b c d e f* be the given figure, and let A B be the given line which is parallel to, and is to correspond with, the side *a b* in the figure. Through the extremities A and *a* draw a line, extending it within the figure, and through B and *b* draw a line to meet it in a point *g*.

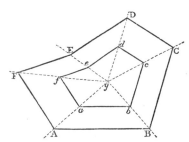

From this point *g* draw lines through each of the other angles, *c, d, e,* and *f,* of the figure, extending them beyond it indefinitely. From B draw a line B C parallel to *b c* (Prob. 8), meeting the production of *g c* in a point C. From C draw a line C D parallel to *c d*, meeting the production of *g d* in D. In the same manner draw D E parallel to *d e*, E F to *e f*, and join F A, which is parallel to *f a*. Then is A B C D E F similar to the given figure *a b c d e f*.

PROBLEM 103.—To make a figure similar to a given rectilineal figure, by means of projections from a diagonal.

Let *b c d e a f g* be the given figure. Draw within the figure the greatest diagonal possible, *a b*; and from each of the other angles let fall perpendiculars upon it (Prob. 3), as *c h, d k, e l, f m,* and *g n*. Draw A B a straight line equal to *a b*. Upon it, from A, measure A *m′* equal to *a m*, *m′ l′* equal to *m l*, &c., until A B

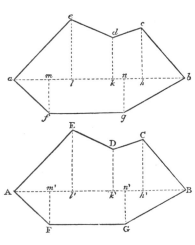

is similarly divided with *a b*. At the points *h′, k′, l′,* raise perpendiculars *h′* C, *k′* D, *l′* E (Prob. 2), equal respectively to *h c, k d,* and *l e*. From *m′* and *n′* on the other side of A B, raise perpendiculars *m′* F, *n′* G, each equal respectively to *m f* and *n g*. Join the points B C, C D, &c., by straight lines; then is is B C D E A F G a figure identical with that given. If the figure is required to be constructed with a side, either greater or less, the line of construction A B must be drawn in the given proportion, and divided similarly with *a b* (Prob. 28); the perpendiculars must also be made proportional, each to each.

It is to be observed, that it is not necessary that the line to which the perpendiculars are drawn should be within the figure; it may be placed anywhere, either within or beyond it; the lengths of the perpendiculars indicating the position of the angles, or other points that may be determined for the construction of the new figure. In this way curved lines of all kinds are very accurately repeated. The following problem depends on the above principle, and the line of construction becomes the axis of symmetry.

PROBLEM 104.—A rectilineal figure being given, to construct another equal and similar figure, but reversed.

Let A B C D E be the given rectilineal figure.
From each of the angles of the figure draw lines parallel to one another (Prob. 8), in the direction towards which the new figure is to be produced, and intersect them by a straight line F G perpendicular

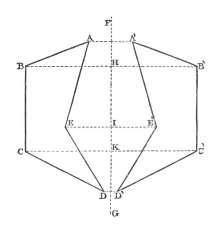

cular to them (Prob. 2). Make F A′ equal to F A, H B′ to H B, I E′ to I E, K C′ to K C, and G D′ to G D. Draw straight lines between A′ and B′, B′ and C′, &c., then A′ B′ C′ D′ E′ will be a figure, equal and similar to that given, but reversed, or the two figures will be symmetrically placed with respect to the axis F G.

PROBLEM 105.—A rectilineal figure being given, to construct another equal and similar to it, by means of parallel lines.

Let a b c d e f be the given figure. From each of the angles of the figure draw parallel lines of inde-

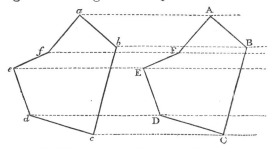

finite length (Prob. 8). Upon each of these measure equal distances from the angular points, as a A, b B, &c.; connect the points as they correspond in the figure, as A B, B C, &c., by straight lines; then A B C D E F will be the figure required. This is a very expeditious method, and has great advantages in practice.

PROBLEM 106.—To construct a rectangle of an area equal to a given rhomboid, upon the same or an equal base.

Let A B D C be the given rhomboid, of which A B is the base. Produce the side D C from C towards E indefinitely. From A and B raise perpendiculars to A B (Prob. 5), producing them to meet D E in points E and F. Then is A B F E a

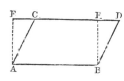

rectangle of an area equal to the rhomboid A B C D. The area of a rhomboid is equal to its base multiplied into its altitude. Let A B = 4, and the altitude B F = 2; then the area = 4, multiplied by 2, = 8, the area.

It is plain that the converse of this problem may also be effected in a similar manner; or a rhomboid may be constructed of an area equal to a given rectangle. Let A B F E be the given rectangle. At A, one extremity of the base line, make an angle C A B equal to any given angle; and from B draw B D parallel to A C (Prob. 8), to meet the production of E F in D; then A B D C is the rhomboid required. The principle of these constructions is, that parallelograms, on the same or equal bases, and between the same parallel lines, are equal; that is, if E D were extended to any length, all the parallelograms that could be constructed upon A B as a base, and between the parallel lines A B and E D, would be equal to one another. This principle is of the utmost importance, since by its means the conversion of all kinds of figures is effected, and their measure obtained.

The conversion of a rhomboid into a rectangle may be effected by means of a species of dissection, which may sometimes be very advantageously applied in practice.

Let a b c d be a rhomboid upon a base a b. Draw b e perpendicular to a b. Make b f equal to a e, and

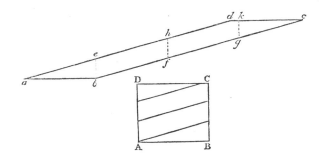

also f g. Draw lines f h and g k parallel to b e. The parts into which the rhomboid is now divided may be placed so as to form the rectangle A B C D, by arranging them so that b f is connected in a parallel manner with a e, f g with e h, and g c with h d.

PROBLEM 107.—To construct a right-angled triangle of an area equal to a given triangle, upon one of its sides as a base line.

Let A B C be the given triangle, and A B the base. Through C draw a line C D, parallel to A B (Prob. 8). From B, one of the extremities of A B, raise B E perpendicular to it (Prob. 5), and produce it 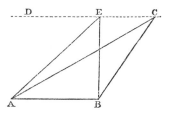 to meet D C in a point E. Join E A by a straight line. Then is A B E a triangle right-angled at B, which is equal to the given triangle A B C.

The area of a triangle is found by taking half the product of the base multiplied into the altitude. B E is the altitude of the two triangles A B C and A B E. Let A B=3 ft., and B E=4 ft., then $\frac{3\times4}{2}$=6 ft., the area of both the triangles.

PROBLEM 108.—To make a rectangle equal in area to a given triangle, the base line being determined.

Let A B C be the given triangle, of which B C is the base line. From A let fall the perpendicular A D (Prob. 3) upon the base B C; this is the altitude of the triangle. Bisect A D in E (Prob. 12). Through E draw a line 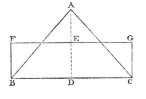 parallel to B C (Prob. 8), and from B and C raise perpendiculars to meet the parallel to B C in points F and G (Prob. 5). Then is B C G F a rectangle of an area equal to the given triangle A B C. It is evident that the area of the rectangle is the base multiplied into half the altitude.

PROBLEM 109.—To make a square of an area equal to a given triangle.

Let A B C be the given triangle, and B C the base line. Draw A D the altitude, and bisect it in

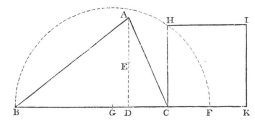

E (Prob. 12). Produce the base B C from C until C F is equal to D E, half the altitude. Bisect B F in G (Prob. 12); and from G, with the radius G F or G B, describe a semicircle. From C raise a perpendicular to B C (Prob. 2), and produce it to meet the semicircle in a point H. Upon C H construct a square C H I K (Prob. 36). This

square is of an area equal to the given triangle A B C. The side of a square which is equivalent to any triangle, is thus a mean proportional between the base line and half the altitude of the triangle. Let B C=6 ft., and A D=4 ft., or D E, the half of A D=2 ft., the square root of 6×2= 3·464, &c., or about 3 ft. 5½ inches, the side of the square sought.

The side of the square may also be found, when the length of the sides forming the triangle are known. Thus, from half the sum of the sides deduct each side successively; then multiply the half sum by the three remainders continually. The square root of the product is the area of the triangle; and the square root of the area is the side required.

PROBLEM 110.—A triangle being given, to change it into one equal to it, but having an altitude or base greater or less in a given proportion.

First, let the altitude be changed. Let A B C be a given triangle, of which A B is the base; and let it be required to construct another of an equal area, but with an altitude equal to *ef*. Produce the base A B from B, towards D indefinitely. Join 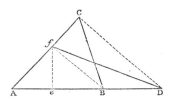 *f* B by a straight line; and from C draw a straight line parallel to *f* B (Prob. 8), extending it to meet the produced base line in a point D. Join *f* D by a straight line. Then is A *f* D the required triangle, equal in area to that given.

In order to increase the altitude of the triangle, or if A *f* D were the triangle given, and that it were required to make the altitude greater, the above process is simply inverted; or C D is first drawn, and then *f* B parallel with it; C and B are then joined, and the triangle is produced.

Next, let the base be changed. Let A B C be the given triangle; and let it be required to construct a triangle of equal area, with a base equal to A D. Join C D by a straight line, and from B draw B *f* parallel with it (Prob. 8); *f* D being joined by a straight line, the triangle A *f* D is that required.

To diminish the base, or if A *f* D is the given triangle, and A B the length of the new base line, the process is inverted, as in the first part of the problem.

Under Problem 106 it was observed, that parallelograms, placed upon the same or equal bases, and between the same parallel lines, were equal to one another. The same applies to triangles which are themselves the halves of parallelograms of some sort. Hence, if a line parallel to A D were drawn through f, all the triangles that could be constructed upon A D as a base, and having their vertices in that line, would be equal to one another. The same applies to the triangles that could be drawn upon A B, with the vertices in a line parallel with it, drawn through C.

PROBLEM 111.—To make a triangle equal to one, and similar to another given triangle.

Let it be required to construct a triangle that shall be equal to a given triangle, D E F, and similar to another, A B C. Make a triangle, D G H, equal to D E F (Prob. 110), with an altitude equal to that of A B C. Find a mean proportional between A B and D H; that is,

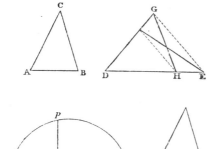

draw L K, and make K m equal to A B, and m L to D H. Bisect K L in o, and describe a semi-circle in it. From m raise a perpendicular to meet the semi-circumference in a point p, then $m\,p$ is the base of the triangle required. Draw R S equal to $m\,p$, and upon it construct a triangle (Prob. 23) similar to A B C, which will be that required.

PROBLEM 112.—To make a rectangle of an area equal to a given trapezoid.

Let A B C D be the given trapezoid. Produce the shorter of the two parallel sides both ways towards E and F. Upon A B measure D C from A to G. Bisect the difference G B in H (Prob. 12), and from A and

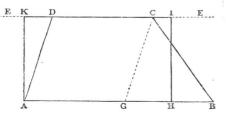

H raise perpendiculars (Prob. 5) to meet E F in points I and K respectively; then is A H I K a rectangle of an area equal to the given trapezoid. The area of a trapezoid is equal to the rectangle contained by its altitude, and half the sum of the parallel sides. This is manifest; for C G B is a triangle, and its area is equal to a rectangle under its base, and half the altitude (Prob. 108); or which is the same thing, to that under half the base, and the whole altitude. Hence A H I K is equal to the area of A G C D, together with the rectangle under G H and H I. Let A B=6 ft., D C=4 ft., and the altitude H I=2 ft., then $\frac{6+4}{2}$=5, and 5×2=10 ft., equal the area of the trapezoid.

Prob. 113.—To make a triangle of an area equal to a given trapezium.

Let A B C D be the given trapezium, and A B the base. Draw a diagonal, D A, and from C draw a line parallel to D A (Prob. 8), to meet the production of the base, in a point E. Join E D by a straight line. Then is E D B a triangle of an area equal to the trapezium A B C D.

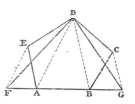

PROBLEM 114.—To make a triangle of an area equal to a given pentagon.

Let A B C D E be the given pentagon. Produce one side, as A B, both ways indefinitely. Draw the diagonals D A and D B. From E draw a line parallel to D A (Prob. 8), meeting the produced base in a point F, and join F and D by a straight line. From C draw a line parallel to

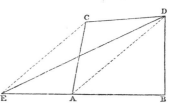

D B, to meet the base produced in G, and draw D G. Then is F D G a triangle equal in area to the given pentagon.

PROBLEM 115.—To make a triangle of an area equal to a given irregular hexagon.

Let A B C D E F be the given irregular hexagon. Join C E by a straight line, and from D draw a line parallel to it (Prob. 8), to meet the production of B C in a point G, and join E G by a straight line; the hexagon is thus reduced to a pentagon, A B G E F, of equal area. Next, join E A by a straight line, and from F draw a line parallel to it, to

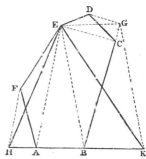

meet the production of A B in a point H, and join H E, which will produce the trapezium H B G E. Now, join E B by a straight line, and from G draw a line parallel to it, to meet the production of A B in K, and join K E; the trapezium is thus reduced to an equal triangle, H E K, which is equal to the given hexagon. Here it is seen, that by the construction of equal triangles between parallels, the figure has been reduced one side successively at each step, and an equivalent figure formed, until at last the triangle is produced. It is evident that a triangle, by this means, may be made equal to any rectilineal figure. The area of any figure may be easily ascertained by this construction; for if it is accurately drawn by a scale, and the process of conversion conducted with care, the resulting triangle may be measured by the same scale, and the area found as indicated in Problems 107 and 109, either multiplying the altitude into half the base, or by employment of the second method, which is that generally used in ascertaining the areas of triangles.

PROBLEM 116.—To make a triangle of an area equal to any given regular polygon.

Let it be required to make a triangle equal to a given hexagon. From the centre, C, let fall a perpendicular upon one of the sides, A B, of the figure (Prob. 3); this is the altitude of the elementary triangle, A B C, of the hexagon. Draw a straight line, D E,

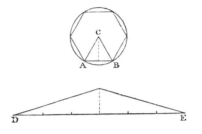

making it equal to the perimeter of the given polygon; upon it construct a triangle whose altitude shall be equal to that of the elementary triangle A B C. This triangle will be equal in area to the given hexagon.

PROBLEM 117.—A regular polygon being given, to construct another, having an equal area, but a different number of sides.

Let it be required to construct a regular nonagon, whose area shall be equal to a given pentagon. Divide a side, as A B, of the figure into nine equal parts (Prob. 24). Upon a straight line D E, equal to five of these parts, construct a triangle D E H, with an altitude equal to that of A C B, the elementary triangle of the pentagon. Construct a triangle, F G L, having its vertical angle, F L G, equal to the angle at the centre of a nonagon which is 40°, and make its altitude equal, also, to that of the elementary triangle of the pentagon. Find the base of a triangle that shall be equal to D E H, and similar to F L G (Prob. 111), that is, find a mean proportional, l n, between D E and F G; this is the side of the required nonagon. Draw N O equal to l n, and upon it construct a nonagon (Prob. 91) which will be equal in area to the given pentagon, as required.

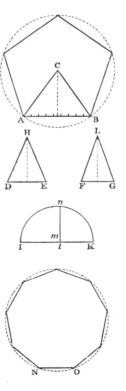

PROBLEM 118.—To make a rectangle equal in area to a given trapezium.

Let A B C D be the given trapezium. Draw B D, a diagonal of the figure, and from each of the angles, A and C, let fall perpendiculars upon B D, meeting it at points f and g (Prob. 3). Bisect B D in e (Prob. 12). Draw a straight line H K equal to B e, the

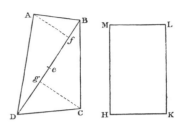

half of the diagonal; and from its extremities raise perpendiculars H M and K L to it (Prob. 5), making each of them equal to the sum of the perpendiculars A f and C g. Join M L by a straight line; then H K L M is a rectangle equal in area to the given trapezium. The area of a trapezium is found by number, by multiplying the sum of the perpendiculars C g and A f by the diagonal, and taking half the product. Let the diagonal of a trapezium=8 ft., and the perpendiculars let fall upon it from the other angles be respectively 2 ft. and 3 ft., then 2×3=5, and 5×8=40, the half of which is 20 ft., the area of the figure.

PROBLEM 119.—To make a rectangle of an area equal to a given regular polygon.

Let A B C D E be a given regular pentagon, of which the centre is F. Draw a straight line H I, and make it equal to half the sum of the sides of the pentagon. Upon it make a rectangle, with an altitude H K (Prob. 38), equal to F G, the perpendicular distance between the centre F and a side of the given figure. Then is H I L K a

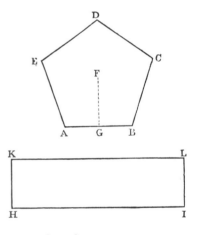

rectangle, equal in area to the given pentagon.

The arithmetical rule for finding the area of the regular polygons is to multiply half the perimeter, or of the sum of the sides of the figure, by the perpendicular, let fall from the centre upon one of the sides. The areas of the first ten regular polygons may be found by multiplying the square of the side, by the corresponding number in the following table:—

No. of sides.	Name of polygon.	Multipliers, or area when the side is 1.	No. of sides.	Name of polygon.	Multipliers, or area when the side is 1.
3	Equilateral triangle	·4330127	8	Octagon.......	4·8284271
4	Square..............	1·0000000	9	Nonagon.......	6·1818242
5	Pentagon..........	1·7204774	10	Decagon........	7·6942088
6	Hexagon..........	2·5980762	11	Undecagon	9·3656399
7	Heptagon........	3·6339124	12	Dodecagon.....	11·1961524

These numbers represent the areas of the polygons with the side 1, and similar figures are to one another as the squares of their sides; hence the rule—Let the side of a pentagon=3 ft., then 3×3 =9, and 9×1·72=15·48 ft., or nearly 15 ft. 6 in., the area of the pentagon.

PROBLEM 120.—To make a rectangle equal in area to a given rectangle, and with a side equal to a given line.

Let A B C D be the given rectangle, and E F the given line, on which it is required to construct a rectangle of equal area. Find a line having the same proportion to the shorter side A D of the given rectangle, that E F has to

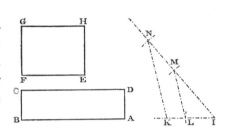

A B; that is, from any point I, draw two divergent lines. Upon one of them make I N equal to A B, and I M equal to E F; upon the other make I L equal to A D. Join L M by a straight line, and from N draw M K parallel with it. Then is I K the side sought. From E and F raise perpendiculars to E F, making them equal to I K, and join G H; then is E F G H a rectangle equal in area to that given. This very useful problem is easily solved by arithmetic. Let A B=6 ft., and A D= 2 ft., and let the given line E F be equal to 4 ft., the fourth side is found by simply dividing the product of 6 multiplied by 2, which is the area of the given rectangle, by 4; the result is 3 ft., which is the quantity sought. Otherwise—

Let C D E F be the given rectangle, and A B the given line. Produce the sides C D and E F indefinitely; produce also the sides C E and D F to G and H, making E G and F H each equal to A B. Draw G F, extending it from F to meet C D, produced in a point L. From L draw L K parallel to D H (Prob. 8), and also equal to it, and join G K by a straight line; then is F M K H the rectangle required, equal in area to that given.

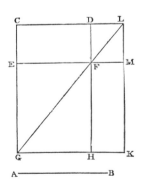

In a similar manner rhomboids may be drawn, equal to given rectangles. The solution of the problem depends on an important property of parallelograms, that if, through any point in a diagonal, lines are drawn parallel to the sides, the figure is divided into four lesser parallelograms. Two of these, through which the diagonal passes, are similar

to one another, and also to the whole figure; these are said to be about the diagonal. The remaining two, through which the diagonal does not pass, are called their complements, and are equal in area, although not always similar figures. This indicates an easy method of making a rectangle similar to a given rectangle, and with a given side. F or G L being the diagonal of G K L C, if G H, any given side, be measured upon G C, and H F and E F drawn, then G H F C is the required rectangle.

PROBLEM 121.—To make a square equal in area to a given rectangle.

Let A B C D be the given rectangle. Produce one side A B from B to E, until B E is equal to B C. Bisect A E in K (Prob. 12), and from K, with the radius K A or K E, describe a semicircle upon it. From B raise B H perpendicular to A E

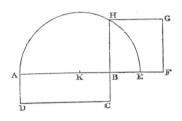

(Prob. 2), meeting the semicircle in H. Upon B H describe a square (Prob. 36) B F G H; this is of an area equal to the given rectangle. The side of a square, which is equivalent to any rectangle, is a mean proportional between its containing sides. If A B=8, and B C=2, then B H is the square root of 8×2, which is 4, and the proportion is 2 : 4 :: 4 : 8, and each area is 16.

PROBLEM 122.—On a given line, to make a rectangle equal to a given square.

Let C D E F be the given square, and A B the given line. Find a third proportional to A B, and a side of the square (Prob. 26); that is, from any point G, draw two divergent lines. Upon one of them measure E F, a side of the square, from G to K; and upon the other measure A B from G to H, and from H to L. Join H K by a straight line, and from L draw a line L M parallel with it (Prob. 8),

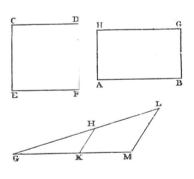

to meet the new line in a point M; then is M K the third proportional sought. Upon A B make a rectangle A B G H, whose altitude A H is equal to K M (Prob. 38). This rectangle is equal in area to the given square. If A B=9 ft., and E F, the side of the square=6 ft., then $A H = \frac{6 \times 6}{9} = 4$, and the proportion is 9 : 6 :: 6 : 4, the area of each being 36. Otherwise—

Let A B C D be the given square, and E F the given line. Produce one side of the square, as D C to G, until D G is equal to E F. Join A G by a straight line, and parallel with it draw a line from D (Prob. 8) to meet the production of B C in H. Through H draw a line parallel to D G (Prob. 8), and to meet perpendiculars drawn from D and G

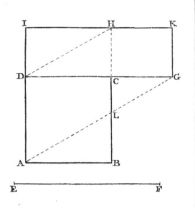

(Prob. 5), in points I and K. Then is D G K I a rectangle equal to the given square; and its side D G is equal to the given line E F. When the given side is less than the side of the given square, the construction must be somewhat modified; that is, let D I be the given side. I K must be drawn parallel to D C, and B C produced to meet I K in H. D H is then drawn, and A G parallel with it, to meet D C produced in G, when K G being drawn, the rectangle is complete.

PROBLEM 123.—To divide a given straight line, so that the rectangle contained by its segment shall be equal to a given rectangle.

Let A B be the given line, and C D E F the given rectangle. Find D G the side of the square, which is equivalent to the given rectangle (Prob. 121). Upon A B describe a semicircle, and from B, one extremity, raise B G′ perpendicular to it (Prob. 5), and equal to D G. From G′, draw a line G′ H parallel

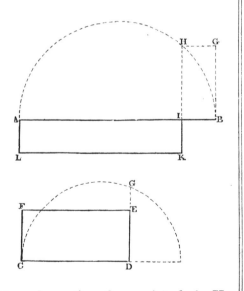

to A B (Prob. 8), and meeting the semicircle in H. From H, let fall a perpendicular H I upon A B (Prob. 3), meeting it in I. Then is AB divided at this point into two parts, A I and I B, which will contain a rectangle equal in area to that given; that is, A I K L is equal to C D E F. The principle of this construction is plainly reversing the process for finding a mean proportional between two lines. The arithmetical computation is, from the square of half the line, to deduct the area of the given rectangle, the square root of the remainder, added to and deducted from half the line, will give the value of the respective parts. Let the area of the given rectangle = 36, and the given line = 15, then $\frac{15}{2} = 7.5$, the square of which is 56·25; and 56·25 — 36 = 20·25, the square root of which is 4·5; this added to and deducted from 7·5, will be 7·5 — 4·5 = 3, and 7·5 + 4·5 = 12, then 12 + 3 = 15, equal to the given line; and 12 × 3 = 36, which is the area required.

PROBLEM 124.—To produce a line, so that the rectangle contained by the whole line produced, and the produced part, shall be equal to a given rectangle.

Let A B be the given line, and C D E F the given rectangle. Find D G, the side of the square that is equal to the given rectangle (Prob. 121). Bisect A B in H (Prob. 12), and from one extremity B, raise B G′ perpendicular to it (Prob. 5), and equal to D G. Produce A B from B, until H K is equal to the distance H G′.

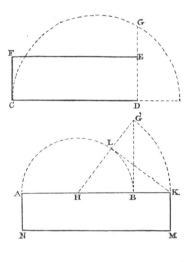

Then is A B produced to K, so that the rectangle contained by the whole line A K, and the part K B, or A K M N, is equal in area to the given rectangle.

The construction of figures that are equal in area to the sum of others is mainly effected by a property of the right-angled triangle, which is one of the most remarkable and beautiful in geometry. This is, that the squares described upon its sides have constant relations to one another; that upon the hypothenuse being always equal to the sum of the other two; and necessarily, that the difference between that upon the hypothenuse and one of the others, is equal to the remaining square; and as the areas of similar figures are to one another as the squares of their corresponding sides, it follows that similar figures of any kind, described upon a right-angled triangle, will have the same relations to one another that squares have, or that the figure upon the hypothenuse will be equal in area to the sum of the other two.

PROBLEM 125.—To make a square equal in area to the sum of two given squares.

Let A and B be the given squares. Construct a right-angled triangle D C E, right-angled at C, and having the sides about it equal each to a side of one of the given squares. The square D E F G, constructed upon the hypothenuse, is equal in area to the sum of those given. By arithmetic, the side of the square that is equal to two others is readily found, being the square root

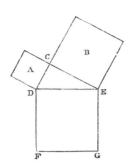

of the sum of the areas; for example, it will be recollected that, in Prob. 6, a method of drawing perpendiculars was given by means of a scale of equal parts, and that the numbers 3, 4, and 5, were employed. Let the side of A equal 3 ft., and that of B, 4 ft.; the areas of the squares will be, respectively, 9 and 16, which, added together, make 25; the square root of which is 5, or the side D C of the equivalent square is 5 ft.

PROBLEM 126.—To make a square equal in area to the difference of two given squares.

Let A and B be the given squares. Construct a right-angled triangle C D E, of which the side C D is equal to a side of the lesser square A; and C E, the hypothenuse, equal to the side of the greater square B (Prob. 22). The square D E F G, constructed upon the side D E of this triangle, is equal to the difference between the given squares. By number, let the side of A = 3, its area will be 9; let the side of B = 5, the area will be 25. The difference between these areas, or 25—9 = 16, is the area of the square upon D E; and the square root of 16, which is 4, is the side D E of the square.

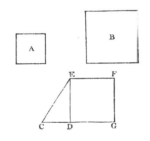

PROBLEM 127.—To make a square equal in area to the sum of any number of given squares.

Let it be required to make a square that shall have an area equal to three given squares A, B, and C. Construct a right-angled triangle F D E, making the sides DF and D E, containing the right angle, each equal to a side of one of the squares, as of B and C respectively. Upon F E construct a right-angled triangle G F E, making F G equal to the side of the third square A. The square E G H K con-

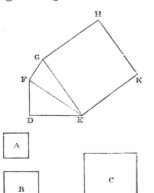

structed upon the hypothenuse G E of this triangle, is equal in area to the three given squares. It is evident that, by proceeding in this method, a square may be constructed, equal in area to any number of given squares; that is, by always adding one to the sum of those already found. By number, the side of the equivalent square is found by simply extracting the square root of the sum of all the areas added together. The same is applicable to any kind of figure, by employing a corresponding side of each, and constructing a similar figure upon the last found hypothenuse.

PROBLEM 128.—To make a square, whose area shall be equal to a given square, any required number of times.

Let A B C D be the given square, and let it be required to make a square of three times the area. Produce two of the sides, as A B and A D, indefinitely towards m and n. Draw the diagonal B D of the square, and make A E upon A n equal to it. Draw E B, and make A F upon A n equal to it. Then the square A F G H, which is constructed upon

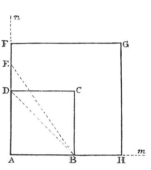

A F, has an area equal to three times that of A B C D. By proceeding in the same manner, always measuring upon A n, the distance between B and that last found, any number of equal squares may be added together. It is to be observed, that the diagonal of a square is always equal to the side of the square which has double the area.

PROBLEM 129.—To make a figure similar and equal to two given similar figures.

Let it be required to make a figure similar and equal to two given similar figures, a b c d and e f g h. Construct a right-angled triangle, A B C, having the sides containing the right angle equal to a b and e f, two corresponding sides of the given figures. Upon A C, the hypothenuse, construct a figure A C D E, similar

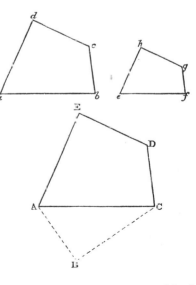

to one of the given figures (Prob. 101); this is equal in area to the two that were given.

PROBLEM 130.—Upon a given line, to make a parallelogram equivalent to two given parallelograms.

Let A B be a given line, on which it is required to construct a rectangle, equal in area to two given rectangles, A C D E, and B C F G. Having constructed (Prob. 17) a triangle, A B C, with the given line A B, and one

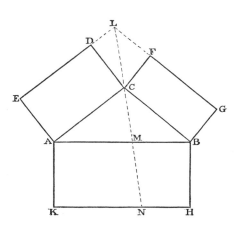

side of each of the rectangles, produce the sides E D and G F of the rectangles, until they meet in a point L. Through L and C, draw a straight line, extending it beyond the triangle until M N is equal to C L. Through N, draw a line parallel (Prob. 8) to A B, and from A and B draw perpendiculars to A B (Prob. 5), to meet the parallel drawn through N, in points H and K; then is A B H K the rectangle required, which is equal in area to those given. It must be observed, that it is not necessary that the parallelograms should be rectangular; they may be oblique-angled, and also dissimilar, the only condition being, that the given line which is to form a side of the new figure, must not be greater than the sum, nor less than the difference of the two sides of the parallelograms employed in the construction. This will show itself by the impossibility of constructing the triangle with the lines.

PROBLEM 131.—To make a square that shall be equal in area to any required part of a given square.

Let it be required to construct a square, equal in area to one-third of a given square A. Find a mean proportional between a side of the square and its third part, that is, draw

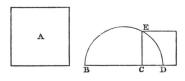

B C equal to a side of the square, and produce it to D, making C D equal to a third part of it (Prob. 24). Upon B D describe a semicircle, and from C raise a perpendicular to it, producing it to meet the semicircle in E. Upon C E construct a square (Prob. 36); this will be equal in area to the third part of that given, as was required.

PROBLEM 132.—A rectilineal figure being given, to make a similar figure that shall be equal to any determined part of it.

Let a b c d be the given figure, and let it be re-

quired to make a similar figure that shall have two-thirds of its area. Draw a straight line, a' b', equal to a b, and produce it to e, until a'e is equal

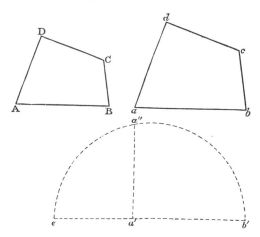

to two-thirds of a b (Prob. 24). Find a mean proportional a' a'' between a' b' and a' e (Prob. 27), and upon this line, or on A B, which is equal to it, construct a figure A B C D, similar to that given (Prob. 101), making A B correspond to a b in the figure, and the area will be two-thirds of the given figure a b c d. The areas of figures are as the squares of their corresponding sides; let a b = 6, then a' a'', the mean proportional between a b and a' e, which is two-thirds of it, or 4, will be 4·9; the squares of these numbers are in the required ratio, or as 24 to 36. By an extension of the problem the side of a similar figure in any ratio may be found, as a' e may be made any multiple of a b, and the mean proportional will be the side of a figure of a proportionally increased area.

PROBLEM 133.—To make a rectilineal figure that shall be similar to one, and equal to another given rectilineal figure.

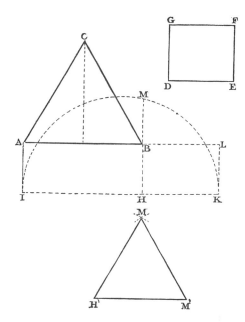

Let it be required to construct a figure similar to A B C, an equilateral triangle, and equal to

D E F G, a given rectangle. Upon A B, the base of the triangle, make a rectangle A B H I of equal area (Prob. 108), and upon the side B H make a rectangle B H K L, equal to D E F G (Prob. 120). Find a mean proportional, H M, between I H and H K (Prob. 27), and upon this line, or H′ M′, which is equal to it, construct an equilateral triangle H′ M′ M (Prob. 15); this is similar to A B C, and equal to the rectangle given.

PROBLEM 134.—To divide a given square into any number of proportional spaces, by means of concentric squares, whose sides shall be parallel to those of the given square.

Let A B C D be the given square, and let it be required to divide it

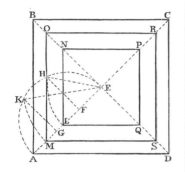

into three equal spaces, by means of concentric squares. Draw the diagonals A C and B D, intersecting each other in E. Divide E A, one-half of the diagonal, into the required number of proportionate parts, which in the present case is three equal parts, E F, F G, and G A (Prob. 24). Upon E A describe a semicircle, and from F and G raise perpendiculars to E A (Prob. 2), meeting the semicircle in points H and K respectively. Make E L, upon E A, equal to the distance E H, and E M equal to the distance E K. From L and M draw lines L N and M O, parallel to A B (Prob. 8), and meeting the diagonal B D. Upon these lines make squares L N P Q, and M O R S (Prob. 36). These concentric squares divide that given into three equal spaces as required.

PROBLEM 135.—A rectangle being given, to divide it so that its parts may form a polygonal band of the same area.

Let A B C D be the given rectangle, and let it be required to divide it into parts that will form a

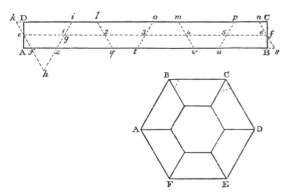

hexagonal band. Bisect A D in e (Prob. 12), and draw e f parallel to A B or D C, and divide it into six equal parts, 1, 2, 3, &c. (Prob. 24.) Upon

e g make an equilateral triangle e g h (Prob. 15), and produce the sides h g and h e to meet D C, and D C produced, in i and k. Make k l, l m, and m n, each equal to twice e g. Make also i o, o p, f q, q v, v s, z t, and t u, each equal to twice e j. Draw l q, m v, and n s, which will be parallel to k f; draw also o t and p u, which will be parallel to i z. The rectangle is thus divided into parts that may be arranged as A B C D E F, into a regular hexagonal band. The rectangle may be divided so as to form any polygonal band, by making the angles i z B, and k f A, equal to the external angle of the polygon, or i z A equal to the internal angle, and then drawing lines alternately parallel through the points of equal division, upon the middle line e f, as in the problem.

PROBLEM 136.—Within a given triangle to construct the greatest possible rectangle.

Let A B C be the given triangle. Bisect two of the sides, as C A and C B, in points D and E, respectively (Prob. 12).

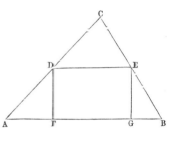

Join D E by a straight line; this line is parallel to A B. From D and E let fall perpendiculars upon A B (Prob. 3), meeting it in points F and G, respectively. Then is D E G F the greatest rectangle that the triangle will contain. The area of the rectangle is always equal to half that of the triangle; it is consequently found by multiplying half the altitude into half the base. It is to be observed, that the character of the rectangle will vary with the side that is assumed as the base, but the area always remains the same.

PROBLEM 137.—In a given triangle to inscribe the greatest possible square.

Let A B C be the given triangle. From any point D, in A C, let fall a perpendicular upon A B (Prob. 3), meeting it in E. Draw

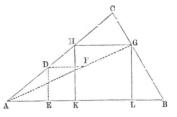

D F at right angles to D E, and equal to it (Prob. 5). Through A and F draw a line, and produce it to meet C B in a point G. From G draw a line G H, parallel to A B (Prob. 8), and meeting A C in H. From G and H let fall perpendiculars upon A B, meeting it at points K and L. Then is K L G H a square, and the greatest that can be constructed in the given triangle. It is plain, that by the same means a rectangle may be constructed within the triangle, whose sides shall have a given ratio; for this purpose D E and D F must be made to have the required ratio, and the construction completed as before.

PROBLEM 138.—To draw a straight line equal to the circumference of a given circle.

Let A B be the given circle. Draw the diameter A B, and divide it into seven equal parts (Prob. 24) 1, 2, 3, &c. Draw a straight line C D, and upon it measure the diameter three times, C 1, 1·2, 2·3, and make 3 D equal to one seventh part of A B; then is the whole line C D nearly equal to the circumference of the given circle.

The absolute measurement of the circumference of the circle has not been effected by geometry; but there are various methods of obtaining an approximate expression of the relation of the circumference with the diameter, and from this the area and other measures are deduced; and any difference that there may be between the results obtained, and the unknown true expression, may be reduced beyond any conceivable quantity, so that, in practice, this want of exactness is of less moment.

In the mensuration of the circle, it is considered as a regular polygon, with sides that are, or may be made infinitely small; by a very simple computation it has thus been found, that the ratio of the diameter to the circumference of a circle, when expressed to ten decimal places, is greater than 1 to 3·1415926535, and less than 1 to 3·1415926536. In practice, there are several modes of more or less accuracy employed for expressing this measure of the circle. For many purposes, the ratio of the diameter to the circumference being taken, as in the construction in the problem, at 1 to 3⅐, or, which is the same thing, as 7 to 22, is sufficient; the ratio of 1 to 3·1416 is employed when greater accuracy is required. It has been found that the ratio of 113 to 355 also expresses the relation with great exactness, being true to six places of decimals. The practical application is very evident, as it becomes a simple question of proportion when the diameter is given in number; thus, as 7 is to 22, so is the given diameter to a fourth proportional, which is the circumference; or, if the given diameter is 12 ft., then 7 : 22 : : 12 : 37·714 ft., which is the circumference nearly, in terms of the unit of the diameter, or any of the other ratios may be employed instead of 7 to 22. The diameter is derived from a given circumference, by inverting the terms of the ratio, or, as 22 is to 7, so is the given circumference to a fourth proportional, which is the

diameter sought. If the circumference is 12 ft., then 22 : 7 : : 12 : 3·81 ft., the diameter. There are also other methods by construction which afford remarkable approximations.

PROBLEM 139.—To draw, by construction, a straight line nearly equal to the given semi-circumference of a circle.

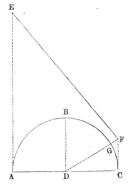

Let A B C be the given semicircle, described on the diameter A C, from the centre D. Raise A E perpendicular to A C (Prob. 5), and equal to three times the radius A D. Draw the radius D B perpendicular to A C (Prob. 5), and from B describe an arc intersecting the semicircle in G. Draw C F perpendicular to A C, to meet the radius D G produced in a point F, and join E F by a straight line; this line is very nearly equal to the semi-circumference given; that is, making the radius D A, 1 the semi-circumference is made equal to 3·14162, instead of 3·14159, &c.

PROBLEM 140.—An arc of a circle being given, to make a straight line equal to it, the rest of the circle not being described.

Let A B be the given arc. Draw the chord A B, and produce it from one extremity B indefinitely. Bisect the arc in C (Prob. 33), and measure A C, the chord of half the arc, upon A B, produced from A to F and from F to D. Divide B D into three equal parts, and make D E equal to one of them. The whole line A E is nearly equal in length to the given arc. This method is very exact for small arcs, but the proportion between the chord of the arc and its height, should not be less than 8 to 1. The arithmetical rule is, from eight times the chord of half the arc, to deduct the chord of the arc, the third part of the difference is the quantity required. By using the above proportion of 8 to 1, the chord of half the arc = 4·1229, which multiplied by 8 = 32·9832, then $\dfrac{32 \cdot 9832 - 8}{3} = 8\cdot3277$, which is the length of the arc.

PROBLEM 141.—An arc of a circle being given of which the centre is known, to make a straight line equal to it.

Let A B be the given arc. From one extremity B draw a straight line through the centre d of the circle, and extending beyond it until e C is equal to three-fourths of the radius. From B draw also a line at right angles to B C, of indefinite length.

From C, through A, draw a straight line, producing it to meet the perpendicular to B C, in a point F; then is B F a line nearly equal in length to the arc A B. A modification of this method has been employed, for the solution of the general problem, for the division of the circumference of the circle into any number of equal parts, and inscribing the polygon.

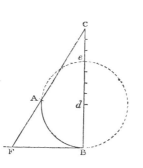

The length of an arc of a circle may sometimes be conveniently found by bending a thin slip of wood round the curve; the length of this, when extended in a straight line, will be very near the length required. Another method is similar to that adopted (Prob. 138), for finding the circumference of a circle, and consists in considering the arc as a portion of a polygon; a small part of it may be taken between the points of a pair of compasses, and this measured upon the curve accurately, as often as it will contain it, either with or without a remainder. The distance may then be repeated the same number of times on a straight line, and the length of the remainder, if any, added; the whole line will then be nearly the length of the arc. It is evident, that the smaller the distance taken by the compasses, the more nearly ought the result to be to the truth.

PROBLEM 142.—To make a triangle equal in area to a given circle.

Let the given circle be described about a centre B, with the radius B A. Let a straight line C D, be drawn equal to the circumference of the circle (Prob. 138), and from

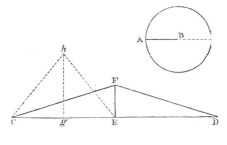

any point E in it, raise E F perpendicular to it (Prob. 2); join F C and F D by straight lines; then is the triangle C F D equal in area to the given circle. If the altitude of the triangle is made as g h, equal to the diameter of the circle, then the base C E must be made equal to the semi-circumference. And in the same manner the base and altitude of the equivalent triangle may be altered; for, if the altitude is increased, the base must be diminished in the same proportion, and the area of the figure will still remain the same.

PROBLEM 143.—To make a rectangle equal in area to a given circle.

Let the given circle be described about a centre B. Draw a radius B A of the circle. Draw also a straight line C D, equal in length to the semi-circumference (Prob. 139), and upon it make a rectangle C D E F, whose altitude, D E, is equal to the radius B A of the circle (Prob. 38). This rectangle is equal in area to the circle. The circumference of

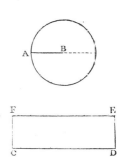

a circle being only approximately commensurate with the diameter, or the half diameter or radius, its area can only be determined with a degree of accuracy corresponding with that of the expression for the circumference. In the problem, the area is made by number to be the radius multiplied into the semi-circumference; or, if the radius is 4 feet, the whole circumference, by Prob. 138, is 25·143 feet, the half of which, or 12·571, is the semi-circumference; and this, multiplied by 4, will give 50·284 feet, which is very nearly the area of the circle.

PROBLEM 144.—To make a square equal in area to a given circle.

Let the given circle be described about a centre B, with a radius B A. Find a mean proportional between the semi-circumference and the radius of the circle, that is, draw a straight line C D, and produce it from D to E, until D E is equal to the radius A B. Upon C E, describe a semicircle,

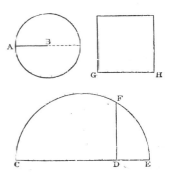

and at D raise a perpendicular to it, to meet the semicircle in a point F; then F D is the line sought. Draw G H equal to it, and upon it construct a square (Prob. 36). This square is equal in area to the given circle. By number, the value of the side of the square is easily ascertained. Let the radius be 4 feet, as in the last Problem. The area was found to be 50·284; the square root of this number, or 7·091 feet, is the side of the equivalent square.

The following very useful rules are derived from the foregoing, and some other Problems:—

1. To find the area of a circle, multiply half the circumference by the radius.

Or, multiply the square of the diameter by ·7854.

Or, multiply the square of the circumference by ·07958.

2. To find the side of a square of an area equal to that of a circle, multiply the diameter by ·8862.

Or, multiply the circumference by ·2821.

3. To find the diameter of a circle which shall contain a given area, divide the area by ·7854, and the square root of the quotient will be the diameter.

Or, multiply the area by 1·27324, and the square root of the product is the diameter.

4. To find the diameter of a circle of an area equal to a given square, multiply the side of the square by 1·1284.

5. To find the circumference of a circle which shall contain a given area, divide the area by ·07958, the square root of the quotient will be the circumference.

Or, multiply the area by 12·56637, and the square root of the product will be the circumference.

6. To find the circumference of a circle of an area equal to a given square, multiply the side of the square by 3·545.

7. To find the side of a square inscribed in a circle, multiply the diameter by ·7071.

Or, multiply the circumference by ·2251.

8. To find the area of an inscribed square, multiply the area of the circle by ·6366.

9. To find the diameter of a circle to circumscribe a square, multiply the side of the square by 1·4142.

PROBLEM 145.—To make a circle equal in area to the ring included between the circumferences of two concentric circles.

Let it be required to describe a circle whose area shall be equal to the circular ring included between the circumferences of two circles, described from a centre A, and whose breadth is B C. From A draw a radius A B of the greater circle, cutting the inner circle in C. Through C draw a line at right angles to

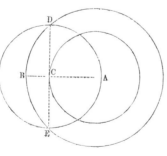

A B (Prob. 2), meeting the circumference of the greater circle in D and E. From C as a centre, with the radius C D or C E, describe a circle. This will be equal in area to the given circular ring. The area of the ring is evidently the difference between the areas of the two circles; and the radius of the equivalent circle is a mean proportional between half the sum and half the difference of the diameters. Let the greater diameter = 12, the lesser = 8, then $\frac{8+12}{2} = 10$, and $\frac{12-8}{2} = 2$, the mean proportional between 10 and 2 is 4·4721, which is the radius sought, and 8·9442 is the diameter. The area may be found by Prob. 144 to be 8·9442 × 8·9442 × ·7854 = 62·832, &c. A more

direct method is to multiply the sum of the diameters by their difference, and the product by ·7854; that is, 12 + 8 = 20, and 12 — 8 = 4, then 20 × 4 × ·7854 = 62·832, the area, as before.

PROBLEM 146.—To make a circle equal in area to two given circles.

Let A B and C D be the given diameters of two circles. Construct a right-angled triangle E F G, right-angled at F, with a side F E equal to A B, and F G equal to C D (Prob. 18). Bisect the hypothenuse E G in H (Prob. 12); and from H as a centre, with the radius H E or H G, describe a circle. This will be equal in area to both the circles of which the diameters were given. The

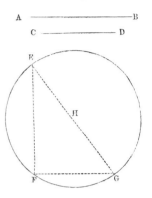

difference of two circles may also be found in a similar manner, proceeding in the same way as for finding the differences of squares, as in Prob 126.

PROBLEM 147.—To divide a given circle into any number of equal or proportional parts by means of concentric circles.

Let the given circle be described about a centre D, with the radius D A, and let it be required to divide it into five equal parts by means of concentric circles. Divide the radius D A into five equal parts (Prob. 24), and upon it describe a semicircle. From each of the points of division upon the radius raise perpendiculars to it (Prob. 2),

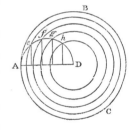

to meet the semicircle in points e, f, g, and h. From D, with radii respectively equal to D e, D f, D g, and D h, describe circles, each of the rings formed will be equal in area to the fifth part of the given circle, and the area of the inner circle will also be equal to its fifth part.

PROBLEM 148.—To divide a given circle into parts that shall be in any given proportion to one another, by means of concentric circles.

Let the given circle be described about a centre D, with a radius D A, and let it be required to divide the circle into parts that shall be in the proportions of one, two, and three. Divide the radius A D into six equal parts, or the sum of the terms. Upon A D describe a semicircle; and from the first and third points of division on it, from the centre, raise perpendiculars to it, to meet

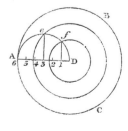

the semicircle in points *f* and *e* respectively. From D, with a radius equal to D *f*, describe a circle, and also from D, with the radius D *e*, describe a circle. The whole circle A B C will thus be divided as required; or the outer circular ring will be three times the inmost circle, and the intermediate will have twice its area.

PROBLEM 149.—To divide a given circle into any number of parts, which shall be equal to each other both in area and perimeter.

Let A B C D be the given circle, and let it be required to divide it into five parts that shall be equal to each other both in area and perimeter. Draw the diameter A C of the circle, and divide it into five equal parts (Prob. 24), at points *e*, *f*, *g*, and *h*. On A *e* describe a semicircle; and, on the same side of the diameter, describe semicircles upon A *f*, A *g*, and A *h*. Next, on the other side of the diameter, describe a semicircle upon C *h*; and, on the same side of it, semicircles upon C *g*, C *f*, and C *e*. The given circle will thus be divided into four parts that are equal both in area and perimeter.

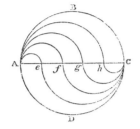

ON THE CONSTRUCTION OF ELLIPSES AND SOME OTHER CURVED LINES.

Those curved lines, formed by the intersection of a cone by planes in different directions, are of the greatest importance in all the arts and sciences, on account of the great beauty of their forms, and the facility of their adaptation. These are extensively employed by the cabinet-maker in many ways, and their introduction into mouldings and other members, confers a graceful variety to the outline, which might not be otherwise attainable. Of these lines the ellipse is probably the most frequently used; it is that figure which is formed by the intersection of a cone by a plane which cuts *both* the slanting sides in any direction not parallel to the base; for it is evident that if the plane were parallel to the base, the section would be a circle. The other conic sections are the *parabola* and the *hyperbola;* the parabola is formed by the intersection of the cone by a plane in a direction parallel to one of the sides, and the hyperbola by any other section that does not cut both the sides.

Different names are given to lines drawn within the ellipse, and to certain points in it, which it is necessary to explain, as they are employed in their construction.

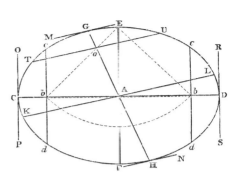

The two most distant opposite points, C and D, in the circumference of an ellipse, are called the *vertices*. And a straight line C D, drawn between the vertical points is called the *transverse axis.*

The middle point A, of the transverse axis, is called the *centre* of the ellipse, and any lines, K L, G H, &c., drawn through the centre to meet the circumference both ways, are called *diameters*. The diameters of an ellipse are not equal, as in the circle, but differ in length; the transverse axis C D being the longest, while the shortest, E F, is that which is perpendicular to it, and receives a particular denomination, being called the *conjugate* axis. The transverse and conjugate diameters, from their being the greatest and least diameters, are also called the *axis major* and *axis minor*. Two diameters of an ellipse are conjugate to one another, when one of them is parallel to a tangent to the curve drawn through the extremity of the other; thus, K L is conjugate to G H, being parallel to M E, a tangent to the ellipse at G, the extremity of G H; and conversely G H is conjugate to K L.

An *ordinate* to any diameter, is a line drawn parallel to its conjugate or to the tangent at its extremity, and terminated by the diameter and the curve; thus, *a* T being parallel to K L or M E, is an ordinate to the diameter G H; and when it is produced to meet the curve in the other direction, as at U, it is called a *double ordinate*. Every double ordinate is bisected by the diameter to which it belongs.

An *absciss* is a part of any diameter contained between its vertex and an ordinate to it, as C *b* or D *b*, also G *a* or H *a*.

There are two points *b* and *l* in the transverse axis C D, which are called the *foci* of the ellipse, and are so situated, that if two lines are drawn to them, from each point in the circumference of the figure, the sum of the two lines will always be the same, or equal to the greater diameter; that is, the sum of E *b* and E *b* is equal to C D. This affords an easy means of determining the points when both the axes of the figure are known; thus, from E, one extremity of the conjugate diameter, with a radius equal to A C or A D, describe an arc of a circle, cutting the transverse axis C D, in points *b* and *b*, which are the points required. The determination of these is of great importance in constructing the figure.

The double ordinate *cd*, which passes through the focus, is called the *parameter* of the diameter *c* D, and it is a third proportional to C D and E F, the conjugate diameter.

PROBLEM 150. — To describe an ellipse, the transverse and conjugate axes being given.

First Method.—Let *a b* be the given transverse axis, and *c d* the conjugate. Draw A B equal to *ab*, and from its middle point E raise E C perpendicular to it, and equal to *e c*, the half of *cd*. From C, with the radius E A,

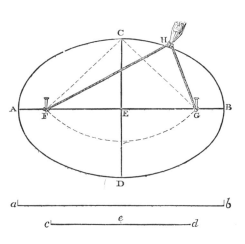

describe an arc intersecting A B in points F and G, which are the foci of the ellipse. In these points let pins of any kind be placed, and to them let the ends of an inelastic cord of suitable thickness be fastened, making its whole length equal to A B. If a pencil or other marking point be now looped in the cord, stretching it at the same time to its full extent, so that it forms two sides of a triangle, as F H G, and the pencil is moved round steadily until it returns to its first position, taking care always to keep the cord fully extended, a curved line will be traced, which is an ellipse, and it will have the given diameters.

Second Method.—Instruments are also constructed by which the ellipse is described by a continuous motion; of these, that most commonly employed is called a trammel. It consists of a fixed and a movable part. The fixed part is generally made of two rectangular bars E G and F H fastened together, so as to have a uniform thickness; on one side of this cross are two grooves, at right angles to one another. The movable part

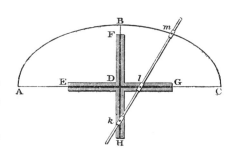

is a rod or bar of wood or metal *k m*, upon which are three sliders, so constructed that they may be fastened securely at any point upon the bar, either by

screws or wedges; two of these, *k* and *l*, are, on the under side, provided with cylindrical pins, which fit exactly into the grooves, so that they may move freely, but without shaking, and the third slider *m* is contrived for holding a pencil or other marking point.

In order to use the instrument, let A C be the given transverse axis, and B D the semi-conjugate axis. Having drawn B D at right angles to the middle point D of A C, let the trammel be placed upon the line, so that the middle of one of the grooves, as E G, may be exactly over the transverse diameter A C, and the other D F over D B in the same manner; the intersection of the grooves will thus be over the centre of the ellipse. The sliders upon the bar must next be arranged. Let the tracing point *m* be fastened at a distance from *l*, one of the cylindrical pins, so that *l m* may be equal to D B, the semi-conjugate diameter; and let the second slider *k* be fastened upon the bar, so that *l k* is equal to the difference between A D, the semi-transverse diameter, and D B, the semi-conjugate, that is, the whole distance *m k* is equal to A D. The pin *l* being now placed in the groove E G, and *k* in F H, by moving the bar round, and keeping the pins in the grooves, the pencil will trace an ellipse. By both these methods the true ellipse is described, but as it is not always convenient to employ them, different means are adopted by which any number of true points of the figure may be obtained, and these connected by a uniform curve, or when less exactness is required, figures approaching to the elliptical form may be produced by arcs of circles.

PROBLEM 151.—To describe an elliptical figure, by finding any number of true points in the curve, the transverse and conjugate axis being given.

First Method.—Let A B be the transverse, and D E the conjugate axis given, and let them be

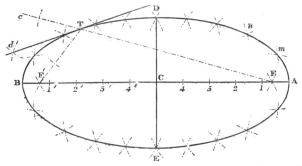

drawn so as to intersect each other at right angles at the middle point C. Find the foci F and F′ of the ellipse, by describing an arc from D or E, with the radius C B, the half of A C. Assume any number of points, 1, 2, 3, &c., in the transverse axis A C, or it may be divided into any number of equal parts. Then from each of the foci as centres, with radii, the sum of which shall be equal to A B, describe intersecting arcs, that is, from F; with the radius A 1 describe an arc, and intersect it at *m* by a second, described from F′ with a radius B 1. From F, with the radius A 2, describe an arc, and intersect it at *n* by a second described from F′ with a radius B 2, and so on for all the points; these points of intersection will all be in the curve, and a line drawn through them will be the ellipse required. A convenient method of drawing the curve where practicable, is to place pins in all the points, and to bend a flexible and elastic slip of wood or metal round them on the convex side, and when it is nicely adjusted so as to touch all the pins, the curve may be drawn on the concave side, repeating the process when the curve is of a length to render that necessary.

The method of drawing a tangent to an ellipse is also shown in the diagram. Let T be a given point, at which it is required to draw a tangent to the curve. From F draw a line through T, producing it beyond the curve towards *c*. From F′ draw F′ T. Bisect the angle *c* T F′ by the straight line *d* T; this line, produced both ways, is a tangent to the ellipse at T, as required.

Second Method.—Let A B and C D be the given axis, mutually bisecting each other at right angles

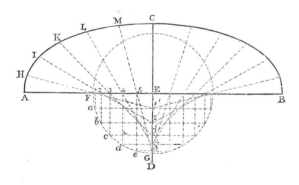

at E. From A upon A B, make A F equal to C E, the semi-conjugate axis; and from E, with the radius E F, describe a circle. Divide the quadrant F G into any number of parts, as into six equal parts at *a*, *b*, *c*, &c. From these points of section draw lines parallel to E G, meeting E F in points 1, 2, 3, &c., marking them from F to E; draw also lines parallel to E F, meeting E G in points 1′, 2′, &c., and mark them from E to G. Through 1 and 1′ draw a line, and produce it to H, until 1 H is equal to A F or E C. Through 2 and 2′ draw a line, and produce it to I, until I 2 is equal to A F. Proceed in the same manner with the other points marked with the same numbers, and the extremities A H I K L M C will be so many points in the elliptical curve, which may be drawn as in the last method; or small arcs of circles may be described through each three of the points. This is an exceedingly useful mode of constructing the ellipse, as the points in the curve may be found

by means of any kind of ruler, or even a piece of stiff paper; for if a distance is marked upon its edge equal to A E, the semi-transverse axis, and A F equal to the semi-conjugate axis, if the points E and F are applied to the diameters A B and C D, drawn at right angles to one another, the third point A is in the elliptical curve, and its position may be marked; the method will be readily understood by reference to the diagram.

Third Method.—Let A C be the transverse axis, and B E the conjugate, mutually bisecting each other at right angles. Draw B F parallel to A D, and F A parallel to B D. Divide F A into three equal parts, and join B 1 and B 2 by straight lines. Divide A D also into three equal

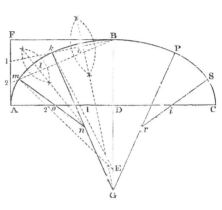

parts, and through the points E and 1 in A D, draw a line to meet B 1 in *k*, and through E and 2 draw a line to meet B 2 in *m*, the points *k* and *m* are each of them points in the ellipse. Bisect B *k* at *h* by a line perpendicular to it, and extended to meet the production of B E in G, and join *k* G. Bisect K *m* in *l* by a perpendicular line, producing it to meet *k* G in *n*, and join *m n*, intersecting A D in *o*. From G, with the radius G B, describe an arc of a circle passing through *k* and B, and extending it to P, until B P is equal to *k* B. From *n*, with the radius *n k*, describe an arc *m k*, and from *r* in P G, with the same radius, describe P *s*. From *o*, with the radius *o m*, describe the arc *m* A, and from *i*, the arc *s* C; a semi-ellipse will thus be produced, and the whole figure may be completed by repeating the same construction on the other side of A C.

Fourth Method.—When the transverse axis only is given, a figure approaching to the true ellipse may be constructed by dividing the given diameter, A B, into to three equal parts at points *f* and *g*; from these points as centres, with the radius *f* A, describe circles which will intersect each other at C and F. Draw the diameters C D, C E, F G, and F H.

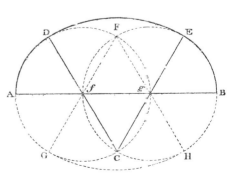

From C, with the radius C D, describe an arc D E; and from F, with the same radius, describe the arc G H. These arcs, with the intercepted arcs D A G and E B H, will complete the elliptical figure. It is not necessary that the line A B should be equally divided, for A *f* and B *g* being made equal, an equilateral triangle may then be constructed upon the remaining space, *f g*,

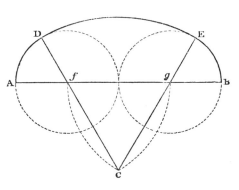

the sides of which are to be produced to meet the circles described from *f* and *g*, and the vertex of the triangle is the centre from which the intermediate arc, D E, may be described. By this construction, the figure produced becomes very irregular, when the points *f* and *g* are placed too near to the extremities, A and B of the diameter.

PROBLEM 152.—Two conjugate diameters of an ellipse being given, to describe the curve.

First Method—By means of ordinates.—Let M R and V H be the given diameters, intersecting each other at the centre C, of the ellipse; and let V H be the greater. From C, with the radius C V, describe a circle. Divide C H, the semi-transverse diameter, into any number of equal

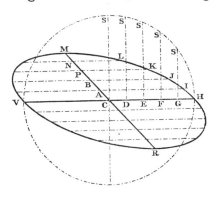

parts, at the points D, E, F, and G; and divide C M, the semi-conjugate, into the same number, in the points A, B, P, and N. From C, draw C S perpendicular to V H, and parallel to it; from the points D, E, F, and G, draw D S, E S, &c., to meet the circumference in points S. Through A, draw a line parallel to C H, and make the ordinate, A I, equal to D S. Draw B J parallel to C H, and equal to E S. Draw also P K and N L parallel to C H, and respectively equal to F S and G S. The points M, L, K, J, I, H, are true points of the ellipse, and other points of it may be found by drawing the ordinates in the same manner for each quadrant; and means may be taken for drawing the curve as indicated in the previous problem.

Second Method—By means of intersecting lines.—Let A B and D E be the given diameters, inter-

secting each other at C, the centre of the ellipse, and let A B be the greater. Through E and D, draw F P and H G parallel to A B, and through A and B, draw G P and H F parallel to D E. Divide A C and G A into the same number of equal parts, in

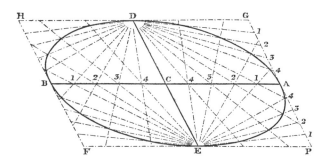

the points 1, 2, 3, and 4. From D, draw lines D 1, D 2, D 3, and D 4, to the divisions in G A; and from E, draw lines through the points of division in A C; these being produced, will intersect the former, and indicate true points of the curve, namely, the intersection of E 1 and D 4, of E 2 and D 3, of E 3 and D 2, and of E 4 and D 1. By proceeding in the same manner with the remaining quadrants, other points may be found, and the curve drawn as already indicated.

PROBLEM 153.—Two equal diameters of an ellipse being given, to describe the curve.

Let A B and C D be the given diameters, which intersect each other at their middle point, and at any angle. From A and B, draw lines A E and B F, intersecting C D at right angles; and from C and D, draw lines perpendicular to A B. These will intersect the first drawn perpendiculars at points G, F, and E, H.

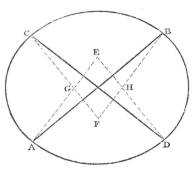

From G, with the radius G C, describe an arc, C A; and from H, with the same radius, the arc B D. From E, with the radius E A, describe the arc A D; and from F, with the same radius, the arc C B, which will complete the figure required. It is evident that if the equal diameters intersected each other at right angles, the construction would cease, and the figure would be a circle.

PROBLEM 154.—An ellipse being given, to find the centre, and to draw the transverse and conjugate diameters.

Let A B C D be the given ellipse. First, to find the centre: Draw two parallel lines, A B and E F, meeting the curve in E A B F. Bisect these lines, and through the points of bisection draw G H, to meet the figure in G and H.   Bisect G H in O; this point is the centre of the ellipse.   Next, to draw the axis : From O, with any sufficient radius, describe an arc of a circle, cutting the ellipse in points C and D ; join C D by a straight line, and

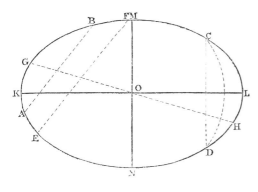

through O draw K L, perpendicular to it, meeting the curve both ways; this is the transverse axis; and a line, M N, drawn at right angles to K L, through the centre O, is the conjugate diameter as required.

PROBLEM 155.—To describe the curve called the ogee, or *cima recta* and *cima reversa*.

First, to construct the *cima recta*.   Let A B and C D be two parallel lines, in which the point A is the point of recess, and C the point of projec- tion of the required curve.   Join A C by a straight line, and bisect it in E.   Bisect C E in F by a line perpen- dicular to it ; and from C draw a line at right angles to C D, produc-

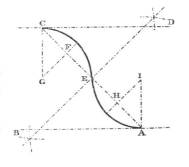

ing it to meet the perpendicular at F, in a point G. Bisect A E in H by a line perpendicular to it, and from A draw a line at right angles to A B, to meet the perpendicular to A E in a point I.   From G, with the radius G C, describe the arc C E ; and from I, with the same radius, describe the arc A E. Then is A E C the required curve.

Next, to construct the *cima reversa*.   Let A be the point of recess, and C the point of projection, in the parallel lines A B and C D.   Draw A C, and bisect it in E.   Bi- sect C E in G, by a line perpendicular to it, pro- ducing it to meet C D in D.   Bisect A E in F, by a line perpendicular to it, and produce it to meet A B in B.   From D, with the radius D C,

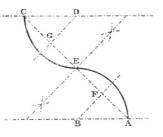

describe the arc C E ; and from B, with the same

radius, the arc A E.   Then is A E C the *cima reversa* required.

It is evident that both the constructions are cap- able of infinite variation, both as to the quickness of the curve, as also to the position of the point of contrary flexure, E ; both of which will very mate- rially affect the character of the line.   The present construction is derived from standard Roman exam- ples.   In Greek ornament, the ogee is usually quirked, and generally also in the Gothic.

PROBLEM 156.—To describe the contour of the *scotia*, or hollow moulding.

First Method.—Let A and C be the extremities of two parallel lines, A B and C D, of which A is the point of recess, and C the point of projection. From A, let fall a per- pendicular A E, upon C D ; and from C raise a per- pendicular to C D, making C F upon it equal to the sum of the half of A E, and two-thirds of C E. From F, with the radius F C, describe a semicircle, G H C.   Through G and

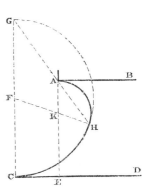

A draw a line, producing it to meet the semicircle in H, and join H F, intersecting A E in K.   From K, with the radius K A, describe the arc A H, which will complete the scotia A H C.

Second Method.—Let A and C be the extremi- ties of two given parallel lines, A B and C D. Draw B D perpendicular to them, and make B N equal to the third part of B D. Draw A E parallel and equal to B N, and join E N by a straight line. From E, with the radius E A, describe the quadrant A F.   Produce N E to G, until E G is equal to the third part of E F.   From G, with the radius G F,

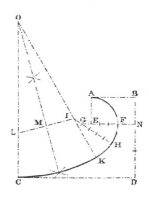

describe an arc F H, whose chord is equal to two- thirds of E F.   Join G H, and produce it to I, until G I is equal to one-fourth part of G H.   From C, raise a line C O, perpendicular to C D, and upon it make C L equal to I H.   Join I L, and bisect it in M, by a perpendicular line produced to meet C L in O.   Through O and I draw a line, and produce it towards K.   From I, with the radius I H, describe the arc H K ; and from O, with the radius O K, describe the arc K C, which will complete the contour of the scotia.

Third Method—By an elliptical curve, drawn by means of ordinates.—Let A B and C D be the given parallel lines. Join A C by a straight line, and from the middle point, E, describe a semicircle upon it. Draw E F perpendicular to A C, and E G parallel to D C, and equal to E F. From any point, H in A C, draw

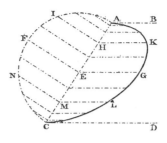

H I parallel to E F, and H K parallel to E G, and equal to H I. Draw M N parallel to E F, and M L equal to it, and parallel to C D; proceed in the same manner for any number of points, and the curve may be drawn through the extremities A, K, G, L, C of the ordinates, as already indicated.

PROBLEM 157.—To describe the contour of an ovolo, the height and projection being given, and the tangent at the receding extremity.

First Method.—Let A B and C D be the parallel lines, between which it is required to describe an ovolo. D A being the height or distance between them, E the projection of the curve, and D F the tangent at the receding extremity D. Through E draw a line,

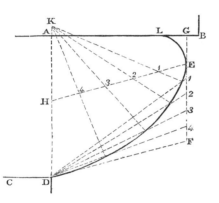

G E F, perpendicular to A B, producing it to meet the tangent D F in F. Make D H upon D A equal to E F, and produce D A to K, until H K is equal to E F. Join H E. Divide H E and E F, each into the same number of equal parts, at points 1, 2, 3, 4. From D, draw D 1, D 2, &c., to the divisions in E F, and from H, through the divisions in H E, draw lines, producing them to meet those drawn from D. The points of meeting of D 1 and K 1, of D 2 and K 2, &c., will indicate a number of points in the curve, corresponding to the number of pairs of lines. Points in the remaining part of the curve, E L, may be found in a similar manner, drawing lines from D, through points of division in H E, to meet lines drawn from K, to points of division in E G, or E G produced. When a sufficient number of points have been found in this manner, the curve may be drawn through them. By this construction, the extremity of the conjugate diameter is between D and E, and gives the moulding a full appearance. By the following method, the

extremity of the conjugate diameter is made to coincide with the receding extremity D, and produces a very beautiful moulding.

Second Method.—Let A B and C D be the parallel lines, D the receding extremity of the curve, E its projection, and D F the tangent at D. Through E, draw a line G E F perpendicular to A B, meeting the tangent D F at F.

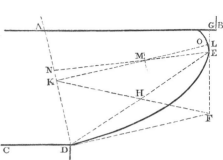

Make D A perpendicular to D F. Join E D by a straight line, and bisect it in H. From F, draw a line through H, producing it to meet D A in a point K. From K, draw K L parallel to D F. From E, with the radius D K, describe an arc intersecting K L in M. From E, draw a line through M, and produce it to meet D A in N. Make K O upon K L equal to E N. Then, with the semi-transverse axis equal to K O, and a semi-conjugate axis equal to D K, construct an ellipse or a part of one; the portion of it contained between A B and C D, will be the curve required. In this manner, by altering the portion of the ellipse, as well as the part of it employed, a great variety may be introduced into the moulding; and the workman's task will show itself in the judicious selection and application of an appropriate part of an ellipse of suitable proportions.

In the Roman examples, the ovolo is usually a quarter of a circle, which is easily described when the height is known; but when the projection is limited, and less than the height, it may be described as follows:—

Let A B and C D be the parallel lines, and let E D be the projection of the ovolo beyond the perpendicular B E. From B, with the radius B E, describe an arc of a circle, and intersect it at F by an arc described from D with the same radius. From F, with the radius F D, which

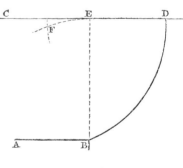

is equal to B E, describe the arc D B, which will be the ovolo required.

PROBLEM 158.—Two parallel straight lines being given, to describe a curve that shall be tangentical to them, at points that are not in the line which is perpendicular to both.

Case 1.—*First Method.*—Let it be required to describe a curve line touching two parallel lines, A B and C D, at their extremities A and C. Join A C by a straight line, and bisect it in E. Through E draw F G, parallel to A B or C D. Make E F upon F G equal to E A, and from F draw F H, intersecting A C at right angles. From A draw A K, perpendicular to A B, to meet F H in K; and from C draw C L, perpendicular to C D, meeting F H in L. From K, with the radius K A, describe an arc A F; and from L, with the radius L F, describe the arc F C. Then is A F C the curve required.

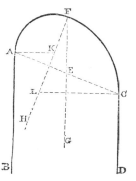

Second Method.—Let A and C be the extremities of two given parallel lines, A B and C D, of which A E is the distance from A to the point where the perpendicular C E, from C, falls upon A B. Upon A E construct the half of a regular polygon, as E *f g h k* A, the half of an octagon whose diameter is A E. Produce C E to L, until E L is equal to the sum of the sides of the half polygon. Bisect C L in *m*, and raise *m n* perpendicular to it, and equal to A E; upon it construct a half octagon, *m r o p q n* A, equal to that upon A E. From *q*, with the radius *q* A, describe an arc to meet the production of *p q* in R. From *p*, with the radius *p* R, describe the arc R S, to meet *o p* produced in S. From *o*, with the radius *o* S, describe an arc S T; and from *r*, with the radius *r* T, describe the arc T C, which will be tangential to C D at C, and the curve will be completed.

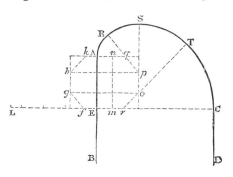

This latter construction, when well executed, produces a very uniform and beautiful curve. It will be understood that all these methods of connecting lines by means of curves, may be employed not only for hollow and projecting members of mouldings, and so forth—as for example, in the upper part of the side-board, Plate XIII., or in the work-table, Plate LVII., Fig. 5—but are also applicable for the determination of larger parts, as, for instance, the form of panelling, to fill irregular spaces, &c. When applied in the Gothic style, they give the contour of the rampant arch.

Case 2.—Let A B and C D be the given lines, and let the curve be also tangential to A C at the point E. From A, upon A B, make A F equal to A E; and from C, upon C D, make C G equal to C E. From E, raise E L perpendicular to A C. From F raise F H perpendicular to A B, to meet E L in H; and from G draw G L perpendicular to C D, to meet E L in K. From H, with the radius H F, describe the arc E F; and from K, with the radius K E, describe the arc E G. Then is F E G the curve required.

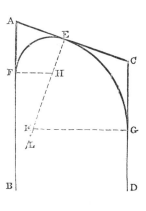

Case 3.—Let A and C be the extremities of two given parallel lines, A B and C D, and let it be required that the curve shall also touch a line which forms an angle with A B, equal to *a b c*. From any point E in the production of A B, let E F be drawn, making an angle B E F equal to *a b c*, and meeting C D produced in F. From E upon E F, make E G equal to E A; and from F, make F H upon E F equal to F C. Join A G and H C by straight lines, which will intersect each other at K. Through K draw L M parallel to E F, and describe the curve, as in the last case, to touch L M in the point K.

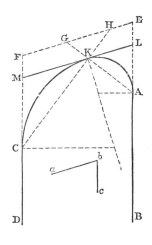

PROBLEM 159.—To construct a spiral curve, of which the radiant is given.

First Method.—Let A B be the given radiant. Divide A B into five equal parts, and from the extremity B draw B C perpendicular to it, and equal to one-fifth part of A B. Divide B C into five equal parts, and draw D C at right angles to it, making it equal to four-fifths of B C. Draw D E parallel to B C, and equal to four-fifths of C D. Join B D and C E by straight lines. From E draw E F parallel to D C, meeting B D in F; from F draw F G parallel to B C, meeting C E in G; from G draw G H parallel to C D, meeting D B in H, and proceed in the same manner for any number of centres required. Next, from B as a centre, with the radius B A, describe a quadrant B I, to meet B C produced in I. From C, with the radius C I, describe the quadrant

I K, to meet C D, produced in K. From D, with the radius D K, describe the quadrant K L, to meet D E, produced in L. From E, with the radius E L, describe the quadrant L M, meeting E F, produced in M. One revolution of the spire will thus be completed, and it may be continued as far as required, or until the radiant is exhausted by the constant diminutions. If it is required to form a scroll of equable breadth, as A N, the spiral

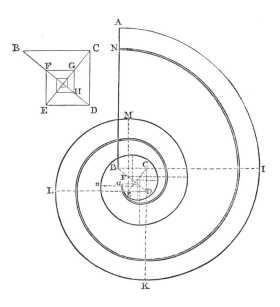

curve must be carried on until the space $a\,n$, between the revolutions, is equal to A N, the breadth of the moulding given; and then a second spiral line, described within the first, from the same system of centres, commencing with the radiant B N, and proceeding in the same manner as with the first line. This second curve ought to maintain an equal distance from the former, and, if properly constructed, will fall into it at its termination.

Second Method.—To construct an Ionic volute.

Let it be required to construct an Ionic volute whose radiant is A B. From B as a centre, with a radius B C, equal to one-ninth part of A B, describe a circle; this circle is the eye of the volute. Draw the two diameters, C D and E F, at right angles to one another. Draw also the chords C F, F D, D E, and E C. Through B draw lines 1, 3 and 2, 4 parallel to them, and divide each of these lines into six equal parts, numbering the first points of division, and then the second in the preceding order, beginning with 5 upon 1 B, 6 upon 2 B, 7 upon 3 B, 8 upon 4 B, 9 upon B 1, &c. Next from the point 1, with the radius 1 A, describe A G, an arc of a circle terminating at G, on the prolongation of a line drawn through the points 1 and 2. From the point 2, with the radius 2 G, describe G H, an arc of a circle terminating at H, upon the prolongation of a line drawn

through the points 2 and 3. From 3, with the radius 3 H, describe an arc H I, terminating at I,

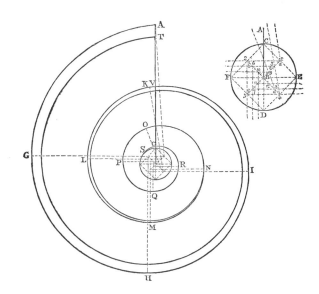

where it meets a line drawn through 3 and 4. From 4, with the radius 4 I, meeting the extension of a line drawn through 4 and 5. From 5, with the radius 5 K, describe K L, an arc terminating in the production of a line drawn through 5 and 6. The same operation is to be continued with the remaining centres, and it will terminate with the last radius 12 R, the arc described with which will fall into the eye of the volute at S, at a very small angle. If a fillet is required whose breadth may be equal to any determined part of the space between the whorls of the spire, as A T, one-fourth part of A V, points $a\,b\,c\,d$ are marked upon the lines 1 3 and 2 4, which are at one quarter of the distances, 1 5, 2 6, 3 7, and 4 8; and the same for the other spaces, 5 9, 6 10, 7 11, &c., to the last 12 B. Then, from a, b, c, &c., as centres, construct a second spiral line within the first, commencing with a radius a T, the point T being marked upon A B, at a distance A T, equal to one-fourth part of A V, the interval between the extremities of the first revolution of the spire. This new line will gradually approach to that first formed, and will fall into it at a point very near its connection with the eye.

There are other methods of constructing the spiral scroll, but those given will be found sufficient. The first is capable of great variation, as the number of revolutions may be increased or diminished at pleasure, by simply altering the proportions of C B to C D, and C B to A B; for it is evident that, as C B is lessened, the proportion of C B and C D remaining the same as in the example, the diminution of the radiant becomes less in the same proportion, and the whorls must be more numerous before the exhaustion of the given radiant. If now C D is increased with respect to C B, a more rapid diminution of the radiant takes place, and there are fewer whorls to the spire. A few trials will make this clear.

On Drawing Instruments.

At the commencement of the present section we described such drawing instruments as were essentially necessary for the construction of the subsequent figures in the problems of practical geometry, and recommended the employment of those alone in the execution of the exercises ; but in making drawings, other instruments are found to be desirable, and greatly to facilitate many operations, when it would be inconvenient to be limited to the straight edge and the compasses.

It will have been observed that two or three of the Problems take a prominent place in the geometric constructions given, such as, the drawing of perpendiculars, of parallel lines, of given angles, &c., and these being of such constant recurrence, in all kinds of drawing, instruments have been devised to obviate the necessity of a repetition of the longer processes of a geometric construction upon each occasion. Of these, the different kinds of squares, of parallel and other rulers, are among the most important for the kinds of drawing employed by the cabinet-maker. Besides these, the draughtsman should be provided with a few drawing boards, which he will find it convenient to have of different dimensions, to suit his work. These should be as smooth as possible on the surface, also perfectly flat and free from warp. The sides should be made at right angles to one another, very accurately, and this is a point on which particular attention should be bestowed, since the edges are much used as guides in drawing lines, and any error is consequently repeated. Drawing boards are better made of mahogany than deal, being less liable to injury from accidental causes, and also keep their shape better. When a board becomes uneven, it is difficult, if not impossible, to draw neatly upon it.

Of Squares.—One of the most convenient kinds of this useful instrument is that called the T square, which consists of a long thin ruler, or straight edge, *c d*, fixed at right angles, into another piece of wood *a b*, called the stock. This second piece is made very much thicker than the ruler, so that when the stock is applied to the side A B of a drawing board, the blade may lie flat on its surface ; the greater thickness of the stock resting against the side will then allow of the ruler being moved up and down

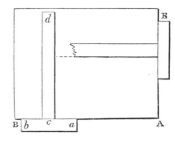

along the edge, so that all the positions of the blade are parallel to one another. In this manner any number of parallel lines may be drawn, and at any distance from one another. If the stock of the square is now applied to another side A E of the board, it is evident that the blade will be at right angles to its former position, and parallel lines being drawn, they will be at right angles to those drawn when the square was applied to the side A B. In using this instrument, the stock should be held in the left hand, pressing firmly, but not heavily against the edge of the board, while a line is drawn with a pen or pencil in the right hand. When the blade is very long, and the line to be drawn is at a distance from the stock end, it may be advisable to hold the blade itself upon the paper, after having arranged its proper position, as a very slight pressure in this case is apt to cause an inconvenient deviation from the direction intended ; also, when the ruler is near the edge of the board, it ought to be so held, because the support is then reduced to only half the length of the stock. It may be observed, that in the execution of a drawing, the error of a faulty square may be rectified by a true drawing board, provided the square be always applied to the same side of the board, and the same edge of the blade employed throughout the drawing ; since the error in this manner being kept constant, and the same for both sides of the board, the lines drawn upon it will always be perpendicular to one another, bearing in mind that the edges of the board are so ; the difference is, that the drawing will be placed awry on the paper. With respect to size, the blade of a T square should be of a sufficient length to extend across the drawing board in its longest direction, but, for general purposes, two feet six inches is a very useful length, with a stock of twelve inches. The blade ought to be thin, say about one-twelfth of an inch thick, with the edge slightly rounded, as the pen runs more freely upon such an edge, and it is, besides, less liable to injury. Some method of verifying the square should always be employed in selecting the instrument; one of the best has been given under Prob. 7, or, a line may be made very carefully perpendicular to another by Prob. 2, making it as long as possible, and then observing whether the line drawn by means of the square deviates from this true perpendicular; the same applies also to the edges of boards.

Another form of the **T** square is that called a *bevel*. In this, the stock is formed of two equal pieces of wood, *b* and *c*; the blade *a*, is fastened flush with one of them, *b*, while *c* is made so that it can turn upon a centre,  and be fixed in any position with a thumb-screw. By this means the blade, and the piece *c*, being arranged at any angle, and fastened, parallel lines making that angle with the side of the board may be drawn, and also any number of other parallels may be drawn from an adjoining side which shall be at right angles to those first drawn.

The *set square* is another exceedingly useful instrument. It consists of a thin piece of wood, about the thickness of the blade of the **T** square, and in the form of a right-angled triangle, as Fig. 1. It is also sometimes made in the form of a trapezium, 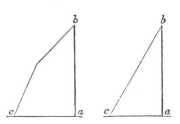 one of the angles of which is a right angle, the other angles being also of some determined and useful measure. Fig. 1 is a good form, having the angle at *a* a right angle, that at *b* equal to 30°, and that at *c* equal to 60°; these angles will be found serviceable in the construction of some triangles, hexagons, &c. In Fig. 2, *a* is a right angle, that at *b* is half a right angle, or 45°, and that at *c* is an angle of 67½°; these are of great use in constructing squares, and octagonal figures. They may be of any size; but one of the most convenient is that in which the longest side may be about eight or ten inches.

The set square will be found a great aid in drawing short perpendiculars, without the trouble of moving the **T** square from one side of the board to the other. For this purpose, one of the sides about the right angle must be laid against the edge of the **T** square, and the other adjusted so that the line drawn along it shall pass through any point. It may also be employed, with the straight edge, for drawing perpendiculars to any line whatever; first bringing one of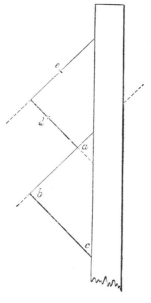

the sides *a b* about the right angle, to coincide with the line, then, placing the ruler against the hypothenuse *a c*, the square must be moved upon the edge until the third side *b c* is in such a situation that the line drawn along it will pass through any given point *d*. The set square affords a most convenient means of drawing parallel lines, not only from its easy application, but also that it is less liable to inaccuracy than most other methods. Let a side *a b* be made to coincide with the given line, and against *a c* let a ruler be placed. If the square is now moved upon the edge of the ruler, until any given point *e* coincide with a point in *a b*, the line drawn along this side will be parallel to the given line; and it is evident that any number of parallel lines may be drawn in the same manner. It need scarcely be remarked, that any inaccuracy in the edge of the ruler will produce corresponding errors in the lines drawn, because, if the side move in a curved direction, the different positions of either of the other sides will no longer be parallel to one another.

There are two or three different kinds of parallel rulers, which may be used sometimes with advantage. One of these consists of a single rule, in which is fitted an axis carrying two little rollers of equal diameters—one at each end, and the instrument moving upon these, its edges will maintain a position parallel to that to which it may have been adjusted. The edges of the rollers are toothed to prevent them from slipping instead of rolling on the paper, which would destroy the parallelism of the lines. Another kind is formed of two plain rulers, connected by two equal pieces of metal turning on centres, which must be equidistant in each;

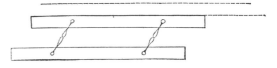

they must also be placed so as to be always parallel to one another, that is, so that the four centres may form a parallelogram in whatever position they may be placed. To use this instrument, the edge of one of the rulers must be brought to coincide with the given line; the other ought then to be held firmly by one hand, while the first is moved until the edge is brought to the place of the required parallel; it is now, in its turn, to be held while the line is drawn. Care should be taken that the ruler does not slip during any part of the process, otherwise error is introduced. These rulers answer their purpose very well for short lines, or where great accuracy is not so much looked to as speedy work; but the T square and the drawing board are always to be preferred, and also the method by means of the set square and ruler.

We have already described the ordinary compasses used for making circles, but it sometimes happens that a circle, or its arc, is required of a larger radius than can be managed with such instruments. In this case, it is necessary to employ the *beam compasses* or *trainer*, as it is sometimes called, and which may easily be formed to describe circles of any size. It consists of a bar of wood C C, generally of well-seasoned mahogany, and of

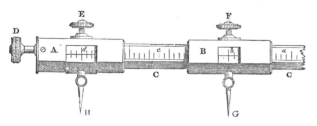

any required length; upon one face of this a slip *a a* of brass, or of some kind of hard light-coloured wood, is inlaid, upon which is marked a scale of feet and inches, with fractional parts of the latter. Two brass boxes, A and B, are fitted on the beam, one of which, B, may be moved throughout its length, and retained firmly, at any required point, by a clamping screw F. The other box, A, has a limited motion, for nice adjustment, by the screw D, and may be fastened by the clamping screw E. Both boxes have points G and H attached, for one of which may be substituted a pencil-holder or a pen. In the sides of the boxes are two openings, *b* and *d*, through which the scale upon the beam may be seen, and the instrument set. The method of using this kind of compasses is easily understood from the description of the parts; for the box A being placed so that the divisions of its scale coincide with that upon the beam, the box B and its point may be placed at any required distance from it. If, again, it is required to transfer a distance with accuracy, the points being placed by hand as nearly as possible, the slow motion effected by the screw D affords the means of perfecting the setting of the instrument to any minute quantity.

Arcs of large circles may also be described by means of the principle pointed out in Prob. 48, and illustrated by Prob. 49. For example, the angle contained by a semicircle is a right angle; hence it may be described by means of a square, the sides of which, B D and B E, are a little longer than the diameter

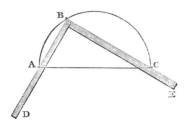

A C. Two pins are fixed at A and C; the square being moved between these, the point B will describe a semicircle which may be traced by a pencil, or marked in any way that is more convenient. In the same way any arc of a circle may be described if its angle is known; that is, if any three points in it are given, merely substituting such angle for the square in the diagram.

Besides the circular curve, the cabinet-maker generally requires others, which, with the exception of the ellipsis, it is necessary to draw by hand. These are of constant occurrence, and in order to facilitate the production of clean and finished drawings, a number of  *sweeps* will be found exceedingly useful. These consist generally of thin pieces of pear-tree wood of different figures, the edges of which are cut into a variety of curves as in the figure. The use of this kind of rule is simple. The drawing having been sketched by hand, and the curves indicated as nearly as possible, some part of a sweep may be found which will nearly coincide, either wholly or in part, with the curve to be described, and it may then be drawn with a pen or pencil in the usual way; care must be taken in shifting the sweep that the ends of the lines nicely unite with one another so as to appear continuous, otherwise a very disagreeable effect is produced, not unfrequently spoiling the whole drawing. A few of these curves, of different forms, being procured, portions of them will generally be found to agree with any kind of line that may be required. This method, it must be observed, ought not to be employed in drawing complicated ornamental work, especially if on a small scale; such should always be drawn by hand, as greater ease and freedom may thus be attained, while stiffness and formality are avoided.

The construction and employment of scales of different kinds, is a matter of great importance to every draughtsman, being one of the chief means whereby drawing is made available in the mechanical arts; without their aid, the workman would scarcely be able to carry into effect any design, with that degree of certainty which is desirable in perfecting his productions. For this purpose, the design or working drawing is always constructed to a scale which ought in all cases to be given, in order that the workman may refer to it, and know the relative dimensions of the different parts. One of the scales most frequently in the hands of the cabinet-maker is that of feet and inches, with their subdivisions; his work is generally designed to this scale, though seldom to the full length of the foot, but a certain space is assumed to represent a foot, as in Fig. 1; and is subdivided into twelve

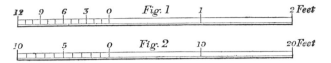

parts, which represent inches; if the scale is sufficiently large to require it, these may be again subdivided into tenth or eighth parts. In this way, Fig. 1 represents a scale of three feet altogether, but it may be extended to any number. Fig. 2 is a scale in which the space assumed is the same as in the former, but is made to represent ten feet, and this is divided into ten equal parts, each of which consequently represents one foot; the use is similar to the last. It ought to be observed that in making these scales, the numbers of the smaller divisions ought to be placed in an order from right to left, and the larger in the contrary direction; this is more convenient for taking off measures, as, for instance, in taking in the compasses a distance of one foot nine inches from Fig. 1, or fifteen feet from Fig. 2.

It is evident that in measuring distances on scales of the foregoing construction, the eye must be depended on when fractional parts of the smaller divisions are required—a method that may be sufficient for many purposes. In drawings on such a small scale as Fig. 2, the principal measures ought to be marked in figures, and the mouldings and other details on a larger scale, if they are to be understood at all. One of the most convenient modes of obtaining minute subdivisions of short lines, is by the construction of what is called a *diagonal scale*. For instance, a scale of feet and inches may be thus simply formed. Draw seven lines equidistant and parallel to one another, containing six spaces of equal breadth, Fig. 1. The length A B, to repre-

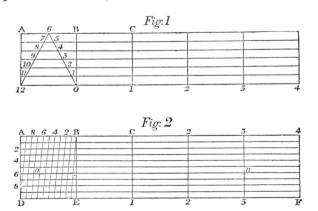

sent a foot, being determined, lines are drawn parallel to one another at right angles to those first drawn, and at a distance equal to A B, a scale of

feet is thus formed. From the middle point of A B, the last division on the left hand, draw the diagonal lines 6-0 and 6-12; these will intersect the parallel lines, and indicate the inch divisions or the twelfth parts of A B, which may be numbered as in the diagram. Another kind of diagonal scale, and one that is very useful for general purposes, particularly where measures are to be subjected to any process of arithmetic, is that called the decimal diagonal scale. This is represented in Fig. 2. Eleven equidistant parallel lines are drawn, containing ten spaces of equal breadth. These are intersected at right angles, as in the former case, by parallel lines A D, B E, C 1, &c., which are equidistant, and indicate the numbers of the assumed unit of measure of the scale. The lines A B and D E of the last division on the left hand, are next divided each into ten equal parts, and, lastly, lines are drawn from B to the first division, from E in D E, from the first division in A B to the second in D E, and so on. The unit of measure, A B, is thus divided into 100 equal parts, or its hundredth parts are known. Thus, if the distance from the perpendicular 3, 3, to the point 6 in A B is taken, it will be 3·6 or $3\frac{6}{10}$; if the distance from n in the same perpendicular, and on the sixth parallel, is taken to o, its intersection with the sixth diagonal, the distance will be 3·66 or $3\frac{66}{100}$. In a similar manner, if A B is 10, then the first measure will be 36, and the second 36·6; or if A B is 100, then the first will be 360, and the second 366, say feet, or any other measure. The ivory or boxwood scales, contained in cases of mathematical instruments, have, on one side, lines divided in this way, generally a half inch and a quarter inch, but the draughtsman frequently requires other scales; these he must construct for himself. On the other side of the same ruler the inch is divided into 15-20, &c., numbers of parts. There is, besides, a scale of chords marked C, which is of use in drawing lines at given angles to one another. The construction and use of this scale will be easily understood from the diagram. The straight lines B A and B C are drawn at right angles to one another, and a quadrant A C described between them with the radius B C. It will be recollected that the quadrant consists of 90°, or the fourth part of 360°, consequently the arc A C, being divided first into nine equal parts, and each of these again into ten, the whole will be divided into ninety parts or degrees. Let the chord A C be drawn, and from C, with a radius equal to the distance

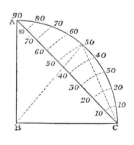

from each point of division in the arc, describe arcs of circles to meet the chord A C as shown. A C is thus converted into a scale of chords, from which angles may be measured in the following manner. Let it be required to draw a line at an angle of 50°, with B C a given line. From B, with the chord of 60° taken from the scale of chords, describe a sufficient arc of a circle, and intersect it by an arc described from C, with a radius equal to the chord of 50° taken from the same scale. Through B and this point draw a line, which will form the required angle with B C. Should the angle be greater than a right angle, the line must be produced, and the supplemental angle of that given, or its deficiency from two right angles employed. By reversing this operation, any given angle may be measured; that is, an arc is to be described, with the chord of 60°, from a scale, and the chord of the intercepted part of the arc measured upon the scale. It must be recollected that the chord of an angle of 60° is equal to the radius of the circle of which it is a part, and hence the reason of the construction.

Angles are also measured and set off by an instrument called a *protractor*. This is simply a semicircular piece of brass or horn, the centre of which is marked; the circular edge is converted into a double scale of 180°, which are marked, in contrary directions upon the instrument, for the purpose of avoiding some trouble in finding supplemental angles. The

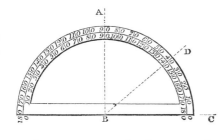

use of the protractor is very easy; for instance, let it be required to draw a line at an angle of 40°, with a given line B C. The centre of the instrument being placed at the point where the angle is required, and the straight side to coincide with the given line, the angle may be marked off with a fine pointed pencil or other sharp point; a line B D is then to be drawn through this and the point B, which will form the required angle with B C; or, if it is required to find the measure of a given angle D B C, the centre of the protractor must be made to coincide with the vertex of the angle, and the straight side with a side of the angle; its measure may then be read off by observing where the other side intersects the edge of the instrument. The protractor is sometimes made in the face of a parallelogram, the scale being marked by lines radiating from the central point to three of the edges, the fourth side coinciding with the diameter. In employing such an instrument, without great care error is apt

to arise, from the great obliquity of some of the lines with its edge, rendering it difficult to mark an angle with any degree of accuracy. The semicircular protractors are generally to be preferred.

The different divided lines that have been mentioned as occurring on ordinary rulers, will be found useful individually; but as they are unalterable, they can only be employed when they happen to suit the scale on which the construction is to be made. The *sector* is an instrument by which this is obviated. This consists of two flat rulers moving round an axis or joint, exactly as in the carpenter's common two-foot rule. The centre of this joint is marked, and from it several scales are drawn on the faces of the rulers, and also some close to the edge or on it. The whole of these scales are not of equal importance to the cabinet-maker, but such as he will find useful we shall proceed to explain. The sector is usually six inches in length when shut, but it is sometimes made of twelve inches, and when fully opened, may be employed as an ordinary measure by the scale of inches and parts at its edge. The other scales which proceed from its centre are double, or each scale is laid twice on the same face of the instrument, once on each leg. The principle of its construction is derived from the proportionality of the sides of similar triangles. Thus when the legs of the instrument are opened to form any angle A C I, a number of similar triangles are

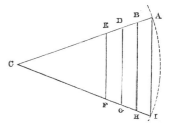

formed by connecting points in each, which are equidistant from C, as E, D, B, in the one, respectively with F, G, H, in the other; the sides and bases of each of these triangles have the same common proportion, or C F : E F : : C G : G D, and the same for the others.

The instrument is used in connection with the compasses, not only for its adjustment, but also for taking the distances from it. Any distance measured on the scales of the sector, from the centre C towards A or I, is called a *lateral distance*; and any space, as from E to F, taken between the corresponding divisions of the scales of the same kind, is called a *transverse distance*.

The radiating scales on the rulers are, on one side, the line of lines, marked L; the line of secants, S; the line of chords, C; and the line of polygons, Pol.; on the other side, a line of sines, S; and two lines of tangents, T. There are also some logarithmic scales on this side. Of these scales, it will be sufficient to explain the use of the line of lines, the line of chords, the line of sines, and the line of polygons. It must be observed that each of the sectoral scales have three parallel lines, across which the divisions of the scale are marked; now, in taking transverse distances, the points of the compasses must be always set on the inside line, or that next the inner edge of the leg, for this line only, in each scale, runs to the centre.

The line of lines is simply a scale of equal parts adapted to the length of the sector. This is divided into ten primary divisions, and these again into ten secondary, which are sometimes subdivided into four equal parts. By this line a given line may be divided in any proportion; proportions may be found to given quantities; and right-angled triangles constructed, or their sides found.

To divide a given line in any required proportion, say that the parts shall be to each other as 2 and 3; these numbers, being added together, make 5. The length of the given line must now be taken in the compasses, and made a transverse distance between 5 and 5 on the scales. The transverse distance between 2-2, and between 3-3, are the lengths of the parts required, as may be seen by dividing the line 5-5 at *a*, making 5 *a* equal to 2-2, the remainder *a* 3 will be found equal to 3-3. In the same manner a line may be divided into any required number of equal parts, say 5. The length of the line being made a transverse distance between 5 and 5, and the sector retained in this position, the transverse distance between 1-1 will be the fifth part of the line, and, being measured upon it, will be divided as required. When a line is too long to be made a transverse distance, it must be bisected continually until it comes within the sector. Thus, if the given line is of such a length that the fourth part only can be made a transverse distance, then the distance between 4-4 will be the part required, and not 1-1. Scales may also be constructed, by this means, of any given length, and containing a given number of equal parts; thus, a scale of fifty feet, to be four inches in length, may be formed by making the transverse distance, from 5 to 5, equal to four inches; then the transverse distance between the corresponding decimal divisions, on the line of lines, will be the scale of feet required. These uses of the line of lines will be found very serviceable, particularly in altering scales in any required proportion.

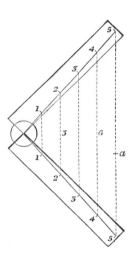

A fourth proportional may be found to three given lines or quantities by the following means. Let the lines given be 2, 3, and 4, say inches; in this case the scales of equal parts on the sector must be considered to represent inches. Make the transverse distance 2-2 of the first term equal to the lateral distance of the second, that is, 3 taken from the scale; the transverse distance of the third term 4-4, will give the fourth term, or the distance 4-4, measured upon the scale laterally, will show how many inches and parts make up the required quantity; here 2 : 3 :: 4 : 6, as in the diagram. This rule is very usefully applied in increasing or diminishing a given line in any required proportion, say to diminish a line of 4 inches in the proportion of 8 to 7. Open the sector until the transverse distance 8-8 be equal to the lateral distance of 7. Next mark the point to where four inches will reach as a lateral distance taken from the centre, then the transverse distance taken at that point will be the line required. A third proportional to two given lines, as of three and four inches, is found, when in an increasing ratio, by making the transverse distance 3-3 equal to the lateral distance 4, the transverse distance of 4-4 measured laterally, will give the third proportional sought, or 5⅓ inches; in a descending ratio, the transverse distance 4-4 must be made equal to the lateral distance 3, when the transverse distance 3-3, measured laterally, will give 2¼ inches, which is the proportional required.

The two scales of lines on the sector may be placed at right angles to one another, by a means employed in the construction of perpendiculars, namely, that any triangle, whose sides are respectively 3, 4, and 5, equal parts, is a right-angled triangle; therefore by taking 5 parts from the scale, and making it a transverse distance between the lateral distance 3 on one scale, and 4 on the other, the two scales will be placed at right angles to one another, and may be used for finding the sides of right-angled triangles; for instance, let the given base be 6, and the perpendicular 5, then the transverse distance between 6 on one scale and 5 on the other, measured on the scale laterally, will be about 7¼, which is the length of the hypothenuse or third side. Or, if the hypothenuse 8 is given, and another side 5, then take 8 in the compasses from the scale, and from 5 on one scale, observe where the transverse distance 8 reaches on the other; then from that point to the centre is the third side, which will be found to be about 6¼.

To find a mean proportional between two lines, as between 40 and 90, the scales of lines must be set at right angles to one another; find half the sum of the given quantities, which is 65, and half their difference, which is 25; then take the lateral distance 65 in the compasses, and placing one foot on 25 in one scale, extend the other to the opposite scale and observe where the transverse distance 65 falls; the lateral distance, in this case 60, is the mean proportional sought.

The sectoral lines of chords are more convenient than the single scale, since they apply to any radius contained within the transverse distance 60-60, at all openings of the sector. To protract an angle of less than 60°, say an angle of 30° at A, on a given line A B.

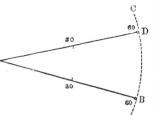

Opening the sector at pleasure, take the transverse distance 60-60, from the line of chords, and with this radius describe an arc B C; set off from B to D, the transverse distance 30-30, and draw the line A D, then is D A B the required angle. When the angle is more than 60°, and less then 90°, set off the transverse distance 60-60 on the arc B C, and also a transverse distance equal to the difference between 60° and the required angle. If the angle exceed 90°, it is better to describe a semicircle, and set off either one or two transverse distances equal to the difference between 180° and the required angle. To protract a small angle, say of 6°, make an angle of 60° and measure off from the arc the transverse distance of the difference 54°.

The lines of polygons (marked *Pol*) are placed along the inner edges of the sector, and are used for the construction of regular-sided figures of from 4 to 12 sides inclusive. They are adapted to the divisions of the lines of chords, and the transverse distance 6-6 is equal to radius. To construct a polygon, say of eight sides, of which each side shall be equal to a given line, make the given line, a transverse distance between 8-8; then take the transverse of 6-6, and with this as radius describe a circle; take again the transverse of 8-8 and measure round the circumference, and complete the figure, by drawing lines from point to point. To describe a polygon within a given circle, make its radius a transverse to 6-6, then take the transverse of the required number of sides, and measure round the circumference as before.

The only other sectoral lines* that we shall describe, are the lines of sines marked S. Their

* In the use of the sectoral lines there is a perplexing discrepancy between the theory, which is perfect, and the practice, which is extremely liable to error. The various lines are never divided with absolute mathematical accuracy; and even if they were, the constant application of the points of the compasses must necessarily widen the divisions. It requires some dexterity of manipulation to compensate the minute errors of excess in deficiency.

principal use to the cabinet-maker is in the construction of ellipses. Let A B be the longer diameter of an ellipsis, and C D the shorter. These must be drawn at right angles to each other, bisecting at E, which is the centre of the ellipsis.

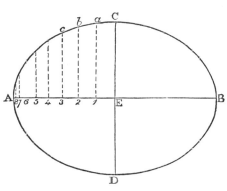

Make A E the half of the longer diameter a transverse distance to 90-90, and take the transverse distances of 10°, 20°, 30°, 40°, 50°, 60°, 70°, 80° successively, and apply them upon A E, from E towards A, as at the points 1, 2, 3, 4, &c. Through these points draw lines parallel to E C, or perpendicular to A E. Next, make E C a transverse distance to 90-90, and take the transverse distances of 80°, 70°, 60°, &c., and apply them successively to the perpendicular A E, as 1 *a*, 2 *b*, &c., and so many points will be obtained through which the elliptical curve will pass. The operation must be repeated for each of the four quarters of the figure.

DRAWING.

Drawing is the art of delineating any object on a plane surface, by so representing its parts in their relation to one another, that a distinct idea may be conveyed of the form of that object, and of such of its properties as may be capable of being expressed by the means employed, as lines, shadows, &c.

Outline is the most important part of drawing; and as more is expressed by this means than any other, it demands so much the greater attention on the part of the designer. Drawing divides itself into two branches—the one executed by the eye and hand alone, without the aid of any instrument except the pen or pencil, this is called *free-hand drawing;* the other is the more exact and rigorous delineation of forms, by the help of scales, measures, and instruments of different kinds, named *geometric drawing.*

Drawing as employed by the cabinet-maker is of easy attainment, requiring only a little pains and perseverance to overcome the few difficulties that lie in the way. Free-hand drawing is not independent of taste, yet consists chiefly in the education of the eye, in judging of lines and distances—and in command of hand to express them. For this purpose, in the absence of regular instructions, a few curves may be drawn, by means of a large sweep, of such a kind as described in page lxi. These may be imitated by hand as accurately as possible, of the same size first; and when sufficient facility and correctness have been attained, they may afterwards be drawn of any greater size, either upon large coarse paper, or upon a black board set upright. This will in time give freedom and boldness of hand, but care must be taken not to hurry, or to pass over inaccuracies. Another very useful exercise for the eye is the division of lines, and judging of distances, &c.; for instance, a line may be drawn and divided into two, three, or more equal parts by the eye, and the correctness of the divisions verified by using the compasses; a line may next be divided into unequal proportional parts, corresponding with those of another divided line, and the exercise verified by Prob. 28 of Practical Geometry. By proceeding in this manner, great precision of hand will be attained. The student may then copy forms more and more complicated, and lastly draw from natural objects, beginning with the simpler forms, and advancing to those that are more intricate. Proceeding thus, step by step, considerable power of execution may be arrived at, but it is always to be borne in mind, that in any progressive acquirement each step must be firmly secured before proceeding to the next; since hurrying, in a matter that depends almost entirely on practice, is a sure way to lose time, and it is far better and easier to bestow pains at first, than to have careless habits to correct afterwards. Figures drawn by free-hand are seldom accurate enough for working drawings; and for detailed proportions, or the formation of different parts intended to unite and concur in the formation of a regular whole, the geometric methods of drawing are absolutely necessary; and as these leave little or nothing to the discretion of the draughtsman, the work is performed with an exactness approaching to mathematical accuracy. The workman ought, however, constantly to exercise himself in judging of the relative measures of objects by his eye; he will thus acquire and retain correct ideas of their forms, which will present themselves as geometric pictures, of which all the parts are known, and be able to produce a representation of them from memory. The workman has frequently to exercise his powers in this way, and he ought to try to put upon paper at once what he has endeavoured to fix in his mind; for objects that are supposed to be indelibly impressed on the memory are sometimes from their very simplicity easily lost.

The repetition of a figure is exact and perfect only when each line of the copy is equal to, and corresponds with, a line in the model, and when the corresponding lines in each contain equal angles. The exact repetition of figures, and their enlargement or diminution, without the aid of instruments, offer no great difficulties to a practised eye. When great exactitude is required, the different methods of constructing rectilineal figures similar to one another, given in Prob. 100—105, may be had recourse to. The application is easy for all figures; since, however complicated a figure may be, by connecting the leading points by straight lines, a number of triangles, or other simple rectilineal figures, are developed, which may be easily repeated, and a corresponding number of points are thus necessarily placed in relation to one another that will regulate the whole reproduced figure. The same remark applies where the outline of the figure is composed of curved lines, since the general direction of these may be indicated by straight lines: for instance, the back of the hall-seat—Plate V., Fig. 4—may be readily copied by reducing the forms to a few straight lines, the direction of which is easily seen, and which will serve as guides for the position of the different curves which make up the outline of the whole. In some kinds of French work, where the forms are of a very indefinite nature, the lines of construction are not easily recognized, but imaginary lines, bounding and determining masses of form, can always be found to aid the draughtsman and designer. Take for example, the sideboard-back—Plate XVI., Fig. 6—in which the ornament presents very few lines that are not, in a great measure, at the will of the designer. The effective part of the ornament, resolves itself into a simple triangular mass, the summit of which is directly over the middle point of the length. The construction of a similar triangle in a like situation, when the design is to be repeated, will afford very efficient aid in making the drawing.

A figure may sometimes be easily copied by drawing a single line in any convenient direction through it, and observing the points where it intersects different parts of the outline. When the object is symmetric, as many of the forms are that the cabinet-maker has to treat, the proper line to employ is the axis of symmetry, or that line which divides the whole into two equal and identical figures. For instance, the pillar and block table—Plate XVII., Fig. 1—may be so divided by a line let fall perpendicularly from the middle of the top line; and the figure may be essentially repeated by the ruler alone, by simply setting off the relative lengths of the lines for the determination of the projecting parts. Sometimes panellings may be easily copied or constructed by dividing the space by a few lines; for instance, the fret at the lower part of the hat-stand—Plate VII., Fig. 3—can be easily repeated, if lines are drawn through the middle of it, parallel with the sides; the different points of contact of the curves may then be marked with the positions of the centres, and the space filled in very readily with the curves. The upper part of the same stand is more complicated, and will be most easily repeated by observing what points lie in the same straight lines, parallel and perpendicular with the sides. Diagonal lines may also be employed with advantage, when the form indicates them; as, for instance, in the end of the occasional table—Plate LIV., Fig. 5—where the little knob below the rosette will be seen to be a central point. The same remark applies to Fig. 6.

It has already been observed that any design intended as a guide to the workman is always drawn to a given scale. The reduction of such drawings, and more especially the enlargment, is frequently necessary. This is usually effected by adopting a second scale, either greater or less in the given proportion; the different parts of the drawing to be repeated are then measured upon the original scale in feet and inches, and the same number of feet and inches are taken from the second scale, and thus a similar figure must necessarily be produced. In full sized working drawings, the foot measure is adopted as the second scale.

One of the most convenient and exact methods of repeating a drawing, either on the same or of a different size, is by determining the relative position of a number of its points by horizontal and vertical lines: thus dividing the surface into a number of squares, and repeating the same, either of the same size or proportionally greater or less; the figure is then drawn upon this, taking care to mark within each square all that is contained in the corresponding square of the copy.

The annexed figures represent the drawing-room

Fig. 1.

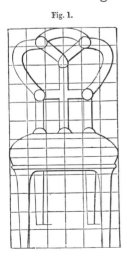

Fig. 2.

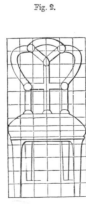

chairs—Plate LXV., Fig. 5—ruled off for reduction in this manner.

It will be readily understood that when the parts of the subject to be copied are very minute or irregular, the size of the squares into which the parallelograms are divided, must be proportionally smaller; or where the intricate part of the drawing occurs, the squares over it fall to be subdivided, to assist the eye in making the outline.

If the design to be copied is too valuable to permit of the squares being actually drawn upon it, the same end may be attained by substituting fine silk threads for the lines. These must be stretched tightly across an open frame, on pins placed at equal intervals, so as to form a network of squares over the open space. By a modification of this method, proportions of length and breadth may be altered, at the same time preserving the design. This is effected simply by altering the proportions of one of the sides of the parallelogram on which the drawing is to be made, dividing it into the same number of parts with the corresponding side of the parallelogram containing the original figure.

When a drawing is not of much value, it may be copied by pricking through the leading points with a fine needle, and using these marks as guides. Tracing paper may also be used sometimes with advantage. This is simply paper that has been saturated with oil or varnish, and dried. It is laid over the drawing, and the outline is traced with a pencil; when finished, the lines may be seen distinctly by laying the transparent paper upon any white surface. Another mode of tracing is by rubbing a sheet of paper, of suitable size and thickness, with black lead or coloured chalk, going over it with a bit of crumpled paper until it ceases to colour the finger when touched lightly; by interposing this with the prepared side next a sheet of blank paper, and placing the drawing above, the forms may be readily traced by any small smooth point passed along the outline. Care must be taken not to press too heavily with the tracer, but a little experience will show the amount of pressure that is necessary. When it is not convenient to fasten the drawings together upon a board by means of pins, a few weights will be found very useful; these ought to be rather heavy—and covered with some kind of soft woollen cloth—to prevent the paper from slipping. The progress of the tracing may be occasionally inspected, to see if any parts have been omitted; but this must be done with great care, as in case of any disturbance of the papers, the re-adjustment is very troublesome.

Another means of enlarging and reducing drawings is by means of an angle, sometimes called the *angle of reduction*. The principle depends on the proportion of the sides of similar triangles. Suppose it to be required to reduce to a third, or to give

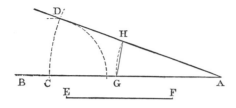

to the lines of the copy a third of the length of those of the subject:—Upon a line A B, mark with the compasses any three equal spaces from A to C. From C, with an opening equal to one of these spaces, describe an arc of a circle, and intersect it at D by another described from A, with the radius A C equal to all three parts; lastly, draw A D, then D A B is the angle required. If, now, E F be a line of the pattern, take this as radius, and from A describe an arc G H intersecting A B and A D at G and H; the chord of this arc is the length required, or the third part of E F. It is evident that the construction may be advantageously applied either for enlarging or diminishing proportional lengths, and that is a very correct method. It may be remarked, that, as a general rule, the correct enlargement of any drawing is rather more difficult than its reduction. This is easily accounted for, since any slight error in measuring the distances is multiplied proportionally to the increase of size; while, on the contrary, an error of the same extent on a diminishing scale may become inappreciable in the reduced copy.

An instrument called the *proportional compasses* is employed for facilitating the process of enlargement or diminution. This is a kind of double compasses, the four points of which may be arranged to any proportion. It consists of two shanks, crossing each other on a centre which is either fixed or moveable. The moveable centre is preferable, since it may be adjusted to give a great variety of proportionals. The construction of the instrument is very clearly shown in the annexed engraving. A B D E are the shanks, and C is the centre, which moves up and down in the slots or openings. On the faces of the shanks are marked divisions of lines and circles, the use of which are best illustrated by examples. By the scale of lines, a line may be divided in any proportion that falls within the range of the instrument. To divide a line into a proposed number of equal parts—say nine, or to find its ninth part; the in-

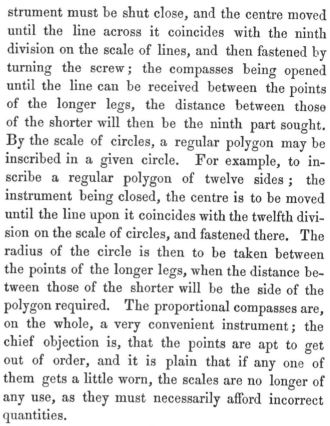

strument must be shut close, and the centre moved until the line across it coincides with the ninth division on the scale of lines, and then fastened by turning the screw; the compasses being opened until the line can be received between the points of the longer legs, the distance between those of the shorter will then be the ninth part sought. By the scale of circles, a regular polygon may be inscribed in a given circle. For example, to inscribe a regular polygon of twelve sides; the instrument being closed, the centre is to be moved until the line upon it coincides with the twelfth division on the scale of circles, and fastened there. The radius of the circle is then to be taken between the points of the longer legs, when the distance between those of the shorter will be the side of the polygon required. The proportional compasses are, on the whole, a very convenient instrument; the chief objection is, that the points are apt to get out of order, and it is plain that if any one of them gets a little worn, the scales are no longer of any use, as they must necessarily afford incorrect quantities.

There are a great variety of instruments by which drawings may be copied mechanically; these are generally called *pantographs*, but our space will not admit of entering on their details. The best instrument of the kind is the invention of the late Professor Wallace, of Edinburgh, called the *eidograph*. None of these contrivances are, however, of much use unless made with a mathematical accuracy that renders them very costly; but even if it were otherwise, the cabinet-maker will find it infinitely more to his advantage in every respect, to depend on himself and his own powers of execution, founded on a correct eye and a ready hand, both of which may be attained by practice.

The copying and repetition of curved lines is effected very much in the same way that other figures are made similar, that is, by determining a number of points which may serve as guides for drawing them. For this purpose, the lines of construction, or those lines that have been used for in-

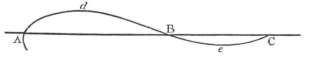

dicating the general form of an object, may be frequently employed, and found sufficient. Thus, if A C is a curved line that it is desired to repeat, a straight line may be drawn in such a direction as to intersect it in the greatest number of points, as at A, B, C. Another line being drawn where the curve is required, and of suitable length, may be similarly divided, and the points of division will be

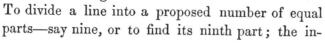

a great assistance in placing the curve properly, and giving its true character. It is of course necessary to observe where the curve is at the greatest distance from the line, as at *d* and *e*, and to make them relatively in the copy. This may be done by measuring, if necessary. One of the best methods of drawing curved lines is that by projections, as indicated in Prob. 152. For instance, let A B be a

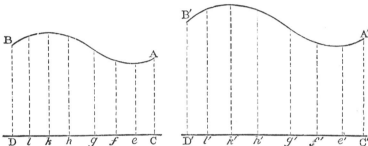

given curved line, a straight line C D being drawn in any convenient situation, any number of perpendiculars are let fall upon it from points in the curve, selecting the most important, which are generally those where the curve is at its greatest projection, and where it changes its direction. The curve line is now easily repeated, either on the same or a different scale, as in the diagram, where it is enlarged one-fourth; the process being simply the division of a line C' D', which is one-fourth longer than C D, into the same proportional parts at the points *e'*, *f'*, *g'*, &c.; from these perpendiculars are raised, each of which is made one-fourth longer than the corresponding lines at *e*, *f*, *g*, &c., in C D. A curve is then drawn through the extremities of these lines, precisely similar to that given.

The rendering of curved lines is one of the nicest operations that the cabinet-maker has to execute, whether in drawing or in his work. This is the case not only in the imitation of a line already drawn, but, in making a design, the selection of an appropriate curve to suit a given situation is one of those points in which taste may be advantageously displayed. For the actual drawing of the line upon the work, when the curve is not given or a pattern used, various methods are employed. One of the best is by an instrument constructed upon the principle in the last diagram. For the line C' D' a long rule is substituted (about five feet will be a convenient length), in this is made an open groove extending to within about half an inch of each end, and for greater strength, there may be a support in the middle. Upon the upper part is a second set of open rulers, which may be moved to any part of the first, and fastened there, by a thumb-screw passing through both. By means of their open grooves, they may be extended, shortened, or set at any angle, with respect to the long ruler. They

represent the perpendiculars D B, &c. At their extremities C A are holders, or notches, in which a long thin slip of steel may be inserted, that may easily be made to assume any given curve by arrangement of the rulers. When this is done, the whole may be moved about without danger of disturbance, and may be applied where required, and the curve drawn with as much facility as a straight line. With such an instrument, it will be found convenient to have more than one steel slip, because the curve is affected by its stiffness. The whole of the rulers ought to be divided to a scale of feet and inches, so that perfect accuracy may be attained in the enlargement of any given curved line, by taking the measures and distances from the drawing. The ingenious workman will have no difficulty in making such an instrument for himself, and in the end it will save him much trouble. There is another very convenient mode, applicable in a variety of cases, and which may be adopted when the curve is in a great measure left to the taste and discretion of the workman. This consists in the employment of a thin slip or rind of elastic wood, about a quarter of an inch square in substance, and seven or eight feet long. When the work is framed, as, for instance, the back of a sofa, the slip of wood is placed on it, and being bent to a curve, is prevented from moving, and may be further adjusted by fastening in small nails where required; when all is arranged to the satisfaction of the workman, a pencil line may be drawn along the edge of the rind upon the framing, which will serve as a guide in shaping. Whalebone may also be advantageously employed in this process, and will be found to possess advantages that wood has not, especially when the curve is quick.

There are some methods for the enlargement or reduction of mouldings, that are more directly applicable to this purpose than others. One of these is founded on the principle employed in Prob. 102, for the construction of figures similar to one another having their sides parallel. Thus, let A B be a moulding, of which A C is the projection, and B C the vertical height; suppose that it is required to alter its dimensions, say to make it one-half larger. Through B draw a straight line B E, parallel to A C, and produce C B from B indefinitely towards F. Next, from each of the points indicating the members of the moulding, or other desirable points, let fall perpendiculars upon B C, meeting it in *d*, *e*, *f*, and from the same points, perpendiculars to D E. From B, as a centre with radii equal to the distance between it and each of the last drawn perpendiculars, describe quadrants meeting B F in g, h, k, F. Next, from any convenient point B' in D E, draw B' C' perpendicular to it, or parallel to B C, making it in the required proportion, as in the present case, one-half longer than B C. This line represents the vertical height of the new moulding. Through C' and C draw a line, extending it to meet D E in E, and through E and F draw a line to meet the production of C' B' in F'. If lines are now drawn from E through each of the points d, e, f, g, h, k, in C F to meet C' F' in points d', e', f' g', h', k', the whole line C' F' will be divided similarly to C F. From C', d', e', f', draw lines perpendicular to B' C', or parallel to D E, of indefinite length. From B' as a centre with the radius B' F', describe a quadrant to meet D E, and from the point of meeting raise a perpendicular to intersect that drawn from C'; the point of intersection at A' will indicate the projection A' C' of the new moulding. Quadrants described in the same way from B', with radii

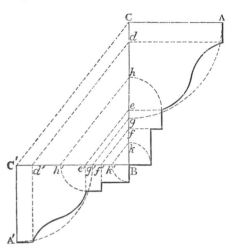

draw a line at any angle with it, as B' C', perpendicular to it, making it equal to two-thirds of B C. From each point of the members of the moulding, draw lines parallel to C A, or perpendicular to B C, to meet B C in points d, e, f. Draw C' C, and from d, e, and f, lines parallel to it, meeting B C' in points d', e', f'. From C', d', e', f', draw lines perpendicular to C' B, of indefinite length. Next from C with radius C A, describe a quadrant to meet C B in g, and from g draw a line parallel to C C' to meet B C' in g'. From C', with the radius C' g', describe a quadrant, or make C' A' equal to C' g'; this will be the projection of the new moulding. From B and e, with radii equal respectively to their perpendicular distance from points in the profile, describe quadrants meeting B C in h and k, and from these points draw lines parallel to C C', meeting B C' in h' and k'. Make the projections from e' and B respectively equal to e' h' and B k', which will afford a sufficient number of points for the construction of the moulding, and it may be easily completed. It is plain that the projection may be made upon either side of C' B, as may be convenient.

The proportions of mouldings may be varied by similar means, that is, a given profile may be altered either in its horizontal projection, retaining the vertical height, or in its vertical height, retaining the horizontal projection, simply by increasing proportionally the lines in the above construction which determine these respective dimensions.

It frequently happens, that in a drawing or design, the only key to the true profile of a moulding is to be found in a mitre, where the members may present themselves under quite different aspects and proportions, the outline of the moulding being produced, in this case, by an oblique section. The true profile may, however, be easily derived from that of the mitre. Let A B be the profile of a moulding, at a mitre of which A C is the horizontal projection, and C B the vertical height. Through

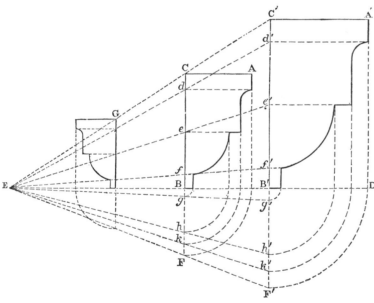

B' k', B' h', B' g', will meet D E, and perpendiculars drawn from these points, to intersect those drawn to C' B', will indicate successively the different points of the members sought, and the moulding may be drawn in the usual manner. If the moulding were required to be reduced, then the vertical line must be reduced in the given proportion, and it would be situated as at G, between C and E. By this method the moulding may be reversed, with the same ease that it is reproduced, by merely reversing the projections, as at G.

The following is another excellent method:— Let A B be the profile of a moulding, B C its vertical height, and A C the projection; let it be required to reduce the dimensions of the moulding one-third part. From B, one extremity of B C,

B draw a line of indefinite length parallel to A C, and from A let fall a perpendicular to meet it in D. From B, as a centre with the radius B D, describe a quadrant to meet the production of C B at E. Draw the chord E D, and from its middle point F draw B F. This line B F is the true horizontal projection of the moulding. From any number of points, as *a, b, c, e,* in the profile, let fall perpendiculars upon B D, to meet it in points *f, g,* &c., and from the same points draw lines of indefinite length parallel to A C. From the points *f, g,* &c., draw lines parallel to F D, and meeting B F in *k, l,* &c. Next, from B with radii equal to B F, B *k,* B *l,* &c., describe arcs of circles meeting B D respectively in points *m, n,* &c. From *m* raise a

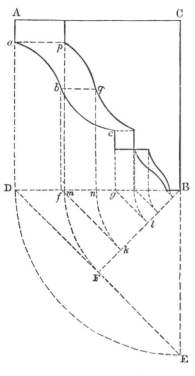

perpendicular to intersect at *p* the parallel to A C, drawn from the point *a* in the profile; from *n,* a perpendicular to intersect at *q* the parallel from *b*; and proceed in the same manner with the remaining points. These will indicate the true projection of the moulding, and it may be easily completed.

It is frequently of great importance to have exact drawings of actual mouldings. There are various modes by which this is effected with greater or less exactitude. One of those most commonly used in practice is to measure a number of perpendiculars to a given line, and to lay down the profile by finding a number of points in it. Thus, if A B is a moulding, a straight-edge C D is held firmly against it, and the perpendicular distance between it and any sufficient number of points is ascertained by actual measurement, at the same time observing the points upon C D, where the perpendiculars fall. The construction then becomes the same as Prob. 103. A good method is to apply a strip of lead, which being pressed against the moulding, will take its form very exactly; it may then be removed, and the line drawn upon

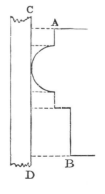

paper by its means. It is needless to observe that the lead must be of a sufficient substance to retain the form when removed, and not so thick as to present any difficulties in taking the impression: when the moulding is large, it may be thicker than when it is of small size. Clay and putty are also sometimes employed when the mouldings are small. The best method, when practicable, is to make a perpendicular saw cut through the moulding; into this a paper may be introduced, and the profile traced. Besides these methods, there is a very beautiful contrivance for taking tracings of mouldings by an instrument devised for the purpose, by Professor Wallis, of Cambridge. This consists of a board, upon which a point is made to trace any moulding by a parallel motion,

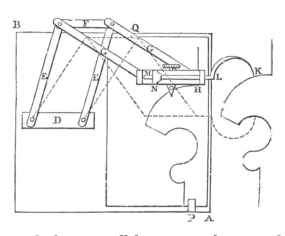

composed of two parallelograms working together. A B is a board of $10\frac{1}{2}$ inches by $11\frac{1}{2}$ inches, D is a plate fixed to the board about the middle of the shorter side. E, E are two arms, each 7 inches long, turning upon centres at the extremities of D, which are about 3 inches apart, and also on F an arm of equal length with D. The first parallelogram is thus formed, the sides of which are movable, and will be parallel to each other in all positions. Two other arms G G, of the same length with E E, are jointed at one end to the arm F, and at the other to the carriage H. This forms the second parallelogram, the sides H and F of which being parallel to one another in all positions, H and D will be so also. By this arrangement, the carriage H may be moved over every part of the board, and all its positions will be parallel to one another and to D. The carriage with the tracer K L M is one of the principal parts of the instrument. The part of the tracer L M is placed in a frame having a pointed screw at M, and a collar at L, so that the whole may be made to revolve upon its axis. K L is nearly a semicircle, and the point K is exactly in the axis. At N there is a button upon the tracer, which serves to guide its motion along the surface of a moulding, as well as to turn it upon its axis. The carriage has a pencil holder O attached. It is plain that, as the carriage and tracer are parallel in every position upon the board, that any point in the carriage will travel in the same path as the tracing point, and consequently if K is made to pass over the profile of a moulding, or other object, the pencil O will mark a line exactly the same upon the board, and of the same size. K L is curved, in order that by its power of rotation it may enter the inflection of mouldings, where a straight tracer would be inefficient, as seen in the diagram. It is necessary that the instrument should be held firmly in one position during the whole process of tracing; to effect this two retaining pieces or supports are attached to the back of the board, which may be adjusted and fastened to any position by two thumbscrews. The paper can be attached to the board by any of the usual means; the best method is by a couple of flat spring-holders, as at P and Q, the latter being placed near the inner upper corner, to prevent the paper from being rubbed up. The instrument does not require very nice workmanship, the essential points being that the arms E E and G G should have exactly the same distance between the joint-holes, as also the holes in the pieces D, F, and H; and that the point K should be exactly in the axis of rotation of the tracer. The parallel motion may be made of thin slips of sheet or hoop iron.

PERSPECTIVE.

Linear perspective is the method of drawing the true representation of objects on a plane surface, through the application of geometrical rules, by which their outlines are determined, and such as they would present themselves to the eye when placed in a known position.

A perspective representation will be easily understood if it be supposed that the eye being placed in a fixed position, a transparent plane is interposed between it and an object in such a manner that the

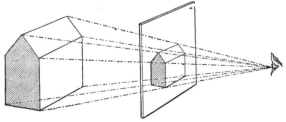

object can be seen through the plane; if the form is then traced upon it, the outline thus produced will be a true perspective delineation of the object. By the rules of perspective the representation of things can be produced whether the objects themselves are actually present, or only their dimensions

and position known. The different planes and lines by which this is effected have received denominations that require some explanation. In every perspective operation three things are to be distinguished, namely, the object to be represented—the observer—and the plane upon which the representation is to be made.

An object is seen by rays which proceed from it in right lines, in every direction, from every point in it. Those which meet the eye of the observer are called *visual rays;* for instance, the rays C A and B A, proceeding from C B to the eye of the observer at

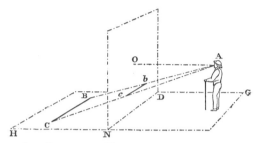

A, are visual rays. These form an angle C A B at the eye which is called the *visual angle*, and the apparent size of any object depends on the measure of this angle, and all objects of the same size appear greater or less according to their distance from the eye; that is, if a line is at double the distance of another from the eye, it will appear of only half the length.

The plane upon which the drawing is to be made is called the *picture*, and is always supposed to be placed between the observer and the object, and the points where it intersects the visual rays, as c and b, determine the perspective representation, as of C B. The picture is always supposed to be placed in a position perpendicular to another

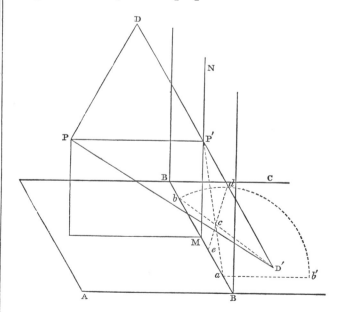

plane, called the *ground plane*, as H G in the former figure, or A C; it is upon this that the objects for representation are placed, and on which the spectator stands. The line of intersection of the ground line and picture, as B B (in the *third* diagram), is called the *base* of the picture; and the point P', the *centre*. The straight line D D', drawn through P, parallel to B B, is the *horizontal line*, which is everywhere level with the eye, and is the *vanishing line* of all the planes parallel to it or perpendicular to the picture. The line M N, drawn through P', perpendicular to D D', is called the *vertical*, and is the vanishing line of all vertical planes that are perpendicular to the plane of the picture. The *points of distance*, D D', are equally distant from P'; and D P', P' D, are each equal to the distance of the observer's eye from the picture. As an example of the way in which the lines operate, draw *a* P' from the point *a* in the base B B, and *b* D from another point *b*; then will *a* P' represent an infinite line perpendicular to the picture; P' *a* B will be a right angle in perspective; and *b a c* a perspective representation of an isosceles triangle.

The preceding may be too severe in theory for a mechanical work, and we shall, therefore, confine our further notices of perspective to a few simple problems, in which points, lines, planes, and solids, are brought into true position and configuration on the plane of the drawing.

Before proceeding to the problems, it is necessary to define terms with reference to their method of construction. This we shall do with the assistance of the annexed diagram, which itself requires some little previous explanation. H L G X is supposed to be a transparent vertical plane, the side

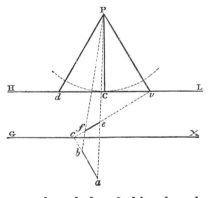

H L being uppermost; the whole of this plane is also supposed to be occupied by so much of the picture as lies between its base and the horizon, or, in other words, it takes in the whole ground view, but no part of the sky. This being understood, G X is the *ground line*, or base of the picture. H L the *horizontal line*, parallel to the former, is that imaginary line which forms the common boundary of earth and sky, and on which the perspective lines of all objects come to a point, or vanish. P is the *point of station*, or the position which the spectator occupies to look upon, or delineate, the view or object; the height of his eye reaches to the top of the transparent plane, and is directly opposite to the point, C, the *centre of the picture*. The *prospective angle*, *v* P *d*, contains sixty degrees, and

includes all that the eye can effectively take in of any prospect without moving the head or changing the position; every picture is therefore, according to strict perspective rule, contained under this angle, and the objects to be delineated must all be brought within it by assuming a proper point of station. The points *v d* are termed the *points of distance*, they being the extreme limits of the picture on the right and left. The point *v* is also a *vanishing point*; in the present diagram it is identical with the point of distance, but this coincidence arises from the mere accident of the line *a b* (of which *v* is the vanishing point) lying parallel to, or in the same angle with, the line P *v*. If the line *a b* be represented by *e f* on the transparent plane, it must be evident that if it were continued, it would pass across the plane, and vanish in the horizontal line at the point *v*. If these definitions be clearly comprehended by the young draughtsman, the following problems will be divested of all difficulty and obscurity:—

PROBLEMS.

I. *To find the place of a given point in the perspective plane.*

Let the given point be A; then as a preliminary operation, draw G X the ground line at a little distance from it, and, parallel thereto, H L the horizontal line; assume the point of station P, and draw from it perpendicularly to the line H L, when C will be the centre of the picture. To avoid repetition, this preparatory operation is to be understood as applying to every problem.

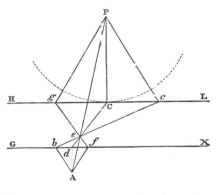

The apparent intricacy of the diagram arises from our having included in it three different methods of finding the place of the point.

1st Method. Draw from the point A in an oblique direction to G X, as A *b*, and from the point of station P draw P *c* parallel to A *b*, and join *b* and *c*; then draw A *d* perpendicular to G X, and draw from *d* to the centre C; the intersection of the lines *b c*, *d* C, at *e*, gives the place of the point A in the perspective plane.

2d Method. Draw A *b*, P *c*, as before, and also *b c*; then draw from the point A to the point of station P, and the intersection of A P by *b c* gives *e*, the place of A in the perspective plane.

3d Method. Draw A *b*, P *c*, as before; draw A *f* at pleasure, and *g* P parallel thereto; join *b* to *c*, and *f* to *g*, and the intersection of these lines *b c*, *f g*, gives *e*, the place of the point A.

II. *To place a line in the perspective plane.*

All original lines *perpendicular* to the ground and horizontal lines, vanish in the centre of the picture; and all lines *parallel* to the ground and horizontal lines, will likewise be parallel to them, when brought into the perspective plane. Thus, D E is represented in the perspective plane by *f g*, and would, if continued, vanish in the centre C; and A B is represented by *b c*, which is parallel to the ground line G X, and the horizontal line H L.

The complexity of the illustrative diagram arises from the line being placed in three positions; but there is a manifest advantage in bringing the several operations into juxtaposition, as we thus see at a glance how variously a line of the same length is represented in the perspective plane, according to the direction in which it lies with respect to that plane.

1st Case. When the line is parallel to the ground and horizontal lines, as A B. Draw P A, P B, from the point of station P, to the extremities of the line A B; join B to the ground line at pleasure, as B *a*,

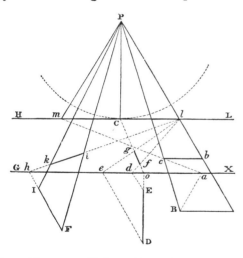

and draw P *m* parallel to B *a*, also draw *m a*; the line *m a* will intersect P B in *c*; draw through *c* parallel to G X, and *b c* will be the representation of A B in the perspective plane.

2d Case. When the line is perpendicular to the ground and horizontal lines, as D E. Continue D E to G X, as D E *o*; draw D *e* at pleasure, and parallel thereto E *d*, and P *l* parallel to both; draw from *l* to *d* and *e*, and from *o* to the centre C; then will *f g* represent the line D E in the perspective plane.

3d Case. When the line lies obliquely to the ground and horizontal lines, as F I. Continue F I to *h* on the ground line G X, and draw P *l* parallel to F I *h*; join *l h*, and draw P F, P I, from the point

of station P to the extremities of the line F I; then is *i k* a representation, on the perspective plane, of the line F I.

III. *To represent a triangle in perspective.*

Let the given triangle be B A D. Continue the oblique lines A B A D to the ground line G X, as A B *a*, A D *b*; draw P *f* parallel to A D *b*, and P *g* parallel to A B *a*, and connect *f* to *b*, and *g* to *a*. The intersection of *f b*, *g a*, gives the angle *e*, the perspective representation of

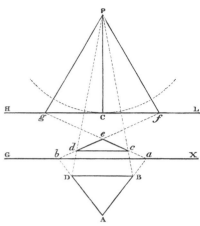

the angle A. Draw from the point of station P, to B and D; and where the lines P B, P D intersect the lines *f b*, *g a*, draw the line *c d*; then will *c e d* be the perspective delineation of the triangle B A D.

IV. *To represent a square in perspective, when placed obliquely to the perspective plane.*

Let the given square be *a b c d*. Continue the sides *a b*, *a c* to G X, as *a b e*, *a c h*; likewise continue the sides *b d*, *c d* to G X, as *b d g*, *c d f*; draw P *n* parallel to *a c h* and *b d g*, and P *o* parallel to *a b e* and *c d f*; draw from *n* to the points *g* and *h*, and from *o* to the points *e* and *f*. The points of intersection *k i l m* define the perspective representation of the square *a b c d*.

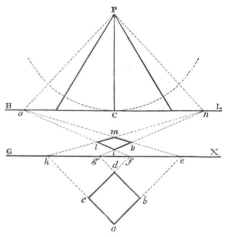

V. *To represent a square in due perspective, when placed parallel to the perspective plane.*

Let the given square be *a b c d*. Continue the sides *a c*, *b d*, to the ground line G X, and draw the diagonal *b c*, continuing it to *e*; draw P *f* parallel

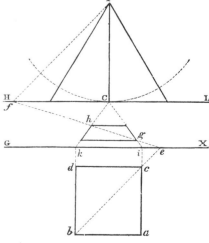

to *b c e*, and join *f* to *e*; also draw from the centre C to the points *i* and *k*; draw lines parallel to the ground line through the points *g* and *h*, where the line *e f* intersects the lines C *i*, C *k*. We have thus obtained the representation of *a b c d* in the perspective plane.

VI. *To represent a pentagon in perspective.*

Let the given pentagon be A B D E F. Continue the lines A D, B E to *a* and *e*, and draw P *f*, P *d*, parallel to B E *e*, A D *a*, and join *a* to *d*, and

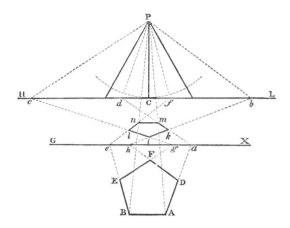

f to *e*; continue the lines D F, E F to *g* and *h*, draw P *b*, P *c* parallel to D F *h*, E F *g*, and join *c* to *g*, and *b* to *h*; and draw from P to the points A and B. The intersection of the lines *b h*, *c g*, gives the angle *i*, corresponding to A F; the lines *b h*, *c g*, are intersected by other lines *a d*, *f e*, in the points *k* and *l*, and *i k*, *i l*, are perspective sides of the polygon A B D E F, that answer to F D, F E; then *a d*, *f e*, are crossed nearer to C, by the lines P A, P B, in the points *m* and *n*, and *k m*, *l n*, are the perspective sides answering to A D and B E; and joining the points *m* and *n*, we obtain the side *m n* corresponding to A B. The given pentagon A B D E F is therefore represented in the perspective plane by *i k m n l*.

VII. *To represent a hexagon in perspective.*

Let the given hexagon be A B D E F I. Continue A D to *a*, E I to *d*, and draw through the points D and F to *b*; the lines A D *a*, B F *b*, E I *d* being parallel, draw P *h* parallel to any one of them; continue B E to *f*, D F to *c*, and draw through the points A and I to *e*; and the lines B E *f*, A I *e*, D F *c*, being parallel, draw P *g* parallel to any one of them; draw from *h* to the

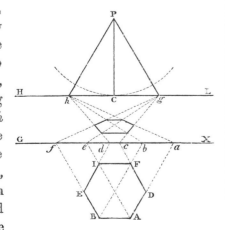

points *a*, *b*, and *d*, and from *g* to the points *c*, *e*, and *f*, and the intersections of these lines from the points *g* and *h*, will give the perspective outline of the hexagon.

VIII. *To represent a circle in perspective.*

Let the given circle be *e a b f d c*. Draw the square A B D E without the circle, and let the sides A B D E be parallel to the ground line G X, and continue A D B E to the ground line. Draw the diagonals B D, A E, continuing them to *g* and *h*; also P *k*, P *i*, parallel to B D *g*

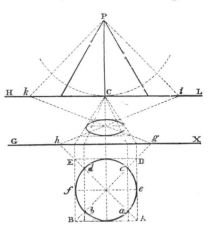

and A E *h*, and join *k* to *g*, and *i* to *h*. Through the points *a b c d*, where the diagonals A E B D intersect the circle, draw the lines *a c*, *b d*, parallel to A D and B E, and continue them to the ground line; draw likewise through the centre of the circle in like manner; and also the diameter *e f*, parallel to the ground line. All the perpendicular lines vanish in the centre of the picture; therefore draw from the point C to all their intersections with the ground line. These lines from C will intersect the lines *g k*, *h i*, in various points; and if from some of these we draw the perspective parallels answering to E D, *f e*, B A, as shown in the diagram, we obtain the points and bounds of a continuous curve which is the perspective delineation of the given circle.

IX. *To represent a cube in perspective, when the original lines lie obliquely to the perspective plane.*

Let A B D E be the base of the cube. This base, or ground plan, is first to be put into perspective by Problem IV. Then from the angular points of the perspective base raise perpendiculars; and on any one of the points *a*, *b*, *c*, *d*, (but more conveniently on *a* or *d*), erect a perpendicular equal to the height of the cube —let it be *a g*, on the point *a*. Draw from *g* to *f*, cutting

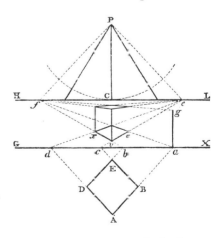

the perpendicular *o*; draw from *e*, through the intersection, cutting the perpendicular *v*; draw from *f*, through this last intersection, cutting the perpendicular *x*; and draw again from *e* to this intersection in *x*. Thus the top of the cube is determined and the whole figure defined, as shown in the diagram.

X. *To represent a cube in perspective, the original lines being parallel and perpendicular to the perspective plane.*

Let A B D E be the base of the cube, which is first to be put into perspective by Problem V. Then on the point *a* erect the perpendicular *a c*, equal to the height of the cube. Raise perpendiculars likewise from the angles of the perspective base. Then draw from *c* to the centre of the picture; and the line *c* C will cut two of these perpendiculars, and form one side of the top of the cube. Draw lines parallel to the ground line, or horizontal line, through the points where *c* C intersects the perpendiculars, and thus obtain the two sides of the top of the cube which lie parallel to the perspective plane. These parallel lines will cut the other two

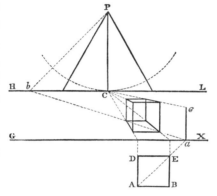

perpendiculars; and a line drawn from C through the intersecting points, will give the fourth side of the top of the cube. And thus the whole figure will be formed, and a cube of the given dimensions be transferred to the perspective plane, as required.

XI. *To represent a pyramid, or solid angle, in perspective.*

Let A B D E be the base of the pyramid, which is to be put into perspective by Problem IV. From *c*, the centre of the base A, B, D, E, draw the line *c a*, parallel to B D and A E; and on *a* erect the perpendicular *a f*, equal to the height of the pyramid.

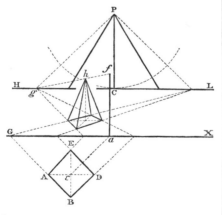

Draw lines from the opposite angles of the perspective base, and they will intersect in the centre of the pyramid, on which raise a perpendicular. Draw from *f* to *g*, and the line *f g* will mark the height, *h*, of the pyramid in the perspective plane. Lastly, draw from the angles of the perspective base to the point *h*, and the figure will be completely formed, and delineated in the terms of the problem.

XII. *To represent a cylinder in perspective.*

Let the circle A B D E be one end of the cylinder.

This is first to be reduced to a perspective plane, by Problem VIII.: then erect on the points *b*, *c*, the perpendiculars *b d*, *c e*, equal to the height of

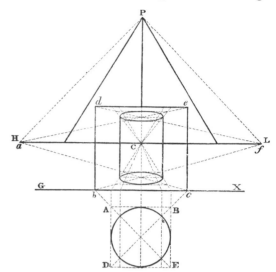

the cylinder, and join *d* and *e*. Draw from *e* to *a*, and from *d* to *f*; and having set off on *d e*, the several divisions or intersections in *b c*, draw from C to the points so obtained in *d e*, and also draw parallels to *d e* to give the top of the cylinder, in the same way that parallels are drawn for the base, according to Problem VIII. The ends of the cylinder being determined, it remains only to draw the parallel lines connecting them, and the figure is completed.

The preceding problems are illustrated by diagrams on a small scale, and that, for the obvious reason, that larger illustrations would have spread over many pages the information which is here compressed within four pages. But, for practice and instruction, it is desirable that the young draughtsman construct his figures on a much larger scale, making each occupy a space not less than the size of our page. The advantages of such enlargement must be apparent; the lines of construction will not crowd together confusedly, and the points of intersection, by which the outlines of figures are determined, will be projected with much greater precision. And, moreover, this mode of practice will enable the draughtsman to introduce much variety of construction, and derive from these elementary problems a thorough knowledge of all the principles contained in them. It may be of advantage to notice in detail some of the variations which may be introduced into each problem.

In connection with the first problem, which determines the position of a point, we may introduce a variation in the height of the vertical plane, or plane of projection. Thus, whilst other portions of the figure are laid down proportional to the diagram, let the space between the ground line G X, and the horizontal line H L, be increased or diminished; or, in other words, suppose the height of the eye, which is measured by the space between the ground and horizontal lines, to be greater or less. It will thus be seen, how the point A takes a different position in the plane of delineation, according to the greater or less elevation of the spectator's eye.

The three cases of the second problem are to be constructed separately, to dispel any confusion that may result from their union in one diagram, and also to admit such variation on each case as may be desirable. Thus, in the first place, take the line D E, which is perpendicular to the ground line G X, and placing it at various distances from G or X, see how it comes into the vertical plane, under these several conditions; and then construct with different heights of the eye, or horizon, and so learn how the position and length of the line are affected by the height of the eye. Treat the lines B A and I F in a precisely similar manner. The young student must not suppose that he has exhausted a problem when he has constructed it precisely as it is shown in the printed diagram; but, on the contrary, he must analyze and vary its details until every elementary principle involved in it becomes clear and satisfactory to him. Indeed, unless this be done, the knowledge of perspective to be derived from the twelve problems is very limited; but if the plan recommended be followed, they will be found to contain all that is necessary in the way of general instruction, and quite sufficient to carry the draughtsman on in the application of the principles to any varieties of objects, under every mode of assemblage.

The third problem presents a triangular area for projection on the plane, and this offers a large field for practice. The triangle may have its base D B parallel to the ground line, yet be situated at any distance from G or X; it may have its base at any angle to the ground line, with the same variation as to distance; its figure may be varied at pleasure; it may be brought nearer to, or removed further from the ground line; and it may be projected with any height of eye, or horizon. And let it not be thought that these variations of construction are profitless repetitions; since from each one new ideas will be obtained, and the general principle more clearly demonstrated.

The fourth and fifth problems give two cases of the projection of a square: in the one, its diagonal is perpendicular to the ground line; and, in the other, its side is parallel to the same line. These problems admit all the variety of construction referred to under the third problem. The side may lie nearer to or more distant from the ground line; it may vary in position with regard to G or X; its side may lie at any angle to the ground line; and it may be projected with horizons of greater or less height.

The seventh and eighth problems project the pentagon and hexagon; and it is most important that all the varieties of construction be employed upon them, since polygonal figures, from the number of lines of which they are composed, come so differently into the plane, according to the point of sight.

The circle completes the series of plane figures, and the method of its perspective projection is shown in the eighth problem. The variations in this case are the removal of the circle nearer to or farther from the base line; placing it more or less obliquely to the point of sight; and viewing it from different heights of the eye, or horizon. With a low horizon, the circle projects very elliptically, as shown in the diagram; but if the point of sight be considerably elevated it loses less of its circular figure, and especially when it comes into foreground, or very near to the ground line.

It is supposed that thus far the young draughtsman will make a separate diagram, on a large scale, for every variation of the several problems that has been recommended, and not attempt to combine two or three projections in one drawing, which would confuse him and frustrate the purpose in view. Having now, however, become conversant with the projection of plane figures under every variety of aspect and position, it is desirable that he should retrace his ground, and familiarize himself with the projection of a number of similar plane figures placed contiguously. Thus, taking the equilateral triangle D A B in problem third, let him repeat it along the ground line, and then draw a line through the angular point A of each triangle, which will thus form a double series, the one filling up the intervals between the other. Let him connect with this line of alternating triangles, two other lines precisely similar. Here, then, he will have a tesselated pavement of triangular pieces closely fitting into each other; and the projection of the whole figure on the plane of delineation will only be a repetition of the operation for a single triangle. In his first trials at these more complicate constructions, it may be advisable that the draughtsman have beside him a number of tints of colour, so that the different steps of his projection may be apparent, and stand out separately from the rest. It must be observed that the projection of a tesselated pavement does not necessarily require a process so tedious as finding the figure and position of every triangle, but it is best to commence on this principle, and, after a little practice, equally certain, but shorter methods, will suggest themselves. Diamonds, squares, polygonal figures, and circles may be similarly combined; and if the young artizan will labour heartily and industriously through this class of projections, he will become a thorough master of perspective, so far as bases and ground surfaces are concerned.

The ninth and tenth problems give the projection of the cube. Its base is a square, and may, of course, be placed, with reference to the ground line, as variously as the square itself. This being a solid, and not a mere surface, the value and effect of a low or high horizon will be very apparent. If the eye be considerably elevated, and the cube lie in the foreground, little more than the top or upper face will be seen; but if the cube is five or six feet high, and the horizon low, the side or sides only will be visible. The student will soon learn, from a variety of projections, what height of horizon is most pleasant to give agreeable form to the object, and avoid those abrupt angles which are termed *violent* perspective.

Problem eleven shows the perspective representation of a pyramid on a square base. This admits all the different modes of projection referred to in the preceding paragraph. If the pyramid be five or six feet high, and the horizon low, only one or two of its triangular sides can be seen; whilst a high horizon, if the pyramid is in the foreground, will lose its altitude, and the area of the base only will be visible with the lines of its angular sides meeting in the centre. Pyramids are not uniformly on square bases; and it will be a useful practice to project them on triangular, pentangular, and polygonal bases. These operations involve no difficulty, since the student is presumed to be thoroughly conversant with the projection of every plane figure under all conditions of aspect and position.

The twelfth problem gives the perspective of the cylinder, and, in connection with this, a patient working out of all the varieties of projection is absolutely necessary, since the most important elementary principles will be demonstrated at every step.

The draughtsman having now grounded himself thoroughly in the *separate* projection of the solids, under all accidents and circumstances, he must proceed to combine them; and, to do this, he must lay down their bases, under all conditions, with reference to the ground line, and transfer them accurately to the plane of delineation, and then raise the solids upon them, according to the rule for the simple figure.

The purpose of the remarks we have offered is to show that the elements of perspective are few and simple, at least for all practical purposes, and that a very sufficient knowledge of the art may be attained, without spending half a life-time in the study of those awful treatises in which lines and angles mix in most admired confusion, and present ingenious labyrinths that few persons have skill or patience to thread. A severe mathematical theory undoubtedly lies at the root of perspective, but the ordinary requirements of mechanical art can safely take the elements it establishes, without all the cumbrous load of proof, however elegant in its demonstrations and captivating to an enthusiast in mathematical science.

LIGHT AND SHADE.

In this department of his art, the draughtsman requires the following materials: a selection of good sable and camel's hair pencils of various sizes; a piece of the best China ink; three cakes of fine water colours,—lake, gamboge, and Prussian blue; and a Wedgewood palette for grinding the ink and colours, with cells to contain the various tints required. Such pencils should be chosen as, when wetted, terminate in a fine point, free from all straggling hairs. India or China ink is tested by the metallic lustre of its fracture, and by a powerful scent of musk; the last criterion is not, however, always decisive of quality, as many of the inferior inks are scented in imitation of the genuine kinds; it is, therefore, safer to rely on the appearance of the fracture, and the smoothness of the ink when ground upon the palette. The lake should be a rich crimson; not the dull heavy colour which, under this name, is usually included in ordinary drawing-boxes. Gamboge can be had at a very cheap rate in the lump, but it is far better to have it in the cake; in the latter form it is purer, and therefore combines more freely with the other colours in the formation of a neutral tint. Prussian blue should be very rich in the tint: this and the preceding colours are also to be tested by grinding; none will work satisfactorily, or mix properly, if gritty particles exist in them. These colours are seldom required by the mechanical draughtsman separately; their principal use is for the preparation of a fine mellow neutral tint, which is much more pleasing in a drawing than the harsh blackness of Indian ink, particularly if it include large shadowed surfaces requiring considerable depth of tone. The method of mixing this tint is to grind down the three colours upon the palette separately; then combine with the Prussian blue as much lake as will compose a rich purple, and add gamboge till a fine pearly gray colour is formed. No drawing can be properly shaded with fewer than three gradating tints, some draughtsmen use so many as five, and hence obtain great richness and depth in their shadows. These are to be prepared in the cells of the palette, and their relative strength properly proportioned; then dip a clean pencil in each, and draw broad strokes side by side on a piece of waste paper; when these are dry, it will be seen whether they have the gradation and depth required for the drawing.

The cabinet-maker may sometimes need to colour his drawings, to see the true effect of the combined materials, and also to give a customer a perfect idea of the intended article. To do this effectively, he must familiarize himself with the colours of woods in their natural state, and also when overlaid with French varnish. He must likewise study the character of the veinings and markings of the woods, and be able to represent these with freedom and richness of effect. Some length of practice and careful observation will be necessary to make the eye and hand skilful in this department; but the workman who has trained himself to this point of art, may fairly claim some precedence in the workshop, as one who has raised himself beyond the mere mechanics of his profession. A box of colours, containing twelve cakes, as ordinarily assorted, will be abundant material for the draughtsman's purposes; and the preparation of the various tints can be thoroughly understood only by continual practice, and training the eye to distinguish the most delicate variations of colour. To become skilful in representing the veins and markings of woods, the young artisan must first learn to outline them with his pencil freely and correctly.

Whatever objects are represented by linear drawing, the appearance of substance, roundness, and distance, may be given to them by an artful distribution of light and shade. If a circle be drawn upon paper, and the interior filled up with any even colour, it will represent a circular plane. When, however, an object has different degrees of shade, the lightest parts appear to come prominently forward, whilst the darker parts apparently recede, in proportion to the variations and depth of shade. For example, draw a circle as before, and, in place of covering the entire surface with an even tint, leave it light in the centre, and deepen the shadows towards the circumference; it will then present the appearance of a ball or sphere. The roundness of a cylinder or column is produced in the same manner. When the draughtsman can give due light and shade to these two solids, he can have no difficulty in imparting apparent substance to all curvilinear forms.

The proximity or remoteness of flat surfaces is produced by even tints of different depths; and in them also the lightest parts approach the eye, and the darkest retire from it. In mechanical drawing the light is usually supposed to come from the top of the drawing, and at an angle of forty-five degrees.

Let us suppose a drawing finished in outline, and ready to receive the light and shade. If China ink is determined on as the medium, grind down a sufficient quantity on the palette, and prepare three tints in so many different cells. The first tint is very light, and is to be applied to plane surfaces which retire from the eye; and all circular forms are to be entirely filled in with it, excepting the central light, which in a globe is a small circle, and in a column or cylinder, a broad, white line; it will also form the projected shadows on the high lights. The second tint must have sufficient strength to separate plane surfaces that retire still farther from the eye, to form the projected shadows on the first tint, and to give roundness to circular bodies; in applying it to these last, care must be taken to leave a portion of the first tint uncovered towards the centre, as a secondary light; and a narrow strip of the first tint is likewise to be preserved at the circumference, as a reflected light. If an ivory ball be held in the hand and the light suffered to glance upon it obliquely, it will be seen that the darkest shadow does not fall upon the extreme circumference, but at a very sensible distance from it; and this fact requires especial attention, for the appearance of roundness can never be properly brought out, unless the faint reflected light be preserved on the shadowed side. The third tint must have considerable strength; it is used for projected shadows on the second tint, and for perfecting globular and circular forms; observing, in this case also, to preserve a portion of the second tint towards the centre, and a smaller portion towards the circumference. If there should be a number of parts in the drawing requiring different depths of shade to discriminate their recession from the eye, intermediate tints must be prepared before we commence, for the strength of the finishing tint will never justify its use as a flat tint of any great extent. If the neutral tint, which we have recommended in preference to India ink, be adopted as the medium of giving shadow, the process of mixing and applying the gradating tints is precisely the same.

Some dexterity is required in handling the pencil, both to produce an even flat tint, and to give a pleasing idea of circular form; and the young aspirant must not be discouraged if, in his first essays, he should fail to give the decisive touch and bold finish of an experienced artist. A conquest achieved without labour is worthless; and all things, that are not practically impossible, can be accomplished by persevering industry. A few hints may obviate first difficulties, and assiduous application will overcome others. Young artists are too apt to work their pencil dry, which always destroys the evenness of the tint, and produces disagreeable seams, and likewise gives a harsh and meagre appearance to the drawing. The true method is, to use as large a pencil as the nature of the drawing will permit, and to keep it well charged with colour, for the largest surface will never be disfigured by a sinking of the tint or by seams, so long as we keep the paper flooded with colour, and thereby prevent the formation of dry edges as we proceed. When laying on a flat tint, the surface should be covered as rapidly as possible, as a farther preventive of sinking; afterwards the drawing should be placed a little aslope, and all the superfluous colour gathered up from one corner of the surface with a pencil that has been moistened in clean water. This done, lay the drawing level again, and on no account touch the tint till it has dried. The shadows of circular bodies and all gradating shadows require skilful management; any sudden transition from light to shade produces a disagreeable effect. Lay on the tint with a large full pencil; then with another pencil moderately moistened with clean water soften off all the edges of the tint. If this be done adroitly, light and shade will blend with each other in such a way that it can scarcely be detected where light ends and shadow begins. It will be obvious that the tint must not at first be laid down to the full breadth of the shadow, as we necessarily extend it by the process of softening off. Every succeeding tint must be softened in the same manner; so that as the light blends with the first tint, so the first tint must blend with the second, and the second with the third. These are all the verbal instructions that can be given for producing judicious and pleasing light and shade; and if the young draughtsman conjoin with them a love of his art and close application, only one more requisite is wanting to insure his success, and that is—*time*.

THE

CABINET-MAKER'S ASSISTANT.

PRACTICAL OBSERVATIONS ON CABINET-MAKING.

INTRODUCTION.

In attempting to furnish some practical observations on the Art of Cabinet-making, one of the greatest difficulties in the outset is to determine at what point to begin; so as, on the one hand, to avoid presuming too much on the previous knowledge of the reader, and on the other, of presuming on it too little. In the one case, the observations are apt to be to some extent unintelligible; and in the other, to be thought commonplace or trivial. Believing that in the greater number of elementary treatises the first of these errors has been the one fallen into, we shall endeavour so to frame our remarks as to render them useful to the inexperienced workman, though it should be at the risk of appearing, to the better instructed, to be descending to greater minuteness than is really necessary; while for him we trust to be able to bring forward some information on the materials, processes, and methods of construction—the result of our own study and experience—which even he may acknowledge to be both novel and advantageous. We therefore submit the remarks that follow to the favourable consideration of cabinet-makers in general, believing that those who have already made the greatest progress in acquiring knowledge, will be found the most willing to receive instruction, and the most ready to overlook any imperfections that may occur in our treatment of the subject.

We have for long been convinced that the vast majority of our artizans bestow far too little thought upon the articles which they manufacture, whether as respects the materials of which they are constructed, the method by which they are made, the purposes they are to serve, or the designs after which they are fashioned. The result of this is, that modes of construction, useful forms, and elegant designs, which have originated with the thoughtful few, are copied and re-copied by the unthinking many, without any intelligent appreciation of why this particular method of construction has been chosen, why this form and proportion of parts is more suitable than another, or of what were the principles of taste and purposes of utility which led to their adoption. And, as a necessary consequence, the articles thus unintelligently copied, have a constant tendency to degenerate in character in the hands of the copyist.

One of the leading causes of this state of things is doubtless the imperfect training given to apprentices. It is too often the case, that while the young workman is instructed what to do, he is seldom told the reason for doing it in the way pointed out to him. Obedience is too much depended on, and thinking intelligence too little. The apprentice thus learns to perform certain pieces of work in a certain manner, and, by steady application, he becomes an active and efficient workman; but his reasoning faculties having been left dormant by his master, and he himself never having had the curiosity to inquire into whys and wherefores, he seldom attains any peculiar eminence in his trade, and rarely becomes an originator himself, or an intelligent copyist and improver of the plans and designs of others. We are glad to think, that though this is the rule, there are many exceptions; but few who have had much experience among workmen will be inclined to deny the general accuracy of these statements. Another cause of this state of affairs is the want, till lately, in this country, of Schools of Design. While in France, and other continental states, the young workman has long had the means within his reach of acquiring such a knowledge of art as would improve and cultivate his taste, and render him capable of more fully appreciating beauty of form, and appropriateness of design, and probably of even himself effecting marked improvements in the articles he produces, the workmen of this country, until a recent period, have been almost wholly destitute of such advantages; and the number of such institutions is still so small, and their range so limited, that a considerable time must elapse before their operation can make any very evident impression on the mass of our operatives. But perhaps the principal cause of the state of matters adverted to, is to be found in the well known fact, that the workmen, generally, have not availed themselves to the extent they might have done, of the means of instruction actually within their reach. Mechanics' Institutes, Schools of Arts, &c. have, during the last thirty years, risen and multiplied in all our large towns, yet how small a portion of our young mechanics have taken advantage of them to acquire that knowledge of mathematics, natural philosophy, and kindred branches of study, that might, through their means, have been obtained. The elevating character of the effects produced on the honourable few who have earnestly profited by the opportunities of improvement thus afforded, make it all the more to be regretted, that a greater number have not been animated to follow their example.

Our readers will, we trust, free us from any intentional want of respect towards those regarding whom the preceding animadversions have been made. We could not refrain from availing ourselves of the present opportunity of stating, freely and frankly, opinions which have not been hastily formed, in the hope that the publicity thus given them may be a means of calling attention to the evils complained of, and lead both employers and employed to be more alive to the importance of adopting such measures as may tend to their removal. The improvement of the art generally, and the happiness and respectability of those engaged in it, are intimately connected with that mental application which we have indicated as necessary to be superadded to bodily labour. Our main object in making the practical observations on Cabinet-making, to which these remarks are introductory, shall be to furnish a stimulus to individual improvement, and thus add our contribution to the means for general progress. And if, in any case, we succeed in inciting the tradesman to careful thought on the nature of the processes in which he is daily employed, and to investigating the reasons why such processes should be performed in their own peculiar manner, our labours will not have been in vain, and we shall feel more than rewarded.

Section I.

On the Nature and Applicability of the various kinds of Wood suitable for Cabinet-work.

Among the difficulties which are experienced by the young employer or foreman, those are not least which attend the selection and purchase of suitable wood. Previously to his being called upon to act in either capacity, he has usually been but little conversant with woods in any other form than their cut up state; that is, as sawn into the various thicknesses of planks and boards, in common use. Although qualified by experience, it may be, to judge of the fitness of material in this condition, for his immediate purpose, in all probability he never has paid any close attention to it in the log; and, consequently, when obliged to become a purchaser, feels great difficulty in determining his choice.

This will not excite wonder, in those who have had most experience in the buying, or judging of wood, in logs. It is true, that the quality and general character of wood is ordinarily expressed in external signs, which experience renders familiar to the observant: but it must be confessed, that a considerable degree of uncertainty attends the opinion formed even by those whose experience is most extensive. But while it is readily admitted, that an amount of hazard always attends the purchase of wood in the log, it cannot for a moment be questioned, that the risk is lessened, in proportion to the experience and attention of the buyer.

What we have just stated, suggests forcibly the wisdom, of all who have it in desire, or in prospect, to become buyers, endeavouring to acquire experience. This all have it in their power to do, who are near a woodyard. Before a log is opened, let the inquirer carefully examine it, and, noting all the peculiarities of its appearance, endeavour to form an opinion of its qualities; the event, as seen in the cut wood, will shew the value of the opinion he had formed: and a repetition of such experiments will certainly conduct an intelligent observer to the attainment of a generally correct estimate of the character and value of wood. In treating of woods separately, we shall endeavour to point out some of the marks peculiar to each kind, which serve to indicate its qualities.

But besides the difficulty, arising from the want of familiarity with the external signs which usually indicate the nature and value of a log, the young buyer is exposed to annoyance from the fact, that in order to purchase advantageously, he must do so at a public sale by auction. Wood, it is true, may be and is bought by private bargain, but this entails the payment of an additional profit to the seller, who intervenes between the importer and the consumer. A limited demand on the part of the buyer may render this the wiser course; but where circumstances admit of it, a public sale, for behoof of the importers, will naturally be preferred, as furnishing the most extensive choice. The disturbing influences to which purchasers at an auction are exposed, arising from personal excitement, prevailing bustle, and the rivalry of opposing bidders, are matters of daily observation. But these are enhanced in the case of a sale of wood, by the comparative uncertainty of the value of the article exposed. Hesitating regarding the worth of the lot, the young buyer is apt to be led by the offers of others, perhaps not better judges than himself, to advance his bidding far beyond his own previous estimate of its value, and far above its real worth. His example acts upon others, until the log, or logs, are raised to a price alike astonishing to the exposer and the more experienced buyers. Few who have attended sales of wood will fail to recal many instances illustrative and confirmatory of what we have described.

In order to guard against folly like this, we would recommend two things; first, make a careful examination, before the sale, of the various lots, and endeavour to fix on several, one or more of which would, from their quality and size, suit your demand; and, second, affix to each a valuation of the price to which you are prepared to bid for it: this done, bide your time—don't bid until one of your marked lots are exposed—bid up to your valuation, if necessary, to get it—but on no account whatever offer more. Some one whom you regard as a good judge may outbid you—let him have it: it is much better that he should, than that, contrary to your own convictions, you should pay a price which, at leisure, you discover to be as far beyond the worth of the article, as it is in advance of your previous estimate of its value. The question arises here, however, How is the inexperienced buyer to arrive at a proper valuation of the lots which he wishes to purchase? To this we answer, By comparing them with similar lots, sold at previous sales, or in the earlier part of the sale at which he proposes to buy. It is much better to arrive at a conclusion after careful and quiet personal observation, than to look to others for advice on the subject of your purchases. They have not what you have, a personal interest in the issue; and hence, are not likely to be so sharp-sighted in choosing for you, as you will be in choosing for yourself. Besides, if you buy at one sale simply on the advice of others, you will, on the next

occasion, feel quite as dependent as before; a predicament which augurs ill for future success.

These hints may, possibly, provoke a smile on the part of those whose experience places them beyond the need of them; but, it is believed, may be of real service to the inexperienced buyer, for whom they are intended.

In treating on the subject of the various woods in use amongst cabinet-makers, our remarks shall be strictly popular, and of such a character as to be easily understood by our readers, of even the most ordinary education. To affect scientific nomenclature, classification, and description, would be unsuitable alike to the practical character of the work, and to the wants of those for whom it is written. We shall therefore take up the different kinds of wood, in the order of their importance to the cabinet-maker, and shall confine our attention to those which are in general use, or likely to become so.

It seems natural to commence with that which forms the groundwork of the greater number of articles manufactured by the cabinet workman, namely,

PINE, OR FIR.

YELLOW PINE.—Of Pines, or Firs, botanists enumerate above twenty distinct species, which it would be foreign to our design to particularize. Of these, we shall content ourselves with mentioning the three varieties which are in common use amongst cabinet-makers. And first, in point of importance, we notice the yellow pine of commerce, known in America as white pine, and denominated by botanists the *Pinus Strobus*. In modern works on trees indigenous, or which have been introduced into Great Britain, we find it called the Weymouth pine, from the fact of its having been planted in great numbers, in Wiltshire, by Lord Weymouth, early in the last century. In this country there have been many instances of this species, after a vigorous growth of sixty or seventy years, attaining a height of from seventy to eighty feet. But generally it has been found to decay much earlier, and to be so much smaller in size, as to render the planting of it unprofitable. Its native country is North America, where the growth of it extends from Canada to Virginia, in almost all varieties of soil, to an extent that seems well nigh boundless. The largest specimens are to be found growing in the soft friable and fertile soils of the valleys, and in the deep black sandy loam of the banks of rivers. In such situations, it sometimes reaches a height of one hundred and eighty feet, and a diameter of fifty-four inches. In appearance it is stiff and formal, of pyramidal growth, having thin and meagre foliage, destitute of that massive richness seen in other species of the pine. Specifically, it is distinguished by having the leaves fivefold, numerous and slender, of a bluish-green colour, and three and a half inches long. The cones are from four to six inches long, composed of smooth scales rounded at the base, and having the apex thinly covered with white resin. The trunk, which tapers considerably from the base to the summit, is free from branches for two-thirds of its height; the limbs, which are short and verticillate, are disposed in stages one above the other, and terminate in three or four upright branches at the top of the tree.

The felling and transporting of this description of timber from its native forests, affords employment to a large number of our British colonists in Canada and New Brunswick. The parties engaged in the work are called *lumberers*, and generally lead a life of extreme hardship and privation, alternated with seasons of riot and indulgence. Hired by a master lumberer, or associated in a party having a common interest in the proceeds of their labour, these men set out in the end of summer for the remote forests which are to be the scene of their winter's toil. Selecting a spot near the banks of a river, and in the midst of as much timber as possible, they divide themselves into three gangs; one of which cuts down the trees, another hews them, and the third is employed in hauling the timber to the banks of the nearest stream, or to the river itself. Rudely lodged in a log cabin, and coarsely fed, they spend the winter, which often lasts until the middle of May, in unremitting toil. The approach of summer, which swells the river with the melted snow, rather increases their hardships, as it then becomes necessary for them to get the timber afloat and rafted; an operation which cannot be effected without the lumberer being day after day, and that for weeks together, wet up to the middle, and often immersed from head to foot. When the timber has been floated down to the seaport, the rafts are taken to pieces and disposed of; which puts the poor lumberers in possession of a whole year's earnings at once. It will readily be conceived, that they often deepen the effects of their lengthened privations, by the brief indulgence in dissipation which follows.

The amount of pine timber annually imported to Britain from our North American colonies, on an average of eighteen years, ending 1841, is 9,634,776 cubic feet, employing upwards of three hundred vessels, the aggregate tonnage of which exceeds one hundred and sixty thousand tons.

Introduced into this country as an article of commerce about thirty-five years ago, yellow pine has almost entirely superseded the red and white pines, or Baltic Timber, which, up to that period, were the only kinds available for the purposes of the cabinet-maker. From its larger growth, its comparative freedom from turpentine and resinous matter, and from its being much softer, it is much better fitted than either of the others for being veneered on, or for interior finishing. The modern cabinet-maker, accustomed to this material, so easily wrought and so free from bias, can scarcely conceive of the difficulties experienced by his less fortunate predecessors; who, for their interior fittings and beds for veneering on, had nothing better than white or red pine, with their innumerable joinings, their flint-like knots, and almost endless shrinkings.

Of the various ports from which yellow pine has been shipped, the popularity has waxed and waned in no common degree. At one time, to advertise a cargo as from Mirimachi, was sufficient to insure its immediate sale; but, whether from the extensive exportation, or from a great fire, which a few years ago destroyed a vast quantity of timber there, recent importations have not obtained nearly the same popularity. The exports from Chaleur Bay for a time successfully disputed the precedency; but these, in turn, have given place to the timber from St. John, New Brunswick, which at present is, on the whole, the best fitted for cabinet-work. The earlier importations of it, we are aware, obtained, and perhaps deserved, a bad name. But more recent cargoes have done much to wipe away the reproach. While the first specimens which met our observation were distinguished by remarkable harshness and strength, accompanied by innumerable black soft knots, what we have met with latterly has been much milder in its character, and entirely free from the kind of knots mentioned. It is, however, by no means safe to purchase, without selection from the importations from any port; for every cargo contains wood of various qualities.

In the case of the house carpenter, there is less need of careful selection; for, from the nature of his demands, a profitable use can be found for timber of any character. If fine, it may be husbanded for interior finishing; but if coarse, can readily be got rid of in large masses for beams, and other covered work. The cabinet-maker, from having no such opportunities of disposing of coarse wood, requires to be more particular in his choice.

The faults in fir, to be chiefly guarded against, are *shakes*, twisted growth, and coarseness. We place the chief evil first, for while wood of twisted growth, or very coarse, may be made something of, when full of shakes it is almost good for nothing. We need scarcely say that the *shakes* to be dreaded are not those visible on the sides of the log, presenting cracks at a right angle to the surface, which are merely the effects of exposure; nor are those in the end of the log, which are seen to radiate from the heart; those most to be feared are *ring shakes*, that is, cracks in the end of the log which follow the grain, or annual rings. These, accompanied by an appearance of damp, show that the log is of a kind that, when cut up and dried, will scarce hold together. But many logs, otherwise fine, are unfit for the cabinet-maker, on account of their twisted growth; that is, from the grain, or fibres, not running parallel to the sides of the log, but being twisted round in the manner of a rope. Boards cut from such a log are sure to twist in drying, and prove troublesome after being wrought. Coarseness, that is, gnarled growth, and numerous knots, which ordinarily render their presence obvious to the most unpractised eye, is also to be guarded against by the careful buyer. In general, a good fir log is to be known by its having the ends dry and firm, and free from the appearance of softness and resinous streaks.

Cutting up.—From the way in which wood is assorted in lots, when exposed for sale, it is not to be expected that all the logs in a lot will be of one quality. On the contrary, as is natural, the indifferent and the bad ones are mixed with the good, and sold along with them. Hence the necessity of attention to the cutting up of the various qualities into thicknesses suited for the purposes for which they are best fitted. If the log be very coarse, it should be cut into boards for packing cases, or the like. If the appearances indicate harshness or strength, it is evidently best adapted for framing, of various sorts. But when a mild and clean log presents itself, it should naturally be cut into thinner boards, for panels, or gables and tops, to be veneered on. The recent introduction of fine fir varnished with copal, as a material for the manufacture of furniture for second or inferior bedrooms, which now obtains rather extensively in large mansions, lends an additional value to timber of this quality. But as every log, however fine, contains more or less of coarse wood near the heart, it is of importance to dispose of this to the best advantage in cutting it up. Many are in the habit of cutting planks of 3 inches, or $3\frac{1}{2}$ inches thick, from the heart, with the view of working up the coarser wood in veneered pillars, or the like; but we regard it as the better plan to take off a few $\frac{1}{2}$ inch, or $\frac{3}{4}$ inch boards, which, however coarse, can be got rid of in drawer shelving, or tops and bottoms of carcases, where quality is of little importance. But in this, as in other matters, experience is the best guide; and, from the varieties of demand, will

conduct different parties to results which, although opposed to each other, are nevertheless best suited to their respective cases. There is one consideration, however, which should not be overlooked in any instance, namely, which way the draughts are to be run through the log. In determining this, regard should be had to two things—the direction of the heart shakes, and the fact that every log has one side finer than the others. It is desirable that the cuts should not cross the heart shakes, and that they should run parallel to the fine side of the wood. When both of these can be attained, it is most profitable; but where they cannot, it is perhaps the least evil to run the draughts in the direction of the shakes.

RED AND WHITE PINES.—We deem it unnecessary to say much regarding red and white pines; but with the view of affording all the information which is likely to prove interesting or useful to the cabinet-maker, shall briefly notice them, in order. The red pine of commerce is denominated, by botanists, *Pinus Sylvestris*, the wild or Scotch fir. It is very extensively distributed over the surface of the globe, being found in almost every country of Europe, and in the more temperate and colder parts of Asia. Although indigenous to this country, and attaining to considerable perfection in various districts, the colder climate of Russia, Denmark, Norway, Lapland, and Sweden seems most favourable to its full development; and in these countries it is to be found of fine quality, and in prodigious numbers. In favourable situations this species of pine attains a height of from 80 to 90 feet, and is from 4 to 5 feet in diameter at the base. The bark is thick and furrowed, the leaves are *in pairs*, of a pale green colour, and from $1\frac{1}{2}$ to fully 2 inches long; the cones thick, short, and not much pointed.

The white pine, or deal, of commerce, is the *Pinus abies*, or spruce fir of botanists. Of this there are three species known in trade, the Norway spruce, and the white and black spruces, or *Abies alba*, and *Abies nigra*, of America. This is a tall and stately tree, reaching sometimes the height of from 150 to 200 feet. The leaves are solitary, scattered upon the branches, and of a dark green colour; the cones from 5 to 7 inches long, and about 2 inches in diameter.

The red pine, although of the highest value in ship building, house carpentry, and all kinds of work exposed to the action of the atmosphere or of water, is, as we have already said, ill adapted to, and almost never used, in the manufacture of cabinet furniture. The white variety, possessing more strength than the yellow, and less charged with turpentine and resinous matter than the red, is better fitted for a number of purposes than either of them. This wood, although grown in Britain, and extensively imported from America, is found in the greatest perfection in the northern parts of Europe, from whence large supplies are annually shipped, for consumpt in this country. Instead of being sent in logs, it is cut up into planks of 11 inches broad by 3 inches thick, and from 18 to 22 feet long, which are called *deals*, and when shorter, *deal ends*; or into pieces of 6½ inches broad by 2½ inches thick, and 20 or 21 feet long, known as *battens*.

There are several sizes to which this variety of fir may be applied, which renders it desirable that the cabinet-maker should have it in stock. Cut into boards of ½ inch thick, it is suitable for plain deal backs; in ¾ inch boards, it will be found useful for bed bottoms; or if cut 1¼ inches thick, it will make excellent tenter frames, or the like, where strength is required. It is very unsuitable for veneering on, as, in the course of shrinking, which it will continue to do after being pretty carefully dried, it will leave the harder veins projecting above the softer, to the great detriment of the appearance of the article for which it has been used.

From its being offered for sale in planks, there is little need for directions as to the purchase of it. We may notice, however, that there is ordinarily the option of buying the planks as they lie, or of picking them. The cabinet-maker will generally find it profitable to pay the small additional charge for having his choice, and so secure the finer timber. This is distinguished by having small annual rings, or being close in the grain. In selecting, care also should be taken to avoid deals or battens which contain the heart of the tree, or which are of twisted growth.

Seasoning.—Every one knows that it is of the greatest importance that wood should be well seasoned, previous to its being manufactured; and that, in attention to this, the quality of the article, and the character of the maker, are alike involved. Let the design be faultless, and the execution perfect, if the material be unseasoned, disappointment to the purchaser, and disgrace to the manufacturer, must inevitably be the result. All, therefore, who seek to attain the reputation of being good cabinet-makers, ought to make certain of the thorough seasoning of their wood. The process of drying may be said to commence from the time that the timber is felled and squared, as either immersion in water, while being rafted down the rivers to the sea, or subsequent exposure to the action of the air, has the tendency to abstract from it the natural sap. This may be

continued, to some extent, while it remains in logs, by taking care to give the air admission on all sides, raising them from the ground on *clean* blocks, and keeping free spaces between; at the same time, noticing that any top covering of slabs is separated from the logs, which it shields from the sun, by fillets of wood. The mention of *clean* blocks may appear trivial, but experience shows, that if these be in a decayed state, they taint the timber which rests on them. If logs are suffered to lie on the soft damp soil of a woodyard, and especially if there are weeds or fungous matter around them, the effect is to impregnate the wood with the seeds of decay, before it is brought into use.

It is, however, not desirable that fir should remain long in the log, as the tendency of the air acting on the surfaces alone, while the body of the wood is unaffected by it, is to produce shakes or cracks, which earlier cutting up would have prevented. When sawn into planks and boards, these should be laid in horizontal piles, with fillets placed at intervals between them, or set upright in racks, divided by fixed fillets. The timber placed upright, will dry sooner than that laid horizontally, but will not generally be found so flat and straight; as the pile, if carefully raised, forms a press to keep the whole in order.

One unacquainted with the subject, would be ready to think that timber would dry but slowly, if allowed to remain exposed in all kinds of weather; but experience proves, that the natural sap is extracted more thoroughly by the action of the external atmosphere, even although accompanied with moisture, than by any artificial means. Wood so seasoned, is much less likely to be the subject of change afterwards, than that which has been dried by artificial heat. All wood used in the manufacture of furniture, should, previously to and in the course its being wrought, be placed in a temperature several degrees higher than that to which the finished article will probably be exposed; this, however, should be preceded by a course of seasoning in the open air. Where heat alone is relied on, it will be found that the outer surface is hardened to a degree that prevents the evaporation of the moisture from the internal part, and that the imprisoned sap will betray its presence, by its subsequent efforts to escape. It is scarcely possible, by any course of treatment, to prevent wood from shrinking and warping under atmospheric influence. We have seen pine that had formed part of a church steeple for between two and three centuries, when taken down and sawn into small pieces, shrink and expand considerably, both in length and width, when exposed to changes of temperature and to the action of the air. So satisfied, by repeated experiment, of the impossibility of rendering any kind of wood impassible by seasoning, was an ingenious watchmaker, who wished to form pendulum rods of it, that he at length found it necessary to char the rods, and in their heated state plunge them into copal varnish, which, by excluding the air, attained the desired result.

The shortness of the time which circumstances allow for the seasoning of material, by the ordinary method which we have recommended, often renders it necessary to expedite the process by having recourse to more artificial means. When a drying room, heated by means of stoves, steam, or hot water, is made use of, it is of great importance that a free circulation of air should be had. Entering at the lower part in a hot and dry state, it escapes at the upper, charged with the moisture which it absorbs in the heated state. When, on the contrary, such rooms are made as air-tight as possible, the wood is then surrounded by a warm but stagnant atmosphere, which retains whatever moisture it may have acquired from the evaporation of the sap in the wood.

As to the time necessary to the proper seasoning of wood, a cabinet-maker of any experience will have little difficulty in determining. The presence of moisture is indicated by a peculiar smell, by the readiness to shrink and warp, and mainly by the weight; for no piece of wood can be said to be thoroughly seasoned, until it cease to become lighter from evaporation. Difference of thickness will of course render it necessary to employ a longer or shorter time in the process; and the purposes to which the wood is to be applied must also be taken into consideration, for it is possible that wood may be rendered too dry.* The fear of this, however, need disturb the cabinet-maker but rarely indeed. If it be objected, that beds for veneering on require to be damp in proportion to the state of the veneer to be laid on them, we will afterwards show that it is very easy to make them so, without having recourse to unseasoned wood, from which the natural sap has for the purpose not been thoroughly withdrawn.

Birch.

It has been common for writers on woods to speak in a very slighting tone of the birch, and to treat of

* We recently saw an instance of this, in an otherwise very well finished public building. In the upper flat, of which on one side the windows were designed to stand open, the floor had been so completely stove-dried, that when exposed to the external air it had expanded, so that it presented a series of curves equal in number to the boards of which it was composed.

it rather as a tree of graceful form and beautiful foliage, than as yielding wood of great utility, and most inviting appearance. While the white birch, or *Betula alba,* and the weeping birch, or *Betula pendula* of Europe, may deserve no higher consideration, it is widely different with the birch of American growth. This, in regard to the cabinet-maker, occupies a place of no mean importance. For a long period it has furnished the staple commodity in use, for almost all the purposes for which hardwood is required: and more recently, the finer specimens of it have been employed in the manufacture of bed-room, hall, and even drawing-room furniture.

Of American birch, there are seven varieties; but of these we shall mention only the three which are commonly imported to Britain, namely, the *Betula lenta,* or mahogany birch, the *Betula excelsa,* or yellow birch, and the *Betula nigra,* or black birch. The *Betula lenta,* or mountain mahogany of America, called also mahogany birch, and sweet birch, is, on account of the excellence of its wood, the most valued. We have seen many specimens, which, in a finished state, rivalled in beauty the finest mahogany. These were of the kind familiarly called *curled:* a descriptive designation warranted by its resemblance to curled mahogany, in having the plane surface variegated by a series of semicircular shades of colour, alternately light and dark, occasioned by the different angles at which the light falls upon the grain of the wood. A figure will most simply illustrate the manner in which this effect is produced. Let the serpentine line represent the undulating growth of the grain lengthways, and the straight line, the saw draught which runs through the log; it is plain, that at each undulation traversed by the straight line the grain is presented at opposite angles to the surface, and hence the variety of colour is produced. The semicircular form of these shades is occasioned by the sawdraught crossing the annular rings of the tree. It is difficult to convey by mere description an idea of the rare beauty of such specimens as we have mentioned: for when finished in French polish, they possess a transparent appearance, suggestive of coloured crystals or precious stones, having the light reflected from a surface polished at different angles, rather than a plane surface of wood. Birch of this quality is well suited for the manufacture of hall furniture, when the design of it is rather plain than enriched with carving: also, for bed-room furniture, when the apartments in which it is to be placed are not large. In a room indifferently lighted, or contracted in its dimensions, the use of birch, from its light colour and transparent surface, has an excellent effect, as the articles seem rather to retire than obtrude themselves, as those in a darker coloured wood appear to do. These remarks will render it evident, that we do not approve of the practice of colouring birch, with the view of making it resemble mahogany. To use colouring matter, whether in the form of vegetable juice, or gum in solution with the polish, is, we apprehend, only to spoil good birch when applied to it; inasmuch as the stain or gum has the effect of destroying that transparent lustre which we regard as its principal beauty.

It may be objected to our strong recommendation of finely figured birch, that it is very liable to shrink and warp. The truth of this will be readily admitted by all who have any experience of its use; but these defects may be counteracted by careful seasoning in the first place, and, further, by avoiding the use of it in the solid, wherever it is practicable to apply veneer. In wardrobe doors, or in the footboards of beds, let both panels and framing be of suitable fir; which will be found, if properly prepared, quite able to resist the natural tendencies of the birch veneer.

Birch logs of the quality of which we have been speaking, bear but a small proportion to the whole amount imported from Quebec, the port from which this variety is shipped for Britain. It is to be found growing not only in Canada, but also in the middle states of Pennsylvania, New York, and the Jerseys; but from these localities the cost of transmission forbids its being sent to this country.

This tree is found to prefer a deep rich soil, is of rapid growth, and when it attains its greatest dimensions, reaches a height of 70 or 80 feet, and a girth of from 9 to 12 feet. It is exceedingly handsome in appearance, budding remarkably early in the spring, when its leaves are covered with a thick coat of down; this disappears later in the season, and leaves them of a bright and lively green. The trunk is straight, and is often clear of branches for a height of from 30 to 40 feet from the ground; the branches are quite smooth, the leaves thin, oblong, tapering to a point, and beautifully serrated. They possess a peculiar fragrance, which they retain after being dried in a stove, affording by infusion an agreeable diluent, superior to some of the common teas of commerce.

YELLOW BIRCH.—The *Betula excelsa* of botanists yields wood much like the last mentioned, but paler in the colour. The trees attain an equal height, but are of smaller girth than the former; rarely exceeding 7 or 8 feet.

BLACK BIRCH.—*Betula nigra* is smaller in size, duller in the colour, and less variegated in the figure of the wood, than either of the species already mentioned, still it is imported into this country in such quantity as to have led to its name being applied to American birch in general. This is, perhaps, to be accounted for by the fact of this variety having been much earlier introduced to Britain than the others. Large quantities are annually exported from St. John, New Brunswick; Pictou, Nova Scotia; and from Cape Breton island. In 1839, the imports of American birch amounted to 336,151 cubic feet, while the consumpt (307,450 feet) nearly equalled them.

Purchase of Birch.—Most of the remarks which we made regarding the purchase of fir, will be found of equal value in reference to birch; we shall, therefore, only make a few additional remarks, which are specially applicable to it. And first, we would recommend the young buyer to select logs in which there is as little sap wood as he can find in the parcel exposed for sale. In birch, the sap wood, even when fresh, is much inferior to the perfect wood, and is peculiarly liable to decay in the course of seasoning in the open air. As in different trees, the sap wood bears very different proportions to the whole, an opportunity for selection is afforded, which it would be unwise to overlook. A glance at the ends of the log will at once enable an observer to judge of the amount of sapwood in it, as there is in colour a marked distinction between it and the matured wood. We would advise further, the purchase of large sized logs, in preference to smaller ones. In birch, the heart, and knots which radiate from it, often form a considerable part of the whole log; and, in a small tree, there is the additional evil, that in squaring and straightening it the best portion of the wood has been hewn away; and hence large timber, though bearing a higher price, will be found the most economical. In obtaining finely figured wood, the difficulty arises not so much from the trouble of selecting it, as from its absolute scarcity. The presence of fine figure is more evident in birch than in almost any other wood, the rough hewn sides of the log showing the transverse semicircular shades almost as plainly as the dressed surface. It is true, that there may be present these external signs, while the figure does not go far into the body of the wood; but the interior never can be fine, without betraying itself externally. Whole cargoes, however, are to be found, in which there are few or no logs of the desired quality.

Cutting up.—In cutting up birch into the various thicknesses in common use, the first thing to be attended to is the character of the log. Should it be of a plain description, it is evidently fitted only for chair rails, sofa stocks and scrolls, and bed stuff. In this case, perhaps the best way of cleaning the heart is to take a 2½ inch plank off each side of the opening draught, then 3 inch or 3½ inch planks for bed-posts; the remainder outwards, to be thrown into thicknesses for rails of common chairs, or for stocks. The heart planks if foul, that is, knotty or shaken, will cut up profitably into rails for easy chairs, or into rails of common chairs with sweeped seats. The rinding of birch, after it has been planked, into the breadths commonly required, for bed stocks and posts, or rails for telescope tables, &c., greatly facilitates the seasoning of it; but this should never be done until the planks are partially dried. When this is not attended to, it will be found much more liable to bend and warp, than it would be after having had a little time to season. It may excite surprise in some, to see sliding rails for telescope dining tables mentioned as one of the uses to which birch may be applied: but we have seen it used for this purpose with great advantage. The dressed surface of birch presents a smoothness, of which oak or Honduras mahogany is destitute; and hence it is much less liable than either of them to become rough from the friction which sliding rails are exposed to. When used for sliding rails, care must be taken to select birch of straight, close growth, free from figure and from tendency to warp, and above all, wood that is thoroughly seasoned. Where these qualities meet in birch, we are persuaded that it will be found nearly equal to Cuba mahogany, in suitableness for the purposes mentioned.

When a log that appears to be curled is to be cut up, it is of importance to examine it carefully, with the view of ascertaining in which way the finest figure is to be obtained. A mistake in this matter may considerably affect the value of wood obtained from a log of the finest quality, and should therefore be avoided if possible. As almost every log has one side of better quality than the others, so every figured log has most of the figure on one side. Various causes have been assigned for this, by different writers, but the fact is unquestionable. Some have supposed, that exposure to the sun of one side more than the other, accounts for its being finer than they; but we are disposed to agree with Duhamel, in regarding the difference as being caused by the tree having had freedom to sway or bend to the side on which the fine wood is found. It is certain that the largest deposit of wood has always been found in the hollow side of a bent log. Our present business, however, is rather to make use of the fact than to ascertain its cause. In cutting a figured log of birch, then, we would recommend that the saw draughts should run parallel to the side which has the greatest appearance of being curled,

and would not regard the crossing of the heart shake transversely, as furnishing a good reason against it. When the wood is so finely figured as to be principally cut into veneers, those planks which are shaken can be rinded into narrow breadths, and sawn into veneers suitable for framing, bases, cornices, or the like. From such a log it would plainly be wasteful to cut thick planks. If used in the solid, it should only be in ⅝ inch, or ¾ inch boards, for clamps or mouldings, to go into work along with fine veneers; or into ½ inch and 1⅛ inch boards, for the seats and backs of hall chairs, or for panels, where these need to be solid, as in the case of French beds.

Seasoning.—We have already remarked, that in birch, the sap wood is peculiarly liable to decay in the course of seasoning in the open air. This indicates the desirableness of using all suitable means to preserve it from those influences which are the causes of decay; and, first, we would recall attention to what is said, in former observations, on the best mode of treating wood while in the log. If true in respect of fir, the hints there given have tenfold force when applied to birch, which deteriorates far more readily when exposed to the soft damp soil of a woodyard, to contact with weeds, or fungus matter. We would further notice the propriety of having the wood piled, or placed in " the horse," *immediately* after being sawn into planks or boards. If allowed to lie close together, as laid off from the saw, especially if the weather is wet, the sap-wood will, in the course of a very short time, discolour and spread the seeds of decay. When piled, care should be taken that the covering is sufficient to prevent the rain from getting in between the boards and lying on the surfaces. It may perhaps occur to some readers, that we are forgetting the cost of the labour which we recommend to be bestowed on the stock in the woodyard. But the experience of the best regulated establishments has shown this expenditure to be the truest economy; while, on the other hand it would, if desirable, not be difficult to adduce numerous instances in proof of the serious loss entailed by a contrary course of treatment.

We would recommend one exception to the rule of carefully covering up birch, namely, when it is to be applied to the purpose of making sliding rails for telescope tables. Here we would suggest the propriety of rinding the planks, which should be cut ¼ inch thicker, and rinded ¼ inch broader than the finished size, and laying out the rinds to the action of the weather. The effect will be, to extract thoroughly the natural sap, to warp the pieces to the full extent of their tendency, and so to secure that no change shall take place upon them after being made up, provided they have been exposed for a sufficient length of time in the open air, and afterwards thoroughly tested in a heated atmosphere.

Planks designed to be sawn into veneers, require to be considerably well seasoned before they are cut; for, if this is not attended to, the damp veneers, on account of their varied consistency of grain presented at many different angles to the surface, will dry so unequally and uneven, that it is hardly possible to lay, without cracking them. Should this occur, notwithstanding care having been taken to avoid it, perhaps the best mode of overcoming it is to place the veneer between two heated boards, and allow it to remain pressed with handscrews for a few hours before it is laid. On the same principle, thin boards that have warped in the course of out-door seasoning, may be flattened before they are wrought. Let them be subjected to a strong and *sudden* heat, and then fixed down to the top of a bench during the night with handscrews or holdfasts; in most cases they will be found much improved on the following morning. But in order to produce the effect, the heat must be sudden, for a moderate and continuous warmth will rather encourage and fix the warping or bent previously acquired.

The seasoning of birch is a process so very tedious, that many cabinet-makers are apt unduly to abridge it, and make use of the material before it is dry. The evidences of this are presented daily to such as have an opportunity of seeing furniture which has been for a time in use. The seasoning process, unduly hastened in regard to the raw material, goes on at leisure in the manufactured article; as little to the credit of the maker as to the satisfaction of the purchaser. This may be made light of by such as seek a profit from single transactions with numerous purchasers, but cannot be too deeply impressed on the tradesman who is anxious to acquire, retain, and increase the confidence of the parties who employ him. This cannot be effected if the seasoning of the material he employs is neglected, or only partially attended to.

BEECH.

The beech-tree, called by botanists *Fagus sylvatica*, if not indigenous to England, must have been introduced prior to the commencement of the written or traditionary history of British trees. It is not a native of Scotland, nor of Ireland, but since its introduction in the middle of the sixteenth century, it has been extensively planted in both countries; and in congenial soils, has arrived at as great perfection, and attained as great a size, as it does in England. The beech is extensively distributed throughout the temperate parts of Europe; and is also found in Asia, and America. In America, as well as in England, it has a very exclusive power of occupancy; the natural forest covering extensive tracts, to the exclusion of all other trees; the growth or interference of which is prevented by its deleterious drip and deep shade.

Of the beech, there is in Britain only one species, " the common;" but there are two varieties, known as the " purple-leaved," and the " fern-leaved." These last are cultivated rather on account of their forming beautiful objects in a landscape, than with any view of turning the wood to profitable use. Of trees grown in Britain, the beech is one of the first magnitude; frequently vieing in dimensions with the oak, the ash, and the chestnut. It is of slow growth for the first few years after planting, but when once firmly rooted, makes rapid progress; and in the course of seventy or eighty years, when it has attained its prime, is frequently from 70 to 90, or even 100 feet high, with a trunk of from 12 to 16 feet in circumference. In trees growing pretty close together, the lower branches die gradually off, or are so much checked in their growth, as not to interfere with the cleanness of the timber in the stems, which run up to a great height, straight and clean. When grown singly, the stem is found of greater girth, but much shorter, and the branches, spread out at acute angles, go to form an expanse of umbrageous shade, the magnificence and beauty of which is rarely paralleled. The bark is thin and smooth, of a pearl or silvery gray colour; the leaves, rather small in size, are thin in texture, and when matured, are of a deep shining green; the mast or seed is an angular nut, contained in a prickly capsule, which, when ripe in autumn, drops from the tree, furnishing an oleaginous kernel, used in many places to fatten swine, and which, in France, is made to yield an oil, not only used for the lamp, but for culinary purposes.

The wood of the beech-tree varies in colour from white to pale brown; the darkest coloured being best in quality, and the produce of the finest soil. It is very durable, when placed and kept under water; and on this account is much used for the keels and planking of vessels, for piles to be driven under water, and the like. But when exposed to damp, or to be alternately wet and dry, it soon rots and decays. From its hardness and uniform texture, it is admirably fitted for being manufactured into planes of every kind in use, and is almost invariably employed for the purpose, as well as for the handles of other tools, chucks for the turning-lathe, and similar articles.

Beech, in consequence of being the wood most

chemically free from foreign matters, is admirably adapted for such articles as require to be stained, in imitation of ebony, mahogany, or rosewood; and when stained furniture was more prevalent than it is now, was extensively used in the manufacture of it. Although, from the change in public taste, little of it is required for this purpose at present, it is still employed in considerable quantity by cabinet-makers. The uses to which it is applied, are, to furnish rails for common and easy chairs, stocks and scrolls for couches and sofas, stocks and posts for beds, &c. For these and similar purposes, it is perhaps superior to birch in some respects, but has the sad drawback of being much earlier subject to decay. That it is so, must be a fact familiar to all who have been accustomed to examine old furniture with any degree of care. It is quite common to find in chairs or tables, in which beech has been used for the rails, that the entire article is in good sound condition, with the exception of such parts as have been made of beech, which are partially or wholly decayed. Again, in bedsteads, or other articles, in which both birch and beech have been used, the beech is frequently found to have been attacked and destroyed by worms, while the birch is quite fresh and good, or only partially decayed where it is in immediate contact with the beech. While these and similar facts are known and admitted, still it is extensively used for the purposes which we have mentioned; and one reason assigned for the preference is not without force, namely, that when cut into tenons, these are not apt to become smooth or slippery in the course of framing, as is the case with birch.

Purchase.—In the purchasing of beech there are three things to be attended to, namely, that the wood is fresh, clean, and of a suitable quality. The tree is sometimes allowed to stand for such a length of time that it has begun to decay before it is cut down; and when this is the case, the wood, it is plain, will be deficient in strength and durability after it is manufactured. This condition of the wood is rendered evident either on examination of the bark, which will be found sitting loosely, and having a discoloured film between it and the wood; or by looking carefully at the end of the tree, in which the grain, instead of having the appearance of being freely cut, will seem rather to be broken or crushed through. The cleanness of the timber is indicated by the absence of protuberances or branches from its surface; and its quality, by its colour and the thickness and width of the annual rings. Where the colour is pale, and the annual rings are so close as scarcely to be distinguishable, the wood is soft; but when the colour is rather dark,

and the annual rings are wide and well defined, the wood will be found to be hard and strong. The purposes for which it is intended to be used, will determine the choice of the purchaser.

Cutting up.—Beech is distinguished by having the transverse septa or fibres, which radiate from the heart, crossing the concentric circles, very distinctly visible. These transverse septa, when presented edgeways to the surface of the article wanted, say a plane, furnish the hardest and most durable sole; which has induced tool-makers and last-makers to cut the wood into lengths suitable for their respective purposes, and then split it with a wedge and mallet in such a manner as to secure this advantage for all the pieces. The cabinet-maker rarely requires to attend to this condition, and, consequently, the tree will by him be cut up into planks of the required thickness in the usual manner. As beech is used for the same purposes with birch, the directions given in regard to the cutting up of the one, will be found equally applicable to the other, and need not therefore be repeated.

Seasoning.—It is a common practice to allow the planks of the beech tree to lie close together for a considerable time after they are sawn, with the view of rendering them more soft and tender, and consequently more easily wrought. Where the wood is very hard and strong, this may be done with great advantage, provided it is not continued for such a length of time as to induce the commencement of decay; but, generally, it will be found most advisable to pile the boards at once, and to keep them exposed to the action of the external atmosphere until the natural sap has evaporated. To attempt to abridge the process, by substituting artificial heat, is particularly unsuited to the nature of beech, which is apt to warp and twist long after the natural sap appears to have left it.

ASH.

The common ash, called by botanists *Fraxinus excelsior*, is one of the most valuable trees indigenous to Britain, whether considered in reference to the valuable qualities of its wood, or the claim it has to the title of a noble and ornamental forest tree. In point of magnitude, it ranks amongst our largest trees, being sometimes found to attain a height of from 90 to 100 feet, and a girth of from 20 to 30 feet at the ground. It is not, however, desirable that it should be allowed to grow until it attain the largest size of which it is capable, as trees of moderate size are invariably found to yield better timber than those of great age and dimensions. The quality of the wood is greatly affected by the nature of the soil on which it is grown; that produced on poor land being stunted and brittle, while that grown in a free loam mixed with gravel, possesses, in the highest degree, that toughness and elasticity which constitute the principal value of the timber. The wood of the ash, though not so durable as the matured or heart wood of the oak, surpasses it and all our indigenous trees in elasticity and adhesiveness of fibre; and is, on account of these properties, universally used in the manufacture of articles where these qualities are particularly required, such as implements of husbandry, wheel carriages, ship-blocks, oars, and various portions of machine work. It possesses the additional recommendation of becoming useful when quite young, the wood being as durable and perfect then, as it is when it has attained its greatest dimensions. Those who have had the most experience, consider it most valuable at the age of from thirty to sixty years.

The ash tree is so remarkable for elegance of form and beauty of foliage, as to have been called the Venus of the forest. The principal stem rises to a great height in an easy flowing line, while the branches, as they lengthen, take generally a graceful sweep; and the looseness of the leaves corresponding with the lightness of the spray, the whole forms an elegant depending foliage. The colour, also, which is of a light and agreeable green, harmonizes and contrasts well with trees of a more sombre hue. It is very late of coming into leaf, rarely before the beginning of June, and its foliage falls suddenly with the first frosts of autumn, however early in the season these may happen. There are three or four varieties of the common ash grown in Britain, which we need not enumerate, as they are cultivated rather on account of their ornamental appearance, than with the view of yielding profitable timber. Guided by the principle of making those trees only which are of importance to the cabinet-maker the subject of special notice, we turn to the ashes of American growth. Of these, botanists enumerate more than thirty distinct species, the most important of which is the *Fraxinus Americana*, generally called the white ash. This species is a native of the United States, and also of Canada; from which it is annually exported to this country in large quantities, varying in amount from 7000 to 25,000 feet. The circumstances most favourable to the growth of this species, are a cold climate, and a moist soil, such as is furnished by the edges of a swamp, or the banks of a river. In such situations, it is found to attain a height of eighty feet, and a diameter of three or four feet, and having the trunk perfectly

straight and undivided often to the height of more than forty feet. On large trees, the bark is deeply furrowed, divided into small squares, and so light in colour, as to have given rise to the name of *white* ash, by which it is known throughout America. The leaves are twelve or fourteen inches long, composed of three or four pair of leaflets, surmounted by an odd one, and present a remarkable contrast of colour, the upper surface being of a light green, while the under side is nearly white. While the timber of this species bears a considerable resemblance to that of the common ash of Britain, it is neither so hard nor so tough; and hence is better fitted for the use of the cabinet-maker. From the time of its being extensively imported, it has gradually and to a considerable extent superseded the other woods used for the interior fittings of chests of drawers, wardrobes, and similar articles of furniture. For the preference, two reasons may be assigned; namely, the entire absence of smell which distinguishes ash, and the ease with which it is wrought as compared with the cedars, &c., formerly in use for the purposes to which ash is now applied.

Purchase.—The principal use to which ash is meant to be put, indicates the desirableness of selecting such logs as are distinguished for the mildness and cleanness of their timber; and the appearances which mark these qualities are obvious to any careful observer. As in the case of most other woods, so in ash, the thinness and closeness of the annual rings, or, in other words, the fineness of the grain, marks the degree in which it is characterized by mildness. An examination of the end of the log will at once furnish evidence on this head.

On turning to the sides, take notice whether the grain is straight and close, and whether there is little appearance of gnarled growth or marked figure. Where these are present, the wood may be expected to be strong and coarse, difficult to work, and liable to warp. Attention should also be paid to the appearances of soundness near the heart of the timber, as it is not by any means unfrequent to find a large portion of it the subject of the dry rot. The existence of this is ordinarily indicated by the soft, spongy, and discoloured appearance of the ends of the tree, especially near the heart.

Cutting up.—As it can scarcely be expected that all the logs in a lot of ash should possess the mildness and cleanness which are desirable in wood to be used for interior fittings, it is of importance to take care that any which are of an opposite character should be cut up for a different purpose. Instead of sawing them into thicknesses for drawer stuff, let them be cut into planks suitable for chair rails, sofa stocks or scrolls, or bed-stocks. For such uses, too, it may be prudent to take a board off each side of the heart draught in a log which, rather coarse at the heart, is on the whole fitted for being cut into thin wood. The main use of ash, however, is to furnish material for drawer sides, bottoms, and *mounters*. By mounters, we will be understood by tradesmen to mean the cross bar of $3\frac{1}{2}$ inches broad by $\frac{3}{4}$ inch thick, which is used to divide into two parts the bottom of a long drawer, for the sake of strengthening it to bear the weight of the contents. The usual thickness for the sides of large drawers is $\frac{9}{16}$ inch, and for the bottoms of such, $\frac{3}{8}$ inch. Where the drawers are of small size, the $\frac{3}{8}$ inch usually employed for bottoms will be found thick enough for the sides, while the bottoms need not be more than $\frac{1}{4}$ inch thick. In determining the order in which these various thicknesses should be cut, we have found it advantageous to take the thickest clefts nearest the heart. This throws the cleanest wood into the bottoms; and should the boards cut for sides prove coarse, they can either be jointed for the purpose, or cut up into the grooved fillets which are extensively used by good tradesmen.

It is of importance that ash logs should be sawn into the various thicknesses for which it is suitable, as soon after it is got into the wood-yard as possible; as we know of no wood which is more liable to crack and shake when exposed in the mass. Nor is it sufficient to avoid this, that it be cut into half logs; for even in this state, the efforts of the natural sap to escape from the centre, will have the effect of producing deep rents on all the sides. In order to prevent this, recourse is sometimes had to the sinking of the logs in ponds of water, where these are available. We regard this as a practice of very questionable utility; for while it is true that immersion will prevent splitting, it is certain to have the effect of inducing discolouration and decay.

Seasoning.—As in the case of beech, so in regard to ash, where it is very strong and hard, it may be of advantage to allow the boards to lie close together for a few weeks after being sawn, with the view of rendering them more tender and easily wrought. But in the case of wood of ordinary mildness, this is not advisable. Generally, it will be found the wisest course to *pile* the boards immediately after they are cut. In doing so, regard should be had to the fact, that, from the nature of the wood and the thinness of the clefts, they are extremely liable to warp and bend in the drying. In order to overcome this tendency, it is of importance that they be laid on a straight and level bed of blocks, closer than is ordinarily required, and that the fillets which separate them should be of equal thickness, and placed exactly above each other, so as to secure the perfect straightness of all the boards in the pile. After being exposed for two or three months, let the whole be turned over, and the boards be laid upside down, with the same care; thus will be secured the fairest chance for the material, when seasoned, being found in a workable condition. Should it be objected that the course recommended is laborious, we can only reply, that the first labour is the least, and that pains taken in the seasoning will prove gain in the working.

ELM.

Although the wood of the elm is now much seldomer used in the manufacture of furniture than it was formerly, we regard it as having a natural claim to be noticed in any account of the woods suitable for cabinet work. The elm, called by botanists *Ulmus*, has been the subject of much diversity of opinion in regard to the number of its species and varieties; some authorities enumerating as many as twelve distinct species, while other writers refer all of these to one species, *Ulmus campestris*, or common elm, and regard the others as varieties merely. This difference of opinion is easily accounted for, by the fact, that the seed of the elm does not all prove true to the tree from which it is gathered, but is apt to produce varieties differing more or less from the parent plant, and from each other. Among the cultivated elms of this country, individuals are found differing as much from each other as if they belonged to distinct genera; and yet there are such a number of kinds intermediate, that classification is found a matter of extreme difficulty, even to those who have paid the greatest attention to the subject. Most botanists, however, are agreed in classifying the elms of British growth under two species, namely, the *Ulmus campestris*, the common, or English elm, and the *Ulmus montana*, the mountain, Wych, or Scotch elm. The first of these is seen in its greatest perfection in the southern and midland parts of England, where it not only forms the avenues of the finest public walks and drives in the vicinity of towns, but forms a large proportion of the timber chosen to adorn the parks and surround the residences of our nobility and gentry. It is of rapid growth, and often attains a height of from seventy to ninety feet, and a diameter of four or five feet. The trunk is tall and straight, and the branches are subordinate to it, throughout its entire length. The leaves are small, doubly serrated or toothed, and are, when matured, of a dark green colour, and rough surface. The flowers, which are of a purple colour, sometimes appear very early in the season, and cover the branches as fully as the subsequent leafy foliage, presenting a singular and beautiful appearance. The common, or English elm, if not indigenous to Britain, must have been introduced at a very remote period; as we find various localities in England to which its name seems to have been attached in the times of the Anglo-Saxons.

The *Ulmus montana*—the Wych, or Scotch elm, is distinguished from the common, or English elm, in having a much more picturesque appearance, attaining a larger size, and yielding timber of a better quality. Instead of a straight continuous trunk of upright and formal growth, it forms a large spreading tree, in which the stem, frequently covered with gnarled excrescences, generally divides itself, at no great height from the ground, into large diverging limbs, which, of free and graceful growth, are rendered pendulous by the weight of foliage they bear. In point of size, too, it considerably exceeds the common elm; for while the largest specimen of that, of which we have any notice, namely, Piffe's elm, in the vale of Gloucester, measured, at five feet from the ground, about sixteen feet in circumference, we find mention made of one wych elm grown in Suffolk, which, at the same height from the ground, was twenty-seven feet in circumference; and of another in the parish of Roxburgh, called the Trysting elm, which, at a height of four feet from the ground, measured not less than thirty feet in circumference. But the principal difference in favour of this species, is in the quality of the timber which it yields; which, by all practical men, is admitted to be superior both in durability and value. This superiority would seem to have been well known in ancient times, for we find the use of the wych elm, in the manufacture of bows, enjoined by statute. The timber of both species, however, possesses in common the quality of resisting the action of water; and hence has long been extensively used for the keels of vessels, for wet foundations, water-works, piles, pumps, and the like. It is also, from its toughness, preferred for the naves of wheels, for the shells of tackle blocks, the gunwales of ships, and all purposes which require a wood that will bear rough usage without splitting.

But the circumstance that principally calls for the present notice of the elm, is its extensive use in the manufacture of furniture up to a very recent date. Although, at present, it is rarely used except for the commoner sort of Windsor chairs and similar articles, not more than twenty years have elapsed since it formed a principal material for drawing-room furniture of the best description. When employed in the manufacture of fine furni-

ture, the large trees of twisted growth, which, when cut, present a fine laced appearance, or waved unevenness, were selected for the plainer parts of the work; and veneers cut from the gnarled excrescences, or curls, for the principal parts, such as table tops, or the surface of cabinets. These excrescences are caused by the stoppage or peculiar diversion of the sap, occasioned by the lopping off large branches or constitutional defect; and annually increasing in size, deposit a curiously veined and marbled wood, which, when cut off and carefully seasoned, are found to yield veneers of rare beauty. Perhaps the main cause of furniture made of this material going out of fashion, is to be found in the fact that, in order to finish it well, an amount of labour was required that the majority of purchasers were unwilling to pay for. This great amount of additional labour was rendered necessary, by the small size, irregular form, and faulty texture, of the pieces of veneer which could be obtained. In order to cover a large surface with small pieces of veneer of an irregularly circular or oval shape, very much more work was needed to join them to each other, than is required in the case of mahogany or rose-wood. But even when this was effected, a greater amount of time was employed in filling up the smaller or larger holes usually found in the veneers, arising from openness of texture, and the admixture of loose bark or gum; all of which required to be carefully filled, in order to produce a solid surface to receive the polish. In the manufacture of such articles, taste, skill, and time, were productive of a result which leads us to regret that work of this description is rarely called for, except for the purpose of matching suits of furniture.

While we think it unnecessary to speak particularly of the purchase and cutting up of elm, it may be useful to call the attention of those who occasionally require it, to the necessity of very carefully seasoning the curls, or wart-looking pieces, usually cut into veneers. If this be neglected, the veneers will not hold together, but, in consequence of their varied texture causing unequal progress in drying, will split in all directions. Even where the greatest care is taken beforehand, the veneers may present, after being cut, a very uneven surface. As in the case of the curled birch veneer, this may be overcome by the sudden application of heat and pressure, which will have the additional effect of shrinking the veneer to its least dimensions before it is laid, and prevent subsequent opening of the joints and pores in the surface. It is scarcely possible to carry too far the drying of the veneer before it is laid, whether as regards the larger pieces, or the smaller bits which are filled into the holes. From the irregular shape of these, it is difficult to join them with sufficient nicety. Any imperfection in this respect, will be greatly remedied by the application of the glue, which will expand the previously dried wood, till it completely fill the space into which it is inserted. In connection with this subject, it may be useful to the young workman for us to notice the propriety of making all his joinings in irregular and waving lines, similar to those which are described by the figure of the wood. It is plain that this will cause more work than making them in straight lines, but the additional labour will be far more than repaid, in their being rendered almost invisible. We would mention further, that the small holes of which we have spoken, should, as far as possible, be fitted with pieces of wood rather than with sawdust and glue, or gum shell-lac; neither of which make such a solid surface for the reception of polish.

Before leaving the subject, we may also notice, that many persons of experience deem it of great advantage to the beauty of the wood, that pieces which are to be cut into veneers, should be buried for some months previously in a heap of horse dung. This is said to have a wonderful effect in improving the show or figure, which we are inclined to credit, from knowing that the same course is followed on the Continent with great benefit, in the case of pieces of the walnut tree intended to be cut into veneers.

From Canada, there is annually imported into Britain, from 40,000 to 50,000 cubic feet of red elm, the *Ulmus rubra* of botany, similar in appearance, but inferior in quality, to the elms of British growth.

Oak.

Of the oak, or *Quercus*, botanists enumerate not fewer than one hundred and fifty distinct species, and it is doubtful whether all are included, even in this large number. Distributed over a large portion of the earth's surface, in almost every variety of soil and climate; and possessing a wonderful power of adaption to these, it presents a wide field for description. But we shall confine our attention to those species which are indigenous to Britain, or which are imported into this country for the use of the cabinet-maker. The *Quercus robur*, or common oak, which is indigenous to Britain, has, by some naturalists of eminence, been divided into two distinct species, namely, the *Quercus pedunculata*, peduncled or common oak; and the *Quercus sessiliflora*, or sessile fruited oak. Externally, the difference between these is marked, by the first

having the acorns supported on short stems, or as it is termed, pedunculated; while the second has the acorns sessile, or without the supporting stems; the leaves, also, of the first are larger, and the bark darker in the colour, than the second. But a more important difference has been asserted to exist, in the qualities of the timber yielded by them respectively; that of the pedunculated, or common oak, being regarded as superior, both in strength, toughness, and durability, to that of the sessile fruited oak. While some naturalists of eminence draw this distinction, others, of not inferior note, contend that the difference is only one of variety, not of species; and that each variety furnishes timber inferior or superior to the other, according to the quality of soil on which they have respectively been raised. By practical men, the difference, if it exists, has been entirely overlooked; for the timber of both kinds has always been used, indiscriminately, for the most important purposes in which oak is employed.

Without presuming to decide which of the two opinions is the more correct, we shall proceed to such observations as apply equally to all oaks of British growth. These would appear to have been held in high estimation in the remoter periods of the history of the island; though, for a very different reason than any of those which now obtain for the oak such an important place amongst our forest trees. During the Saxon rule, and even after the time of the Norman conquest, the oak was valued chiefly for the acorns which it yielded, and which were used, not only in general, for the fattening of the herds of swine, which constituted a great part of the wealth of our Saxon ancestors, but also, in seasons of scarcity, were rendered available for human food. Strange as this statement may appear to modern readers, it is rendered less wonderful on referring to the experience of our British troops, who, in the absence of a well-supplied commissariat during the Peninsular war, were sometimes glad to satisfy the cravings of nature with this humble fare. Of such importance, in respect to the food which they yielded, were the oak forests considered, that we find some of the Saxon kings passing laws for their preservation; and others rewarding their powerful military retainers, or dowering their daughters, by settling on them the produce of a certain portion of oak forest. But an advancing civilization soon elevated the oak to a higher place in the national estimation, and connected it intimately at once with the maritime superiority, and the religious sentiment of the British people. We find indications of the estimate which, at a very early period, had been formed of its fitness to supply material for sea-going vessels; in the remains of large and rudely-fashioned canoes scooped from the oak, which have been at different times disinterred in various parts of the country. The construction of these vessels, which are common only to the earliest stages of society, would seem to prove the use of the oak, for such a purpose, to have commenced at a date, perhaps, earlier than the Roman invasion. What was thus early begun, has been continued down to the present day; and whether, in the oared galleys of the Saxons, the three-masted vessels of the times of the Tudors, or in the first-rate Indiaman, or British ship of war of our times—the oak has formed the staple material. So identified, indeed, is the oak with naval architecture, that the British government has long deemed it necessary to commit to the care of the same department in the public service, the rearing of the timber, and the superintendence of the dock yards. There are three qualities possessed by the oak, which procure for it the distinction of being regarded as the fittest material for shipbuilding; namely, strength, toughness, and durability. Any one of these qualities, taken singly, may be found, in an equal degree, in some other species of timber: but in no other species are all three found combined in the same degree. Another recommendation to the ship-builder is the crooked growth in oak, which, forming short turns and elbows, furnishes pieces suitable for what is called *knee-timber*. But the extensive use of oak timber, in early times, was not confined to the ship-carpenter; for we find that, in all the older ecclesiastical edifices, it furnished material not only for the heavier timbers, but also for the beautiful interior decorations, many of which have excited the admiration of all succeeding ages. So invariably has it been employed in the religious buildings reared by the piety or superstition of ancient times, that it has, from the association of ideas, come to be regarded as the only material congruous with the nature of any of the more expensive structures erected for religious purposes. The matchless screen of the minster at York, the stalls of the cathedral at Gloucester, and the shrine of the chapel of Edward the confessor, in Westminster Abbey; all were of oak. The practice of modern times would seem to sanction the canon of taste here implied; for we have invariably, in the circumstances, if not the same material employed, at least an imitation of it given by the painter. In the interior fittings of our ancient baronial halls and castles, and in the furniture with which they were provided, the exclusive use of oak prevailed to an equal extent. Although the successive introduction of walnut, mahogany, rosewood, and other fancy woods, may, for a time,

have rendered oak less popular in the private mansions of the great, recent years have shown a revival of the taste which prefers it as the most suitable material for the furniture of the hall, and the library, if not of the spacious dining-room. For these purposes, the wainscot, imported from Dantzig, Memel, and Riga, has, in modern times, been employed almost to the exclusion of British oak. The grounds of preference are, that the wainscot is milder in its character, and more easily wrought than the British oak; but, chiefly, that in it the grain is finer, and more interspersed with the ornamental markings or flower, from the septa or medullary rays in the wood. In common phrase, "*the champ*" is better. We have often heard these qualities, in wainscot, attributed to a particular process of steeping which it is said to undergo after being cut; but, after careful inquiry, are persuaded, that the difference between it and common oak does not arise from any peculiar mode of treatment, but from an original difference in the species, and, in part, from the nature of the soil on which it is raised. The name wainscot, is derived from the purpose for which it was extensively employed, before the introduction of plaster as a finishing for interior walls, in Germany, Holland, and on the Continent generally. It is composed of two words, "*wandt,*" a wall, and "*schot,*" a defence; which, at first descriptive of the use to which oak was extensively put, came, at length, to be applied to the wood itself. The common name given in England to the panelled lining of an apartment, was "the wainscot" or "wainscotting," which generally consisted of oak. The name thus acquired, has been retained to the present day; and, although not correctly descriptive, is serviceable in distinguishing the article referred to, from the oaks of British growth, and those which are imported from America.

In external appearance, there is a considerable difference between the common or British oak, and the *Quercus cerris*, the Turkey or mossy-cupped oak, which is imported into this country under the name of wainscot. While the common oak has ordinarily a short trunk of from six to twelve feet high, which divides itself into large crooked limbs, but little inferior to the main stem, the Turkey oak is of a pyramidal growth, having a tall straight trunk, which often reaches a height of forty or fifty feet, and to which the branches are subordinate, rarely assuming the large size, or tortuous form, of the limbs of the common oak. In illustration of the remarkably straight growth of the oak which is imported under the name of wainscot, we may mention, that it is a common practice to split the trees into two halves, simply by boring a hole in the top, at the beginning of winter, and filling it with water, which, expanded by the action of frost, forms a wedge sufficiently powerful to split the tree in two throughout its entire length. The occasion for thus dividing the trees, seems to be the necessity of reducing them in bulk to fit them for being floated or rafted down the rivers Dwina, Niemen, and Vistula, from the mountain sides where they are grown, to Riga, Memel, and Dantzig, the ports from which they are shipped to Britain. Of the importations from these three ports, the wainscot of Riga is the most valuable for the purposes of the cabinet-maker, and brings by far the highest price. They, however, are not of uniform value, but distinguished by the names "crown," and "common," into a fine, and an inferior quality. Although in respect of strength, toughness, and durability, wainscot is decidedly inferior to the common oak, it possesses all these qualities in sufficient degree to warrant the employment of it in furniture and interior finishings, for which its ornamental appearance renders it much more suitable. We accordingly find that, for such purposes, it has almost entirely superseded the oak of native growth. Nor is it the sole rival with which our indigenous timber has had to contend; for there is annually imported, from Quebec, from 200,000 to 300,000 cubic feet of oak of American growth. Upwards of seventy distinct species of oaks have been enumerated by naturalists, as indigenous to America; varying in importance from a lowly shrub, to the loftiest forest tree. Of these, we shall mention only the two which, in value, approximate to those of European growth. The *Quercus virens*, or live oak, is that which, in the quality of its timber, bears the closest resemblance to our common British oak, and is, in the United States, regarded as the most valuable for shipbuilding. The general Government has at different times laid out large sums in the preservation and establishment of plantations of live oak, with the view of supplying the naval dockyards with suitable materials. This species being confined to the southern States, has not, we believe, been imported into Britain as timber, nor has the attempt to cultivate it in this country been successful, the climate being too cold to permit its growth, except in very warm and sheltered situations. The *Quercus alba*, or white oak, which is abundant in the northern States of the Union, is that which is imported from Quebec, to supply the British market. Inferior to the common or British oak in strength and durability, and to wainscot in fineness of grain and beauty of figure, it is nevertheless extensively used both in carpentry and cabinet-making. Costing not more than one-half of the

price of wainscot, it is often employed in the manufacture of hall furniture of an inferior description, for plate chests, gun cases, and similar articles. When it is of fine quality, even good tradesmen employ it for the inferior or subordinate parts of furniture, of which the principal surfaces are in wainscot; but in all cases, a practised eye can readily detect the difference. It is also extensively used for the rails and slides of telescope dining-tables, and other purposes which requires toughness and strength in comparatively small bulk of wood. Like all the other species of oak, it holds a large amount of natural sap, with which it parts very slowly, and the evaporation of which shrinks the wood to the extent of about one thirty-second part less than its original size. It is also very liable to warp and twist in the course of drying, which points out the great necessity of carefully selecting for purchase such logs as are straight grown, and avoiding such as have the grain twisted after the manner of a rope. Where this is the original tendency, scarcely any amount of seasoning is sufficient to counteract it; on the contrary, it will show itself not only in the course of working, but even after being manufactured, when exposed to a variation of temperature. This is peculiarly mischievous when it is used for the purpose of making sliding-rails; which, requiring to be wrought at intervals, are found to be out of order just when they are wanted, and when there is not time to adjust them.

In purchasing a lot of American oak, it may not be possible to avoid including one or more logs of the twisted growth which we have described. But care should be taken, that pieces of this nature are cut up into thicknesses suited for purposes where the tendency to warp will be productive of the least harm. Indeed, we are persuaded that less loss will result from using it as common hardwood, than from applying it to uses which its cost would render desirable, but which it is unfitted to serve. Where, from the necessity of economy of production, it is found requisite to employ American oak for finishing purposes, attention should be given to the selection of such pieces as have least of the oaky appearance; or, in other words, which are closest in the grain, and have the best figure, or *champ*, and, in consequence, most closely resemble wainscot. In the selection of wainscot for purchase, it is also needful to have respect to the same rule; for entire lots of it are to be found which are of strong oaky growth, and possess but little of the mildness, closeness of texture, and beauty of figure, which render it valuable in preference to British or American oak. It is also of importance to choose lots in which the logs are straight, and of considerable size. When they are small, and much bent, they are necessarily less economical in the cutting out, and require, for most purposes, an additional number of joints. As we have already said, wainscot is, to a considerable extent, imported only in half logs; and hence, few boards cut from it are found to be straight at a greater breadth than eleven inches. The half logs are of a greater breadth than this, it is true, but they can only be cut in one way, to secure the beauty of the wood; that is, the draughts must run from the split side to the round side. This takes them either perpendicularly or obliquely through the silver grain, or medullary rays, which yield the ornamental marking, or *champ*. This will be found in the greatest perfection in those planks, the surfaces of which are at a *small* angle with the lines of the silver grain; these should be selected for cutting into veneers, or for fine ½ inch or ⅝ inch thick boards, for panels or the like. A cut will most simply illustrate our meaning. We have, in the figure, a section of a half log of wainscot, in which the annular rings are represented by the semicircular lines, and the silver grain, or medullary rays, are seen radiating from the heart 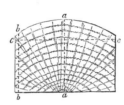 to the circumference. A draught run from *a* to *a*, as in the dotted line, would present a more showy surface than a draught from *b* to *b*, in which the silver grain is presented more obliquely. A glance at the figure will furnish another reason for running the draughts from the split side to the round side of the half log, namely, that it avoids the waste which would be occasioned at the round side, were they cut in the direction of the dotted line from *c* to *c*. But before leaving the subject of the silver grain, or medullary rays, we would earnestly invite the attention of young workmen to a careful study of the laws which regulate the show or figure of the timber which they are engaged in working. Many, from not having had their thoughts directed to the results which can be produced by an intelligent acquaintance with these laws, are guided in their mode of treating a piece of wood, by a simple regard to ease or convenience. In consequence of this, it is regarded as a matter over which they have no control, whether, when finished, it shall be showy or plain. Whereas, on the contrary, the result, in all cases where a piece of wood can be worked in two ways, is entirely in the hands of the workman. Suppose he is called on to run a moulding in oak; if he run the plane parallel to, or at a small angle with, the silver grain, he is sure to bring out all the show which the wood possesses; but should he run the plane on the edge of the silver grain, he will render the moulding as plain

as the wood is capable of making it. The knowledge of this alternative resting with him, ought to be sufficient to induce any young man, desirous of rising in his business, to make the subject a matter of careful study. It is, perhaps, not going out of our way to remark, that the union of mental effort with physical toil, of which we have specified an instance, is the natural way to render bodily labour less irksome while it lasts, and, eventually, to raise the workman above the necessity of engaging in it. But to return to the cutting of wainscot from the log, it may be observed, that as it is impossible to get all the logs in a lot, or even all the planks in the same log, equally showy, the plainer wood should be cut into the thick planks required for bed-posts, truss-legs, table-pillars, the feet of hall chairs, and the like. In articles of such bulk, although generally plain, it will ordinarily be found practicable to turn the showy side to the front, or prominent part of the job.

But the main thing to be attended to, in the treatment of oak or wainscot, is the seasoning; for, if manufactured before it is dry, it will split and open in every direction. This tendency will only be increased, and the evil aggravated, by attempting to hurry the process by any application of artificial heat, with which we are acquainted. From the extent of the shrinking which takes place in drying, when the outer part is dried, while the damp heart remains undiminished in bulk, the outer rind must necessarily crack. Should an attempt be made to fill these cracks with thin slips, however neatly inserted, they are sure to show themselves in course of time. The inner part, when reduced to its least bulk by drying, will carry the previously seasoned outer part with it, and eject, as intruders, the slips which have been inserted before the seasoning was complete. To prevent this, there is nothing for it but to subject the material to a course of thorough seasoning in the open air; the tediousness of which will be amply compensated by the result.

It would be improper to close our notice of oak, without adverting to what is called *black oak;* that is, timber which, from long-continued immersion in water, or from being imbedded in a moist mossy deposit, has changed from its natural colour to black, or an intermediate hue. Salt water has the effect of changing the colour of oak, which has been submerged in it for a sufficient length of time, to a deep black, but the process would appear to be very tedious; for the timber of the "Royal George," which sunk with Admiral Kempenfelt, and a numerous crew, in 1782, when fished up about seven years ago, was found to be but very partially affected, the heart of it being but little changed, although at each end, and on the outsides of the various pieces, the discoloration had reached to a bluish green. We had an opportunity of examining the wreck of part of the Spanish Armada, which, after lying nearly two and a half centuries under water, was recovered on the north-east coast of the island about twenty-five years ago; and in this, as in the former case, the natural colour of the wood had changed to a jet black. In both cases, the timber was unchanged in quality, remaining as firm and sound as ever it had been. Most, although not all of the specimens of black oak disinterred from bogs and mosses which we have seen, have been less firm and sound in quality, and not so deep in the colour as the last mentioned of those recovered from the sea. Indeed, there is perhaps no material presented to the cabinet-maker, which is the occasion of so much trouble and annoyance in the manufacture, as the moss or bog oak. Proprietors on whose land it is found, are naturally fond of having it made into articles of furniture, but are little aware of the difficulty of the task. Although, on being dug up, it may seem perfectly firm and compact, yet on being exposed to the action of the air, in the great majority of instances it shakes and cracks to an extent that is scarcely conceivable by those who have not witnessed it. And in pieces which are more compact, the tendency to warp is so great, as to render it almost impossible to work it in bulk, with the hope of its remaining *fair*. The only chance of making credit-able articles of furniture from it, is first to dry it very slowly under cover of a cellar or outhouse, and then to cut it into veneers; which, if dried with equal care, may stand pretty well when laid on a proper bed. Of course, this rule must be taken with the exception of retaining as much of the wood solid, as may be required for mouldings or other portions, such as chair feet, and turned or carved work, which cannot be veneered. It will be found of advantage in lending cohesion to the naturally open texture of the wood, to rub in *size*, or weak glue, into such parts of the surface as can be conveniently cleared afresh after the glue has dried. This, by shutting out the air, will lessen the chances of the article cracking after it is manufactured. To attain the same end, it is of importance that the French polisher should, immediately after the surface is cleaned, fill up the pores with blackened plaster of Paris.

Maple.

Of Maple, called in botany *Acer*, there are about thirty-six distinct species, of which two are indigenous to Britain. The first of these, *Acer pseudo-platanus*, the great maple, sycamore, or mock plane tree, is a robust hardy tree, which grows to a size equal to that of the oak, ash, and other trees of the first rank; and is little affected by exposure, whether from the sea breeze, or the highest winds in inland situa-tions. It has an erect stem, which, diverging into large angular limbs, with a strong spray supporting a large unbroken mass of foliage, affords an impene-trable shade from the rays of the sun, and a shelter from the blast. This recommends it as an excellent break-wind for mansions in exposed situations, and as a companion to other trees of a less hardy nature. From early spring till late in autumn it is covered with leaves, which at first of a yellowish tint, deepen into positive green, giving place, at the close of the season, to a bright reddish brown hue, not less beau-tiful than either. The bark is of a fine ash gray colour, broken into patches of different hues by the casting off old flakes, which tend to increase the picturesque appearance of the tree. The second species of maple indigenous to Britain is *Acer campestris*, the common or field maple. Ordinarily placed in hedge-rows or copse-woods, and cut over as a bush or shrub of inferior growth, it is in many districts of the country very rarely planted and treated as a tree; and hence, few specimens of it are found which have attained the magnitude that, in an appropriate soil, it is capable of reaching. In favourable circumstances, and under proper treat-ment, it arrives at dimensions but little inferior to that of trees of the first rank, and presents a very handsome outline, and picturesque appearance. Of the foreign species which have been introduced and extensively cultivated, the most important is the *Acer platanoides*, or Norway maple. As its name implies, it is a native of Norway; but is also found growing extensively in Russia, Germany, Switzer-land, and France. Like the great maple, it is hardy and robust, withstanding the effects of the sea breeze as well on the coast of Britain, as it does on its native shores of the Baltic and western coast of Norway. In size and general appearance it is very similar to the great maple, although its foliage is not so heavy; and its leaves are, when fully expanded, larger in size, and lighter in the colour. The timber of these three species is similar in appearance and quality; being of a whitish colour, close and compact in the grain, easily wrought, and little liable to warp. These qualities have recommended them as a suitable material for turnery, patterns for foundries, the soles of mangles, cutting boards, and for various pieces of machinery. Except in rural districts, European maple has been used to a very small extent in the manufacture of furniture, and would scarcely have called for notice here but for its affinity to the American species, which yield the wood known as *Bird's-eye maple*, one of the most beautiful materials employed in the manufacture of cabinet furniture.

Bird's-eye Maple is the wood of *Acer saccharinum*, the sugar maple, rock maple, or hard maple; it is indigenous to America, and is found in greatest abundance between the forty-third and forty-eighth degrees of latitude. In the northern parts of the States of New York and Pennsylvania, it is said that there are not fewer than ten millions of acres which produce these trees, at the rate of about thirty to an acre. It is also abundant in Canada, New Brunswick, Prince Edward's Island, and Nova Scotia; and is thence imported in considerable quantities into Great Britain. In America, it is less valued on account of its timber than for the saccharine juice, which it yields in such quantity as to furnish a large proportion of the sugar used by the inhabitants of the rural districts and back settlements of the country. The process of collecting this sap, and manufacturing it into sugar, is worthy of passing notice. In the end of February, or beginning of March, while the ground is still covered with snow, on a site conveniently near to the trees from which the sap is to be collected, a shed is raised to shelter the sugar boilers from the weather. Their implements and utensils are few and simple, consisting of a few augers, tubes, troughs, buckets, and boilers. Operations are commenced by boring holes of $\frac{3}{4}$ inch diameter, and $\frac{1}{2}$ inch deep, obliquely, ascending into the trunks of the trees, at about 18 or 20 inches from the ground. Into these holes are fitted tubes of elder, or sumac, which convey the sap, to the extent of from one to three gallons per day, into the troughs placed to receive it. These are, once every day, emptied of their contents, which are placed in barrels near to the boilers. The evaporation is effected by means of a brisk fire, during the application of which to the boilers the contents are carefully skimmed; and when the liquid has been reduced to a syrup, after being strained, it is poured into moulds, and the molasses drained from it. The result is the production of a sugar, which, when refined, may even compare with the finest used in Europe. The quantity produced must be very large, for single trees are often found to yield as much as 30 lbs. weight in a season.

But it is as an ornamental wood that the maple calls for our attention; and in this respect its claims are considerable. The figure in maple of highest repute is that known under the name of 'bird's-eye' —a designation which it has acquired from the small dots, or little conical projections, with a small hollow in the centre, which, in the finished work, bear a strong resemblance to the eye of a bird. The cause of these appears, on examination, to be the existence of internal spines or points in the bark, on which the successive layers of wood are moulded in a series of abrupt curves, corresponding to the spine or point which causes them. A simple figure will illustrate our meaning.

Let *a b* be the saw-draught, which runs in a straight line through the fibres of the wood, curved by the projection of the spines from the bark *c d*; this renders apparent the cause of the seeming projections. But in order to account for their beauty, it must be noticed that at each intersection of a curve the fibres are presented at a different angle to the light which falls on the surface, and hence the variety of light and shade, transparent and opaque. Another beautiful figure in maple is that known familiarly as *fiddle-back figure*, from pieces of that kind being usually chosen to form the back part of violins. It may be described as consisting of a series of small undulations in the grain, which, as in the case of the *bird's-eye* figure, are transformed into varied beauty when traversed by the straight line of the saw-draught. In the plane finished surface it resembles closely the undulations on the sands of the sea shore, caused by the ripple of the waters. There is a marked difference between this and the *bird's-eye* figure, in this respect, that while the one is peculiar to maple, the other is found in mahogany, and various other woods.

The maple would appear to have attained celebrity, as an ornamental wood, even amongst the Romans; for Pliny dilates at length on the beauty of the specimens furnished by that which grew in Istria and Rhætia, and says that it exceeded in loveliness even the *citrus*—a tree which was regarded as of such value, that instances are on record of single tables formed of it being sold for sums varying from £8000 to £11,000 sterling. While in modern times, which have rendered us familiar with the products of the western hemisphere, this estimate may justly be deemed extravagant, still it will readily be admitted, that for a variety of purposes, this material is eminently suitable. In mirror and picture frames, or other articles, in which it is associated with gilding, there is, from its pale colour and transparent lustre, a congruity and suitableness which is not possessed in the same degree by any other wood with which we are acquainted. The qualities specified render it also a very appropriate material for the manufacture of furniture for a drawing room, which happens to be imperfectly lighted, or which is from any cause sombre-looking and dull. In such an apartment, with an exposure to the north, and a paper and carpet of rather dingy hue, we have seen it employed with the happiest effect. Nor is it less appropriate to the requirements of a well-furnished bedroom. It will be found of the greatest service as furnishing a variety to the " mahogany room," the " oak room," or the " birch room," in a large mansion. Let the chamber be rather small or dark, if maple is used for the entire suit of furniture, its size and cheerful aspect will apparently be greatly increased. But irrespective of dimensions and light, there is in maple a peculiar adaptation to the adornment of an appropriately-furnished sleeping apartment. Suggestive to the fancy of purity and happiness, it seems to combine in furnishing, to as great an extent as mere accessories can do, the subordinate elements of an agreeable bed chamber.

Maple veneer is also well adapted for the interior fittings of Davenport writing-desks, or similar articles of drawing-room furniture, which require to be nicely finished internally; as it not only presents an agreeable contrast in colour to the rosewood, walnut, or mahogany, used for the external surface; but also, from its pale hue, gives the appearance of cleanness, and serves to reveal more perfectly than a darker material would, the contents of the article when it is placed in the shade.

Unlike most other woods, maple is very liable to shrink *lengthways*. Inattention to this peculiarity may be productive of considerable inconvenience in the subsequent widening of mitres, or butt joints, which were perfectly close at the time they were made. The cause of the evil is easily explained. By a reference to our figure, it will be seen that the grain of the wood, from its frequent undulations lengthways, partakes nearly as much of the character of side wood as of end wood. The bed on which the maple veneer is laid, say mahogany, on the contrary, from the straightness of its grain, is not liable to any sensible decrease in length in the process of drying, after being subjected to the action of moisture in the application of the glue with which the veneer is laid. In order to prevent such a result, it is needful that the veneer should in every case be shrunk to its least dimensions before it is laid down.

The pale colour of maple has led to its being frequently used for the bordering of surfaces, of which the main body is veneered with walnut or rosewood; and also to its being employed to furnish the alternate squares in draught boards, where they are introduced into the tops of tables made of the same material as the darker squares. The effect of this is very good, but is frequently greatly marred in the polishing; by the use of French polish made of dark gums, or which contains colouring matter. This

polish, which, in so far as the dark veneer is concerned, is beneficial, or at least harmless, has a very bad effect on the maple; as it not only dulls the lustre of its bright spots or undulations, but substitutes a dirty reddish tint for the naturally pure colour of the whole. In the lighter-coloured woods generally, but particularly in maple, it is of importance that the polish used should be as transparent and colourless as possible. Even where they are combined with a darker material, we would recommend that this rule should be adhered to; for it will be found that the purity of the lighter parts of the article, will more than compensate for any loss which the darker sustain from the absence of colouring.

The quantity of maple imported into Britain is so very limited, as to leave the purchaser but little choice of different growths; the finest we have had an opportunity of examining was brought from St. John, New Brunswick. It is of importance that the buyer be on his guard against trees which are of impure colour, or disfigured by stains; as it is not uncommon that such as have the finest figure are rendered valueless by the presence of dull greenish streaks, the result of the tree having died before being cut down, or of improper exposure afterwards.

SATIN WOOD.

Although much less popular now than formerly, as a material for furniture, satin wood is so pretty in itself, and is still so extensively used, as to render it needful to notice it in a work like the present. The finest kind of this wood was found, growing in great abundance, in Hispaniola; an island so named and first discovered by Columbus, and subsequently known as St. Domingo and Hayti. A thirst for gold seems to have been the master passion of the early navigators, and appears to have left the majority of them little leisure and less inclination to observe the wonders of the vegetable kingdom, which the New World presented before them. The Spanish colonists who succeeded them, and the French bucaneers who, a century later, effected a settlement on the island, were equally regardless of the immense forests of mahogany, satin wood and other timber, which have since proved a source of wealth to the exporters, and furnished a supply of new and beautiful materials to the manufactories of Europe.

The selecting and cutting of timber for the purposes of exportation, was induced by a series of occurrences, in themselves of a calamitous nature. Previously to the Revolution in the mother country, towards the end of last century, the French colonists had confined their attention to the production of sugar, coffee, cotton, and indigo, and exported these in large quantities. Encouraged by the liberal policy pursued by the French Government, the colony rapidly attained a degree of prosperity altogether unprecedented. Though occupying little more than one third of the island, it far surpassed in opulence not only the Spanish part, but the whole Spanish West Indies. This thriving state of commercial affairs experienced a severe check in consequence of the revolutionary struggle in France. The promulgation of republican doctrines in St. Domingo, containing a numerous coloured population, many of whom were in a state of slavery, led to a war of races, marked during its continuance by extreme ferocity, and leading eventually to the massacre or expulsion of the white population, the cessation of industrial pursuits, and the ruin of commerce. But this change in the state of society, had one effect of more importance to our present subject than any of the social or political changes at which we have felt it necessary to glance, in so far as it led to the more extensive cutting and exportation of the fine woods with which the island abounded. The black population, disinclined to the continuous labour of the plantations, allowed these to go to waste, and had recourse to the spontaneous supply of commodities for export furnished by their almost interminable forests. Amongst the other woods thus brought into notice, satin wood was exported in large quantities into Britain, and rapidly rose into general favour. Close in the grain, of a pale yellow colour, and elegantly veined, it presented an agreeable variety to the more sombre coloured woods, of which drawing-room furniture had been commonly manufactured, and for a number of years it was extensively used in preference. That it did not retain this eminence is to be accounted for partly from the caprice of fashionable taste, and partly from the fact that when polished with bees' wax, the mode then in use, it speedily gave off its colour and presented a pale blanched appearance. This defect has been remedied by the introduction of French polish, which preserves the colour; but the wood had fallen into disfavour before the remedy had been discovered, or rather, before it had found its way to Britain. Another cause of the comparative neglect into which satin wood has fallen, is its greasy nature, which renders it liable to part from the bed on which it is glued in veneer, or at joints where it is framed or wrought solid. This oily matter, held in the cellular tissue of the wood, gives it a highly aromatic odour, and renders it very inflammable. Although fallen into disrepute as a material for entire suites of drawing-room

furniture, it is still employed for articles of ornament, interior finishings, picture and mirror frames, and such purposes as maple is used for. The reasons which recommend maple for these uses, apply with nearly equal force to satin wood. Lightness of colour, beautiful figure, and a silken lustre, which has given rise to its name, all indicate its fitness for being *associated* with gilding and mirror plates; or for being *contrasted* with the darker woods, where variety is desired. In addition to what is used for furniture, a considerable quantity of satin wood is employed in the manufacture of brushes and fancy turnery. The supply is drawn not only from St. Domingo, but also from Porto Rico and Nassau in the West Indies, and from Singapore and Bombay in the East Indies. The relative values of the different growths will appear from a statement of their present prices. St. Domingo wood costs in London £14 per ton; Porto Rico wood, £10; Nassau wood, and those of East India growth, about £8. The wood of India and Ceylon is paler in the colour and less handsomely figured than that grown in the West Indies, but is of the same species. The name given by botanists to this wood is *Chloroxylon swietenia*. It is a variety of the same family to which the mahogany tree belongs; is *leguminous*, or bean-bearing, and yields an oleaginous matter known as *the oil of India*.

A fuller account of the natural appearance and habits of this wood would have been desirable, but hitherto there has not appeared any full account of the botany of the West Indies from which such information could be drawn.

WALNUT.

The common walnut, or royal walnut, named by botanists *Juglans regia*, is a native of Persia, whence it was brought by the Greeks. It appears to have been early introduced into Italy, and was known amongst the Romans as the Nut of Jove. We have no authentic information as to the time of its introduction into Britain, but mention is made of it in the earliest botanical records. Its fruits furnished the first inducement for its cultivation, and afterwards the useful and ornamental character of its timber secured for it permanent attention. In ancient Italy, it was highly valued for its beauty, and, according to Strabo, great prices were paid for tables and other furniture manufactured from it. In France and other continental states, from an early date, every encouragement has been given to its increase and cultivation. Evelyn, whose *Sylva* was written in the seventeenth century, says that it was abundant in Burgundy, and that 'in several places betwixt Hanau and Frankfort in Germany, no young farmer is permitted to marry a wife till he bring proof that he is a father of such a stated number of trees; and the law is inviolably observed to this day, for the extraordinary benefit the tree affords to the inhabitants.' In Britain, walnut appears to have been the first wood which superseded oak as the material for furniture of an expensive description; and it is not difficult to account for the preference. Closer in the texture and susceptible of a higher polish, softer, and hence more easily wrought, differing in colour, and often curiously veined, it naturally came to be regarded as the appropriate material for the furniture of apartments of which the interior finishings were in oak. The introduction of mahogany and other exotic woods, it is true, effected a great change in the general taste, and caused walnut for a long period to be regarded only as a material for gunstocks; for which its specific lightness and strong lateral adhesion rendered it eminently serviceable. The quantity required in Britain for this purpose, during the late war, greatly enhanced the price, and led to the cutting down of a large proportion of the trees growing throughout the country; and in France, it is said, that about the year 1806 not fewer than 12,000 trees were annually required for this purpose alone.

Within the last few years another change has taken place, and walnut furniture has again become popular. Fine old specimens of chairs, cabinets, tables, &c. that had been quietly resting in the lumber rooms of our large mansions, have been brought to light, repaired, and polished, and either reinstated in their former places, or sold at prices that would have astonished their long-departed makers. The great demand for these antique specimens of furniture has naturally led to the resuming of the manufacture of similar articles; and hence we find that in drawing-room furniture especially, walnut is now very extensively employed. One circumstance that has contributed to the renewed popularity of walnut, is the revival of a taste for marquetry or inlaid work, for the lively and variegated colours of which this wood forms a very appropriate ground. Of an olive brown colour, interspersed with darker and lighter veins, it acts as a foil to the light and parti-coloured ornaments, which, in the form of centre-parts, corner ornaments, or borders, are inserted in it. Of the common walnut grown in Europe, the qualities are various, some yielding much finer veneers than others. The importations from Italy are most valued, and at present are sold in London at prices varying from 9d. to 1s. per superficial foot. The growths of France are next in value, particularly those of Auvergne, in which the black and red veins are almost invariably found distinctly marked. We had recently an opportunity of examining a parcel of planks brought from Smyrna, which were very pale in the ground, and inferior in the marking; they were sold at 7d. per foot. There are some very fine trees, of large size, to be found in the parks of our nobility and gentry, but they are not numerous, and are seldom exposed for sale. In order to increase the limited supply from these various sources, recourse has been had to the black Virginia walnut, or *Juglans nigra*, a considerable quantity of which is now imported into Britain from America. It is denominated *black*, to distinguish it from the white walnut, or *Juglans alba*, of which there are several varieties, known under the general name of hickory, the wood of which is much lighter in the colour, and less valuable than the black walnut. The importations of black walnut, since the increased demand for it in this country, have been considerable. In quality, it is decidedly inferior to that of European growth, as is indicated by the price, which is only about $4\frac{1}{2}d.$ per superficial foot. What we have seen is of a dull uniform brown, having little of the figure which is necessary in ornamental furniture. It is, however, serviceable when wrought in the solid, for the inferior parts of articles of which the principal parts are veneered with finer wood, and for chairs, couches, pillars, brackets, balls, or the like. Finely-figured veneers of this wood are considered so valuable as often to be sold at from 2s. to 3s. per foot. These are the produce of trees that have grown upon rather dry and poor soils, and which are, in consequence of their slower growth, closer and firmer in the grain, than those which have been more quickly raised on rich and deep soils. The most beautifully marked specimens are yielded by cutting the large roots of such trees into veneers, after placing them in heaps of dung for a considerable time, which has a wonderful effect in deepening the markings and enriching the ground. At a recent public exposition of furniture, &c., in Paris, a *secretaire*, veneered with this material, excited universal admiration.

Although walnut is at present a fashionable material for furniture, we are disposed to think that there is little probability of its continuing to be so for any great length of time. We arrive at this conclusion on the ground that it is destitute of one of the three elements of beauty in wood, namely, *lustre* or *transparency*. It possesses the other two, *colour* and *figure;* but these enter more largely into the character of other woods, as mahogany, maple, satin wood, &c., which possess the additional recommendation of being lustrous and transparent in a high degree. It is inferior also, we think, in colour and figure to rosewood, which has not the advantage of being lustrous or transparent. For these reasons, we expect that it will speedily decline in public estimation, but in the meantime it is necessary for every tradesman who would keep up with the times, to direct his attention to the manufacture of it.

ROSEWOOD.

Rosewood is the produce of the Jacaranda, of which there are several varieties. It is indigenous to the East Indies and the Canary Islands, to Africa, and Central America; but the principal importations into Britain are from Brazil, where it is grown of the finest qualities, and in great abundance. Of the quantity imported into this country, on an average of the five years from 1840 to 1844 inclusive, we find nearly 2000 tons per annum entered for home consumption. The importations from Rio de Janeiro furnish the largest-sized and best-figured wood, and bring a considerably higher price than those from Bahia, the other principal seaport, situated about 800 miles to the north of Rio de Janeiro. Amidst the profusion of beauty and grandeur which distinguish the vast virgin forests of Brazil, the Jacaranda is too striking to be overlooked by the traveller. Von Spix, a German naturalist, who visited them, says, 'Among these sovereigns of the forest, the rosewood tree attracts the eye by the lightness of its double feathered leaves; the large gold-coloured flowers dazzle by their splendour, contrasted with the dark green of the foliage.' The name commonly given to this wood, *rosewood*, is descriptive of the fragrant smell of the wood itself, and not of any odoriferous properties possessed by its foliage or flowers. It has furnished occasion for frequent remark, that it is almost always exported in *half logs*, and not in whole trees. The reasons for thus *splitting* or *sawing* up the trees (for the division of them is commonly so rudely effected, as to partake of the characters of both) seem to be, that in the absence of navigable rivers, or roads of easy passage, it is necessary to reduce the weight of the pieces, for the purpose of facilitating their transport from the interior of the country to the sea coast; and further, that the trees are generally so faulty in the heart, that little, if any, loss arises from dividing them. The trees, unlike most other woods, are never squared, and for this reason, that the best wood is always found at the outside. The rudely-halved, unsquared, and crooked appearance of the planks,

forbid the idea of the wood being sold by measurement, and accordingly it is purchased by the weight, as ascertained and stamped on the ends at the custom house. The prices at present current are, for good *Rio* wood, in lots, about £20 per ton; and for *Bahia* wood, about £12 per ton. Single planks are to be found worth double the highest price we have quoted, and inferior lots are to be had at a lower figure than the lowest mentioned; but in order to get good lots of large-sized wood, with a mixture of veneer planks included in them, it is necessary to give the prices stated. An inferior kind is occasionally imported from Honduras, and sold at about £7 per ton; but it is so soft, porous, and ill coloured, as to be fit only for the manufacture of ordinary furniture.

In selecting rosewood for purchase, it is of importance to attend to the size, soundness, colour, and figure, of the planks, of which the various lots are composed. Planks of a small size, although bought at a lower price than larger wood, will be found less profitable to the cabinet-maker. For the manufacturer of picture frames, or of brushes, the narrow breadth is less objectionable; but in purchasing it as a material for furniture, the full-sized wood, although it cost more money, will be found the most economical. It is a matter of greater difficulty, in general, to secure *sound* wood, than to get it of a proper size; since, in importations of a fine quality, it is not uncommon to find the greater proportion of the planks, or half logs, scooped out on the heart side as if designed for pumps or canoes; and this may be the case to a considerable extent, even although it does not appear at the ends of the wood. Pieces that are marked by sudden bends lengthways, are to be avoided as suspicious, where there is no opportunity to turn over and examine them. But the *colour* is of more importance than either size or soundness in rosewood. Much of it is to be found of a dull light brown colour, resembling nothing more than a dried peat; whereas in wood of good quality, the ground is of a clear sharp colour, varying in depth of shade from orange to dark red, having the graining or figure distinctly marked in black. In seeking to ascertain the colour, it is desirable to learn what it is near the heart; for often a thin rind of good coloured wood is found on the outside, enclosing a very inferior heart. The value, of course, is greatly increased when the wood is well coloured throughout. In seeking for wood of a fine figure, special attention is to be paid to the appearance of the annular rings, as seen in the ends of the planks. When the concentric circles of red and black are found regular, or only slightly irregular, much show or figure is not to be expected. But when, on the contrary, they are found in waving and tortuous lines, a good figure is certain to be found. Another indication of fine figure is the plank being marked by knobby protuberances, which, when pierced, are found of a light colour. These, when intersected by the straight line of the veneer saw, produce an abrupt dash of light, which contrasts very agreeably with the sober aspect of the general surface; and, therefore, planks having these knobs, and other indications of figure, should be carefully selected for veneers, while the plainer pieces are reserved for chair wood, couch-feet and scrolls, table-pillars and claws, and solid work generally. In cutting up veneer planks, regard must be had to the form of the concentric circles, in order to bring out the best figure which the plank is capable of exhibiting; and this object will be best secured by making the saw-draughts run as nearly as possible parallel to the circles. The annexed figure exhibits a transverse section of a plank, in which the concentric rings present the irregular form necessary to produce a fine show or figure. If this plank 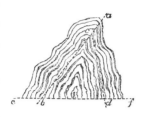 were sawn in the direction of a line drawn from *e* to *f*, the surface would show the smallest amount of figure of which it was capable, and would consist of a series of nearly straight lines of red and black alternately. But if a draught were run from *a* to *b*, and then another from *c* to *d*, the surfaces would present a beautifully variegated figure, the richness of which would be greatly increased were the knobby protuberances found elevating the grain lengthways. Rosewood, in this respect, presents a remarkable contrast to mahogany; for in it the finest figure is secured by causing the saw-draught to go right across the concentric rings, instead of parallel to them. The cause of this difference is, that in rosewood the medullary rays, or transverse septæ, are hardly distinguishable; and hence, there is almost none of that lustre or transparency which lends the chief beauty to mahogany, maple, birch, and other woods, in which the medullary rays are large. Rosewood is remarkable for the large quantity of gum and oleaginous matter which it contains; is, consequently, difficult to dry or shrink to its least dimensions; and is less easily held by glue than most other woods. Hence it is desirable to cut up such planks as are to be used in the solid, into thicknesses suitable for the various purposes to which they are to be applied, as long before using them as possible. If intended for chairs, a plank next the heart will be most profitably cut into front-leg thickness; a thickness for two or three back-legs in depth, say $4\frac{1}{2}$

inches or $6\frac{1}{4}$ inches, may be taken next, and the remainder, which will be narrow, may be thrown into clefts for clamps or mouldings. It may be found profitable to take up another plank of nearly the same quality and colour, and cut a thickness for claws off the heart, and then one to serve for chair-top rails, couch-feet, and scrolls; the remainder, if any, to be cut into $\frac{3}{8}$-inch stuff for fret work, beads, and the like. In order to secure the quicker and more thorough drying of the material, we consider it profitable, in establishments where the uniformity of the demand justifies it, to cut up the planks not only into thicknesses, but also depthways, into the various pieces of work which retain pretty nearly the same outline edgeways, although the facial lines may require to be varied, as patterns change. This mode of cutting will be found conducive to the more speedy and complete seasoning of the material, and will also, by careful *lining*, effect a considerable saving. Any difficulties to which this mode of breaking out wood may give rise, in settling for work done by *the piece*, may, we apprehend, be readily overcome by a judicious foreman in dealing with reasonable workmen.

In drying rosewood, it is of importance to take care that it is neither exposed unsheltered to the rays of the sun, nor suddenly to artificial heat; for either will have the effect of producing cracks, which, even although they close, cannot be concealed in the finished work. To make good furniture of this wood it is especially necessary that it be gradually and thoroughly seasoned; otherwise it is sure to betray the neglect afterwards.

Another peculiarity of rosewood is, that much of it is very porous, and that the pores are elongated on the surface, in a way that renders it difficult to produce a good solid body of polish on it. To remedy this, various plans have been tried. Size of various kinds has been employed to fill in the pores; but although well papered off, it furnishes a very harsh and ungenial surface to polish upon, and shrinks below the surface afterwards. Blackened bees'-wax has been rubbed in, and then cleaned off; but this has the effect of preventing the polish from getting properly riveted in the wood, and causes it, when the article is in use, to peel off on the least friction. The best remedy yet discovered, is, after the surface has been finished by the cabinet-maker, to rub it carefully in with plaster of Paris, coloured with rose-pink, which, after being *set*, is to be carefully papered off. This does not shrink like the size; and has the effect of preventing the oil used with the French polish from finding a hiding-place in the pores, whence it afterwards exudes on exposure to the air, and eats off the polish like rust on a metallic surface. The dull brown colour of a large portion of rosewood, has led to a variety of experiments to improve its appearance. Some have tried the dyeing of it with successive coatings of an infusion of logwood, but the effect is so unsatisfactory as not to repay the trouble. Others have used a strong solution of gum-dragon, or dragon's-blood, as it is commonly termed. This produces a very enlivening effect, in superinducing a rich purple hue on the dull brown of the wood; but it always presents the appearance of a thick coloured or painted medium being interposed between the spectator and the wood. We think it decidedly preferable to make use of a vegetable colouring, such as the extract of camwood, or other dyewood of the required tint; which, in solution with spirits of wine, produces the desired change on the colour of the wood, without suggesting the idea of its being painted.

Although it has had recently some rivals to contend with, we regard rosewood as being likely to furnish a permanently fashionable material for drawing-room furniture. Besides being intrinsically beautiful, it contrasts admirably with the materials usually employed in drapery; whilst mahogany, maple, satin-wood, and walnut, are apt to lose by comparison with the stuffs with which they are associated, or may have the effect of depriving these of their proper effect. We are not acquainted with any drapery material which can interfere with the beauty of rosewood, or any for which it does not present an appropriate foil, and setting. The only well-founded practical objection to its use has been the difficulty of keeping it in order; and this may be met by an increased attention to the careful finishing of the polish, which is often but very imperfectly effected.

Zebra-Wood.

Zebra-wood, like rosewood, is indigenous to Brazil, and is found in great abundance in the virgin forests which cover that territory, and whose profusion and variety of vegetable riches excite the admiration of European visitors. It is the produce of *Omphalobium Lamberti,* and apparently also of a second species, for one of the trees yielding this wood is, in Portuguese, named *Burapinima,* and another, *Goncalo de para;* both of which are of considerable size, and frequently furnish planks, or half-logs, twenty-four inches in breadth. Of the amount imported into Britain during five years, we find, on an average, nearly 145 tons per annum entered for home consumption. The price current at present, in London, for wood of this kind, of fair sizes, sound, and of good figure, is about £10 per ton. Of course inferior pieces are to be had at a lower price, and selected planks are charged higher. Zebra-wood, as its name implies, is striped in a manner resembling the skin of the zebra. On a ground of a pale buff colour are imposed, in straight lines, veins of a dark brown hue, clouded with black. This wood has a lively and rather gaudy appearance, but is destitute of lustre or transparency, and presents none of that agreeable variety of configuration which distinguishes rosewood. It has long been extensively used in the manufacture of drawing-room furniture, for which, in apartments that are imperfectly lighted, its smart and gairish colouring renders it peculiarly suitable. In such circumstances, we are disposed to think it preferable to walnut or rosewood, but do not regard it as equal to maple or satin-wood; the pale colour and transparency of the latter rendering them much more easily lighted up. When zebra-wood is employed in furnishing a drawing-room, we think it important to the general effect that a material of one colour only be used for covering the furniture, and draping the windows; since a chintz or party-coloured damask either loses on comparison with the wood with which it is associated, or, on the contrary, makes the wood itself appear tame and poor. Indeed, the effect of all our furniture woods is greatly dependent on the colour of the materials employed in connection with them; consequently, tradesmen should endeavour to acquire such a practical acquaintance with the harmony of colours, as shall enable them to furnish a hint on the subject, and determine the choice of a purchaser in the right direction. It is by no means uncommon for the most laboured efforts of the cabinet-maker to be defeated, by the colour of the drapery being injudiciously selected. This might ordinarily be obviated by his showing, in contrast, the opposite effects of an appropriate and an inappropriate association of materials.

Zebra-wood has become much less popular than it was a few years ago; the variableness of public taste will account for this to a considerable extent, but another cause is to be found in the fact, that many of the articles veneered with it have given way. We have seen tables whose tops were cracked throughout, in parallel lines about $1\frac{1}{4}$ inch apart, and in which there was scarcely as much of the veneer adhering to the bed as sufficed to hold the rest. This was evidently the result of using the wood in a damp state; and when exposed to the action of the air it shrunk, in virtue of a natural law, to its least dimensions; but in consequence of the bed on which it was laid being drier than itself, the shrinking could be effected only by its splitting up into fragments. Hence the necessity of attending to the thorough seasoning of the wood, whether in the solid or in veneer, before it is used. The density of the wood necessarily renders this a tedious process; but it can be neither omitted nor abridged without compromising the character of the manufacturer, and deteriorating the quality of his work. In cutting up zebra-wood, care should be taken to select the planks which have the finest figure for veneers. The plainer planks must be used in the solid for chair-wood, couch-scrolls, table-pillars and claws, and mouldings of fret pannels for cabinets. The cleft next the heart, if unsound and faulty, may be most profitably cut into thicknesses suitable for the front legs of chairs, which, from their shortness, may be lined so as to leave the smallest amount of refuse or *broke*. A plank of 4½ inches thick will be found a convenient size, furnishing either two back feet for chairs, the scrolls of French couches, or turned feet of Grecian couches. A three-inch plank will furnish spiral columns for commodes, or claws for loo tables, which in the present mode require to be of this thickness at least. We have found a few two-inch planks useful for the claws of smaller tables, and for spiral work in cheval screens, and similar purposes. It may be added, however, that different schemes of cutting up material will be chosen by different makers, in accordance with the class of articles on which their work principally runs.

MAHOGANY.

We now come to treat of mahogany, the chief of furniture woods, whether considered in regard to beauty, utility, or durability. Alike suitable for the purposes of the machinist, the ship-builder, and the cabinet-maker, it has been employed, from the time of its first introduction, to a greater extent than any other wood of equal value. Various accounts have been given of the discovery of this beautiful wood, and its introduction into Britain; but of these we shall instance only such as are duly authenticated. The first mention made of it is by Sir Walter Raleigh, one of whose vessels touched, in 1595, at the island of Trinidad, to undergo needful repairs. In his search for wood, the carpenter brought on board a quantity of mahogany, which, on being wrought, astonished all who saw it by that beautiful variety of appearance which has since rendered it so famous. It does not appear, however, that this wood excited attention in England until nearly a century later, and the circumstances which called it into notice were purely accidental.

Dr. Gibbons, a physician of some eminence, had a brother, a West India captain, who brought over some planks of this wood, simply as ballast. The Doctor was then building a house in King Street, Covent Garden, and his brother thought the planks might be of service to him; but the carpenters found the wood too hard for their tools, and it was laid aside as useless. Soon after, Mrs. Gibbons wanted a candle-box, and the Doctor employed Wallaston, his cabinet-maker, to make it from the wood that lay useless in his garden. He again complained that the material was too hard; but the candle-box was made, and it appeared so beautiful that Dr. Gibbons insisted on having a bureau made of the same wood; and this, when finished, became quite an object of curiosity, and was shown to many visitors. The Duchess of Buckingham saw and admired it, and ordered Wallaston to make another bureau for her. The approbation of her Grace was sufficient to render the wood famous and fashionable, and in consequence the use of mahogany became general. Thus, from a circumstance trivial in itself, arose a most extensive branch of British commerce, and a complete revolution in the manufacture of cabinet-furniture. Before the introduction of mahogany, oak, elm, and walnut, had been the only materials available for the manufacture of the more expensive, as well as the plainer articles of furniture; but speedily thereafter, these fell into almost entire disuse, and were, for nearly a century and a half, entirely superseded by mahogany. If the latter wood has more recently given place to any of the former, it is owing not so much to any intrinsic superiority which it possesses, as to the caprice of public taste, which seems to be ever seeking change, although it should be a change for the worse. These capricious changes in the taste of the public must be looked for as a matter of course; and those whose business it is to furnish articles designed not merely to supply the wants, but also to meet the wishes of the community, will find it wisdom to adapt their productions to the varying phases of the popular demand for novelty.

Mahogany is of such importance in cabinet-making that we are justified in giving a more extended account of its appearance in the forest, and of the mode of cutting and transporting it from its native soil, than we have found necessary in the case of woods of minor importance. We apprehend there are few who have been engaged in the manufacture of this wood, who have not desired some knowledge of these particulars. Known in botany as *Swietenia mahogani*, or common mahogany, it includes the varieties of Spanish mahogany, Cuba mahogany, and Honduras or Bay mahogany, all of which are commonly imported into Britain. These, however dissimilar, are not distinct species, but varieties of one species, whose qualities are determined by the soil on which they have respectively grown. The harder, more compact, and beautiful varieties, are the produce of dry and rocky soils; while the larger and softer wood is grown on low and marshy grounds. The mahogany tree of Honduras is a most magnificent and splendid object, compared with which the largest oak, the king of our forests, dwindles into insignificance. The enormous size and height of the trunk, the vast spread of its branches, and the space of ground covered by its roots, are alike remarkable. Some idea of the magnitude of the growing tree may be formed from the measurement and weight of the logs which are occasionally cut from it. The largest of which we have any account was seventeen feet long, five feet four inches broad, and four feet nine inches thick; it weighed fifteen tons, and contained 5136 superficial feet of one inch thick. The tree is often found 100 feet in height, rising nearly sixty feet in column from the spur to the limbs, which diverge into numerous branches that form a large and handsome head, covered with shining green leaves, and spotted with tufts of flowers, of a reddish or saffron hue. The leaves are about eight inches long, divided into leaflets about two and a half inches long, which are in pairs from three to five in number. The fruit is of an oval form, about the size of a turkey's egg. The tree is easily raised from the seeds, and it thrives in most soils, varying in grain and texture with the characters of each. It is almost impossible to give more minute circumstances attending the growth of this valuable tree, as its progress to maturity is scarcely perceptible within the life of man; we may state, however, that not less than 200 years is regarded as the average period which it requires to reach its full maturity.

In Honduras, the season for cutting mahogany usually commences about the month of August. The labourers employed consist of gangs of from twenty to fifty men, having a conductor, who is styled captain, and an intelligent observer, named the huntsman, whose duty it is to search the woods to find labour for the whole. Cutting his way through the woods to some elevation he ascends one of the highest trees, and minutely examines the country. At this season, the leaves of the mahogany tree are invariably of a yellow reddish hue; and a practised eye can readily discern, at a great distance, the spots where the wood is most abundant. These ascertained, the huntsman descends, and, unaided by compass, or any other guide than the recollection of his observations,

proceeds, with almost unfailing accuracy, to the scene of promise. Should the nearer view confirm his expectations, his next care is to retire without leaving any traces of his discovery behind him, that might enable competitors in the same pursuit to profit by his labours. Despite of his care, however, it not unfrequently happens that his track is perceived, and others take the promised spoils out of his hands. When the treasure is found and secured, the operation of felling commences, and as many trees are cut as will occupy the gang during the season. These are commonly felled at about 10 or 12 feet from the ground, the axe-man being elevated on a stage of convenient height. The man thus employed appears to be in a situation of some danger, but an accident is of rare occurrence. A sufficient number of trees being cut, the gang rear habitations for themselves on the banks of the nearest river, down which the timber is to be floated to the port of shipment, and in the construction and arrangement of these dwellings, much taste is frequently displayed, whilst the rapidity with which they are raised is equally remarkable. The next operation—and that one of great toil—is to form roads from the mahogany village to the spot where the wood is cut, the main road being directed as nearly as possible to the centre of the cuttings. Each man clears about 100 yards of road per day, clearing away the under-wood with his cutlass, and employing his axe or fire to level the larger trees; and these last he employs in the construction of bridges, for transit across the streams that intersect his road. If the trees lie much dispersed, miles of road and many bridges have to be made, branching out in various directions from the main road. The road-making is usually completed by the month of December; and then commences the cross-cutting of the trees into logs, and the squaring of the logs, with a view to lessen their weight, and render them more manageable in their transit from the forest to the river. By the month of April all is ready, and the ground in proper condition for carrying the logs to the river. This operation must be completed during the months of April and May, the earth being softened at all other periods of the year by heavy rains, and made impassable by trucks heavily laden. To this task, therefore, the whole force of the gang is directed, some being employed in loading, others in driving the oxen, and the remainder in cutting food for them. There are usually seven pairs of oxen, with two drivers to each truck, and six trucks to a gang. The labour of loading and driving, on account of the intense heat of the sun during the day, must be performed in the night-time, and by torch light; which renders the scene extremely picturesque and interesting to a stranger. The six trucks, extending to a length of nearly a quarter of a mile on the road—the great number of oxen—the half naked drivers, each bearing a torch—the wildness of the forest scenery—the rattling of chains, and cracking of the whips—and all this at the hour of midnight, present more the appearance of some theatrical exhibition, than of the sober industrial pursuit which has fallen to the lot of the wood-cutters of Honduras. On arriving at the river side, the logs, marked with the initials of the owner, are thrown in, to await the rising of the flood in sufficient strength to float them down to the sea. Nor is long delay necessary; two or three weeks of the heavy rains which now prevail, being sufficient to swell the rivers to a height more than sufficient to float the logs. The gangs follow in a kind of flat-bottomed canoes, called *pitpans*, to guide and facilitate their progress, until they are intercepted by a boom, placed at the mouth of the river. Here each gang claims its own logs, and, forming them into large rafts, floats them to the wharf of the owner; where they are taken out of the water, and subjected to a more particular trimming, to fit them for shipment. A large proportion of the entire exportation from Honduras is sent to Britain, which, on an average, amounts to nearly 4000 logs per annum. This variety of mahogany is commonly called *Bay-wood,* and is now used by cabinet-makers chiefly for veneering upon, for inferior parts, or for articles of solid furniture. The earlier importations were distinguished from the present, by containing a much larger proportion of hard showy wood, much of which was cut into veneers, and was well worthy of being used for finishing purposes. Thirty or forty years ago, bay veneers were nearly as much used as those cut from Spanish wood, but they have since been almost entirely superseded by the latter. Two causes have contributed to the change, one being the inferior quality of the wood now imported; and the other, that while Spanish wood improves in appearance after being manufactured, bay-wood loses its colour and force of expression from lengthened exposure. But not only has it almost entirely ceased to be cut into veneers, it is also much less used for solid work, such as chair frames, dining-table tops, and the like. This may be in part accounted for, by a considerably increased demand for it by machine-makers, coach-makers, carpenters, and ship-builders, which has had the effect of raising the price of large-sized and good firm wood: and further, the increased importations of small-sized Spanish logs, sold at a moderate price, have furnished the cabinet-maker with a harder material, equally suitable

for many of the purposes for which bay-wood had been employed, and not more expensive. Still, for panels, door-framing, and table-tops, which are to be veneered upon; and also for all pieces of work that are required to be specially free from warping or change, we have no material equal to good bay mahogany. Whether in instruments that are to be submerged in water, or those which are to be exposed to atmospheric change, we have no wood equally impassible: and hence, for levelling-rods, tide-gauges, and similar articles, it is the material almost exclusively employed. Mahogany, of all kinds, possesses another valuable property, namely, durability; and in this respect it is equal, if not superior to, any other wood with which we are acquainted. Although, while in the tree, it is subject to the attacks and ravages of various insects, we have never seen nor heard of any instance, in which, after being manufactured, it has suffered from this cause. It cannot be reckoned an exception to this statement, that when planted in thin clamps or veneers on any of our home-grown hardwoods which fall speedily to decay, it should be perforated by the insects which destroy them; for we never find it attacked when detached from other woods. A remarkable proof of the durability of mahogany was furnished in June 1846, when several competent judges met to inspect various specimens of timber, which, six years before, had been placed in a fungus pit, for the purpose of testing their powers of resistance to dry rot. Of the various woods which had been subjected to this test, comprising English and American oak, African and East Indian teak, elm, ash, mahogany, and other woods, every description of timber, except the mahogany, was in a greater or less state of decay; but it was found to be in a perfectly sound state. While experience has shown that mahogany possesses, in a high degree, the qualities which we have mentioned, the main cause of its becoming and continuing so extensively popular as a material for furniture, is its beautiful appearance. The general colour of even the plainest kind is agreeable, and the finer sorts are distinguished by a variety of beautiful configuration and transparent lustre, that claim for this the first place among our furniture woods. Of the earlier importations, those from the island of Jamaica furnished a great proportion of the largest and most beautiful wood, of which we have seen several specimens in old furniture, marked by a wild irregular figuring and deep colouring, more resembling tortoise-shell than the mahogany in use at present. The trees nearest the sea were cut first, those near streams capable of floating them to the sea followed, until all the mahogany which would repay the cost of its transmission had been removed. We learn from missionary intelligence and books of travel, that many noble trees are yet standing in different parts of the island, which the difficulty of removal alone has preserved. It is surprising that no attempt has been made to continue the supply of accessible wood, by planting the waste lands, of which every proprietor has some within his range, and which, although unfit for almost any other purpose, would nevertheless be quite suitable for nurseries or plantations of mahogany.

Mahogany is imported in large quantities from the island of Cuba into Britain. On an average of five years we find nearly 1200 tons per annum entered for home consumption. It is sold under the name of Cuba mahogany, to distinguish it from Honduras and St. Domingo mahogany. It is much closer in the texture and harder than Honduras wood, and, in these respects, is nearly equal to Spanish or St. Domingo wood, to which it bears a considerable resemblance. It is generally paler in colour, and even when well marked with figure, wants the force of expression which distinguishes good Spanish wood. Unlike the latter, Cuba wood does not improve in the working, nor does it acquire the same rich mellow appearance from lengthened exposure after being manufactured. But the main defect of Cuba wood lies in the dark brown spots and streaks with which a great part of it is disfigured, to an extent that forbids its use for finishing purposes. The cause of these peculiar markings we cannot explain, but we have heard them attributed to the attacks of insects, whose perforations of the earlier and more tender layers of the tree, had, either from some colouring properties in themselves, or from the introduction of external air and moisture, produced the blemishes described. We are inclined to favour this idea, from having found many logs thickly marked near the heart, while the outer layers, to the thickness of five or six inches, was wholly free. But however caused, the liability of Cuba wood to this defect, renders the purchase of it uniformly troublesome and hazardous. Where the blemishes are distinctly marked externally, the purchaser will of course offer only such a price for the wood as the purposes it is fit to be used for will afford. But it is no uncommon occurrence to find a log giving strong indications of show or figure, and having no appearance of the dark spots or streaks, which yet, when opened, proves to be worth a far less price than has been paid for it. This uncertainty of value involves, on the other hand, the possibility of procuring really good logs at a price far below their value. When

this wood is found free from the fault described, it is very useful. If plain, it may be advantageously cut into bed pillars, chair wood, table legs, sofa feet, &c. For these purposes it is not necessary that the logs be of a large size, as wood of 18 inches deep, or less, will cut out quite as well, and cost less than logs of a larger size. When 19 inches deep and upwards, and of fair quality, the logs are called *table-wood*, and are cut into thicknesses suitable for dining-table boards, dressing-table tops, and ledgings. For dining-tables made on the old principle, whether on legs or on pillar and claws, it was deemed necessary to have the boards about 24 inches deep, or even broader. But since telescope dining-tables have come into general use, boards of a less breadth are found to suit quite well. Indeed, we are disposed to think boards of 20 inches or 22 inches deep are preferable to those of a larger size. They are lighter, and, consequently, more easily added to or taken from the table, and therefore less liable to injury; besides, the most convenient enlargement of a table is by boards, each of which are fully the breadth of a chair, for in this way the size of the table can be exactly suited to the number of the company. In selecting a table log, it is important to observe the length of it, whether it is long enough to yield two boards, or is not much longer than one board. Either of these is preferable to a log of an intermediate size, which would necessarily leave a considerable portion of the wood to be used for inferior purposes, and thus enhance the price of the table-boards. But good table-wood is often so scarce, that the purchaser must frequently buy logs, which otherwise suitable for his purpose, are yet of an inconvenient length. In cutting up such logs, it becomes a question of importance whether they should be cut the whole length into thickness for table-boards, leaving a number of short lengths after cross-cutting the boards. This question will be answered differently by different persons, according to the varying nature of their demands; some finding in the manufacture of small articles, ample use for all their cuttings of seven-eighths or one inch wood, while others find it more profitable to cross-cut the boards at the proper length, and to leave what wood is beyond in thick plank, which can afterwards be cut into chair-tops, rails, &c. Where this latter plan is resorted to, it is necessary, in cross-cutting the boards, to be very careful to prevent their splitting, which they are very apt to do. To effect this, a cramp should be put on each side of the saw-draught, only one board taken off at a time, and that carefully covered on the newly-cut end with canvas, glued, to exclude the air, before the cramp is removed. Each board in succession should be treated in the same way until the whole are cut off, when the thick cutting which remains should also be glued and covered with canvas. It will be noticed that we have spoken of the thickness of table-boards as seven-eighths of an inch or one inch. These different thicknesses are made use of in different localities, and while we would not presume to decide authoritatively on the matter, we may be allowed to express our opinion, that in tops which *are not* clamped, seven-eighths of an inch wood is thin and meagre in appearance, while in tops that *are* clamped, it may suit very well. For the tops of dressing-tables of a plain description, the usual thickness is five-eighths of an inch; while for those of a better kind, three-fourths of an inch, or even seven-eighths of an inch thick tops are used. The ledgings are usually half an inch thick; but the ledgings of washing-tables, in consequence of their greater depth, require to be of five-eighths of an inch wood. When practicable, it is important that the ledgings should be of the same log with the tops; and this can ordinarily be attained without loss, by using for them the faulty or shaken boards, which are unfit for tops. When a log is cut into boards of the thicknesses specified, there can be no difficulty in working it up into mouldings or clamps of one kind or another, if it should prove unsuitable for the purposes designed. But Cuba wood may be of a quality fit for cutting into veneers; and occasionally considerable prices are paid for it with this view. As in treating of Spanish or St. Domingo mahogany we shall have occasion to mention the different kinds of figure, and their external appearances, the hints we propose to give regarding the purchase of veneer logs will be found equally applicable to Cuba wood, and need not be anticipated.

When, instead of being fit for veneers or good solid work, a Cuba log is found much spotted or streaked with brown, perhaps the best use that can be made of it is to cut it into thicknesses suitable for the sliding rails of telescope tables. For these, we know of no material equally free from liability to warp; and in them the discolouration is of no consequence whatever. We have also seen it cut with advantage into five-eighths of an inch and three-fourths of an inch thicknesses, to be used as beds for veneering. Where the veneer employed has a strong tendency to warp and draw, Cuba wood will be found to offer a greater resistance, and to stand better than even Bay mahogany.

Before referring to Spanish mahogany, we may briefly notice, that, about twenty years ago, there was a considerable importation into this country of what was called African mahogany. It was a native of Western Africa, shipped from Gambia, and designated by botanists, *Khaya Senegalensis*, of a genus very closely allied to the *Swietenia*, or true mahogany, to which its wood, when cut, bore a strong resemblance. When first introduced, and before its true character was known, a considerable quantity of it was bought and manufactured into furniture. A very short experience of its qualities, however, served to drive it out of the market; and it has now fallen into entire disuse. Brief, however, as was its term, it did serious damage to several makers, who had used it largely, in ignorance of its qualities. When new and fresh, it had a fleshy colour, which, on continued exposure, deepened into a dirty purple, of a most disagreeable appearance. Nor was it only in colour inferior to genuine mahogany; it altered much more in drying, did not hold glue so well, and, consequently, the furniture made from it gave general dissatisfaction.

Spanish or St. Domingo mahogany is grown in the island of St. Domingo or Hayti; from which the annual exportations have greatly increased since the beginning of this century. In the year 1801, the whole amount exported was only 5217 feet; in 1821, the export amounted to 55,005 feet; while in 1841 it had increased to 7,525,461 feet. Since that date, the exportations have undergone but little variation. Of the whole amount exported from Hayti, about one-sixth part is imported into Great Britain, where the consumption seems to have kept pace with the supply; for on comparing the consumption of 1831 with that of 1837, we find it increased nearly fourfold, the amount in 1831 being 280,000 feet, and in 1837, no less than 818,900 feet. Of the whole amount imported into Britain, nearly a half is brought to Liverpool; which is resorted to not only by the chief buyers and consumers of the United Kingdom, but is also visited by purchasers from the Continent. From the Liverpool market, France, Germany, Russia, and even India, have of late been drawing supplies of Spanish mahogany. The large supply in this market naturally attracts purchasers; and an additional reason for preferring it is the liberal mode of measurement. Mahogany is not sold by weight, like the finer fancy woods, the irregular shapes of which forbid measurement; nor is it measured by the cubic foot, like the more common woods, but by the superficial foot. In other words, the contents of the log are stated in the number of square feet of boards, each one inch thick, which it will yield. To do this fairly, an allowance of fully one-eighth of an inch ought to be made for each saw-draught that would be necessary to cut the log into one-inch boards. A further allowance should be made for the loss in taking the slabs off the sides of the log, to straighten and clean it; and further, should there be unsound and faulty wood at the ends of the log, such as *shakes* or *rots*, an allowance should be made for these also; the result of the whole being to make the purchaser pay for the number of superficial feet of one-inch wood which the log will yield, and no more. These allowances on the measure are generally believed to be more liberally given in Liverpool than elsewhere, and hence its popularity amongst buyers; of whom those who come from the greatest distance are often heard to say, that the extra allowance on the measurement of their wood is more than sufficient to cover the expense of their journey to purchase it. We have made these remarks on measurement with the view of furnishing a useful hint to our less experienced readers, many of whom may not have a demand great enough to warrant their going to purchase at Liverpool. When it is expedient to resort to a nearer market, the buyer should either purchase by the Liverpool measure, giving a profit to the middleman who has brought it within his reach, and whose trouble must be repaid; or examine carefully for himself, by the directions we have given, whether the log or logs will yield the number of superficial feet which they are said to contain.

It is worthy of remark, that the mahogany imported under the name of St. Domingo wood is of varied quality, and is the produce of widely-distant localities. From the celebrity attained by the exports from St. Domingo city, it has become customary to carry the growths of other localities coastwise thither, and ship them for foreign markets under the common name. The cargoes thus collected are ordinarily of less value than those which consist of wood grown in districts more adjacent to the city; the latter is therefore usually distinguished by the name of city wood. Good quality consists in the wood being close in the grain, and of firm texture; or fine, in opposition to coarse; and of a kind nature, in contradistinction to the harsh and brittle hardness which is frequently found in mahogany. Bad quality is marked by the grain being porous, and of a gray and smutty appearance; and also by the specific lightness of the wood. The *colour* of mahogany is a principal element in determining its value, and varies in shade from a pale yellow, resembling pine timber, to a deep red. The colour most esteemed is a medium between the extremes, rather nearer the pale than the dark shade mentioned. Wood from the city is chiefly of a rich generous hue, varying from gold colour to ruby; but its superiority over other importations, consists principally in the transparency and beauty

of figure by which it is distinguished. *Figure*, in mahogany, may be divided into two kinds, namely, *roe* and *mottle*. Roe is that alternate streak, or flake, of light and shade running with the grain, or from end to end of the log. If the streak be regular in size and unbroken, it is little thought of; but if the flakes be broad, and if the light and dark parts have a tendency to blend, yet strongly contrast with each other, and are variedly broken in their progress, then it is considered fine. Mottle is that mark in the wood which, in a polished board, at first view appears like something raised upon the surface, and leads an observer to feel if it be a plane or not. This figure is much varied in form, and has had distinctive names given to the various kinds, of which we may mention the following:—*Stop-mottle* mostly arises from angular grains, and is in broad flashes, frequently diverging from a centre, like the foot of a bird; *fiddle-mottle*, so called from its resemblance to the figure often seen in the wood used for the backs of violins, and the cause of which we have endeavoured to explain in treating of Maple. *Rain-mottle* is another variety of this figure which is greatly valued; it is somewhat similar to fiddle-mottle, but is in larger and longer marks. These last are rarely found to penetrate into the heart of the log, and hence in cutting it is usual to take a plank for veneers off each of the four sides. Another well-known figure is the *plum-mottle*, so called from its resemblance to a section of a plum-pudding. It is rather hazardous buying logs giving indications of this figure, as the spots, which arise from indentations of the grain, often turn out disagreeably dark in colour. But this is by no means invariably the case, many specimens being found quite free from this blemish, and variegated in a most agreeable manner. Another variety is the *peacock-mottle*, so called from the eyes in it, resembling the spots in the tail of the bird after which it is named. A log, strongly marked with this figure, was sold in Liverpool for nearly £1000. Of all the varieties of figure, however, stop-mottle is the most esteemed; and, when united with broad roe of good quality and fine colour, constitutes the highest perfection in mahogany. It is not uncommon to find a price as high as 12*s.* per superficial foot paid for a log which possesses these recommendations; and on rare occasions, 15*s.* and even 20*s.* per foot has been given. Another variety of figure, but now much less popular than formerly, is the *curb*, or that peculiar feathery marking, which is caused by the log being cut above where it has diverged into two separate hearts, each forming the centre of a limb of the tree. The wood deposited between these two, before they finally separate into the forked shape, is often found very beautiful, and was, till lately, highly prized for veneering panels, sideboard backs, and moulded fronts, for drawer fronts, and round table tops, on which the curls radiated from the centre. Plainness or variety in the appearance of mahogany depends essentially, and chiefly, on the position of the fibres as presented to the light. When they lie parallel to the axis of the tree, the wood has a uniform and plain character; and the more contorted, interwoven, and, at the same time, regular in their distribution the fibrous masses are, the greater the beauty and richness of expression. The comparative abruptness of these transitions in the fibre, constitutes the chief distinction between roe, mottle, and curl.

The longitudinal and transverse sections of the fibre, or the *rip* and *cross cut* in plain wood, present the extremes of condition and of distinction of shade. Between the right angle which these sections form with each other, there is a varying range in degree of dip and direction of fibre, which developes the characteristic appearance of fine mahogany. The weather-seasoning and sunlight, and also the polish on finished surfaces, beautifies the wood, by intensifying the difference of shades produced by this variety in the fibrous arrangement. Good wood, besides its permanent expression of figure, when seen from a single point of view, exhibits a varying beauty as the observer alters his position, the lights and shades dissolving into, and alternating with each other. This illusion of change defies the imitation of the painter, and is unconsciously one of the chief attractions which mahogany furniture presents.

A practical knowledge of cabinet-making is indispensable in the selection of woods, particularly those of the more expensive sorts. In addition to the quality of logs, the consideration of their length, in connection with their breadth, determines their fitness for the various uses of the trade. Attention to this circumstance is of especial importance in buying mahogany.

Table wood is amongst the most useful, and considering the quantity with its required quality, it is the most expensive. Telescope table tops are made from 4 feet 6 inches to 5 feet 6 inches long ; and the breadth of the leaves or slip tops from 21 inches to 30 inches. These dimensions determine the selection of a log not less than 5 feet long by 22 inches in depth. If the tops are mounted on pillar and claw, they are usually wrought in three breadths, and consequently a log of less depth, say from 19 to 22 inches, will suit. If the log exceeds what is above stated, by 6 or more inches, the over length will clear away faults, or may be wrought up into clamps for the moulded edges of the tops. If the log be an

expensive one, and more than one length of tops, it is obviously more economical that it should be one or more exact additional measures of the length required, so that the wood may be wrought up without loss. Under such circumstances, the greater the length of a log it is the more valuable, as it can be cut up more advantageously ; besides, if faults do occur in a long length, there is room for selection, and avoidance of blemishes ; whereas, a log 5 feet long, which appears adapted for tables when opened, is frequently found to be a little shaken at one or both ends, however sound it may have appeared externally, and probably not one table board can be got out of it. In selecting wood for Pembroke tables, the same considerations have to be kept in view ; their usual size is from 3 feet 6 inches to 3 feet 9 inches. The bed portion of the top is from 22 to 24 inches wide, and each of the wings about half this breadth. Quality, colour, and figure are here requisite also, but this being a less expensive kind of table than the telescope, it is customary to make them of wood inferior in these respects. Defective tops of longer length may be wrought up in these tables, and this is the more conveniently done, as in them only one and the same side of the wood is at any time exposed. These tables are not now so common in good houses as formerly, a smaller size of turn-over table, on pillar and claw, having taken their place. As the quality and figure of wood varies considerably in different parts of a log, in cutting up table wood the boards should be marked in the order in which they lie to each other in the log, by numbering them on the edge, beginning at the one side, and proceeding to the other. This is of less importance if the wood be intended for telescope tables, as in them the loose tops are so adjusted as to fit whichever sides are brought together ; but in turn-over tables where the boards are permanently joined in forming the tops, it adds much to their appearance that the grain, colour, and figure of the parts be well matched; and as there is always greater likeness in these respects between the nearer than the more remote boards of the log, the marking guides in making such adjustments more perfectly and rapidly.

The apparent direction of the heart or centre should be carefully attended to in the selection of a table log. If the tree, when growing, has been crooked, the heart of course retains its original divergence from the direct line, when the timber is cut straight in forming the log.* The bend, in such case, may have been so great as that the heart in its

---

* The necessity of compact stowage is one of the chief reasons for squaring the logs.

course will crop out on the side of the log, and again dip into and traverse it diagonally. As the wood surrounding the heart is usually plainer, and is easily distinguished, this oblique direction of it through the breadth of the log, invariably deteriorates the quality of the timber.

This condition of the heart renders the wood unfit for tables, from its unequal shrinking, and consequent liability to warp and split in seasoning. It is, besides, less fit for telescope tables, where the tops are loose, than for tables on pillar and claw, where the fixed joints and the bars below keep the boards under constraint.

There is a further objection to the use of wood of this character for the sort of tables last referred to, that as the boards in the top should match together in their general figure and quality, this, from their irregularity of expression, is done with difficulty, or very imperfectly. In laying open such a log, the saw-cut should be made as nearly as possible in the same plane as the wandering heart, and not at right angles to it. By this means the plainer wood, with any defects or blemishes at the heart, may be planked off by the saw, whereas, if it be cut the opposite way, these defects will be dispersed through all the boards.

Chair-wood logs require less attention to size in their selection than to colour, straightness of grain, and firmness of texture. This is especially true in regard to wood intended for front legs, and in this less when they are turned than when sweep-moulded. Till lately the profile of the most common pattern of back-leg required it to be cut out the flank-way, and the broader the wood there was the less waste of material; but this style of chair, in mahogany, is now falling into disuse. The profile in the most prevalent pattern of back-leg is a segment of a circle, the wood being cut the deep way, and the style of the chair presented in front. The log selected for this purpose is first laid open, to ascertain its quality, and, if found suitable, it is then cross-cut into blocks the proper length of back-legs, and sent to the saw-mill. There is, by this means, no waste, as formerly, in intermediate cuttings, the saw-draught at once separating the wood into sweeps, the required thickness. Chair logs should not square less than 16 inches, so that if laid open through the centre, the sweeps may present such a breadth as to admit at least three legs being moulded on their face. This should be regarded as a minimum size of chair log. In the event of its turning out faulty in the centre, it may come in for bed-pillars; it will also pretty evenly divide for turned legs of the ordinary size. This eventual use of a log, supposed to be suitable for

chairs, will determine the safest lengths to be selected in purchasing. Lengths of 8 feet, 8 feet 6 inches, or 9 feet, or multiples of these, are the most suitable.

Veneer logs require more skill and greater knowledge of cabinet-making for their selection than those for any other purpose in the trade. The expected quality of the veneers will determine the use they are likely to serve, and will consequently regulate the considerations of price, and the choice of dimensions. It is a good general maxim to be kept in view, in the selection of woods, that the lengths chosen should be determined by the diameters; for this the practical skill of the buyer must find application; but, generally, this relation of the dimensions is not so important in a veneer as in a table log, and less in chair wood than in either. The cross section, or the end of logs, is the best criterion of their general character; by the inspection of the wood in mass it can be judged pretty accurately whether the quality indicated on the side is continuous throughout. This is especially true in judging of veneer logs from the arrangement of the fibres of the wood, which fits it for veneers, and the indications of its quality from this reason are the more decided, the richer the wood. The reason of this may be briefly explained. In cross-cutting a *veneer* log, the general mass of the wood is cut at right angles to its length, but the fibres of the wood, whose contortions and overlappings give richness to its expression, are not cut at the same, but at very varying degrees of angularity. From this reason, the end of the log presents the characteristic appearance of the wood pretty faithfully, the various shades being shown on the end, from the same cause as those on the side, if not with equal distinctness. The different kinds of figure are not discovered with equal facility on the end view, and in most cases it requires a practised eye to distinguish them. Roe or shade is always easily observable; mottle frequently, but with greater difficulty; the roe by a strong deep colour, and the mottle by faint flakes running from near the centre to the outside. It is further important to observe whether the indications of figure are uniform throughout the log, or otherwise; if they become indistinct, or fall off towards the heart or centre, the rich or veneer wood will be confined chiefly to the outer side; and, on the contrary, when greater depth and variety of shade are apparent toward the centre, the outside may be expected to be the plainer wood. Such irregularity in quality depreciates the value of the timber, and limits its use to fewer and inferior purposes.

Curls.—In selecting a log for curls, particular attention should be paid to the width between the two centres or hearts, with the view of ascertaining the probable length of the figure. When the centres are unusually wide, a long length of curl may be expected suitable for the panels of wardrobes; and, on the contrary, when the centres are near, the curl is likely to be fit for short panels only, or for the star tops of tables. A defect in the quality of the curl is frequently caused by the ordinary circumstances in the growth of the tree, which go to form it. This is due to partial detachments of the branches, at short intervals, before their complete divergence from each other at the top of the stem. The formation of *in-bark* at these points is destructive of the value of the curl. The external indications of this fault are generally not very decided. The most certain and conspicuous mark is when there is the appearance of bark, imbedded or interposed between the concentric rings of the exposed sections of the several branches. This defect may exist in the absence of this symptom, as the log may have been cross-cut at a point where the branches are solidly united. Upon this supposition, it is important to observe whether the concentric rings of the wood at the contiguous parts of the branches are regularly formed, or whether they are distorted, as if by mutual pressure, in their growth. There is a greater probability of the existence of this blemish in the curl in the former case, than in the latter. Their dimensions and soundness are the chief considerations to be kept in view in examining the more common kinds of wood. In the ornamental sorts, in addition to these, other qualities claim attention, and, accordingly, greater discrimination is necessary, as those are increased in number and varied in character. Required excellencies are met by their corresponding defects, and the distinct perception of the indications of both is necessary to a correct and well-balanced judgment. An excellent preparative to the study of wood, is a general knowledge of structural and physiological botany. An acquaintance with the character of woody fibre, and with the chief circumstances that attend its growth, will impart greater acuteness and accuracy to observation, while a knowledge of the distinguishing names of the different parts of the stem of trees, and of the uses which these serve or express in their structure, will furnish the language of distinction and description.

A correct opinion of the quality of timber might be readily formed, if the general appearance of the outside of the log correctly indicated its entire character; but when even an approximation to a correct judgment depends so frequently on a variety of obscure hints, carefully collected, which blend their influence in forming a general impression of its nature, it is the more necessary to sharpen the powers of observation by careful and attentive study.

It is well known that good judges of timber are rare, and that it is always a great recommendation to a workman to possess a thorough knowledge of these materials of his trade, while to an employer or foreman, who conducts or superintends an extensive business, an acquaintance with woods, their several varieties, particular qualities, and usual prices, is all but indispensable. None of the woods deserve or require such particular attention as mahogany. In it great loss may be incurred through ignorance, while it is well known that a successful purchase has often given a decisive turn to the fortunes of a business. The risk of loss on the one hand, and the uncertainty of a profitable purchase on the other, are reasons sufficient to induce an attentive study of this the most important wood used in the trade. Competent skill removes this uncertainty; and while it imparts greater security, it also alleviates much of that anxiety of mind which arises from a hazardous investment. From the number of different woods used by the cabinet-maker, and the variety in dimension and quality of the several specimens of each which present themselves, no precise rules can be given for their selection. Suggestions of a general sort are all that can be offered; the practical knowledge and peculiar skill which qualifies for purchasing safely, can only be attained by personal observation and attentive study. This valuable acquirement has hitherto terminated with the individual possessor, and no attempt has been made to preserve and disseminate the results of mature experience. Much that is dependent on personal sagacity and acumen is of course incommunicable, but many useful hints and existing maxims for the selection of woods thrown together after some system, would assist the inexperienced, and add to the general stock of intelligence in the trade. A methodic inspection of woods has the recommendation of directing the attention to a series of particulars in succession, so that the observer, instead of resting in an indefinite general impression of any specimen under examination, may come to form a distinct and positive judgment of its qualities. No wood extensively used in cabinet-making is better suited thus to exercise the judgment of the workman than mahogany. This wood embraces three great varieties, possessing different properties, which adapt them for various general uses in the trade; in addition to this, there is the further diversity of the several specimens of each in quality and dimension, which points out their respective fitness to particular kinds of work. The inspection of the wood in log should go far to predetermine these conclusions, and, accordingly, the requisite skill required for this purpose. The circumstances which give this wood the appearance of fineness, have been already referred to. Observation may be further assisted, by pointing out and classifying the defects incidental to mahogany. The consideration of unsuitable form or dimension in the log is here purposely avoided; both faults being obvious, and their importance easily determined; attention is chiefly directed to those less apparent blemishes in the timber, which arise either from peculiarities in the growth of the tree, or from external causes affecting it.

These defects may be severally designated General, Local, and Accidental.

GENERAL.—When the blemish is not partial and limited, but extends to the whole or the greater part of the log, such as—

Colour—when this is of a pale unvaried character, approaching that of American birch, or Havannah cedar, or of a deep red.

Coarseness of Grain—the appearance of which is often such as no quality of finish can ameliorate; it is, besides, frequently accompanied with defective colour and harshness in the figure.

Dotted—when the wood wears a fungoid appearance, or that of extreme age, as if the tree had been fast decaying, or perhaps was quite dead when cut down.

Brittleness and Softness in the Fibre—the usual accompaniments of that appearance of the wood previously referred to.

Wandering Heart.—The character and external symptoms of this blemish have been already referred to. Although the quality, colour, and figure of the wood be in general good, its use is limited, and its value lessened by this defect. It is not uncommon to find the heart so crooked in its course in an otherwise fine log, as to prevent it yielding one sound board.

LOCAL—when the defects are confined to a portion of the wood, or distributed at considerable intervals through its mass, leaving the greater part sound, such as in the occurrence of

Knots.—These, when large, are often accompanied with much plain wood. They are more injurious when they occur in the depth than in the thickness of the log. If in the depth, the log must be cut on the side, so as to clear off the knots on one or more of the boards. This causes loss, as the thickness of the log thus determines the breadth of the boards. When this fault occurs on the edge of the log, it is of less consequence, as the breadth is then preserved.

Spots occasionally accompany some peculiarity of figure in the wood, as in plum mottle, already referred to. These blemishes, in this figure, are sometimes offensively dark; and frequently they break out into numerous small fissures, with *in-bark*, which are widely diffused over the sides of the wood, and so render it valueless.

List.—This, in figure and distribution, is like straight roe, running with the general direction of the grain, and is of a dark cloudy colour. It appears to be caused by the irregular deposition of the secretions in the wood. This also frequently occurs, but in minute degree, and of the same colour with its other defects, in wood with plum mottle figure.

Stains are of various hues, and are often irregularly dispersed throughout the log; frequently, from their dingy colour, they appear to be the incipient symptoms of decay in the wood.

Cork centre, with its almost constant accompaniment, *worm-holes*, the soft, spongy character of the wood rendering it easily penetrable by worms. This defect frequently extends considerably round the centre, and is of a pale colour. The logs in which it occurs are generally raw in grain, and specifically light—the usual indications of rapid growth in the tree.

Curls, when of useful dimensions, and of suitable quality, rank next in value after table and veneer wood; but when formed on the stems of trees, in the growth of branches, they are a serious blemish in the timber. The indications of their presence in the log are quite decided, and easily observed. If at the top of the trunk the tree has spread out into many branches, curl may be expected in connection with each, and on the end of the log the medullary centres, with their concentric layers, are the symptoms of its presence. These indications are still more decided from the oblique section of the branch made on the side of the log, exposing, with greater certainty, the character of the surrounding timber.

ACCIDENTAL DEFECTS are those which arise from external circumstances, affecting the timber in the tree when growing, or after it is cut down, such as—

Shakes.—This defect presents two varieties, one of which runs with the grain of the wood, and the other directly or obliquely across it; each is commonly accompanied by a distinct and characteristic difference in the appearance of the wood. In the straight shake, the wood, for most part, is otherwise sound in colour and fibre; but in the cross shake it is usually defective in both these particulars, being brittle, and of a dull, dark colour. In the former case, the defect is confined to the heart or its vicinity; in the latter, it extends irregularly through the mass of the wood. Local disease in the tree, and a consequent arrestment of its growth in the parts affected, may account for the lengthwise rending of its timber, but the cross and irregular fractures, apparently destructive of its vitality, are most probably caused by the disruptive action of electricity, and the defective quality of the wood may be a consequence of the subsequent decay of the tree.

Rot.—The occurrence of this on the outside of a log, either on the end or side, is a conspicuous fault, and liberal allowance in the measure is usually given for clearing it off. It sometimes lurks in the timber without any distinct external indication either of its existence or extent. Large cavities and decayed masses are frequently found in the heart of logs, while very faint and indistinct symptoms of these appeared on their outside. This defect, in most cases, may be considered the consequence of soft centre, and its decay. Interior rots are frequently caused by decayed branches, exposing the inside of the tree to atmospheric influence and the attack of insects; knots are frequently accompanied with decayed wood, and their soundness on the outside, taken together with apparent firmness of heart in the log, are the only certain indications of the absence of rot internally. This defect occurs in St. Domingo wood more than in Honduras, and less in Cuba wood than in either.

Worm-holes are common to all kinds of mahogany, but they occur less frequently in Cuba wood than in the others. This defect is easily seen when it appears in the sap, or on the edge of the log, but the indications of its existence in the heart are much less decided, and its occurrence much more injurious; wood partially affected with this blemish, may be wrought up as a bed for veneering on, when only the veneered side is exposed, as in the tops of loo-tables; probably, also, in the veneered gables and ground-framing and panelling of the doors in rosewood cabinets, the insides of which are imitation grained.

Adzing of logs, beyond what is necessary in forming them, is a deception practised for the purpose of concealing plainness, or of exaggerating the appearance of figure in the wood. This has the character of a defect in logs having a hollow side, as there is greater waste than might otherwise be in clearing the timber of the adze marks. It is also a proper reason for sharp inspection, and of claim for more liberal measure on the part of the buyer, to cover the loss from this intentional irregularity in the surface.

A good practical method of prosecuting the study of mahogany, or of the woods in general, may consist in first carefully attending to the several external indications of the quality of the timber in the log, and from these predicating a distinct judgment

of its character; and when the log is laid open, a comparison between this original opinion, and the now disclosed character of the wood, should be made. Such exercise sharpens the power of observation, and tests the judgment.

A STATEMENT *of the* IMPORTATION *into* BRITAIN, *with the* CONSUMPTION *and* STOCK *of the different sorts of* MAHOGANY, *for the last Seven Years, ending Feb. 1.*

	IMPORT.			CONSUMPTION.			STOCK.		
	Average from 1845-1849.	1850.	1851.	Average from 1845-1849.	1850.	1851.	Average from 1845-1849.	1850.	1851.
Honduras Logs.....	3,651	3,379	4,030	3,619	2,351	4,561	1091	400	869
St. Domingo Logs..	12,408	18,815	21,152	11,615	20,095	21,029	3220	2959	3082
Cuba Logs	4,329	1,567	2,296	4,402	1,459	2,257	939	127	166

TABLE *of* IMPORTS *of* MAHOGANY *of every description, into the* UNITED KINGDOM, *for the Years* 1838 *to* 1849 *inclusive; and of* MAHOGANY *from* ST. DOMINGO, CUBA, *and* HONDURAS *respectively, into the* PORT OF LIVERPOOL *for the same period.*

	IMPORT INTO LIVERPOOL, FROM				Total Imports into the United Kingdom.
	St. Domingo	Cuba.	Honduras.	Total.	
Year.	Tons.	Tons.	Tons.	Tons.	Tons.
1838	2360	270	3666	6,296	23,336
1839	2540	972	4121	7,633	25,859
1840	1630	373	2716	4,719	23,115
1841	1865	200	2479	4,544	19,502
1842	2080	180	1128	3,388	16,938
1843	1510	765	2726	5,001	20,284
1844	3215	1766	4473	9,454	25,622
1845	5127	4458	4891	14,476	38,351
1846	3480	2819	7503	13,808	40,238
1847	3836	888	4045	7,769	34,009
1848	1603	2139	1757	5,499	31,668
1849	5121	1025	4911	11,057	29,012

Relative Number of Feet to Weight.—Returns are made to the custom-house, for statistical purposes, upon the estimated ton. The ton weight, if from the city of St. Domingo, in logs, usually yields *for sale* from 290 to 310 feet, and from 270 to 290 feet in curls; from other parts of Hayti, from 300 to 320 feet in logs, and from 290 to 300 feet in curls. From Cuba, the average is 290 to 300 feet to the ton; and from Honduras 330 to 350 feet to the ton.

CEDAR.

This name is given to several trees which differ much from each other in their botanical characters and relations, and in their properties and value in the arts.

The *Cedar of Lebanon* (*Pinus cedrus*), by the sanction of ages, and from many interesting associations, is unquestionably the most celebrated tree which bears the name. It is equally distinguished for its vast size, and for the irregular grandeur of its form. It is superior in picturesque effect to all other evergreen coniferous trees, and when arrived at maturity, or approaching those gigantic dimensions which it acquires in its native climes, may be justly considered as one of the most magnificent of the vegetable creation. The growth of the cedar is not confined to Lebanon, but extends over the whole range of mountains which girdle the northern and eastern shores of the Levant, known as the mountains of Taurus, Amanus, and Libanus of antiquity, and also over the mountainous regions of the north of Africa.

It thrives well in English soil, but, from its slowness of growth, it has not been extensively planted for its timber; such trees as grow here have been introduced chiefly from a feeling of novelty or for ornament. The specimen of this tree reputed to be the highest in Britain is one at Strathfieldsay, measuring about 108 feet high; and one at Syon, said to be the largest, the height of which, in 1837, was seventy-two feet, and the diameter of the trunk at three feet from the ground, eight feet.

The trunk of the cedar has a massive columnar character, being of large diameter in proportion to its height. At a few yards up it usually divides into three or four limbs; these frequently grow together like a cluster of Gothic columns for ten feet more, when they begin to spread out horizontally. No experiments made on the quality of its timber, grown in England, go to sustain its ancient reputation for strength, durability, or appearance. Climate and situation may impart to the wood of the cedar grown upon Lebanon, properties which it can never acquire in the plains of England. The cross section of the trunk resembles that of the silver fir, and the wood in plank is little different from common deal; it is of a pale reddish white, light, spongy, and soft in texture, easily worked, but apt to warp and split in drying, and by no means durable.

The general texture and grain of the wood grown upon its native mountains, appears to be superior to that found elsewhere. In the *Histoire du Cèdre*, it is mentioned of some cedar wood brought from Mount Lebanon by Dr. Pariset, in 1829, that when wrought into a piece of furniture it presented a compact surface, and was agreeably veined and shaded.

The associations of religion and of history may lead to the occasional use of the cedar of Lebanon, but from the scarcity and inferiority of its timber, it is not likely to come into general repute as a cabinet-wood.

Pencil Cedar, so called from its extensive use in the manufacture of pencils, is known to botanists as the *Juniperus Virginiana*, and is of the same natural order as the pines. It is a native of North America, of the West Indies, and of Japan. It is not of large growth, seldom exceeding forty-five feet in height, and is imported in logs, averaging about fifteen feet by nine inches square. The matured wood is of a reddish chestnut brown; it is uniform and straight in the fibre, soft, brittle, and light, and has a pleasant odour. Its use in furniture is chiefly confined to the interior work of small cabinets, for which it is peculiarly adapted from the silky smoothness it takes, and from its colour, odour, and small size.

The wood is durable, and not liable to the attack of insects. The faults incidental to it are the want of uniformity in the shape of the log, frequently aggravated by the irregular and imperfect transformation of the sap-wood into true wood; this last defect is not confined to the outside of the timber, but frequently appears in large white spots throughout. Knots and shakes in the heart, extending through the entire length of the log, are of common occurrence.

The rejection of the sap-wood together with the shakes and other blemishes, causes great waste in working. It is sold by cubic measure, the price varying between 2s. and 4s. 6d. per foot. The average annual importation of pencil cedar into Britain, taken over seven years, ending February 1, 1851, was 17,545 cubic feet. The consumption in the same time, was 17,198 cubic feet. The average stock on hand over the same period, was 27,612 cubic feet. On comparing the last two years of the average with those preceding, the consumption of this wood seems declining.

Havannah or *swamp Cedar*, called also *bastard cedar*, is the *Cedrela odorata* of Linnæus, and belongs to the same natural order as mahogany. It is destitute of figure, and paler in colour than mahogany, and is also coarser in the grain, more brittle, and softer. It is a native of North America, and of the West India Islands; it grows rapidly, and attains a vast size in the lower grounds of Florida and Louisiana, and in the rich valleys of the mountains of Cuba. There have been many instances of single trunks of trees of this wood being hollowed out into canoes about 40 feet long, by 6 feet broad. It is used in inferior furniture, for the ground framing and panelling of veneered doors, and in carcase-work for the gables and inside work of sideboards, wardrobes, commodes, and chests of drawers. It is better suited for the bottoms of drawers than for their sides, as the wood wears rapidly, being too soft for use when the drawers are either large or heavily loaded with their contents. The highly resinous character of some specimens of this wood unfits it for cabinet-work, as the gum oozes out, rendering the surface adhesive to the touch. It is sold by the superficial measure, 1 inch thick, from 5½d. to 6½d. per foot. On comparing the two years ending February 1, 1850 and 1851, the consumption of this wood seems greatly on the increase. The quantity imported in these years, respectively, was 360 and 492 logs; the consumption in the same time, 462 and 504 logs, leaving on hand a minimum residue of former importations.

Himalaya Cedar, the *Cedrus deodora* of botanists, is one of the pine tribe. It is a native of Central Asia, and of the Himalayas, growing on the mountains of Nepaul, and the upper terraces of Bengal. Its ordinary dimensions, at mature growth, are 150 feet in height, with a trunk 30 feet or more in circumference. It is a hardy tree, and grows at great elevations. The quality of its timber, as reported, seems to adapt it well for cabinet-work; it is said to be compact, resinous, highly fragrant, and of a deep rich colour, which has been compared to polished brown agate. The grain is remarkably fine and close, and capable of receiving a beautiful polish. In respect of durability, "the Deodar wood of India is all but imperishable."*

This timber, employed in buildings which have stood for 200 years, when taken down was found in no way impaired, but fresh, and fit for further similar uses. It has been recently introduced into Britain by the transmission of seeds from India, but its timber has not yet been imported in any considerable quantity.

New South Wales Cedar, the *Cedrela Toona* of botanists, resembles Havannah, but is coarser in the grain, and of a deeper red colour. The bark, leaves, and fruit of the tree have an offensive smell, like assafoetida; but the timber has a pleasant odour. It is found in the East Indies, and is there much used in joinery work. The packing cases containing importations from Australia, are usually made of this wood. It is enumerated in the list of woods ordinarily on sale in Liverpool, but the supply is limited. It is sold by superficial measure, at from $4\frac{1}{2}d.$ to $5\frac{1}{2}d.$ per foot.

Bermudas Cedar (*Juniperus Bermudiana*), a native of the West Indies, is one of the loftiest trees in Jamaica, and attains to a large diameter; it has the same colour and odour as pencil cedar, but it is of a firmer texture, harder, and heavier. It was formerly much used in shipbuilding.

THE YEW (*Taxus baccata*),

Is indigenous to Britain and to most European countries, and to the North of Asia; a variety of it is found in the North American continent. It grows in rocky and mountainous wooded districts, and is found in such elevated situations within the tropics.

There are many specimens of this tree existing in England, of venerable age and of vast size, several exceeding thirty feet in circumference. It is of comparatively slow growth, and frequently many centuries have elapsed before it has shown any symptoms of decay. It is a common saying that a post of yew will outlast one of iron. This feeling of its durability, along with the constancy and freshness of its foliage, has led to its selection as an ornament to churchyards. The trunk is irregularly formed, not round or smooth, but deeply grooved longitudinally. The wood is remarkable for closeness of grain, and for elasticity and toughness of fibre— qualities which eminently fit it for heavy strain and active wear; and in bygone times, recommended its use in the construction of that formidable weapon the long bow, so destructive in the powerful and skilful grasp of the English archer. The colour of the matured wood is a rich, light, chestnut brown, deepening into tints of darker shade, and illumined by flashes of orange. Near the root, and at its ramifications, it is variegated and veined, so as to vie in beauty with the finest foreign cabinet woods. The sap-wood, which is of a light yellow, and scarcely inferior in texture to the true wood, when wrought up and judiciously intermixed with the other shades, adds greatly to their novelty and variety.

The wood of the burrs or excrescent growths of the yew, resembles and is often as beautiful as Amboyna wood; the figure is usually larger, and the ground colour equally fine. If we add to these qualities its extraordinary durability, and that when used in bed furniture it is never approached by insects, the yew may be safely pronounced as not only one of the most valuable of our native trees for general use, but also to be scarcely at all inferior, for cabinet-work, to the most costly woods of foreign growth that have been introduced. The importance attached to this wood, and the chief inducement to its cultivation in former times—the manufacture of bows—have now ceased for centuries. It has unfortunately fallen into undeserved neglect, and has not been extensively planted with a view to its use in the arts. At present it is not to be procured in sufficient quantity, to be made generally available for the larger articles of furniture.

The cost of this timber is high, and varies exceedingly, from £20 to £40 per ton, and for superior specimens as high as £60 have been occasionally paid. Good veneers of the burr of the yew cost from 10$d.$ to 1$s.$ per foot. An excellent quality of yew-tree is obtained from the neighbourhood of Lochlomond.

SNAKE WOOD, LETTER, OR SPECKLED WOOD.

Its botanical characters are uncertain, but it is supposed to be the *Tapura Guianensis*, a native of the northern parts of South America, of Demerara,

---

* Lindley's *Vegetable Kingdom.*

Surinam, and the banks of the Orinoco. It is the heart of a tree sheathed in sap-wood three or four times its own diameter; is called by the Indians *Bourra courra*, and is used by them in the manufacture of bows, for which it is particularly suited, from its highly elastic character.

It is exceedingly hard, and close in the texture; in colour a reddish brown, like red hazel, varied by lighter and darker streaks running with the grain throughout; with numerous black spots, fainter and fewer towards the heart, but increasing towards the outside. The appearance of the wood from these spots, by a little aid of the imagination, may be supposed to resemble letters, or the scales of the reptile whose name it bears. The wood, when fine, is very beautiful. It is imported in round sticks, averaging 7½ feet long by 5½ in diameter.

Its selling price is from 3*d*. to 9*d*. per lb. Its adaptation to cabinet-work being much restricted by the smallness of its size, it is principally used in veneering picture-frames and in turnery, and in the more expensive kinds of walking-sticks.

Teak Wood.

Teak Wood (East Indian) is the timber of the *Tectona grandis*, which is the most important tree belonging to the order of the *Verbenes*, and grows to a vast size, having a rough prickly trunk, with ash-coloured bark, and deciduous foliage. It abounds in the mountain parts of Malabar, Burmah, and in the Rajahmundry Circars, and also in Java, Ceylon, and on the Tenasserim coasts.

It is justly styled the oak of the East, from the durable and strong character of its timber, the fibres of which are wavy and interwoven, giving them great tenacity. In mercantile shipbuilding it is esteemed superior to all other woods. In colour it is minutely streaked of two near shades of a light brown, and in general appearance resembles a plain and inferior kind of mahogany.

The banks of the Godavery, in the Deccan, yield a variety of this wood, closer in the grain and heavier than the common kind. This is beautifully veined and well adapted for furniture. Burrs, or excrescent growths, are sometimes found on the older trees, the wood of which is finely variegated, resembling in quality and colour similar products of the yew or Amboyna wood.

Teak is sold by cubic measure, at from 3*s*. 9*d*. to 4*s*. 6*d*. per foot.

Purple Wood.

Purple Wood, called also Amaranthus, is a product of Brazil, and, like most other woods of small growth and irregular shape, is imported in the round

state. In dimension, it varies from 8 to 10 feet in length, and from 6 to 9 inches in diameter. In toughness and rigidity of fibre, it resembles rosewood, but is harder, much finer in texture, and heavier. It is wavy and irregular in grain, but has very little variety in figure, and is irregularly coloured in various shades of purple, lighter near the outside, and gradually darker towards the centre. Like most woods that are extremely hard, this is commonly pipy and unsound at heart. When cut up and exposed, the colour deepens; and when, from the decay of the heart, the interior wood has been for a long period accessible to the air, it acquires a dark rich wine colour.

The mature wood is surrounded by a thick coating of sap, of a brownish yellow, about three-quarters of an inch in thickness.

Purple wood is sometimes confounded with King wood and violet wood, but these are frequently figured, whereas purple wood is usually plain. It is used for buhl-work, for marquetry, and turning, and is sold by weight.

King Wood.

King Wood, also called Guiana wood and Violet wood, is imported from Brazil and the neighbouring provinces of South America, in round sticks, averaging 4 feet in length, by 4 inches diameter. In general appearance it resembles rosewood, but is much finer in the grain. In colour it is minutely and alternately streaked in purple and violet, and is perhaps one of the most beautiful of cabinet woods.

Its size, along with the frequency of heart blemishes, confines its use to small cabinets and turnery.

It is sold at about £8 per ton.

Ebony.

Of this wood there are three kinds imported, which differ much from each other in dimension of timber, in colour, and grain. They are severally known as Mauritius ebony, East Indian (which grows in Ceylon and the Indian islands), and African ebony, shipped from the Cape of Good Hope. The Mauritius variety (*the Diospyros Ebenus*) is the finest in the grain, the hardest as well as the blackest and the most beautiful of the three, and also the most costly. The best specimens of this kind of ebony vary from 6 to 8 inches in diameter; in this size the colour is more uniformly and intensely black, and the wood more sound. When it rises to from 16 to 18 inches diameter, blemishes abound, and the colour is a dark steel gray. Ebony is uncommonly apt to split on exposure to sunlight or rapid seasoning. This occurs in all woods in varying degree; the fibres on the sides and ends contract in drying, while the wood in the heart, continuing saturated with the juices of the tree, retains its original dimensions, and the outside rends in consequence. The harder the wood the more slowly and unequally it parts with its moisture, and the disruptive action is, in consequence, more energetic. This constant tendency in all woods is intensified in ebony, from the dark colour of the true wood absorbing heat more readily than any other. These facts, taken with the generally straight direction of the grain, are the chief causes of the blemishes that are found in this wood. The Mauritius ebony, when first cut, is usually quite sound, and, with a view to its preservation, it is immersed in water for many months; and when taken out, the two ends are secured from splitting by iron rings and wedges.

When split, ebony presents a lustrous silky appearance, and when viewed in extended surface, a faint yellowish hue is diffused throughout. It is used principally in cabinet and general turnery; in musical instruments for flutes and piano-forte keys; and in cutlery for knife-handles. It is sold at from £16 to £20 per ton.

There are, besides, two other varieties, under the same genus, found in the Mauritius, one known as white ebony, which, in most of its characters, resembles box wood; and another, called young ebony, that in texture resembles the white, but of an ashy tint, irregularly coloured, and streaked of iron gray. It appears as if the wood were in the course of being transformed to black.

East Indian Ebony (*Diospyros ebenaster*), which grows in continental India, Ceylon, and the Indian islands, has greater range in the dimensions of its timber than the former. It varies from 6 to 20 inches, and even to 28 inches, in diameter; that from the continent of India is imported chiefly from Madras and Bombay. In grain, colour, and figure, the Indian ebony is inferior to Mauritian, but it is less liable to split in seasoning, and more free from interior blemishes. Besides the *Diospyros ebenaster*, there are other Indian species which yield ebony, namely, the *Diospyros tomentosa* and the *Diospyros Roylei*. Altogether, there are nine different sorts of *Diospyros* known; of these only the two above referred to are black. Ceylon or East Indian ebony sells at from £9 to £10 per ton.

African Ebony is imported in billets ranging from 3 to 6 feet long, 3 to 6 inches wide, and from 2 to 4 inches thick. It is inferior to the two former in colour and grain, but there is less proportional waste in its working than in the others. The African, besides, stands better, being more inert under varieties of moisture and temperature. This latter property leads to its use in the construction of theodolites, sextants, quadrants, and generally in mathematical and philosophical instruments. It is sold at from £7 10s. to £10 per ton.

Green Ebony is a product of the West Indies generally, and is imported chiefly from the island of Jamaica, in pieces from 3 to 6 feet in length. The tree is smoother and thinner in the bark than the principal variety of Cocus, which it resembles in grain, and also somewhat in colour. The heart wood is of a brownish green, and is highly resinous, like rosewood; and, like black ebony, it is straight-grained, and cleaves easily. It is used in turnery and marquetry, and also for rulers, as it stands well.

Calamander or *Coromandel Wood.*—A beautiful species of timber brought from Ceylon, and the Coromandel coast of peninsular India. It is not well known what plant produces this wood, but it is believed to be a species of *Diospyros* or ebony. Some accounts would limit its production almost exclusively to Ceylon, where it is said to grow in clefts of the rocks, whence it is difficult to extract the roots, which, of any part of the tree, yield the most beautiful kind of timber. From the variety of colour exhibited by different specimens of Calamander wood, it would almost appear evident that the timber is the product of several different species of plants, though, as already stated, probably all belonging to to the genus *Diospyros* or ebony. Generally expressed, its appearance is something between rosewood and zebra wood, with a red hazel or chocolate brown ground, figured with black stripes and marks. The darkest kind of wood is that most seen in this country, and is known alone as Calamander; a lighter coloured variety, somewhat striped, is called Calemberri; and a third kind, almost as light in shade as English yew, but possessing a ruddier hue, and partially veined and marked with darker tints, is called Omander. All these timbers, whether the produce of different trees, or of the same tree in different states, are very hard, but still they are easily cut by the veneer saw, and as easily wrought upon the turning lathe, for which, indeed, they are peculiarly well adapted; and all of them form very elegant furniture woods.

The duramen or heart-wood of the Calamander, like all other hard woods, is surrounded by a thick sap wood, which, in this timber, has a light yellow colour, and is of equal hardness with the heart, but has a coarser, opener fibre.

It is imported in small logs of about 3 feet long, and 3 to 6 inches diameter, though some logs, at times, are to be met with having a diameter of 9 inches. It is irregularly shaped in the log, but sound, and not subject to rend while seasoning. Being in considerable request in ornamental turnery, and frequently scarce in the market, its price fluctuates, but, generally speaking, it sells from 8*d.* to 1*s.* per lb.

Mountain Ebony is a general popular designation for the different species of Bauhiniac, but the term is chiefly confined to one, *Bauhiniac porrecta*, which grows on the higher grounds of Jamaica. The wood is hard, and veined with black.

SANDAL WOOD.

Sandal Wood is the timber of the *Santalam album,* and found chiefly on the coast of Malabar, in Ceylon, and generally in the Indian Archipelago. By the Cingalese it is called *Handium.* It is usually distinguished into white and yellow sandal wood, both being products of the same tree. The yellow is the interior and matured wood, and is the most valued from its colour and firmness of texture, but chiefly for its fragrance. It exists in greater proportion, according as the tree has reached maturity. The most fragrant part of the tree is near, and at the root, where the colour of the wood deepens to a yellowish brown. The exterior part is the white, and corresponds in character to sap, this, higher up, is found in greater quantity, and is less firm, and without fragrance; and, consequently, of comparatively little value. Sandal wood sells so high, that the tree is seldom allowed to grow more than a foot in diameter. An oil, extracted from it, is extensively employed as a perfume in the funeral ceremonies of the Hindoos. The Brahmins form a pigment from the dust, which they use in giving the *tilac* or frontal mark to the god Vishnu.

A decoction of the bark yields a red or light claret-coloured dye, which, when used simply as an infusion, fades rapidly.

The wood is imported in trimmed logs from 3 to 8 inches, and very rarely 14 inches, diameter; it is softer than box wood, and more easily cut. It is used in the manufacture of small cabinets, and the interior work of escritoires for boxes, musical instruments, fans, &c.

Another tree, called red sandal wood, yields a deep red dye; its native Indian name is *Rukta-chundum.* It is known to botanists as the *Adenanthera pavonina.*

AMBOYNA WOOD.

Amboyna Wood, known also as Kiabooca wood and Lingoa wood, is a product of the Spice islands of the Eastern seas, Amboyna being one of those islands, and hence the name of the wood. It is from Ceram, another and a larger one of the group of islands, that the chief supply of this wood is obtained; Singapore is the mart, from which it is imported to Europe. It is the product of an excrescent growth or burr of a large tree, whose botanical characters are uncertain, supposed by some to be the *Pterospermum indicum,* by others the *Pterocarpus draco.* The wood of the tree is of a plain character, lighter in colour than the burr, and, in grain, resembles mahogany.

Amboyna wood is imported in oblong, irregularly shaped slabs, ranging from 2 to 4 feet long, from 4 to 24 inches wide, and from 2 to 8 inches thick. In its general expression it resembles the burr of the yew tree, it is much softer in the wood, and is more minutely and uniformly figured, being full of small curls and knots. It is also more yellow in colour than the yew, and ranges between an orange and chestnut brown, and frequently red brown. It is an exceedingly beautiful and highly-ornamental wood. Its available size, figure, and colour recommend its use in the manufacture of small cabinets. It is, besides, frequently used in veneering more extensive surfaces, such as loo table and tea table tops. In such cases, from the irregularity of form in the wood, and from the abrupt and transitory character of the fibre, the joinings require to be waved and indented. Considerable skill and care are requisite in the surface finish of this wood. It is generally, but not uniformly, soft; and, in consequence, does not present a firm or equable resistance to the action of tools. In working it, a keen edge, little bite, a quick and steady hand, are important points to be attended to. A chief difficulty in bringing this wood to a perfectly smooth or flat surface when polished, arises from irregularities in its expansion, caused by its general softness, and unequal absorption of moisture.

This is usually remedied by reducing these asperities and inequalities by the action of pumice and oil. This process darkens and deteriorates the appearance of the wood in some degree. Amboyna wood is now of less frequent use than formerly. It is sold at 1*s.* 6*d.* per foot of veneer.

PARTRIDGE WOOD.

Partridge Wood, sometimes called Cabbage wood, is brought from Guiana, the Brazils, and the West Indian islands, chiefly Cuba. There are several commercial varieties of this wood, distinguished as red, brown, black, and sweet partridge. The first three names are founded on the prevailing colours in the specimens. From the uncertainty respecting its botanical character and relations, it is highly probable that the wood of several trees is included under this name. The red sort is called *Angelim* and *Cangelim* in the Brazils, and Yava, in Cuba. The West Indian partridge wood is said to be furnished by the *Heisteria coccinea* of botanists, a small inelegant tree, about 20 feet high, growing by water courses. The variety imported from Guiana is the product of a tree which attains a height of 60 feet, whose native name is *Boco*.

Partridge wood resembles rosewood in weight, and closeness of grain; and it has an odour like log-wood. In cross section, the annual rings are distinguishable by their colour, by different degrees of hardness, and porosity. The darker they are, the harder and less porous, and *vice versa*. This circumstance is the chief cause of the peculiar figure in the wood when seen in plank, giving it the general appearance of an endogen, or of one of the palm tree woods. In the most valued examples, it has a dark and variegated appearance, resembling the plumage of the bird whose name it bears; and, according as it varies in complexional character, it is denominated Pheasant wood or Partridge wood. The predominating colour is a reddish brown, irregularly mingled, and minutely veined, and hatched in various shades of a deeper tint, approaching black. Besides these more decided colours, feathery and evanescent hues of blue and red faintly light up and beautify the general expression. It is imported in large planks; in square, but, for the most part, in round logs, ranging from 9 to 18 and 27 inches diameter; and is sold by weight at £5 per ton.

It was formerly used by the Brazilians in ship-building, and is known in British dockyards as Cabbage wood. By the cabinet-maker it is chiefly used in small cabinets, and general turnery,—in making chairs and couches; also for veneering picture frames and brush backs, and for making walking sticks, umbrella, and parasol handles, &c.

COCUS WOOD.

Cocus Wood, or *Cocoa Wood*, is a product of the West Indies, and is imported chiefly from the island of Cuba, in logs of from 3 to 6 feet in length, and from 3 to 9 inches in diameter. The stem of the tree is irregularly figured and modulated. It is finer in the grain than rosewood, but resembles it in weight and fibre. A thick coat of sap wood, varying from $\frac{3}{8}$ to $\frac{3}{4}$ of an inch in thickness, resembling ash in colour and fibre, surrounds the true wood. Cocus wood, in cross section, presents the concentric rings of growth, alternately and minutely coloured in yellow and brown. These colours, although easily distinguishable on the end view, are seen in the plank section to be so mixed and diffused as to give the wood in mass a pretty uniform yellowish brown colour, which is intermixed with streaks of a darker hue. It deepens on exposure to a dark brown, and sometimes to nearly black.

This does not possess the necessary qualities of a good cabinet wood; its small size, frequency of heart faults, general inferiority in figure, and, above all, its liability to change in colour, unfit it for extensive use. It is, however, very suitable for turnery of all kinds, and is much used in the manufacture of tubular musical instruments, such as flutes, flageolets, &c. It is sold at from £5, 10s. to £6, 10s. per ton.

There is another wood bearing the name, and considered to be a variety of cocus wood, which is chiefly used in ship work, for tree rails, pins, and the wheels of blocks. This sort is smaller than the former in the size of its timber, varying from 2 to 7 inches diameter, a large proportion of which is a hard sap of the colour of beechwood. The interior wood is coarser in the grain, but presents greater variety and beauty of expression; its predominating colour is a chestnut brown, inclining to red, but veined with deeper tints. This wood is also suitable for turnery, and veneers of it are used for brush backs. It is sometimes called brown ebony. Cocoa wood is exogenous, and must not be confounded with the cocoa-nut tree, as they are widely distinct in their characters, the latter being a palm tree. Notwithstanding the long and frequent use of these woods, their botanical characters are unknown, and some uncertainty exists as to the localities of their growth.

MANCHINEEL TREE (*Hippomane mancinella*)

Is a native of the West Indies, growing chiefly on the shores of the Caribbee Islands, and on the northern coasts of the neighbouring continent of South America. At mature growth, this tree is of vast size, its leaves are ovate, serrated, and very shining. The fruit, foliage, and sap are highly poisonous. The whole tree abounds in a milky juice, of a most venomous description, which, when dropped upon the skin, produces a sensation of severe burning, followed by a blister. It is said that the Indians poison their arrows with it. The fruit is like a small apple, appearing so tempting and like the English fruit, that many strangers have been poisoned by it. The workmen who fell the trees, first kindle a fire around the stem, which causes the juice to become so thick as not to flow or disperse from the blows of the axe, otherwise they would run great risk of injury from its deadly properties.

The wood is a most beautiful material for furniture, being finely variegated with yellowish brown and white; it is very close and hard, and susceptible of a high polish.

CANARY WOOD.

Canary Wood is a product of Brazil, chiefly obtained from Para, one its Northern provinces; it is found also in the other adjoining regions of South America. In the several places of its growth, it is variously named; at Darien it is called *Amarilla*. Nothing is known of its botanical character. It is sometimes imported as squared timber, but most frequently in round logs, ranging from 9 to 14 inches in diameter. The wood is straight and close in the grain, about the texture of American birch, but much heavier; its general colour is a golden yellow, or light orange; on end section, the annular ranges are waved and of slightly varying shades; this circumstance imparts a minutely veined expression to the wood in plank, which much enriches and beautifies it. The characteristic and finer colour, is frequently intermixed with dingy streaks of a yellowish brown, and fissures and cracks often occur, extending considerably round the heart. Were this wood uniformly coloured, and free from defects, it would be a very valuable cabinet-wood.

Canary wood although suitable from colour and texture, as an ornamental cabinet-wood, yet its small dimensions, faults in colour, and heart blemishes, confine its use within narrow limits; it is little employed except in marquetry and turning.

A wood called *Vigniatico* which resembles canary wood closely, and by some supposed to be identical with it, is also imported from Brazil. This name appears to be a corruption of a general term, *Vinhatico*, given by the Portuguese to several yellow woods, besides the variety in question under that name, imported from Brazil.

CAMPHOR WOOD.

Camphor Wood is the timber of the *Laurus Camphora*, and is found in Japan, China, India, and Brazil. It grows to a considerable height, dividing into many branches, and covered with smooth greenish bark; the leaves are ovate and lance shaped.

The root, wood and leaves, have a strong odour of camphor; this substance is found to lodge everywhere in the interstices of the wood, also in the pith, but most abundantly in the knots and crevices. It is obtained by dry distillation and sublimation. The camphor is often found concrete in cavities and fissures in the heart of the tree. This secretion is obtained from several others of the *Lauraceae*. Camphor wood is imported in logs and planks of large size. It is a light soft wood, frequently spongy, coarse in grain, of a dirty greyish yellow colour, irregularly interspersed with streaks of iron grey. Its dimensions, but chiefly its fragrance, are its sole recommendations for cabinet-work, and that only for internal finishings. It is used also in turnery.

JAPAN WOOD.

Japan Wood or *Bukkum Wood, Caesalpinia Japan*, is a product of China, Siam, Pegu, the Coromandel coast, and the Islands of the Eastern tropical seas. It is found also in Brazil, and is obtained from a tree of the same genus as Brazil wood.

It is imported in sticks 1 to 4 inches in diameter, and 3 to 8 feet long; it is close in grain and heavy, and abounds in defects, chiefly from the growth of the wood, being crooked, and deeply indented.

The colour is a beautiful orange, which deepens on exposure to a rich reddish brown; it is used in turnery, but its faults limit it to small articles; it is exported abundantly by the Chinese for treenails in ship building. It also yields a beautiful red dye.

TULIP WOOD.

Tulip Wood is imported from S. America, chiefly from the Brazils, in round sticks, trimmed and cut like King wood, which it resembles in figure and in general dimensions, being usually from 2 to 7 inches in diameter. The prevailing colour is a flesh-red, varied by streaks of a deeper tint of the same. These blended colours are very beautiful, but not permanent; the wood besides, from its frequent unsoundness at heart, and other blemishes, is very wasteful. It is used in the smaller articles of cabinet work, and in turnery.

It is often scarce, and sells at about £25 per ton.

A wood, bearing the name of the French tulip wood, which comes from the East Indies, chiefly from Madras, appears to be an excellent cabinet and turnery wood, and is held in great esteem by French cabinet-makers. It is much straighter in the grain, and softer, than the Brazilian wood of that name; the darker streaks present a more decided contrast to the ground colour, which is an orange-red. This wood is resinous, but has no odour.

HOLLY.

Holly (*Ilex æquifolium*), is found in most parts of the northern hemisphere, being dispersed throughout Europe, North America, Japan, Cochin-China, &c. In Britain it is one of the most beautiful native shrubs or low trees.

Although ordinarily seen as shrubbery, and as forming hedge-rows, yet there are many examples in England and Scotland of hollies 40, 45, and 50 feet high, with trunks varying from 2 to 4 feet in diameter. Holly is an evergreen, having beautiful deep green glittering spinulose foliage; this prevailing colour is prettily contrasted with the coral hues of its berries, and in some of its varieties by a white and gold border on its contorted leaves. The wood of the holly is white, very hard, uniform and close in grain, and susceptible of a fine polish. It admits of being dyed of various colours with great facility. It was formerly much used, chiefly in the white state, or when dyed black, for lines or *stringing* in cabinet work. It is used also in cross-veneering portions of the case work inside of pianofortes, in the construction of harps, and extensively in the manufacture of painted Tunbridge ware. Holly is exceedingly apt to split when newly cut, and when exposed in seasoning; it is, at the same time, liable also to become spotted and stained from the mutual chemical action between its sap and the constituents of the atmosphere. To prevent the occurrence of these blemishes, the wood, when felled, is cut into the form and dimensions required for its several uses, as veneer or other planks, or as round blocks for turning. With a view to extract the sap, and to preserve and improve the whiteness of the wood, these pieces are then boiled in water for many hours. Immediately after boiling they are placed into a compact heap, and closely covered up, to prevent the wood from splitting from the too rapid action of the air in cooling and drying. A species of fermentation now takes place, and a fungoidal growth of a greenish hue, and to some depth forms on the wood. As the heap dries, after the lapse of several weeks, the covering may be gradually removed, and the mildewed appearance brushed off. As the boiling necessarily operates superficially on the wood, from surface to centre, it will always vary in its efficiency and completeness, and that the more decidedly according to the duration of the process, and as the masses acted on are large or small; the larger pieces requiring longer time, that the effect may penetrate to a greater depth. Under all circumstances the heart is but partially affected, and is still liable to stain if the wood, when newly cut up, is again immediately laid together. For this reason veneers, when newly cut, should be kept asunder for a day or more, and thicker wood for a much longer period; for resting in contact for a few hours will cause stains to appear. By suitable care, holly will be fit for use in five or six months.

Lime Tree.

Lime Tree or Linden Tree. Most of the species of the order *Tiliacea,* to which this tree belongs, are found generally distributed within the tropics, forming diminutive plants, shrubs, or trees, with elegant flowers, usually white or pink. A few species are peculiar to the northern parts of either hemisphere, where they form timber trees of stately growth. Of the lime tree there are two great varieties, the European and American, severally known to botanists as the *Tilia Europea,* and the *Tilia Americana.* The former has been long naturalized, and by some affirmed to be indigenous to Britain; its geographical distribution embraces a great portion of the middle and north of Europe. From its graceful form, rapidity of growth, and highly odoriferous flowers, it is a favourite avenue tree in Holland and Germany, and also in England. Honey procured from the flowers of the lime tree is esteemed the finest in the world.

Among native trees, the lime ranks in the first class in point of magnitude, frequently attaining a height of 80 or 90 feet, with a trunk of corresponding dimensions. In Switzerland and Germany there are lime trees of an enormous size, and one in the county of Norfolk is mentioned by Sir Thomas Brown as being 90 feet high, with a trunk 48 feet in circumference at $1\frac{1}{2}$ feet from the ground.

The smooth bark of this tree furnishes the materials from which bast mats are made. After being macerated in water, the bark separates into layers. These mats are mostly fabricated in Russia and Sweden, where the fibre is also sometimes manufactured into nets; and in Carniola it is even woven into a coarse cloth for ordinary clothing. The American variety of lime present few points of distinction from the European. In foliage and dimensions they are very similar: in the character and uses of the timber they are identical. It is found in Canada and the northern parts of the United States, but in Virginia, Georgia, and the Carolinas, is only met with in the Alleghany mountains. The wood of the lime tree is very light in colour, approaching to white, or yellowish-white; it is close and straight in grain, of a fine texture, and nearly as soft and light as deal. It stands well after being properly seasoned, but is not suited to any use wherein it might be exposed to frequent alternations of moisture and dryness.

From its inert character it makes an excellent ground for japanned and inlaid work, and is used for the frames of the best japanned chairs, inlaid with mother of pearl. This wood, from its even texture, capacity of sharp outline, freedom from knots, and general facility of working, is well suited for carving. The works of Gibbons at Windsor Castle, and St. Paul's, London, are of lime tree.

It is employed in general turnery, and also used in the sounding boards of harps and pianofortes, and the key levers of the latter, and in various parts of other musical instruments; it is also used in panelling carriages, and in the manufacture of toys.

It is sold at an average price of from 1s. 6d. to 2s. per cubic foot.

ALDER.

Alder (*Alnus glutinosa*), possesses very wide geographical distribution, being found throughout the whole of Europe, by the margins of streams, or in marshy grounds. It is widely dispersed in similar localities throughout Asia and Northern Africa, and a species, said to be identical with it, grows in Canada and other parts of North America. It is indigenous to Britain, and is one of the most common trees. In dry soil it frequently does not grow beyond the dimensions of a large bush, and, even under more favourable circumstances, seldom rises above 30 or 40 feet in height. The wood of the alder is soft, and of a homogeneous texture, and not capable of enduring much lateral strain. When growing, the timber is of a white colour, but upon being cut down and exposed, it changes to a deep red; this afterwards fades into a flesh-colour of different shades, which it retains. The timber of old knotty trees, and that of the root of others, is often beautifully veined, and chairs and tables made of it possess all the beauty of the curled maple, with the addition of a deep rich reddish tint.

In Scotland and the north of England, this wood is frequently used in furniture; suitable specimens are, however, comparatively rare, and they are usually sought after and employed by those who have a partiality for articles made of native grown timber.

From its durability under water, the alder is sometimes used for piles, pipes, and the barrels of pumps, and in inferior turning, such as toys, powder boxes, brushes, bobbins, &c., and also in making patterns for founding.

CHERRY TREE.

Cherry Tree (*Cerasus Sylvestris*). This tree has various other popular and also local names, such as Gean tree, Merry tree, Wild Black Cherry, Merries, &c. Pliny relates that Lucullus, the conqueror of Mithridates, introduced it into Europe from Asia, now nearly 2000 years ago. From Italy it was speedily propagated to most European countries, so that " other lands had cherries, even as far as Britain beyond the ocean." The cherry is, however, considered by some to be indigenous to many parts of Europe, and to be also a native of England, where it is cultivated chiefly as an ornamental tree, and for its fruit.

In average and moist soil the cherry, or gean tree, in little more than half a century, attains a height of from 60 to 70 feet, with a diameter from 20 to 24 inches. The wood of the mature tree is thus large enough for general purposes. It is, besides, in texture and colour suitable for ornamental work, being close grained and firm in fibre, in colour approaching a plain and pale mahogany; and in durability second only to the oak. The cherry tree is another of several instances wherein the culture and use of a valuable native timber has been superseded by foreign imports. In Britain, cherry wood is little used by cabinet-makers, and specimens of furniture made of it are rare; but in France, and other parts of the Continent where this tree abounds, it is extensively used by the cabinet-maker, turner, and musical-instrument maker.

LOCUST WOOD.

Locust Wood. This name is common to three great varieties of timber of considerably dissimilar qualities, the products of trees of widely different botanical characters. They are known to botanists as the *Robinia pseudacacia, Hymenea courbaril,* and *Gleditschia triacanthos.*

The *Robinia pseudacacia* is a native of North America, growing most abundantly in the Southern States, and generally diffused throughout the whole country. Of this tree three varieties are common, popularly distinguished as the red, green, and white locust wood. They are so called from the prevailing colour of the duramen or heart-wood. These variations in the appearance of the timber, are probably due to difference of soil, situation, and climate. The locust tree grows rapidly; and under favourable circumstances sometimes reaches a height of 70 feet, and 4 feet in diameter. As it is very branchy, the bole is usually short, and seldom straight for any considerable height. The branches often contain as many cubic feet of timber as the main trunk, and are armed with strong hooked spines. It is remarkable for the smoothness of its leaves, which close themselves at night, and for the more enduring freshness of its verdure as compared with many trees. In its most attractive period, bunches of white and yellow flowers hang gracefully from the branches, and contrast beautifully with the deep shining green of its luxuriant foliage.

Locust tree has been extensively propagated in Europe, especially in France and England. In the latter country, specimens of considerable size were growing in the year 1640. Its growth in a good sandy soil is so rapid, that it has been known to attain a height of sixteen and even nineteen feet in four years. In ten years it gains a height of 20, 30, and even of 40 feet. When at mature growth, which it reaches in about forty years, it is not of more than the average dimensions of timber trees, yielding then between 40 and 50 cubic feet of available timber.

The wood is close grained, very hard, of a greenish-yellow, with a slight tinge of red in the pores, and finely veined. It is exceedingly tough and durable, having been known to remain quite unimpaired, although entirely exposed to extremely varying atmospheric influence for nearly a century. As the result of numerous and carefully conducted experiments made in the Government dockyards and elsewhere, locust wood was found to be "heavier, harder, stronger, more rigid, more elastic, and tougher, than the best English oak."

In shipbuilding, tree-nails made of locust wood are esteemed superior to bolts of iron, in consequence of which it is imported for the Government and other building-yards. In North America it is more highly valued by the cabinet-maker and turner, than any other native timber. The locust is one of the very few trees planted by the Americans.

Hymenea Courbaril, the second tree enumerated, whose timber bears the name of locust wood, is found in the West Indies, Guiana, and Brazil. The usual dimension of this tree is from 60 to 80 feet in height, and 5 or 6 feet in diameter; it sometimes attains to a vast size, several varieties of it, when at mature growth, being the giants of the South American forests. Martin describes some specimens seen by him in Brazil, of such enormous dimensions, that fifteen Indians with outstretched arms could only barely enclose one of them. Close at the root, they were 84 feet in circumference, and 60 feet where the boles became cylindrical.

In good and characteristic specimens, this wood has a veined and variegated appearance. The prevailing colour is a rich reddish brown, diversified by streaks of a lighter and darker hue. These last frequently expand into irregular flakes, which deepen to nearly black, and by presenting a varying contrast with the lighter tints, enhance and beautify the general expression.

This wood possesses all the important qualities of a valuable cabinet-wood. In dimension of timber, in colour, figure, and texture, it is well suited to the manufacture of the larger and more expensive articles of furniture. It has hitherto been comparatively little known to British cabinet-makers, but from the elegant and ornamental character of the articles of furniture, manufactured of this wood and shown by the Austrians in the Great Exhibition, it is probable that it will soon be introduced into general use in this country.

Gleditschia triacanthos, the last of the three trees, whose timber has been called locust wood, is better known as the honey locust. It is a native of North America, and is found chiefly in the Carolinas and Virginia. It attains a height of 50 to 80 feet, and when young, its trunk and branches are covered with prickles, which, hardening as the tree becomes older, form a formidable defence. Its foliage which is of a light green colour, is very elegant, and its seeds which are covered with a sweet pulp, yield, when infused and fermented, an intoxicating liquor, much prized by the American Indians. The wood is coarse grained; it splits with great ease, and is little used.

SAUL, or SAL TREE,

Shorea robusta, is one of the largest timber trees of India, common over the eastern and western peninsulas, and the adjacent islands, and extending northwards to the foot of the Himalayas. Saul is esteemed the best, as it is the most extensively used timber in India, for beams, rafters, and various other building purposes; and in the north-western provinces, it is employed in all government works. It is stronger and tougher than Sissoo or Teak, yet not so passively durable as the latter, but for heavy strain or active wear, it surpasses any other Indian timber. The wood is close grained, heavy and of a uniform light brown colour, and in India is extensively used for furniture. The tree yields a balsamic resin, used in the temples of India, under the name of ral or dhoona, as an incense; by Europeans, under the name of dammer, for the same purposes as many other resins, and in the dockyards in Bengal as a substitute for pitch.

SISSOO.

Dalbergia sissoo is a tree well known throughout the Bengal Presidency, and highly valued on account of its timber, which furnishes the Bengal shipbuilders with their crooked timbers and knees. The trunk which is generally crooked, is lofty and frequently 3 or 4 feet in diameter. The sissoo has numerous spreading branches, pinnate leaves, with small drooping leaflets, imparting with their foliage, and the tree generally, a light elegant appearance. It is universally employed both by Europeans, and natives of the north-west provinces, where strength is required. In structure, it resembles the finer kind of teak, the Godaverian variety, but is tougher and more elastic. *Dalbergia latifolia* another and superior sort of sissoo, is a product of the Malabar coast. It is much darker than the former, being of a greenish black, with lighter coloured veins running in various directions, and takes a fine polish. This variety, called by the English Indian rosewood, and black-wood tree, and by the natives, *sit sal*, is one of the largest trees in India, attaining a circumference of 15 feet. Both sorts possess the qualities of good cabinet-wood, in dimension of timber, firmness of texture, and average appearance.

Sissoo with Saul is, for general purposes, more extensively used in Bombay and the north-west of India than any other timber.

JACK WOOD.

Jack Wood is the timber of *Artocarpus integrifolia*, and is a variety of the bread fruit tree. This tree is a native of India, and belongs to a class of trees that are extensively distributed over East India, both continental and insular, and also over the islands in the South seas. It is likewise extensively cultivated in the West Indies; its fruit being a favourite food with the negro population.

The specific character of the tree, as its scientific name imports, is founded on the entireness of its leaves, which are undivided, not lobed, or sinuated. The fruit, the production of which gives such importance to this class of trees, is pear shaped, of varying size, and grows on the trunk and larger branches. That on the branches, and farthest up the tree, is about the dimensions of the human head; but it gradually becomes larger the farther down it grows, till, on the stem near the root, it attains to the bulk of the body of a full grown man. The fruit is luscious, and has a powerful smell, of the flavour of strawberries. Its edible quality appears to be owing to the presence of starch, in its succulent heads. These at first contain a very tenacious milky juice, which subsequently hardens into the consistency of newly-made bread, and is as white as snow. The taste is insipid, with a slight sweetness, somewhat resembling wheaten bread. The natives prepare it by boiling or frying in palm oil. Europeans use it at dessert, with salt and water, like olives.

Jack wood, in colour and grain, resembles a rather coarse and inferior variety of mahogany. In cross section, the concentric rings are seen to be variously and alternately coloured in different shades of brown, the wood in plank presents a minutely streaked appearance, which, at near view, imparts to it considerable richness and elegance.

The general colour of the wood, when first cut, is yellowish brown, which deepens on exposure into a reddish brown. It is harder and heavier than mahogany, and abounds in white, gritty, silicious particles in its pores.

In India, jack wood is extensively employed for all purposes in house carpentry and furniture; and in England for cabinet work, marquetry, and turnery.

BEEF WOOD.

Beef Wood.—This name, obviously depending on the colour of timber, ceases to be distinctive among red woods of otherwise uncertain character, and of near or uniform shades. Accordingly, many woods have this name, but that sort which is most commonly designated beef wood, is known also as Botany Bay oak, and is imported from New South Wales, in round logs about 9 feet long, and from 9 to 14 inches diameter. In general colour, it is more intensely red than mahogany, with occasionally dark veins, small, slightly curled, and minutely dispersed throughout the entire surface. Some specimens are pretty. It is used in turnery, in veneers for bordering and for small cabinets and brush backs, and in the manufacture of Tunbridge ware.

The descriptions given in the foregoing pages by no means exhaust the woods that might have been brought under notice; but, intentionally, the list has been restricted to those best known, and most extensively used, as little advantage could accrue to the practical man from vague notices of timbers whose nature and qualities are imperfectly known. The endeavour has been to assist the cabinet-maker in estimating the qualities, and recognizing the kinds of timbers by their appearance and properties, and, at the same time, to indicate the most suitable purposes for which they may be used, the method of treating them, and their commercial value. A few additional particulars have been added concerning the growth of the trees, and where they flourish; but it is to be regretted that, especially respecting many tropical woods, so little precise information exists; a desideratum which might soon be supplied, were importers to procure from the producing countries accurate intelligence of the growth and habits of the trees, with portions of their inflorescence, fruit, and foliage. By inspecting these, scientific men would be enabled to tell to what class of plants the trees belong, and thus a flood of light would be thrown on a subject which, at present, is admittedly very obscure.

VENEERING.

Veneering is the process of overlaying a prepared surface or ground with thin wood. This art was known to the ancients; Pliny speaks of it as a recent invention, in his time, and descants on thus converting the cheaper into the most valued woods, by plating the former with the latter. He praises the ingenuity evinced in cutting a tree into thin slices, and thus selling it several times over. The citrus, the terebinth, various kinds of maple, box, palm, holly, and the root of elder and poplar were the woods then employed for this purpose. As at present, glue was used in fixing the veneers. At this period, furniture so embellished, was esteemed as a luxury; and, from its great expense, was confined entirely to the mansions of the most affluent persons. The skill possessed did not apparently extend to veneering continuously a large surface, but was chiefly confined to patch-work and inlaying; the desideratum felt then, and for a long time afterwards, being the means of properly cutting and laying veneers of large dimension. It is only in modern times that veneering has had that extension which makes it a matter of public interest. Its general use dates from a period considerably later than that of the introduction of tropical woods into Europe, for the manufacture of furniture. The comparative scarcity and consequent expense of the finest furniture woods, their unfitness, in general, for being wrought in the solid state, from their fibrous structure, usual dimensions of timber, and difficulty in working, together with the inconvenient weight given to many articles of furniture, made of them, seem to have suggested the notion of employing the finer woods in overlaying others which were cheaper, lighter, less liable to warp or fracture, and of greater facility in working. Improvements in veneer-cutting, and veneering have powerfully contributed to beautify, extend, and economize cabinet-making, and thus to disperse the products of this manufacture through all ranks and conditions of society.

In veneering, the chief particulars demanding attention are, the suitable character of the ground, its preparation, with that of the veneer, the general process of working, with the attendant circumstances proper or incidental to the operation. These will be considered in their natural order, along with various practical examples of important cases of frequent occurrence in the experience of the workman.

The proper quality and condition of the timber forming the ground for the veneer must, in all cases, be carefully attended to. The choice of the cabinet-maker is here confined within narrow limits, as comparatively few woods are suitable for this purpose; particularly if, under the condition of fitness, we include also the comparative expense of material and of facility in working. The American yellow pine and Honduras mahogany are highly esteemed, and most extensively used; the latter wood is well adapted, from its firm texture, for undulating surfaces and shaped-work; both are straight in grain, large in size, and usually sound; they do not readily warp or split, are free from offensive juices, and are easily wrought. Woods possessing great strength of fibre, and closeness of grain, such as white pine, birch, beech, or elm, do not suit well for veneering on, especially for large purposes; being comparatively difficult to work, and more resisting and intractable under the application of remedies to any defects in the wood or faults in the workmanship that occur. Woods which abound in unctuous or resinous juices, such as red pine or rosewood, are also unsuitable; their exudations interfering with the action of the glue. American oak, and Havannah or swamp cedar, are frequently used as a ground for veneering on; the former suits well, the latter, indifferently, being too soft, brittle, and raw in grain. Black Virginia walnut, extensively used by American cabinet-makers, is well adapted, from its size and other qualities, for the veneered gables, door frames, and panels of cabinets, or for massive shaped-work. But no original quality in the timber will relieve from the necessity of its suitable preparation for veneering purposes; it must be properly weather-seasoned (for a year at least, the time required depending much on the thickness of the timber), and afterwards, for a short period, fire-dried. The latter process tones the wood to the temperature of a dwelling-house, and ensures that residuary shrinkage consequent on the escape of the aqueous vapour always present in the out-of-door atmosphere, with which the wood continues to be saturated after it has been seasoned. The glue employed in veneering on such timber dries properly, the water in it being readily absorbed by the pores of the wood, and the thin gelatinous layer interposed between the surfaces speedily hardens, giving them the due adhesion to each other. Otherwise, if the ground be wet, the wood being already saturated, the water of the glue is not taken up, while the continued exudation of moisture from the ground maintains the glue in a liquid state, till it decomposes or putrefies, when it loses its adhesive power, and the veneer in consequence peels off. This occurs only in extreme cases, when the wood yet retains its natural juices, or has been wrought too soon after being cut up. Partial, but imperfect seasoning, is attended with consequences of a like kind, although less mischievous; in this case the glue may dry, and the joined surfaces apparently adhere sufficiently, but the ground in a dry apartment soon shrinks to its minimum dimensions, when the veneer becomes either blistered, by starting from the ground at intervals, or becomes shrivelled and uneven on the surface. This defect becomes particularly conspicuous when the shrinkage is unequal, from any irregularity in the form of the ground, or from some imperfection in its timber. In the selection of wood for veneering, especially if the surface be large, choice should be made of a piece free from knots, shakes, and strong figure.

When the surface to be veneered is broad, such as in the case of tables, sideboard tops, or of door panels, the veneer should be laid on the side of the ground which is next the heart of the tree; this side in any case may be easily observed, by inspecting the end of the board, and noticing the direction of the growth rings of the wood. The annexed cut will serve to explain the propriety of this preference of the heart side for veneering on. *Fig.* 1 represents a cross section of an exogenous tree,

Fig. 1.

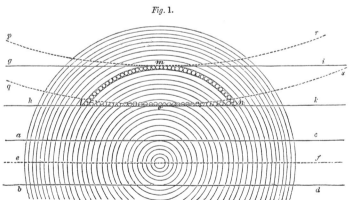

with its concentric rings. A plank *a, b, c, d,* cut diametrically, presents the rings equally disposed on opposite sides of the line *e f* drawn through the pith centre; the fibres forming the ring segments being thus similarly circumstanced in respect of shrinkage; the board, if equally exposed in seasoning, remains flat across. A plank *g h i k* cut out of any other portion of the tree, will be found, as an effect simply of drying, to curve outwards, presenting the heart side of it convex. This arises

from the contracting force being greatest in the longest continuous lines of fibres, as will be explained on referring to the diagram. The number of fibres, and consequently their contracting power in the line *l, m, n,* proportionally exceeds the number and force of the fibres in the line *l, o, n,* the same amount which the curve of the segment exceeds its chord in length. The plank accordingly tends to take the form indicated by the dotted lines *p q r s.*

A veneer, therefore, when laid on the heart side of the board is resisted in contracting, while drying, by this natural convexity of the ground; whereas, when it is laid on the outer side, the energies of both ground and veneer unite in drawing the veneer surface hollow. Where a perfectly flat surface is required, or where the ground has to be veneered on both sides, as in the folding tops of card tables, it is customary to cut up the board into narrow breadths, and alternately reverse the pieces, and join them together so as to equalize and distribute their different tendencies to curvature.

Fig. 2.

The ground, of whatever form or extent, must be uniform and smooth, free from sudden irregularities or fibrous roughness. Where the planes of direction are meant to be straight, they should be strictly so; when curved, they should be regular. The veneer is thus more easily laid, and from its extreme thinness it does not admit of the reduction of any inequalities of the surface afterwards. In preparing a flat ground, it is first planed; any remaining irregularities are then wrought off with the toothing plane; the blade or iron of which is grooved, lengthway on the face, so as always to present a serrated edge, whose projections or teeth dig into the wood, and work off its minute inequalities of surface.

Fig. 3 presents a form of toothing plane, better adapted for working large surfaces than that ordinarily in use. The plane should be provided with two irons, one having finer teeth than the other; the coarser being required for the ground, and the other for the veneer. The cannel, or grinding bevel of the irons, should not be longer than that of other planes, as otherwise the irons are apt to vibrate in their action, and tear or dig out portions of the surface. The toothing action takes

Fig. 3.

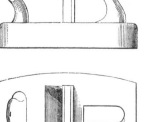

place first in the direction of the grain, then obliquely across it, cutting off any irregularities, and thus flattening the surface. Besides the general use of smoothing the ground, the toothing process increases the extent of glued surface by the indentations of the teeth in the ground and veneer, and ensures the retention of a sufficiency of glue between them, when they are acted on by the caul or the hammer, in extruding the excess of glue. A round soled plane, similar to the ordinary hand-plane of that form, is used in toothing the hollow segments of circles, such as the veneered sweeps of table blocks, &c. Quick and varied curves, on being wrought to outline, are toothed with a rasp, or with the toothing plane iron detached. On the ground being toothed, it is sized over with thin glue, wrought into it with a sponge or the hand. The size, on drying, stiffens those fibres of the wood raised by the previous operations, so that they are easily shaved off by a steel scraper, or by the toothing plane short-set for the purpose.

When the surfaces are large, such as in the tops of loo tables or side boards, and the wood, dry previous to the operation of sizing, the side of the ground next the veneer requires to be soaked with water to expand it. As the moisture must penetrate the wood some distance, the board may be laid for a few hours on a bed of wet sawdust, *Fig. 4.* This expansion of the ground serves to counteract the

Fig. 4.

shrinkage of the veneer, and is especially necessary when the ground happens to be very dry, and the veneers are hammer laid. It is usual to swell and veneer loo table-tops in halves, and panels in pairs. When the wood is deemed sufficiently swelled, it is then sized, and allowed to harden just enough to fix the fibres raised by the toothing and damping. This method is practicable only when the ground is finished plain on the edge, no mouldings at this stage of the work being planted on it; otherwise the mitres and joints are apt to be forced open. To avoid this the ground and veneers are treated differently; the former is allowed to remain straight, and the veneers are dried and pressed between heated boards, to preserve them straight, and then cauled. The ground may be secured by bars screwed on below; these are slightly rounded on the edge, and are left on until the veneer is completely dry; the bars may also be used as a security when any of the methods referred to are adopted.

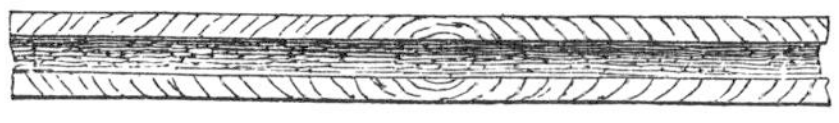

The perfection to which the cutting of veneers has now been carried, leaves little to be said on their preparation or treatment before they are laid. Veneers should not be kept in a very dry atmosphere, more particularly the richer varieties of them; an out-house or ground floor, where they are under the ordinary moisture and temperature of the seasons, is most suitable. Before they are laid, the traces of the veneer saw should be toothed off; this gives greater pliancy to the veneer, and ensures its closer approximation to the ground. When the veneers are stout and resisting, and are to be hammer-laid, or cauled on a curved or convex ground, they may be reduced thinner by the toothing process.

Two methods are ordinarily resorted to in veneering such curved surfaces as occur on the pillars and blocks of tables, fronts of sideboards, or on mouldings in general; the one is to strengthen or support the natural tenacity of the veneer on its being bent; the other, to increase its flexibility. The former is effected by glueing on the outside of the veneer canvas or calico, to preserve it from fracturing under the unequal pressure of the caul, while the veneer is being pressed down; the latter, by subjecting the veneer to the action of moist steam, a process similar in principle to that employed by shipwrights, in bending their planks to the required curvature. Veneers having a strong roe or curl, from the extreme irregularity of their grain, suffer by being subjected to a sharp heat, or to extreme moisture, their contractions and expansions being so very unequal that they speedily fracture; accordingly, they require to be carefully covered with canvas whenever they are laid on a curved surface, and in all circumstances must be cauled down. When the veneer for any surface consists of several pieces, and these marked by a waved or extremely irregular figure in the wood, as frequently occurs in rosewood, or without any decisive indications of grain or direction of fibre, as in Amboyna-wood, yew-tree, oak root, or birds'-eye maple, it is customary, in forming the joints, to follow the prevailing direction of the figure in the wood, or to join the pieces together, in lines which are least likely to be detected by the eye in the finished work. To effect this, the edges of the veneers are lapped on, and glued to each other; after the glue is dried, a fret saw is made to pass through both thicknesses together, tracing by the cut the intended line of the joints, which, on the superfluous wood on both pieces being chipped off, are quickly and perfectly formed. These waved joints in the veneers, when the required conveniences are at command, are better, and as expeditiously made, by this method, as those that are straight and wrought by the plane; they are, besides, often more economical than the others in the saving of veneer, and, under the circumstances supposed, always more elegant. The joints after being prepared in the above manner, are put together in the dry state, and connected by slips of cloth glued over them. On these being dried the veneers are then cauled down.

Veneers are laid by two methods—by the hammer or by caul. Hammering is a process of easy application when the veneer is of a mild and pliant nature. For some work this method is more convenient and expeditious than cauling—such as for border finishing, for slipping, for cross or feather banding, the laying of sweeps, and generally for small work. Some extensive surfaces, not otherwise easily accessible, are best to be done by the hammer; such as the tops of sideboards, or commodes, when these are clamped to thickness from under. Hammered surfaces are not generally so secure in standing as those that are cauled, in consequence of the veneer requiring to be moistened on its upper side with water or thin glue, to counteract its tendency to curve up from the ground, and also to admit of the hammer gliding easily over the surface. The form of the hammer is given in *Fig.* 5. The handle is fixed into the head, low down, so as to give the operator greater leverage power over it. A blade of steel, $\frac{1}{8}$-inch thick, is inserted into the head below, having its under edge rounded

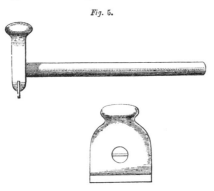

Fig. 5.

along its length, so as to concentrate the pressure exerted on the hammer, and assist the smoothness of its action. The form given to the head above, furnishes at once a good hold, and an easy rest for the hand. In laying a large veneer with the hammer the assistance of several hands is required; the ground and veneer are gently heated previous to glueing; the glue is then spread on both, and the veneer, on being laid on the ground, is coated over with thin glue, and rubbed down with the outstretched hands of several persons. The hammers are then applied, at first, in sweeping over the whole surface, to reduce any undue swellings of the veneer, and to exclude the air. The more close and effective action then commences of two persons or more, on opposite sides, proceeding from the middle towards the sides and ends; the head of the hammer is urged against the veneer with one hand, while the handle receives a rapid horizontal motion to right and left, being made to travel from centre to side with a wriggling step, carrying a wave of the superfluous glue under the veneer before it. The veneer is, from time to time, coated at

the parts requiring it with hot size, to maintain the warmth, and relieve the friction of the hammers. Greater flexibility is given to the veneer by keeping up the wet and heat; it is thereby prevented from cracking and curling up at the sides. The glue becomes stiff on being chilled, and the pressure of the hammer behind the wave is apt to break the veneer, from the abrupt bend to which it is subjected. If, by slowness in the operation, arising from the extent of surface, fewness of hands, or the temperature of the workshop, the glue under the veneer becomes cold and stiff, its warmth and fluidity may be quickly restored by passing a hot smoothing-iron swiftly over it. The use of the iron should not be prolonged after the glue has been forced out, otherwise the continued heat is apt to raise the veneer. The quality of the process gone through is now tested by smartly tapping the veneer surface all over with the extremity of the hammer handle; if the sound is hard, the contact is complete; if dull and hollow, the application of the hammer must be renewed. Occasionally veneers are met with which in certain parts of them, from heart wood, or peculiar conformation of grain, are extremely difficult to lay perfectly; such parts, after some hours, may be easily reduced by the partial application of the caul, when the surrounding portions are cooled and contracted. In very dry workshops it is often advantageous, at the conclusion, to lay the veneered board face-down on the floor, and covering it with shavings or sawdust, to prevent too rapid drying.

The process of cauling veneers is distinguished from that of hammering them by the pressure, which is necessary to urge the veneer into close contact with the ground, being applied at once over its whole extent, and maintained until the parts united cool and consolidate. Cauls may be described as a means of conveying heat, and of transmitting pressure to the whole surface of a veneer at once, in laying it; they must vary in form and dimension, corresponding with the ground to which they are applied, requiring to be perfectly parallel to it, and the force exerted on them must be uniform in its distribution over its entire extent. They are generally made of pine-wood, sometimes of wood with canvas continuations for abrupt curves. Cauls, formed of bags of suitable size, partially filled with hot sand, are frequently employed in veneering hollow and irregular surfaces; canvas or girth web is commonly used in cauling cylindrical grounds, such as table pillars, round pedestals, or potstands. The pressure exerted on the caul is ordinarily by screw action, variously applied; for general purposes the common hand-screws are suitable; but in the treatment of broad surfaces these are inefficient or tedious. *Fig.* 6 presents an apparatus which is found very effective; it consists of a rect-angular frame of hard-wood, 3½-inch thick, formed of two pillars, with two cross rails framed into them. The upper rail is tapped by a series of screw holes, through

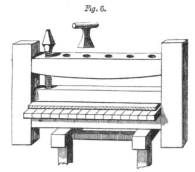

Fig. 6.

each of which a wooden screw is made to pass, the ends of the screws act together on bars, which cross the caul, and transmit the combined force of the screws to it, and thence to the veneer. The screws have a square tapering head, which fits into a hollow iron key, the upper end of which is wrought into a bar, to give it sufficient leverage, for turning the screws. Several such frames are required; their breadth between the pillars and their number depend on the dimensions of the sur-face to which they may be applied. When at use they are sufficiently effective if set apart from each other nine or ten inches. The caul, *Fig.* 7, con-sists of a number of separate planks, four or six inches broad, and two inches thick, which are slotted to-

Fig. 7.

gether, by cross bars morticed at exactly equal distances through the whole series; by this arrange-ment the breadth of the caul may be varied at pleasure, according to the character of the work. Two such cauls are necessary when the ground is to be veneered on both sides at once, or when the ground is thin wood, such as in door pannels; but, when the ground is stout, one may be sufficient, in which case the veneer is laid face-down, as shown in *Fig.* 6, with the bars crossing the back of the ground. In proceeding to lay veneers on both sides of a board with this apparatus, the caul screw frames are mounted on a suitable trestle or stool, and set apart from each other at equal intervals; one at each end of the board to be veneered, and the intermediate space equally divided between the others. A slip of deal is then run edgeway along the top of the upper rail, and fixed by hand-screws to the projecting top of the pillars; this keeps the screws in their places, and maintains the whole steady. The cauls being prepared flat and smooth in the surface, are rubbed over with linseed oil or grease, and then heated; the oil prevents the caul from adhering to the veneer, by means of any glue which may ooze through its joints or elsewhere.

The under caul is then, keeping the heated side up, slid quickly through the frames along the top of the under rails. On this under caul the ground with the veneers are laid, and upon them the upper caul is now placed. The bars are then adjusted under the screws, and the centre course of screws, taken lengthway along the several frames, is now rapidly urged home with a moderate force, so as to express the superfluous glue from the centre of the veneer, towards the sides and ends. The course of screws next in order on each side of the centre one are now wrought, and so with the others on to the two outsides. All the screws are now strongly tightened up, and the pressure is maintained for about four hours; by the end of which time the veneer and ground will have cooled, and adhered securely to each other. The screws should not be left on with full tension over night, as they and the frames are likely to be impaired by such continued action; besides, in cases where it is not desirable, a permanent flatness is thus apt to be given to the veneered ground. It may be more convenient that the cross bars be screwed to the upper caul per-manently, more particularly if the usual dimensions of the grounds veneered are large, and generally uniform. The upper caul alone is necessary when the ground is thin, and veneered on one side only; the under caul, in such case, serving to resist the pressure merely. In absence of an apparatus of the above sort, broad flat surfaces are laid by means of cross bars, and the ordinary hand-screws aided by cramps, as may be. Deficiency and inequality of pressure, and comparative slowness of manipulation, by which heat is lost, are the chief objections to this method. Flat surfaces are generally easily laid, the pressure required being simple in direction, and acting parallel to the plane of the surface. In curved grounds, circular or various, there is greater difficulty, the pressure necessary being often com-pounded of several directions of force, requiring, from the peculiar shape or condition of the piece of work under operation, some exercise of skill in the workman to resolve these into two or more single forces of available direction, whose joint action will be effective. On these uneven surfaces it is fre-quently found convenient to employ several cauls in succession, or those having canvas continuations of them to carry the veneer over abrupt changes of outline or return curves. Mr. John Meadows, of London, has recently patented an apparatus, by which the same veneer may be carried continuously without break or joint, over all forms of curved surfaces, or of angles. This is effected by a series of cauls hinged to each other, and acted on by direct screw pressure, and by lever power, supported by ratch-work. Mouldings, flutes, and reeds of columns, or of bed-posts, all varieties of curves, or sudden inequalities of surface occurring in general cabinet-work, may be veneered by this arrangement. Several excellent examples of its efficiency were displayed in the Great London Exhibition of 1851. This apparatus, a drawing and detailed description of which is given in the *Repertory of Inventions for 1850, vol. xv.*, consists of a series of distinct and similar combinations of screws, levers, and connected cauls, which are arranged along, and fixed to a bench, and set apart at such intervals as may be deemed necessary from the extent of the work to be performed, or from the amount of pressure that may be required. One of those is presented in *Fig.* 8; *a* is the bench to which the fixed cramp *b* is attached by screws and nuts; *c* is a fixed metal tubular caul resting on the bench; *d* is a moulding in the process of being veneered; resting on the back of the moulding is a block, *e,* on which the

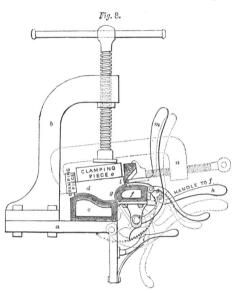

Fig. 8.

force of the cramp screw is brought to bear vertically; another caul also, metal and tubular, *f*, hinged to the first, urges the veneer into the hollow member of the moulding *g*, by means of the hinged lever *h*, and maintained in position by the ratch *i*; a third caul *k*, attached to the caul *f* is applied to the square member of the moulding *l*, and forced home by the lever *m* and the hand-cramp *n*, acting from the back of the block *e*. These several forces are made to bear in quick succession.

The cauls shown at use in *Fig.* 9 are suitable for one sort and dimension of moulding only; for other forms additional cauls are needed; these are fitted to the original caul and the ground respectively, and interposed between them. Two other forms of mouldings, *a, b*, with their appropriate cauls, *c,d*, are shown in the course of being veneered, in *Figs.* 9 and 10. In veneering with the lighter

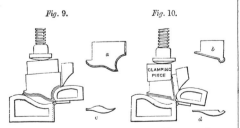

Fig. 9.   Fig. 10.

coloured woods, the patentee recommends the use of a glue prepared from parchment cuttings, boiled down to a strong size, and mixed with this a quantity of whitening, to bring the glue to the consistency of a stiff paste. It was also found advantageous to introduce between the veneer and caul heated sheets of very thin brass, with a layer of paper between them and the veneer, to prevent the former from adhering to the veneer. The tubular metal cauls, when used alone, may be heated by steam injected into them.

This invention seems best adapted for veneering surfaces (of mouldings or other) of such frequent use, and determinate form and dimension, as would warrant the preparation of a fixed series of cauls adapted to them.

When mouldings are cross-veneered with rich wood, of small and diversified figure, their appearance is much improved, and the general beauty of an article of furniture is thereby greatly enhanced. For this purpose mahogany curl veneers are often used, with the best effect. The mouldings around the front of the stage and on the back of sideboards are suitable points for the display of this method of veneering. It is, besides, employed with advantage on the cornices of wardrobes and book-cases, and on the ends of posted or French beds. The process may be exemplified in the method of veneering a sideboard front, whose mouldings are of the form shown in *Fig.* 11. The mouldings

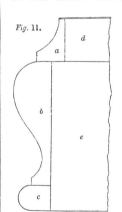

Fig. 11.

are put on the front from below up, beginning with *c*, then *b*, both of which are planted on the ground, *d e; a* is planted on the edge of the top, *d*, before the latter is veneered. The utmost nicety of adjustment is necessary to preserve the veneer continuously over all the parts.. The curl veneers require to be sawn much thinner than usual, taking not fewer than thirty-two thicknesses out of the inch. The total length and breadth of the surface to be laid being first determined, the veneers are then cut up. They require to resemble each other as nearly as possible in the figure of the wood, and, consequently, in breadth of surface, which amount is determined by the quantity of available rich wood that the veneer contains. Accordingly, a cross section of the whole veneers in the plank is made, cutting off as many pieces as will, by their united breadths, cover the surface to be veneered. The length of the cut is determined by the surface-breadth of all the mouldings on the front, making due allowance, in both measures, for waste in working. Before cutting the veneers, the rich wood in the curl is centred by a pencil-mark, and the half-breadth is set off on each side of this point, and squared over the ends of all the veneers at once. By adhering to these marks in sizing the veneers, the greatest possible uniformity in their figure is obtained. As the veneers taken from opposite sides of a plank usually differ considerably from each other, to preserve a general uniformity in their character, they should be arranged so that the richest outside veneer may occupy the centre of the front, and the others in succession to the right and left of this, on towards each end. The change in the character of the veneer is thus equally dispersed, and serves rather to enhance than impair the appearance of the work. The veneers are now joined on a flat board, edge to edge, with the ground side up, and in such lengths as are required for the different parts to be laid. The edges of them are then lapped over with narrow slips of paper, glued on. After the slips are dry, and the joints secure, the veneers are turned upside down, and the ground on which they rest is chalked, in order to increase the friction or partial adhesion of the veneers to this bed or surface. The side of the veneers now exposed is carefully toothed, by a plane having extremely fine teeth, and short set; after which, the surface is scraped and then completely overlaid with tough writing-paper, by means of thin glue, care being taken that there are no overlappings of the paper. The superfluous glue is forced out by a smooth, straight edge of steel, bone, or hard wood, suitable for the purpose. The whole is now left to dry, after which the veneer is again turned over, and the slips of paper formerly glued on are moistened, and in a little time scraped off. On this, its ground side, the veneer is now increased in its flexibility, from reducing its thickness by the toothing plane. The thickness suitable for curved surfaces is less according to the degree of curvature; and where this, from the character of the mouldings, is considerable, it is better, rather than to reduce the whole veneer to the extreme condition of thinness, that those parts only be so treated which most require it. However, in general, the thickness of the veneer must not exceed that of No. 3 glass-paper, used in the trade, or should be such as would require between fifty and sixty thicknesses to make one inch. The veneers, after being thus prepared, are cut by a fine saw into slips, of such breadths as are suitable for each of the mouldings, taken in succession from below up, care being had that the parts so cut be put on the several grounds so exactly over each other as to maintain the figure of the veneer continuously. The saw by which the veneers are cut requires to be extremely fine; the teeth, from the centre towards each end, are set in opposite directions, so that it cuts both ways. Its application must be close, light-handed, and slow.

The mouldings to be veneered must be carefully wrought, with their contour or outline strictly uniform throughout their entire length. An equal accuracy is required in the cauls, that they be proper counterparts of the mouldings; the latter are first completely wrought, and the cauls are made to correspond to them. Whatever slight inequalities may remain on the cauls after they are made, are completely removed by covering a piece of the corresponding moulding of each with No. 3 glass-paper, and forcibly rubbing these asperities off. The ground and caul, by this means, come to apply to each other with great exactness, so that when the veneer is interposed, no portion of its surface is free from the required contact and pressure. The glue employed must be stout and clean, and the cauls hot and well oiled. Several days should elapse after the veneers are laid before they are cleaned; the paper is then moistened with water and rubbed off, and the mouldings are entirely finished before they are planted. The mitres are struck by the plane, acting against the fibres, to prevent the veneer from chipping. Sharp corners, of moderate angularity, may be laid with the same veneer; one side of the angle being first cauled, leaving the veneer for covering the other side to project. After the part first laid is dry, the projecting veneer is slightly cut under by the saw, then folded over and cauled down.

The method pursued in this process is adapted to the cross or straight veneering of curved surfaces in general, and demands, for its successful application, considerable skill and experience.

At page 42 of this Work, the method of veneering the star tops of loo tables is briefly noticed, along with other particulars of their construction. In addition to what is there stated, several details in connection with the laying of these tops with curls, or other veneers of similar shape, fall to be introduced in this place. The curl veneers on star tops are of equal size, and always an even number; they are seldom fewer than ten, or more than sixteen; twelve is the most common number. This diversity in quantity depends on the dimensions of each top, taken with the available amount of rich wood in the veneer. The veneers selected must be all of apiece, and they should be numbered in the order in which they lie in the plank, beginning from one to twelve, or other number, according to the quantity to be laid. A pencil-line is then drawn through the centre of the rich wood in each veneer, as in *Fig.* 12; along this line, from the tapering end of the veneers, other pencil lines are swept across, with a compass, at equal distances on each veneer, passing through the parts that are alike and most striking and characteristic in the figure of the wood. These cross lines serve to identify the parts so marked with certainty, and assist much in matching the veneers on the ground. The divisions of the top being now drawn on the ground, a tapering mould of thin wood, half of the determinate size of the veneer, is then made. The shape of this half-mould is drawn on the veneers, the mould being applied, in succession, to both sides of the centre line on each veneer, having its tapered end adjusted to the centre point from which the cross sweeps were struck. The two outside veneers of the quantity selected always differ most from each other in their figure; this difference is often so great as to render it necessary, for the proper effect, to distribute the veneers on the top after a particular order. Ordinarily, the top one of each pair of veneers is simply turned over, and brought side to side with its fellow; and all are laid according to their numerical succession, the last and first being thus finally brought together. The other method referred to is shown in *Fig.* 13, where the first

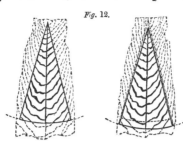

Fig. 12.

and last pair of veneers in the series are laid opposite to each other; the next two most remote pairs are placed on the alternate sides of these first, being the continuous numbers. Following the same order,

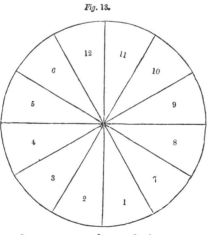

Fig. 13.

the others that remain are put into their proper place, and thus the circuit is completed, any diversity in the figure is thus more equally distributed. If the veneers are cauled, and laid in close succession to one another, each must be left to dry completely before the succeeding one is put down. That first laid, after it has dried, is carefully stripped on both sides, and the adjoining veneer is fitted to it. To support this veneer to the joint, a thin slip of deal is temporarily sprigged

to the ground, along the outer edge of the veneer, between which slip and the veneer first laid the one now in process is inserted, and urged home like a wedge; and so on with all the others. It is obvious that as little moisture as possible should be applied to curl-veneers in laying them.

The glue used by the cabinet-maker is a jelly made of the refuse portions that are pared off the hides of animals, before they are subjected to the tan-pit for conversion into leather. Good glue is translucent in the cake, of a clear amber colour, and, when dry, hard and brittle. Inferior varieties are more or less opaque or muddy in appearance, arising from their mixture with impurities incidental to their preparation, such as lime or other mineral ingredients, or from errors in the process of manufacture. Glue made from animal matters in a state of partial putrefaction is inferior in strength, and, when moistened, emits the odour, while it retains the peculiar qualities of such a condition. On this glue being boiled, gases are disengaged from it which become entangled with the glue, and give it a frothy consistency. An apparently similar effect may also arise from the mixture of the glue with other gelatinous substances, with which, on boiling, it does not coalesce, such having a less specific gravity than the other materials, and consequently boil at a different temperature. Glue very recently made, although of good quality, exhibits, in some degree, this frothiness of appearance when boiled; it is, for this reason, better that the glue be some months old before it is used.

In extensive workshops, glue is prepared in large quantity at once, for general use. The cakes are broken into small pieces and put into a large boiler, and soaked for some hours with as much water as will cover them. On the application of heat, the glue dissolves and boils; the boiling is continued for an hour or more. Water is added from time to time, to replace that evaporated in the process, and the glue is finally diluted to a degree rather greater than is suitable for general work. During subsequent heating by the workman, the excess of water is soon dissipated, and the glue thickens to the proper consistency. The boiler may now be removed from the fire, and its contents left in it to cool; or the glue may be poured into an iron trough, or one of wood, tin lined, from which source the workmen can replenish their glue-kettles as needed. To prevent dust or other impurities mixing with the glue, the kettle should be provided with a metal lid, notched in the edge to admit the brush handle. Frequently the glue is boiled in the workman's kettle, and that over an open fire. This circumstance causes the frequent preparation of the glue in small quantities, involving a loss of time, and, besides, the fuel usually at command in a workshop, chips of wood and shavings, flames up and soils and chars the glue, while the temperature necessary within a limited time to dissolve the glue, requires that energetic boiling of the water which is constantly attended with the inconvenience of its effervescence and overflow.

Glued surfaces are considered to cohere from the joint action of several forces, and these are, the pressure of the atmosphere, the adhesion of the glue to the wood, and its own proper tenacity. None of these forces, taken singly, will explain the strength of a well-made glue joint, which greatly exceeds the known energy of the first of these, the strength of a joint being often greater than that of solid wood; for when it is fractured, the separation does not at all times occur through its complete length, and even when this does take place, some of the fibres of the wood are almost invariably torn out. For the full efficacy of the second of these forces, certain qualities in the wood itself are necessary, seeing that to some woods the glue adheres better than to others; of these mahogany and deal are examples. The tenacity of the glue, or that force with which its particles adhere to each other, is the proper measure of its quality; if deficient in this, either from original inferiority in the substance itself, or from its being diluted too much with water, the joint will be deficient in strength, however good the workmanship.

The *rationale* of the action of glue in joining wood appears to be, that the fluid gelatinous matter interposed between the surfaces, in adhering to the wood, penetrates also its pores for some distance, where it hardens, and thus articulates the parts together. This saturation of the pores forms over each surface in contact an air-tight layer, by means of which the supplementary force of the atmospheric pressure is obtained, while the incremental tenacity of the glue, or the mutual adhesion of its particles, consolidates and secures the whole. This view explains the necessity of having the glue of a certain consistency, and of keeping the surfaces warm for the operation. If the glue is too thick, its adhesion to the wood is lessened, as it does not penetrate the pores sufficiently; if too thin, the capillary action of the pores solicits the glue into the wood of both surfaces, and partially ruptures the connection between them. That the surfaces should be hot is more necessary in the former case than in the latter, in order to maintain the liquidity of the glue, and to expedite its drying. These considerations apply equally to veneer surfaces as to those of solid wood.

WOOD-CARVING.

In the following observations on wood-carving, no description will be given of the tools and benches used, as the learner will acquire a knowledge of these more readily and efficiently under a master, than from the most lengthened treatise. It will be taken for granted that the young carver is already skilled in the ordinary mechanism of his art; and an attempt will be made merely to lay before him certain principles, attention to which will enable him to detect the errors of the ordinary routine, and assist him to elevate himself from being a mere workman, to the higher position of a thinking artist.

Sculpture falls into two great divisions—

1. THE ROUND, OR FIGURE COMPLETE ON EVERY SIDE;—

2. SCULPTURE IN RELIEF, that is, wrought on a ground and rising from it. Of this there are three degrees—high relief (*alto-rilievo*), in which the objects are highly raised, and often almost detached from the ground, having a prominence of one-half or more of the natural projection; low relief (*basso-rilievo*), where the objects merely swell out on the ground, and project but little; and sunk relief, or countersunk, where the outlines are sunk below the surface, and the objects do not project above the level.

Carving in the round is applicable to the human figure and the whole animal creation, and such inanimate objects as may be introduced as accessories. In copying complete forms, there is no perfection short of the realization of living nature; no bar but that of the artist's power, which he may extend day by day: the gallant hound, with pricked ear and eager eye, and every straining muscle quivering with intense energy, and the bird's ruffled plumage, will tax to the utmost the cleverest hand. These, however noble a field for the wood-carver, can scarcely be considered ornament, and are generally introduced but sparingly. As the earth is specially adorned with verdure, so the more fitting materials for ornament are to be found in the vegetable kingdom; and as here we see, in fact, each plant rising from and supported on its mother earth, so in ornamental carving, plants require to be employed on a ground, and should never stand alone; they must, therefore, be referred to carving in relief.

Carving in relief is not an entire truth, like carving in the round, which actually produces the form as it exists in nature; there we see that the foliage is distinguished from the ground by colour; here both are the same in colour and material. Hence it becomes a conventional or partial view of nature; and consequently, the perfectly free study of nature as we see it, is checked, until we can determine the limits of the sphere still open to our endeavours.

We must make no arbitrary rules, but seek only for those natural principles which are calculated to guard the learner from error. Such laws and traditions of the workshop are as numerous as the prejudices and mistakes of their masters; but true laws are few, and their only object is to save the student from being misled.

The most essential thing in every art is to consider what means we have at our command, what it is possible to produce with those means, and what the inherent properties of the material forbid. We thus place a definite goal before our view, and do not lose time in attempting what is beautiful and appropriate in one art, but impossible in our own.

The material is solid wood, which it is impracticable to carve into forms almost as slight and delicate as the flowers of the field. Against such an attempt its extreme fragility would almost be argument sufficient. But carry patient care to the utmost, and you produce a form still clumsy when compared with its original; where now are the varied colours which distinguish flower from leaf, and both from the ground, or the climber from the tree round which it twines? You have done your utmost to sever its connection with the ground from which it has been hewn, but the strength and elasticity of the real plant are wanting, and a touch will break it into a thousand pieces. The aim of art is not deception, for the common scene-painter or wax-flower modeller will easily imitate a curtain or a bunch of grapes, so that birds and men shall be deceived for a short space. True art is an adaptation of natural beauties to the material employed. Thus, carved foliage must not pretend, by any quality, to be other than a part of the wood from which it has emerged; it must possess the necessary strength of material to

fit it for the daily use to which it is to be subjected, nor must any part be made, to appear even, as if detached from its support. The true idea would seem to be, that the material from which it springs is so pregnant and teeming with beauty that it bursts spontaneously from its ground, like the rich vegetation heaving and swelling up from its moist bed of the primeval earth; and accordingly it is always most beautiful to see the leafage swelling up in one part softly from the ground, while another is thrown boldly up, as if caught by the breeze.

To copy nature too closely, leads thus to a neglect of other and more essential qualities; and a modified treatment is necessary; for even if we go as far as the strength of wood will allow us, it will still look frail to the eye. A good practical rule seems to be, to leave the wood as thick as you would be obliged to model it in clay, that is, in good working order. You will find that no great portion will stand alone without extraneous support. In applying this rule, the nature of the work must guide us as to the greater or less strictness with which it is to be enforced. It must be closely attended to in large and important pieces of furniture or decoration, but in more capricious and lighter objects we may relax in our severity, and allow more or less play of tendril or spray; but in all cases there should be a sufficient portion massed upon the ground, to show that these lighter parts are playful stragglers from the general design. Again, if the carving is to be gilt, the apparent change into a solid metal will allow greater license.

The power of representing space is also denied to sculpture; drawing is an abstraction; and, by linear perspective, objects can be shown gradually receding into the distance; but it only professes to be a partial delineation, and no actual form is there present to show the deceit. Painting, indeed, simulates the real form, but colour and aerial perspective, by making the diminished objects and their shadows appear dimmer and grayer, as in nature, complete the illusion. Sculpture is impotent to produce this effect; for, however the forms may be diminished in true linear perspective, the colour is as positive on the smaller as on the larger foreground figures; no atmosphere can intervene in the few inches of extra depth, and thus to the educated eye every attempt to reproduce pictorial effect is a failure, however palliated by skilful execution. No figure or portion of the sculpture can be represented as apparently farther removed than the actual plane of the ground on which it rests, and one part cannot be represented nearer to the eye than its real projection. This is a rule constantly violated since the *renaissance* of the art. Ghiberti introduced this false element into the reliefs of his celebrated gates of the Baptistery at Florence, and the example has spread till we have seen architectural compositions and pictures—such as Da Vinci's Last Supper, and Raphael's cartoons—copied in wood and in metal. This is a false road for sculpture, from which the works of Flaxman have done much to rescue it.

There is one general rule which applies principally to designing; but should here be mentioned, as a skilful carver is often called upon to design, or at least arrange details. No decorative adjunct should be allowed to become an essential constructive part, or assume the place of a real support in any work. Every good design should be constructed in the simplest and most natural manner, the lines good, the parts well-proportioned, and the general form graceful; so that, were no ornament added, it would still remain simple and elegant. Hence all figures and animals used as supports are bad; and though, by altering the lower part, you ensure that the caryatid shall not run away, you only produce an unnatural monster, as unfitted as ever for the purpose. The easy remedy is to introduce a bracket column or pilaster as obviously the real support, and then the figure becomes an ornament to the design. So again, all imitations of trees or reeds, used as columns, chair-backs formed of actual stems, curtain-rods with ends like flowers, are bad; they are lies. If real, they would be absurd, and, being put to do real duties, they are shams; whereas, let the column, chair, or pole-end exist with the foliage and flowers overlaying, twining around or gushing out of the solid wood, and you recognize them at once for what they are—ornaments. The worst and vilest instances of this bad taste, though bepraised by guide-books, and stared at in faith by sight-seers, are the huge pulpits in the Flemish churches, where the priest discourses from a leafy arbour, inhabited by parrots and monkeys, his head over-canopied by a carved tree, as large as life, loaded with fruit, flowers, and cherubs.

As a branch, severed from its parent stem, is an imperfect and now useless object, so a literal copy of a plucked sprig does not form a legitimate ornament. Before it can be ranked as ornamental art, it must show evidence that man's intellect has acted on it, and reduced it into harmony and fitness with the purpose to which it is applied. This harmony manifests itself in the two qualities of symmetry and proportion; whose presence, indeed, is essentially necessary, before an imitation of nature becomes transmuted into art.

Symmetry is an equal harmony, or balancing of the parts which form the whole; and proportion, the relative differences between all the parts. In a well-grown tree each branch varies in size and shape from every other, gradually decreasing in regular proportion from the base to the top; while the mass of branches on the one side counterbalances the mass of those on the other, and the tree is equipoised, or symmetrical. Symmetry, without proportion, produces monotony; and proportion, without symmetry, confusion. The whole of composition lies in the harmony of these two qualities. Proportion requires that there should be variety in the parts, and symmetry, that one side, or division, should be equivalent to the corresponding one. Every leaf and group may be different, and a large mass may be balanced by several small ones; but there should be the same general contour and weight of masses. Artistic expression depends on the adjustment of these two principles; as, on the predominance of one or other, the severe or playful character of the ornament depends.

Ornamental carving depends, for its principal effect, on light and shade, and here she reigns supreme; for, however inferior the form may be, light and shade are nature's own, and lend themselves to a thousand expressions. The general rule should be to produce soft and rounded masses, swelling up in one part like the hills and mountains in nature; in another spreading out like the plains at their feet, and contrasted here and there by a sharp, cutting edge or bold projecting-line; while, in parts, the points may be thrown up to catch bright sparkles of light. Of course, the changes are infinite, according to the effect to be produced; but generally, hard, sharp, cutting lines should be used with discretion, as contrasts to the prevailing ornament, otherwise the carving will become poor and hard. The modern plan of cutting the ornaments for panels and small pieces of carving separately, and fixing them on the ground when polished, is one great source of hardness and tameness; for the junction of the ornament with the ground must everywhere show a hard angular line, detaching the carving from the ground. Indeed, it is impossible to produce the effect of good Gothic carving, without cutting it out of the solid wood, a point which has been closely attended to in the new Houses of Parliament.

A very beautiful instance of the contrast of successful treatment is the architrave of Ghiberti's gates, at Florence, of which a portion is found in every drawing-school; where the leaves of the egg gourd are thrown up as if caught by the wind, and contrast with the smooth oval fruit and broad-winged birds.

If garlands are introduced, let them be such as could be formed of twined flowers, and not solid masses of flowers and fruit, stuck as closely as possible together, without stalks, or of leaves stuck in a solid lump, which could never exist without needle and thread.

In ornamenting mouldings, the lines must always cross the moulding, in order to exhibit the profile, and never run in the same direction. The forms used should not be too positive or deeply cut. The Greek mouldings are a good study of well-adapted ornamentation: they are never so deeply cut as to interfere with the profile, nor to allow the shadow of the ornament to prevail over that produced by the general form. In Roman mouldings, on the contrary, the ornament usurps too much importance; the leafage is coarse and deeply cut, and the indentations so many that the outline is apt to be lost; and, in place of long and well-defined lines of light and shade, a confused richness is the only effect produced.

All woods that are tolerably close-grained, and of uniform colour, are suited to carving; but handsomely-figured woods, such as finely-mottled rosewood, zebra-wood, mahogany, or bird's-eye maple, on the contrary, lose their own beauty, and destroy the effect of the workmanship. Pear, lime-tree, and chestnut, being tough, moderately soft, and close-grained, are the best suited of all woods to the carver's tools; but, unless stained, they want colour to fit them for general use in ornamental furniture. Those best qualified, by their colour, for decorative purposes, and for exhibiting, at the same time, beauty of modelling, are holly, oak, walnut, and similar woods, which retain a moderate polish, and have no strongly-marked figure to interfere with the most delicate light and shade: they are also the woods best adapted to the Gothic style, where the parts are generally small, and rectangular forms and angles prevail, and where the carving is often delicate and in low relief.

Mahogany has a smooth grain, well suited to the carver; but the style of ornament should be broad, and the forms round and smooth, to display fully its rich colour and smooth grain, which is susceptible of a very brilliant, and yet soft polish. Finely-figured wood is entirely thrown away on elaborate work, and accordingly, for such, colour is the great quality we must select. Maple, satin-wood, and figured birch, are not desirable, for the same reason; besides which, the alternate layers of hard and soft wood render them difficult to cut. Rose-wood is the least fitted for carving of all the woods used in furniture; its long open grain requires filling up with so much polish, that every curve shows a sharp dash of light like polished metal; while its dark and rather dull colour, when cut across the grain, absorbs the light, and entirely obliterates the distinction between half-tints and shadows; so that all we should aim at, in ornamenting rose-wood, is to produce sharp sparkles of light, glittering like dew-drops on a dark ground. Elaborate modelling is entirely lost; a bold free ornament, opposing strongly the black deep shadow against bright sparkling lights, is best suited to it; when the wood is very orange in colour, then these objections are lessened.

Ebony, in spite of its dark colour, takes such a soft smooth surface, free from metallic glitter, that it is well adapted to objects of moderate dimensions; its great hardness and the labour of working it, together with constant flaws and defects in colour, cause it to be generally replaced by pear-tree, which, if well stained, is of a richer black than ebony itself.

Having now mentioned those great principles which distinguish the functions of an artist-carver from that of a mere workman, let us impress on the young student the importance of an attentive study of drawing and modelling in clay, as the only means by which he can rise to eminence. Drawing is the first training of the hand, and the means by which he can take memorandums of the beauties he may fall in with, and of the ideas that arise in his mind; but modelling, above all, must be his daily study and guide. It is the only means of acquiring freedom of hand and bold sweeping curves, before his fingers have been cramped by long years of toil, and of preserving that power when once gained.

The great reason why the French have hitherto excelled us in wood-carving is, that they always model their ornament completely before beginning it in the wood, by which means they judge of the effect, and easily make any alterations. It is much more economical; there is no uncertain trying, or fear of boldly cutting away the waste; the carver saves half his time, and the work is better done; nothing has to be done twice over. In England, how much carving, too costly to be abandoned as destroyed, has already, when half done, lost all beauty of proportion, from the wood having been cut away during a few hours' absence of the directing head; the workman is dispirited, and the work is turned out, at last, deformed with clumsy gluing on, in the attempt to restore its original character.

CABINET-MAKER'S ASSISTANT.

DESCRIPTION OF THE PLATES.

PRELIMINARY REMARKS.

IN commencing the description of the Plates a few words may be offered on their arrangement, and the manner in which the descriptions will be treated. The designs for the furniture of each apartment, or series of apartments of a similar character, are numbered consecutively, so as to form a distinct group, and be of easy reference. These groups are arranged in the order in which the apartments to which they refer usually present themselves in houses of the larger size. Thus, as being the entrance apartment, *Hall furniture* naturally comes first; this will be followed in order by *Dining-room and Parlour furniture*, as being the rooms next approached; after these *Library furniture* will be taken up, to be followed in succession by *Drawing-room furniture*, *Bed-room furniture*, and a short section on general details and *miscellanies* which do not properly classify under the heads into which the subject has been divided.

The descriptions will mainly relate to the practical construction of the several designs in the plates, and be so treated as to explain and obviate any difficulties that may occur to the tradesman in carrying the designs into execution. While, to avoid tediousness, many things must either be stated as to be done *in the ordinary way*, or else passed over in silence, it will be our endeavour fully to explain the parts of construction, regarding which any doubt or difficulty is likely to arise. Sometimes several methods of construction will be given, with remarks on the advantages and disadvantages of each, leaving the tradesman to adopt the one best suited for the quality desired, and the price to be obtained, for the article in hand. To avoid repetition throughout the descriptions of a series of designs, parts similarly constructed, after having been once described, will not be noticed in the succeeding figures, or else merely by reference to the description of the figure under which a notice of the part in question is to be found. Sections and diagrams of construction will be introduced wherever they are deemed necessary for the elucidation of the text.

HALL FURNITURE.

The furniture, painting, and decorations of the hall, lobby, or entrance room of any mansion, whether large or small, or by whatsoever name it may be called, should be rather of a quiet and sober description, than have the least tendency to gaudiness; for it is obvious that much show, particularly of positive colouring and gilding in the hall, staircase, or approaches to the more important rooms, tends to destroy the richness and brilliancy of these apartments, and to lessen the effect they would otherwise have by contrast, were due relation preserved between the furniture and decoration of the approaches and that of the more important rooms. In large and well arranged mansions, this principle is steadily kept in view; and though the rooms throughout be decorated with bright colours, gilding, and pictures, these are either entirely excluded from the approaches to the apartments, or else used very sparingly. Sculpture, and articles of taste and *vertu*, of quiet and unobtrusive colouring, are employed as hall decorations, which, while they impart a feeling of comfort and a certain richness of effect, do not detract from the splendour of the public rooms of the mansion.

Armorial bearings, so frequently displayed on hall furniture, may, with advantage, be blazoned in their true colours, and gilding introduced where gold forms part of the blazon. Such an introduction of gold and colours supplies an agreeable point of relief, and tends to give sprightliness to the piece of furniture to which they are applied; but the employment of positive colour throughout, or the hatching of the ornaments with gold, should rather be abstained from, or if employed, it should be but sparingly.

The Elizabethan style, in which the greater part of our series of hall furniture is designed, has been much in favour, and is well suited for this purpose. It possesses a degree of gravity and solidity of expression, and is easily enriched and rendered ornamental, with comparatively little labour. This, in a mercantile point of view, is of material advantage, seeing that comparative cheapness of execution can be achieved in a style of so marked a character, and having such richness of effect.

HALL TABLES.—PLATE I.

These tables are of the usual dimensions suited to houses of moderate size. As they stand to the wall, and the back legs are but little seen, two plain pilasters are usually employed for the back supports; for these turned legs are sometimes substituted. The true top has the united thickness of the two upper mouldings; for this fir wood, veneered on, is often used: but, considering the rough treatment to which hall tables are exposed, it is more judicious to form the top of $\frac{5}{8}$-inch board, and to clamp it of fir to the proper thickness; the top is thus rendered more firm and resisting, and when dents or scratches occur on it, the solid wood admits of their being erased or removed without any trace of damage. The rails are wrought plain, and framed in the ordinary way; the front and end ones are veneered, the back rail being made stout, to receive the pilaster, which is morticed into it. The front rails of figs. 1 and 3 require to be kept back from the flush of the leg about $\frac{3}{8}$ inch, to admit of the large bead on their under edge being mitred round it; by this means also the framing is strengthened, from the rails being inserted more towards the centre of the legs. One or two bars should be dovetailed between the rails from back to front; with these the clamps on the top should correspond in position, and rest upon them, thus strengthening the framing and supporting the top. The panels on the front rails of all the designs are planted on. In paning the legs, they should first be wrought in the turning-lathe to the outline; at the parts of greatest diameter it is not necessary that the round be completely formed. The outline so formed comes to be the mitre-angle or margin-line of the panes, after they are wrought; accordingly, to maintain the pattern true, the projections must be brought further out, and the hollows deepened more in turning than is shown on the profile of the panes. This amount varies with the number of panes in the inverse order; the fewer the panes the greater the prominence or depth must be given to the members.

Taking the depth of the moulding on the pane as one, the depth of the turned outline should exceed it; for figures of from 4 to 12 panes, the following amounts nearly:—

4 panes $\frac{4}{10}$	7 panes $\frac{1}{8}$	10 panes $\frac{1}{20}$
5 „ $\frac{1}{4}$	8 „ $\frac{1}{12}$	11 „ $\frac{1}{23}$
6 „ $\frac{1}{6}$	9 „ $\frac{1}{14}$	12 „ $\frac{1}{27}$

that is, if the number of panes is 4, and the depth of the moulding 1 inch, the mitre or turning-depth is $1\frac{4}{10}$ inch, and so of the others according to the table, the same proportion being maintained in all sizes of mouldings. When great accuracy is required, and the panes and mouldings large, attention must be given to these measures in turning before paning.*

Fig. 1. The detail A, is a cross section of the top, front rail, and panel. The panels taken together should be at least $\frac{3}{4}$ inch in thickness, and of rich wood. They may be variously finished on the edge; in the drawing they are represented as if formed of three thicknesses laid together. This appearance is made by rebating the face down, or otherwise the lower part may be reduced to $\frac{1}{4}$ inch in thickness, forming the apparent ground, and the remainder may be fielded on the edge, as B, or what is more lively in appearance, a hollow may be wrought on it all round, as C. The large centre and small side and end ornaments are finished a veneer thickness thinner than the edge of the raised panels, and made to abut with them. The most common method for bringing out high projections, such as the greatest diameter of the leg, is by clamping. Although material and labour are in this way saved, the method is hazardous and seldom succeeds well, particularly if there is any difference between the pieces joined in respect of seasoning. If the clamps are of wet wood the joints open, and the pieces curve out at their edges from shrinkage; again, if the block of the leg is not well seasoned it also con-

---

* The difference between the depth of the moulding $a\,c$, and its mitre $a\,b$, is expressed by the difference between the base of a right angled triangle and the hypothenuse. This relation is expressed and computed by the following formula:—

As radius : Secant of comp $b\,c\,a$ :: Depth of the moulding : Depth of mitre. On allowing 90° to the right angle, the principle upon which the value of the angle of the panes is computed, may be understood by reference to *Euclid*, B. I., Prop. xxxii., Cor. 1.

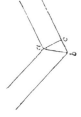

tracts, the glueing is then snapped, and the clamps drop off; besides, wherever there is much moisture the glue undergoes putrefaction, and the parts joined soon cease to cohere. For similar reasons, when the leg is solid and entire, and the mouldings large and deeply wrought, the wood employed should be thoroughly and uniformly seasoned, otherwise the subsequent irregular shrinkage causes numerous shakes and blemishes. This is strikingly exemplified in oak, where the medullary rays being the parts of least cohesion, rend readily, appearing like so many planes of cleavage. A further objection to clamping arises from the constant difficulty of matching the figure and grain of the parts, so as to conceal the joints, and avoid the appearance of patchwork. This defect may to some extent be hid by cable-carving or vermiculating the member so treated; this is frequently done. Where it is practicable, it is better to form the mouldings of largest diameter, by grooving that part of the leg and inserting a piece of wood for the purpose. The ring-moulding or flat ball of the leg A, may be formed in this way, by grooving the leg at the part down to the diameter B, and forming in the ring a hole C, of

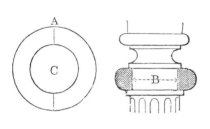

the same diameter: the ring, which is of cross wood running with the grain of the leg, after being planed so as to fit within the lips of the groove, is dexterously split into two pieces, and then glued into its place on the leg, and afterwards turned; or the ring may be formed of two cross pieces, planed to a joint, and a semicircular hollow being cut out of each, they are then glued together on the leg. The nodules or buttons in the hollow, at the upper part of the leg, and also those on the ball, are dowelled in. The listel, which terminates the upper end of the panes, is to be kept round; and when the panes are formed, the drops or pendants are inserted into them, under the projecting lip of the listel. Previous to glueing, the drops should be let into their place, and the profile of the panes drawn on their edges; then, on being detached from the leg, they may be finished more easily and accurately. In turning the leg, care must be taken that the hollow at the upper end of the panes be not formed too quickly, as by so doing the marginal line of the panes cannot be maintained without destroying the listel; or otherwise, that the listel cannot be preserved without deforming the panes.

Fig. 2 is similar to fig. 1 on the front rail. The

fret ornament on the square of the legs should be planted on subsequent to framing the table. The wood for the frets should be prepared $\frac{1}{4}$ inch thick, the pieces first wrought to size, and then cut either singly, or, with a view to greater speed, they may be glued together with a layer of paper interposed between their surfaces, and all at

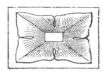

once perforated and wrought to pattern. The small bevelled panels on the frieze of the leg are separately wrought, have their facets hollowed, and the edges laid open.

In fig. 3, the legs are finished square in cross section. To effect this, the blocks should first be dressed square and parallel, and laid side by side; the profile of the pattern, in full size, should then be formed on the edge of a piece of thin wood, and drawn on the perpendicular outsides of the legs as they lie, keeping them flush with each other at the bottom end; the legs should then be firmly held together by cramps at each end, and lines drawn across them, corresponding to the facial dimensions of the mouldings and members to be formed; these lines guide the direction of the saw, or other tools, while the profile lines determine the depths. The mouldings may thus be easily relieved by cross cuts, and then accurately and expeditiously wrought into shape upon two sides of each leg. The other sides must be profiled singly, and the diameter measures of all the parts are set off from the centre. The panels on the shaft of the leg may be variously formed, either by planting their margins, and so recessing the shaft to form the fields of the panels, or by working the leg to the full size, and grounding the panels down, or by retaining the panels flush with their margins, and forming their outline by running a gutter or groove $\frac{1}{4}$ inch broad all round; or, lastly, by planting on a small raised moulding. Either of these two latter methods is more expeditious than the first, although not so elegant. Small facetted panels are planted on three sides of the frieze part of the legs. The drop ornaments which depend from the frieze, should be kept $\frac{1}{16}$ inch beneath the flush of the listel which overlies it.

In fig. 4, the panels on the rails are finished as in fig. 1, with the addition of prism-shaped ornaments being planted on their fields. As previously stated, the shoulder ornaments on the leg should be separately prepared and fitted, and then cut all at once; this ensures perfect uniformity in the pattern, and is, at the same time, more safe and expeditious in working. Two large oval-shaped pateras, with raised centres, are shown on the square of the legs end way. The under edge of the rails is finished with a square fillet; in other respects, this differs little from the preceding. Several members in the turning of the leg are kept round; this, besides being a saving of labour, gives considerable additional elegance to the pattern.

HALL TABLES.—PLATE II.

Fig. 1 has the front and end rails straight lengthwise, and hollow on the face, as shown in the annexed section of the top and rails. The panels are grounded to the hollow in front, wrought parallel to its surface, and made to sweep at their ends with the adjoining foliage. The large centre ornament should be roughly adjusted to the frame previous to being profiled for carving; any remaining irregularity in 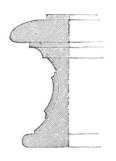 the grounding may be corrected while profiling; when prepared, a bed of fir wood should be made for the ornament to rest on, to which it is to be temporarily glued, so as to support the weaker parts during the carving. The trusses should be wrought out of wood not less than $3\frac{1}{2}$ inches in thickness. They are lined out to a mould, and made to shoulder with the under side of the frame, and dowelled to a block within the corner. The line of rest $a\ b$ is determined by the proper attitude of the truss, which, as a general rule, requires that the toe and swell of the truss in front be in the same perpendicular line $a\ d$, to which the line $a\ b$ is drawn at right angles; or otherwise, the position of the truss may be adjusted to the eye, and then the line $a\ b$ is drawn parallel to the ground line, $c\ d$. The foliage  at the top of the truss, shown as curving out in the hollow of the frame, is wrought on the solid, and grounded to the frame behind. The back supports may be made of $1\frac{1}{4}$-inch wood, profiled to the shape of the truss, and wrought on the exposed side to the same pattern. The back outline of the truss, where it joins with the carved ornament under the rail, is indicated by a band which sweeps from the frame to the toe. The ornament under the rail may be most conveniently fitted to its place, by making a half-length mould of it, and adjusting it to the inside of the truss; then fit a rod of wood tightly between the hollows of both trusses, and transfer this exact measure to the board from which the ornament is to be cut; draw two lines square across at the points laid

down, and the mould is then applied to each of these in succession and drawn. The ornament is not pierced under the rail, but wrought solid, and relieved on the face. It is fixed to the rails and trusses by screws passing through it at the narrowest parts.

In Fig. 2 the front and end rails of the frame are plain across, but sweep lengthwise with the fore corners canted, as shown in the annexed plan sketch. Greater strength is given to the rails by building them up of thin wood. The sweeps a and $c\ c$, with blocks inside $d\ d$, to which they are dow-

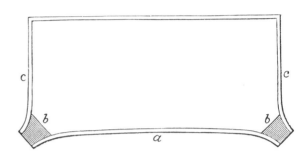

elled from the canted corners. The panels are grounded to the sweep of the rails; the shield requires $1\frac{1}{2}$-inch wood; it is carved separately, and planted on. The trusses stand obliquely to the front, and rake from before backwards with the under edge of the frame; they are dowelled to the corner blocks. The small panels in front of the trusses are grounded down. The centre of the rail below is pieced, to give sufficient breadth for grounding the shield. The fillet and listel below the rail are not planted on the face, but are together formed on sweeps of sufficient breadth to clamp on the under edge of the rail; the jagged portion around the bottom of the shield is formed of one piece, of the thickness of the moulding, joined to the ends of the straight parts, and glued on the face.

In Fig. 3, the rails are framed in so as to project the panes formed on the square of the leg; three panes are shown in front, and three on the end, the outer corner pane being common to both views; in forming them the two outside squares of the leg are divided off each into four equal parts, 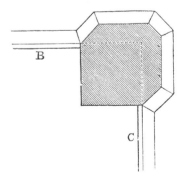 with one division set off on the adjoining sides of the other squares, and the two middle divisions of the four on each square go to form one pane that is direct and parallel to the front and end rails and large. The small oblique panes are then formed by planing off the three corners to a gauge line drawn through the outside points of division. The moulding, corresponding with that on the rail, is then planted on the panes.

The foliage and panelling on the rail and legs are wrought out of solid wood. The panelled brake in the centre is grounded to the rail, and stands out about ¾ inch from its surface. The drop D below is dowelled into a block within the rail; its position is determined by the necessity of maintaining the profile of the brake and vase uniform, whether seen from the front or end. The fret is pierced through and fixed by screws, it is kept back so as to fall in the same plane as the extremity of the drop.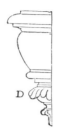

HALL CHAIRS.—PLATE III.

These chairs require to be strong and massive, and, like most hall furniture, are usually made of oak. The style of the back is their chief distinguishing feature. The seats are framed and boarded with a moulding, carried round the upper edge of the front and side rails; the backs are wrought separately, and screwed to the seat rail, with a recline of about 1½ inch.

Fig. 1 has the back plain, and profiled on the edge, with the scrolls raised by clamping, the shield planted on, the moulding at the top planted on also, and the ornament resting on it screwed down.

Fig. 2 has the interior of the back, within the band, grounded down flat, forming the panel. The band is scrolled backwards at the wings, and has a small hollow moulding carried round its inner edge; the pieces forming the scrolls abut against, and are dowelled to the outside of the back; the top scrolls are brought out by clamping.

Fig. 3 has the back framed and the panel checked in behind. The front and side rails are shaped below, with a band planted round their edges.

Fig. 4 is flat on the back, with the side scrolls planted and profiled with the ground; the centre scroll is brought out by clamping, and the shield is planted on.

Fig. 5 is flat in the centre of the back, with the wings dowelled on and wrought concave to the front. The circle, with the shield inserted in it, and the hanging panel, are clamped on.

Fig. 6 has the ground of the back plain, with the mouldings at the side and top planted on the face; the other ornaments are clamped on the centre. The seat rails are wrought to shape out of thick wood; the legs are rounded on the knees, and finished flush with the rails.

Fig. 7 has the wings of the back scrolled back-

wards, similar to fig. 2. The drops on the under edge of the side scrolls are let in with a pin. The centre ground is plain, and the shield and panel are clamped on. The mouldings on the back below are planted, and then carved. The feet under the rail is screwed on.

Fig. 8 has a plain ground on the back, with the ornaments clamped on. The top moulding is planted on the face, and the back above profiled to correspond. The tie in the centre is let into the moulding.

HALL CHAIRS.—PLATE IV.

Fig. 1 has the seat frame made of 1-inch wood. The legs are mitred together, and blocked inside. Fillets of wood are glued and screwed within the rails, crossing the grain, to strengthen the framing. The seat is dowelled down on the four corners, and screwed to the fillets from below; the legs within are then profiled, and the band round their edges is relieved by grounding the legs. The medallion on the backs is planted on. The back is attached to a bar which crosses the frame under the seat.

Fig. 2 has the ornamental parts of the back wrought out of solid wood 1½ inch thick; the side scrolls and lower end are maintained at the greatest thickness; the ground round the shield and panel is reduced to about ¾ inch. A pin is turned on the end of the spiral column, and the back is dowelled on it. The hind legs stand out from the frame, to receive the back between them. The front legs, with the scroll resting on them, are wrought of one piece, and the front and side rails are dowelled into them, and afterwards wrought to pattern. The frame is further strengthened by dowelling the seat to the top of the legs.

Fig. 3 has the ground of the back plain; side pieces of greater thickness are glued on to form the scrolls. The top scroll is brought out by clamping; the moulding and shield are planted on; the square heads of the front legs are reduced in size to bring out the turning into greater relief, and are wrought in with the band on the front and side rails. A hollow moulding is planted on the frame under the seat; the ornaments on the legs are wrought on the solid wood.

Fig. 4 has the seat framed, and clamped on the top with ½-inch board. A block is screwed on under the seat behind, and wrought flush with it for attaching the back; the ends of the block are concealed by profiling them to the back scroll of the seat supports. The shaped ends are dowelled into the seat, with the stretching rail shouldered between them, and bored through and wedged on the opposite side; a patera is then planted on to cover the part.

Fig. 5 has the moulding on the top and the side

ornaments of the back planted on a flat ground. The fret is sunk into the back, its border stands out about ⅛ inch past the flush of the ground. The seat rails require 1¼-inch wood, and to be of sufficient breadth to work in with the carving on the legs. The side rails have the character of a half length of the front, but longer. This chair would be improved by the foliage of the ornamental parts being lightened and simplified.

Fig. 6 has the back formed out of a single piece 3 inches in thickness. The circle is hand-wrought, or it may be turned, after partially carving out the surrounding parts; the interior of the circle is slightly convex, with the crest and shield formed on it. The panel below is sunk ½ inch. The truss legs are entire. The seat rails require to be stout, and the frame is dowelled together.

Fig. 7 is flat on the back, with a band planted on, having a hollow wrought on its inner edge. The initials are cut in fret, and may be relieved by gilding. The front legs stand out from the rail ⅜ inch. A hollow moulding is carried round the seat, and mitred on the projecting square of the legs. The ornamental parts of the front rail are pierced, and the members are bevelled on their edges. The legs are wrought square, and sunk panelled on the can and shaft.

Fig. 8 has the back perforated behind the side scrolls, and under the top moulding, with two triangular openings on each side of the circle. The circle, with its overhanging foliage, is planted on. The initials may be relieved by gold or colour.

HALL SEATS.—PLATE V.

The form of the examples given freely admits of more or less variety in ornament. The back, a conspicuous and important part, is in each case fixed by screws to the back rail of the seat, with a recline of about 1½ inch. The breadth of the seat is about 23 inches.

Fig. 1 has the back framed; the top rail extends the entire length of the back, and is morticed down on the ends; the under rail is framed between the ends, and requires to be of sufficient breadth to pass to the under edge of the seat rail. The ornamental members are dowelled in with the framing. The moulding along the top is rounded, that on the ends is flat, a hollow is wrought on the inner edge of these throughout. The tie on the top is fitted on. The circular moulding in the back is planted on, and the shield, which is inserted within it, has the ground perforated at its sides and top. A small moulding with plinth is planted on the back, and made to rest on the seat. The seat framing should be strengthened by cross bars. A stout board, ⅞ inch thick,

having a moulding carried round it, forms the true seat.

When the legs are paned, the scroll and other ornaments are planted on. The panels above the legs are formed of a single piece, and dowelled on. The front rail is not cut through at the linking of the band on centre and ends, as it would be weakened thereby.

In fig. 2 the back is wrought out of a single piece. The back legs are entire, extending from the floor to the under edge of the scroll on the back. The part above the seat is centred for turning, by leaving a notch of wood a on the leg in cutting it from the plank, or by screwing a piece on. The legs behind are framed in, so as to stand out about half their thickness from the rail, to admit the back between them. The band and tie ornaments on the back are similar to fig. 1. The interior of the back is cut out to receive the frets; they are let in from behind for this purpose: a rebate is wrought all round the opening, leaving a lap in front ¼ inch thick. The appearance of the back would be much improved by red cloth, or a polished panel being shown behind the frets. The shell on the back is principally wrought out of the ground, and, partly from a piece planted on.

In fig. 3 the back consists of three distinct parts, two of which, the ends, are a rather novel adaptation of hall chair backs; the other, the top rail and ornament, which fills the space between them. On the chair-back ends the perforations at the margin of the shields within the circle, and those beyond it, towards the outside, serve to lighten the general expression. The small panels below are sunk 7⁄16 inch, with a small hollow moulding carried round their inside. The vase which surmounts the back is dowelled down. The top rail is scribed between the ends and lapped in and screwed behind. A strap of wood forms the listel on the upper side of the rail; this is made removable, so that when glued down it conceals the screws, which are made to pass through the rail on fixing the fret.

In fig. 4 the back is in three parts, another rendering of the same idea as fig. 3, but is more consistently maintained, the centre being of the same general character as the ends, but enlarged with modified details. The several portions are first dowelled together at their points of contact, and then screwed to the seat. The irregular shaped panels that are around and under the shields are perforated; the marginal lines of these openings have a small hollow wrought round them. The grain of the wood in the back stands at right angles to the seat. The configuration of the front and ends of the seat with the spring of the truss require that the rails be wrought out of 2½-inch wood. If the rails are veneered, the raised parts may be pieced on, and consequently thinner wood will suit the framing.

Hat and Umbrella Stands.—Plate VI.

To present a surface within a limited space whereon hats may be hung; that the points of suspension be easily accessible, numerous, and suitably arranged; and that this distribution of the points be accompanied, and, as it were, concealed by ornamental embellishment, seem to be the essential considerations in designing and making a hat stand. The additional convenience of an umbrella stand is provided for and suggested by the necessity of finding a supporting base for the hat stand. The examples here given are constructed of one or three upright bars fixed to the side of a stout rectangular box; to these are attached arms of varying length, straight or curved. The standards, from the great leverage due to their length, and any depending weight, must be securely fixed to the back rail of the box; for this reason also the box must be strongly made. To hold the drip water, the box is lined with a movable tinned case, provided with a perforated shelf resting about 1½ inch from its bottom. Over the box, and attached to the stands in front, are brass rods, as in the first three examples, or wooden poles with ornamental ends, as in the last three, against these the umbrellas lean when set into the box; this circumstance determines the height proper to the rods measuring up from the shelf within the box.

In fig. 1 the cross arms, with their ornamental supports, should be first framed together before they are fixed to the vertical bar; by so doing, the joints of the framing can be more easily made, and better preserved from strain, and also the exact points for checking in the arms may, at once, for the whole, be more accurately determined. The arms and upright should be mutually checked, so as to pass into each other freely; otherwise, if they are too tight, the upright bar is bent forward, and the cross arms are thrown irregularly backwards. The ornamental brackets which support the under cross arm are first attached to it and to the upright bar, and then dowelled down on the box.

Fig. 2 is best adapted for mahogany; the arms require the same thickness of wood as the upright, and are dowelled to it. The required height of the lower cross arm determines the length of the trusses. The top ornament is dowelled down.

Fig. 3 resembles fig. 1, and is more easily made, the ornamental parts being simpler. The centre upright is much strengthened by the attachment given to the lower cross arm to the standards in the back corners of the box.

Fig. 4 differs from the preceding in having three standards, all connected at their upper end by an ornamental arched top. This affords the convenience of more numerous points for hanging than the others, has greater firmness in the standards, and is altogether stronger. The carved ornament is let in and grounded on the middle standard and top at their junction. The arms are dowelled on. The brackets with the pole are screwed on from behind. The ornamental ends of roller are formed separately from the shaft; the shaft has a pin turned on each end, and is made to shoulder exactly between the brackets; a pin and shoulder is also turned on each of the ends. The brackets are bored quite through, and the shaft inserted between them before they are finally screwed; the ornamental ends of the roller are then cramped on. The scroll brackets which abut against the foot of the middle standard are dowelled on. The thickness of wood required for the standards is 1¼ or 1⅛ inches.

Fig. 5 is similar to fig. 4 in its framework, excepting the semicircular top and the details of ornament. The round top is half checked on the standards, and for the sake of strength it should be wrought of three thicknesses, having the fibres of the wood crossed. The frets should also be prepared of three thin layers, and stand finished ⅜ inch thick. The top ornament, excepting the drop below, is formed of one entire piece.

Fig. 6, in its general character, resembles fig. 4. The brakes on the base, with the spiral columns which stand on them, give this design the character and appearance of greater stability and firmness than any of the others. The arched top is formed of one entire piece, and dowelled on.

Hat and Umbrella Stands.—Plate VII.

Fig. 1 stands obliquely to the plane of the picture, presenting the end in profile. The essential particulars of form and construction in this are similar to those of figs. 1, 2, and 3, Plate VI. The trusses, with the pole fitted between them, are screwed to the end standards, and dowelled down to the top of the box. The standard should not be less than 1½ inch thick, and the arms 1 inch thick. The latter would be much strengthened by being wrought of two thicknesses of wood clamped together, with the grain of the pieces crossing each other obliquely. The tapering hollows carved in the front of the arms should be wrought half the depth of their varying diameter; the arms towards their extremities are tapered slightly in their thickness. This is effected by grounding them down in the face, so as to relieve a band which is gradually formed on their outer edge, and terminates its greatest depth at the scroll. The two lowest arms, at their under edge, are united with the ornament overlying the cross rail; the parts are wrought separately, and then joined.

Fig. 2, in its under part, resembles several of the preceding. The large circle in the upper part supplies the place of the centre and side standards, and cross arms in the others. The rim should be wrought of four segments, and made up of three thicknesses, forming together 1⅛ inch thick. The joints of the segments are made to pass each other, for strength, and the middle thickness is made of cross wood. The face of the rim is cross banded. A hollow moulding is carried round the inner and outer edges of the rim. The diagonal bars, ¾ inch thick, are half checked into each other, and fitted into the circle, and fixed by dowels passing through the rim into their ends. The rim is fitted and dowelled to the top of the centre standard, and fixed to the side standards, by screws passing through the hollow at their top into the rim; the outer edge of the rim is slipped with veneer. The centre ornaments are planted on at the crossing of the bars. The top ornament is formed of three pieces, carved separately, and screwed on.

Fig. 3, in configuration and ornament, combines the elements of several of the preceding, with some varieties and additions. The frets are grooved in; the standards are first framed together by the cross bar, and the frets are slid into the grooves from the upper and lower ends. The arched top, formed of a single piece, is then fitted down, and the standards are let into and fixed to the box; the vases on the top of the side standards are let in with a pin; the tie in the centre of the arch is scribed into the moulding; the coronet with foliage is then planted on.

CLOCK CASES.—PLATE VIII.

These examples are designated wall clocks, as they are supported on a bracket, or hang on the wall, instead of resting on the floor. Besides being an article of hall furniture, they are of frequent use in public offices, places of resort, &c. They are usually made of oak, frequently of mahogany, and sometimes of satinwood, or deal painted in flat tints, and the carving hatched with gilding. The style of the design and character of the apartment for which the clock is intended, determine the material and manner in which it should be executed.

In fig. 1 the head is of one piece, and extends to the bottom of the truss-shaped ornaments on each side, where it joins with the framing of the door opening: it is wrought of 2¾ or 3-inch wood. The bissel surrounding the dial is turned on and gilt; a brass ring, glazed, is hinged to the bissel and secured by a lock. The door moulding is checked to receive the fret from behind. A thin panel, with coloured silk, is put in behind the fret, and a plate of glass in front preserves the silk from dust. The drops at the bottom of the case are let in with a pin, and the torus moulding is broken round them and carried back. The ornament below is formed of three pieces, which are joined behind the drops, and fixed to the sides and bottom of the case. The front of the clock is attached to the casing behind, which encloses the works.

Fig. 2 has the front of the head formed of ¾-inch wood, and fretted with coloured cloth shown behind the openings. A hollow moulding is carried round the front margins of the frets on both edges, and gilt. Within the fret a circular ground is formed for planting the bissel moulding. The head stands out from the body of the case 1½ inches; the door is glazed; the side ornaments below are kept back ¼ inch from the line of the case front; the large moulding and bracket at the bottom go back to the wall.

Fig. 3 has a plain ground, with the ornamental parts of the head and lower end planted on the face. The side mouldings, with their overlying foliage, are attached to the side of the door opening. The icicles, under the sweeped moulding on the top, should be gilt. The bissel is brass, and gilt. This pattern might be executed in rosewood, and would be much enriched by the mouldings and carved portions being hatched with gilding.

Fig. 4 may be wrought out of fir wood, and either painted in flat tints relieved by gilding, or entirely gilt; the head requires 3-inch wood. The side mouldings and bottom ornament are attached to the door frame. The door is glazed, with a silk covered panel behind the fret.

CLOCK CASES.—PLATE IX.

These examples have the front of the head formed of one entire piece. The clock work is enclosed within a circular casing behind, which is built of fir wood, and veneered round; this casing follows the general outline of the front, and is attached to it; it is perforated on both sides, for emitting the sound when the hours are struck. The head, so formed, is fixed to a frame, on which, in figs. 2 and 3, the upper part of the cornice mouldings are planted. The inside of this frame is grooved, and made to correspond with the outside dimensions of the body of the case, so as to receive its top within it; hardwood fillets, which work into the grooves, are screwed to the sides of the case, and on these the frame, with the attached head, slides off or on as required. The entire back is enclosed by a board, which is shaped at the upper end to the interior of the case containing the mechanism. The interior of the case must be clear for the descent of the weights. The usual depth of the case inside, from back to front, is 6 inches, but some bulky compensation pendulums, such as the mercurial, require 8 or 9 inches, to allow sufficient room for the weights to pass.

In Fig. 1, the case is entire, extending from below the head to the base. The front, containing the door opening, is framed up the whole length. The sides are feathered into the front with a plough, and checked behind to receive the back; the whole is then wrought flush and veneered. The ornaments on the front and sides are planted on. The door is glazed, and opens at the second band above the shield. The interior of the back, opposite the door, should be veneered or covered with cloth. The feet are wrought in three pieces, the front and the two sides: they are mitred at the corners in front, and afterwards carved; the back connecting them is lap-dovetailed in, the moulding above is wrought separately, and planted on.

In Fig. 2, the head is made of wood $1\frac{3}{4}$-inch thick, and has the bissel turned on the solid. The frame which connects the head with the body overlies the egg moulding at the top of the case, forming the block of the cornice. The pedestal and body are wrought separately, and afterwards joined. The pedestal is hollowed in the front and sides with the fore-corners canted. The method of constructing

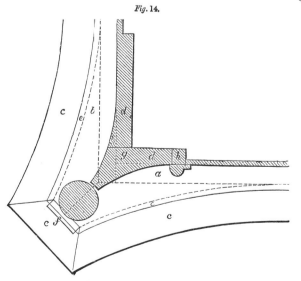

Fig. 14.

the pedestal and the adjoining parts is shown in *fig.* 14. The front, *a*, and the side, *b*, collectively

expressed by the dotted lines, are clamped up of deal, upon a ground of the same, $\frac{7}{8}$ inch thick, dovetailed together, and afterwards hollowed to a radius of $16\frac{1}{2}$ inches; the clamps are 2 inches thick, where they mitre at the front-corners. The top moulding, *c*, rests on the top of the pedestal, and projects beyond it $1\frac{3}{4}$ inches; the hollow member below stands beyond the flush $\frac{1}{4}$ inch; the space behind the moulding is pieced out so as to finish flush with the inside of the pedestal ground, and join with the body of the case, *d*, where it is fixed within the pedestal. The canted corners, *f*, are clamped with solid wood, $\frac{3}{8}$-inch thick, to form the sunk panels. The front, *g*, forming the door opening, is framed up of solid wood; the stiles are $2\frac{1}{4}$ inches thick, and taper in breadth from $1\frac{5}{8}$ inch at top, to $3\frac{3}{4}$ inches at bottom; the cross-rails are $\frac{7}{8}$ inch thick. As the body of the case requires, for secure attachment, to pass about 2 inches within the pedestal, the sides must be made so much longer, and the under cross-rail broader. The frame is wrought flush behind, where it applies to the case, the difference of thickness in the stiles being thrown to the front. The upper ends of the stiles are reduced to the thickness of the cross-rail, and wrought flat across; and their inner edges, all down, are brought to the same thickness, as a ground for the door to act on; the side pieces are then gradually scooped hollow, from above downwards. The sides of the case must be of solid wood, $1\frac{1}{4}$ inch thick, so as to work in with the sweep of the mouldings on the top of the pedestal. The door, *h*, is glazed. The base block is formed of one solid piece, 2 inches thick, and the scrolls are glued on to the required depth; the back scrolls, *d* (*fig.* 15), must be wrought so as not to project behind, that the case may stand close to the wall. The shell in front of the block is set in between the carved scrolls.

Fig 15.

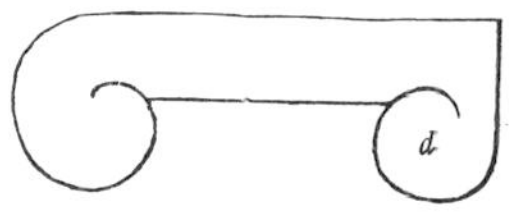

Fig. 3, in the chief points of construction, is identical with the preceding. The body of the case at the top is rounded over to where the head is attached, and then veneered. The foliage on the upper corners is planted on. The moulding on the top of the pedestal is mitred round after the pedestal and body are joined. The panel, with its mouldings, is formed of one piece, and fitted to the hollowed front of the pedestal, then carved and planted on. The base includes the carved moulding, the square block, and feet. The feet are each separately wrought of one piece, and screwed on.

Fig. 4 requires $3\frac{1}{2}$ or 4-inch wood for the head. The bissel is turned on the solid. The position and character of the pilasters, on the body of the case, gives it greater breadth across than any of the others. The case, with its pedestal, is shaped, as shown in the plan sketch (*fig.* 16), so as to present a ground for planting the trusses and pilasters. The door acts on pivot hinges, and sweeps under the cornice and over the pedestal mouldings.

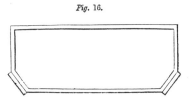

Fig. 16.

DINING-ROOM AND PARLOUR FURNITURE.

Dining-room furniture should be characterized by three qualities—convenience, solidity of construction, and absence of gaudiness. In the furniture of a family apartment in daily use, strength and solidity of construction are absolutely necessary for tear and wear; and any structural form, ornament, or decoration that interferes with comfort is to be discarded. Richness of effect, rather than showiness, is to be aimed at, and that by the use of good materials, and by masses of colour judiciously harmonized, without being monotonous; decided contrasts should be but sparingly used. The sideboard being the chief article of furniture in the room, the other articles of plenishing ought to be kept in subordination to it, and consistent with it in style and decoration. Having to contrast with plate, the sideboard should have a species of richness that looks well alone, and, at the same time, sets off the service of plate to the best advantage. Positive contrasts of various-coloured woods, gilding, decorations in brass work or ormolu, tend to interfere with unity of design, and disturb the effect of plate; such modes of ornament should be therefore avoided. Sufficient effect may be obtained by the use of beautiful woods, carefully wrought, and enriched occasionally by carving, inlaying, or fret-cutting. For variety, woods of different shades, but not of different colours, may with advantage be used together, and ornaments of bronze employed instead of carving.

Pedestal Sideboard.—Plate X.

The dimensions of the pedestals, with the proportional length of the drawer between them, are the principal determining measures of the sideboard. The usual height of the top is 39 inches, the width from 26 to 30 inches, and the length from 7 to 9 feet, according to the size of the room. The example here presented is plain in style, and simple in construction. The doors are flush panelled and veneered over, the mouldings and shields being clamped on. The back, between the pedestals, is closed in by a panelled frame, with the projection of base carried round it; this is screwed to the back edge of the inner gables, which, in consequence, are kept the thickness of the frame narrower than the outside gables. The pedestals are adjusted to their position by two pins glued into their upper ends, which pass into the top. They are then screwed firmly to their places, so as to support and regulate the action of the drawer fitted between them. This drawer has the sides grooved, and is made to act upon fillets screwed to the inner gables. A piece, forming a field for the centre ornament, is planted on the middle of the frieze drawer; it is fitted exactly between the listels of the upper and under mouldings, and wrought flush with them. The moulding, which is carried round the gables, is attached to the top; it is formed on a fillet of wood, clamped on the edge of a strap of deal 3 inches broad. The top is veneered and finished square, and slipped with veneer on the edge. The ground of the top is made of $\frac{7}{8}$-inch deal, clear of knots, and sound; the required thickness being made up by clamping below, lengthwise, and across at the ends and middle. If the top, in drying after being veneered, remains convex on the upper side, this can be easily rectified by cutting at intervals through the cross clamps, under the most convex portions of the top, small pieces of a wedge form, and chipping these parts out, and increasing their breadth by inserting at their edges thin slips of wood, then glueing and driving the wedges home, and so forcing the top straight. Should the top happen to become concave on the upper side, from the contraction of the veneer in drying, this may be remedied by running grooves, an inch apart, into the cross clamps, and fitting freely into them fillets of wood with strong glue. The top is then forcibly bent, and maintained slightly convex on the upper side till the glue in the grooves is thoroughly dry. The back is let into the top the thickness of the ground, and screwed; the bevelled moulding of the back rests on the top. The end view shows the top moulding in profile, the required projection of the top behind, and the centre drawer, indicated by dotted lines.

Pedestal Sideboard.—Plate XI.

Fig. 1 is of a simple character, and in construction resembles the example given in Plate X. The top may be formed of $\frac{5}{8}$-inch solid wood, clamped with deal to the required thickness: the ovolo moulding on its edge is planted on, and placed so as to present the listel above of the proper depth. The part of the moulding on the ends of the top, and also the returns of the brakes, should be formed of cross wood, so that the grain of the wood may be continuous with that of the top itself. The pieces for this purpose must be carefully seasoned, and should be grooved and feathered on the top. They are not mitred, at the fore-corners, into the front mouldings, but are put on before them, and planed flush with the square edge of the top, and then butt-joined with the mouldings in front. The hollow below the top is separately prepared and planted on. A block ½-inch thick is planted on the drawer front, and the mouldings on its upper and lower edge are carried round it; small side trusses, ¼-inch thick, are joined to the edge of the block, and in front they are made to finish flush with the lip of the upper and lower mouldings. The drop below is let in with a pin. The brackets under the ends of the drawer are fixed by screws passing through the inner gables. The doors are wrought flush as a ground for the shaped panels, ⁵⁄₁₆-inch thick, which are planted on them; on these again the small fielded centre panels are glued down, and the mouldings carried round their edges. The general appearance of the design may be improved by increasing the breadth of the straight portion of the back to six inches. The ground of the pediment, above this part, may be formed of deal, pieced on the edges to show solid wood, when it is profiled with the top moulding, which is planted on the face. The ground and fret are both completely finished before they are glued together. The semicircular ends are formed of deal, veneered on the face, and the mouldings, which are turned, planted on: their upper edges are then slipped with veneer.

Fig. 2.—From the enriched character of this design, no great extent of plane surface is presented; it is consequently not so well adapted for wood possessing large or striking figure, as for that of a minutely variegated and plainer character, such as oak. The stage is framed and fitted with drawers. The exact measures of the stage being determined, those of the ground frame are so much less by the greatest depth of the mouldings planted on it. The position of the cross rails are regulated by the same condition, which again determines the spaces from the frieze drawers. The stage frame in plan and vertical section is shown in *figs.* 17 and 18; the dotted line, *a a*, marks the outside of the mouldings, which are carried round the front and ends of the ground frame; the lines *b b* the ground, with the thickness of the wood employed—the front portion of the ground being the three drawer fronts. Four blocks, *c c c c*, 1¼-inch thick, are

planted on the extreme ends of the two outer drawers, and around these the frieze mouldings are

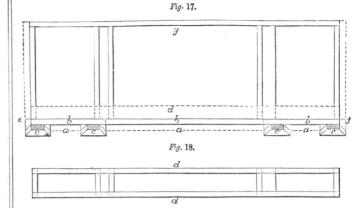

Fig. 17.

Fig. 18.

carried, forming the brakes shown in the drawing. The six cross rails of the frame are cross headed with solid wood. These headings are tenoned into the long rails, *d d, fig.* 18, and they show solid wood on the drawers being drawn out. By this means, also, the action of the drawers is rendered more smooth, and the cross rails are kept from warping. The drawers are made to abut against the frame in the line *c f*. The back rail of the frame, *g*, should not be finally glued till the drawers are fitted, as any irregularity in breadth, dimension, or workmanship, may thus be more easily remedied. The large moulding on the drawer fronts must be of solid wood, as the panelling shown on it is formed by grounding down. The doors, which are sunk panelled, have their stiles, the united breadth of the pilaster grounds, and door framing. The circular head of the door is formed by piecing up the inner corners (*fig.* 19). The pieces are mitred together, and glued to the adjoining parts of the stile and rail—the grain of the wood being made to run with these parts: the whole is then flushed off and veneered. The mouldings stand out beyond the flush, are glued to the inner edge of the frame, and form a check for the panel. The pilasters are ⅝-inch thick, and solid; the drops at their top and bottom are planted on ⁵⁄₁₆-inch thick. The back is formed of two thicknesses—the one in front of ⅜-inch solid wood, the other of ⅝-inch deal. The front board is wrought to pattern, and perforated in the centre. This figured opening is traced on the board behind, and the space marked is veneered and polished; the two thicknesses are then glued together. The top moulding, which forms the profile of the back, is planted on the face, and has a hollow moulding wrought on its inner edge. The prism-shaped panels, with the ground

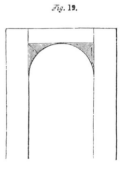

Fig. 19.

on which they rest, are made of two pieces separately wrought, glued together, and planted on. The fret pediments are of $\frac{5}{8}$-inch wood, and dowelled on.

Fig. 3 has the top resting immediately on the pedestals, as in Fig. 1. The corners of the pedestals are canted, and recede from the line of the doors at an angle of 45°, or $\frac{1}{2}$ a square mitre; consequently the cant is thrown equally on the doors and the gables. The pilasters, of solid wood, are $3\frac{1}{8}$-inch broad, and $\frac{5}{8}$-inch thick. From their position, the doors require to stand beyond the front edge of the gables $2\frac{1}{8}$ inches. The inner pilasters are attached to the doors, and the outer ones to the gables; to these last the doors are hung. The propriety of fixing to the gables the outside pilaster of each door is obvious, as otherwise the trusses on them would prevent the doors from opening to the square. The ground for the moveable pilaster is glued to the side of the door frame before the latter is veneered. On veneering the door, the edge of the veneer on the stile is made to join with the pilaster. The frets on the pilasters are wrought $\frac{3}{16}$-inch thick, and planted on a ground $\frac{5}{16}$-inch deep. The doors are in all respects similar to those of Fig. 2, excepting the upper rail; the greater breadth of which serves as a ground for planting the bordered fret. The moulding on the ring is similar to that on the door stile, but smaller. The length of the drawer is determined by the distance between the trusses on the inner pilasters; that being the space within which it must act. The drawer opens at the outer ends of the fretted panels, in the manner shown in *fig.* 20. The breadth of the moulding on the base determines the projection of the frame around the front and sides of the pedestal. The canted corners are wrought flush with the face of the shaft of the pilaster, and dovetailed into the front, D, and side of the frame, E, *fig.* 21. On this ground a block, C, is glued down—being made the proper thickness and breadth for carrying round the base moulding. The upper edge of the base is bevelled, and slipped with veneer, before the moulding is planted on. The back is pieced on the upper edges and ends with solid wood, and veneered on the face. The ornament at the centre and top of the back is separately wrought, and the scrolls terminating the top moulding are fitted into it. After the front of the back is finished, the fret is planted on. This last consists of five pieces—two, forming the top, which are butt-joined in the centre,

Fig. 20.

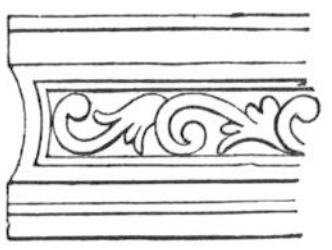

Fig. 21.

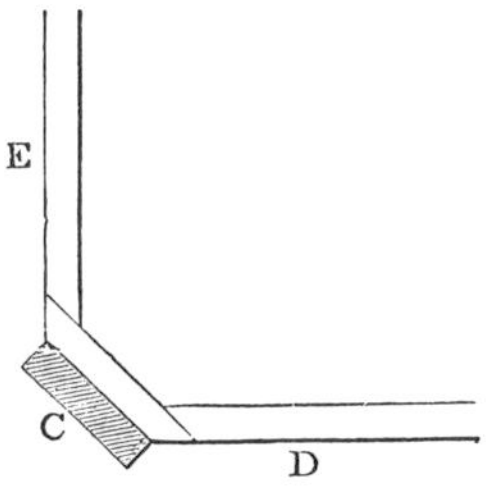

the two ends, and the straight portion at the bottom. These several parts are profiled and adjusted at the points of contact previous to fret cutting.

Fig. 4 has the pedestals tapered on the sides. They are two inches narrower at the top than at the bottom. The doors are sunk panelled, and the moulding (*fig.* 22) is made to lap on the stile. The pilasters are $\frac{1}{2}$-inch thick, and the small panels on their front are $\frac{3}{8}$-inch thick, and fielded on the edge. The trusses are formed of two pieces—the scrolled portion and the foliage below it being separately wrought. Between the pedestals behind, the space is filled by a frame flush panelled and veneered over; a base is formed on its under edge corresponding with that of the pedestals, and mitred in with it.

Fig. 22.

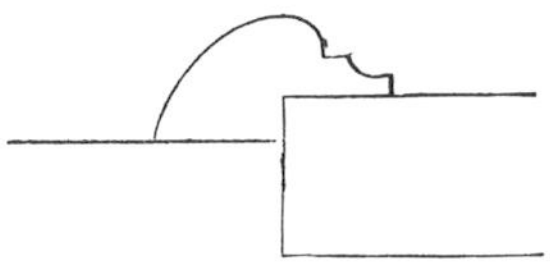

The back has a mirror in the centre, surrounded by a rim, with a moulding planted on its edge. The lip of the moulding projects within the rim, forming a check in which the plate rests. The rim is made up of segments of two $\frac{7}{8}$ thicknesses of deal $2\frac{1}{4}$-inch broad. These are cut of various lengths, so as to strengthen the rim by making the pieces lap over the butt-joinings on the sides alternately. The ends of the rim are connected by a bar, *a* (*fig.* 23), which is $\frac{7}{8}$-inch thick, and in breadth $\frac{3}{8}$-inch less than the depth of the check which the thickness of the sideboard top forms behind. The bar is checked flush with the fore-edge of the rim, and glued and screwed. The semicircular moulding, *b*, which is turned, is then planted on, and the outer edge of the rim is afterwards veneered. After the rim is polished, the plate, *f* (*fig.* 24), is laid

Fig. 23.

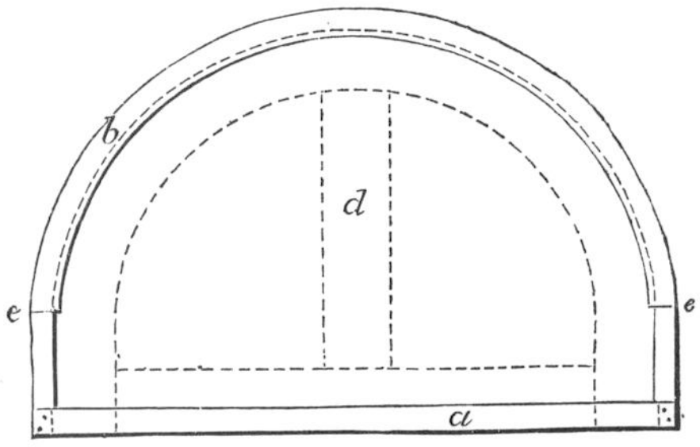

Fig. 24.

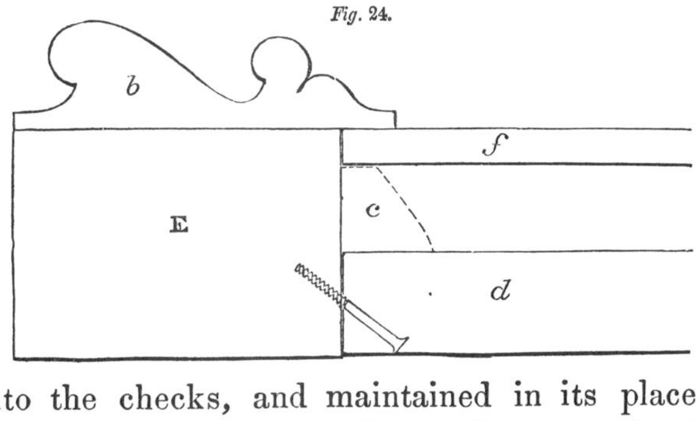

into the checks, and maintained in its place by blocks, *c*, three inches long, that are glued at short intervals around the inner edge of the rim. The mirror has a framed back, made of $\frac{3}{4}$-inch deal,

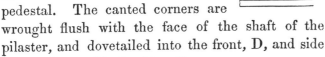

and panelled. It is fitted within the rim, as indicated by the dotted lines, and made to rest on the blocks, and is fixed by screws passing through it obliquely into the rim. The entablatures, which adjoin the mirror at each end, have their ground formed of 2-inch deal. They are made to stand in advance of the rim ⅜-inch. For this purpose they are in front checked on the sideboard top, and at their inner ends behind, the rim is checked into them, leaving a lap of ⅜-inch thick in front of the mirror. The rim moulding abuts on the top of the entablature at *e e, fig.* 23. The moulding at its base may, for the protection of the plate, be carried along the front of the mirror. The bar, *a*, would, in consequence, require to be made of sufficient breadth, as a ground for the moulding, which should lap over like that on the rim, forming a check for the plate.

Pedestal Sideboard.—Plate XII.

This design, in construction and embellishment, differs considerably from any of the preceding. The ground of the back is of deal, 1-inch thick, and of one piece, checked and screwed at the ends into the adjoining sides of two pedestals. The centre of the back is increased in breadth, and projected 1¼-inch in front by clamping. On this part a ground panel, with an ornamental scrolled border, is planted. The panel and border may be wrought together of one piece, 1½-inch thick. The panel being grounded down, and the small raised panels planted on its field; or, otherwise, the larger panel may be separately wrought, and of sufficient thickness to project, as shown in section Fig. D, and the scrolled border formed of four separate pieces, fitted round it. The scrolled head of the clock is made of wood 4-inch thick. The bissel is separately wrought, and let into the upper moulding of the back, then applied to a ground formed for it on the head, and fixed by screws from behind. The dial and clock-work is let in from the front, and behind a space is cut out to admit the work. The bracket and shelf shown in the profile, Fig. C, are fixed by screws passing through the back. The fret pediments on the ends of the back are made of 1-inch wood, and the band on their edges is formed in relief. Before veneering the top, the ovolo moulding on its edge is planted on. The projecting centre part of it, having the rounded ends, is first planted. It is formed of a piece whose finished breadth is 3½ inches. The end pieces are then mitred with or scribed to this. In the drawing, the frieze drawer is shown as straight in front, but, from the projection over it of the brake on the top, it would be more elegant to project the drawer also,

so as to correspond in outline with the parts overlying it: in this case, the drawer front would require to be built at the ends. Two designs for the decoration of the pedestals are given. The pedestal door, to the right, shown in section Fig. F, is flush panelled, and veneered over with the shield and mouldings planted on. Ornamental pieces of rich wood, ¼-inch thick, are fitted within the brakes of the mouldings, and glued down on the door. On the left-hand door a raised panel is planted: it is made to lap on the framing all round, as shown in section Fig. K. The coved and torus mouldings are mitred round the panel in succession, after which the field is veneered. The carving round the panel is formed of four pieces 1½-inch thick, which are fitted to the edge of the mouldings and glued down, or they may be screwed on from behind. Any slight inequalities in the joinings may be remedied after the parts are fixed. The grain of the wood, in all the parts, should run lengthwise with the door. The coved moulding of the raised panel on the gables, is pieced out on the corners to form the brakes. The cabinet between the pedestals, including the base on which it stands, is separately made. The doors are flush panelled and veneered over. An elliptical bead attached to the right-hand door laps over the left at their joining. The distance between the trusses on the inside gables, determines the united breadth of the doors—that being the space available for their opening. Two stiles—whose breadth slightly exceeds, say ⅛-inch, the greatest depth of the trusses, are fixed—one at each end of the cabinet; and to these the doors are hinged. The ring moulding on the doors is shown in section Fig. L. The hollow side of the triangular corners is made to sweep from the same centre with the ring. These corners are formed of mouldings on the door to the right; and on the left by small bevelled panels, with rebated margins.

Pedestal Sideboard.—Plate XIII.

This design is well adapted for oak; and, from its rich and massive character, it should be executed of a large size, that sufficient space may be given for combining boldness with delicacy in the details of its decoration. The pedestal doors require wood 1⅜-inch thick: they are sunk panelled, and the mouldings are checked, to recess the door ⅜-inch, and are made to lap on the stile. The trusses are dowelled to the sides of the frame; and, together with it, form the true breadth of the door. There are two panels in each door, that in front is 1 5/16-inch thick, and fretted; the large figured spaces in the corners being cut through, and their edges bevelled; the interior smaller spaces may either be grounded down ¼-inch into the panel behind, and the scrolled frets planted close: or inlaid with darker wood, and the ornament produced upon it by inlaying with wood of a lighter colour. *Fig.* 25

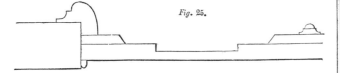

Fig. 25.

presents a cross section of the pedestal door, half-width, in a line passing through, and including the nodule above the ring in the centre. The ring is turned and cut into four equal pieces, between the ends of which the ties, which are solid, are interposed and fitted. The head is fixed by screws passing through the panel from behind. The four trusses should be profiled together out of a single piece, and the tie on the shaft of each afterwards planted on. The stage frame is made similar to that of Fig. 2, Plate XI.; the exact measures being determined by the dimensions of the sideboard, and the greatest depth of the front mouldings. The large ovolo moulding may be variously made, according as the panelling and foliage on its front are wrought in relief, or planted on. If in the former manner, it may be wrought in the solid, or clamped with 1¼-inch wood, and then veneered over; in the latter, it may be made of fir, and veneered, and pieces forming the ornamental parts may be glued up of three thicknesses, and cauled together to the curve of the moulding as a ground, and afterwards cut to figure and planted on. The rosettes on the end drawers, and the husk and leaves on the centre one, are separately wrought and let into the front. The top is veneered after the moulding on its edge is planted on. The back is formed of deal 1¼-inch thick, pieced with solid wood on the ends and centre, and veneered, as represented in the drawing, with wood of a lighter and darker shade; the former being the margins of the panels, the latter their fields. The mouldings are made to lap over the sides of both veneers. The mouldings on the top of the back, extending from the semicircle towards the ends, may be each formed of a single piece; and also the upper mouldings of the panels, which are parallel to them; all these mouldings are planted on the face. The semicircular moulding, and its overlaying ornament, are together wrought out of the solid; they are formed of three separate pieces; the centre or top part, which is fitted between the scrolls and checked, so as to be flush behind, and lap down in front; and the two segmental side pieces which are scribed edge-on to the ground, and from above down, for about ⅓ of

their length, are made to lap 1½-inch on the front, to form the scrolls and foliage, and below to mitre in with the adjoining ends of the top moulding. The thickness of wood required for these parts is about 2¾ inches.

The two similar carved ornaments on the top of the back, on the opposite sides, and at the base of the semicircle, are each formed of two pieces; the head portions, with their scrolled extremities, rising obliquely from behind, and resting on the outer end of the flat parts of the top mouldings, which mitre in with the semicircle; and the scroll shown in front as connectedly passing from under the mouldings, and recurved from before backwards. Small ornamental cylinders, laid horizontally, are made to fill the space between the semicircle, and the insides of the scrolls, where they are butt-joined, and the parts fixed by dowels. The other extremity of the ornament is fixed by screws passing through from behind; wood 3 inches thick is required for these parts. The shield is wrought of wood 2¾-inch thick; the ring is turned on, and its inside flattened as a ground for the head, previous to which the carving on the shield is blocked out. The head is carved separately, and screwed on from behind.

The cabinet between the pedestals is recessed 5 inches, measuring from the fore-edge of the inner gables. This space on the outside of these gables is clamped with wood, solid or veneered, 1⅛-inch thick. In the front, and towards the centre of the clamp, a hollow is wrought to a radius of 3½ inches; the line of which sweeps from the outer edge to within 1½-inch of the back of the clamp, where a flat border of that breadth is left. If the clamp is veneered, a panel is formed on the bottom of the hollow, by planting a small moulding on the face; if solid, a groove ¼-inch deep may be carried round to mark off the panel. Pendant foliage is shown above the panel, which may be wrought in high relief by inserting a piece into the ground of the hollow. The clamp forms a check behind, which determines the position of, and forms an attachment to, the cabinet between the pedestals. The base, with its moulding, must correspond with the outline of the clamp. The doors are flush panelled, and the ornamentation of them may either be produced by fret cutting—a piece of cloth being introduced behind the fret—or by inlaying the ground of the pattern with wood of a darker colour.

SLAB SIDEBOARDS.—PLATE XIV.

Slab sideboards differ from pedestal sideboards in being more fitted for the display of plate or articles of *vertu*, and less for a place of deposit.

Fig. 26 shows the manner in which the stage frame, and that of the base, should be wrought;

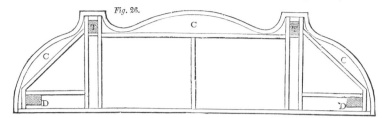

Fig. 26.

the rounds and hollows of the outline of the ground are formed by clamping with deal, *c, c, c,* upon a frame so constructed. The operation is guided by moulds of the ends and front, previously formed, and must be accurately done. The clamps for the frieze moulding are wrought by the same mould, and must be 1¼-inch thick; the centre clamp may be cut out of two lengths, and butt-joined in the middle; the carved ornament in the centre of the rail will cover the joining. The scrolls, shown on the end mouldings, are wrought on the solid. The foliage under the rail, and between the front trusses, consists of three pieces, the centre and two sides; these last are cut out to the sweep of the front rail, and made to work in with the top of the trusses; corresponding pieces are cut out, but of shorter length, and fitted to the outsides of the front trusses. The carving shown on the frame, over the front trusses, is wrought on the solid and apart; the advancing hollow sweeps of the front and end mouldings are flushed with the ground frame, and the carved parts are planted on. The top is clamped to thickness the usual way; and, when wrought to shape, the mouldings, which are hand-wrought, are dowelled on; care being taken that the dowells are bored parallel to each other, and, as nearly as possible, at right angles to the surface into which they are driven; few dowells, judiciously inserted, are quite sufficient to adjust and secure the mouldings firmly to their place. As considerable difficulty may be experienced in bedding the mouldings properly, after being nearly fitted, they may be temporarily glued to their place; and, when dry, a smooth and broad bow-saw blade may be carefully passed between the moulding and the ground, so as to cut off any little inequalities on either, and thus bring them more expeditiously to a joint; the same method might be resorted to with the frieze moulding. The front and end top mouldings should be fitted, mitred, and glued down first; and the short pieces, for the brakes, after. The listel above the moulding should be afterwards slipped with veneer, and any slight defect in the joints of the mouldings with the top, may be concealed by bringing the veneer to join edgewise with the moulding above. The front trusses are fixed by dowells passing

through the blocks, T, T, on the frame. The back trusses are placed so as to stand clear of the framed back; they are dowelled to blocks, D, D, fixed within the frame. In both, the high projections may be brought out by clamping. The top of the base is in all respects treated as the stage top in framing, and boarded above; the edges of the board being previously slipped, and the mouldings planted on them, it is then glued and strongly blocked to the cross-rails, and afterwards veneered. The frame enclosing the back is flush panelled, and checked and screwed into the back of the base and stage frame; the mouldings, with their carved corners, are planted on the veneer.

The back is formed of two thicknesses of solid wood, that in front requires ⅜-inch, that behind may be ⅝-inch thick; the front portion is veneered over, and then cut through to the figure of the panels; the ground behind is polished at the exposed parts, and the pieces cut out are reduced to size, moulded on the edge, and clamped down; the carving on the corners, excepting the small scrolls, is separately wrought and fitted on. The scroll work and foliage, around the edges and in the centre, are planted on the face. The heart-shaped carved work surrounding the initials, is shown as hooked on the descending sweep of the top scrolls; the parts in contact alternately under and overlaying each other. This arrangement is produced by keeping the scroll rather full in thickness, and thinning off the part below, so as to make it appear to dip under, emerge, and overlay the other. The whole centre carving is formed of one piece, and is first planted down; the top mouldings, the ends of which terminate in a calyx from which the foliage seems to issue, are afterwards fitted on.

Fig. 2 resembles Fig. 4, Plate XI., in the stage, which may be fitted with drawers. The hollow curve of the frieze moulding, on the return of the brakes, is formed of two solid pieces, mitred in the angle; the pieces are slip-dowelled together, and, when profiled, are afterwards taken asunder, and the large moulding is formed on them separately; they are then, finally, glued together, and their surface is wrought off. The centre drawer opens, and the end drawers abut, at the spring of the curve. It may be most convenient to form the top of ½-inch board, clamped to thickness; the ovolo moulding, in such case, being kept down, so as to leave the listel to project. The trusses are wrought of 3½-inch wood, and are fixed by dowells to the stage and base. The frame enclosing the back is sunk-panelled; the mouldings on it are checked on the framing, and the panels are let in from behind.

The ground of the back may be of solid wood, or of deal, and in either case veneered; labour is saved by making it solid, in consequence of the shaped ends and perforated centre requiring the exposed edges to show solid wood; if made of deal, the ends of the ground, and also the centre, must be pieced with solid wood; that on the centre must be inserted into the ground, with the edges feathered and grooved into it; the surface, after being flattened and prepared, is veneered over. The centre ornament is wrought of 1¼-inch wood, and, when completely finished, is clamped down; the back is then perforated, and wrought to profile of ornament. The top moulding is wrought of a piece with the upper part of the carving on the ends, and is clamped on the face. The panels on the back are formed by planting the shaped mouldings on the face of the veneer.

SLAB SIDEBOARD.—PLATE XV.

This design is well suited for oak; and, to give it proper effect, should be executed of a large size. The pillars are blocked out square, and are profiled, as stated under Plate I. They are then framed up with the ground of the stage, and the drawers are made to act between them. The brakes on the front and ends are formed on the square heads of the pillars, which stand out beyond the line of the frame 1½ inches. The large moulding is solid, so as to admit of the panelled foliage, and other ornaments, on its surface, being wrought in relief. The moulding is carried round the entire front and ends; in the order of work, it should be first planted on the heads of the pillars, between which the parts forming the fronts of the drawers are afterwards scribed in. The ends of the drawer fronts so shaped, are made to lap beyond the drawer, the body of which is, as usual, square wrought, and made to act between cross rails morticed in from back to front, as shown in the diagram given under Plate XI., Fig. 2. The top is formed of ⅞-inch deal, and clamped to thickness. After the top is wrought to size, pieces forming the ground, for the projection of the brakes, are glued on its edge. The moulding is then mitred round, and the whole surface is flushed off and prepared. A board of solid wood ⅜-inch thick, after being wrought to the proper shape, is clamped on the top, and forming, by its thickness, the upper member of the top moulding. The frame of the base, if made of solid wood, requires to be 1⅛ inch thick, and must be lap or mitre dovetailed in the fore-corners; if made of deal and veneered wood, 1¼ inch thick is necessary. The top of the base is boarded over with wood of the same thickness as that of the frame;

this part must be recessed from the front and ends, to form a check for the moulding, which is carried round its edge; it is also kept within the line of the back rail, the thickness of the upright framing behind. The base must be strongly made, and the top firmly blocked down, so as to form a secure and unyielding attachment to the pillars in front, and to the back framing. This last consists of three distinct frames, flush panelled and veneered, which are severally checked into the adjoining sides of the four pilasters at the back, and made flush behind with the stage and base. The pilasters are morticed into blocks that are glued within the back rails of the stage and base frames; small fielded panels are planted on their fronts. The ground of the back is prepared of two thicknesses, similar to that of Plate XI., Fig. 2. The front board should finish ⅜-inch thick, and solid; that behind, ⅞-inch, and of deal. The mouldings bordering the frets are fitted into the prepared openings, and should stand out beyond the ground ³⁄₁₆-inch. The pieces for forming the frets are fitted to their place before being cut; after which, and when completely finished, they are planted. The small ornamental pedestals are first planed up square, and the vases on their top turned on the solid, and carved. Previous to planting the mouldings on them, the pedestals are fixed to their place on the back; the two at the ends are dowelled on, the others are half checked, and planted on the face, and the top mouldings are abutted on them. Small panels, ⁵⁄₁₆-inch thick, with bevelled edges, are planted on the body of the pedestals. The wood forming the foliage which surmounts the semicircle, requires to be 1½ inch thick; it is fitted to outline, and maintained 2 inches broad for carving; when completely finished, it is fixed by screws. The frets require ¾-inch wood, and are dowelled down. The ring is turned separately, and the shield is planted within it.

SIDEBOARD BACKS.—PLATE XVI.

From the examples here given, backs may be selected suitable for several of the designs of sideboards contained in the preceding plates, or the elements of their configuration and ornament may be variously blended together, or partially modified and adapted to other designs; care being taken, in such adaptation, to preserve unity of style and harmony of proportion.

Fig. 1 is formed of a board of deal, veneered, with the mouldings planted on the face, and slipped with veneer on the ends and upper edge. The block resting on the scrolls is a solid piece, with the mouldings returned on the ends. The tie is let into the block. The shield, which is veneered, has the grain of the veneer laid in the direction of its length.

Fig. 2 has the ground pieced on the upper edge, at the centre, before it is veneered. The centre ornament, including the scrolls on the top moulding, is wrought of one piece. The ornaments on the ends are checked, and made to lap on the front, so as to butt against and work in with the top moulding, the straight part of which is separately wrought.

Fig. 3, like the preceding, has the ground formed of deal, and veneered, with the top mouldings and centre ornaments planted on the face. The small pedestals at the ends are dowelled on, and in horizontal section appear as in (Fig. 27).

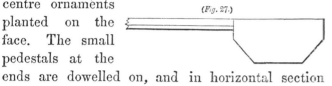

(Fig. 27.)

Fig. 4 has its centre projected by clamping with a piece ¾-inch thick, around which the mouldings above and below are mitred. A panel ⅜-inch thick, having a small hollow wrought around its edge, is planted on the face of this raised portion; overlying this is an ornamental border, inclosing a panel separately wrought, and of a single piece—the panel within being grounded by cutting through the border, which is thinned off inside. This construction is shown by a vertical section through the centre of the back (Fig. 28). The panels on each end are ½-inch thick, and veneered with rich wood on a ground of solid wood, with their edges fielded down. The ornamental pediment is dowelled on, and requires wood 1½-inch thick.

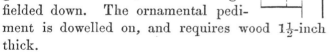

(Fig. 23.)

Fig. 5 has the ground solid, and may be veneered or not, according as the wood is plain or figured. The carving is planted on the face; the centre part with the scrolls may be formed of one piece; the stem from which the latter appear to issue, and the end scrolls are entire, and wrought together. The shield is planted on.

Fig. 6 has the ground solid and veneered; it is pieced, on the upper edge, so as to profile with the carving on the ends and centre, which is planted on it. The panels on the ground are ⁵⁄₁₆-inch thick, and veneered with rich wood. The shell carving, on the centre, requires 2-inch wood; it is of one piece, and distinct from the flowers on each side; the latter, with the flowers at the ends and the top moulding between them, are wrought of one piece, 1¾-inch thick. The scrolls which form the ends are planted on the face, and butt-joined below the flowers.

PILLAR AND BLOCK TABLES.—PLATE XVII.

In pillar and block tables the dimensions of the block are variable; the breadth across its centre, and the expansion of its limbs, severally, depend on the diameter of the base of the pillar, and the size of the table top; ⅔ of the breadth of the latter is usually taken as the measure of spread for the block. The form and construction of block, suited for five of the examples here given, is shown in (Fig. 29.) Fig. 4 differs from the others. The block is framed up of three pieces of deal A B B, 4½ inches broad, by 2½ inches thick; batten wood at half breadth is frequently used for this purpose. Diagonal pieces C C for forming the sweeps are let into the limbs of the frame, and the inner corners D D are blocked up with short wood; the top surface is then flushed off, and, afterwards, if the block is to be finished plain, as in Fig. 1, it is clamped with deal ⅝-inch thick, before the sweeps are cut out; but if, as in Figs. 2, 3, 5, and 6, the mouldings on the blocks are formed on the clamps, which are solid, the blocks are sweeped out and veneered on the edge before the clamps are glued down. Besides the above method, the blocks are frequently formed from three thicknesses of wood glued together, the grain of the centre one being, for sake of strength, made to cross that of the others. The wood, in this case, must be well seasoned, as, from the irregular mixture of end and side wood, the shrinkage will be unequal, and apt to show through the veneer. When the sweeps are to be carved, solid wood has to be planted on, and in such cases any defect in seasoning is not so readily apparent. A mould for making the block in this way is of especial advantage in piecing up and economising the wood.

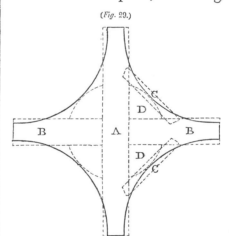

(Fig. 29.)

Fig. 1 has the pillar four-sided, and paned on the corners; the panes are of equal breadth throughout, the taper being altogether formed on the sides. The body of the pillar is made up of four pieces of deal, 1¼-inch thick, and of the entire length shown, with about 5 inches additional for forming the tenons on each end, by which it is attached to the upper and lower blocks; two of the pieces are cut out full to the diameter and taper of the pillar, the two other pieces have the same taper, but are made narrower than the preceding by twice the thickness of the wood so employed. This arrangement is shown in cross section (*Fig.* 30); the narrow pieces *a a* are first glued edge-on and flush with the edges of one of the broader pieces *b*, a cavity is thus formed, which is closely filled in at each end with short pieces of thin wood, from 7 to 9 inches long, expressed by the dotted lines; lastly, the side *c* is clamped down. After the pillar is wrought to

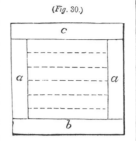

(*Fig.* 30.)

shape, the panel veneers are laid, and a raised border, ¹⁄₁₆-inch thick, which defines the ground of the panel, is planted on; within this border, and glued to it, a fillet, which encloses the fret, is carried round; this fillet is ¹⁄₁₆-inch broad, and stands out ⅛-inch beyond the flush of the border. The paned corners are then veneered, and the pillar is shouldered in the lathe, at both ends, for framing. The pillar and block are framed together before the mouldings at the bottom are planted on.

Fig. 2 has the pillar solid and turned; the profile given to it in turning is shown in (*Fig.* 31); it is afterwards formed into an irregular octagon.

(*Fig.* 31.)

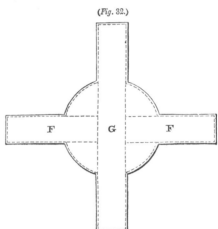

The four scrolled sides are of uniform breadth, and flat; the others are wrought slightly hollow, and are irregular in figure; the former are wrought in relief, presenting an edge thickness of ½-inch, by grounding the adjoining sides down; the ornamental parts on the latter are wrought out of the solid; the wings of the shield extend round and unite with the corresponding parts of the shields on the other sides. The heads of the trusses are fitted on to the hollow sweep of the pillar, and the leafage on their upper sides is made to curve up under the scrolls. The ribbon, shown as hanging from the scrolls, is formed of cross wood, and indented into the block; its facial outline, waved form, and points of contact with the adjoining parts, may be taken off by lead moulds, and transferred to the wood from which it is to be cut; the apparent termination of the ribbon, shown as crossing the hollow of the truss, and over-hanging the block, is separately wrought and indented. The band on the edge of the block below is planted on, and made to sweep in with the carved feet; these last are first profiled together out of one piece, and then cut asunder and separately carved.

Fig. 3 has a form of pillar, which may either be made solid and of one piece, or the lower part alone may be made solid and turned, the upper portion

being fir wood veneered, and shouldered and dowelled within the carved calyx from which it rises. The scrolls on the block and pillar are fitted on and fixed by screws passing through them at the most convenient points of contact; the holes of the screw-heads being concealed by plugging them with wood. The carved balls under the extremities of the block are hollowed out in the lathe to receive the castors, and are fixed by screws to the block.

Fig. 4 has the limbs of the block framed up similar to those of the preceding examples. The body of the block, as shown in (*Fig.* 32), is formed by quadrants of a turned circle of solid wood, moulded on the edge, which fill the angles of the limbs. The quadrants are first dowelled to the pieces F F, and with them are framed into the longer piece G;

(*Fig.* 32.)

the mouldings on the limbs are then scribed end-on to the quadrants, and mitred round. The pillar has the outline of the carved portions formed by turning; the leaves on the shaft are then laid open, and the band on the ball is wrought to figure. The scrolls behind are let into grooves formed in the pillar, and they are fixed to the block by screws passing through from below.

Fig. 5 has the block, in all respects, similar to Fig. 3. The trusses, which rest on the ends, are fixed by dowels. The pillar is solid, and may be formed of two pieces, butt-joined above the ball, where the leaves diverge; the parts may be dowelled together, or securely braced by a bolt passing through both, with a nut acting on its extremity, below the block. The bottom of the pillar is paned, forming a ground for the large moulding which is planted on.

Fig. 6 has the part of the pillar above the shield turned to outline, before it is paned; it is at the same time shouldered in the lathe at both ends, for framing. The lower end of the pillar is hand-wrought, and made to spread out on the block; its butt joins with the scrolls on the ends of the block, and is wrought off with them; at the sides, the pillar sweeps out below, so as to project the bottom of the shield a little beyond the flush of the block. The flowers on each side of the shield, and the leafage between the scrolls at its bottom, are indented into the block.

TELESCOPE DINING TABLES.—PLATE XVIII.

Tables of this sort have received their name from the slide action by which their length is varied. The compactness of their minimum size, their capability of speedy extension, and the facility with which they may be adjusted to various measures, intermediate, between their extremes of length, are their chief recommendations. From these qualities, they contrast favourably with the other varieties of dining tables, which they have in a great measure superseded. The least and greatest dimensions required in a telescope table, together with the form of the ends, determine the number and length of the slides. In addition to the available length of each pair of slides, a constant measure of 8 inches is necessary, as an overlap, at each end, so as to secure sufficient strength in the frame, and also to maintain the mutual attachment and steady action of the slides when drawn out. In execution, it is important to attend to the dimensions of the loose boards of the top, more particularly their breadth, which serves as a unit of measure, and, within certain limits, governs the consideration of length in the table.

Fig. 1 shows the frame of a telescope table, with the slides drawn out; Fig. 2 shows the same, with the slides pushed in; in Fig. 3 the frame is shown bottom upwards, presenting the cross bars and points of attachment for the supporting pillars. In these figures the outline of the top is indicated by dotted lines. Fig. 4 represents the action of the slides with the form and articulation of the checks. In Fig. 5 the slides are shown in cross section, on an enlarged scale; and Fig. 6 shows the method of adjusting them within the rounded ends of the table. The slides, necessarily, consist of two sorts, those which move either way, and those which are fixed, and serve to support and regulate the motion. The slides a a and b b, at one end, with their correspondents a' a' and b' b' at the other, are fixed, and are severally the outside and inside slides; the former are fitted and screwed within the rounded ends; they must be exactly parallel to the side rails and to each other; the latter are dovetailed on the ends of the bar c, which is screwed to the side of the leaf-holder, in the centre of the table Fig. 2, and made to stand out at right angles to it, and parallel to each other. To distend the frame and steady the action of the slides, cross bars f, g, h, are screwed on the under edge and inner ends of the moveable slides. The bar f is fixed flush with the ends of the slides, to which it is attached; the next in order, g, is kept within the flush the full breadth of the bar f; and, again, the

bar h, the united breadth of both the preceding bars; by this arrangement, when the table is at smallest size, the several bars come together as shown in dotted lines, Fig. 2. The slides are hook-checked together, or, as this method of attachment is sometimes called, T grooved. The body of the slides requires to be 4½-inches broad, by 1¼-inch thick, and may be made of birch, oak, or Bay mahogany—the last is preferable; the wood must be thoroughly seasoned, and straight in grain, as any shrinking or warping of the slides will render their motion difficult or impracticable. The pieces forming the checks should be separately wrought, as greater convenience is thereby given for properly finishing the friction surfaces, and, consequently, of insuring greater accuracy and smoothness of action. The alternate lip and groove of the slide-checks should be of the same dimensions, and the breadth of the two interior hooks, formed of one piece d, Fig. 5, should be equal to the united breadth of the two exterior ones, e, e; these measures, besides the more equal distribution of strength in the parts, afford, also, greater facility and accuracy in working. The checks require wood ¾-inch thick; they should first be all wrought accurately of the form and dimension of the portion d, Fig. 5; the rebates may be run out with a plough, or, what is more suitable, by a plane, made for the purpose. To prevent jamming in the action of the slides, the lips of the checks should be formed with a slight taper outwards. In putting on the checks, the parts e, e, Fig. 5, are first glued down and screwed with the part d loose between them, the condition of their action is then ascertained, and any stiffness remedied; the several pieces are then together carefully flattened across, and the part d is fixed to its place on the adjoining slide, and so on with the others.

A space is formed for holding the loose tops securely within the table itself. This is a very convenient and somewhat novel arrangement; but is unsuitable when the top projects more than 1½-inches, and when the boards exceed four in number; as in the one case there would be an inconvenient depth of brake in the top, while in the other the leaf-holder would be rendered so deep, as to interfere with the use of the table. Another and very neat contrivance for disposing of the loose tops is shown in Plate XXII., where they are placed in the back part of dining-room side-tables.

A stout board of hardwood, 1¼-inch thick, forms the bottom of the leaf-holder, and is screwed on as shown Fig. 3; to this the centre pillar of the table is attached; this bottom board is cross-headed at the dotted line k, which serves to strengthen the side framing, and form a proper attachment for the hinges of the flap door ; hardwood fillets are screwed to the sides within, forming, by their interspaces, grooves into which the loose leaves are slid ; the sides and bottom are then wholly cloth covered. The flap door is made of solid wood, 1⅛-inch thick, and cross headed ; tenons or dowels are inserted into the exposed ends of the sides of the holder, and corresponding mortices, or bores, *m, m*, into the inside of the flap ; these assist in supporting the sides of the leaf-holder under the action of the slides. The top of the leaf-holder has the same projection all round as the rounded ends of the table-top ; it is moulded on the ends and returns of the brake, and clamped below, so as to mitre-in with the other mouldings. The rounded ends are built up of sweeps of deal 1½-inch broad, and veneered. The mouldings on the edges may be formed of cross wood planted on, or, if the grain is to be lengthwise, the mouldings, after being wrought, may be rendered flexible by immersion in moist steam, and then bent to the round of the table. The fixed portions of the top are screwed to the rounded ends and leaf-holder ; the former recede from the inner ends of the rim exactly the amount of projection given to the sides of the latter. The ends, *l, l*, are boarded below with hardwood, 1¼-inch thick, so as to form a secure attachment for the supporting pillars ; these bottom boards are kept back from the flush of the ends of the built frames the united breadths of the three bars *f, g, h* ; they abut against these bars when the table is at its least size. Continuous with the hardwood bottom, the outer part of the round is boarded with deal ¾-inch thick ; both boards are finished flush below, the difference of thickness being thrown to the inside. The supporting pillars have hardwood blocks dowelled on their upper ends, and are finally fixed on by screws passing through the blocks into the bottom boards.

The joints of the tops are slip dowelled ; the pins and bores are formed on alternate sides, and are made exactly to correspond to each other in number and position. The number is usually five— one in the centre of length, from which the others are set off equidistant, two towards each end ; those nearest the ends are placed over the catch. By this arrangement it is indifferent what boards are made to join, the dowels and boards being made to fit each other in any arrangement.

In working the tops, they are first planed up, brought to the requisite thickness and breadths, and squared in the ends ; they are then surface-finished below, and clamped for the moulding ; they are afterwards carefully jointed and dowelled, and the catches put on. The fixed portions of the tops are first brought together, wrought off, and trimmed flush in ends ; the slides are then drawn out, and the leaves are individually in succession put in, wrought flush with the previous parts, reversed and adjusted in the surface and ends ; the slides are then drawn out the entire length, and all the leaves are placed in and braced together. The moulding on the edge of the top is then wrought, and finally the surface of the table is glass-papered and finished.

Small-Sized Telescope Dining Tables.

The frame and slide construction of an elliptical telescope table are shown in (*Fig.* 33). This table, at least size, is 5 feet 2 inches, by 4 feet 10 inches, and is capable of being extended to 14 feet : it

(*Fig.* 33.)

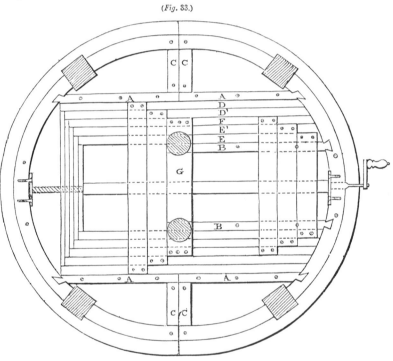

stands on six turned legs, for which two pillars with claws or blocks might be easily substituted. In this, as in the preceding example, the outer slides are shortened, on account of the ends being rounded ; consequently both designs are better suited for tables of small size than those having square ends, wherein all the slides may be of equal length. The figure presents the under side of the table, showing the position and attachment of the legs and slides, the form of the rim, and projection of the table top, drawn to a scale of ¼ of an inch to the foot. The two outside and the two inside slides, A A and B B, are fixed by screws, which pass through them into the top ; they are also dovetailed into the rim ; the outer pair is so at both extremities, and cut in the middle at the opening joint of the top, where transverse bars C C are dovetailed into the adjoining ends of the slide and rim; this supports the rim, and strengthens the parts so connected against the traction of the *screw expander*. Between the fixed slides five other pairs D D′ E E′ F are made to act; two of these D D′ move in connection with the outer fixed pair, and two, E E′, with the inner; the middle slide F is, relatively to these, stationary, and maintains the connection between them. The several pairs of moveable slides have a stretching rail dovetailed into their inner ends; these rails, as shown in the cut, come together when the slides are pushed entirely

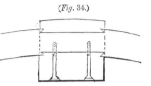

(*Fig. 34.*)

in; they are bored in the centre, so as to allow the screw to pass freely through them. A bar G is screwed to the under edges of the middle pair of slides F, into which the two centre legs are morticed; the other legs are let into the rim by regulated dovetails, and screwed from the inside, as shown in plan, (*Fig.* 34.) The mutual attachment of the slides is shown in (*Fig.* 35); those marked D and D′ are T grooved, as when drawn out they are not so well supported at their extremities as the others, which are feathered and grooved only. The slides are conveniently moved by an apparatus

(*Fig. 35.*)

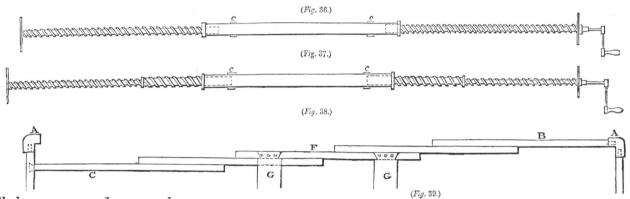

(*Fig. 36.*)

(*Fig. 37.*)

(*Fig. 38.*)

(*Fig. 39.*)

called a *screw expander*, examples of which are shown in (*Figs.* 36 and 37); these severally, are suitable for tables which extend 12 and 15 feet. This arrangement consists, essentially, of a screw and tube-nut, which are fixed centrally within the ends of the table frame, and parallel to the slides, so as to make the line of traction in the screw to be exactly at right angles to the joints of the top. The tube is fixed in position, but is free to revolve by the action of a crank handle. The screw is supported lengthwise on the top of the table pillar, or on bars crossing the table, and, in either way, secured to its place by holdfasts, which brace it down. To suit large tables, one or more additional screwed tubes are introduced; these act alternately, as nut and screw, penetrating each other like the parts of a common telescope.

Large-Sized Telescope Dining Tables.

The plan of a telescope table with square ends is shown in (*Fig.* 38), drawn to a scale of ½-inch to the

foot. The slide action of this table, when extended, is shown in (*Fig.* 39), on a scale of ¼-inch to the foot, and a cross section of the slides in (*Fig.* 40), on a scale of 1½-inch to the foot. With an equal number of slides, square-ended tables are capable of greater extension than when the ends are rounded as the curves encroach upon the length of the slides. This table is supported on four legs, A A A A, which are framed in with the ends of the rim ; the sides of the rim B B form the two outside fixed slides, and are at one end morticed into the legs ; at the other they abut against the legs opposite, and are free to pass out or in as the table is being extended or contracted. The two inside fixed slides, C C, are dovetailed into the end rail. Two cross bars G G are dovetailed into and screwed to the centre pair of slides F F ; to these last the *screw expander* is attached, and greater breadth is given to F F (*Fig.* 40), to admit of the cross bars being partially sunk into their edges. When the slides are drawn out,

(*Fig.* 40.)

they are apt to droop in the centre of their united length; to counteract this tendency they should each be wrought slightly convex on the upper edge about ⅛-inch. The sum of this convexity is considerable on the whole length ; and by thus giving an arched form to the slides, they are maintained at their proper level.

TELESCOPE TABLES.—PLATE XIX.

Fig. 1 is a design for a telescope table, in the Gothic style. The stand is so made that, on extending the table, the columns, which appear an integral part of it, are drawn away in connection with the ends, leaving the middle portion alone as the central support. The transverse block, to the ends of which the columns are adjusted, is formed of three pieces framed together ; one of these is the entire length between the columns, the two others are half lengths, and morticed into opposite sides of the first, in the same line, and at right angles to each other. All the corners of the block are plain stop-chamfered. From the extremities of the block spring four curvilinear buttresses, the upper ends of which abut against, and are dowelled to the top of a small octagonal pillar, which is introduced between them rather to form a point of attachment than as a means of support—a separate support being unnecessary. The buttresses and pillar are fixed to the table by a cross bar of hardwood, which is first dowelled down on their ends, and afterwards screwed below to the middle pair of slides, and to the rim of the table. The buttresses below must be wrought flush and square up with the ends of the base block, so that when the columns are withdrawn, the parts may present a finished appearance, as in (*Fig.* 41), a tudor rose, or other flush ornament, being carved on the extremities of the block to relieve the plainness.

Each column is in one piece throughout its length, and is clamped at the lower end to form the moulded base, the profile of which is afterwards

(*Fig.* 41.)

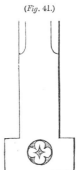

formed at once on all the columns placed together : they are left square at the upper end, where the mouldings forming the capitals are mitred round them. Before paning the shafts of the columns, the corners are chipped in the lathe, and the beads at both ends are at the same time formed. The vandyking, which overlaps like tiles on a roof, is drawn on the panes, and cut ; each lap, as shown Fig. 2, is formed by bevelling the part below it upwards and inwards. The elongated drops at the bottom of the rounded laps, formed on the alternate panes, are planted on ; they are turned from a cylinder of wood, temporarily glued together in halves, and afterwards split asunder. At their lower end the pillars present the appearance of being strongly united with the base block, by the ends of the latter passing through and projecting beyond them. This expression is given to these parts by pieces dowelled endwise on the front of the pillars, which continue the direction of the lines of dimension in the arms of the base block : before they are finally fixed, the pieces are ogeed on the ends, and separately carved. This illusion is rendered more perfect by the apparent insertion of wedges, with ornamental ends, at each side, into the neck of the projecting parts. Fig. 3 shows the moulding on the top, the square block below it is formed by clamping. On extending the table, the rim parts in three, opposite the lines of junction of the tops—the middle piece of the top being fixed and stationary. The rim is shown enlarged in Fig. 4, and has the fore angle of its lower edge stop-chamfered and wrought into a double ogee, and at the ends a leaf sunk carved. The cross rails, which form the ends of the rim, are finished below like the sides ; they are morticed between the latter, leaving the carved ends of the sides to project beyond them. As the Gothic style is rather stern and angular, depending much for its effect on bold light and shadow, oak, walnut, and our home-grown furniture woods in general, are better suited to it than mahogany, or most foreign woods, whose brilliant colour and high polish are better shown in smooth curved surfaces.

As a general rule in carving Gothic leaf ornaments, the carver should procure leaves of the tree he intends to adopt, and observing not the form of any single leaf, which may be defective, but the general form common to all, carefully follow it, exaggerating the size and relief of the large ribs and projections, and suppressing the smaller and less marked features. The sycamore or plane-tree leaf, with its pendulous fruit introduced between the interstices, is that which has been selected for this design.

Fig. 5 is a table on the same plan as the foregoing, and is shown extended. The ornamental work is a modification of the Italian style, and is carved out of the solid wood. The pillar of the stand is the chief central support, and is larger in proportion to the others than those of Fig. 1. At the bottom, it is let into and shouldered on the large ring-moulding, as marked by the dotted lines, (*a, a, Fig.* 42). This con-

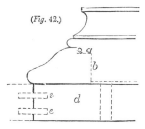

(*Fig.* 42.)

struction is necessary to strengthen the projecting lip of the hollow and bead below. The body of the pillar passes through the ring, in the line *b*, and is morticed into the circular block, *d*, on which the ring rests. Four flat stretchers are fitted and dowelled, *e, e*, to the edge of the circular block, and wrought flush with it above and below, before it is finally fixed to the pillar. The wood forming the stretchers must be sufficiently thick to allow for the relief carving on their upper side, and for the greatest diameter of the turned ends which join with the scrolled supports. A projecting moulding is formed on each end of the turned part of the stretchers, that on the extremities of the latter forms the shoulder against which the scroll joins. At their upper end, the scrolled supports are fitted and screwed into the angles of a four-sided cap, which is turned, paned, and fitted on the pillar.

When the table is closed, the bottom curve of the scrolled supports is made to abut against the hollow of the base of the columns, as in (*Fig.* 43). The stand rests on eight castors, four of which are fixed in the extremities of the scrolled supports, which, in consequence, spread suddenly out, as in (*Fig.* 44); and four are screwed to blocks, fixed under the stretchers at the line of their greatest breadth. The columns are turned, leaving sufficient wood for the carving, which, both on these and on the centre scrolls, should be in moderate relief, and carefully rounded, so as to present no hard outlines, and with scarcely any undercutting, as that would prevent the foliage from forming one harmonious mass with the curves, on which it is wrought. The upper moulding of the top is wrought on the boards; the others are

(*Fig.* 43.)

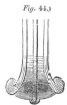

Fig. 44.)

formed on the rim, and extend the entire length of the table, the loose tops having portions of the rim continued on them.

TELESCOPE DINING TABLES—PLATE XX.

Fig. 1 is a side elevation, and Fig. 2 an end elevation, of a telescope table in the Italian style, enriched by natural foliage. A sketch plan, corresponding with Fig. 1, and showing the position and arrangement of the supports, is given in Fig. 3. The scroll supports are each of an entire piece, and require wood 5 or 6 inches thick; but for economical working, a piece to form the small scroll at bottom, with its appendage, may be dowelled on. The lower ends of the supports rest in capsules, turned and carved separately, and screwed on with the castors sunk into them. The centre part of the rail is stuffed, to serve as a foot-cushion, the ground of it being a box without bottom, the sides of which are of deal, 1 inch thick, and the ends formed of stout blocks, fixed by dowels passing through the sides. This construction admits of the rail being either spring or cushion stuffed. A small moulding which borders the stuffing is carried round the box. From the inside of the end of the box, screws are sent through into the dependent scroll of the supports, by which the latter are strongly braced to their places. Additional strength may be given to these dependent scrolls, and to their attachment to the stuffed rail, by connecting these parts by a strap of iron beneath. The scrolled supports are slightly tapered upwards, and their upper ends are dowelled to a rail, which is screwed to the under edge of the table frame. The leafage in front is carved, and lies on a double ogeed moulding; and the back is gently rounded to the band—see section, (*Fig.* 45). The centre pillar may be introduced or not, according to the length of the table. The large ring-moulding on the pillar is turned and fitted on; and the lower extremity of the pillar is paned square as a shoulder for the claws, which are dowelled on it.

(*Fig.* 45.)

Fig. 4 is a side elevation, and Fig. 5 an end elevation, of a table in the Gothic style. The legs are wrought in with the table-frame, and should not be of less than 3-inch stuff. Their edges are chamfered, either with a double ogee or plainer chamfer, according to the degree of richness required. In the centre of the rail, the chamfer is carried up, and a leaf is carved in the hollow. The end rail is carried through the top of the legs, and projects sufficiently to receive the cap of a columet, which descends the leg and pins the end of the stretcher, the drop below appearing as the end of the column. The stretcher is a solid piece, the centre being sunk down to receive an inch or so of the stuffing.

SIDE TABLES.—PLATE XXI.

Fig. 1 has the top framed of deal with a large veneered moulding carried round the front and ends; the brakes are formed on blocks planted on the ground; the scrolled ornaments are first fitted to ground and profiled, then indented into the front, and afterwards separately carved, finished, and fixed in. The shaped pillars are made of wood 2 inches thick; a band or border, ⅝-in. broad and ⅜-in. thick, is planted on both sides of each pillar. This border is projected beyond the flush of the pillars edgewise $\frac{1}{16}$-in., so as to present a border on both edges, the space inclosed by the borders on all sides, may be fretted or inlaid. The pillars are framed together side to side by three cross rails, the two lower bear the shelves, and the upper rail is dovetailed into the heads of the pillars, and screwed to cross bars fixed in the under side of the frame. The middle cross rail is morticed in; two fillets are shown on its edge, the upper one being formed by the projecting end of the shelf which rests on the rail. The front of the shelf is similarly finished by clamping below. The lower cross rail is dowelled in, and is moulded, with a check formed below, into which the shelf is screwed.

Fig. 2. The top frame is similar to Fig. 1; the moulding on it must be solid if the frets are wrought in relief, and if they are planted, the wood forming them must be glued up of three thicknesses, and cauled to the profile of the ground previous to being cut; or, better than either, the figure of the ornament may be formed by inlaying. The shaped supports may be made of two pieces, each forming one of the arched feet and pillars; the former being of solid wood 1½-inches thick, laid horizontally, the latter of fir wood of the same thickness, slipped on the edges and morticed into the feet; both are afterwards flushed off and veneered on the sides. Or otherwise the supports may be made entirely solid, and the feet dowelled to the side of the upright, in this case the scroll brackets above are wrought out of the solid. In either method, the trusses below are separately wrought and planted on. A groove is wrought on the inside of the supports to receive the ends of the arched fret; the shelf below is dowelled in between the ends. Two cross rails are dovetailed within the top frame from back to front, between which the pillars are tenoned and screwed.

Figs. 3 and 4 are similarly made. The legs are shaped out of square blocks, and wrought flush with the rails of the top frame; the large moulding is then carried round the front and ends of the frame. The cabled panels and small trusses on the squares of the legs, Fig. 3, are planted on. The spandrels on both figures are fixed to the legs and rails by screws.

RISING SIDE TABLES.—PLATE XXII.

These tables present the convenience of varying the number of shelves, by means of a telescope slide action formed in the supporting pillars. The first three examples have four shelves when drawn out, which number may with facility be reduced to three or two. Each of the supporting pillars consists of three distinct parts, and the shelves are attached to the corresponding divisions in these pillars. The lowest and middle portions are chambered, and receive within them the parts they support, so that when the table is depressed to its least height, the two upper portions of the pillar disappear, the highest part passing into that below it, and both together into the lowest part. The two upper shelves A B, (*Fig.* 46), move with the slides E F, the two lower C D, are permanently fixed; the lowest shelf is wrought into a groove and dowelled between the pillars; all the other shelves are dowelled on the ends of their supports. Openings are cut through the shelves B C, to allow the slides to pass. The slides must be fitted accurately, and made to move freely within the receiving chambers; their motion is regulated, so as to assist their easy ascent, and prevent their too rapid descent, by counterpoising weights of lead *g g g g*, cast to a convenient shape; of these there are four to each pair of slides, the sum of whose weight is equal to that of the shelf and slides together. The weights are attached to the edge of the slides, and are shaped to suit the space within which they are to act. To obtain the proper weight for each counterpoise, weigh each shelf and its two slides together, and take a quarter of this amount for the weight of a single counterpoise, there being four of them.

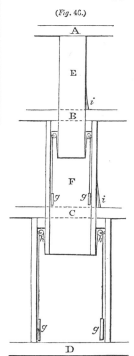

(*Fig.* 46.)

The weights are suspended by cords attached to the bottom of the slide, and are carried over pulleys *h h*, fixed in the upper end of the chamber in which the slide acts. The pulleys are of brass ½-inch diameter. Besides facility of motion, the slides must be kept from passing out, and also maintained at their proper height; the former is effected by glueing thin blocks of wood to the edge of the slides within the chamber; the latter, by springs formed of wood or steel, *i, i,* sunk in the slide behind, which, when the slide passes down is depressed, and when drawn up, starts out and rests on the top of the shelf.

Figs. 4 and 5 are a convenient combination of the dining table leaf-holder, with the rising side table. The leaf-holders here designed are cases consisting of two panelled frames, forming the front and back, bound together by a top and bottom of deal dovetailed into their edges. The front frame of Fig. 4 is wrought flush, with a raised panel planted on; the corresponding part of Fig. 5 is sunk panelled, with a moulding carried round the frame. The receiving or chambered slides of the side table are dowelled on the edge of the front, and wrought off with it. Fillets, cloth covered, are screwed on the top and bottom of the case, leaving intervals between them into which the loose table tops are slid; in Fig. 5 these interspaces are divided the whole height, by dovetailing pieces edgeways into the top and bottom. This method has the convenience of suiting any difference of breadth in the leaves. The leaf-holder is rendered more accessible by having a door at each end. The bracket and moulded pilaster on Fig. 4 are wrought together, and the lying trusses are both joined to the pilasters. The corresponding parts of Fig. 5 are wrought out of one piece. The movable shelf, in both examples, has a moulding planted on its fore edge and ends, which is of a breadth to lap down and receive the top of the leaf-holder within it, when the shelf is depressed. In Fig. 4 this is done completely; but, in Fig. 5, the upper member only of the top moulding is concealed.

DINING-ROOM CHAIRS.—PLATE XXIII.

All the designs here given have their seats fixed. Figs. 1 to 4 inclusive, have the back legs framed up parallel to each other; these, along with Fig. 8, are straight across the back; the others in the plate, as ordinarily, have the back hollowed, with the back legs diverging at their upper end.

In Fig. 1 the semicircular top is dowelled down on the legs and scroll rounded from before backwards. The panels are formed by grounding, and are rounded on the face, their field being sunk carved. The cushion behind is separately stuffed on a frame which is made to fit within the back; it is let in from behind, and fixed by screws passing through the frame into the legs. The back of the frame is then covered and gimped round the edges. The shaft of the front leg is parted by grooves, $\frac{1}{8}$-inch broad, terminating in a bore at both ends. The moulding on the seat frame is cross wrought on the squares of the legs.

In Fig. 2, the back legs at the seat rail are $2\frac{1}{2}$-inches broad. The top, which is dowelled down on them, forms the greatest breadth of the back. In framing these parts together, the proper position and exact depth of the dowel holes must be carefully attended to, so as to prevent their appearance when the looped openings on the sides are cut out. The front legs are shaped so as to spread out below, in front and on the sides; they are framed in, flush with the seat rails, the latter being clamped on their lower half, and with the legs form a ground for planting the moulding on the seat frame.

Fig. 3 has the stay in the centre of the back tenoned into the seat rail; the top is dowelled down on it, and on the legs, and afterwards cut out to figure. A small hollow moulding is carried round all the inner front margins of the chair back. The seat frame and front legs are wrought similarly to Fig. 2.

Fig. 4 has the back executed similarly to Fig. 1. The front legs are framed in with the seat rails, and the moulding on both is sunk carved or inlaid, and planted on.

Fig. 5 is framed up in the usual manner of vase-backed chairs. The seat rails are $3\frac{1}{2}$-inches broad; of this breadth $2\frac{1}{4}$-inches are of hardwood, slipped on the lower edge, with $1\frac{1}{4}$-inches of solid wood, to show as such on forming the sweeps below the seat. On their lower half the rails are cross-clamped on the face with $\frac{3}{8}$-inch solid wood, thus making the grain of the rails to run with that of the front and back legs, and affording depth of wood for grounding the triangular spaces on the adjoining parts of both; and also for forming in relief the leaf ornament on the centre of the front rail. A small hollow moulding may be formed on the inside corners of the legs, and continued around the under edge of the seat rails on the sides and front.

Fig. 6, the back is framed up similarly to Fig. 5. Its projecting sides, formed by pieces dowelled on the legs, are curved forward so as to sweep with the stay and top rails: the latter is dowelled on the legs after the side pieces are put on. A raised bead or fillet is carried round the inner margin of the back. The seat frame is made separately from the fore legs; the latter are checked and shouldered in front, under the edge of the frame, and pass up within it behind, and are there glued and screwed.

Fig. 7 is in all respects wrought like Fig. 5. The top is dowelled to the legs at the point of their greatest width, so as to give sufficient strength to the frame. The stay, from its deep curvature, requires to be fitted and framed up without resistance or strain, as it would otherwise be easily fractured.

Fig. 8 has the back wrought separately of a single piece, similar to a hall chair. The interior of the back is grounded down around the margin of the cushion, which is highly stuffed on the solid wood. The seat rails require to be $3\frac{1}{2}$-inches broad, for sweeping out below. They *(Fig. 47.)* are cross clamped with $\frac{3}{8}$-inch wood on the under half, similar to Figs. 5 and 7. The bead on the front rail is wrought on the solid. The manner in which the front leg must be framed in is shown in (*Fig.* 47).

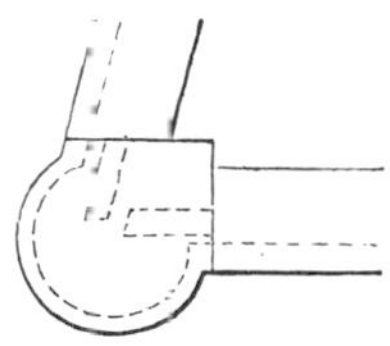

DINING-ROOM CHAIRS.—PLATE XXIV.

The designs in this Plate are, in their outline and general construction, similar to vase-backed chairs; and, excepting Fig. 3, are all loose seated.

Fig. 1.—A projecting moulding, carried round the seat frame, is planted on the rails, and cross wrought on the squares of the legs, which, before being framed up, are pieced out by ⅜-inch clamps on the front and sides, to form the projection.

Fig. 2 has the panel in the back made of solid wood ⅝-inch thick, with a raised border in front ⅜-inch deep, planted around its sides and bottom; the top portion of the band, along with the carving, requires 1-inch wood. The panel is let in from behind, and made to join with the apparent stay, the ends of which are formed on the legs; it is fixed by screws or dowels passing through the apparent stay, and through the seat and top rails. The back cushion is stuffed on a loose panel ½-inch thick, previously fitted within the band on the ground panel, and fixed by screws sent through the latter from behind.

Fig. 3.—In this example the top rail is not cut through but grounded at the ends, where the marginal moulding inside is carved and scrolled. The back stay is shown as in advance of the legs, its scrolled ends being carved on them, and its middle portion shouldered between; or otherwise, the stay may be of one piece, separately carved, and grounded on the legs, and on another stay framed between them. The seat rails are shaped out, and clamps ½-inch thick, of a corresponding form, are planted on them. The truss legs are carved after being morticed and adjusted to the seat rails.

Fig. 4 has the frame of the back cushion let in from behind, and fitted between the seat and top rails, to which and to the legs it is screwed from behind.

Fig. 5 has the back panel fitted, finished, fixed, and stuffed, similarly to Fig. 2. The carved ornament on the front rail is profiled, then indented; separately carved, and lastly glued down.

Fig. 6.—The top rail joins down on the legs at the greatest breadth of the back, forming with them the carved shoulders of the side scrolls. The looped openings are afterwards cut out, and the border of the cushion is formed in relief on the legs. The triangular space between the seat, scroll, and band below, is not perforated. Fillets are screwed on the inside of the legs to carry the stuffing. The back is cloth covered.

Fig. 7 has the back stay framed in, leaving a space between it and the seat rail for the stuffing of the seat to pass. The frame for the back cushion (*Fig.* 48), is fitted between the legs; at the top it is shaped so as to support the general outline of the stuffing, and is fixed by dowels *a, a,* to the scrolled ends of the legs, below; it is dowelled to the stay at *b,* and on the sides screwed to the legs at *c, c, c, c.*

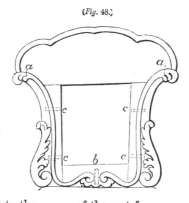

(*Fig.* 48.)

The truss legs are dowelled to the corner of the seat frame.

Fig. 8, in the back, is made similarly to fig. 7. The cushion frame extends down to, and is dowelled on the back rail of the seat. The seat moulding is wrought similar to that of fig. 1.

CHAIRS.—PLATE XXV.

The designs on this Plate are well suited for either the dining-room or the library. The contour of the first three examples approaches that of the hall chair, to which, with minor modifications, they might be easily adapted. Fig. 4, besides its fitness for the dining-room, presents the chief elements of the devotional chair. They are all loose seated.

Figs. 1, 2, and 4, have the back cushion stuffed on a panel ½-inch thick, previously fitted within a raised border, ⅜-inch deep, formed on a ground panel, which last, in Figs. 1 and 2, is framed in between the pillars. The corresponding part of Fig. 4 is dowelled from under the seat rail, and from above fixed by screws passing through the semicircle. The loose panels are fixed to the others by screws passing through from behind.

Fig. 1.—The semicircular top is turned and chamfered on the outer and inner edges; a moulding is mitred round its ends, where it joins down on the columns. When the semicircle is in its place and before it is fixed, the pieces forming the frets are accurately fitted in, then lined out and fretted. The frets are finished and fixed on before the semicircle is finally dowelled on the pillars. A screw passing through the top of the semicircle, connects the cushion frame with it.

Fig. 2.—The semicircle is turned and planted on the face of the ground panel of the back. The back legs may be made the entire length, or the part surmounting the capitals of the columns may be dowelled on.

Fig. 3 has the back rail of the seat pieced with solid wood, and made of sufficient breadth to admit of its upper edge being wrought in with the band, around the inside of the back legs. The back cushion is stuffed on a frame previously fitted in; it is fixed by screws. The truss legs are dowelled to blocks fitted within the corners of the seat frame.

Fig. 4.—The capitals of the spiral columns are separately turned and carved; they are fixed by pins, turned on the ends of the spiral columns, which pass through them into the semicircle. The front feet at the top are projected so as to recess the seat rails $\frac{3}{16}$-inch.

EASY CHAIRS.—PLATE XXVI.

Easy chairs, as their name imports, are especially adapted to those sedentary and reclining attitudes of person which are most favourable to repose or relaxation. They are usually large, low-seated, and spring-stuffed, with a sloping back. In executing Figs. 1 to 4 inclusive, thin profile moulds of the front and back legs and haunch rails are at first made, and according to these, the wood for the chair is lined out full, on the board. When sawn out and faced up, the wood is again more accurately lined, and the framing-shoulders, with the position and length of all the mortices, previously marked on the moulds, are set off on it. A little over wood is left on the profile of the legs, above and below the several side mortices, which is wrought off after the sides are framed together. When the legs are shaped out, they should be carefully adjusted, parallel to each other, across the haunch mortices. This is necessary to preserve the seat frame parallel, and, besides, from the great length of the back legs, a slight inaccuracy at the seat rails becomes, when the chair is framed up, increased, and quite apparent at the top of the back.

Fig. 1.—The frets are dowelled down on the haunch rails, and are fixed above, by screws passing through the elbow rails, after the latter have been framed into the back legs. The seat cushion may be either fixed or loose; if the former, fillets must be screwed to the inside of the haunch rails to carry the stuffing; for a similar purpose, fillets are fitted between the cross rails of the back; they are screwed along the side of the back legs, following their general outline, but narrower, so as to form a uniform check for the stuffing; if the seat cushion be loose, a separate frame resting on the back and front rails of the seats, as in ordinary cases, is required to support the stuffing.

Fig. 2.—The front legs and elbow stumps are of one piece, and, so also, the back legs; the latter, however, may be formed of two pieces, butt-joined in the line of the seat, and dowelled together. The elbow rails are framed in with the sides of the chair. A panel, cloth covered, is let into the space between the seat and elbow rails; it is supported behind by fillets, screwed on the rails, forming a check for its sides. The circular ends of the panel lap on the elbow stumps and back leg, which are grounded down. A moulding, which laps on the panel, is planted around the space between the rails. The fret, after being completely finished, is screwed on the face of the panel.

Fig. 3.—The scrolled elbow stumps are dowelled down on the seat rail; on the top of these the elbow rails, on being framed into the back legs, are screwed down. The space between the side rails is filled by a cloth-covered panel, around which, and lapping on it, a moulding, planted on the rails, is carried.

Fig. 4.—In tapering the front feet, downwards, the scrolls on both sides of the toe, are wrought in relief below, and on the turn at the hinder part of the leg, upwards, terminating in a leaf ornament under the seat rail; the extremity of the leaf is formed by piecing it out below the rail. The elbow rail is formed of two thicknesses, the lower of which is solid and made to project, forming with that above it, a check for the stuffing; the projection is rounded into a bead, which, at the inner end, joins in, with a similar moulding planted round the opening between the seat and elbow rails.

Fig. 5 is circular in the back, with the fore feet set obliquely to the front. The general method of construction is shown in (*Fig.* 49.) The front rail is fitted and clamped with solid wood, on a hardwood ground; it shoulders with the feet in the lines *a*, *a*. The back feet *b*, *b*, are framed up between the ends of the circular seat rails, being dowelled in. Two hardwood standards, *c*, *c*, forming a part of the back frame, are strongly tenoned into the back feet, before the latter are framed up. The standards are made to incline back at the top, an amount depending on the profile form given to the back. A hollowed cross rail, *d*, is dowelled down on the standards; on this the top rail of the chair is glued down. The moulded band, which borders the stuffing, extending from the leafage on the top to the front feet, is formed of three pieces; the part forming the elbow stump, joins down on the foot, at the line *e*, and unites with that on the elbow rail, at the joint *f*; this part, in the order of work, is first dowelled on; it is clamped behind with deal, and receives into it below, at the back, the stuffing rail *g*; and above, the elbow rail is checked into it and into the standard *c*; on this rail the part *f*, *i*, is clamped, and at the line *i* it unites with the ascending side piece *i*, *k*, which last is clamped with deal and dowelled to the standard *c*, and receives down on it the ornamental top rail. The top rail and the band, down to the line, *f*, require 2½-in.

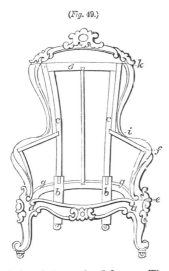

(*Fig.* 49.)

solid wood; the elbow stumps, from *f* to *e*, require 3-in. wood. All the carving is executed after the chair is framed together.

Fig. 6.—The front is framed up, and all the parts of it are carved at the same time. The elbow, scroll, and leg are of one piece, requiring 3¼-in. wood. Standards are inserted into the hind feet, to form the back framing, as in Fig. 5; on the sides and top of these the pieces forming the carving are dowelled.

TABLE AND CHAIR LEGS.—PLATE XXVII.

In this Plate are shown, Figs. 1 to 5, designs of turned and truss legs for hall and other tables, with the depth of framing and form of top and rail moulding proper to each; and Figs. 7 to 12, designs of chair legs, the larger and more massive suitable for oak or mahogany; the smaller and lighter, for rosewood or satinwood.

Fig. 1 has the ball of the leg formed of a separate piece, which is indented, turned, and then paned; the small panels on the panes may be formed in relief, or they may be face moulded in one piece together, then profiled separately and indented. The buttons on the band on the top of the shaft are let in with a bore, and the dart shaped ornaments below are indented.

Fig. 2 has the profile of the carving on the ball, formed in the lathe. The shield on the square of the leg, and the panels on its lower extremity are planted on.

Fig. 3 has the ball of the leg square wrought. The leg is first wrought out in the lathe immediately above the ball, and below it, from the drop downwards, leaving a square block from which the ball with its appended decorations is profiled.

Fig. 4 requires not less than 3½-in. wood. On being profiled, it should be adjusted and fitted to the frame before being carved; it is attached to the frame in the ordinary manner.

Fig. 5 has a check cut out of the top of the truss, on the bottom of which the table frame rests; this part extends backwards, and is carved and wrought in with a moulding under the rail. The frame abuts against the side of the check, which part is wrought into the carved foliage, that curves out under the top moulding. The ear-shaped opening on the side is not perforated, but grounded down.

Fig. 6, from its form and plainness, is suitable for satinwood (which, from its light colour, does not shade well in small mouldings, or surface carving), but may also be made of mahogany, if the diameter measures of the design are enlarged.

Figs. 7, 9, 11, and 12, are best adapted for oak, but the first three may also be made of mahogany. Fig. 12 is for a hall chair, and is alternately square wrought, and turned along its length, from the bead under the rail to the top of the shaft; the leg is turned, and the ball paned. The shaft, with the drapery on it, is profiled square, and the latter afterwards carved on the face; the drops below are indented. Fig. 8 and 10 are for drawing-room chairs, and should be of rosewood, walnut, or satinwood.

SOFAS.—PLATE XXVIII.

All the figures here have the seats square framed, with the hind feet turned, and the backs separately wrought and screwed on. Figs. 2 and 3 have the hind feet shaped and framed in, with the rounded corners. The backs are fixed, being wrought on the frame.

Fig. 1.—The elbow stumps are dowelled down on the feet, with an incline back of 4 inches at the top; below they are square with the feet, and recede $\frac{1}{8}$-in. from the flush, on the front and sides; towards the top they gradually wind outwards to give the top scroll an overlay at the ends of the sofa. The stumps require solid wood, $3\frac{1}{2}$-in. thick, and are clamped behind with deal. Two pieces of hardwood, $1\frac{3}{4}$-in. thick, *a*, (*Fig.* 50), corresponding in facial outline, and breadth, with the stumps, are dowelled on the back feet, with an incline backwards of $2\frac{1}{2}$ inches at the top. The back, on being screwed to these pieces, receives a corresponding slope with them. Three cross bars, *b, c, d,* are fitted between the front and back stumps; the upper bar, *b*, is checked in, and nailed down on the stumps, forming the elbow; the others are let into grooves; the lowest bar, *d*, is kept $1\frac{1}{2}$-in. above the seat rail; to this the cloth in stuffing the end of the sofa is nailed. The frame for the back is made of deal 1 in. thick, and consists of two long rails *e, f,* and four cross ones, of which *g, h,* are two. The end bar, *g*, is made flush with the outer edge of the stumps *a*, to which it is screwed. The moulding on the back is planted on the face, and the upper edge of the back is veneered. The hind feet are made to stand out beyond the back rail $\frac{3}{4}$-in.; on this projection the back is made to rest.

(*Fig.* 50.)

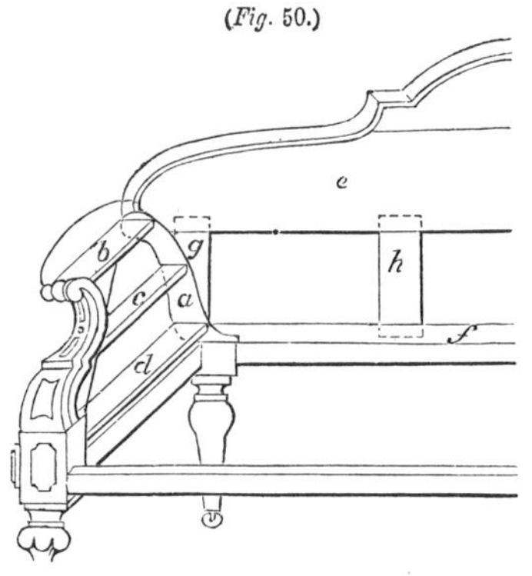

Fig. 2.—The ends of the frame towards the back are carved of a parabolic form, which in outline sweeps with the position given to the elbow scrolls. The mould for working the ends may be easily traced by the hand, but if greater accuracy is required, a parabola may be drawn, by the method of ordinates, whose diameter and altitude are severally 24 and 18 inches, the vertical half of which curve is the form given to the ends of the sofa (*see* Practical Geometry, page 51). The elbow scrolls are dowelled down on the feet with an incline backwards of 5 inches at the top. They have a face breadth of $3\frac{1}{2}$-inches, with a depth of 14 inches. The hind legs *a* (*Fig.* 51), are dowelled between the adjoining ends of the back and end rails *b, c.* A standard *d*, which forms a part of the back frame, is strongly tenoned into each leg, having an incline backwards of $2\frac{1}{2}$-inches at the top. The top rail of the back, *e*, is morticed down on these standards, and also on two others that are framed into the back rail of the seat. The elbow is built on a curved rail *g*, the ends of which are checked into the back of the elbow scroll, and standard *d*. The pieces *h*, after being butt-joined to the standard, and glued down on the rail *g*, are fixed at the ends by dowels sent obliquely through them into the standard. The whole is then wrought off, and the joinings are overlaid with pieces of canvas, saturated with glue. Stuffing rails *i, i, i,* are carried round, parallel to, and $1\frac{1}{2}$-inch above, the back and ends of the seat frame; these have their ends inserted into the back of the elbow scroll, into the top of the back leg *a*, and into the framing of the back *f.*

(*Fig.* 51.)

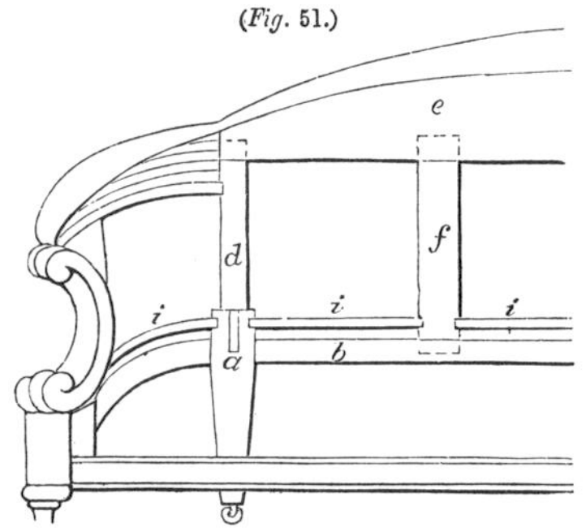

Fig. 3 has the ends wrought similarly to Fig. 2. Two upright pieces, terminating the curve of the ends, are morticed between the seat and elbow rails: the latter are dowelled down on the top of the balusters.

Fig. 4 has each of the front feet, with the elbow stumps, of one piece. On the feet being turned, the front half of the parts forming the stumps are sawn down, and cross-cut above the square of the foot; the exposed surfaces are cleaned, and the detached pieces are temporarily glued together, turned, carved, and polished; then split asunder, and planted on the parts from which they were originally cut. In other respects this example is finished similarly to Fig. 1.

Sofas.—Plate XXIX.

The upper design is framed in the usual manner. The moulding on the seat rails and back is similar in character, being rounded, (as shown in the section figure), and planted on the face. The elbow stump has an incline back of $2\frac{1}{4}$-inches at the top; its appearance from above, along with its connections, is shown in a separate figure, on an enlarged scale. The decorations on all these parts are intended to be formed by inlaying, but a somewhat similar effect may be produced by grounding and sunk carving.

The lower figure has the spiral pillar and front foot of one piece. The fore-edge of the end stuffing is attached to a plane pilaster, behind the pillar, and tenoned into, and between the seat and elbow rails, as shown in section. The scrolled cap of the pillar is separately carved and dowelled on.

Sofas.—Plate XXX.

In the upper design, the seat being first framed up, the ends are then formed, and the back is afterwards separately made, and fixed by screws. The elbow scrolls are $1\frac{1}{2}$-inch thick, and clamped on a hardwood ground; after being carved they are dowelled down on the feet. An ogee presented obliquely to the front, as shown in section A, is formed on the face of the scroll: (*Fig.* 52) shows the latter in section, where they join down on the feet. The centre ornament of the back, with the moulding on which it rests, is formed of one piece, $2\frac{1}{4}$-inch thick, which extends to, and mitres with the hollowed sweep of the end portions of the moulding. These last are $\frac{7}{8}$-in. thick, and planted on the face, or otherwise, as shown in section C, the centre ornament may be dowelled on; the recurved ends of the leafage being separately made, carved, and indented.

(*Fig.* 52.)

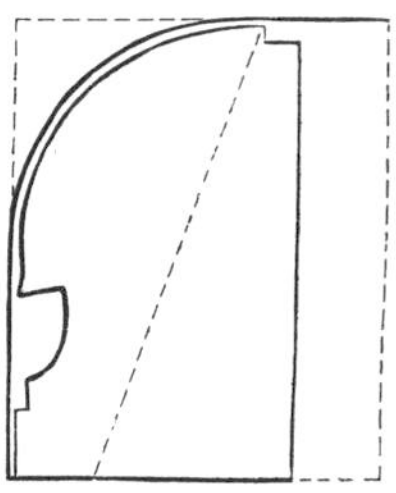

(*Fig.* 53.)

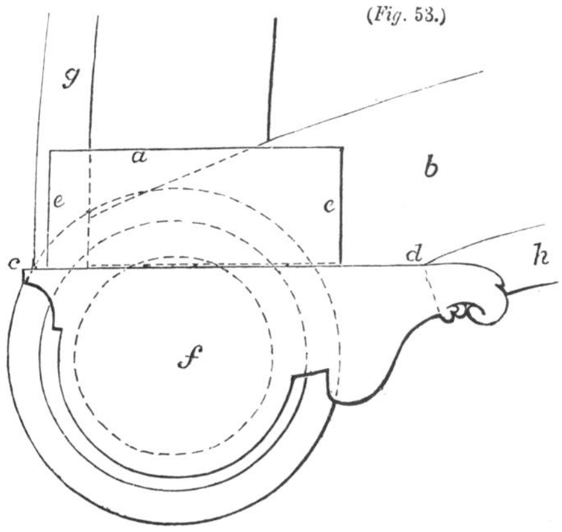

The lower design has the framing of the back, and of the seat behind, made as described under Plate XXVIII. A method of framing up the scrolls and front feet is shown in (*Fig.* 53).

The end rail, *a*, is joined on behind, and dowelled to the front rail *b*. The corner so formed, is cut off in the line *c*, *d*. The hardwood ground, *e*, *e*, of the scroll is dowelled down parallel to the line *c*, *d*, and flush with the centre corners, thus forming, with the depth of the seat rails, a ground on which the elbow scrolls are clamped and dowelled. The scrolls require 3-inch wood, and the moulding on them is shown in section G. The bottom of the elbow scroll is wrought off flush with the under edge of the seat rails, and the feet are dowelled to them; the position of the feet is indicated by the lines on the wood-cut, and the form and depth of the carving on them in section F. The clamp forming the moulding on the front rail is fitted, glued down, and wrought before the elbow scrolls are fixed on; it is made in two lengths, which are butt-joined in the middle behind the centre ornament. The elbow scrolls abut on the ends of the rail moulding, and the small scrolls terminating the latter are wrought on the former. The carved ornament on the centre of the front rail is formed of two pieces, joined vertically in the centre, and indented; it is shown in section E.

Sofas.—Plate XXXI.

The upper design has the seat frame dovetailed together in the fore corners, and the feet glued and screwed on after: or, otherwise, the front rail may be framed in between the extremities of the end rails, and the latter then tenoned into the front feet. The hind feet are framed up with the seat rails. The elbow scrolls, and the ends of the sofa, are wrought like those of Fig. 1, Plate XXVIII. The flowers which hang from the scrolls are, after being carved, partially indented into their place and dowelled on. The front and end rails are similarly finished, but the latter are not recessed; they are ground, veneered, or clamped, with thin wood, and, when polished, the fret, which is $\frac{5}{16}$-inch thick, is then glued down; the ornamental lentils and dots are afterwards planted on. A projecting square fillet is planted on the upper edge of the rail, and a torus, or other moulding, on the lower. The centre of the back, extending, on both sides, to the curve of the moulding beyond the leafage, is wrought from one piece of solid wood, 3 inches thick; the further portions of the moulding mitre in with the centre, and are planted on the face, and veneered on the top. The ring surrounding the head may be turned and planted on; the ornaments on its edge may be shaped facially, in the lathe, and then profiled. The head is separately carved, and, when finished, is screwed on from behind.

The lower design has the upper end of the front feet checked down to the ground of the carving; they are then framed in flush with the ground of the seat rail. The front and end rails are similarly finished; the enriched round moulding on them is separately wrought of $\frac{1}{8}$-inch solid wood; it extends the whole length and breadth of the frame, and is planted on; the border, on both edges of the round, being mitred and glued down after. The scrolls adjoining the feet, and below the rail, are separately carved and screwed on. The elbow scrolls are made of 1-inch wood, clamped on a ground of hardwood, the flowers suspended by an apparent ring, from the scrolls, are fitted to the latter, and fixed by dowels. The carving on the back is of one entire piece, 3½-inches thick, extending on each side to the mitre angle, at the extremity of the leafage; the further parts are mitred in and planted on. This design may be executed either in mahogany or in rosewood; if, in the latter, the thickness of the material employed may be less than that above indicated, and the recessed and delicate parts of the carving may be hatched in gold, or gilt.

Details of Sofas.—Plate XXXII.

Figs. 1 to 5, have the front of the sofa first formed. The hardwood grounds for the elbow scrolls are checked in flush with the face, and also shouldered on the upper edge, of the end of the seat rail, where they are glued and screwed. The feet, which are solid, are dowelled on the under edge of the rail, and also flush with it in front. These parts serve as a flat and a uniform ground for the clamps of solid wood which form the carving.

In Fig. 1, the elbow and foot are clamped with one piece, which unites to the adjoining part on the seat rail previously glued down; from the cant given to the scroll above, and the form of the foot at the bottom, the thickness of wood required is 1¾-inch; that on the rail being $\frac{7}{8}$-inch.

Fig. 2 is wrought similarly to Fig. 1, and of wood 1¼-inch thick. In this example the foot need not be clamped, but made of the entire thickness, and projected in the framing, beyond the ground of the adjoining parts, an amount equal to the thickness of the clamps on them. The clamps of the rail and scroll abut together, and join down on the foot.

Fig. 3. The clamp, on the elbow and foot, consists of two pieces; that, on the former, joins to the rail at the lower extremity of the wing; that on the foot has its upper end, on which the leafage is formed, scribed into the clamps on the rail. The trefoil figure in the centre of the foot, from the neck upwards, is a separate piece, which is first profiled and indented into the rail, and the line of depth, for the carving, accurately marked on its edges; it is then detached, carved, and finally fixed in its place. Wood, 4-inch thick, is required for the elbow, and 1½-inch thick for the clamp on the foot.

Fig. 4 is clamped similarly to Figs. 1 and 2, and requires 2-inch wood. The flower festoon, which overlies and hangs from the neck of the scroll, and the eagle's beak, may either be carved on the solid, or procured, in embossed leather or gutta percha, from the manufacturers of these articles.

Fig. 5 is wrought in the same manner as the foregoing, requiring also wood 2 inches thick. The column is half thickness, and is planted on the recessed ground of the scroll, the lower members on it mitre in with the moulding on the front rail.

Fig. 6 has the feet framed in flush with the ground of the rails, and the moulding on the latter is carried round the front and the ends. The scrolls are dowelled down on the rails.

Figs. 7, 8, and 9 are the free ends of rosewood couch backs, the solid wood is feathered, or dowelled end on, to the deal framing of the back, and extends below the bottom line of the carving about 3 inches, so as to present the latter above the seat cushion. The thicknesses of wood required for these severally are 2-inch, 1¾-inch, and 2¼-inches. Corresponding to each of these, and immediately below them, on the Plate, are three examples of couch feet; they are framed up with the seat rails, the mouldings on which are wrought in with the carving on the feet.

Figs. 10 to 14, inclusive, are examples of the fore feet and elbow scrolls of rosewood couches, with the front rails shown in cross section. The foot and scroll in all these, excepting Fig. 11, are together formed of one piece. The projecting leafage, overlieing the rail, or under it, as in Figs. 10, 13, and 14, is indented or fitted on, after the parts are framed up. The thickness of wood for these varies from 3½ to 4 inches.

LIBRARY FURNITURE.

The library, the name of which sufficiently indicates its distinctive use, may be described as the gentlemen's drawing-room; for, as the ladies receive their friends in the drawing-room, the gentlemen, in like manner, generally receive those visitors having business with themselves individually, in the library. As a matter of convenience, also, on occasions when the formalities of fashion may with propriety be merged in the free and easy intercourse of friendship, that apartment is not unfrequently converted for the time being into a drawing-room, and still oftener it is used also as a parlour. Consequently, it should be alike free from the heavy stateliness of the dining-room, or the gaudy and formal, because studied, disorder or negligence of the drawing-room; but nevertheless allied somewhat to the one in its sober hues, and to the other in the richness rather than the lightness of its furniture. By this means its protean character will be well maintained; and by keeping the decorative always in subjection to the useful, it will be rendered, what it ought to be, the most comfortable room in the dwelling. Oak is a favourite wood for the furniture of the library, and suits admirably for carrying out the character of the room above indicated; but mahogany, rosewood, &c., may likewise be used, according to taste; that employed in making the book-case determining the general character of all the other pieces of furniture.

It may be observed, however, that in some houses the library forms one of the drawing-room suite of apartments; opening into it, when occasion demands, by folding doors. In such cases the woods employed in making the book-cases and the general decorations of the room, though they ought not to be the same as those of the drawing-room, should, in every respect, harmonize with the furnishings of that apartment. By following such a course, not only is a great scope allowed for the exercise of taste, but a unity of design and feeling is maintained throughout the series of apartments, contributing, in a high degree, to produce that pleasing elegance which ought to be the aim of all concerned in the furnishing and embellishing of a house.

BOOK-CASES.—PLATE XXXIII.

Figs. 1 and 2, are designs of book-cases, similar in plan, but differing in the details of ornament. The body, or carcass of each, is formed in two heights, connected together by a framed surbase, interposed between them, to which they are severally screwed. Each of these main divisions, again, consists of three distinct parts, which are separately made and screwed together. The outside gables, with the exposed parts of the others, are of solid wood; all the rest being of deal. Previous to framing the carcasses, and after the wood for them is surface wrought, it assists accuracy and expedition in working to set off the full and exact profile of the whole job, with that of the mouldings and other parts, on a slip of deal; and, at the same time, the cross measures over the gables, doors, and pilasters, on a single rod; this serves as a sure reference for measurements, and as a constant check on the accuracy of the work. The doors of the upper centre carcass are hinged to the gables; the left hand door is shut by slip bolts, sunk in the ends and edge of the inner stile, which pass into perforated brass plates sunk into the cornice and surbase. The right hand door locks on the left; the line of junction in Fig. 1 is concealed by an ornamental bead, planted on the right door, which projects ¾-inch, and is checked to lap on the adjoining stile of the left. The doors on the wings lock on the gables of the centre which projects beyond the former 3-inches. All the pilasters, on the upper part, are attached to the doors; the stiles of the latter being made of sufficient breadth as a ground for them. Before being glued to the doors the pilasters are veneered and polished on the face; and the bordered frets, when finished, are planted on them, to conceal the joints; the inner edges are then slipped with veneer. After the pilasters are planted on, they, along with the doors, are flushed and veneered on the outer edges. In Fig. 2, the pilasters are ornamented with small panels and rosettes, the former being veneered with rich wood, and inlaid. The doors are glazed, either with a single plate in each, or as represented in the drawing with several; in which last case, the astragals are mitred into the stile mouldings, and grooved and feathered behind, to form the checks for the glass. With a view to strength, the slips or feathers are glued into the grooves, with their ends inserted into the back of the stile moulding, and also fitted tightly between the stiles. The doors on the under part of both designs are sunk panelled. The panels of Fig. 2 are inlaid, those of Fig. 1 have a raised, sunk carved, or inlaid panel planted on them. A raised border is formed on the body of the pilasters, within which the carving, after being finished, is, in both cases, planted; that of Fig. 1 is fixed by screws passing through the pilaster from behind. The two outside pilasters, on each design, are fixed to the doors; the two inside are fixed to the centre carcass; the ground, for the latter, is formed by the frame, to which the curtain and fringe are attached. This frame is made of deal, 1-inch thick, and consists of two upright stiles, and one cross rail at top; the stiles are sunk flush into the fore edges of the top and bottom of the carcass, within which the frame, after being shaped out and slipped with veneer on its inner edge, is fitted and blocked behind: the frame is then veneered on the face. The fringe is attached to the inside of the frame, and the curtain is suspended from rings which move on an iron rod, the ends of which are bent, and made to hook into staples or eyes, screwed on the frame within. The enclosed space is designed for depositing maps, globes, specimens, &c. The inside of the book-case is provided with movable shelves, resting on serrated racks or on pins, attached to, or inserted loose, into the gables. Two varieties of the former, along with one of the latter, method of support are shown in (*Fig.* 54). The first consists of pairs of toothed slips, *a, a,* 1¼-inch broad by

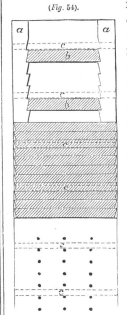

(*Fig.* 54).

$\frac{3}{8}$-inch thick, exactly similar to, and equidistant from, each other, that are glued on along the insides of each pair of gables, and flush with their fore and back edges. Cross bars b, b, of the same thickness, bearing the shelves c, c, are fitted between the slips, and made to rest on the projecting teeth. The slips are prepared from a single piece by a plane for the purpose. The other method is by serrating the gable the entire breadth, by means of the plane referred to, and bevelling the ends of the shelves c, c, to fit; here the wood of the gables should be not less than 1-inch thick, and of Bay mahogany. The same sort of wood is most suitable for the gables when the shelves are supported on pins, as the bores for them are more smooth and resisting. The pin holes should be equidistant, and similar in height on both gables, and to stand out $\frac{1}{2}$-inch, with their exposed ends slightly rounded.

The books in the shelves are arranged in a decreasing scale from below up; the largest books occupying the bottom shelves, and the next less those in succession upwards; the propriety of this arrangement is obvious. From the particulars of the length and breadth of the largest books, along with the required number of ranges, the absolute dimensions of the book-case are deduced; these being conditions which must be fulfilled whatever modifications the views of stability in the structure or elegance in the design may require. The usual dimensions and sorts of books are the following:—

Large folio, 18 × 14 in.	Large 8vo, 10 × 7 in.	Large 18mo, 7 × 5 in.
Small do., 16 × 11½ „	Small do., 9 × 6 „	Small do., 5½ × 4½ „
Large 4to, 14 × 10 „	Twelves, 8 × 5 „	Large 32mo, 5 × 3½ „
Small do., 11½ × 9 „	Small do., 7½ × 4½ „	Small do., 4½ × 3 „

The base, surbase, and cornice, are each, in both examples, framed up the entire length. The base proper is that part which is the ground support in the direct line of descending pressure; from the cornice downwards, solid below solid is the true principle of construction. The ornamental parts are mechanically non-essential, but are superadded for the purposes of beauty and effect.

Book-Cases.—Plate XXXIV.

Fig. 1 has the body or centre of the book-case recessed 3 inches; the doors, on this part, are, in consequence, pivot hinged. In (*Fig.* 55), this method of hinging is shown, as it appears on removing the cornice. A and B are the carcasses of the centre part and wing, which are screwed together; C, C′, are, respectively, the door when shut and open; e, is the pivot, or pin on which it turns, which is tightly driven into the door stile, in the centre of its thickness: it passes through,

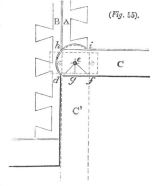

(*Fig.* 55).

and is supported by a small brass plate sunk into the wood. The position of the pin is exactly determined by the half thickness of the door stile, and by the length of the side of a right angled isosceles triangle, d, e, f, whose perpendicular height, g, e, is equal to that half thickness. A gauge set to these measures in succession, and run on the end of the stile, from its face and edge, will give, where the lines intersect, the proper point for inserting the pivot. The stile on its outer edge, d, h, is rounded to the radius e, d; it describes the curve, d, h, i, on the door being opened or shut. This curve is wrought out of the adjoining gables of the centre A, and of the wing B, on the edge and side of these severally. It may be

convenient to screw the gables first together, and draw the curve on the parts at once by a mould. The curve may be freely wrought out, but as exactly as is compatible with the smooth action of the door; for by giving too much space in the curve, the door stile in the centre being unsupported, is apt to yield backwards, and expose the joint in front. On the book-case being temporarily screwed together, the base, surbase, and cornice, are centred for the door pivots by means of a veneer mould of the door top applied to the parts. The pins pass through, and are secured to their place, by brass plates sunk into the wood.

The upper doors have their mouldings checked and lapped on the frame: the rounded corners of the moulding are turned, and butt-joined with the other parts. As these doors are glazed, each with a single plate of glass, they must act smoothly; their framing must be perfectly parallel, and made of wood not liable to warp. A bead, screwed on, is carried round within the door frame behind the plates, keeping them in their place; it should first be temporarily screwed on, and a slip of wood, the exact thickness of the plate, made to pass round the frame, gauging the space between the door moulding and the bead, wherever the screws are inserted. On the screws being withdrawn, and the bead removed, the plate is put in, and the bead is then replaced, and finally screwed on. The under doors, on the wings, are flush panelled, and the mouldings on these, and on the centre doors, are planted on the face. Panels, cloth covered, are shown behind the frets. The cornices on the wings are separately made; that on the centre being a detached piece, fixed to its place by screws passing through a block glued on it behind; or otherwise, the several cornices may be framed together, the centre one being tenoned between those on the wings, and the under moulding carried round the whole. The carved ornament requires 2½-inch wood in the centre, and is dowelled on. The circular pediment on the wings are dowelled on; they, along with the vases at their ends, should recede from the front to the line of the cornice frieze; if, in this position, from the projection of the cornice mouldings, the pediments appear too low, they may be raised by blocks, or by increasing their breadth on the under edge. The mouldings which border the pediments are turned, and with the other ornaments in front, are planted on the face.

Fig. 2.—All the pilasters on this design are inlaid with a raised border; those on the wings are attached to the door frames. The centre is without doors; the pilasters on it, after being finished, are dowelled on the edge of the middle divisions; similar half pilasters are fixed on the gables of the upper part; the rounded corner and cross mouldings being planted on after the pilasters are glued down. The exposed shelving in the centre may be draped with cloth. The curtains below, with the rods from which they hang, are treated as those of Fig. 2, Plate XXXIII.

Book-Case.—Plate XXXV.

In the execution of this design, the body, or carcass work, is similar to that of the foregoing. The middle portion of the book-case is projected beyond the wings 3 inches; the pilasters on it are fixed to the gables; those above are grounded on haffits to which the doors are hinged, and on their outer edge finished flush with the latter, and with the gables. Corresponding haffits are fixed on the adjoining gables of the wings; these, from oversight have been omitted in the drawing. The paneling, and other decorations on the shaft of the pilaster, are $\frac{5}{16}$-inch thick. The under middle doors are hinged to the pilasters, those on the wings, above and below, to the gables. The under doors are sunk panelled: the frets on those in the middle part are $\frac{3}{8}$-inch thick; the ornamental panels on the others are $\frac{1}{4}$-inch thick, and have a border formed on them by bevelling the edges. Sections of the cornice and base mouldings are presented in figs. 56, and 57: the panels, on the frieze of the cornice, are $\frac{5}{8}$-inch thick. The vases, on the top, are fixed in the perpendicular line of the frieze; their under part must be of sufficient height to bring them full into view, as seen from the front. The top ornament is clamped on the face, for the centre scroll work, on a ground $\frac{7}{8}$-inch thick.

(*Fig.* 56.)

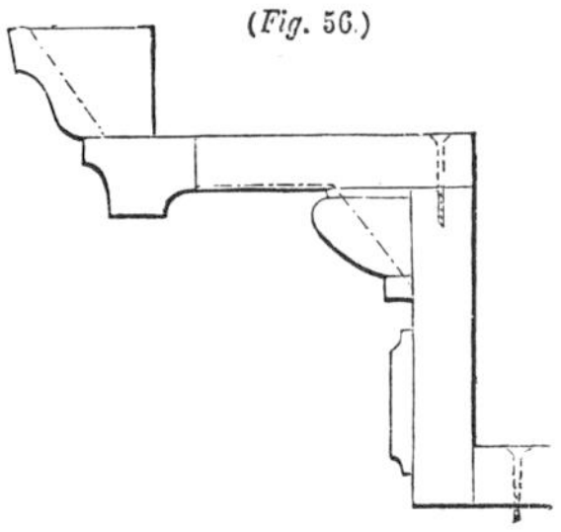

(*Fig.* 57.)

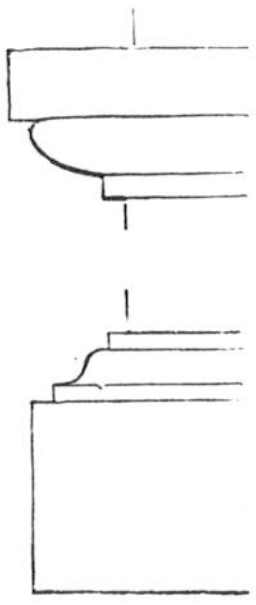

Book-cases.—Plates XXXVI. and XXXVII.

These two Plates, with others in the series about to be referred to, furnish designs whereby a library may be fitted up in a neat and uniform manner, the several portions of its furniture agreeing with each other in their style of design. Plate XXXVI. shows the book-cases for one side of the room, with a design for the chimney-piece, surmounted by an appropriate mirror; the cases for the second side of the room are shown in Plate XXXVII., with a suitable design for the door of the apartment; the cases for the third side of the room would be a simple adaptation of those shown in the drawings to the proper length; in the fourth side of the room the windows would occur, and if a case is desired on the pier between them, it would be merely a repetition of two compartments of one of those shown in the drawings. The table, Plate XL. (*Fig.* 1); the chairs, Plate XLII. (*Figs.* 1, 2, 3), and the window cornices, Plate LXXI. (*Fig.* 1), are well suited to accompany these book-cases in the same apartment, being all designed in a similar taste.

Plate XXXVI.—Both book-cases here given are formed in two heights, of a single carcass in each. They are divided inside by two upright divisions into three nearly equal compartments. The two outside doors are hinged to the gables, and lock on the middle door, which again is hinged to the division on its right, and is stopped on that on its left, where it is slip bolted into the cornice and surbase: consequently the middle door can be opened only after the others have been opened. Or, otherwise, the middle door may be feathered in the ends, and made to move freely to right and left, in grooves formed in the cornice and surbase: the parts grooved must be clamped with solid wood. A bead, or slender half column, with a capital and base, is planted on each of the outside doors, and made to lap on that between them. The base and cornice mouldings are shown in section (*Fig.* 58), along with the method of glueing them up. The decorations on the pilasters are $\frac{3}{8}$-in. thick, those on the upper doors $\frac{1}{4}$-in. The vases surmounting the cornice are turned and carved, and the wings are afterwards fixed on them.

(*Fig.* 58.)

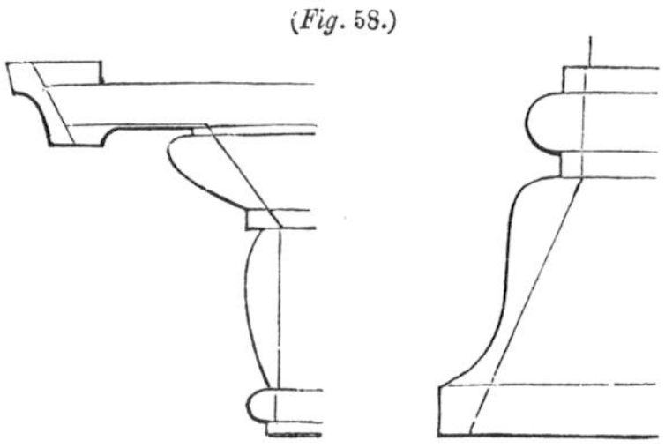

The ground of the mirror frame on which the mouldings and other ornamental parts are planted, is two inches thick; it consists of a cross rail at top, tenoned into two upright stiles. The inner edge of the ground all round, is checked for the plate; leaving a fore lap, $\frac{5}{8}$-inch thick, to which it is applied. The belt that borders the frame inside may with advantage be gilded; consists of four pieces, two on the sides on which the scrolls are formed, and two across above and below, which are checked into the others. The supporting ties along the sides and top of the belt are half checked into it, and into the fore lap of the frame, the rounded ends being wrought off.

The glass plate below rests on a rail, $\frac{7}{8}$-inch thick, which connects the pilasters, being dovetailed into them from the under side. A moulding similar to, and mitreing in with that forming the base of the pilaster, is planted on the edge of the rail, lapping on the plate. This arrangement is not shown in the drawing. The fillet which crosses the plate below might be supported by ties checked into the upper member of the moulding on the bottom rail. The trusses on the ends of the frame below are $1\frac{1}{4}$-inch thick. A panelled frame, $\frac{3}{4}$-inch thick, fitted and screwed within the checks, protects the glass plate behind.

Plate XXXVII.—This book-case has its upper part made in four carcasses; of which the centre or body constitutes two, and the wings one each; and the under in three, the centre being in one piece. Both heights are divided inside into six compartments. The pilasters on both divisions are similarly fixed; those at the ends are attached to, and move with the doors; those in the middle are dowelled on the gables of the centre part; being made flush with them outside. All the end doors are hinged to the gables, the others on the lower part to the fixed pilasters; the upper doors may be similarly hinged if the decorations on their corners are dispensed with, otherwise they must be pivot hinged. The corner ornaments of the latter are $\frac{1}{4}$-inch thick; the pivots, in consequence, must be inserted that amount, fully, farther in on the end of the door stiles, so as to permit the door to open. A hollow corresponding to this increased radius of the door must be wrought out of the parts which adjoin it.

The figure to the left is the work of the joiner, being a door for the apartment, having its architraves and other decorations designed in keeping with the book-cases.

Secretaire Book-cases.—Plate XXXVIII.

This piece of furniture is adapted either for a library, a parlour, or a bedroom, according to the use to which it is put. It consists of two heights; that above is suited for containing either a small library, or a particular selection of books. The under portion is filled with drawers; the upper one of which is provided with a hinged front which folds down, forming a writing board; the interior of this drawer is fitted up with small drawers and pigeonholes. The under drawers, according to the room in which the secretaire is placed, may furnish a convenient deposit for maps, philosophical instruments, or mineralogical or botanical specimens; or they may be devoted to general use, as a repository for body-clothes or napery.

Fig. 1 is in the Moorish or Alhambra style. It has the upper part divided inside into two compartments. The doors require 1⅛-inch wood; they are first framed up with a small hollow wrought on the stiles and bottom rails; the upper corners inside are then bosomed, to form the round. The face of the door frame, from the top down to the spring of the curve below the circle, is next checked down ¼-inch, and this part is then veneered. The triangular corner spaces are further grounded down ¼-inch, and veneered in the bottom with wood darker than that of the door frame, or otherwise, according to taste. The spaces and frets are entirely finished before the latter are glued down. The circle is turned, and made to lap on the door frame; below, it mitres-in with a curved piece, which is butt-joined to, and laps on the stile. The pilasters consist each of a half column, surmounted by a vertical panel, with a raised border; the panels are grounded on the recessed part of the door frame. The middle pilaster is attached to the door on the right, and laps on that on the left. In the under carcass, there are below three true drawers; those above them project 1½-inch, and are only apparent, being *shammed* on the hinged fold, forming the front of the secretaire drawer. The body of the drawer is strongly made, the ends requiring ⅞-inch Bay mahogany; into these the bottom is checked and screwed, and the top and back dove-tailed. The fold acts between the pilasters, being of the same length as the drawers below. The method of hinging it is shown in (*Fig.* 59). The fold a,

(*Fig.* 59.)

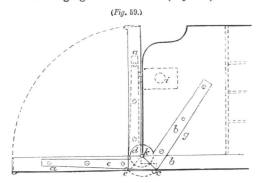

and the bottom of the secretaire b, require to be of the same thickness; at the hinge, they are half-checked into each other, the breadth of the check being equal to the thickness of the wood; by this means the point c is kept in the same plane, whether the fold is open or shut. The fold is supported by a strong iron hinge d, the two limbs of which e, f, are respectively sunk flush into the ends of the fold a, and secretaire g, and abut against each other in the mitre line k c. In addition to the hinges on its ends, the fold is supported towards the middle of its length by two small edge hinges. When the fold is closed, as shown by the dotted lines, it is caught and fixed by a spring-catch i, sunk within the ends of the secretaire. The small drawer casing and the pigeon-hole divisions may be fixed in the surrounding parts of the secretaire drawer, or they may be formed in a separate case, and fitted in from behind. The

(*Fig.* 60.)

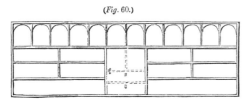

small drawers and pigeon-holes may be variously arranged; the example given in (*Fig.* 60) is generally approved of. Here the

pigeon-holes are ranged above the drawers, the space in the centre is closed by a small door opened and shut by a secret contrivance, and is fitted up with drawers and pigeon-holes for depositing cash or important documents. The door is hung on pivots inserted into its sides, at about ⅜-inch from the top. The divisions forming the pigeon-holes are barely ⅛-inch thick; those between the drawers are ¼-inch full; both are slipped with solid wood on the edge, and moulded with a bead plane. The upright divisions adjoining the sides of the small door, present the same fore-edge thickness as the others; these require ½-inch wood, checks being formed on them within, by which the door is stopped in locking it. As shown in (*Fig.* 61),

(*Fig.* 61.)

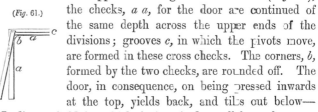

the checks, a a, for the door are continued of the same depth across the upper ends of the divisions; grooves c, in which the pivots move, are formed in these cross checks. The corners, b, formed by the two checks, are rounded off. The door, in consequence, on being pressed inwards at the top, yields back, and tilts out below—affording a hold by which it is raised parallel to the cross checks, and thrust into them.

The decorations on the frieze and pilasters may be carved or inlaid. Figs. A and B show, on an enlarged scale, the details of the ornamental capitals; figs. E E' the drawer nob in front and profile.

Fig. 2 is in the Elizabethan style, and very similar in construction to the preceding. The doors have raised mouldings; the frets on their upper corners are fitted and fixed to the moulding, and also flush with it inside, so as to apply properly to the glass; the front of the secretaire includes the two upper apparent drawers. Figs. C and D present two designs for the profile of the pilaster brackets; Figs. F F' show the drawer nobs in front and profile.

Each of these examples may be provided with a secret drawer in the frieze, forming a convenient place for drawings or private papers. The front of the drawer forms the frieze, and may be made to extend over, and finish flush with the gables; in such case, the mouldings immediately under the top are planted on the drawer front, and the sides of the drawer act on the gables. The drawer is locked by means of a catch or spring, formed of an elastic slip of wood, fixed on the under side of the bottom, at right angles to it; the slip at the inner end is obliquely indented into, and screwed on the bottom, leaving the other end free, and standing out; it is so placed, that the drawer, on being pushed in, is locked by the spring starting out and abutting against the inner edge of the fore-edge below. To raise the spring, the secretaire has to be opened, and the spring pressed up from below.

PANELS IN FRET-WORK.—PLATE XXXIX.

Frets, for decorating panels, usually consist of duplicated halves, whose figured parts are symmetrically arranged along a central line or axis; the effect produced being made to depend on the connection, equipoise, and harmonious distribution of similar elegant forms and profiles. Frets should agree in style, and in other general characters, with the piece of furniture in which they are employed—being sober or playful in delineation, bold or slender in details, according as the latter is formal or fanciful, massive or delicate, in its treatment. The proper thickness of frets varies with the character of the wood employed; and should be greater when the wood is soft and brittle, as in mahogany or oak, and less when it is hard and tough, as in rosewood, zebra wood, or satin wood. When a fret is very tender and delicate in its parts, it may, to preserve it from risk of fracture, be planted upon a polished ground prepared to receive it; and, to give greater richness and relief, the ground may advantageously be made of a darker or contrast colour.

Fret-panels are ordinarily wrought of three thicknesses, the middle one being made to cross the grain of the others; in frets of rosewood, stout veneers are considered sufficiently thick, in those of mahogany, the centre thickness is most frequently ¼-inch beadwood. In glueing up the pieces, the surfaces should first be well toothed, and the glue employed should be rather thin; the cauls require to be well heated and powerfully screwed down, and left on for about four hours, till the glued surfaces are cooled and consolidated.

Figs. 1 and 2 are in the Moorish or Alhambra style, and are suited only for a piece of furniture designed in the Moorish taste. They may be finished by gilding and painting in positive colours in the manner peculiar to that style; and, in such a case, the other parts of the work in which they are employed should be carried out in a similar manner, that unity of purpose may pervade the whole. They require a tough and hard wood, owing to the delicacy and tenderness of many of the parts.

Figs. 3 and 6 are in the Louis XV. style, and are well suited for rosewood. They require to be made of stoutish wood, owing to the veining of the leaves, which may be done partly by the fret-saw, but chiefly by surface-working.

Figs. 4 and 5 are in the Elizabethan style, and, from their massive character, are well suited for oak or other light-coloured wood. Towards the upper part of Fig. 5 several small horizontal bands are planted on after the fret is cut.

LIBRARY TABLES.—PLATE XL.

Fig. 1. The supporting pedestal in this design requires to be strongly made. It is provided with a door in front; the sides and back are sunk-panelled, and made so as to appear framed; the method of construction is shown partly in Fig. 2 on the plate, but more completely in the annexed cut (Fig. 62). The gables of the pedestal are two upright boards of deal, ⅞-inch thick, into the ends of which a top and bottom are dovetailed; one similar board forms the back. The boards, at the same time, form the fields of the panels, and are, in consequence, veneered in the centre; they are also the ground on which the frames d, d, d, which surround the panels, are planted. The frames are ⅝-inch thick, have a moulding carried round their inner edge, and are veneered on the face; they are joined to the boards, forming the carcase of the pedestal, before the latter is framed together. The interior of the pedestal may be left a free space for maps or portfolios, or it may be shelved for general purposes. The back may, at first, be temporarily sprigged to the gables, as at g, and then blocked inside, k k; the corners are afterwards planed off in the line h i, making equal angles with the sides and back. Blocks, also, are glued on along the fore-edge of the gables, inside, with which they form the canted corners in front; they require to

be of solid wood, as the door acts between them. On the corners being formed, the pilasters, b, b, b, b, are planted on. The ornamental brackets are screwed on from the inside of the canted corners.

(Fig. 62.)

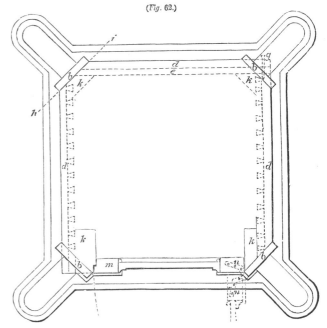

The door is framed, sunk-panelled, and pivot-hinged. The door-stile, m, is bevel-checked on the block k; n, n' present the appearance of the other stile and hinge when the door is shut and open. The projecting decorations of the door-stile determine the position of the pivot on which the door revolves. This point, for practical purposes, cannot be accurately marked on a figure of so small a scale; suffice it to say, that it lies in the line of the block k, parallel to the gable—its exact position being where that line, if produced, intersects the front line of the decoration. The panelled fret is let in from behind, and applied to the door-moulding; the rhombus on its centre is veneered and inlaid.

The tops of library-tables are usually made of deal, being framed and flush-panelled; they are moulded around the edges with solid wood, and bordered on the face with veneer; the interior of the top is leather-covered and embossed. In this case, from the character of the moulding on the top, it may be more convenient, that instead of flush-panelling the frame, it be overlaid at one breadth with deal, ½-inch thick, having the upper member, a, (Fig. 63), previously planted around its

(Fig. 63.)

edge. Before glueing down the board, the moulding on the frame is planted and wrought. The rim, c, under the top, is separately wrought and fixed by screws. The top is connected with the pedestal by means of a frame which crosses both diagonally; this frame is first screwed to the top, and is so placed as to maintain the latter parallel to the pedestal; the extremities of the frame rest on, and are screwed to, the corner brackets; additional strength may be given to the connection of the parts by screws sent through the top of the pedestal into the frame.

The base is formed of two pieces, crossed at right angles, and half-checked into each other; the angles are bosomed by diagonal pieces dovetailed in. On the ends of the base being rounded, its edge all round is cross-bordered with veneer; the moulding on its top is separately wrought on a clamp ⅝-inch thick, which may be of solid wood, or of deal, and veneered on the top.

The second design on the Plate, like the ordinary consulting-room table, consists of two pedestals supporting a connecting frieze-frame and top, and having two fronts, with drawers, entering from each. The drawer in the frame over the knee-hole is provided with a writing-board, hinged within its front. The frieze-frame is entire, extending the whole length; the four corners of it are morticed into blocks, 4-inch square, which extend down to, and rest on, the capitals of the rounded pilasters; it projects beyond the body of the pedestal ¾-inch all round.

The method of forming the outer corner of the frieze-frame, with that of the pedestal under it, is shown in (*Fig.* 64). The true lines in the cut represent the frame, the dotted ones the under-lying part of the pedestal. The front and end rails, *a*, *a*', are tenoned into the corner block, B; on the latter, a quarter round is formed in front. The gable of the pedestal, *c*, recedes from the fore-edge of the carcass top *d*, 2½ inches; the projecting part of the latter is cut-in an equal amount, from the line of the gable—thus forming a rectangular corner. An upright fore-edge, *f*, is dovetailed into these cornered ends of the top and bottom, into which, and into the opposite gable, the horizontal fore-edges between the drawers are dovetailed. A diagonal piece, *g*, connects the edge of the upright with that of its adjoining gable, forming a ground for planting the rounded pilaster. The block, forming the corner of the frieze-frame, is made to lap down in front of the pilaster-ground; for this purpose the block is cut out behind in the line *i*, *k*, *l*. The frame is made to pass down similarly on the pilasters adjoining the knee-hole—the pieces forming the lap being dowelled on its under edge. The inner pilasters are planted on a ground of deal, ⅞-inch thick, which is slipped with solid wood on its inner edge, and is half-checked on the fore-edges, and sunk flush with them, and with the edge of the adjoining gable. The pilasters are returned on the corners of the pedestal; they are sunk-panelled by means of a raised border planted on; the carving in front is separately wrought and glued on. The decorations on the rounded pilasters, and on the frieze-frame, are carved in relief.

All the drawers are recessed with a moulding planted round their fronts. The upper drawer of the pedestal has its front broader than its sides, an amount equal to the depth of the arch on the former. An ornamental key and drawer handle, in keeping with the design, are shown in Figs. 3 and 4; these should be executed in bronze or else bronzed with the veining gilt.

(*Fig.* 64.)

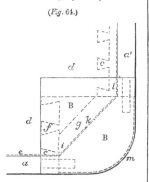

Writing Tables.—Plate XLI.

Figs. 1 and 2 are Davenports—the desk parts of which are made in the ordinary manner—requiring wood ¾-inch thick for the body and hinged fold; the latter may be made of deal, or of Bay mahogany, cross-headed—the solid wood forming the mouldings being planted around its front and ends; it is afterwards veneered below, and bordered above with veneer, and leather-covered. Fig. 1 is either mitre or lap dovetailed, according as it is made of solid wood or veneered. A small drawer, *a*, (*Fig.* 65), for holding pens, ink, &c., is fitted into the right end of the desk towards the back; it is usually about 10 inches long, and hinged to a block, *b*, which moves with the drawer in the space *c*. On the drawer being pulled out, it is stopped by the attached block, and folds in conveniently to hand, along

the end of the desk. The fretted ledges, which are formed of three thicknesses, are dowelled down on the desk-top. In Fig. 1, the base is a flat frame of hardwood, 1¼-inch thick, which is bordered on the edge with veneer, and overlaid by a ⅜-inch clamp of solid wood, having mouldings wrought on its edge all round. The pillars are turned and then carved; they are fixed in position by pins formed on their ends. The general effect of this design may be considerably enhanced by hatching the carving on the pillars in gold, by substituting gilt-tooling for blind-tooling on the leather covering, and by bordering the ornaments of the fretted ledge with a narrow gilt outline.

(*Fig.* 65.)

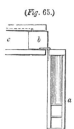

In Fig. 2 the sides are framed up, and panelled similarly to those of Fig. 1, Plate XL. The pedestal drawers are recessed and moulded around their fronts. The left end of the pedestal is distinguished from the right, by being closed with a single panel having a moulding carried round it, and a small carved ornament planted on its centre. The ends of the desk are panelled by a planted, raised border; the leaf ornament and the panel on which it is planted are both finished before they are glued together. The base is footholed in front like that of Fig. 1, it is lap-dovetailed together, and clamped on the top, its projecting ends form a rest for the supporting scrolls. The scrolls require 3½-inch wood, and are fixed by screws sent through the top of the base and the bottom of the desk. The effect of them may be much heightened by partial gilding.

Fig. 3. In this writing-table the plinth is made of deal, dovetailed together, and veneered; the brakes in front are glued on, and the mouldings mitred round. Cross-rails or corner blocks of hardwood must be sunk into the base below to receive the castors. The outside gables are framed—the inside ones are plain and dovetailed together, with divisions for drawers; the latter are dovetailed into the gables, and the grounds for the columns are half-checked on them, and made flush with their edges. The pilaster-grounds must be lined up of a sufficient breadth to receive the columns in front, and to admit the drawers to pass quite clear. The top should be of Honduras, and veneered, with the mouldings planted round and made to project sufficiently to rest on the caps of the columns. The columns are flattened a little behind on their greatest projections, so as to apply to the grounds to which they are screwed from within. The cases for the top are made separately, and screwed on—one may be with pigeon-holes, and one with shelves for books; the desk must also be made separately and screwed on, a small ledge should be fixed on it behind. The centre shelf should be hinged at the back, and either let down with a rack or with small spring bolts at each end. The gallery may either be of fret-work or of bronze. This design is well adapted for mahogany, with the mouldings and portions of the columns ebony or ebonized—the ornaments containing the handles ebonized—and the handles either of bronze or silvered.

Library Chairs.—Plate XLII.

The first three figures have their top rails dovetailed on; this, considering the depth of sweep cut out of the rails below, is the strongest and most secure mode of fixing them. All the decorations on the back legs are wrought on the solid, excepting the small bevelled panels, which are planted. The ornamental work on the front rail of all the designs, from the moulding on the seat frame downwards, is formed by pieces varying in the several cases, from ¾ to 1½-inch thick, which are fitted and dowelled under the seat rail, and shouldered and tongued between the legs; the pieces are first fitted, then detached, profiled, carved to pattern, and finally fixed on.

Fig. 1 has the mouldings on the seat-rail planted on, after the chair is framed up; the mitred corners of the mouldings are blunted by slightly rounding them; the small knob in the centre of the back is placed in a sunk channel, and does not project beyond the flush of the back.

Fig. 2 has the upright stay in the back scribed under the top rail, and dowelled between the latter and the cross stay: the apparent bottom-end of this part is wrought on the cross stay. The moulding on the seat is cross wrought on the front legs; the square heads of the latter are reduced, to give the moulding greater prominence.

Fig. 3.—The under edge of the cross-stay joins on the back rail of the seat: the stay is perforated after the back is framed up. The front legs are framed in flush with the seat-rails; and the moulding around the seat, and the decorations of the legs, are planted on.

Fig. 4 is flat across the back. The frame surrounding the cushion is formed of two stiles and a bottom rail; it is below dowelled between, and framed up with the back legs. The top rail requires 2-inch wood; it is first joined down on the spiral columns, and on the free ends of the cushion frame; it is then detached, shaped out below, and carved on the face. The shell is carved out of the solid. The bordered fret surrounding the cushion is planted on: it is formed of five pieces, the curved and the straight piece on each side, and the bottom piece, which mitres in with the others. A frame carrying the stuffing of the cushion is fitted in from behind, and fixed by screws.

Fig. 5.—The top rail joins down on the legs, through the centre of the brake on the back; at this part, the curve on the back leg may be pieced out by clamping. The back legs and top rails are bordered, on both edges, by a bead wrought on the solid; the interspace being carved on the face. The stuffing of the back may be effected on checks formed on the legs and top rail; or, on a separate frame, fitted in, and screwed on from behind. The two borders surrounding the front legs and rail, with the enclosed carving, are severally wrought apart, and planted on.

Fig. 6 has the back made similarly to that of Fig. 4. The top rail, from a line across the top of the columns, being of one piece, and dowelled down; it requires 3-inch wood. The cushion frame may be supported, in the centre, by screws sent through the pillars; the screw heads being covered by pateras. The carving on the front-rail is separately wrought, being first mitred on the seat frame; it is bordered on both edges by a square fillet carried round the seat.

DRAWING-ROOM FURNITURE.

THE drawing-room being the principal apartment of a house, and appropriated to the elegancies, refinements, and amusements of modern society, its furniture and decorations afford full scope for the display of taste in the owner and of ingenuity in the artists or tradesmen he may call to his assistance. The uses of the drawing-room naturally suggest that its furniture and decorations should wear a light and cheerful aspect, and that its general colouring should be gay rather than grave. Beauty and elegance of expression being the main features to be studied in this apartment, there is not the same necessity for subordinating the ornamental to the useful, as in furniture intended for the dining-room or library; ornament may, consequently, be more freely introduced, richer materials employed, and greater license taken, both in the forms and in the colours adopted. Variety of form is very desirable, and playfulness of design may be freely introduced in such articles as are more for show or amusement than for actual use, and of these a drawing-room usually contains a fair share; but while aiming at variety of form, consistency of style should be maintained, and no piece of furniture introduced obviously at variance with the prevailing character of the furnishing of the room. This would be a gratuitous remark, were not such improprieties so frequently committed, often resulting in giving an expensively furnished apartment very much the appearance of a curiosity shop. Variety and brilliancy of colouring, but without theatrical display, is very appropriate to the drawing-room, and, when properly managed, is productive of the best effect. Through fear of offending good taste, or of producing an effect verging upon tawdriness, neutral tints and colours, slightly removed from white, relieved by gilding, have been extensively adopted for the walls; and the various draperies have been made to match one another in colour so nearly as to give but little relief and variety. While such treatment seldom produces jarring and incongruity, it is generally wanting in liveliness of expression, and frequently marred by insipid uniformity. In many instances, a bit of decided contrast colour, introduced in small quantity into a room treated in this manner, is of great value in giving clearness and decision to the general effect. Were the principles of harmonious colouring more generally understood, the selection and arrangement of colours for the drawing-room would soon assume a more decided and artistic character. It is therefore evident that to this result the cabinet-maker ought to work in co-operation with the upholsterer and decorative painter; and that all, in due relation to the architect and to each other, should combine to produce a whole, in which the harmonious arrangement of the parts, as to form, position and colour, is as carefully observed as in a skilfully painted picture; the rules applicable to the one being equally suited to the other.

It is the more necessary to insist upon this intimate connection of the various branches of the decorative art, from its having, of late, become so extensively subdivided—an arrangement, in some respects, advantageous, from the superiority of execution obtained by it, combined, in many cases, with diminished cost of production; but liable, from the want of co-operation, to produce the grossest violations of propriety and taste. Among the more glaring instances of such violations, we need only refer to many of the carpets, and other decorations now in use, attractive to the uneducated eye by their extreme elaboration of design and brilliancy of colour, but which, when placed in their proper position, only serve to destroy the purity and tone of every other colour associated with them, and effectually disturb the repose and harmony so essential in a well-furnished drawing-room. The same want of propriety is as frequently seen in the work of the cabinet-maker, where hard and persistent forms are made to obtrude themselves on the eye with most unpleasing effect, instead of quietly blending with the other decorations, and forming part of a pleasing and well-compacted whole.

Straight lines, with their necessary sharp and angular convergencies, should, as much as possible, be avoided; substituting, in their stead, graceful and flowing curves, gently varied in their character, so as to avoid abrupt transitions, or monotonous uniformity. If this holds good in relation to the more massive and stationary portion of the furniture, it is still more applicable to those articles that are immediately intended for luxurious repose, where any sense of hardness and angularity should never be tolerated, but lines expressive of the softest and most pliant curves, aided by the skill of the upholsterer, should here be made suggestive of all the comfort and ease that such combinations can convey.

The woods most in favour at present for the ornamental purposes of the drawing-room, are rosewood and walnut-wood. The former is so well known as to require little or no comment, except that its usual dark and heavy character is frequently felt to be incapable of harmonizing with some styles of decoration in which lightness is essential; on this account, therefore, and also from the peculiar beauty of grain it frequently exhibits, walnut-wood has of late been very extensively used: it associates well with almost any style of decoration and colour of material, without either detracting from them, or intruding upon the eye. For the purposes of carving, it has many advantages; it is more easily worked, and the lights and shadows are more clear and effective than in rosewood; while, in flat surfaces, some of the finer specimens of veneer, from their great variety of figure, admit of most elegant combinations. In large and important work, in this wood, where relief and effect are required, gilding, judiciously introduced, is productive of the best results.

CHIFFONNIERS.—PLATE XLIII.

The chiffonniers represented on this Plate are, in point of construction, very similar to each other; and much that has been said on the construction of sideboards, is applicable to them. The plinths and friezes should, for the sake of convenience, be made separate from the carcasses. The breaks may be formed on the plinths, by gluing on the grounds blocks of from 1½ inch to 2 inches in thickness, according to the projection of the pilasters; they are then veneered and finished off, when the top moulding, previously worked in a length, is mitred round, and, for security, blocked from beneath. The friezes may be provided with a drawer the whole length, on the front of which, the moulding, after being worked to its character, is mitred round, and then finished by the carver. The carcasses, from their simplicity, require no explanation. The tops, or slabs, are, in these designs, intended to be of marble; but, if made of wood, deal may be used, with the mouldings first planted round, and flushed off, and the surface veneered.

Fig. 1 has the doors flush-panelled and veneered; the circles, enclosing the carved heads, may be turned, and the rest of the moulding mitred into and around them to the design. The two smaller panels, enclosed in the angles of the doors, may be defined by mitring a ¼-inch bead, or other suitable small moulding, to the shape required. The field of the inner panel is grounded down ¼-inch; and a piece of fret-work, ⅛-inch in thickness, is inserted. The carved heads in the centre require wood of 2 inches to 2½ inches in thickness, to produce the necessary relief and effect. They are secured from behind by screws. Heads moulded in plaster, similar to those in the design, may readily be procured, and if either bronzed, or tinted to the colour of the wood in which the chiffonnier is wrought, would form a cheap and effective substitute for carving; or electrotypes in copper might be taken from those in plaster, and employed in their stead. The pilasters, which are affixed to, and open with the doors, should be about 4½ inches broad *(Fig. 66.)* in their widest part; they are shaped at the sides, and also in front, as shown in the profile, (*Fig.* 66). The top and bottom ornaments of the astragal dividing the doors, may be turned in one piece, and afterwards cut in half. The best construction for the back is to frame its lower division of deal, and veneer it; the moulding should then be mitred round the inside of the frame, forming a check for the veneered panel, which is put in from behind; on this, a smaller raised panel of solid wood, ⅜-inch thick, having a moulding wrought round its edge, is veneered and planted. The shelf, if not solid, should have the moulding planted round before veneering; and, when finished, can be fixed to the lower back by screws from above. The upper part of the back, having to be shaped to the carving, should be veneered on solid wood, otherwise the edges, after being shaped, will require to be veneered. The brackets which support the shelf should not be less than 1-inch in thickness, rebated behind to admit the back, thus avoiding unseemly joints; they are fixed by screws from behind, and by dowels at top and bottom.

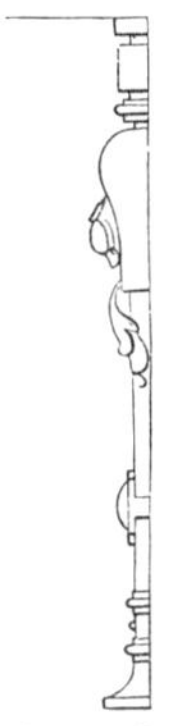

Fig. 2 differs from the above in having plate-glass introduced into the back, the rebate for which is formed by the moulding, that is, planted on the stile, being allowed to project ½-inch beyond the inner edge of the frame. In all other respects the construction is similar to that of Fig. 1.

Fig. 3.—In this design the doors are sunk-panelled, the panel being let in from behind; on the fields of these, raised panels, ⅜-inch thick, are planted. The carved pilasters having, in some parts, a bold projection, require to be about 3½ inches thick, to produce the necessary effect. The brackets supporting the shelf are carved in the solid, and have their ornamental terminations dowelled on. The decorations of the frieze are wrought separately, and planted.

Fig. 4.—The doors are flush-panelled, and veneered over; the mouldings on them are mitred to the shape, and planted on the face. The columns, after being turned and carved, require to be flattened at the back, removing nearly one-fourth of their diameter, so as to bring them under the caps, and close to the grounds on which they are planted.

CHIFFONNIER.—PLATE XLIV.

This design is similar in construction to those on Plate XLIII., but has more importance given to the back, which here forms a very conspicuous feature. In order to insure the requisite firmness and stability, the back should be framed in one piece, extending the whole height; the top part, behind the shelves, being flush-panelled, and the mouldings planted on the face. The shelves have the mouldings on them returned on the ends, to preserve uniformity; the middle shelf is screwed on from behind. The shelves are ¾-inch thick, and the brackets require 1½-inch wood; they may be treated as described under Plate XLIII. Fig. 1. The members of the fret-work pediment have their edges bevelled throughout, thus giving additional force and richness, by forming a double outline to the figures; the brackets may, with advantage, be treated in a similar manner. The pediment requires ¾-inch wood; the spear-heads on it may be wrought separately, and dowelled on. The details of mouldings, &c., given on the Plate, render those portions sufficiently intelligible without farther description. The fret-panels of the doors are of different designs, that selection may be made, according to taste, not that two designs so different are intended to be introduced in the same chiffonnier; an additional design for the fret-panel is also given in Fig. 3. In the end view, for the same reason, a design for the brackets is given different from that in the elevation, and it is in some respects the better of the two. The design of this chiffonnier would not be marred were it made with one shelf instead of two; in that case, it is the upper bracket and upper shelf that should be left out; the fret-work pediment would then be placed on the lower shelf.

CHIFFONNIERS.—PLATE XLV.

This Plate contains two examples of winged chiffonniers, which, in some parts of their construction, differ from those already described. They are each formed in one carcass, the top and bottom of which extend the whole length, are recessed in the centre part, and receive, at the proper distances, the two inner gables, which are morticed in. (*Fig.* 67.)

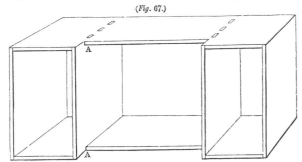

(*Fig. 67.*)

Fig. 1.—The several parts of the friezes and inner gables, forming both angles A of the recessed centre, are clamped so as to sweep together in the curve which is formed on them. The construction of the plinth is shown by (*Fig.* 68), being simply dovetailed together in deal; blocks are fitted into the inner angles at A A, and shaped out; after which the whole is

veneered, and the moulding, of solid wood, formed on the edge of a slip of deal, is planted on its upper edge. The frieze frame is similarly constructed, solid wood being planted round to

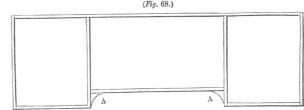

(*Fig.* 68.)

form the moulding. The carved ornaments at the angles are formed by working a single piece of solid wood, sufficient for the whole of them, to the exact curve of the moulding, then mitring portions together to fit the angles, after which they are carved upon a saddle of soft wood. As the carved back is intended for the reception of plate-glass, and being, at the same time, light in character and delicate in decorations, it should, for sake of strength and sharpness of outline, be made of Bay mahogany, or some other hard and straight-grained wood. There being no brackets in front to steady and support the mirror with its frame, this is effected by continuing the ends of the ground frame, 4 or 5 inches, below the bottom rail, to allow of their being screwed to the back of the frieze, as shown in (*Fig.* 69). This frame should be made ⅝ths or ¾ths of an inch

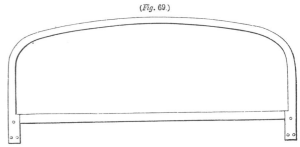

(*Fig. 69.*)

narrower than the carving; so that, when the latter is screwed on from behind, it will project over the inner edge of the frame, forming a rebate for the glass.

Fig. 2 is so similar in construction to the above, that any additional remarks are unnecessary.

CHIFFONNIERS WITH HIGH MIRRORS.—PLATE XLVI.

Fig. 1.—This design is well adapted for being executed in dark oak or walnut, with the ornamental parts throughout relieved and heightened in effect by partial gilding. The ornament is in the Byzantine manner, a style of decoration that has rarely, if at all, been applied to the purposes of modern cabinetwork. Though possessing considerable resources, and great variety and beauty of expression, its distinctive merits, and susceptibility of adaptation, have been too long overlooked or neglected by decorative artists. The ornamental details of the remains of Byzantine architecture in Italy, especially in the oldest edifices of distinction in Venice, and the illuminated manuscripts of the Byzantine period preserved in our museums, supply the designer with suitable materials for decorations in this style. The chiffonnier is simple in construction; the base and frieze are separately made; the ornament on the latter is first shaped to the ground, then profiled, carved, and planted. The gables are sunk-panelled, and finished ornamentally like the door. The ground of the panel forms the true gable on which the bordering frame, ⅝-inch thick, and the other decorations, are planted. The doors require 1⅛-inch wood; and are also sunk-panelled, and bordered around the frame by a fillet, which, along with the moulding, are planted on the face; a hollow, or other small moulding, is carved round the inner edge. The carved panels of the doors require 1-inch wood; these, after being profiled and perforated, are carved to pattern, and fixed by screws from behind; coloured silk or velvet, covering the panel, is introduced behind, to give richness and effect to the ornament. The outer pilasters are attached to the doors; that in the middle is dowelled on the centre division of the carcass. The moulding on the glass frame is separately wrought, and planted on a ground frame, 1½-inch thick; the carving is wrought in pieces, and dowelled or screwed on, at the most convenient points; the portions of the foliage which overlie the moulding, are separately made and fitted on.

Fig. 2 is decorated in the Moorish style, the ornamental details being based on those of the palace of the Alhambra. This style has, as yet, been but little employed in this country for cabinet-work, though the French have produced some very excellent adaptations from it. It is admirably suited for gilding and polychromatic embellishment; and, if the style of the Alhambra be fully carried out, such enrichments are really necessary. Moorish ornament may, however, be adapted to our domestic requirements, and very rich and agreeable effects produced in it without the application of colour. Those who wish to study this style, and satisfy themselves of its capabilities, will find valuable assistance by consulting Murphy's *Arabian Antiquities of Spain*, and the works on the Alhambra, by Owen Jones and by Girault de Prangey.

The design Fig. 2, may be entirely executed in deal, and painted in the polychromatic style, using the primary colours on the ornamental parts, and relieving them by gilding. Were the painted surfaces enamelled, it would give greater permanence and value to the colours, and impart to the whole a lustrous and highly-finished appearance. Such treatment, however, would require a special or complementary arrangement of colour for the room in which this piece of furniture is placed; and also, that similarity of design and treatment, though in a modified form, be carried out in the rest of the furniture of the apartment, to preserve consistency. This design may also be effectively wrought out in woods of various colours; in which case the chiffonnier would have a more subdued effect, than if treated in the manner we have just described, and would also approach more nearly to the character of drawing-room furniture commonly in use. For example, the plinth, the frieze, and the carved pilasters, may be made of walnut wood; the doors veneered in satin wood, with their mouldings also wrought in wood of light colour, with exception of the inner member, which should be dark; the ornaments on the panels inlaid in lime-tree, dyed in bright colours, the ground for the ornaments being a dark neutral colour, produced in the same manner, making the general effect of the panel be, to tell dark on a light ground, the dark mass being relieved by the radiant form and colours of the inlaying; the ornaments on the frieze inlaid in various colours, like the panels, but made to tell light on a dark ground. The effect may be further heightened by bordering the leaves of the inlaid parts by a fine gilded outline, and by hatching the carved pilasters in gold. The mirror-frame may be wrought in deal; but better in lime-tree, and gilded; the gilding being relieved by a good deal of burnished work, and by the partial introduction of colour. Several variations of this method of treatment will readily suggest themselves.

CABINET.—PLATE XLVII.

This cabinet is decorated in the French style, and, if executed in rosewood, would form a very useful and elegant article for the ante-drawing room. The character of the design would be maintained with equal effect if worked out in walnut or mahogany, where these woods are employed in the furniture of the apartment. In construction it is similar to a chiffonnier, having a secretaire drawer in the frieze, with the upper carcass shelved for books, &c.; the latter part is made and finished separately, and, as usual, is fixed in its place by dowels and screws. The doors require wood not more than ¾-inch thick. The rebate to receive the plate-glass is formed by planting the carved mouldings on the face of the door, as shown in the section B, which presents also the character of the moulding on the front of the brackets. A break, corresponding with the projection of the bracket, is formed on the cornice, as shown at section A. The pedimented ledge on the top is of solid wood ½-inch thick, on which, as a ground, the carved ornaments are planted. The space enclosed by the carving in the centre of the ground is perforated, and so also the figured spaces or panels on each side of it; the two end portions of the ledge, shown in side view, are, at their points of contact with the back and top, dovetailed into the one and dowelled on the other. The secretaire drawer opens between the end panels, and is similar in construction to that described under Plate XXXVIII., but different and simpler in its interior arrangements; one plan is given (*Fig.* 70) which, in a cabinet of this kind, will in most

(Fig. 70.)

cases be found suitable; but the arrangement may of course be varied as circumstances and convenience dictate. The drawer front is veneered flush, and the panels and carved work surrounding them planted on the face;—of the character of these mouldings, as well as those forming the frieze, section D will be found sufficiently explanatory. The lower part is so similar to the chiffonniers already described, that little explanation is needed beyond what is furnished by the design itself and the sections accompanying it. The gables or ends are panelled to correspond with the front, simply by planting on in the usual manner. Both carcasses are closed in behind by panelled frames of deal; that on the book-case may be cloth covered, inside, or flush-panelled, veneered, and polished. An agreeable variation of this design may be made by omitting the doors on the lower part, enclosing it instead by silk curtains, enriched with ornamental needlework, suspended from a brass rod, the ends of which would be inserted in the upper part of the pilasters.

CABINET.—PLATE XLVIII

This is another cabinet on the same plan as the one just described, and differing only in the style of its decorations, which is Elizabethan. The fret-work pediment on the top is ½-inch thick; that on the doors not more than ¼-inch. The frets are prepared, in the usual manner, of several thicknesses; each of them, along with the portion of the band connected with it on the top and sides of the door, is formed of a single piece; the sides mitre in with a corresponding piece at the bottom. The frets and bands attached to them are fitted into the rebate formed by the door-frame and moulding, and glued to the projecting lip of the latter. Another good method of fixing the frets is to rebate the inner edge of the doors, on the front, for the thickness of the fret-work, which, when the doors are veneered, then is fixed in its place, and the mouldings,

(Fig. 71.)

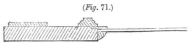

being planted so as to lap over, effectually secure it, and also cover the joints—as the section of the door style (*Fig.* 71) will sufficiently explain. The glass panels in the doors may be secured from behind by beads in the usual manner. The plinth in this design has the inner angles of the breaks hollowed into a curve, as shown in the plan section F, which greatly improves the appearance.

MIRROR FRAMES.—PLATE XLIX.

Fig. 1 is a design for a mirror-frame, in the French style, suited for the back of a chiffonnier, and intended to be entirely gilt. It is wrought as a fret, but so relieved and enriched by carving as to have much the appearance of a carved frame. The square-moulded frame is first made and finished. The moulding is planted on the edge of a ground frame, 1½-inch thick, and 2 inches deep, which is dovetailed together at the upper corners, and below, the sides of the frame are tenoned into a bottom rail, whose ends project laterally, to serve as a ground for planting the base mouldings of the fret and frame. A moulding, corresponding to and mitring with the two under members of the base, is planted on the edge of the bottom rail, and made to lap on the glass-plate. The fret, to be well relieved by the carver, requires 1-inch wood; it is dowelled on the frame. The wood for the fret being prepared, before cutting out the figure, the points of contact most convenient for the insertion of the dowels should be set off on the frame and fret, at which points they are bored, and the parts are then slip-dowelled together; at the same time, the top and sides of the fret, in the line of the ends of the frame, are also dowelled together; any inequalities of surface being smoothed off after the parts are finally glued up. Cloth of scarlet or other suitable colour is intended to be introduced at the back of the fret, which would much enhance its effect and richness.

Fig. 2 is a design for a mirror-frame, in the Elizabethan style, to be executed in rosewood, oak, &c. The rounded corners of the frame are formed on the ends of the top rail, which are dowelled down on the sides. The moulding is, as in the previous case, planted on, and the frame is slipped with veneer around the edges. The surrounding fret-work is rebated into the frame, and screwed on from behind; it will be sufficiently strong if made ½-inch thick; the centre part of it, however, requires to be thickened up to about 4¼ inches, to allow for the projection of the scrolls; the shield and small prism-shaped ornaments are planted on, and the vase over the centre ornament is flattened at the back, leaving three-fourths of the circle, and let into a bore. The side pieces may be worked separately from the top, which, after rounding the corner, joins down on them, where the parts are united by dowels.

CHIMNEY-PIECE MIRROR FRAMES.—PLATE L.

Fig. 1 is a design for chimney-glass frames in the French style, for gilding, with a shield in the centre, to be blazoned with armorial bearings, in proper colours. The panels on either side are perforated, and filled up with brass lattice-work. Both the scroll and shield at the top should cant well forward, and the backs be kept free and clear—the sides and top are half-checked on each other in the upper corners, and the joints are concealed by the ornaments.

Fig. 2 is another design in the same style, also to be carved and gilt. This frame is made of deal, and pieced out at the prominent parts; it is made up in two thicknesses—of a ground frame 1½-inch thick, and the carving which rests on it—the ground following the general outline of the carving on the outside, being wrought off with it; on the inside it is overlapped by it, to form a rebate for the glass. The carving of the top consists of three pieces—the straight centre, capped by

a moulding, and the two ends, which are scribed to it. The perforated top ornament is separately made; it is dowelled on the centre, and, below, scribed on the face. The sides may be formed each of one piece, or the moulding may be separately wrought, and planted, and the scrolls afterwards fitted on.

Fig. 3 is a bold and effective composition in the Flemish style, to be executed in oak and hatched in gold. The frame is wrought entirely out of solid wood, 2 inches thick; the chief projections of the carving being formed by clamping the several parts to the required thickness: the centre should be pieced up 5 inches additional, at least; other parts, on the top and sides, about 2 inches. The frame, before it is put together, is rebated all round for the glass; at the upper corners, the top and sides are mitred, and at first slip-dowelled; the inner angles being previously bosomed, to form the curve of the moulding; care must be taken, that the dowels are inserted so as not to come out in the profiling, or carving. After being fitted in the joinings, the top and sides of the frame are separately profiled and carved; leaving the upper corners in the rough (*Fig.* 72) till the frame is finally cramped up. Additional strength may be given

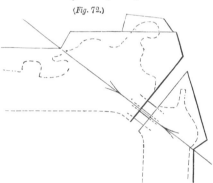

(*Fig.* 72.)

to these parts by crossing the joints behind with an iron plate. The shield is carved separately, and screwed from behind. The scrolls at the sides, with the drops depending from them, should have a projection of about 3 inches from the face of the frame. The parts to be gilt are, the centre of the shield, the moulding round the small open panels, the most prominent parts of the scrolls, the raised members and points of the leaves, and the flat moulding next the glass. The frame is fixed to the wall by an ornamental piece of brass, screwed on behind, and projecting at the sides, in continuation of the design; through this and into the wall, a large brass-headed screw is passed.

CHIMNEY-PIECE AND MIRROR.—PLATE LI.

This design for a drawing-room chimney-piece mirror, is to be executed in Bay mahogany, and gilt. The ground thickness required for the frame is about 4 inches; the chief prominences of the carving, as in the previous case, being brought out by clamping; in the centre of the arched top an additional thickness of 3 inches is required, as this part has to be canted well forward; the upper and under corners are pieced up with 1½-inch wood. Before the wood is profiled for the carver, a rebate for the glass is formed all round on the sides and top, leaving in front a lap 2 inches thick, and of sufficient breadth at the top to allow the inner profile edge of the carving to lap on the glass, and similarly on the sides, so as to admit a portion of the moulding, with the interior parts of the winding foliage, to project inwards. The spaces to be perforated on the sides, between the moulding and the foliage, are sawn out, after the parts are defined, and roughed out in the carving, which is entirely finished before the frame is put together. The top is joined down on the sides; at the junction, paned blocks of wood, with a moulding wrought on them, are interposed between the parts; they are first screwed to the top, and then dowelled on the sides. The vase, with flowers surmounting the sides, is separately made, and dowelled on. Much of the beauty of this frame will depend upon the skill of the gilder in burnishing, and properly tipping the leaves and flowers. The chimney-piece was executed for Robert Napier, Esq., the eminent engineer. It was made in four parts, the sides each in one piece, as far as the top of the capital of the pillar, where the upper parts joined on to them. The upper portion was in one piece, and the shelf made separately in the usual manner.

PIER TABLES WITH MIRRORS.—PLATE LII.

Fig. 1. This pier table and mirror-frame is intended to be carved and gilt throughout. The ornaments are adapted from natural foliage, the plants employed being the wood sorrel, the convolvulus, and the ivy. The table top is of marble, $1\frac{1}{4}$-inch thick, and moulded on the edge. The carved moulding, immediately under the top, is formed on the edge of a flat frame, made of deal, or of lime-tree, according as the moulding is planted on, or wrought and carved on the solid: this frame rests on, and is screwed to, the legs and ornamental rails. The ornamental rails are also of lime-tree, and require to be $1\frac{1}{2}$ inches thick; they are shouldered and dowelled between, and wrought off with, the scrolls of the legs; after being shouldered and fitted to the legs, they are profiled below, then framed up, perforated to pattern, carved on the face, and thinned off from the inside, around the profile edge of the several openings: the centre of the front rail is brought out by clamping with 1-inch wood. The body of the truss legs in front, requires $3\frac{1}{4}$-in. wood, and towards the top they may be pieced out $4\frac{1}{2}$-inch or thereby, additional; the top scroll, also, may be eked out behind and on the sides by clamping. The bottom scrolls may be pieced on the leg, the joints being braced up and secured by working the thread of a stout screw into both surfaces, on gluing them together. The back legs are about half the thickness, and have a profile, similar to those in front. They are connected together behind by a plain rail of deal, $1\frac{1}{4}$-inch thick, which forms the back of the table-frame. The stretchers are also of lime-tree, and require $2\frac{1}{2}$-inch wood; they are wrought in two pieces, with half of the circular centre on each; by these parts they are dowelled together, and they are fixed to their place on the leg by screws let in from below.

The glass-frame is wholly made of lime-tree; the arched top and bottom rail are half checked on the stiles; the latter extend down to, and are screwed on the back rail of the table. A moulding, planted on the face of the bottom rail, is made to lap on the glass, and mitre in with its correspondent on the stiles. The pendant wreaths are separately made, and fixed in with wire or screws. The glass rests in a check formed in the frame, and is protected behind by a panelled back, as formerly described.

Fig. 2. This pier table and mirror-frame is adapted either for being entirely gilt, or for being made of walnut, or other solid wood relieved by gilding. It might be rendered peculiarly rich and effective, by treating the flat members and simpler parts in white and blue enamels, and relieving merely the ornaments and smaller mouldings by gilding. If intended to be gilt or treated in colours, the parts that are to be carved should be of lime-tree. We shall describe the design as if executed in walnut:—

The table top is of marble, $\frac{3}{4}$-inch thick, resting on a frieze frame on which the mouldings and other decorations are planted; the straight part of the frieze may be solid, or of deal, and veneered with blocks of solid wood glued on at the ends to form the projections. The centre circle on the frieze requires 3-in. wood for the relief of the head, and the other ornaments on the face 1 to $1\frac{1}{2}$-inch wood. The foliage on the curve of the end blocks, and that on their side, shown in Fig. 3, is wrought in relief, and carved on the solid. The base is made similarly to the frieze; the pedestals on which the figures stand are

wrought out of blocks of solid wood, and are glued and screwed to a ground formed on the base. The semicircular projection, supporting the base, is turned and planted on. A clamp of solid wood, having a moulding wrought on its edge, covers the top of the base, and abuts against, and mitres in with, the back portion of the pedestal mouldings. A veneered frame, panelled with glass, encloses the back. The arched brackets, of solid wood, shown Fig. 3, as resting on the base, and supporting the frieze, are dowelled on the ends of the frame; these, for strength, may be made of two thicknesses of wood, whose fibres slightly cross the hollow sweep in front, being veneered. The brackets are sunk-panelled on the outside, and a small carved ornament is planted on their fields.

In gluing up the solid wood for the figures, care must be taken as to the direction of the grain in the prominent and delicate parts, such as the expansion of the foot, extension of the arm, or fingers, or in any pointed or depending parts of the attire; so that in these parts the fibres of the wood may correspond, as nearly as possible, with the direction of their length; this is necessary for facility in working, and smoothness of finish, and for giving the parts sufficient strength under the operations of the workman's tools, and also to prevent them from being easily injured, after the work is finished.

The ground frame of the mirror is plain, and veneered on the face and edges, the decorations being planted on it. The top arch must be thicknessed up, so as to project and rest on the caps of the columns, the ornamental cornice moulding being planted on it. The spandrels on the arch are sunk on the face and veneered, an enriched moulding being carried around their inner edges: the ornaments in the spandrels are carved separately, and planted. The columns are in one length, plain and spiral turned, and the several parts are then paned and carved. A perforated gallery, of $\frac{1}{2}$-inch wood, is dowelled, or blocked and screwed on the top of the cornice.

LOO TABLES.—PLATE LIII.

Throughout the whole range of cabinet furniture, there is probably no article which requires so much care and experience in the manufacture, as the Loo Table. The top, especially, presenting to the eye a large level surface, under such circumstances, that the slightest irregularity, or imperfection, is brought distinctly into notice. The ground, and veneers,

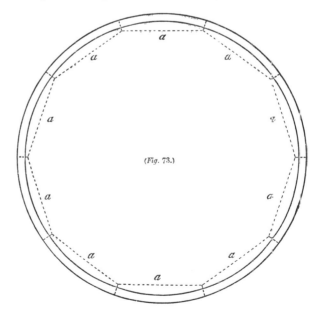

(Fig. 73.)

in consequence, must, in respect of their quality, preparation, and seasoning, be carefully adjusted to each other, having, in all cases, due regard to their relative capabilities of expansion and shrinkage, both during the process of working, and in the subsequent use of the tables. Previous to veneering the top, the moulding has to be planted round the ground-work. We shall describe two methods of doing this. The first is, to reduce the top to a polygon of as many sides as convenient, *a, a, a,* (*Fig.* 73), and, on the edges thus formed, groove and tongue the solid wood for the moulding, as shown in (*Fig.* 74), great care being taken that the joints or mitres of the moulding are perfect and true throughout; when these are dry, and flushed down, the top may then be prepared for veneering. It is obvious, that, with a top so prepared, the veneering should be conducted in as dry a manner as possible, as any warping tends to start the joints. Another method, and one much used where the moulding is not. intended to be enriched by carving, is to divide the edge into a great number of small angles, as in (*Fig.* 75); then bevel

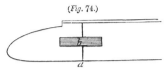
(*Fig.* 74.)

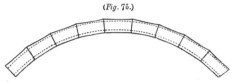
(*Fig.* 75.)

them, and, on the bevels so formed, place fine ½-inch solid wood, cut cross way of the grain (*Fig.* 76), where the lines of shading indicate the direction of the grain. Previous to planting the ½-inch wood in its

(*Fig.* 76.)

position, it should be carefully baked, so as to avoid all risk of shrinkage, and should then be laid in alternate pieces, which, when dry, will admit of the other pieces being tightly fitted between; when dry, and flushed off, the top may be veneered.

Fig. 1 has the veneers on the top formed so as to radiate from a centre, an arrangement which displays to great advantage the rich figure found in the burrs of walnut, oak, yew, amboyna wood, and is also well suited to the usual form and figure in the curl portions of mahogany. The ground of the top being prepared in the manner already described, and the division, or joint-lines of the veneers, carefully drawn on it, the veneers may then be wrought to the lines, and fitted together in the dry state, to be cauled in one, two, or more portions, as convenient; or they may be laid by the hammer in two operations, one-half being laid in alternate sections, and, when dry, the others carefully fitted in between, the joints being secured from the air by slips of paper glued over them. The rim is formed of three thicknesses of inch pine, cut to the required sweep, and built up in the manner shown (*Fig.* 77). The principal thing to be observed, in this operation, is to place the joints as far as possible from each other, otherwise the strength

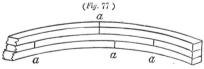
(*Fig.* 77)

of the rim will be endangered. When properly shaped to the required circle, and veneered, the pieces to form the scrolls shown on the bottom edge, may be fitted in lengths sufficient to form either one or two scrolls, and afterwards carved, the joints being formed at the terminations of the scrolls. The clamps should be made of 1½-inch bay wood, and about 2½ inches in depth, the cross clamps being framed into the others, with double tenons. The heads of the screws, by which they are secured to the top, should be sunk about ½-inch, and the holes either plugged up and levelled off, or a

neat turned button fitted into them; great care is necessary in screwing on the clamps, so to regulate the depth of the holes, that the screws may not penetrate too far, and so injure the veneer of the top.

In this design, the pillar may be blocked out of the solid, or glued up in bay wood, and shaped to the curves, as shown in (*Fig.* 78), which is a cross section of the upper portion of

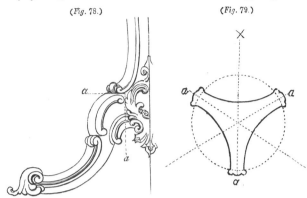
(*Fig.* 78.)   (*Fig.* 79.)

the pillar; the scrolls *a, a, a,* being fitted to the angles, after the sweeps are veneered, and surface finished. The claws require wood 4 inches in thickness; they may either be dowelled on, or, as shown (*Fig.* 80), dovetailed into the base of the

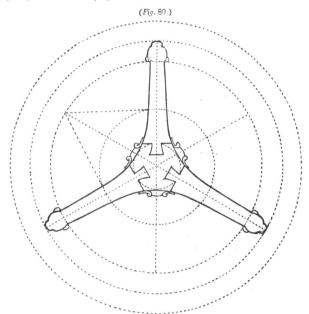
(*Fig.* 80.)

pillar. The position in which the joints will be least apparent is shown at *a, a,* (*Fig.* 79). The centre ornament on the bottom of the pillar should be carved separately, and afterwards dowelled on, and, with a little management, it may be made to conceal the connection of the claws with the pillar.

Fig. 2 is so similar in its construction to the table just described, as to need little further explanations, beyond what relates to the construction of the pillar, which should be of solid wood, and in three portions, the joints of which are arranged as shown *a, a, a,* (*Fig.* 81), those for the claws are presented at *b, b,* (*Fig.* 82).

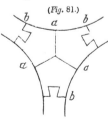
(*Fig.* 81.)

Fig. 3. The top in this design is intended to be laid in different coloured woods. In planting the solid wood on its edge, care must be taken that the butt joints fall in the indentations of the moulding. The rim is built, and its decorations planted as described in the preceding examples.

The pillar should be solid, and made to extend down as in Fig. 1, to give attachment to the claws. After the body of

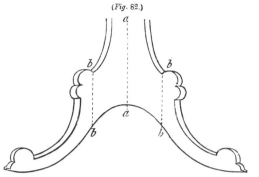

(*Fig.* 82.)

the pillar is shaped out, it is shouldered in the lathe in the line *a, a,* (*Fig.* 83), the under portion is reduced by the turner,

and then paned to receive the claws, which are dowelled, or dovetailed on. The brackets *b, b,* are separately made, and dowelled on. When the whole is properly fitted together and shaped, it is ready for the carver, from whose hands it will receive the enrichments shown in the design.

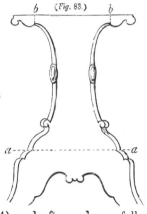

(*Fig.* 83.)

Fig. 4. In this design, the rim is built up in the usual manner; the ogee moulding should be either veneered on clean fine pine, or, if solid, first wrought out of clear ⅜-inch wood as shown at (*Fig.* 84), and afterwards carefully bent round; or, otherwise, the ground of the rim may be cross

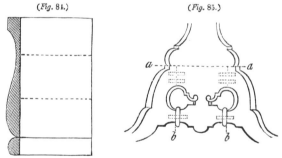

(*Fig.* 84.)　(*Fig.* 85.)

clamped with short lengths of well-dried and rich wood ⅜-inch thick, on which the moulding is afterwards wrought. The bead is separately wrought, and bent round the rim. The pillar, as far as *a, a* (*Fig.* 85) should be of solid wood; the lower part being dowelled to the claws in the manner shown at *b, b.*

Occasional Tables.—Plate LIV.

Fig. 1 is an Occasional Table, in the Elizabethan style, of large and massive proportions, suitable for a library or business-room. It should be executed in oak. Each of the supporting ends consists of four distinct and principal parts, which are separately made and finished, before they are joined together —the base, the shaped block, which rests upon it, the pillars which are dowelled into this, and the arched top, with its connected brackets, which joins down on the pillars. The shaped ornaments between the pillars is separately made, and dowelled on the block below, and fixed at the sides by screws sent through the pillars, the screw heads being covered by a pateras. The feet are profiled in one piece, then cut asunder, tapered towards the front, carved, then wholly finished, and screwed on.

The stretcher is intended to be stuffed, which should be done before it is finally fixed in its place. The moulded edge of the frame is intended to fold down, revealing the fronts of the drawers; when closed, it is kept in its place by a spring in the rail.

Fig. 2 is a design for the end support of an Occasional Table, adapted for rosewood. The construction will be understood by the accompanying plan of half the table (*Fig.* 86).

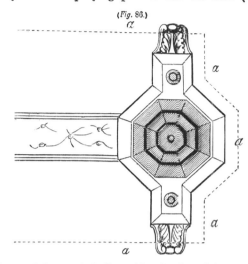

(*Fig.* 86.)

The shape of the top is indicated by the dotted line *a, a, a,* &c. The pillars are first turned out of the solid, then paned, and afterwards carved. The cap of the pillar may be separately

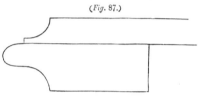

(*Fig.* 87.)

made of bay mahogany, or deal, with a rosewood moulding planted round its edge. The top is of ⅞in. mahogany, with the first member of the moulding planted round before veneering. The other moulding is formed on a clamp glued on below, as shown in (*Fig.* 87).

Fig. 3 and 4. Another design for rosewood, Fig. 3 being the end view, and Fig. 4 the ground plan. This table is, in its construction, so much like Fig. 1 as to require little farther explanation. In the plan, the circular centre between the stretchers, is intended for a small brass-wire paper-basket; or a neat vase or twisted pillar may be there introduced with good effect.

Fig. 5 shows the end of a table, of the same kind, to which the stretcher of Figs. 1 and 2 may be applied. It is intended to be executed in oak, with the standards, or shaped end of one piece, 1½-inch thick, perforated to the design. As it is sometimes difficult to procure wood of sufficient breadth for such purposes, the standard may be jointed in the centre. This defect is compensated by the convenience which is thus furnished of profiling the four halves of the standard together at once; each pair requires to be afterwards carefully and strongly dowelled together. The standards are secured at the top by a flat frame of hardwood, to which they are dowelled or screwed; on the edge of this frame the under moulding of the top is planted and formed. The table frame may be rendered more firm and secure by inserting into and shouldering between, the shaped ends, as high as the rosettes, a turned ornamental stretcher, the ends of which may be carried through and wedged, from the outside, and then covered by the rosettes.

Fig. 6 is a variation of the design, Fig. 5, and may be wrought in a similar manner. The stretcher may also be varied, shaping the edges to any neat design.

Either of the two last Tables may be so modified as to be

suitable either for a Drawing-room or Bed-room; and, with a little variation, would make effective Work-Tables.

Loo Tables.—Plate LV.

This Plate contains four designs for Loo Tables, in styles differing greatly from those previously described, and exhibiting a marked originality in the combination of parts and general treatment.

Fig. 1. The moulding on the top, being free from carving, it may be treated by the second of the processes given in the introductory part of the description of Plate LIII. The lower part should be made in three portions, namely, the pillar, the collar, and the claws. The pillar is turned and afterwards finished by the carver, and the upper portion of the collar is also turned, and the lower part afterwards shaped in the manner shown in (*Fig.* 88) elongated over the claws. The

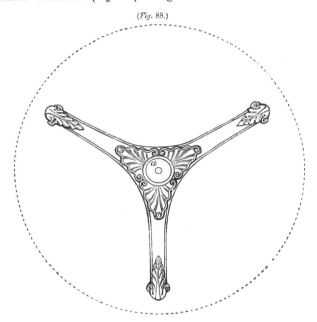

(*Fig.* 88.)

claws may be dovetailed into a centre-piece, in the manner shown at (*Fig.* 79).

Fig. 2. The arrangement of the lower part of this table requires that the upper block be made somewhat different from those of the tables previously described, in order to provide a sufficient bearing for the three smaller pillars; this may be accomplished by framing the block of 2-inch Honduras or birch, 3 or 3½ inches in width, as shown at (*Fig.* 89).

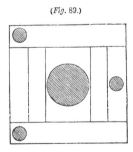

(*Fig.* 89.)

Fig. 3 presents a simple and effective mode of enriching the rim, which in this instance is first veneered and finished off as if intended to be left plain; the shaped work previously prepared and shaped is then laid on, and may be either solid or veneered, but in either case should not exceed ¼ or ₁⁶₀-inch in thickness; the carved ornaments are finished separately, and then glued in their places. The standards of the lower part require to be about 2¾-inch thickness when finished, they are tenoned or dowelled to a centre-piece, as shown at (*Fig.* 90). This figure is a section of (*Fig.* 91) on the line *b, b, d* represents the centre-block, *c* the standards, and *a, a, a,* the position of the joints; or, the joints may be formed at *e, e* (*Fig.* 91), in which case the piece of wood required for the centre-block

would be of much smaller dimensions. Oak, or walnut, are the woods for which this design is most suited.

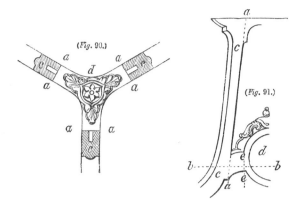

(*Fig.* 90.)

(*Fig.* 91.)

Fig. 4 presents a table in which gilding may be introduced with good effect, associated with any of the more choice woods. From the arrangement of the lower part, this table does not admit of the top being turned up in the ordinary manner. The top block being connected with the scrolls rising from each limb of the base-block, it, in consequence, exceeds considerably the usual dimensions of this part in other tables. It should be secured to the clamps by four thumb-screws, as shown at (*Fig.* 92). In constructing the lower block, the

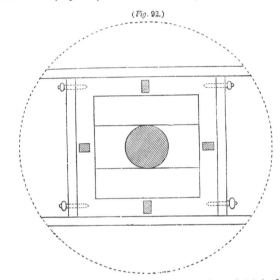

(*Fig.* 92.)

ground should be framed or halved together of 1½-inch pine, as shown at (*Fig.* 93), a process which has been before de-

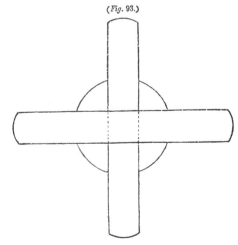

(*Fig.* 93.)

scribed under Plate XVII. This ground should be accurately shaped to the proportions required and veneered; the moulding has to be placed on it, the simplest method of doing which is to turn the centre part *b* (*Fig.* 94) out of solid wood, the moulding being accurately described on its edge; four other

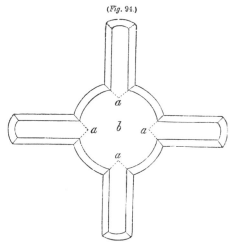

(*Fig.* 94.)

pieces of solid wood should then be carefully shaped to the limbs of the block, and the moulding accurately worked on their edges—they may then be mitred into the circle in the manner shown at *a, a, a, a.* These mitres are in a great measure concealed by the base of the table-pillar. If the nature of the wood renders this plan inexpedient, a counterpart of the block *b* (*Fig.* 95), may be made, smaller in size, an amount, equal to the projection of the moulding, all around. This piece *c* should be firmly glued on to the other, and in the rebate so formed the solid wood for the moulding should be planted, the joints being concealed by the upper square of the moulding *a*, formed by a clamp of ⅜-inch solid wood covering the whole. The swan-necked scrolls may be of bronze, with the leafage tipped with gold; they may be fixed by screws sent through the upper and lower blocks.

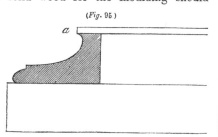

(*Fig.* 95.)

Occasional Tables.—Plate LVI.

Fig. 1.—As this small table depends for its effect on sharp and well-defined shadow, it is not suitable to work it in woods of varied colour, or in those whose lustre is only shown to advantage in smooth rounded contours. We shall therefore assume that it is made of solid wood, having the top made of inch stuff, with a thickness glued on beneath the outer edge, and the moulding worked out of the solid. In forming the ornament depending from the under surface of the top, four square blocks, with their lower ends turned or canted, should be prepared, into which the intermediate ornaments are doweled at the ends; these are finally cut on the curve out of solid wood, then shaped and carved, and the whole is doweled into the under side of the rim; small blocks may be glued at the back of the pendant squares to stiffen them, if thought necessary. The four standards are then shaped out of 1¾-inch stuff; the foliated ornament at their foot is relieved by the carver on each side. The circle in the centre is turned out of 2¼ wood; the moulding carved or not. It should then be carefully notched out to receive the standards, the notch being ⅜ less than the width of the standard, which must be grooved in so that the circle goes slightly into the standard, to conceal the joint. The standards must then be screwed to a bearing-piece at the top, and

doweled below to the top of the plinth. The plinth is made of ⅝ stuff, on the edge of which the moulding is worked, with a thickness glued on below, and shaped. The feet are shaped out of solid wood, carved, and a sinking made, if requisite, to receive the castors.

Fig. 2.—This table is suited, from its greater richness, for an inlaid, marble, or marqueterie top. The ground of the top should be got out of mahogany, thicknessed up beneath, and the wood for the moulding planted on all round; the square edges being banded with veneer, and the top veneered. The rail is shaped as in the design, and carved leaves placed on it as brackets where they are shown. The centre column must be got out right to the bottom, the upper part turned, and pieces doweled on for the three scrolls. The standards and claws must then be shaped, as shown in the section (*Fig.* 96), and

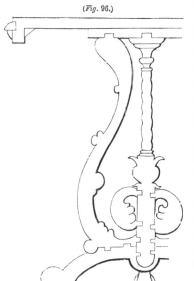

(*Fig.* 96.)

doweled together without gluing first. It is now ready for carving, after which it must be glued up fast, and the joints are afterwards trimmed by the carver. The scroll supports may be of from 2½ to 3-inch stuff, and the claws 3-inch towards the foot, of course, widening towards the centre.

Fig. 3.—The top is made of Honduras, and veneered, with a moulding planted on it. Below, and at each end of the top, is a wide rail, forming a rim, to receive the columns, and the siderails are dovetailed into them. If the wood be expensive, the rail may be veneered with a bead planted round the lower edge, or clamped with a thickness of ½-in. to 1-in. stuff, on which a moulding may be worked. The columns must be fitted and turned, leaving wood for the wreaths; gluings may be put on the caps to form the projections, but the better way is to shape the whole top ornament with the two caps out of one solid piece, and then put long dowels through it into the columns. The stretcher is turned, and the claws shaped out of 3-inch solid wood, tapered on each side towards the feet, with a piece of ¾ stuff, which is shaped and moulded on the edge, and laid on their tops; it is then doweled and glued together, the stretcher being tenoned into the claws. The castors are, as usual, sunk in the feet.

Fig. 4 is made exactly like Fig. 3, excepting that the end standards join down on the arched feet in the straight line drawn between the angles which their profile makes with the feet. The carving which completes the bottom of the standard, is wrought on the feet. The standards require 2½ to 3-inch stuff, and are doweled on; the feet are shaped out of solid 3-inch wood.

Ladies' Work Tables.—Plate LVII.

Fig. 1 is a design intended to be executed in mahogany; the bag to draw out from the end, being in this way much more convenient for a lady's use when sitting before the table. The part shown in the design above the bag is the front of a drawer, the interior of which is fitted up in the usual manner, and provided with the proper requisites for needle-work. (*Fig.* 97) presents a convenient method of dividing off the interior of a rectangular work-table drawer. The divisions are made of pencil-cedar, and may be silk covered; their edges are frequently embellished by silver lines. The drawer is pulled out by means of the scrolls at each end, which serve the purpose of handles. The

(*Fig. 97.*)

top, being made to lift up, should be furnished inside with a small mirror, inclosed within a tastefully ornamented border. The four scrolls which support the top should be finished before they are fixed, except at that part where they join the pillar, to which they are secured by means of screws. The pillar is turned the whole length, the claws being dovetailed or doweled into it.

Fig. 2 is a design to be executed in ebony, relieved by silver lines, &c. The top is well suited for mounting in a mosaic work of fine spars or marbles, inclosed within a Buhl border, executed in ebony, silver, and tortoiseshell. The body of the table is hexagonal or six-sided; the top is made on a ground of $\frac{5}{8}$-in. Honduras; it is hinged, with a moulding planted around it. The inside of the frame under the top is provided with a movable tray, furnished with the requisite fittings, or these

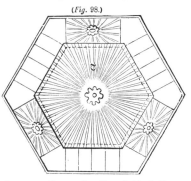
(*Fig. 98.*)

may be fixed as shown in (*Fig. 98*), where the usual manner of setting off the interior of a hexagonal work-table is presented. The part corresponding to the drawer, in Fig. 1, being fixed in this example, access to the bag is obtained through the centre space *a*, which is covered by an ornamental lid; the upper end of the bag, as shown by the dotted lines, passes up within the top frame, and forms a check on which this lid rests. The bag is formed by working a piece of sufficient thickness and length to form the six sides to the sweep required, and then mitring these together, and afterwards panelling them. Or the wood forming the bag may be made up of three thicknesses, of stout veneer, glued together, and cauled down on a mould, having the required outline of the bag; when the gluing is completely dry, the gores are cut out, and mitred together. Two pieces of deal, shaped to the inside size and figure of the bag, above and below, may be temporarily employed, to form a ground on which the mitring is effected; the bottom piece may, however, be permanently fixed, as a means of attaching the bag to the pillar. The mitres are strengthened by keying the angles outside; this is done by inserting slips of veneer with glue into slant cuts of the saw; on these being properly dry, the surface of the bag is smoothed off, and the panelled openings are then cut, and moulded around the edges; the mitre cuts are concealed, by afterwards veneering the borders which surround the panels. The upper portion of the table is shouldered to the pillar within the calyx, the interior of which is outlined and bottomed by the turner; the parts are fixed together by a strong screw from the inside of the bag. Down the stem of the pillar a silver line should be inserted. The tips of the flowers and ends of the fruit should be relieved in the same manner.

Fig. 3 furnishes another design for hexagonal tables, to be executed in rosewood. The top part of this table is supported by three scrolls springing from the pillar, much in the same way as Fig. 1. The bag is made in the same manner as in the table just described. There are six leaves on the upper portion of the pillar, one running up each scroll, and one intermediate. The divisions of these leaves may be so managed, as in a great measure to conceal the joints.

Fig. 4 is designed for rosewood, with the upper part made in the same manner as the others. The scrolls, in this instance, re-

(*Fig. 99.*)

quire to be made each in one piece, from the top to the insertion of the claws; they are joined in the centre, and doweled together, and the claws fitted under each; the scrolls are secured by screws, as in (*Fig.* 99), *a*. The upper part of the table is secured to the lower by a screw bolt, *b*, *b*, which, passing from the inside of the bag through the pillar, is tightened underneath by means of a nut. The leaves, at the bottom of the bag, touch the scrolls, which arrangement affords an additional means of strength, by admitting of a screw being passed from the inside of the bag into the scrolls.

Fig. 5 is a design suitable for maple-wood, relieved by ebony mouldings and inlaying, and, in construction, is similar to those already described. The inside should be fitted up with coloured silk, and the fret work on the panels relieved by the same material.

Fig. 6—a design suited for rosewood and satin-wood, relieved by gilding. The top to be inlaid with various coloured woods, inclosed within a circle, the angles being filled up with Buhl-work, executed in tortoiseshell, &c.; the first and third moulding on the top, the mouldings around the panels of both frame and bag, portions of the scrolls and foliage, and the mouldings on the block, are the parts to be gilt. The panels of frame and bag being of satin-wood, these parts are, in consequence, separately made, and the upper part is screwed to the lower by means of a bolt, as described under Fig. 4.

DRAWING-ROOM SOFAS.—PLATE LVIII.

The details of construction given in the description of Plate XXVIII., and several following Plates, are equally applicable to the sofas figured here. It will be only necessary to notice the peculiarities in the ornamental details, in which alone the difference consists. The frames are made, the solid wood planted on the fronts, and the feet doweled underneath, precisely in the manner formerly described.

Fig. 1.—In this design the lines of the foliages, with a little care, may be so arranged as effectually to break or conceal the joining of the feet to the frame. The peculiarity of execution consists in a portion of the foliage which springs from the end of the front rail being made to clasp, as it were, the base of the elbow; it will only be necessary, when planting the solid wood on the front rail, to make provision for the additional thickness required, when the whole can then be carved and finished together.

Fig. 2 differs simply from sofas already described, in the styles of the ornament, the mode of execution being precisely similar.

Fig. 3 presents a marked contrast to most of the preceding designs, both in arrangement of lines, and details of ornament. It is, however, doubtful, whether the broad and decided angularity observed in the treatment of some of its parts, may not be objectionable. In such case the difficulty

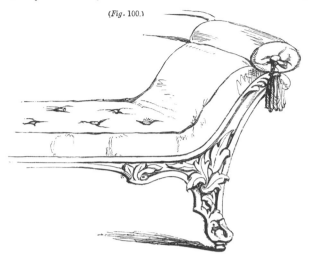

(*Fig.* 100.)

may be surmounted by softening the lines, and modifying the angular features of the design, in the manner shown in the accompanying figure.

Fig. 4.—This design is so similar to those figured in Plate XXVIII., as only to require an explanation of the ornament in the centre of the back; the solid wood for which is doweled firmly to the deal framing, and afterwards carved, care being taken to preserve an easy graceful line for the edge of the stuffing.

DRAWING-ROOM SOFAS.—PLATE LIX.

Fig. 1 is a sofa designed in the French style, in which the various members are doweled, and skilfully relieved, as to render it admirably suited for satin-wood and gold, or for gilding entirely. The same design, carefully wrought in rosewood, will also prove very effective and pleasing. In constructive details it is similar to the designs on Plate XXXI. The centre of the back is in one piece, as far as the dip in the moulding, where the end pieces are mitred up to it. The solid wood on the front rail is also in three pieces, arranged in a similar manner.

Fig. 2 bears so close a resemblance to Fig. 2, Plate XXXI., that a reference to the description given for that design will furnish all the information required.

DRAWING-ROOM SOFAS.—PLATE LX.

Fig. 1 is another very graceful design, in the French style, eminently suited for gilding, or finishing in white and gold. In this design the seat frame is first made of birch, to the shape of the design; upon it the back is built up of birch and pine, in the manner shown and described under Plate XXVIII., Fig. 2. Around the ground framing of the back, the solid wood required for the carved work is carefully and securely planted: great attention being paid to the security and soundness of the joints. It will be found in practice, that, after the various pieces are fitted in these places, much of the heavier parts of the carving may be more readily roughed out before being finally fixed, which is also desirable for this further reason, that the risk of jarring and disturbing the joints will be thereby considerably lessened.

Fig. 2 requires to be built up in the same manner, observing,

of course, the same precautions in fixing and working the mouldings, &c. The clusters of leaves and fruit may be separately wrought and indented.

COUCHES.—PLATE LXI.

The couches on this Plate will be readily constructed from the descriptions already given.

COUCHES.—PLATE LXII.

The general construction of these couches will be readily understood.

Fig. 1 is best suited for execution in the lighter coloured woods, such as maple, or satin-wood, or birch, and the character of the ornament is such as to admit of its being considerably improved and illuminated by a judicious introduction of gilding.

Fig. 2 is a design better adapted for rosewood or mahogany, in either of which woods it would prove a very effective and elegant couch.

DRAWING-ROOM CHAIRS.—PLATE LXIII.

It is presumed the general construction of vase-backed, or drawing-room chairs, is sufficiently understood, as to render any particular explanation in this place unnecessary, especially as many of the remarks in page 25, relating to the dining-room chairs on Plates XXIII. and XXIV., are equally applicable to those now under notice—as a rule, however, drawing-room chairs should be smaller and decidedly lighter in character, than chairs intended for dining-room purposes—grace and elegance being requisite in the one case, solidity and strength essential in the other.

Fig. 1 exhibits a simple design framed together in the usual manner of vase-backed chairs, but from the quick sweep of the under part of the stay, it is necessary that the joint should be formed in the manner shown in (*Fig.* 101) *a, a*. The moulding on the face of the back is simply three beads, as shown in (*Fig.* 102):

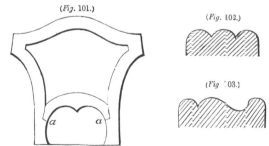

(*Fig.* 101.)   (*Fig.* 102.)

(*Fig.* 103.)

that on the legs being made to correspond. This back may be either stuffed into a rebate, sufficient wood for this purpose being left on the inside, which serves also to give additional strength to the back; or the space may be fitted with a loose panel, which, when stuffed, is put in from behind, and secured by screws.

Fig. 2 is another vase-backed chair, framed upon a light coloured wood, inlaid with a darker one. In other respects it is similar to the one just described.

Fig. 3 differs only in ornamental details, the construction being similar.

Fig. 4 has the back moulded, the character of the moulding is shown at (*Fig.* 103).

Fig. 5 exhibits considerable novelty in the character of the back, and requires great care in the arrangements of the joints and the position of the dowels, in order to secure the necessary strength when the perforations are made.

Fig. 6 is finished flat on the face, the enrichment being either inlaid with a dark wood, or sunk into the face; the stay is framed into the seat, as well as the back, and the small panels shown in the design, either sunk or pierced through.

Ottoman Seats.—Plate LXIV.

Fig. 1 is well adapted for gilding, and is, in construction, simply the lower part of a cabriole chair; with this difference, that all the sides are finished alike. This being the case, further explanation is unnecessary.

Fig. 2, being supported in a different manner from the above, requires some little attention, in order to secure the necessary strength and firmness. In order to do this, it is better to make each end of two separate pieces, cut length way of the grain, and cross-lapping them together, by which means, firmness is obtained with economy of material.

The framing of Figs. 3 and 6 needs no remark, except that the perforated brackets in the latter are more conveniently made separately, and fixed in their places after the stool is framed together.

Figs. 4 and 5 will necessarily require the rails to be deeper than in the former examples, on account of the pierced work at the bottom. The former is well adapted for ebony, relieved by gold; and the latter suitable for walnut and oak.

Fig. 6 has a decorated ovolo moulding carved around the seat-rails, which are framed in flush with the legs. The figuration on the moulding may be carved on the solid, or the moulding may be made of deal, and covered with an inlaid veneer.

Drawing-Room Chairs.—Plate LXV.

Fig. 1 is intended to be executed in a light coloured wood, the only difficulty consists in properly securing the stay; in all other respects the construction is simple. The enrichment on the feet is sunk into the face, after they are sloped and otherwise finished.

Fig. 2.—In this, as in the chair, Fig. 5, Plate LXIII., the chief care required is in working the stay, which is framed up entire and cut out after. The leaves, in contact with the back legs, are each secured by a dowel. The leaf under the stay may be doweled on from below, after the latter is framed in its place. The top rail joins down on the legs in a line, passing through the middle of the two lower circular openings.

Fig. 3.—From the complicated character of the back in this design, the simplest plan, if not the best, is to make the lower part of the chair separate, and form the back from a solid piece of wood, of sufficient thickness to allow of the necessary sweeps, making also allowance at the bottom for its being doweled and screwed to the seat-frame; otherwise the material and time required to frame up the various parts composing the back, would be so great as to add considerably to the cost.

Fig. 4.—The construction of the back in this design is simpler than appears at first sight. If the banister be doweled to the top and to the seat, it will scarcely need securing at the sides. The beads shown on the fore legs are wrought on the solid; the legs are, in consequence, projected in front, and on the side; the tops of the legs are reduced flush with the seat-framing.

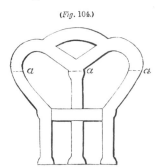

Fig. 5.—Some little nicety is required in framing up the back of this chair. The cross forming of the stay is first framed; the joint of the top is shown at (*Fig.* 104), *a, a, a ;* the moulding on the face is simply a bold hollow finished on either side by a square border, the centre of the hollow being relieved by sharp clean channels, or grooves terminating in bores, as shown in the design.

(*Fig.* 104.)

National Emblem Chairs.—Plate LXVI.

The designs on this Plate exhibit the national emblems—the Rose, the Shamrock, and the Thistle —treated in a conventional manner, and furnish a striking example of how much originality may be produced from most familiar objects, when treated in a true artistic spirit.

The three first designs are, in construction, similar to chairs already described, Plates III. and IV., wherein the back, being carved from one solid piece, is secured to the back rail of the seat by means of dowels, or screws. The effect of these chairs mainly depends upon the thorough consistency of the general design with its decorations, and upon the skill of the carver in rendering, with fidelity and spirit, the conception of the artist.

Fig. 4 is made in a similar manner to the above; but as it is intended to have a stuffed back, arrangement must be made for that purpose by forming a rebate, into which the stuffing is secured.

Fig. 5.—The back of this chair is constructed in the ordinary manner of vase-backed chairs, with either a loose panel for stuffing, or a rebate left for the purpose.

Fig. 6.—This back is also carved out of the solid, and the rebates left for the six small panels to be stuffed into.

Chairs from the Great Exhibition.— Plate LXVII.

The designs on this Plate severally possess a distinct unity of character and decisiveness of expression, along with considerable elegance of outline and of originality and beauty, in the details of decoration.

Fig. 1 is constructed in the ordinary manner; it may be executed in lime-tree, and done up in gold and colours; or of walnut, with the bordering and leafage gilt. The cushion of the back is stuffed on a separate frame, and let in from behind.

Fig. 2 may be made of oak or walnut, with the decorations gilt. The stay of the back is cut to outline after it is framed up; it shoulders with the legs along the border of the band, being, at first, wrought flush with them, the carving and borders on it being afterwards wrought in relief. The leaflets surrounding the cushion are separately executed and indented. The knees are sunk carved; the bed for the leaf on the front rail is grounded down, and the leaf is separately carved and planted on it.

Fig. 3 is adapted for rosewood, and constructed in the usual manner; the banister is doweled between the stay and top rail: the connection between these parts is much concealed by the inlaying. The several openings of the back are bordered by a bead wrought on the solid.

Fig. 4 may be made of oak or mahogany; if—as is most suitable—of the former, the leafage may be partially gilt. The triangular stay is formed from a single piece, having the grain running upwards, on which the mouldings are worked to outline, and in relief: it is framed below in with the back legs, and, along with the latter, receives the top rail down on its upper end. By relieving the mouldings a rebate comes to be formed, for the stuffing, all around them.

High-Backed Chairs.—Plate LXVIII.

This is a variety of chair in which great scope is given for taste and embellishment. In most cases they are intended for covering with embroidery and needle-work. It is, therefore, obviously desirable that the character of the needle-work and of the chair should, as far as practicable, be in keeping with each other. On this account, and for the purpose of selection, several designs, in various styles, are given in this and following Plate. Much will of course depend upon the situation in which the chairs are intended to be placed, whether they be wholly or partially gilt, or executed in any of the various woods used for decorative purposes.

Fig. 1 is a design, the elements of which are drawn from various styles—French, Flemish, and old English—each of which contributes to certain of its parts. The twisted pillars in the back are each in one piece, from the ground to the top of the capital; the stay forming the lower part of the back panel is framed in between, on this, the uprights forming the sides of the panel; and on these and the spiral pillars the top is securely doweled on. The scroll in the centre of the top will have to be pieced up to obtain the necessary relief. This back may be stuffed into a rebate left for that purpose. The fore feet are framed in after the usual manner, and the seat-moulding is wrought around their upper part. This design is well adapted for rosewood hatched with gold.

Fig. 2 is framed in a similar manner, the principal difference consisting in the style of ornament. The cushion-frame joins down on the seat. The mouldings around the cushion are planted on an under frame, the inner edge of which extends within the mouldings to furnish attachment to the stuffing. The moulding around the seat is wrought on the square of the front feet, the portion of the square below the moulding being reduced to work in flush with the seat-rails.

Fig. 3.—Here the back feet form the margin of the panel, the top being doweled direct down upon them. The carved ornament running up the sides should be well set back, otherwise the effect on the edges will be heavy.

Fig. 4 is similarly constructed. The outline in this design being less angular than the last, is more suited to work partaking of the French style of ornament.

Antique State Chairs.—Plate LXIX.

These chairs are of a similar character to those just described, but elaborated in their treatment in order to adapt them to situations where considerable display is required.

Fig. 1 has the back feet entire, from the floor to the coronet: at this part the piece forming the top is jointed on. The thickness of the wood required to produce the necessary relief in the carving, is about 3½ inches. The margin round the panel projects about ⅜-inch from the general surface. The cushion frame is joined up with the back; below it is doweled on the stay, which, again, while it is attached to the seat rail, is, at the same time, framed in between the scrolls on the legs. At the sides and top the frame is fixed by dowels at several of its points of contact with the carving. The stuffing is effected from the front, on a rebate formed on the frame. The flowers at the side lie well in a deep hollow. The front legs stand at an angle with the seat, the rails on each side being finished in the same manner as the front. This chair may be executed in oak, further heightened, if required, by gilding.

Fig. 2 is constructed similarly to Fig. 1. The panel of the back is, below, attached to the seat rail; at the top it is doweled into the caps of the columns. The attachment in the middle of its length may be most securely made by screws which pass through the pillar, the screw heads being covered with pateras. The arched moulding and scroll work, forming the top, are separately made; the former consists of two pieces, which abut in the centre against a block to which the top of the panel frame is attached. This design may be made of oak, with partial gilding.

Fig. 3.—The hind feet rise a few inches above the seat, and terminate in two scrolls which are wrought in with the curve of the back. The latter, including the panel, is executed from one solid piece, 3½ inches thick. Below, the back fits in between the hind legs, and, for strength of attachment, passes down to the bottom of the seat-rail, which for this purpose is recessed. On these fittings being made, the back, at this part, is shaped out and finished, as shown in the design. By another method the hind feet may be wrought flush with the top of the seat, and the back strongly doweled down on the feet and seat-rail. The pendant fruit and foliage on the sides of the back are executed separately, and, at convenient points, attached by dowels: several other decorations along the sides may be fixed on after the latter are profiled. The deep curvature given to the front legs may require that they should be supported by a strip of iron, sunk in from behind, which may be concealed by a veneer glued on the back of the leg.

Antique High Back Chairs.—Plate LXX.

This Plate furnishes three designs intermediate in character and enrichment with those already described.

Fig. 1.—The pillars in this chair are also a continuation of the back feet, and the top is framed in precisely the same manner as Fig. 1, Plate LXVIII. The ornament below the front rail is doweled on after the seat is framed.

Fig. 2.—The back of this chair is in one piece, or in two jointed together in the middle, as in Fig. 2, Plate LXIX. The chief peculiarity in this design consists in the perforated supports substituted for the front feet; these should be of wood 1½-inch thick, the scrolls being pieced up in the usual manner.

Fig. 3.—This chair also has the back carved out of the solid, as before described.

Window Cornices.—Plate LXXI.

Window cornices should correspond, in character, with the dimensions, use, general outfit, and tone of the apartment for which they are intended; and the materials of which they are made should, in colour, present only a mild contrast to their dependent drapery.

All the designs on this Plate may, with little variation, be adapted to either the dining-room or drawing-room, the first three more especially to the former; and may be executed in mahogany or in oak, with the decorative portions partially gilt. The two last, Figs. 4 and 5, are best suited for the drawing-room, having their upper mouldings and flat portions approximately tinted to the prevailing hues of that apartment; an enamelled light blue, or a French white, if otherwise suitable, consorts well on these cornices, all the other decorations being done up in dim and burnished gold. Each cornice is supported and attached, by slip catches, to a lathe or narrow board of deal, 4 inches broad, which rests on iron brackets screwed to the architrave of the window. The ends of the cornice are returned at right angles to its length; the depth of the return is such as to admit it to abut against the wall of the apartment, covering in, at the same time, the end of the lathe, and the thickness of the window architrave. The two curtain rods are attached to the under side of the lathe, and the drapery border or valance is tacked on around its edge.

Fig. 1.—The fretted portion is made up of two ⅜-inch thicknesses, crossed; the front thickness has the grain running lengthway. This part of the cornice is of sufficient depth to extend up, and form the ground on which the carved moulding is planted and mitred; the top moulding is separately made, and screwed from above.

Fig. 2 is similarly treated to Fig 1. The scrolled ornament and its intermediate carving are separately made, fitted together, and planted. On the ground being profiled under, the centre ornament, after being shaped, is checked out on its upper half so as to lap on the ground, leaving the lower part to pass in below the under edge. To each side of the centre carving the ends of the adjoining scrolls are fitted, and the overlay of the centre foliage is fitted to the ground and indented into the scrolls; and so on with the other parts, in succession, towards the ends. The perforations of the ground have a small hollow wrought around their edges, and are clothed behind. If the carving is wholly gilt, the cornice may be made of deal.

Fig. 3 is, in its chief features, similar in construction to Fig. 2; the profile below being wrought out, the projecting foliage on the under edge, at both ends, is then carved on the face out of the solid. The other decorations are then planted on in succession, from the centre to the ends. The corner scrolls are formed of two pieces mitred on the angle, and planted on the face: they join to the sweeps on the upper edge of the overlay on the foliage. The upper member of the mouldings is separately made, the others are planted on the face.

Figs. 4 and 5, if gilt and coloured, are wholly made of deal; if not, the ground must be of solid wood, and the decorations, as in the preceding examples, after being wrought, are planted on. The clustered leaves and fruit, depending from the centre and ends of Fig. 4, may be formed of *papier maché*, or carved in the solid; the corresponding embellishment, in the centre of Fig. 5, may be similarly formed, according as the corner is to be gilt or otherwise. The wood for the corner carving of both examples, after being partially wrought, is planted on both sides of the angle, and mitred together.

Window Cornices.—Plate LXXII.

The first three figures on this Plate are best suited for mahogany, or for rosewood: the two last for oak.

Fig. 1. The ground is framed in between two small square blocks, which form the ends; into these, also, the returns are mortised; the ground is then profiled under, and may be perforated, according to the design, with cloth shown behind the openings; or it may be left entire, with a raised border of the same outline, planted around it. The large moulding is carried round the projecting heads of the blocks; thus forming a brake, which is carved. The top moulding is separately made, and screwed on from above, and the centre and end ornaments, resting on it, are doweled on.

Fig. 2 has, similarly to Fig. 1, the corners formed by solid pieces, into which the front and returns are mortised; these pieces are made to project sufficiently beyond the ground to give relief to the carving—about 2 inches. They are wrought off flush with the ground, inside, so as not to interfere with the drapery; and are rounded on the angle, in front, and also within, for strength to the part. The carving is planted on the face, and in the following order:—the centre ornament is first glued down, the pieces adjoining the carved corners next; and the scrolled pieces intermediate, after their overlaying portions are indented, are lastly put down.

If this cornice be made of rosewood, gilding might be introduced with advantage on all the carved parts.

Fig. 3 blends the prominent features of both the preceding examples, and is treated similarly to them.

Fig. 4 has the ground perforated by panelled openings that are filled with frets, behind which cloth is shown. The frets are set in from the front, and supported behind by small blocks glued, at intervals, around the edges of the openings; in other respects, this cornice is made similarly to the preceding.

Fig. 5. The ground here is entire, with a bordered fret planted on it; the fret is $\frac{1}{16}$-inch thick, and has a small hollow wrought on it around its inner edges. The large moulding on the top is screwed on from above, and the hollow under it is planted on the ground.

Whatnots.—Plate LXXIII.

The whatnot is a piece of furniture which serves occasional or incidental use, and belongs, indifferently, to the dining-room, drawing-room, or parlour; but when especially designed for either, it should coincide with the proper character and general outfit of the apartment.

Fig. 1 is suitable for the dining-room, and should be executed in mahogany, or better in oak of a light colour. The ends are shaped out of a board of 1¼-inch wood, and bordered in relief on both sides, around all the edges of the general profile and the openings. The relieving is effected by bevelling the ground into the edge of the border, and then smoothing off, on the interior surface, the consequent inequality of level. The decorations are formed by inlaying or indenting wood, oak, or other of a darker colour than the ground. The shelves are doweled between the ends; the framing of them may be additionally strengthened by screwing at once to the ends and lower shelves under small blocks of wood or knee brackets of iron; a similar treatment of the upper shelves would be apparent, and offensive to the sight.

Fig. 2 is for the drawing-room, and may be made of rosewood or of walnut. It consists of four principal and separate parts, which are doweled together; these are the tripod base, and the three similar divisions which rest on it, and on each other, and are surmounted by a pedimented ledge. The back leg of the tripod consists of two halves, glued together side to edge, forming a right angle; the half, whose side is glued, must be broader than the other, an amount equal to the thickness of the edge which applies to it: these halves are framed into the fore legs of the tripod. In forming the angle, all the other divisions lap on each other in a similar manner. The shelves are interposed between the divisions, and have the mouldings, on their edge, carried completely round: they are screwed down on the divisions, and these again, in succession, doweled on the shelves; or, otherwise, the divisions may join directly down on each other, and the shelves may be fixed by screws sent through from behind, or supported by blocks from below. If this design be executed in dark wood, the shelves should be veneered with satin-wood, bird's-eye maple, or other light wood; the carved mouldings on the edge of the shelves should be dark, or they may be done up in dim gold. The small ledges around the upper shelves may be of bronze. The decorations on the legs of the tripod are formed by grounding the surface down, and planting on a fret of richer and lighter wood than the border which surrounds it, or of wood similar in character to that used on the shelves.

Fig. 3, like the preceding, is formed of separate parts; but these do not all rest vertically on each other; the two upper portions recede backwards, so as to bring, in succession, the several shelves, which gradually diminish in size from below up, to rest on the upright brackets. The stability of the whatnot, from this arrangement, is secured by the outward spread of the back feet of the pedestal. The brackets are doweled on, at the proper angle, to the edges of the mirror frames. After the wood-work is wholly finished, the mirrors are fitted, and blocked in from behind, and protected by a panelled back.

MUSIC SEATS.—PLATE LXXIV.

These should correspond, in richness of style and in the materials of which they are made, with the instrument in connection with which they are most frequently used. The backs of all the designs in this plate are separately executed; and, excepting that of Fig. 5, are wrought in with the framing of the seat, similar to those of chairs. The true seat may be of a determinate height, and fixed, or it may be made movable, and capable of being elevated and depressed, within a range of several inches, to the convenience of the sitter. This is effected by means of a nut and screw action within the pillar, and by which also the pillar is connected with the seat.

A longitudinal section, presenting the construction and the arrangement of the several parts of a movable music seat, is shown in (*Fig.* 105); *a*, is the supporting pillar of the seat, which is tubular; *b*, is a small cylindrical wooden pillar, also tubular, which acts in the larger pillar, completely filling its tube, and made to move steadily and smoothly in it. The small pillar, *b*, is tenoned at the top into a cross bar, *c*, which is mortised between, or screwed to, the rails of the seat; its diameter is determined by that of the nut, *d*, of the screw, *e*, which shows the end of the pillar, the bore of the nut being continued through the pillar, so as to admit the pin of the screw for its entire length. The inner pillar is sometimes wholly iron, being then a tubular nut, having the screw made to work in its whole length. The tube of the larger pillar is bored in the turning-

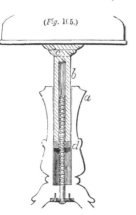

(*Fig.* 105.)

lathe, and the pin of the screw is let into it from below, its head being shouldered and screwed on the bottom of the pillar. When the form of the outer pillar admits of it, the upper end is surrounded by a virrel to strengthen the lip of the tube; when this is impracticable, a ring of brass or iron, for the same purpose, is indented into the end of the pillar and smoothed off flush with it.

Fig. 1.—The expansion of the pillar at the top may be a separate piece, connected with the seat and centre pillar, the line of separation being made at the hollow, immediately above the leafage, on the pillar. The claw feet are doweled on the prolonged extremity of the pillar, the joint being concealed by a leaf ornament afterwards planted on.

Fig. 2.—The paned part of the pillar may be separately made, and shouldered within the leafage by the turner. The ball terminating the bottom of the pillar, is doweled on after the screw has been fixed to its place.

Figs. 3 and 4 are, in all important particulars, alike. The decorations on the pillars, when they join to the claws, are fitted on after these parts are united. The seat frames are, in front, mortised together, the rails being made of a breadth sufficient to admit of the required shape being given to the seat. The pieces for the mouldings of the seat are shaped cut after the ground is formed; they are then separately wrought and planted. Fig. 4 may be wholly gilt.

Fig. 5.—The back of this design is made differently from the others on the Plate; the scrolled sides of it, together with the rail connecting them below, have the same curvature as the round seat, and are let into, and screwed to it. The mouldings on the seat are carried completely round it, and the bottom rail of the back is cloth-covered behind. In making the back, the scrolls, which require 3-inch wood, are profiled, and the top and bottom rails are shouldered and temporarily doweled between them. The bottom rail is first fitted and cramped up dry; the top rail is then accurately adjusted between, and shaped out to, the top scrolls. The piece for the fret is prepared in the usual manner, of three thicknesses, making together ¾ in.; it is brought to the required shape by gluing the veneers down on cauls moulded to the form of the back. The piece must remain several days under pressure, when, after being properly set, it is taken out and brought to a size, a little more than the opening of the back. The design of fret is now drawn on it, after which it is accurately fitted into its place, and, at its points of contact with the scrolls and rails, marked and doweled. After the fret is completely finished it is framed up with the back.

Fig. 6.—The back is wrought out of the solid; the ring-moulding, in its centre, is turned with a check formed inside to receive the stuffing. The carving on the edge of the back is wrought on the solid. The double scrolled ornament below is separately made, and fitted within the back; it is fixed by pins sent into the circle from under, and similarly attached to the back rail of the seat. The pillar is treated similarly to that of Fig 2.

Fig. 7, in the back, is made similarly to Fig. 6, being of one piece. The cushion is stuffed separately, and fitted in and screwed to its place from behind. The carving on the claw feet and pillar is wrought after these parts are framed up. This design may be done up in colours, with the foliage gilt.

Fig. 8 has the back made of one piece also. The claw feet are, by the scrolls, strongly doweled to the pillar, and to each other. The bottom scrolls are pieced out on the side, so as to rake with each other, on the three sides alike; and, also, that they may receive down on them the bottom end of the pillar, which is scribed on. Their connection may be strengthened by an iron plate, screwed on below.

Canterburys and Fire-screens.—Plate LXXV.

The first of these consists, essentially, of a drawer-case, on the top of which is placed a series of divisions, either in an inclined or vertical position, for holding music books; while the drawer, which extends the whole length, is a convenient deposit for loose sheets or manuscript.

The first of these consists, essentially, of a drawer-case, on the top of which is placed a series of divisions, either in an inclined or vertical position, for holding music books; while the drawer, which extends the whole length, is a convenient deposit for loose sheets or manuscript.

Fig. 1.—The drawer may be made to act within the ends of the case, with its front lapping over the edges and finishing flush with the outside. The divisions are grooved into the circular ends, and the latter are dovetailed into the back, and, with it, doweled down on the case. A bordered fret, $\frac{3}{16}$-inch thick, is planted around the margins of these parts, and the interior surface of the round ends, outside, is inlaid. The feet are wrought out of a piece of $\frac{7}{8}$-inch wood, and doweled on; they are grounded $\frac{1}{8}$-inch down for the fret, which is planted on them.

Fig. 2.—The divisions are connected together by a turned roller, pieced and shouldered between their ends, and are doweled down on the case. The two outside divisions are perforated, and the decorations, on their exposed sides, are planted on the face. The bracketed feet require $1\frac{1}{8}$-inch wood. The stretcher is shouldered between, and passes through, the feet, and is wedged from the outside. The exposed ends are covered by pateras.

Fig. 3 has a large moulding carried round the drawer-front and the ends of the case, the drawer being made to open like that of a sideboard. The divisions on the top are inclosed, on the ends, by a piece shaped out of the solid and doweled between the two outsides. The decorations in front, after being carved and finished, are planted on. The circular centre is turned: it and the carving around it are formed of one piece. The interior of the circle is perforated, and the decorations within it are separately made and set in. The feet are doweled on.

Fig. 4.—The drawer is made to act between the pillars, which extend the whole length, having the parts of the case framed into them. The mouldings on the top are doweled on the pillars, and connected together by a turned roller, shouldered between the scrolls, at each end. The other decorations shown in front, with their correspondents on the opposite side, are doweled between the case and top mouldings. The frets, at their points of attachment, are checked in from behind. The interior divisions are doweled on the case, and their upper corners are notched into the cross-roller.

Figs. 5 and 6 are fire-screens resting on claw feet; those of Fig. 5 are doweled to the paned sides of a square block. In Fig. 6, the feet are joined together by an intermediate piece, to which, and to the feet, the pillar with the scrolls at its base is doweled. The poles, in both designs, are shouldered on the pillar, and let into it by a bore. The ornamental top requires to be slip doweled, a pin being turned on the pole which passes into it. The screen is suspended by a circular spring sheath of brass, lined with leather, which is screwed on behind, in the centre of breadth, and near the top; a ring, of equal diameter, is similarly fixed near the bottom; through both these the pole is

made to pass: a pinching screw acting on the spring maintains the screen at any required elevation. The frames of the screens are $\frac{5}{8}$-in. thick, and made up in the usual manner of frets. The front thickness of Fig. 5 requires to be stouter than the others, so as to admit of the round moulding, which borders it, being wrought in relief. The scrolled sides of Fig. 6 are doweled on to the fret frame; the ornamental border, around the top and sides, is inlaid. The sewed piece is let in from behind and secured by a veneered panel, surrounded by a neat small moulding.

Fire-screens.—Plate LXXVI.

Fig. 1 is a screen having a fixed centre frame, into which three other slide frames are made to act; two passing out to right and left, and one drawn out from the top. The centre part is made of 1-in. solid wood mitred dovetailed together, and to receive the slides, it is grooved inside above and below, and slit through on the sides and top (*Fig.* 106). The side slides pass each other, having the rising one between them. The frames forming these are $\frac{5}{16}$-in. thick, and bordered around the edge by $\frac{5}{8}$-in. solid wood. The cloth covering the frames is sewed

(*Fig.* 106.)

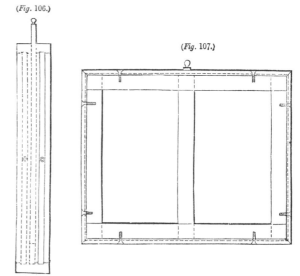

(*Fig.* 107.)

on around their edges, and the wood forming the border is grooved to receive the cloth and frame, and mitred and screwed on, the screw heads being afterwards plugged and slipped over with veneer (*Fig.* 107). The sewed pieces shown on both sides of the centre are also stretched on similar frames, which are checked into the frame flush from the front, and their edges are overlapped by the mouldings on the frame, which are planted on after. Before this last operation, a block is glued on the inner border of the frame of each slide, to prevent it from passing entirely out; these blocks abut on the divisions of the fixed frame. The frame and pillar are united by means of the carved piece between them, which is doweled to both.

Fig. 2.—The frame surrounding the panel is alike on both sides; the mouldings on one side are fixed, and form a check into which the panel is laid; the other mouldings are then glued on, and maintain the panel in its place. The ground frame for the cloth is of $\frac{3}{8}$-in. wood, and made similarly to the preceding. The screen frame is doweled between the pillars at the top and bottom, and is let into the turned mouldings at these parts. Below the pillar is reduced in diameter, and flattened to receive the claw feet, which are doweled on.

Fig. 3.—The screen is carved out of one piece $1\frac{1}{2}$-in. thick; it may be made of solid wood or of deal and gilt; if the latter, the vase must also be gilt, and the leafage on the pillar, the scroll feet and drip below.

Fig. 4.—The panel frame is a fret $\frac{5}{16}$-in. thick, having a flat ground around its inner edge, on which the moulding is planted and made to lap on the cloth. The cloth is put on from behind, and may be closed in by a plain panel, secured by a small moulding.

BED-ROOM FURNITURE.

THE character of the furniture proper to the bed-room, with its related apartment, the dressing-room, is strongly marked in its general qualities, and strikingly distinguished from that of the other parts of a dwelling. Here the bedstead, wardrobe, dressing and wash tables, &c., convey, in their several names, peculiar and recurring uses and obvious adaptations. Utility is a predominating sentiment in this section of house furniture, but the feeling of beauty is not therefore excluded; this may be decidedly evinced in decoration, being, however, rather subdued in expression, and qualified and limited in application. The bed-room being an apartment devoted to seclusion and repose, all its appointments should sympathize with this, its essential nature. Its prevailing hues should be toned into consistency with the feelings of rest and retirement; a mellowed light, whether natural or artificial; an absence of gaudy colour, and of striking contrast; a dignified soberness and stability of expression, should belong to its most conspicuous pieces of furniture. This apartment seems to require that these conditions be fulfilled for its suitable treatment.

FRENCH BEDSTEADS.—PLATE LXXVII.

The designs on this Plate may be executed in mahogany, walnut, satinwood, or maple; they are finished plain on the side which stands next the wall, the exposed parts alone being decorated. Spring mattresses are frequently used for this sort of bedstead, in which case, the lathe bottom should be kept about 6 inches down from the top of the sides.

Fig. 1.—The end consists of three distinct parts separately made and doweled together; these parts are severally indicated on the pilaster as corresponding to its base, its body and the carved ornament which surmounts it. The base is dovetailed together out of 1½-in. hardwood, and veneered; it is clamped on the top by a solid piece of the same thickness, having a moulding wrought around its edge. The front and back pilasters are of hardwood, 3-in. thick, and veneered on the face; they are joined together by a board, inclosing the end, whose breadth is equal to their whole length. This board is of deal, 1¼-in. thick, and is feathered in between the pilasters, and finished flush with their outer edges; it is strongly blocked to the pilasters inside, and along with them is veneered over on the outside: the mouldings and other decorations on this part are planted on the veneer. The square block forming the cap of the pilasters is a board which extends across both, and strengthens the end, and it also serves as a ground for the orna-

mental top. A cross rail is also dovetailed into the pilasters under, and assists in securing their connection with the base. The scrolled top pieces are profiled together, and doweled on the pilaster before they are glued; the space between them is filled by two pieces of solid wood, which mitre together at the top, and are made to margin within the outer edge of the scrolls where they are doweled; the overhanging leafage at the top is framed of a separate piece, which is profiled, indented, and separately carved. The entire inside of the end is stuffed. The sides require 1¼-in. hard wood (birch or wainscoat.) The necessary breadth at the ends is produced by doweling pieces on; they are veneered on the face, and the various decorations are planted on the veneer; the upper edge of the side may be cross bordered with stout veneer. The sides may be tenoned into the edge of the pilasters, or strongly slip doweled, and secured to them by French screws; see Fig. 7, Plate LXXXV.

Fig 2.—The end of this design is also formed in three parts; the two lower join together in a line with the upper edge of the sides. The lowest portion forms on side view a pedestal to the pilaster, and extends down so as to admit of the base being formed on it by clamping. The ends are enclosed and panelled, and all the top scrolls and other decorations are treated similarly to Fig. 1. The corner pieces are slip doweled to the side rails, and also to the edges of the pilasters.

Fig. 3 differs considerably from the preceding in some particulars of design and construction; the end consists of three principal and of two minor parts; the latter are the supporting base and scrolled top, both of which are screwed on. The undermost of the larger parts is wrought in uniformly with the sides, as in Fig. 2; on the top of this part a moulded portion is made to rest, consisting of a block of deal or hardwood, on the outside and front end of which the mouldings after being wrought are planted: the end of the block thus apparently makes a part of the pilaster. The portion resting on this block is fixed to it by dowels, and strengthened by a cross rail, which is mortised into the ends of this upper section of the pilaster; this part of the end is inclosed similarly to Fig. 2; a piece of solid wood is glued on the upper edge of the board, to admit of the hollow at the neck being wrought on it. The end is stuffed inside and on the top.

Fig 4 is a bedstead well adapted for oak; it is framed and double screwed in the common manner, the foot and sideboards being doweled between the posts, and made to extend down and cover the hardwood rails, which for this purpose must be kept within the flush of the posts the necessary amount. The head and footboard tops are formed of two pieces, mitred in the centre, and doweled down on the sides of the frame. The frets are planted on a sunk ground, before which they and the ground to which they are applied are both finished.

Fig. 5.—The sides and foot end of this design are similarly finished; the scroll supports are turned on the feet, and then carved; a pin is wrought on each, by means of which the scrolls are attached; they are, besides, slip doweled on the side. A roller of deal, conforming to the shape of the scrolls, is doweled between them, and from the inner edge of this roller a piece, forming the footboard, is carried right down and fixed to the inside of the end rail: the whole is stuffed over. The headboard and corner pieces are let into grooves, wrought out of the pillar before the latter is turned. The feet are separately wrought and doweled on.

HALF TESTER BEDSTEADS.—PLATE LXXVIII.

Bedsteads of this character are in frequent use, and are very suitable for moderately-sized apartments. Their style is intermediate between French and tester bedstead, being less expensive than the latter, and esteemed more elegant than the former.

Fig. 1.—The head-posts are square, measuring on the side about 4 in.; they are made up of birch, 3-in. thick, clamped on their exposed sides, namely, the front and its adjoining inside, with solid wood, 1-in. thick. At their upper end, the posts terminate at the cap below; they extend to the under edge of the side rails, where the turned feet are doweled on them; they are chamfered on three corners, and their decorations are planted on. The short foot-posts are of solid wood, 6-in. square; the ball of the turned feet may be brought out by clamping. The side and end rails are made of birch $2\frac{1}{4}$-in. thick, and are veneered on the face. On the surface of the veneer being finished, the bordered frets are glued on the veneer; these require to be $\frac{5}{16}$-in. thick, the outside layer being thicker than the others, as the frets are relieved on the front by the carver. Around the frets a raised border, $\frac{3}{8}$-in. thick, is then planted; the upper edges of the side rails are afterwards veneered.

The frame of the footboard requires solid wood, 3-in. thick. The side rails of the frame are doweled between the top and bottom; the lines of the joints being the upper edge of the bottom rail, and the diameter line of the circle along the brakes. The border, surrounding the outer edge of the frame, is $\frac{5}{8}$-in. thick, and is planted on the face; the straight portion of this border below extends down, on both sides, to the bed rail, forming a ground on which the bottom moulding of the footboard is planted. The panel of the footboard is made of $\frac{7}{8}$-in. deal, and laid with a choice veneer; it is let in, from the outside, into a check formed for it on the frame: in this process the panel is first profiled, and its outline drawn on the face of the frame, the thickness of the panel is then gauged on the inner edge of the frame, and the space, to form the check, is cut out true to these lines. The panel being thus kept exactly flush in front, a small moulding, planted on the frame, is made to lap on it, covering the joint. The front and sides of the frame for the canopy are of solid wood, $\frac{7}{8}$-in. thick, and dovetailed together; these parts are panelled by means of a raised border, $\frac{3}{8}$-in. thick, which is planted on; the frets, as in the case of the rails, being previously glued down. The apparent blocks, forming the corner ornaments of the cornice, are each made up of two pieces, clamped on the face, and mitred on the angle. The canopy behind is connected with a vertical frame of deal, $1\frac{1}{2}$-in. thick, which, in length, extends across, and rests on, both posts; while its breadth corresponds with the depth of the arch of the canopy. This frame is fitted, and doweled between, and is, behind, wrought off flush with, the sides of the canopy. A block of solid wood is glued within each angle, formed by the two frames where they join; by this means the canopy is slip doweled on the posts.

The canopy is maintained in position by a strong straight bar of iron, which is screwed to the head-posts and vertical frame behind. A flat frame, or lathe, is fitted within the cornice, leaving a space between of $\frac{3}{8}$-in. broad, for the valance, which is nailed to the edge of the lathe. Two right-angled iron brackets, screwed to the posts, serve to support the lathe, which again is connected to the cornice by tongued catches screwed on from above.

Fig. 2 is made like the preceding; the head-posts and canopy are similarly treated; the apparent prolongation of the former, above the cap, is a thin piece planted on the frame. The ground, for the canopy frame, is dovetailed together; in front, it may be pieced out on the upper edge with deal to receive on it the cornice moulding. The thin pieces, forming the margin of the panels, are mitred together on the fore corners of the frame; and so conceal the dovetails. The framing of this bed may be connected by screws in the ordinary manner; the heads of which may be concealed by the oval pateras.

Half Tester Bedsteads.—Plate LXXIX.

The principal difference in construction, between the designs here given and those on the preceding Plate, consists in the character of the footboard; in both the present examples it is let into the foot-posts; a groove being mortised out of each. This is effected before the posts are turned; the grooves being temporarily filled tightly with a piece of wood, to prevent their lips from chipping in the lathe. The footboards are framed, and flush panelled, with a moulding planted on the face. The panels may be inlaid, or covered, with figured cloth; they are let in from the outside, and applied to a cheek cut out of the framing; with a view to greater strength, they may be strongly blocked from the inside, and are stuffed over. The head-posts extend the whole height, and may be of hardwood, veneered or clamped, on the exposed sides, while the decorations are all planted on. The bed rails are sunk panelled by means of a raised border which is planted on them. The decorations, under the rails of Fig 2, are slip doweled, and are brought near to the outside, so as to admit the curtain pawn to pass behind them. Both these beds should be framed together by the screw, Fig. 7, Plate LXXXV. The cornices of both designs are similarly constructed; the supporting brackets may be slip doweled, or secured to their place by screws sent through the cornice from the top, and also through the posts from behind.

Half Tester Bedstead.—Plate LXXX.

In all essential particulars of construction, this design resembles either of the preceding. The head and foot posts are wrought square, and the panels are grounded down and veneered. Their mouldings and frets are, after being wholly finished, planted on. The triangular ornaments on the top of the foot-posts are carved on the solid. The small panels below are made to cover the screw heads, and are movable. For other methods of bracing the posts, and framing together, the reader is referred to the description of bed-pillars, under Plate LXXXV. The mouldings in the four posts are carried around the rails; the top edge of the latter is veneered. The footboard is sunk panelled, and doweled, between the posts; the ornament in its centre is inlaid. The cornice is mitred into the capitals of the pilasters, into which the head-posts are formed. The back of the cornice is screwed to a cross rail, which is dovetailed edgeways into the top of the posts. The fret brackets, supporting the cornice, are fixed as described under Plate LXXIX.: these may be of bronze, or of wood, made up in three thicknesses. The frets, on the angles of the posts and rails, are slip doweled on these parts.

Bedstead (medieval).—Plate LXXXI.

The woods most suited for this style of design are oak, birch, and walnut; or any light-coloured wood may be used, but not mahogany, which, to show the full beauty of its grain, requires broad and rounded surfaces. The corresponding ends of the bed and canopy are framed permanently together; they at once join on to the side rails, and the ridge rail of the bed, and are secured by ordinary bed screws. Each of the two centre standards is mortised flush into the end rail of the bed, which again is tenoned into the posts. The latter are 3½-in. thick, and project, on each side, ¼-in. beyond the rails; the standards, rails, and shaped arms, are wrought flush, and are 3-in. thick; to this thickness, also, the foot-posts are made to taper at the tops, where the arms, which have been previously shouldered into, and doweled on to, the standard, are adjusted and doweled on; the line of the joints on the side may be partially concealed by a sunk patera and leafage. The arms on the corresponding part at the head of the bed are made to join down on a straight cross rail, which is tenoned into the posts. The standards sensibly taper, both on the thickness and breadth, from where the lower arms join to them up to the top. This expression of taper is shared by the upper supporting arms and the arch of the canopy, giving to these parts greater lightness of appearance. The upper arms are tenoned into the standard, and shouldered on it obliquely, as shown in (*Fig.* 108). From the upper part, *a*, the standard is further reduced to a breadth which it maintains to the top. The arch may be formed of two pieces doweled together, and then joined down on the standard; or the latter may pass up and receive on its sides the two segments forming the arch; the latter is the better method. To assist the action of the cramps, in framing the parts together, a notch of wood should be left on the upper edge of each segment; these may be wrought off after.

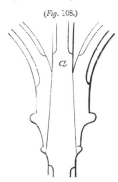

(*Fig.* 108.)

In addition to the ends, the wood-work of the roof consists simply of three rails, one on each side below, tenoned into the segments of the arch, and also the ridge rail; all of which are secured by screws passing through the ends. The ridge rail may be continued to any depth that may be deemed necessary for stiffness to the bed, as this will depend much on the close and secure abutment of the rails, and on the strength of the screws. The contour of the roof may be completely maintained through its entire length by ribs spanning the distance between the side and ridge rails; two such ribs will require to be screwed to the inside of each of the ends, to distend the cloth.

The poles for the curtains must be fixed outside, being supported by passing through the ends of the curved arms at the head and foot. The ornament is extremely simple, the carving being merely sunk in the solid wood. It may vary in richness from simple outlining, leaving the figure almost flat, to the most careful modelling, in which, however, under-cutting must be avoided, or any such depth as shall interfere with its presenting a surface in harmony with the predominant idea of flatness. Most of the wood-work is also chamfered lengthwise, either with plain chamfering or ogeed, still preserving the square profile in section, as in the cross rail at the head and foot. The panels of the head-board are represented as stuffed; those of the foot-board as covered with tapestry, stained light. The draperies, whether rich or not, should have a pattern treated in flat unshaded colours; all chintzes, or silks, with flowers shaded and drawn in close imitation of nature, are inadmissible, as they violate the principle which guides the ornament of the wood-work throughout. The valances may be embroidered if there be any difficulty in finding a pattern suited to their form; but with a pattern merely powdered with fleur de lis, crosses, or diapers, this is likely to be unnecessary. Gymps should be sparingly introduced on the edges and principal lines; they may, however, be run with good effect on the circular canopy from the divisions of the valances to the ridge, as in the design. In summer, the effect of this bed would be lightened by substituting white muslin for coloured curtains around the foot.

POSTED BEDSTEADS.—PLATE LXXXII.

The designs on this Plate are similar to each other in all the chief particulars of construction. The head and foot posts are of equal length; those at the head, when exposed, are of a square form, and of solid wood, or of hardwood laid with stout veneers, and are finished ornamentally; they are usually of birch, 3½-in. thick, tapering to 2½ in. at the top, and cloth covered, the head piece of the curtains being carried round and tacked on them behind. The foot-posts of the figure to the left are square wrought; and clamped at the parts of greatest diameter. The capitals, including the square blocks on which the cornice rests, may each be formed of a separate piece from the posts and doweled down. The panels on the square of the posts are removable, being fixed to the post by catches, so as to cover or expose the framing screws as needed. The foot-posts of the other design on the Plate are turned above and below the square, and afterwards carved. The foot-board is framed and panelled; the top and bottom rails being tenoned into the ends. The wood of the frame requires to be of a breadth to admit of the figure of the panels being cut out of it. When the panel openings are profiled, checks are wrought around their edges inside to receive the panels, the forelap of the check has a hollow moulding wrought in its edge. The panels are cloth covered. After the top edge of the frame is profiled, the top mouldings at the ends are fitted on. The scrolls at the centre of the top are separately prepared, then planted and wrought off. The foot-board of the figure to the right may be joined up in one breadth of solid wood, and cross-headed at the ends; or it may be made of 1¼-in. deal, and veneered over; the top moulding is planted on the face on both sides, and veneered on the top. The shaped panels, ⅜-in. thick, with the other decorations, are planted on the face. The foot-boards are doweled into the posts.

The head-board is framed, fitted between the head-posts, grooved in the end, stuffed inside, and slid into its place on tongues mortised into the posts.

The cornices are supported by a frame lathe of 1-in. wood, which rests on the top of the posts. This lathe, when the curtains are suspended from iron rods attached to it below, is distinct from the cornice, with a space of ⅜-in. between them around the sides and foot end, to admit the valance, which is tacked to its edge; in such case the cornice is attached to the lathe by tongued catches.

In the present examples, the lathe *a*, as shown in (*Fig.* 109,)

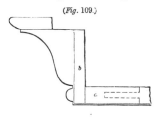

(*Fig.* 109.)

is glued permanently to the cornice *b*, and, with the cornice, is veneered below. The sides of the lathe, at the foot end of the bed, are tenoned, and joined to the corresponding part of the cornice; they receive on them the end which is fitted, and glued to the cornice within the returns; this arrangement is necessary when the curtains are suspended from poles fixed into the head of the posts, as in these examples, wherein those parts are wholly exposed to view. The poles are let full into the posts for two or more inches.

The cornice consists of three separable parts—the end with its returns of about 8 in. long attached, and the two sides, which abut against the returns. When the cornice is framed together, these ends approach, but not so closely or firmly as is necessary for the strength or elegance of appearance. A simple device is commonly resorted to for bracing home the joints. The abutting ends are tongued and slip-doweled together, so as to maintain the various parts and members of the mouldings flush and uniform with each other. As shown in (*Fig.* 110), a slip of hardwood, 1½-in. broad, and ⅜-in. thick, is glued and screwed on within half-an-inch of the joints, across each of the four adjoining ends of the returns and sides of the cornice; each pair of slips taken together when screwed on is slightly wedge-shaped and tapered from below up. Another piece, ¾-in. thick and 3-in. broad, is checked out to the form and depth of the pieces screwed on, and made to pass on them tightly from above down, so as to force home the joint and maintain it secure. Brass catches, of a suitable construction, are frequently employed for this purpose; the method referred to, however, is cheap and efficient.

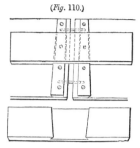
(*Fig.* 110.)

The decorations surmounting the cornice are put on in the usual manner. Posted beds should be mounted on French castors; these are completely concealed from view when the bed is fully mounted, and their action is easy and smooth.

(*Frontispiece*)
STATE BEDSTEAD.—PLATE LXXXIII.

This design, in its lower parts, does not differ materially in construction from the ordinary four-posted bedstead: it is square-framed, having four short posts or pedestals in the angles. The pedestals in the body are not less than 6 in. square, the panels on them are grounded down, the mouldings of the base and capital are mitred around them, and the carving at their upper end is planted on the face, the pieces being mitred together on the several angles. The four columns on each pedestal are centred, as shown in (*Fig.* 110); they are fixed by a pin and bore, having their bases, which are 4 in. in diameter, just touching each other. The caps of the columns are separately made, each being fixed by a pin turned on the column; their diameter is such that they require to be flattened where they come into contact with each other; they are connected together by small iron plates, which are sunk and screwed into them from above. A solid piece, wrought ornamentally, is doweled on the top of each group of columns, forming a support for the cornice. These pieces at the foot of the bedstead are turned, and each is decorated with four small inverted trusses, which rest on the several columns, and are fixed to the turned piece. The corresponding pieces on the head posts are shaped, carved, and perforated from the front in the form of a Gothic arch. The bed rails are recessed from the front, on the sides, and foot end, thus making the pedestals to appear in relief. The foot-board laps down in front of the end rail, covering it completely, and presenting on its under edge the same finish which is given to the lower edge of the side rails. The head-board is framed up strongly of 2½-in. deal, having its upper edge pieced with solid wood to form the figures. The piecing may be variously affected; two methods are shown in (*Fig.* 111). According to one of those methods, four principal pieces are required—two on each side *a*, *a*, (6-in. thick), forming the lower half, and the attire of the reclining figures; the moulding connected with this part may be wrought on the solid, or, if esteemed as more convenient, it may be separately wrought and planted on a prepared ground. Another piece, *b*, 8-in. thick, joins down on the head-board and side pieces in the line *c*, *d*, passing under the arms of the figures; the joint and the opposition of the grain of the wood in the parts should be hidden as much as possible by the folds given to the dress in

(*Fig.* 111.)

carving. A fourth piece, *e*, 10-in. thick, is joined on the last in the line, *f*, *g*, to form the middle-winged figure, as the head

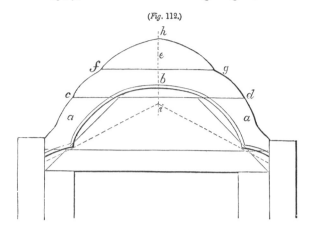
(*Fig.* 112.)

is in advance of the wings, and both parts project inwards, overshadowing the sleepers; additional pieces may be clamped on the face, to give the due projection to the parts. The dotted lines on the cut suggest another method of gluing up the wood; for the carving in this case, the line *h*, *i*, is that of a butt joint of two pieces, which is formed in the medial line of the centre figure. It may be desirable to execute the centre figure separately, and to adjust and fix it on from behind. The cornice consists of four principal parts, which are separable, the two ends and two sides; those parts at the angles being slip dovetailed together, and secured by angle plates. The ground on which the cornice mouldings are planted is formed of deal 1-in. thick; the semicircular parts of it are made in two thicknesses; the ends of the semicircles are half checked on the short horizontal pieces, which again being dovetailed into the sides, with them form the angles of the cornice. At the head, square blocks are glued on the ground to form the brakes; the turned blocks on the corresponding parts at the foot may be scribed on. The depth of these brakes and blocks is about 3½-in. measuring on the top moulding of the cornice. Attention to this is necessary, as the valance, which is nailed to the roof, passes between the two inner columns, on its being carried round to the ends. After the mouldings on the cornice are planted, the turned blocks may be notched on the angles of the ground, and then mitred in with the adjoining part of the moulding, and finally screwed to the end of the cornice; this latter particular is important, as in dovetailing the ground the pins of the dovetails are formed on both ends of the sides, which parts in consequence are first put on the bed, the ends being driven home after. The ornamental brackets on the angles of the cornice below are doweled on, and are let in by the end into the ornamental pieces which are fixed on the pillars. The vases are turned, separately carved, and slip doweled on the top. The leaves on the cornice should be profiled from one or more long pieces shaped to the ground, and then separately carved. The roof of the bed is made with straight horizontal sides, and arched ends dovetailed at right angles into them. These ends are not apparent in the drawing, from being cloth-covered on their upper edge; they follow the general outline of the tops of the arches, and are at both ends kept apart from them about ⅜-in., so as to admit of the valance being interposed between. The ornamental ridge pole of the roof is tenoned between the ends of the cornice; a block is carried along its under edge on each side for attaching the cloth of the roof; the apparent convexity of which is formed by straining the cloth stiffly between its points of attachment, the centre of the curve being supported on each side, by a stretching rod mortised between the circular ends.

BED PILLARS.—PLATE LXXXIV.

Fig. 1.—This design is for mahogany pillars; being suitable for the common thickness of wood for posts of this description, namely, five inches. The can is turned by itself, and joined round the pillar. Excepting the can and buttons, and the clamps of the base, this pillar is solid throughout. The panels covering the bed-screws are fastened by ball and plate catches, as shown in (*Fig.* 112), or by two screw nails, which fasten like dove-tails upon the post.

(*Fig.* 113.)

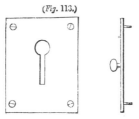

Fig. 2.—The pillar shown in this figure should be made of oak. This wood being less costly than mahogany, it is better to have it the whole thickness, since the labour of clamping and mitring will not be compensated by any saving thereby effected in the wood. The drops under the can, and the decorations above the base-moulding, are planted on. The pillar is turned the whole length of the twisting, and a third of the capital: the remainder of the capital being wrought square. If no twisting lathe is at command, the spirals may be hand-wrought, and, as preparatory to this, take a piece of girth-web, and tack it to the front and centre of the pillar, just above the can; then wind the girth round it spirally, making eight turns between the can and the capital; taking care to terminate the spiral on the front side, as otherwise the capital will appear to *throw*, for want of support. When the girth is fixed, draw the spiral lines along its edges with a pencil, after which it may be removed and the work begun. A flat twist is made, in the first place, which the carver afterwards deepens and finishes. This design does not admit of panels on the surbase to cover the bed-screws.

Fig. 3.—This pillar is for mahogany, and is turned its whole length. The can is put on in the same manner as Fig. 1.; and the buttons and drops are sunk in. The slide panels on the surbase are also fixed as in Fig. 1.

Fig. 4.—The design exhibited in this figure is adapted either for oak or mahogany. If made of oak, whole wood is to be used, for the reason given under Fig. 2; and the pillar is to be turned its whole length, leaving *wants* for the octagonal sides. If mahogany is used, the mouldings above the surbase, and also the base mouldings may be planted and mitred. As this pillar tapers to the top, as much wood may be taken off the thickness, at that part, as will make all the small mouldings. These last are wrought the cross way of the wood; and the best method is to cross-cut them at their breadths, and plant them continuously on the edge of a board, and work them all in one length. This pillar must be fastened by the patent screw, Fig. 7, Plate LXXXIII., as the design is not suitable for panelling.

Fig. 5.—This is intended for mahogany, and is turned from the upper mouldings of the surbase, all below which is square. The large bead or can is planted as in former cases; and the base and upper mouldings are mitred on. The slide panels are the same as in Fig. 3, and other examples.

BED PILLARS.—PLATE LXXXV.

Fig. 1.—This pillar is intended to be made of Bay mahogany, veneered with Spanish wood. It is turned the whole length of the shaft and surbase. The base moulding is made separately, and fixed on with dowels; and the mouldings constituting the can above the surbase are formed from a ring of wood, separately

made, and let into a groove turned on the pillar; as shown in Plate I., Fig. 1; the inserted piece being afterwards turned and carved on the pillar. The capital is also of Spanish wood, carved separately, and is fixed upon the shaft by a tenon. This pillar must be covered with a strong mottle veneer, which, when polished, gives it a clear, plain, light effect, being its principal beauty. The portions of the pillar above and below the can are separately veneered, and each with one piece. In proceeding to lay the veneer it is first brought to its proper breadth at each end, allowing, besides the absolute measure, $\frac{3}{16}$ in. more for one of the sides to overlap the other; it is then stripped straight on the edges, and laid by means of girth web rolled tightly around it on the pillar. As the process is a little tedious, and during it the glue is apt to cool, after the web is wound round the pillar the glue is heated, and, at the same time, the web is tightened strongly up, by moistening the whole surface with hot water before a blazing fire; turning the pillar, and exposing all parts of it in succession to the heat. The whole is allowed to dry for a day, after which, the girth web is unwound, and the veneer is washed clean; the overlapping side is now carefully stripped back by a rebate plane, until the edge of the underlying side begins to appear; a hot iron is then coursed along the veneer at this part, to dissolve the glue retained under the projecting side, and so to reduce the inequality of surface: the two edges of the veneer being thus brought to abut together, and the joint accordingly formed. Sliding panels, usually placed on the surbase to cover the screws, are not applicable to this pillar; and their use is obviated by adopting the patent screw, Fig. 7, the construction of which is so simple as to require little explanation. It consists of a strong iron screw, which deeply penetrates the posts from the inside of the framing, at an angle of 45 degrees. The body of the screw passes through the centre of an arch of iron, which, while its extremities act on both rails, urging them home, re-acts equally, and at the same instant, against the screw, the action of which solicits the post powerfully inwards. The ends of the arch are resisted by their partial insertion into the wood of the rails, where, also, for the same purpose, iron plates crossing the rails are screwed on. The head of the bracing-screw is formed into an eye, through which a lever is made to act in turning it.

Fig. 2.—This pillar is also to be made of mahogany, and turned the whole length from the square, or top of the surbase. The can is octagonal; the moulding on it is separately made, being worked in one length and mitred round. The ground for the moulding is formed on the original thickness of the wood for the pillar; which, at this part, is not entirely turned, but has merely the corners chipped off. The screw heads are covered with sliding panels. The base mouldings are mitred and clamped; as much wood as will serve this purpose may be cut down from the several sides of the post at the top before it is turned.

Fig. 3.—In this design the turning commences at the top of the surbase. The can is formed, fixed, turned, and carved, as in Fig. 1; and the ornamental part above the can is gorged out, the pillar being left so much thicker for the purpose. The base mouldings are mitred and clamped as in Fig. 2. As the effect of the surbase would be injured by the sliding panel, this pillar must be fixed like Fig. 1, by the patent screw, Fig. 7.

Fig. 4.—This is adapted either for oak or mahogany, and is wrought in the same way as Fig. 3. The buttons on the can, and the small detached ornaments in the cavetto, above it, are sunk in.

Fig. 5.—This pillar is to be made of mahogany, and to be wrought in the same manner as Fig. 2, all above the surbase being turned, and all under it square. The shaft is octagonal, and starts from the round above the can. The method of starting and finishing the panes, shown in this example, has a very good effect. The surbase has sliding panels for the screws, the button above each panel being sunk in.

Fig. 6.—The design here given is intended for oak, and the whole pillar is solid except the can, which is split and put on as in Fig. 1, and the base moulding which is blocked from one piece and fixed with dowels. The pillar is turned the whole length from the base moulding to near the scrolls of the capital, and to preserve the octagonal form as large as the wood will admit, the turner must leave, on the greatest diameters, *wants* or flat spaces nearly the size of the panes. To enable him to do this, suitable wood must be given to him, and, for guidance, a full-sized draught of the design. After the wood is turned, draw on the lines for the octagon in the usual way. This is done by fixing the pillar in what is termed a *reeding* box (*Fig.* 114), which is a long box without top or bottom, about

(*Fig.* 114.)

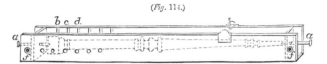

nine inches square inside, and about nine feet long, and made of inch and quarter deal. It is provided with movable ends, through which pivot-centres *a*, *b*, are driven for suspending the post when under operation. Grooves *b*, *c*, *d*, &c., are wrought in the sides of the box, into which the end *a*, may be slid, to fit different lengths of posts. The ends may be varied in height to suit the requirements of work, and, in such case, the sides are braced together by a wooden screw, *f*, which, passing through one side, acts in the other opposite. On the pillar being laid in the box, divide its circumference into eight equal parts with the compasses; then with a reeding gauge draw pencil lines through the points of division along the entire length of the pillar; this being done, the octagonal sides on it are formed by flattening the surface between these lines.

This pillar is screwed to the stock in the same way as Fig. 1. In place of the patent screw, Fig. 7, however, the contrivance shown at Fig. 8 may be used, which is quite as simple and efficient. The exact breadth of the stock B is drawn on the side of the post at the proper height, and a second breadth, D, with about an inch additional, immediately below the first. Then work out of this lower measure a groove 1½-in. broad, and of a depth equal to the intended length of the tenon, continuous with this mortise, and of the same depth a receiving dove-tail is wrought out of the upper breadth, which widens inwards and narrows towards the top; with this a dove-tail, formed on the end of the stock, is made to correspond. This construction is shown by A, Fig. 8, and by section A B, Fig. 9. The framing is effected by inserting the dove-tail of the stock into the groove, and raising it into the receiving part, where it is maintained by the block *d*, which fills the groove, and is urged home, either by cramp or hammer, after the wedge *c* is driven in. When the bed is to be taken down, on driving out the wedge *c* the whole framing will come asunder readily.

Cots and Cradles.—Plate LXXXVI.

Fig. 1 is, in the body and head, framed and sunk panelled. The side framing is wrought to shape; it is 2¼-in. broad, by ⅞-in. thick, with the end rails mortised into the sides; the latter only are veneered before the frames are put together, the end rails being cross-veneered after. The two end frames are each formed into quadrant curves, which are half checked on each other below, and above are tenoned or checked into a cross

rail. The end frames abut on, and are glued and screwed to, the ends of the side frames. They are made to project so as to form a ⅜-in. raised border on the side, which is cross-veneered. The panels are cloth covered and set in from the outside; they may be supported behind by fillets, sprigged on the framing, or by a check wrought out of it before it is put together; the panel mouldings and frets are afterwards planted on. The sides are connected at the bottom by a keel-piece, which is screwed on them and on the ends. The head is formed of three pieces, the two sides and top; these are made up as frets in three thicknesses, making together about ½-in. The proper curve is given to the pieces by cauling them on suitable moulds. The back of the head is similarly prepared, and, after being shaped and panelled, is doweled down on the body. The sides of the head are then fitted to the back and body, and doweled on the latter. The circular top is then joined down on the sides, and keyed to them from the inside, and canvassed over at the joints. After all these fittings are made, and before they are finally fixed, the panelled openings on the head are cut out, and the mouldings around them mitred in. The pieces cut out form the panels, which, after being trimmed and cloth covered, are restored to their original position. After the head of the cot is attached to the body, the moulding around the upper edge of the latter is planted on. A square fillet is formed around the head in front, by planting on the face a cross band ¼-in. thick, which works in with the upper member of the moulding on the body. The upper edge of the moulding and of the fillet, is cross-banded. The cot is suspended by looped brass rods screwed to it at each end, and carried over strong studs fixed into the supporting pillars. It may be necessary that the stretching rail below be made more massive and stronger in its attachment to the pillars than is shown in the Plate. The length of this rail is obviously determined by that of the cot, including the greatest projections on the pillar. The cot is stuffed inside.

Fig. 2, in the body, is built of ⅞-in. deal. The segments should generally go completely round the end, their joinings being effected chiefly on the sides; each layer might be independently formed, and the pieces for strength made to half lap on each other at their abutments. On the whole being glued up, it is then wrought to shape on the outside, and smoothed off within. The body may be cross-veneered or done up in colours, with the mouldings and other decorations gilt. The panels on the sides are cloth covered. They may be either formed flush, the cloth being nailed on the body, or the pieces may be cut out, covered, and, after the mouldings are planted, replaced from the inside and blocked. The mouldings may be wrought to shape out of the solid in quarter lengths, and butt joined; or they may be wrought in half lengths, and steam bent around the ends, and butted in mid length. The fret ornament around the bottom is ₃⁄₁₆-in. thick; it is by the upper edge checked into the body, and then lapped over by the moulding. The bottom is checked in from below. The head in front view is semicircular, and is formed of seven ribs to the two in front, which together form the semicircle; a piece of solid wood, for the carving, similarly shaped, is glued on to the ribs and edge of the body. The carving is executed and the parts fitted before they are finally fixed; after which the other ribs are adjusted, the whole being brought together at the top, and secured by screws, and by cloth glued on. The head is cloth covered outside, and stuffed within. The crown, which surmounts the head, is gilt, and rests on a crimson tasselated cushion.

Fig. 3.—The body of this cradle is a large moulding, of solid wood, thin wrought and adjusted to the overly, and mitred in the four corners. The mitres, on their upper and under edges, are secured by small iron plates, which are sunk flush into them, diagonally, and screwed on. The carving on each corner is formed of two pieces, which are grounded and mitred together. The bottom is formed by a board screwed on, upon the edges of which the mouldings, shown in the design, are planted; to this bottom the rocking feet are doweled or attached by screws sent through from within. The head is built of staves of solid wood, on which the carving in front is wrought. The ends of the staves are made to project, so as to form together a fillet round the back of the head.

Fig. 4 is, in all important particulars, similar in construction to Fig. 3.

WARDROBES.—PLATE LXXXVII.

The sort of wardrobe, of which the designs on this Plate are examples, is usually made in a single carcass, with a loose cornice and base; frequently they are made in two carcasses, the interior adjoining gables of which are screwed together; in such case, the moulding shown between the doors, which in the single carcass is glued on the door stile, is of a breadth corresponding to the thickness of both inner gables, and is planted on one of them, flush with the inside, and projecting beyond the outside so as to lap on the edge of the other gable, which is brought close up behind the moulding, before both gables are screwed together. Whatever method is adopted, the wardrobe, interiorly, is divided into half, if not, by the construction of two distinct and separate divisions; then by one centre division, mortised between the carcass, top and bottom; most frequently this centre division is stopped short below, being mortised into a horizontal division, dove-tailed into the gables at about 10-in. from their lower end; by this means, a drawer space, the entire length of the wardrobe, is cut off, which forms a convenient deposit for small clothes or napery. Of the two upper spaces, that to the right is fitted with drawers and trays; there are usually three drawers and four trays, the drawers being under; the latter are separated from each other and from the trays, by fore-edges and shelves. The trays are made to run on fillets screwed to the gables. The space to the left and also the carcass back, which is framed and panelled, are cloth lined, and provided with hooks at the top for hanging dresses.

Fig. 1.—The four corners are wrought into a quarter round on the gables of about $2\frac{1}{2}$-in. radius. The rounded corners stand in advance of the top and bottom edges of the carcass about $\frac{1}{2}$-in., and the doors which fit between them are, in consequence, sunk this amount, and stand out, their remaining thickness forming a long brake in front; the base and cornice are made to correspond with the outline thus given to the carcass.

Fig. 2 is made like the preceding, but is square in front, and embellished by two ornamental columns, $\frac{3}{4}$ of the round, which are doweled on the doors or screwed on from the inside.

Fig. 3.—The pilasters on the doors are sunk panelled by means of a raised border planted on, within which a small moulding is afterwards mitred and fitted. A block and vase, continuous of the pilaster, are planted on and above the cornice. The doors are sunk panelled. An ornamental panel, with a moulded border, is planted on the field of the door panel. The ornaments on the angles of the doors are together wrought out of one piece, then cut asunder, and planted on.

Fig. 4.—The fret on the door, enclosing the moulding on the top, is formed of two pieces, mitred together in the centre; each pair may be glued and fretted together, then separated, fitted, and planted. The top ornament is formed of $\frac{1}{2}$-in. wood; it is slip doweled on the top, and afterwards cut.

WARDROBES.—PLATE LXXXVIII.

These designs are of a plain character, and require, for effect, that they be executed in rich wood; each should be constructed in three carcasses, the two outer of which, or wings, should be entirely a free space within, for hanging dresses, and cloth lined, or furnished below with one drawer, each about 12-in. deep; the centre part is provided with drawers and trays. The cornice and base of each design are entire.

Fig. 1 has a projecting centre, on the gables of which the doors on the wings are made to lock. The panel of the centre door is a mirror plate; the door frame, in consequence, must be of $1\frac{1}{2}$-in. wood; the plate is protected from behind by a panelled frame $\frac{3}{4}$-in. thick. The two inner pilasters move with the centre door; the outer pilasters are attached to the doors of the wings. The block in the centre above the cornice, along with the frets at each end of it, are set back parallel to the front of the cornice frieze, and fixed by screws.

Fig. 2 has the doors all in one plane, with the centre one pivot-hinged; they are flush panelled, with a raised panel planted on each. The two centre pilasters are fixed, and those at the ends are, as in Fig. 1, attached to the doors of the wings. They are stop chamfered on the corners to within $\frac{3}{16}$-in. of the door stile, and the other decorations on them are inlaid.

WARDROBES.—PLATE LXXXIX.

The general construction of this wardrobe is sufficiently apparent from the design; the wings are made and adapted similarly to those of the preceding. The doors are flush panelled and veneered over; two styles of decoration are shown on them. The mouldings and relievo figures on both are planted on the face. The pilaster on the door to the left is wrought from one piece of solid wood, the truss and base are made to abut to and lap on it; the tie ornament in the centre of the shaft is planted on. The carving around the circular moulding on the door to the right, is formed of two pieces of 2-in. wood, joined together in the centre. The drawers and cabinet between the wings are separately made, and in the ordinary manner. The cabinet doors are pivot-hinged; a slip of wood $\frac{3}{8}$-in. thick, moulded on the fore edge, is interposed all around, between the cabinet and the top of the drawers, so as to make the doors sweep clear of the drawers' top; this, although not apparent in the design, requires to be introduced. The two interior gables of the wings may be of solid wood, or veneered only as far as they are exposed, the continuation backward being of deal. The mouldings on the cabinet doors are planted on the face of the door framing, and made to lap inwards, forming a check for the frets, which again are closed in from behind with a panel, cloth covered; the heads on the centre of the frets are screwed on from behind. The several parts of the large moulding on the cornice are first mitred, then carved and planted; the angles are trimmed after the whole is glued down.

WARDROBES.—PLATE XC.

The designs on this Plate are formed in two heights, which are united together in the bottom line of the columns and pilasters. The upper portion is divided interiorly, as described under Plate LXXXVII.; the under part is a case containing a large drawer, which acts between the base and surbase, and extends the whole length, between the gables, with its front lapping over their edge. Sometimes, and more ingeniously, the drawer front is made to pass within the gables, being stopped flush with them; and the pilasters are hinged to the edge of the gables, and made to lock on the drawer.

The doors on the figure to the right are flush panelled; on the panel of each, as a ground, an ornamental panel of solid wood, 1¼-in. thick, is laid; the ground panel might be dispensed with by increasing the breadth of the doors' framing, and making the ornamental panel to lap on it. A hollow moulding is wrought on the solid around this panel, and its edges are pieced out to form the brakes on its sides. After this raised panel is shaped and glued down, the mouldings of the door frame are mitred and planted around its edge; the field of the panel is veneered with rich wood; the panel on the drawer front is similarly treated. The pilasters are separately made, and, on being wholly finished, are planted on the door frame. The cornice ground, in the centre of its front, is pieced out and veneered, forming a ground on which the top mouldings are planted.

The other design, on the Plate, has the doors also flush panelled, with an ornamental panel planted on. The columns are slightly flattened behind, and applied to, and screwed on, the door stile. The shaft of the columns is veneered. The capital and base of the column are doweled on; the moulding surmounting the former is paned. The carved top of the door moulding is of one piece, 2-in. thick, of cross wood, and includes the curves which join on to the ends of the stile moulding, the grain of both pieces being made to run alike. This part, in the order of work, is first planted, and the adjoining parts are abutted to it. A raised panel, ⅜-in. thick, is planted on the drawer front, and the moulding is carried round it; on this ground the other decorations are successively glued down. (*Fig.* 115) presents the cornice in cross section. The ornament, on its top, requires 2-in. wood, with the chief projections of the carving brought out by clamping.

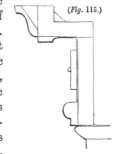

(*Fig.* 115.)

PILASTERS AND BRACKETS.—PLATE XCI.

The pilasters and brackets, designs of which are shown on this Plate, are principally intended for wardrobes; they might also be employed on bookcases, or adapted to decorate the front of other carcass work. Each example is surmounted by an appropriate entablature, which may be considered either as forming part of the pilaster, or as separate from it, and suggestive of a style of cornicing becoming the piece of furniture on which the pilaster or bracket might be displayed. In executing the profile of any of these designs, when several pieces are required, it is more expeditious to cross work them all at once out of a single piece, or to glue the pieces temporarily together for this purpose; those for the top and bottom together, and severally apart, any projections on the sides being afterwards brought out by clamping.

Fig. 1 is adapted for oak or mahogany; it is relieved behind and also around the scrolls by various perforations; the turned drops on the under part are doweled or screwed on.

Fig. 2 is suitable for mahogany or rosewood; it is also well adapted for gilding, if this should accord with the character of the piece of furniture on which it is introduced.

Figs. 3 and 4 should be executed in oak; the latter may be partially gilt.

Figs. 5, 6, 7, 8.—These brackets may be detached from connection with any more extended design, and employed as an independent means of support. In such case they should be treated freely, according to taste or fancy, and may be executed in solid wood, and partially gilt, or in deal, and done up in gold and colours. They may also be employed on a pilaster ground, with a base or bottom piece to correspond, as in the other designs on the Plate.

WASH-STANDS AND DRESSING-TABLES.—PLATE XCII.

Fig. 1.—This design, with its decorations, is founded on the Moorish style of the Alhambra. The top and ledges should 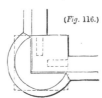 be of marble, resting on a moulded frieze, the ground of which is framed into the top of the legs, as shown, (*Fig.* 116). The legs, after being turned, are reduced in the square at the top, so as to work off flush with the rails; the turned corner-caps, and the mouldings which mitre with them, are then fitted and planted on. The order of operation being thus, the caps are first notched on the corners; they are then mitred, and the mouldings on the front and ends are afterwards adjusted to them. The ledges are, as usual, pinned down on the marble top; the back and returns are united at the angles by means of small pillars of wood or marble, surmounted by carved vases; if the pillars are of wood, the back is checked into them behind, and secured by screws sent through the marble into the wood; the returns being let into grooves, wrought into the front. The bracket for supporting the water bottle is fixed on from behind. The stretcher is of solid wood, and is doweled from under to the bottom of the legs, the stump feet being afterwards doweled on.

(*Fig.* 116.)

Fig. 2 is a Gothic wash-stand, well adapted for oak of a light or dark variety, the top and the ledges to be of marble; the latter may be of wood. The frame under the top is separately made, and the moulding is planted on around it; at the ends it is doweled down on the shaped cross-bar, which again is similarly fixed to the pillar. The stretcher below is mortised between the bottom blocks.

Fig. 3.—The top is of marble, and forms about two-thirds of a circle: the rim under it is of solid wood turned and doweled down on the supports; and, as the back is straight, a cross rail, the thickness of the moulding, unites the ends of the rim behind, being half checked into them. The two shaped supports behind are doweled together, edge to edge, in the same plane, the one in front being fixed to these at right angles. The back may be of solid wood and attached to the rim by screws, or it may be of marble, and made to rest on a check, formed by the projecting back rail, being also attached to the top in the usual manner.

Fig. 4.—The top, with its ledge, and also the mirror sole, may be of marble; the moulding under the top is formed on a flat frame, consisting of a front and two ends of solid wood; the back rail may be of deal. The pedestals are separate; and on the table being fitted up, they are united together by the bracket which crosses the knee-hole and supports the drawer; and by the fore-edge that borders the drawer above, which is dovetailed into the gables, but chiefly by the moulded frame which crosses, and is screwed to, the top of both pedestals.

The mirror supports, on being profiled, are fitted to the sole; they are attached by screws, wrought into the standards, which are made to pass through the marble, and secured by nuts from under. They are afterwards separately carved, finished, and finally fixed; if the sole is made of wood, the supports are simply doweled on. The mirror frame is built up of two ½-in. thicknesses of mahogany; the fret on it is made up in the usual manner, and checked in flush from the fore-edge of the frame; the moulding is then planted on, and made to lap on the glass; the outer edge of the frame is slipped with veneer.

Fig. 5.—As in this design the moulding under the top is planted on the body of the pedestals; the top itself, in consequence, rests immediately on both. The pilasters intersect the moulding, and pass up to the top; they are planted on a ground formed for them on the pedestals, and are chamfered on the angles, the other decorations on them are carved out of the solid. The frame supporting the glass is made entire, and formed of two equal thicknesses, that behind, for sake of strength, being made to cross the front thickness obliquely. At the top, the pieces do not mitre, but lap on each other, and, during the process, the frame is stiffened below by a cross rail temporarily screwed on the bottom. The standards, on their outer edge, are chamfered from both sides to the joint line in the middle. They are made to lean backwards, and are supported from behind by a piece shaped like the other feet, so that the standards have a tripod support. The position of the mirror may be made secure and permanent by pinning the standards into the top. The glass frame is made similarly to that of Fig. 4, the moulding being planted on and made to lap within a ground frame, forming a check for the plate, the outer edge being slipped with veneer.

MOULDINGS.—PLATE XCIII.

The mouldings, the designs for which are here given, are all of full size. The assemblage, arrangement, and relative dimension of the parts, forming each of the examples in the series for cornices, may be considered as judicious and elegant, but arbitrary; other and equally suitable combinations may be made of the various members or elements, dispersed throughout the several designs; requiring the exercise of judgment and taste in the cabinet-maker for their selection and adjustment. The various entablatures may be wrought in such parts, separately, as are most suitable either for the economy of materials, or for convenience of working. Lines are drawn behind several of the mouldings, suggestive of the thickness and breadth of solid wood required for their execution. If the mouldings are to be veneered, the reader is referred to p. 56 of this work, where that process is considered in detail.

The other mouldings on the Plate are adapted to the stiles of doors that are sunk-panelled, or for bordering the edges of raised panels; the particular character and dimension of each of the mouldings will readily suggest its adaptation for one or other of these purposes.

MOULDINGS.—PLATE XCIV.

The various combinations of mouldings shown on this Plate, are presented in full or available size, along with their profile and perspective expression; the absolute dimensions given may, however, be easily modified and adapted, while the same form and proportion is preserved among the *parts*, or, as previously stated, other groupings of the forms may be effected, according to taste, or the character of the work on which the mouldings are to be displayed. Besides the uses of the mouldings for table tops, with their rims, and for chiffoniers, &c., as suggested in the title, the profiles are generally well adapted for turnery, where the mass is considerable, and the members are bold and expansive.

PORTABLE BED CHAIR AND OTTOMAN SEAT.— PLATE XCV.

The piece of furniture variously shown, in the design here given, is admirably adapted for the military man or traveller,

when subject to circumstances wherein the conveniences which it furnishes are not otherwise easily attainable. It is so contrived as to admit of three distinct uses, with a corresponding change in the arrangement and appearance of its parts suitable to each; it may, with facility be converted, on occasion, either into a chair, bed, or open seat; and in this last, which is its most compacted shape, it may be stowed into a stout trunk, of moderate dimensions, and easily carried.

The seat is square framed; its front is made in the ordinary manner. The haunch rails, being exposed on both sides, should be of solid wood 1¼-in. thick; they require to be about 3¼-in. broad, as they have to receive within them the bed-frames when folded; they are in front mortised into the prolonged upper end of the legs, flush inside, and are, at the back, lap-dovetailed into a cross rail of the same dimensions; the under edge of this quadrangular frame being made to correspond in height with the upper edge of the front rail; the dimensions of the interior space requires to be about 28 inches, measuring between the sides; and, from back to front, 25 inches.

A drawer case, made of ⅞-in. wood, corresponding exactly in form and dimension with the outside of the chair seat, is glued and screwed to the rails from under, and wrought off flush with them; the case extends forward, close to the inside of the front rail, to which it is fixed by screws sent through it from within. The sides and closed ends of the case, and the edges of the drawer opening, are of solid wood; its top and bottom are of deal. The moulding around the case below is partly scribed on to the back of the front legs, and a screw is sent through each corner into its adjoining leg. The turned back feet are doweled on. The bed frames are of solid wood and cane woven in the centre. The frame, within the seat, is permanently fixed, and made to rest on the top of the drawer case. The second in order is hinged to that first named, having the knuckle of the hinge to the upper side, and half pin up, so that these two frames may fold directly down on each other; the third frame has the knuckle of the hinge down, requiring this frame to fold to the under side of the second, on that being raised to fold on the first; when so arranged, they come to be adjusted as they should be shown in Fig. 1—there being an inadvertency in the drawing at this point, three pairs of hinges being apparent, whereas only one, and that the under pair, can be shown. The supporting legs are secured to their position by iron screws, wrought into their upper end, which are made to act in plate-nuts that are sunk under the outer sides of the second and third frames, as shown in Fig. 2. These legs, when the piece of furniture is altered from being a bed to being a chair or seat, are stowed away into the drawer. The mattress for the bed consists of three separate pieces, corresponding to the three folds; these also are united edge to edge, and by ties or buttons, so as to fold on each other and conveniently stow into the drawer; when the article takes the form of a chair, one portion of the mattress is used as the seat cushion. The elbows are framed in the ordinary manner; they are hinged to the side rails, and when folded down as in Fig. 3, the scrolls require to pass in behind the front feet; and, in consequence, they must recede from the front the full thickness of the feet. The top is hinged to the upper edge of the back rail of the seat; it is stuffed inside and also without, where it is covered with a sewed piece, as shown in Fig. 3. When the top and elbows are erect, they are locked together by spring catches or hooks.

Fig. 4 is a trunk for containing the chair, and opens on the side; it may be of oak, with japanned corner clasps, or of deal, and leather covered.

Steam-boat Railings and Clock.—Plate XCVI.

The fretted rails, designs of which are here shown, are intended to surmount the first tier of berths in a steam-vessel, and to enclose and form the front of the second tier, being made to pass along the sides and around the stern. The rails consist of parts, whose lengths correspond to those of the several berths, and whose adjoining ends are united, by means of small pillars, into which the rails mitre above and below; the pillars rest on, and are doweled to, the elbows of the sofas of the lower berths.

Fig. 1.—This railing is in the Flemish style, and should be made of rosewood; the fret is, as usual, made up in three thicknesses, and relieved on the face by carving; it is put in and secured by a stout panel from behind; sometimes there is a groove made in the upper and under moulding to receive the fret, as shown in section at A.

Fig. 2 is in the Elizabethan style, and for oak; this rail is made similarly to the last, being different only in detail; it is presented in section at B.

Fig. 3 is in the same style as the preceding, but to be executed in rosewood; here there are two portions of the rail presented, the smaller of which is at the stern, and over it the ornamental clock is placed; it being fixed on a veneered ground formed on the rudder case. The pendant flowers and fruit on the rail are gilt; and so also the small moulding in contact with the fret; the vases are hatched with gold. In all other respects this rail resembles the preceding. The clock case requires wood 6½-in. thick; it is made of deal, and entirely gilt; the dial may be white or silvered. This rail is shown in section at C.

Details, &c.—Plate XCVII.

The sketches on this and the two following Plates, although detached from the connections in which they were originally presented, will readily suggest to the experienced cabinet-maker their particular use or easy adaptation.

Figs. 1 and 2 are well suited for the corner ornaments of the doors of such cabinets, as are shown in Plates XXXVIII. and XLVIII.; or the carved part may be wrought in relief and fretted, or the figure alone may be inlaid.

Figs. 3 and 5 are truss brackets, suitable for the top and bottom of pilasters; the foliage on both is similar to that on Fig. 1; the moulding which borders the latter is similar to that which caps the upper trusses; this uniformity of style would adapt these parts for being displayed on one common ground.

Figs. 4 and 6 are brackets which might be employed for supporting the upper and under shelves of a chiffonier respectively.

Figs. 7, 8, and 9, are key-hole ornaments; the first two of which may be inlaid, or the whole may be separately carved and planted.

Figs. 10 and 11 are panelled ornaments, and may be employed of greater dimension, according to surface.

Details, &c.—Plate XCVIII.

On this Plate are shown the front and side views of four details of a massive character; the designs are wrought out by the fantastic combinations of animal and vegetable forms, and are highly novel and ornamental.

Figs. 1 and 2 represent a truss support suitable for a hall or bagatelle table, slab side-board, or under part of a book-case or other cabinet. It may be done up in oak or in colours, and partially gilt.

Figs. 3 and 4 are two views of a design intended for being attached to fixed pilasters on an open cabinet, and generally also can be made to serve purposes similar to the preceding.

Figs. 5 and 6 exhibit a bold and effective design for the front of a sofa, couch, or easy chair; it might also be introduced with good effect on the bottom ends of a half tester bedstead. A form, approaching to this, is sometimes given to the ends of sofas for the saloons of steam-vessels; such require to be very massive, and the grain of the wood in the head must run so as to preserve the greatest possible strength in the parts having least support.

Figs. 7 and 8 display a striking and highly original treatment of the pilaster of a cabinet below, and the subjacent portion of the base by the introduction of a griffin figure, the body and appended carving of which unites the pilaster and base, and passes down to near the bottom of the latter.

Details, &c.—Plate XCIX.

All the details on this Plate are so approximately related in general style, that they might be displayed together on one piece of furniture.

Fig. 1 is a top ornament suitable for a bookcase, wardrobe, sideboard, or chiffonier; it is also well adapted for a mirror, in which case it should be gilt.

Fig. 2 might be employed as a decoration for door panels.

Figs. 3 and 4.—A pair of either of these might be displayed on the top of the wings of a wardrobe or bookcase, one at each end of Fig. 1.

Figs. 5 and 6 are appropriate devices for ornamenting the grounds of pilasters.

Ornaments adapted from Nature.—Plate C.

Fig. 1 is a study of leaves and berry of the hawthorn (Crataegus oxyacantha).

Fig. 1, a.—In an adaptation for a circular compartment, the centre group of berries must rise semicircularly, the stalks and leafage to lie flat upon the ground, with the large leaves swelling gently up in rounded forms towards the middle of their broader parts. The outer group of berries must have the lower layer in half relief only, with those above lying on them, fully rounded, so as to induce, from their numerous convexities, a sparkling reflection of light.

Fig. 2 is the common pea (Pisum sativum), of which Fig. 2, a, is an arrangement, for the spandril of an elliptical arch; the lower pods must lie in high relief on the ground, the large leaves immediately above them rising in rounded masses, where they are not repressed by the stalks. Each pair of leaflets must be arranged so that the lower one is in very low relief, while the upper swells up considerably.

Fig. 3 is a study from the Sonchus oleraceus, being a variety of the sow thistle, of which Fig. 3, a, is an adaptation for a capital, having the stems carrying buds between the leaves; smaller leaflets are arranged symmetrically around the ovolo.

Fig. 4 is a study of rye-grass (Secale cereale), of which Fig. 4, a, is an application to a frieze, along with the common ground ivy (Glechoma hederacea), festooned between it. Here the leaves of the latter must rise in full rounded masses, contrasting with the more angular forms of the grass; one side of many of the leaves should nearly disappear into the ground, and the back leaves and leaflets near the grass should be but faintly detached from it.

Fig. 5.—Studies of Penicillaria spicata, the bulrush, and the leaves of a water plant; the latter is very common in ponds and ditches.

Fig. 5, *a*, is an ogee moulding, ornamented with both the above; the cylindrical head of the bulrush is shown as shrouded by the folding leaves of the water plant.

ORNAMENTS ADAPTED FROM NATURE.—PLATE CI.

Fig. 1.—A study from nature; it is a small plant found commonly in hedges.

Fig. 1, A.—Adaptation of the above as a perforated gallery, the application of natural forms to this purpose represented merely by outline on a flat surface, requires a more rigidly geometric treatment than where the surface is relieved by carving; it is also necessary that the points should be protected by being made to touch; otherwise it would be too liable to be broken. The rounded form of the mushroom is introduced below to support the leaflets, and by its semicircular curve, to contrast with the rigid, straight lines. The novel and agreeable effect produced by the introduction of this humble plant, serves to prove that no objects in nature, however simple or insignificant, should be considered as beneath the attention of the ornamental designer.

Fig. 2.—Study from the sow thistle.

Fig. 2, A.—Part of a support for a small table. The capital composed of the sow thistle, with leaflets arranged around the necking. The shaft is worked out of a circular turned piece, with a panel sunk on three faces, each containing a grass or some other simple upright plant. At the base, tendrils of the convolvulus bend over, like scrolls, with a leaf between them. The rib, carried up the angle, connects them as a stem with the leaves which bend over at the top. The bulb is ornamented with ivy leaves and berries, which must be kept in low relief, so as not to destroy the contour.

Fig. 3.—A screw mount; the outer part is perforated; the forms are adapted from a very beautiful plant, which is seen climbing in the hedges, with dark green shining leaves, and red berries. The centre part has an inlaid ornament, composed of ivy leaves and berries twined round a geometrical arrangement of lines. The peculiarities of the ivy are all indicated, even to the small roots which support it.

PLATE I.

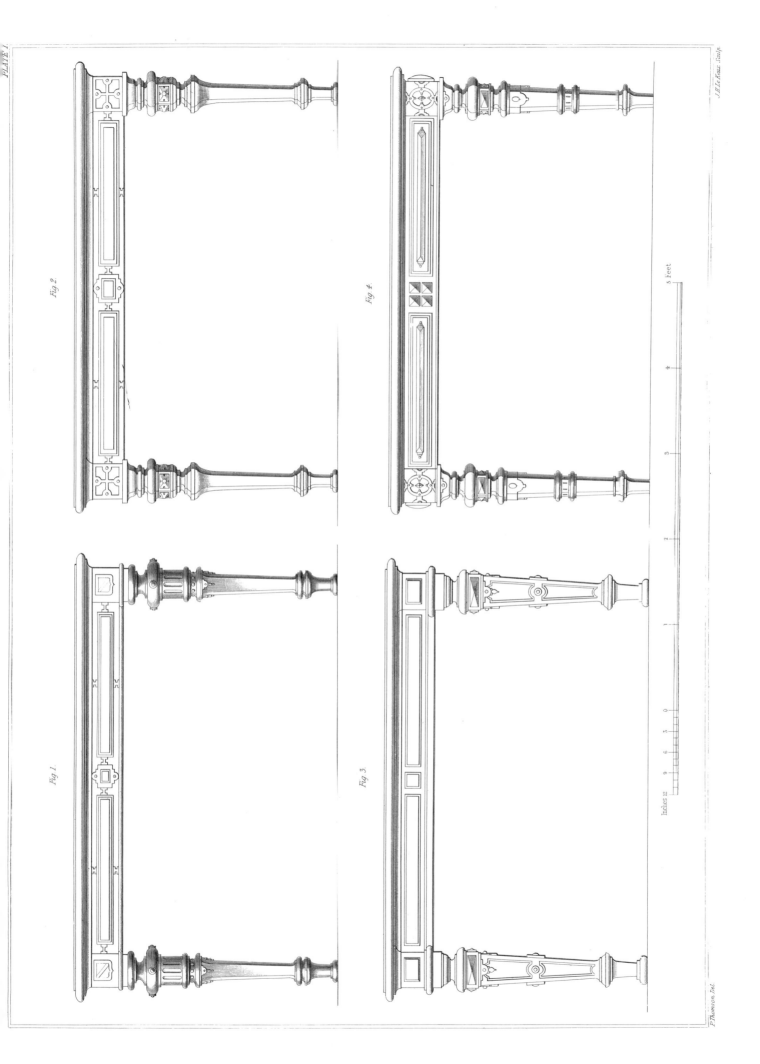

Fig. 2.

Fig. 1.

Fig. 4.

Fig. 3.

Inches 12 9 6 3 0 1 2 3 4 5 Feet

P. Thomson. Del.

J. H. Le Keux. Sculp.

Fig 1

Fig 2

Fig 3

P. Thomson Del.

J. H. Le Keux Sculp.

PLATE III

Fig 4.

Fig 3.

Fig 2.

Fig 1.

Fig 8.

Fig 7.

Fig 6.

Fig 5.

Inches 12 9 6 3 0 1 2 3 feet.

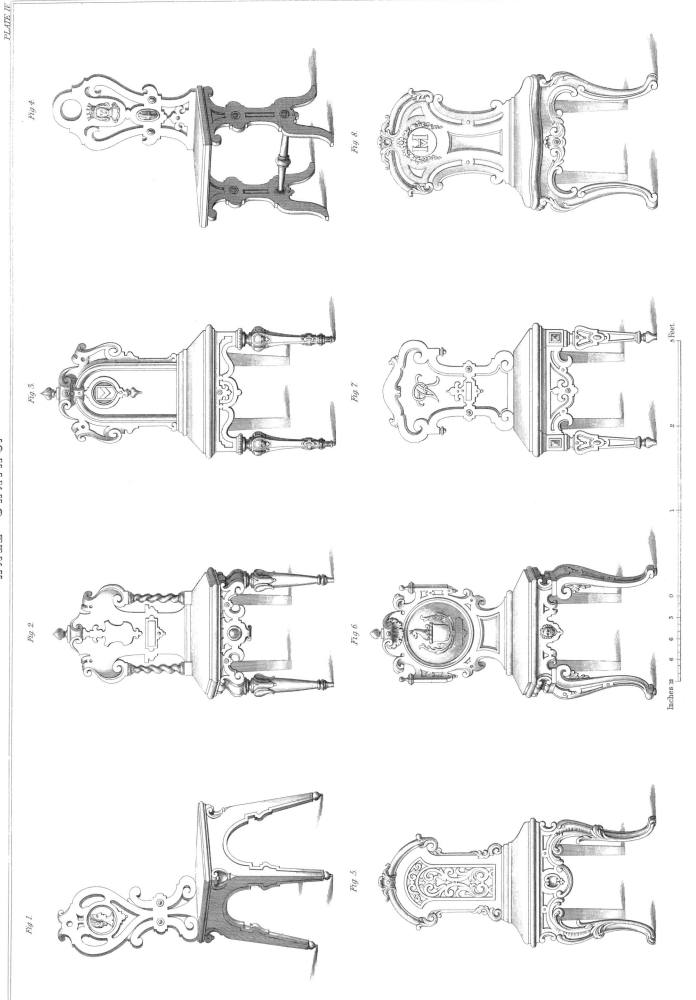

PLATE IV

HALL CHAIRS.

Fig 1.

Fig 2.

Fig 3.

Fig 4.

Fig 5.

Fig 6.

Fig 7.

Fig 8.

Inches 12   9   6   3   0   1   2   3 Feet.

P. Thomson, Del.

J.H.Le Keux Sc.

PLATE V

Fig. 1.

Fig. 2.

Fig. 3.

Fig. 4.

inches 12   6   0   3   1   2   3   4   5 feet.

P. Thomson. Del.   J. H. Le Keux. Sculp.

PLATE VI.

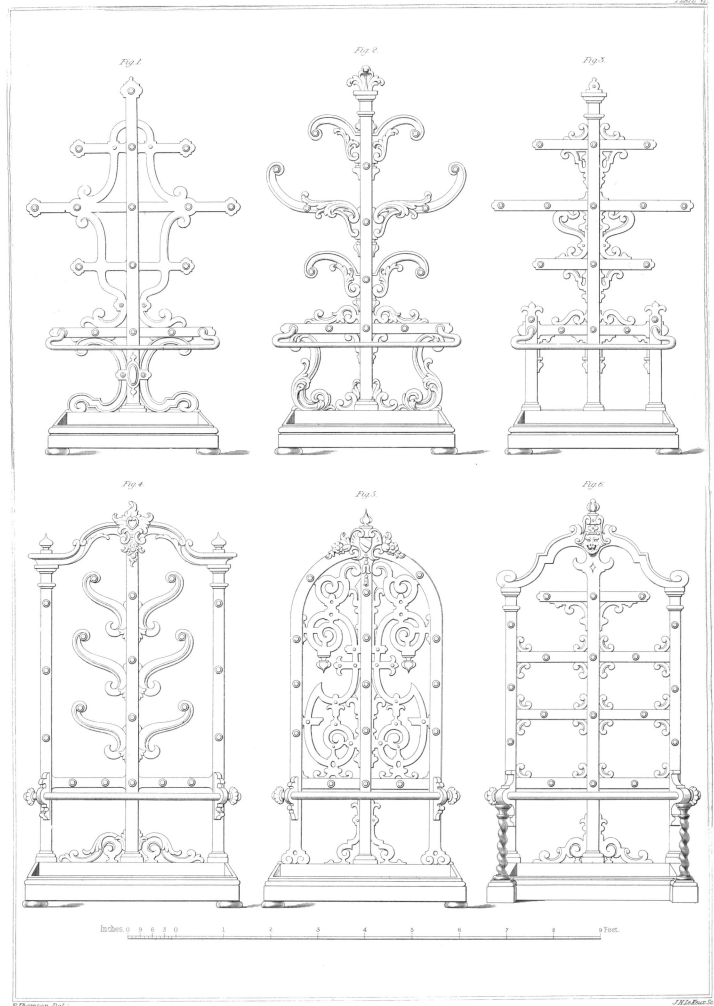

Fig. 1.   Fig. 2.   Fig. 3.

Fig. 4.   Fig. 5.   Fig. 6.

Inches. 0 9 6 3 0   1   2   3   4   5   6   7   8   9 Feet.

P. Thomson Del.

J. H. le Keux Sc.

PLATE VII.

HAT AND UMBRELLA STANDS.

Fig.1.

Fig.2.

Fig.3.

Inches. 12 9 6 3 0 1 2 3 4 5 6 7 Feet.

P. Thomson, Del.

J.H. Le Keux. Sc.

PLATE VIII

CLOCK CASES.

Fig. 4.

Fig. 3.

Fig. 2.

Fig. 1.

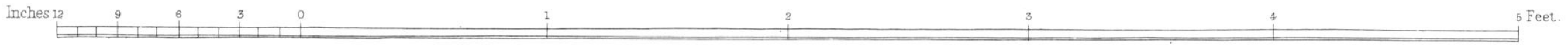

Inches 12   9   6   3   0   1   2   3   4   5 Feet.

F. Thomson Del.

J. H. le Keux Sc.

PLATE IX

CLOCK CASES.

Fig. 1.

Fig. 2.

Fig. 3.

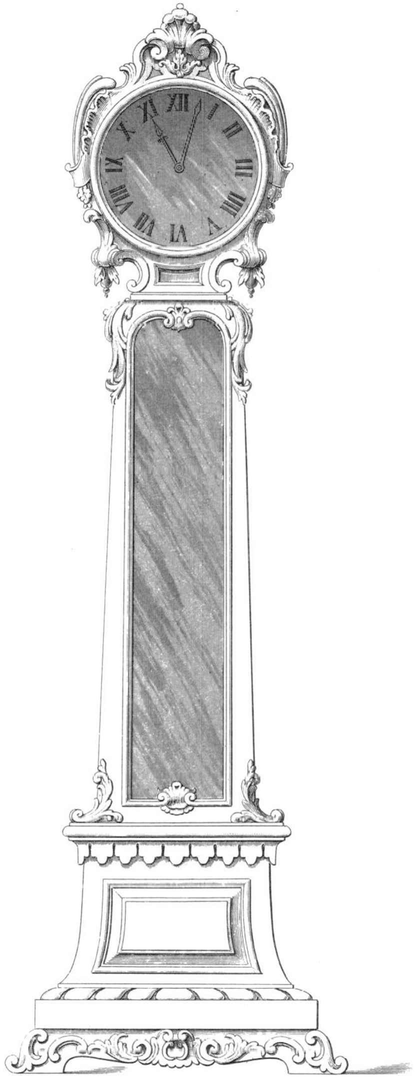

Fig. 4.

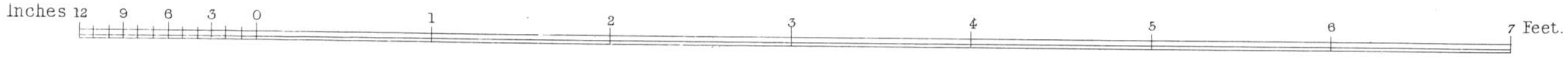

Inches 12 9 6 3 0   1   2   3   4   5   6   7 Feet.

A. P. Thomson del.   J. H. Le Keux Sc.

PLATE I.

PEDESTAL SIDEBOARD.

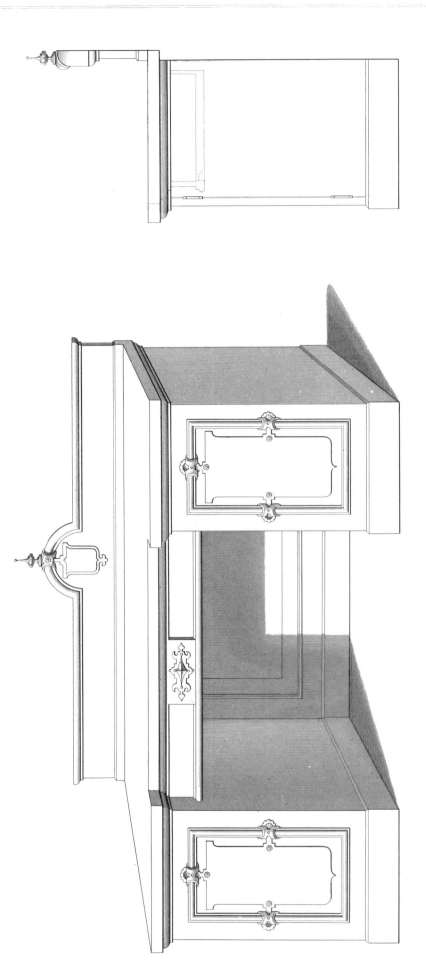

J. Thomson Del.

J.H. Le Keux Sculp.

Inches 12   9   6   3   0   1   2   3   4   5   6 Feet.

PLATE XI

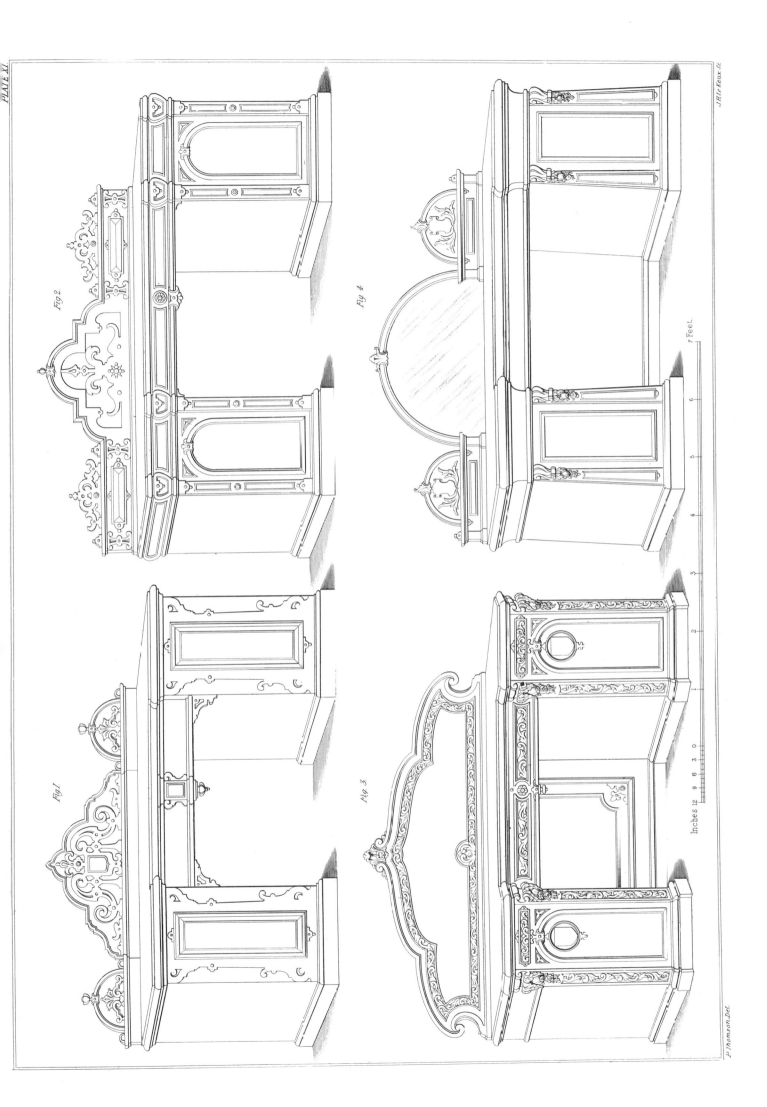

Fig 1.

Fig 2.

Fig 3.

Fig 4.

Inches 12 9 6 3 0   1   2   3   4   5   6   7 Feet.

P. Thomson. Del.

J. H. le Keux. Sc.

PLATE VII

PEDESTAL SIDEBOARD.

Scale for the Details.

J. Thomson Del.

PLATE XIII.

PEDESTAL SIDEBOARD.

Inches 12   9 6 3 0   1   2   3   4   5 Feet.

Inches 12 9 6 3 0   1   2   3   4   5   6 Feet.

PLATE XV.

SLAB SIDEBOARD.

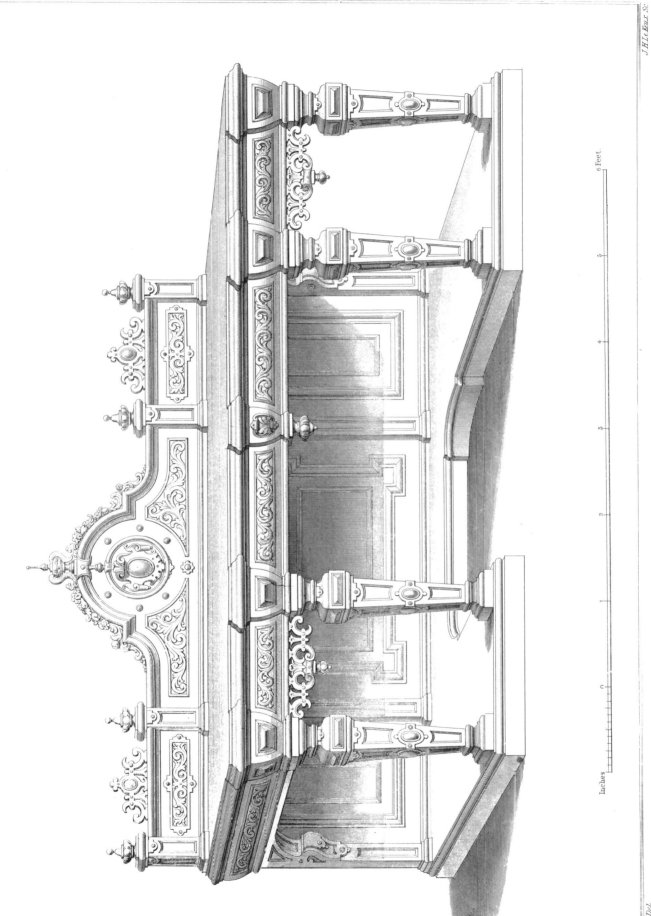

Inches

6 Feet.

Fig. 1.

Fig. 2.

Fig. 3.

Fig. 4.

Fig. 5.

Fig. 6.

Inches. 12   9   6   3   0   1   2   3   4   5   6 Feet.

P. Thomson Del.

C. Wands Sc.

PLATE XVII.

PILLAR AND BLOCK TABLES.

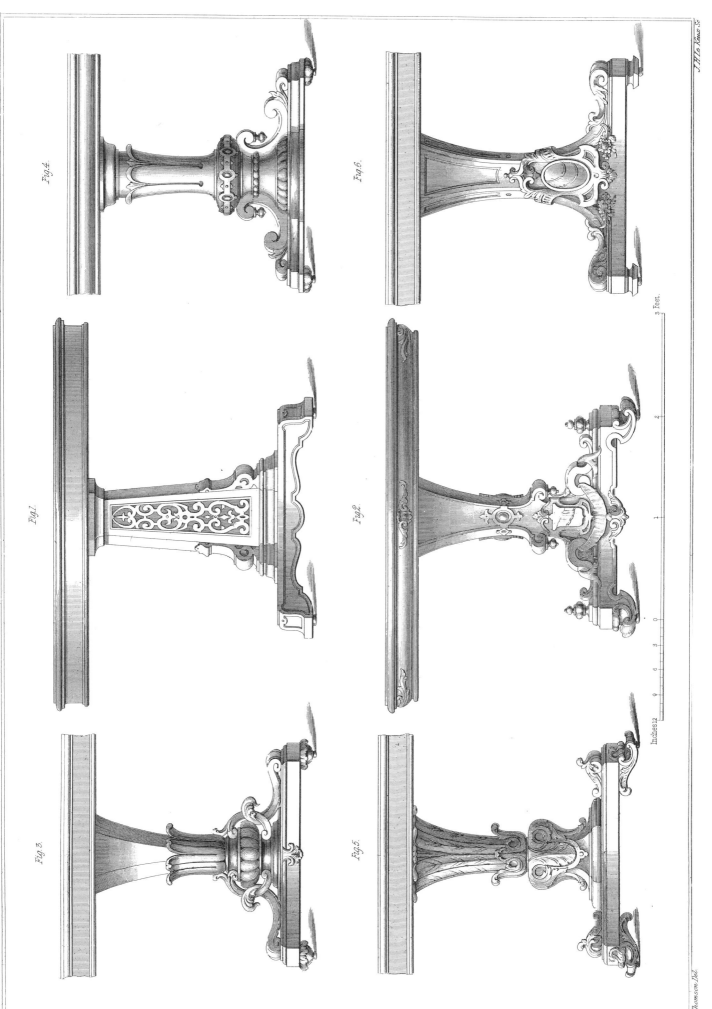

Fig. 4.

Fig. 1.

Fig. 3.

Fig. 6.

Fig. 2.

Fig. 5.

Inches 12   9   6   3   0   1   2   3 Feet.

P. Thomson, Del.   J. H. Le Keux, Sc.

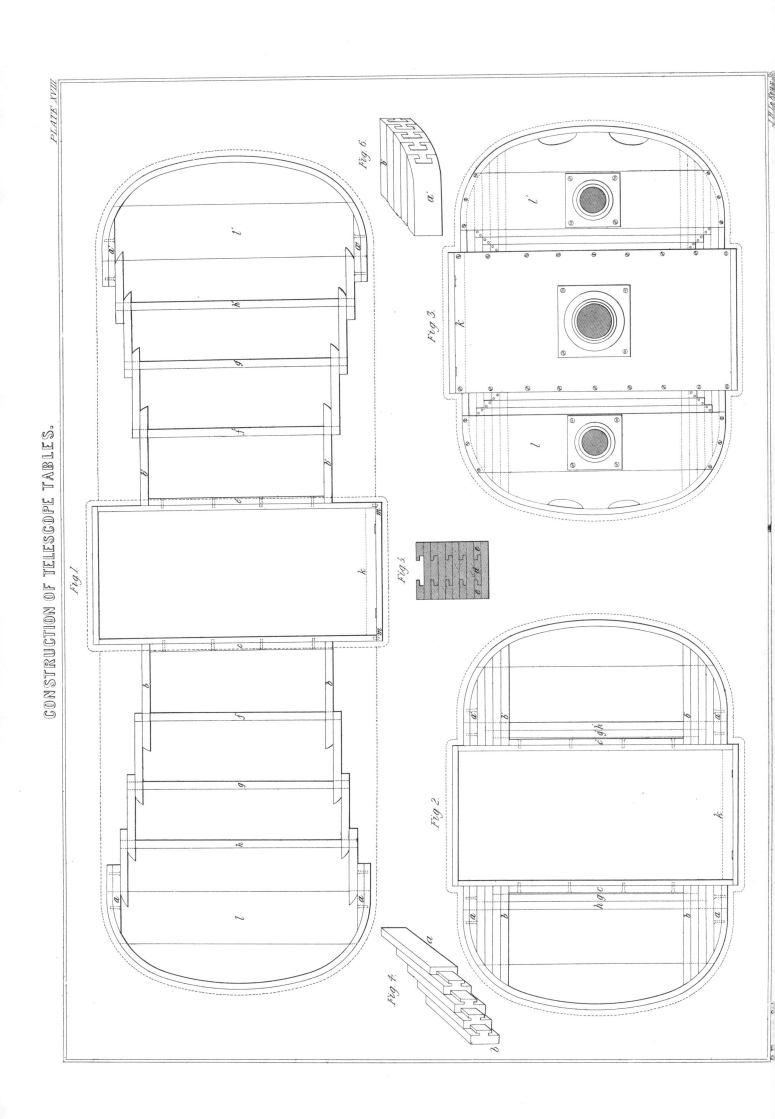

CONSTRUCTION OF TELESCOPE TABLES.

PLATE XVIII.

Fig. 1.

Fig. 2.

Fig. 3.

Fig. 4.

Fig. 5.

Fig. 6.

PLATE XIX

TELESCOPE TABLES.

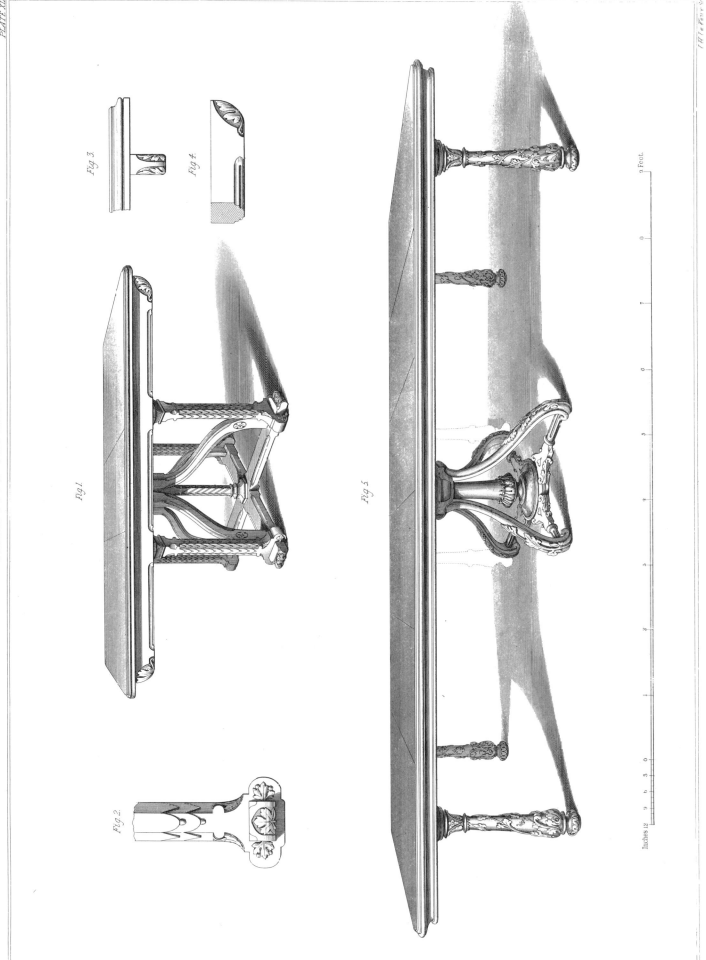

Fig. 1.

Fig. 2.

Fig. 3.

Fig. 4.

Fig. 5.

Inches 12 9 6 3 0 1 2 3 4 5 6 7 8 9 Foot.

PLATE XX.

TELESCOPE TABLES.

Fig. 1.

Fig. 2.

Fig. 3.

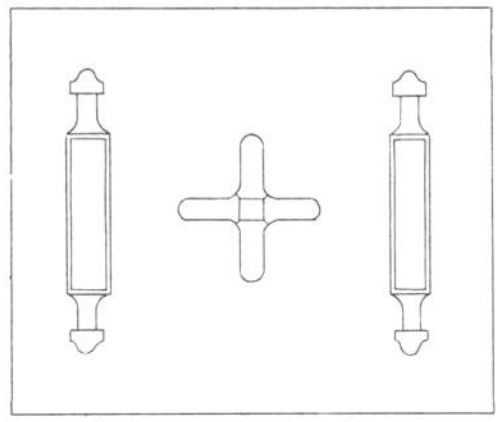

Fig. 4.

Fig. 5.

Inches 12 9 6 3 0   1   2   3   4   5   6   7 Feet.

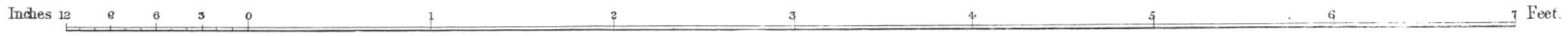

G. Inglis Sc.

PLATE LXI

SIDE TABLES.

Fig 2.

Fig 1.

Fig. 4.

Fig 3.

Inches 12 9 6 3 0   1   2   3   4   5 Feet.

P. Thomson, Del.

J. H. Le Deux Sc.

PLATE XXII

RISING SIDE TABLES.

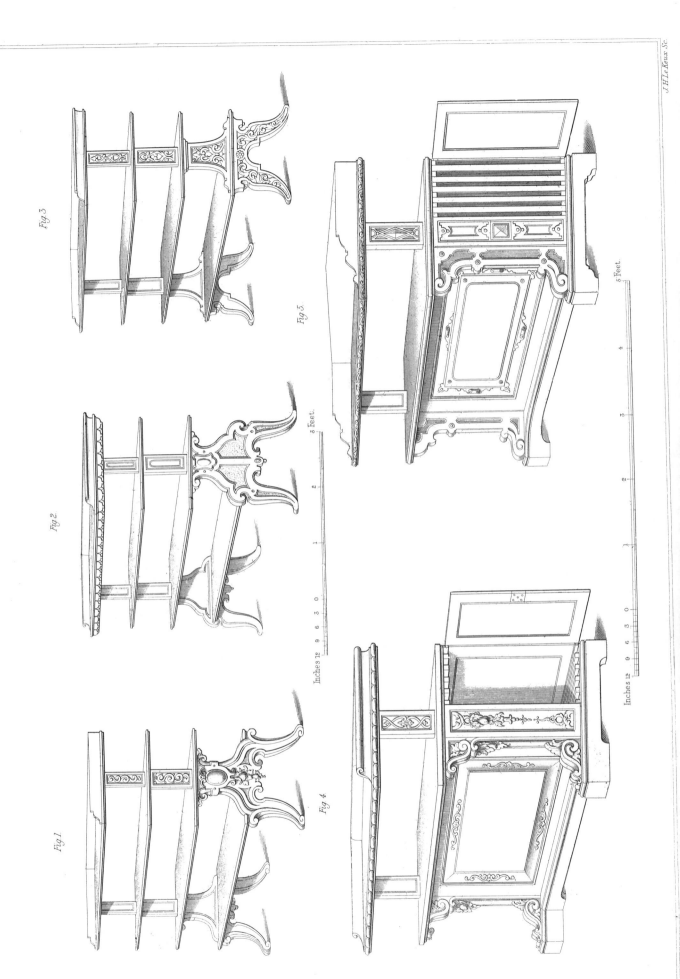

Fig 3.

Fig 1.

Fig 2.

Fig 4.

Fig 5.

Inches 12 9 6 3 0   1   2   3 Feet.

Inches 12 9 6 3 0   1   2   3   4   5 Feet.

J.H.Le Keux Sc.

PLATE XXIII.

DINING ROOM CHAIRS.

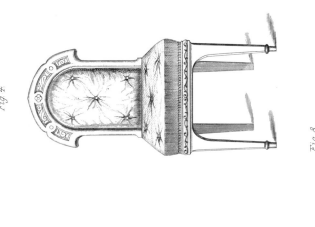

Fig. 1.

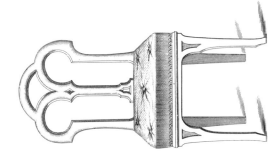

Fig. 2.

Fig. 3

Fig. 4.

Fig. 5.

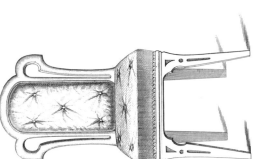

Fig. 6.

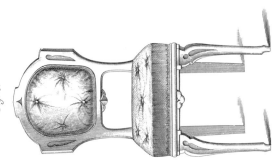

Fig. 7.

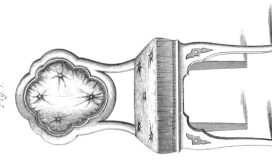

Fig. 8.

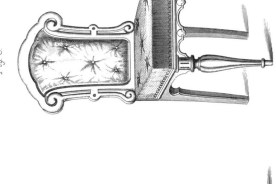

Inches 12   9   6   3   0   1   2   3   Feet.

P. Thomson and Carl Hamburh. Del.

J. H. Le Keux Sc.

PLATE XXIV.

DINING ROOM CHAIRS.

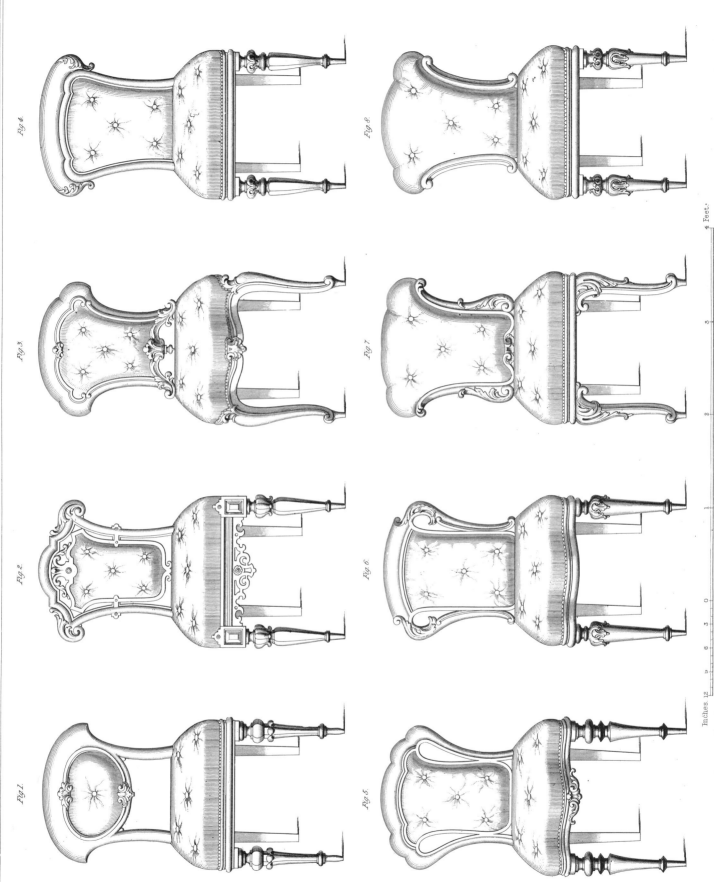

Fig. 1. Fig. 2. Fig. 3. Fig. 4.

Fig. 5. Fig. 6. Fig. 7. Fig. 8.

Inches. 12 9 6 3 0 1 2 3 4 Feet.

PLATE XXVI.

Fig 1.

Fig 2.

Fig 3.

Fig 4.

J. Dibdin Del.

J. Le Keux Sc.

PLATE XXVI.

EASY CHAIRS.

Fig.2.

Fig.4.

Fig.5.

Fig.6.

Fig.1.

Fig.3.

Inches.12   9   6   3   0   1   2   3   4   5 Feet.

PLATE XVII.

TABLE AND CHAIR LEGS.

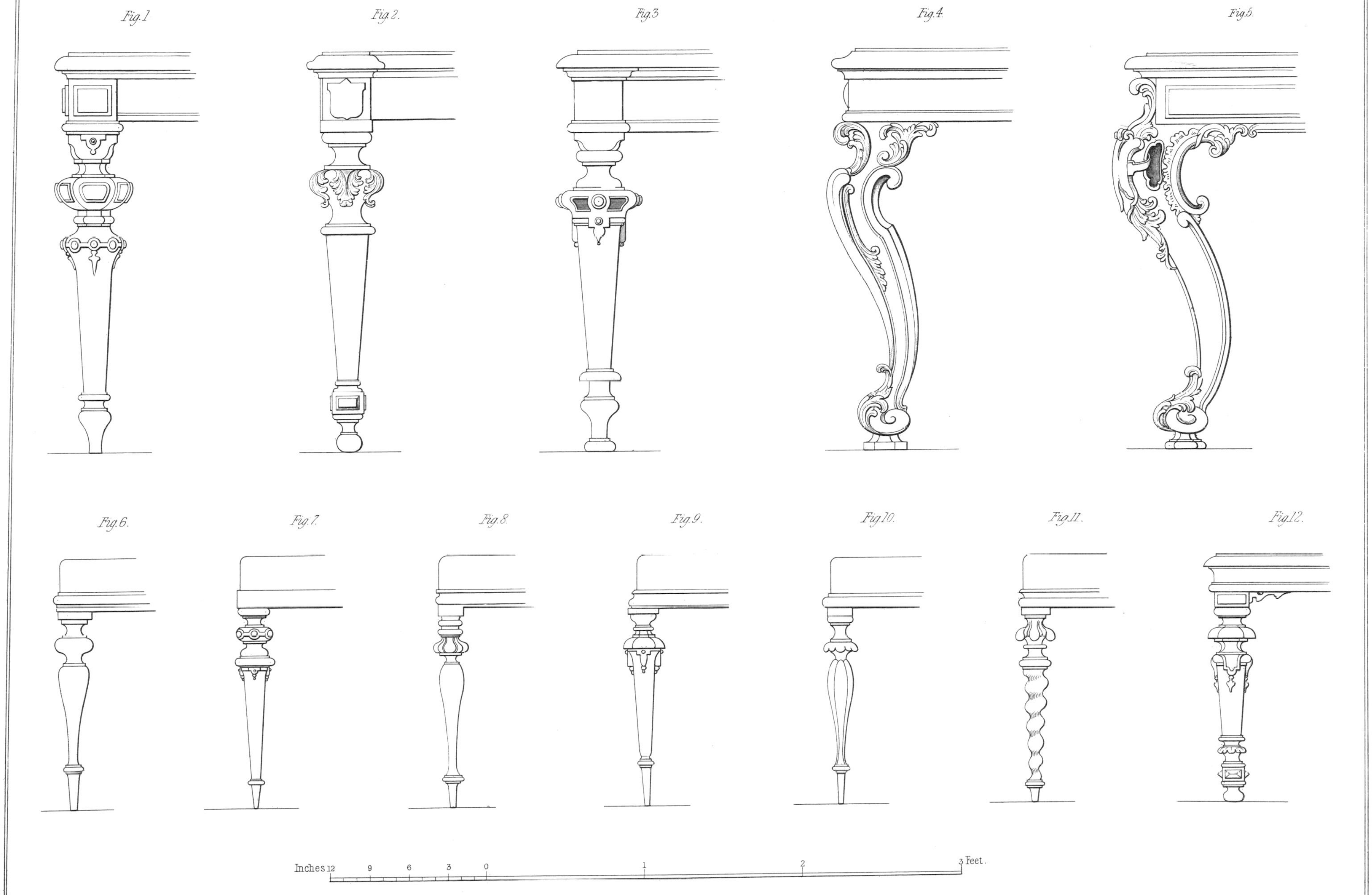

Fig. 1

Fig. 2

Fig. 3

Fig. 4

Fig. 5

Fig. 6

Fig. 7

Fig. 8

Fig. 9

Fig. 10

Fig. 11

Fig. 12

Inches 12   9   6   3   0   1   2   3 Feet.

P. Thomson Del.

PLATE XXVIII.

S O F A S .

Fig. 2.

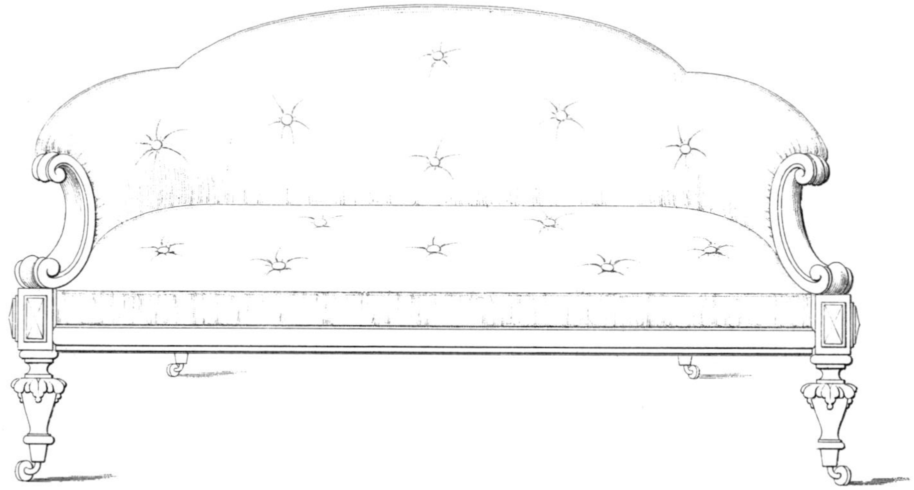

Fig. 4.

Fig. 1.

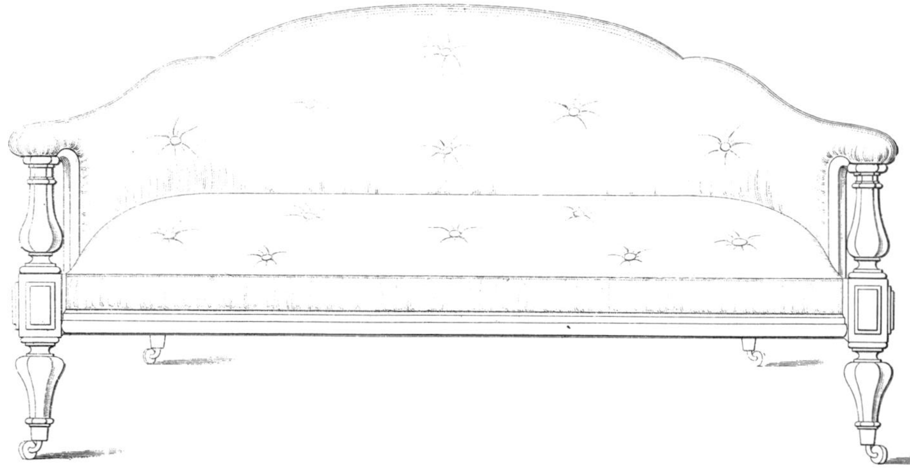

Fig. 3.

Inches. 12   9   6   3   0   1   2   3   4   5   6   7 Feet.

P. Thomson, Del.

J.H. Le Keux. Sc.

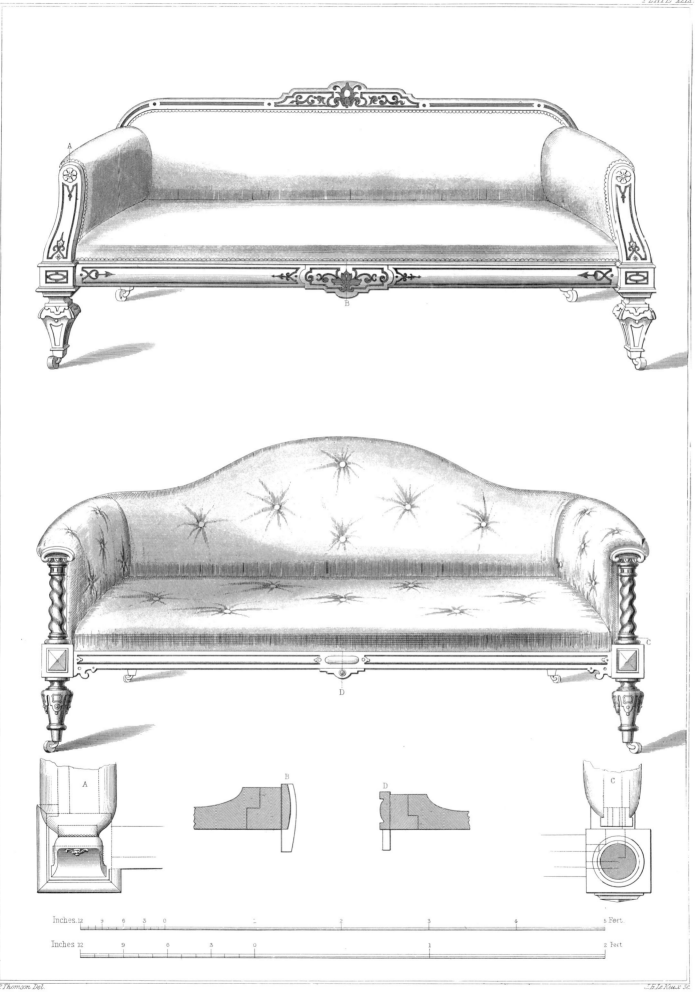

PLATE XXXI.

Inches 12   9   6   3   0   1   2   3   4   Feet.

F. Thomson Del.

J.H. Le Keux Sc.

PLATE XXII

DETAILS OF SOFAS.

Fig. 1.

Fig. 2.

Fig. 3.

Fig. 4.

Fig. 5.

Fig. 6.

Fig. 7.

Fig. 8.

Fig. 9.

Fig. 10.

Fig. 11.

Fig. 12.

Fig. 13.

Fig. 14.

Inches 12   9   6   3   0   1   2   3 Feet.

PLATE XXVII.

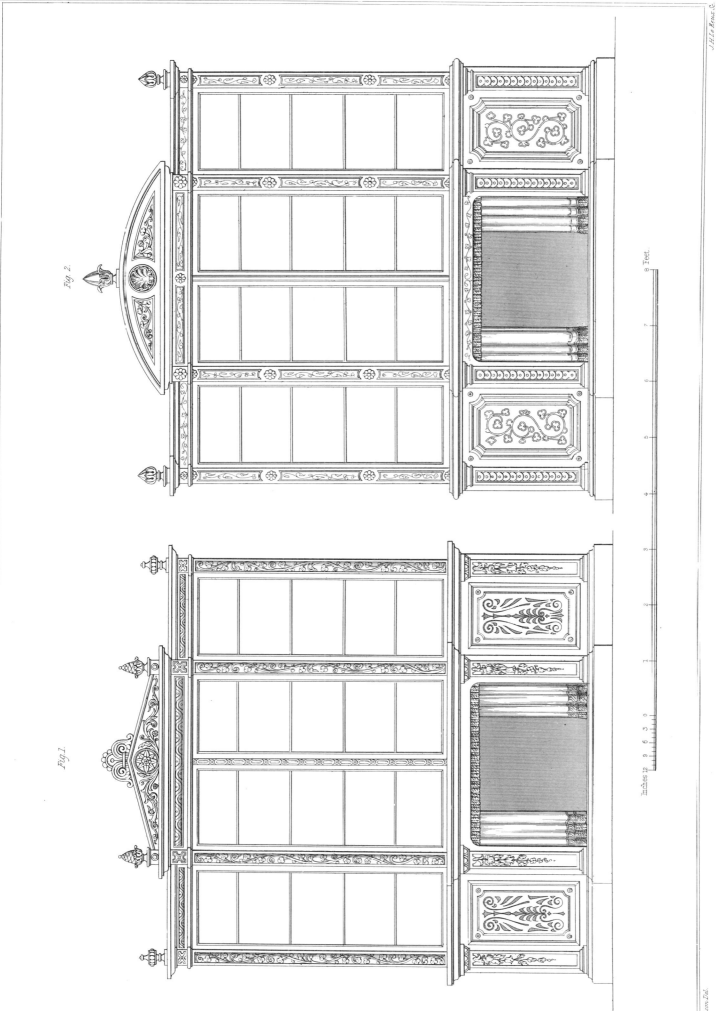

P. Thomson. Del.

Fig. 2.

Fig. 1.

J.H. Le Keux. Sc.

Inches 12   9   6   3   0   4   5   6   7   8 Feet.

PLATE XXXIV

Fig 1

Fig 2.

Inches 12 9 6 3 0   1   2   3   4   5   6   7   8   9   10   11 Feet.

P. Thomson Del.

J. H. Le Keux Sc.

PLATE XXIV.

Inches 12 9 6 3 0   1   2   3   4   5   6   7   8   9 feet.

PLATE XXXVI

BOOKCASES WITH CHIMNEY PIECE AND MIRROR.

W. J. Brewer Sc.

F. Thrupp Del.

Inches 12 9 6 3 0   1   2   3   4   5   6   7   8   9   10 Feet

PLATE XXVII

P. Thomson Del.

W. A. Beever Sc.

Inches 12 9 6 3 0

10 Feet

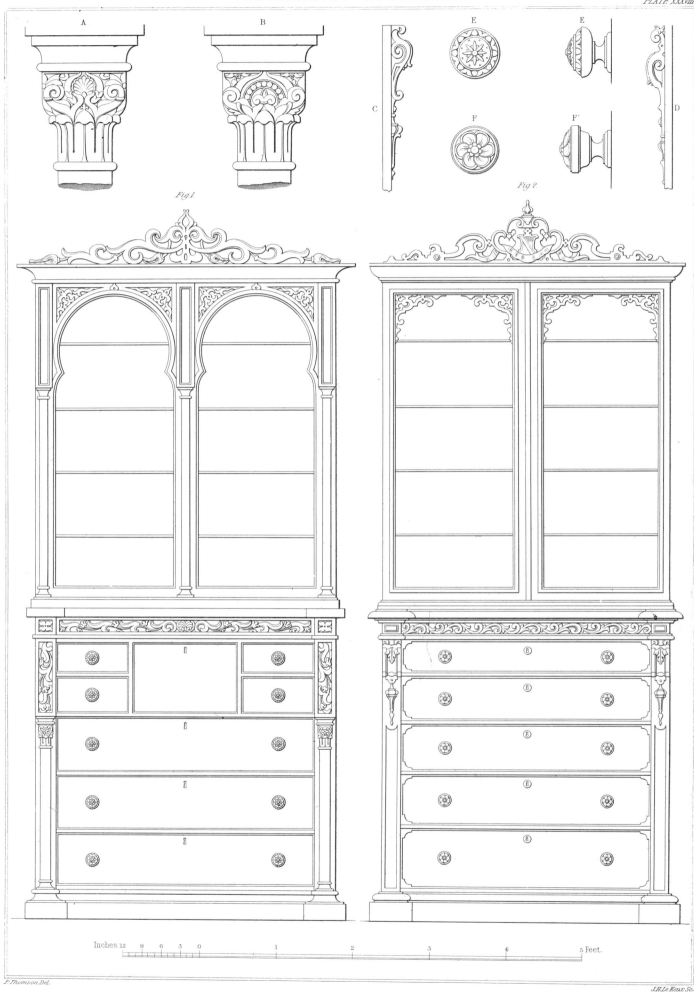

Fig.1

Fig.2

Fig. 1.

Fig. 3.

Fig. 2.

Fig. 4.

Fig. 5.

Fig. 6.

Inches 12   9   6   3   0   1   2   3   4 Feet.

LIBRARY TABLES

Fig. 1.

Fig. 3.

Fig. 4

Fig. 2.

Fig. 5.

Inches 12 9 6 3 0 1 2 3 4 5 Feet.

J. H. Le Keux Sc.

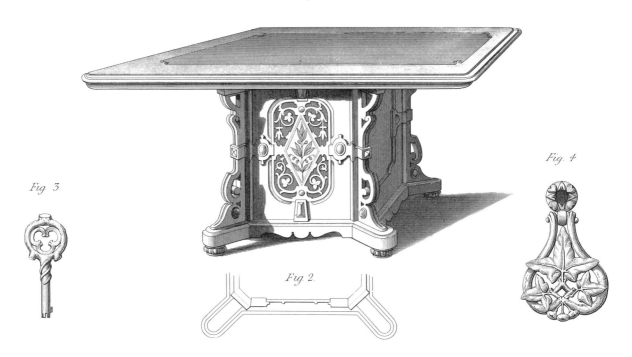

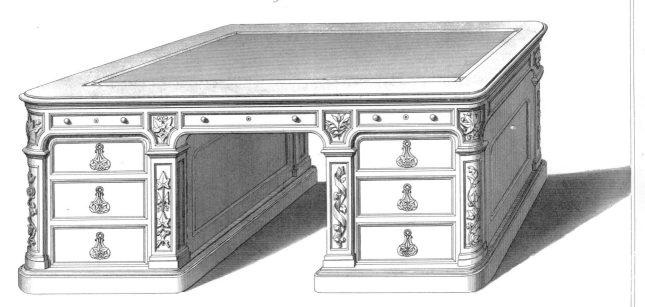

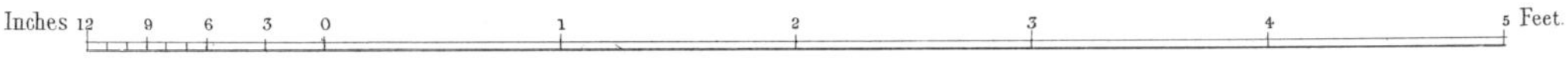

WRITING TABLES.

PLATE XLI.

Fig. 1.

Fig. 2.

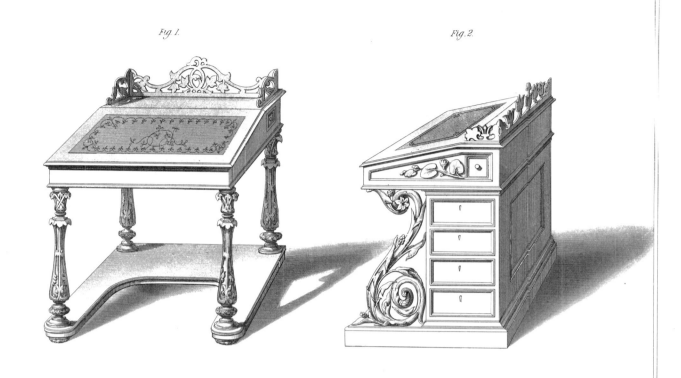

Fig. 3.

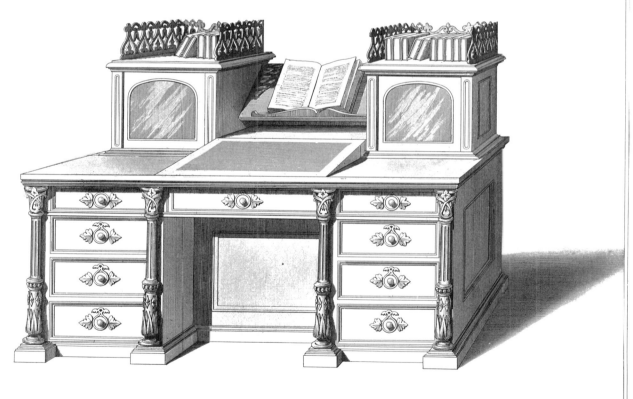

Inches 12 9 6 3 0 1 2 3 4 5 Feet

J. H. Le Keux Sc.

PLATE XIII

LIBRARY CHAIRS.

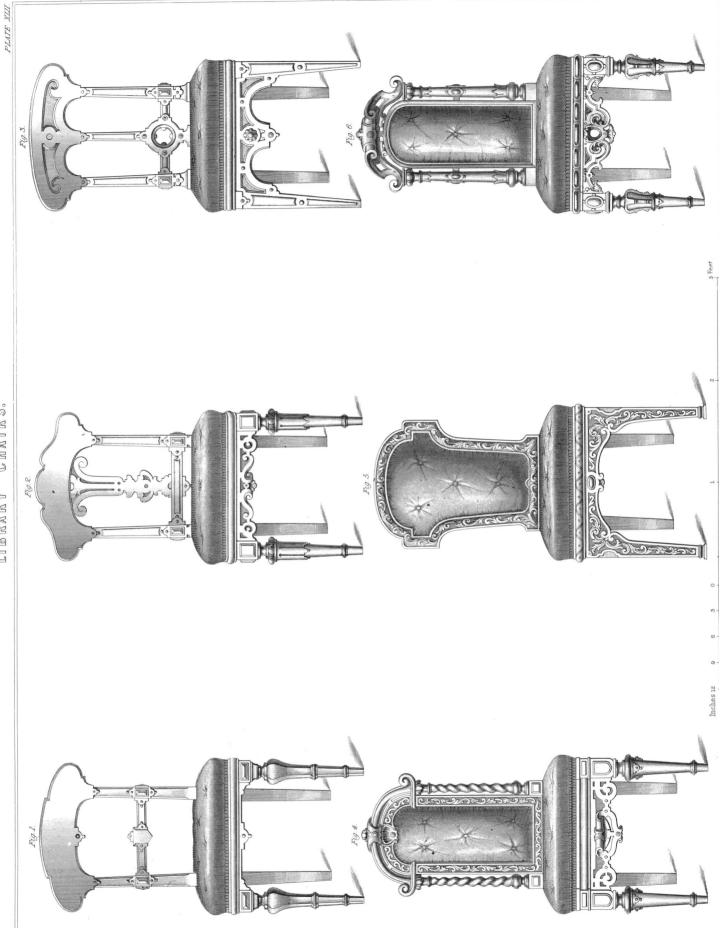

Fig. 1.

Fig. 2.

Fig. 3.

Fig. 4.

Fig. 5.

Fig. 6.

Inches 12   9   6   3   0   1   2   3 Feet

PLATE XXIII.

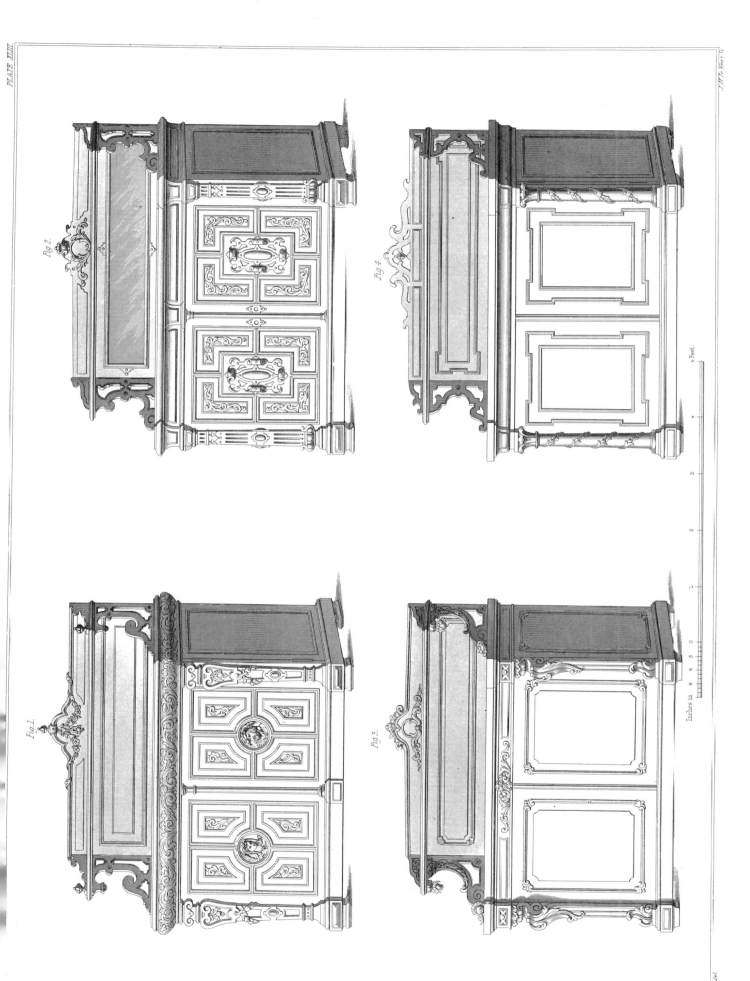

Fig. 1.

Fig. 2.

Fig. 3.

Fig 4.

Inches 12 9 6 3 0   1   2   3   4   5 Feet.

PLATE XLIV

CHIFFONNIER

Fig. 3.

Fig. 4.

A
B
C
D

Scale for the Details.

0   3   6   9   12   6 Feet

Inches 12   9   6   3   0   1   2   3   4   5   6 Feet

J. Thomson Del.

J. H. Le Keux Sc.

Fig. 1.

Inches 12   9   6   3   0   1   2   3   4   5 Feet.

Fig. 2.

P. Thomson Del.   J. H. Le Keux L.

PLATE XLVI.

CHIFFONNIÈRES with HIGH MIRRORS.

Fig.1.

Fig.2.

Inches 12 9 6 3 0   1   2   3   4   5   6   7   8 Feet.

PLATE XLVII

CABINET.

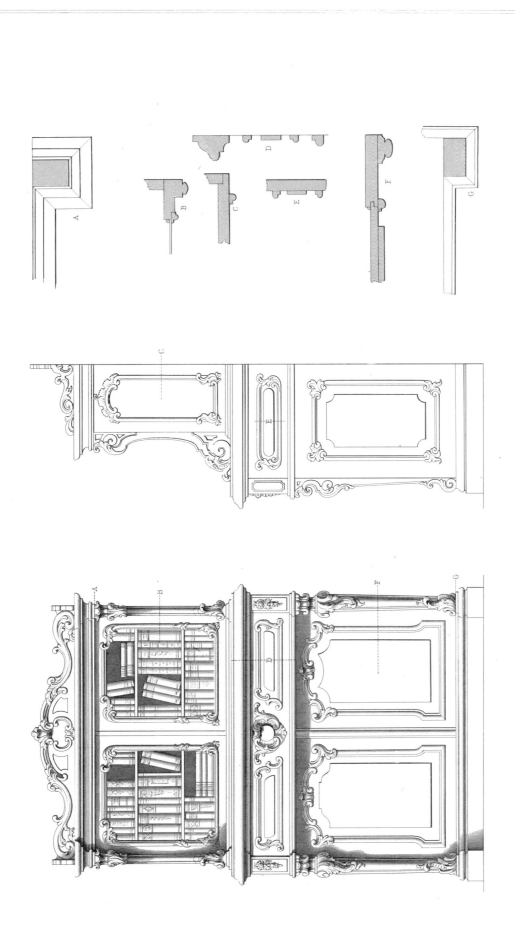

P.Howard Del.

J.H.Le Keux Sc.

Inches 12 9 6 3 0 1 2 3 4 5

Inches 12 9 6 3 0 1 Foot.

Scale for the Details.

PLATE XLVIII.

CABINET.

A

B

C

D

E

F

P. Thomson Del.

J. H. Le Keux Sc.

Scale For The Details

Inches 12   10   6   3   0   1 Foot.

Inches 12   9   6   3   0   1   2   3 Feet.

Fig.1

Fig.2

Inches 12 9 6 3 0 1 2 3 4 Feet.

P.Thomson.Del.

J.H.Le Keux.Sculp.

Fig 1.

Fig 2.

Fig 3.

Inches 12   9   6   3   0   1   2   3 Feet.

Sketch plan of Jambs.

P. Thomson Del.

J. W. Lowry Sc.

Inches 12 9 6 3 0   1   2   3   4   5 Feet.

PLATE III.

PIER TABLES WITH MIRRORS.

Fig. 1.

Fig. 2.

Fig. 3.

Fig. 4.

PLATE LIII

LOO TABLES.

Fig. 2.

Fig. 1.

Fig. 4.

Fig. 3.

Inches 12 9 6 3 0   1   2   3   4   5 Feet.

T. Thomson, Del.   J.H. Le Keux Sc.

PLATE LIV

OCCASIONAL TABLES.

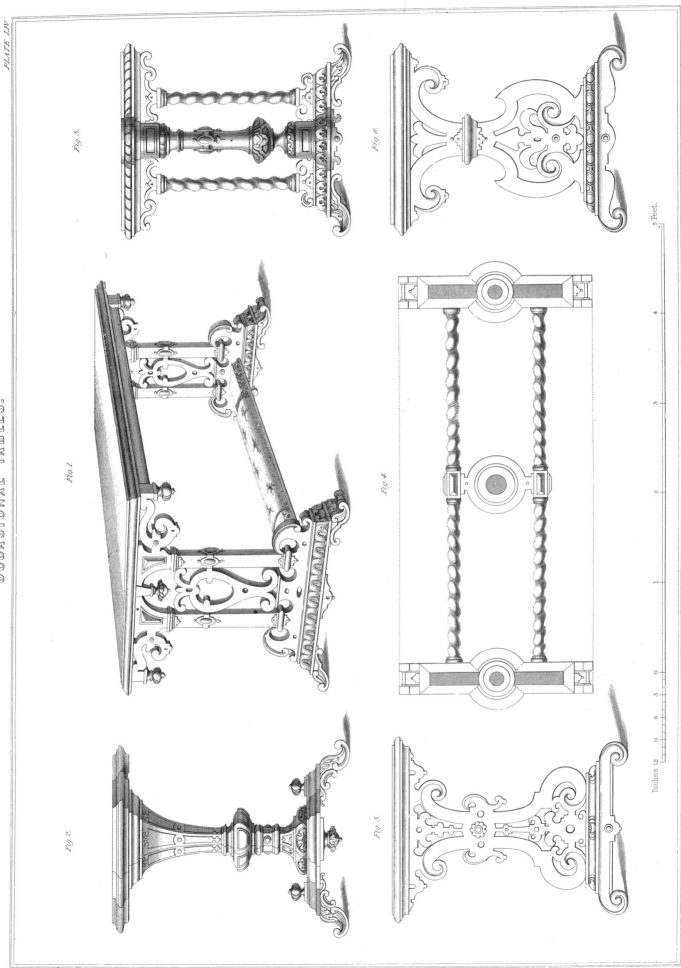

Fig. 3.

Fig. 6.

Fig. 1.

Fig. 4.

Fig. 2.

Fig. 5.

Inches 12   9   6   3   0   1   2   3   4   5 Feet.

PLATE LV

LOO TABLES.

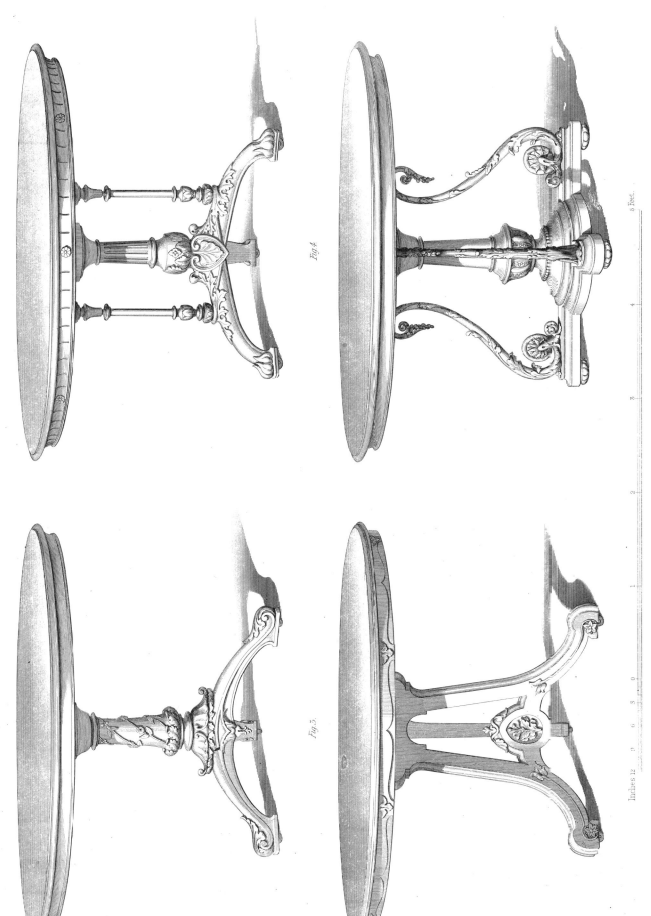

Fig 1.

Fig 2.

Fig 3.

Fig 4.

Inches 12   9   6   3   0   1   2   3   4   5 Feet.

PLATE LVI

OCCASSIONAL TABLES.

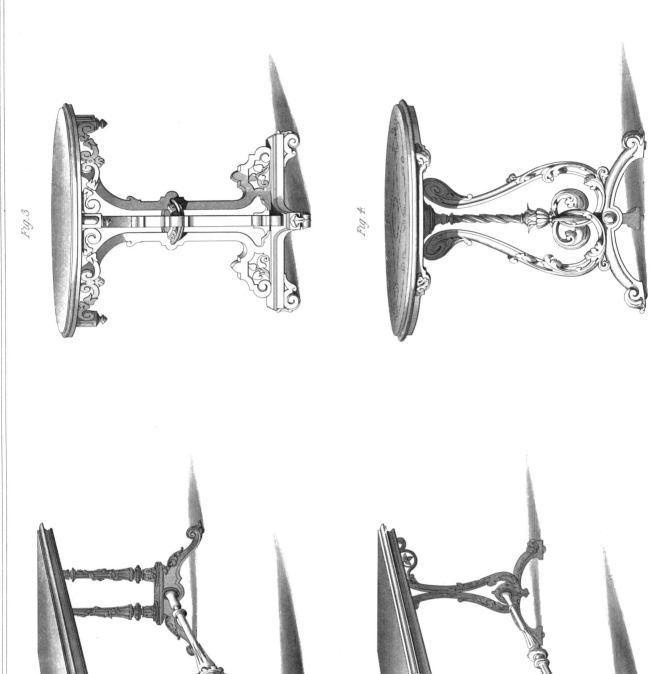

Fig.1.

Fig.2.

Fig.3.

Fig.4.

Inches 12   9   6   3   0   1   2   3   4   5 Feet.

PLATE LVII

WORK TABLES.

Fig. 1.

Fig. 2.

Fig. 3.

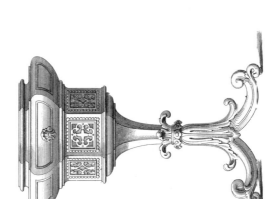

Fig. 4.

Fig. 5.

Fig. 6.

Inches 12   9   6   3   0   3 Feet.

J. Thomson. Del.   J. H. Le Keux. Sc.

PLATE LVIII.

DRAWING ROOM SOFAS.

Fig. 1.

Fig. 2.

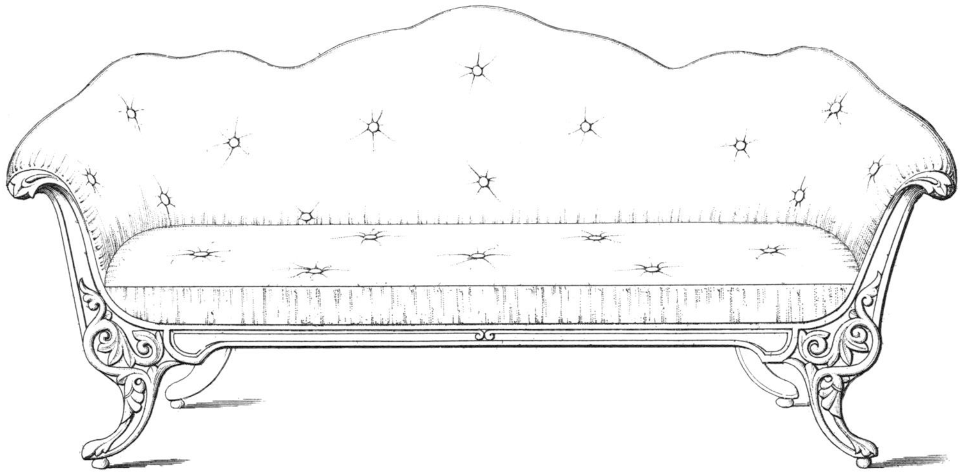

Fig. 3.

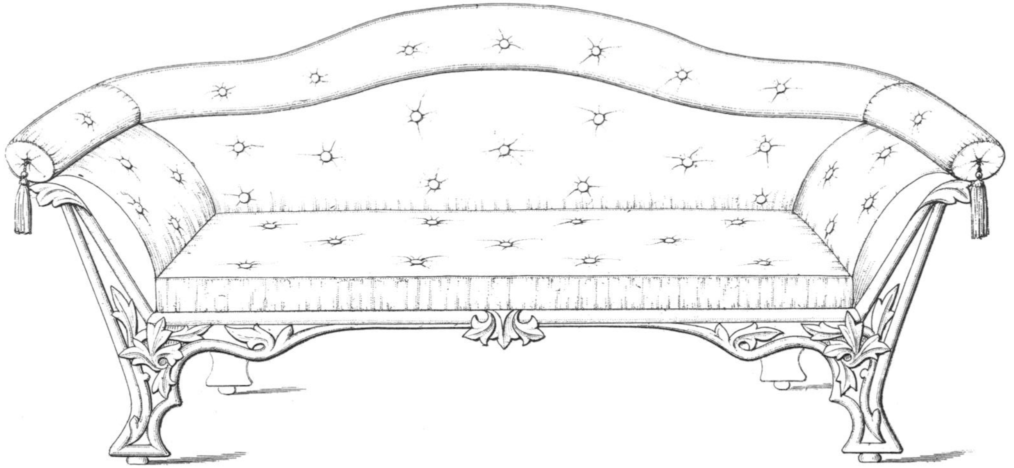

Fig. 4.

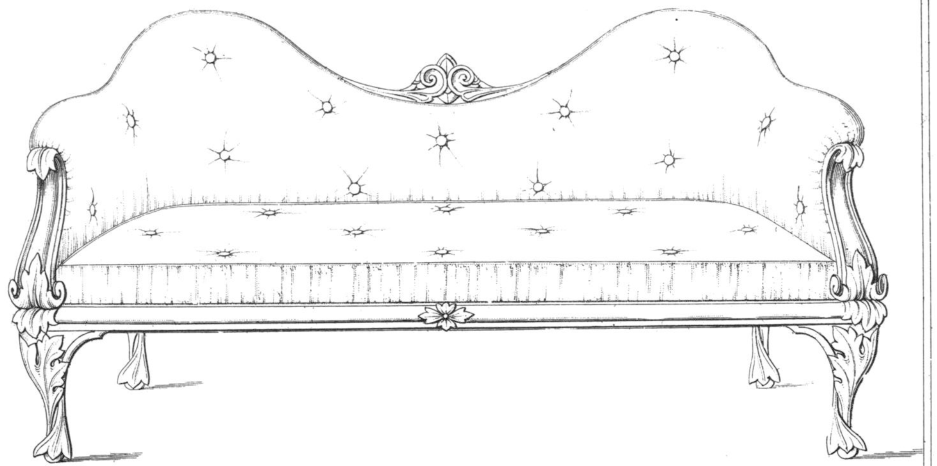

Inches 12   9   6   3   0   1   2   3   4   5   6 Feet.

P. Thomson. Del.   J.H. Le Keux. Sc.

Fig 1.

Fig 2.

Inches 12   9   6   3   0   1   2   3   4   5   6   7 Feet.

Fig. 1.

Fig. 2.

Inches 12   9   6   3   0   1   2   3   4   5 Feet.

P. Thomson Del.

J.H. Le Keux Sc.

PLATE LXI.

COUCHES.

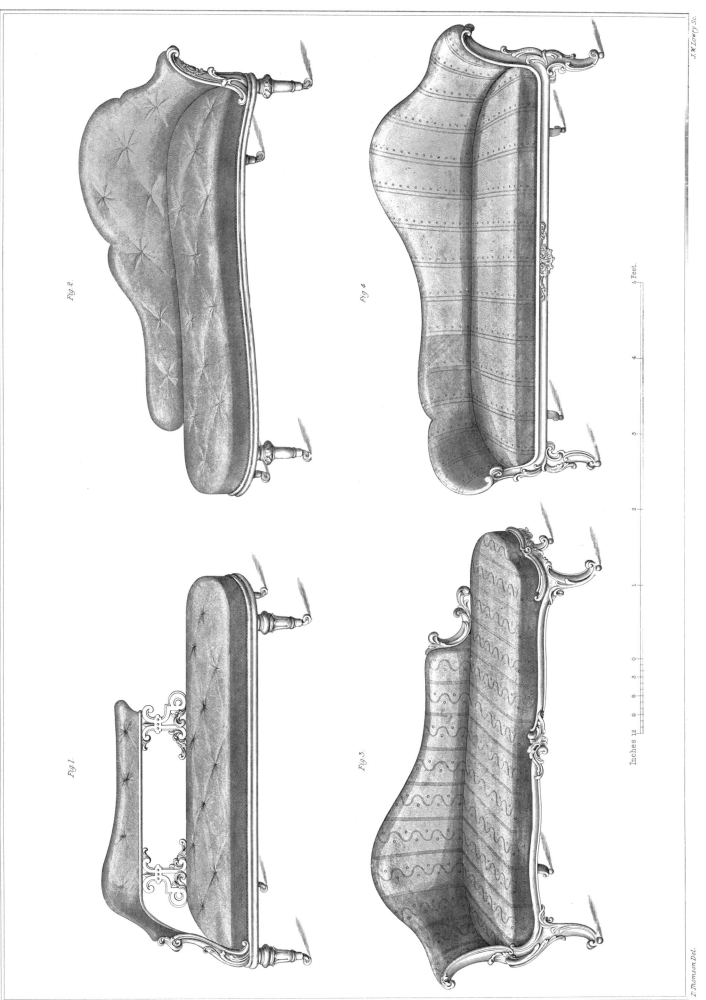

Fig. 1.

Fig. 2.

Fig. 3.

Fig. 4.

Inches 12 9 6 3 0 1 2 3 4 5 Feet.

P. Thomson Del.   J. W. Lowry Sc.

PLATE LXII.

Fig 1.

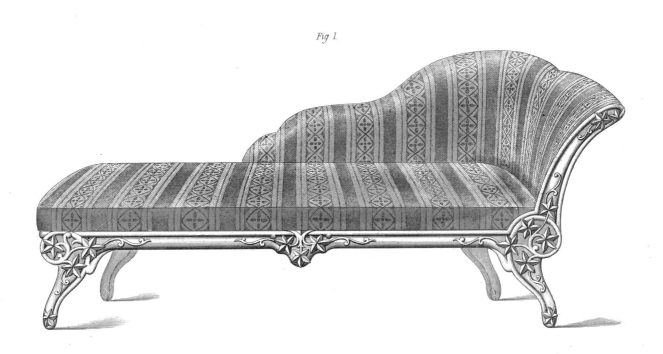

Fig 2.

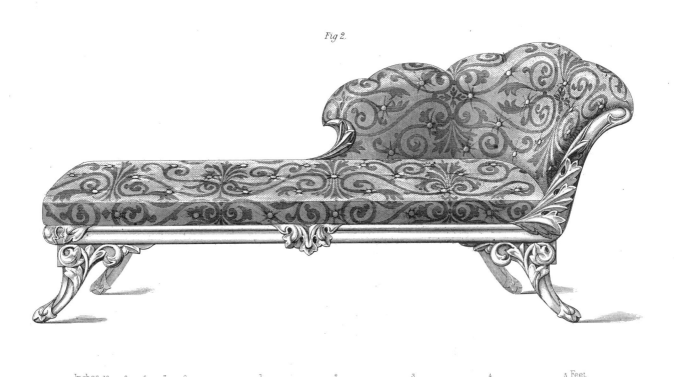

Inches 12 9 6 3 0   1   2   3   4   5 Feet.

PLATE LXIX.

Fig. 3.

Fig. 2.

Fig. 1.

Fig. 6.

Fig. 5.

Fig. 4.

Inches. 12   9   6   3   0   1   2   3   4. Feet.

PLATE LXIV

OTTOMAN SEATS.

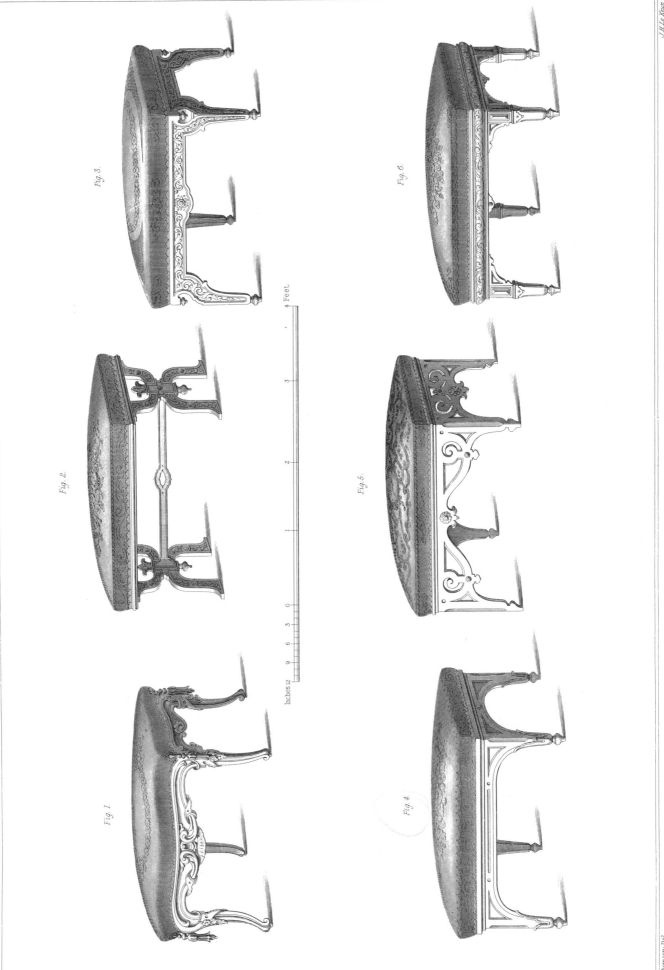

Fig. 1

Fig. 2

Fig. 3

Fig. 4

Fig. 5

Fig. 6

Inches 12 9 6 3 0   1   2   3   4 Feet.

P. Thomson. Del.   J.H. Le Keux Sc.

PLATE LXIV.

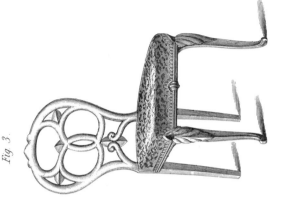

Fig 3.

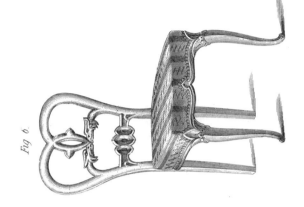

Fig 1.

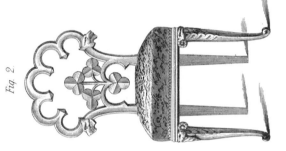

Fig 5.

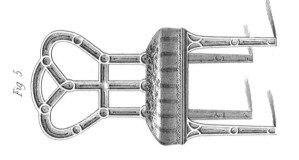

Fig 6.

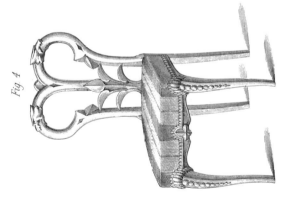

Fig 2.

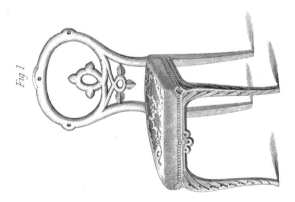

Fig 4.

Carl Hambuch. Del.

J. H. Le Keux Sc.

Inches 12 9 6 3 0 1 2 3 Feet.

PLATE LXVI.

NATIONAL EMBLEM CHAIRS.

Fig. 1.

Fig. 2.

Fig. 3.

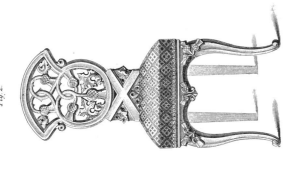

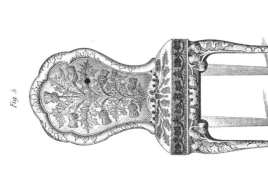

Fig. 4.

Fig. 5.

Fig. 6.

Inches 12   9   6   3   0   1   2   3 Feet.

Carl Hambuch Del.

J.H. Le Keux Sc.

Fig. 1.

Fig. 2.

Fig. 3.

Fig. 4.

Inches 12   9   6   3   0   1   2   3 Feet.

J.H.Le Keux Sc.

PLATE LXVIII.

HIGH BACKED CHAIRS.

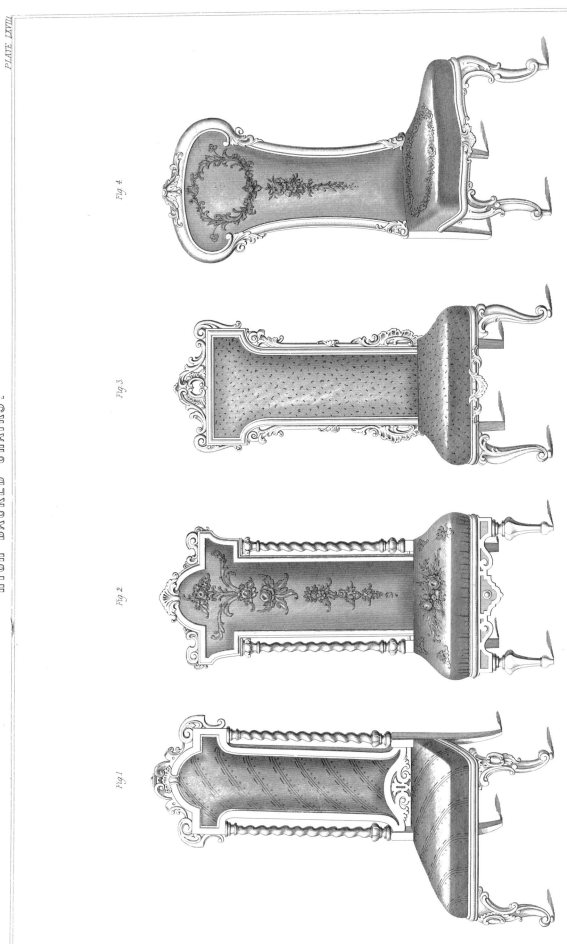

Fig 1

Fig 2

Fig 3

Fig 4

Inches 12   9   6   3   0   1   2   3   4 Feet

P. Thomson Del.

J. W. Lowry Sc.

PLATE LXIX.

ANTIQUE STATE CHAIRS.

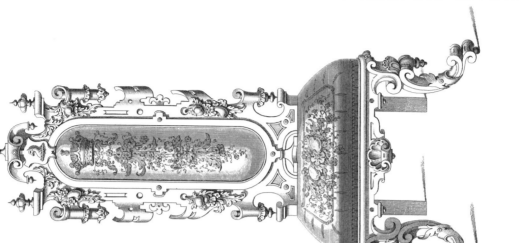

Fig. 3.   *Fig. 2.*   *Fig. 1.*

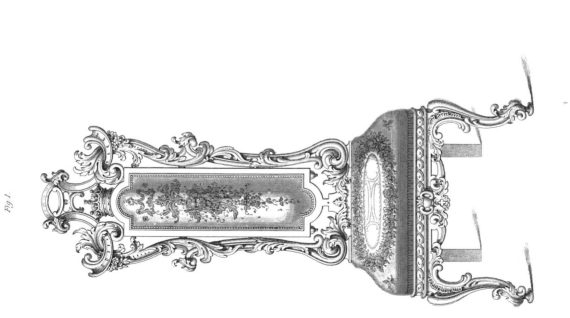

Inches 12   9   6   3   0   1   2   3   4   5 Feet.

F.Thomson del.   J.Watt Sc.

PLATE LXX.

ANTIQUE HIGH-BACKED CHAIRS.

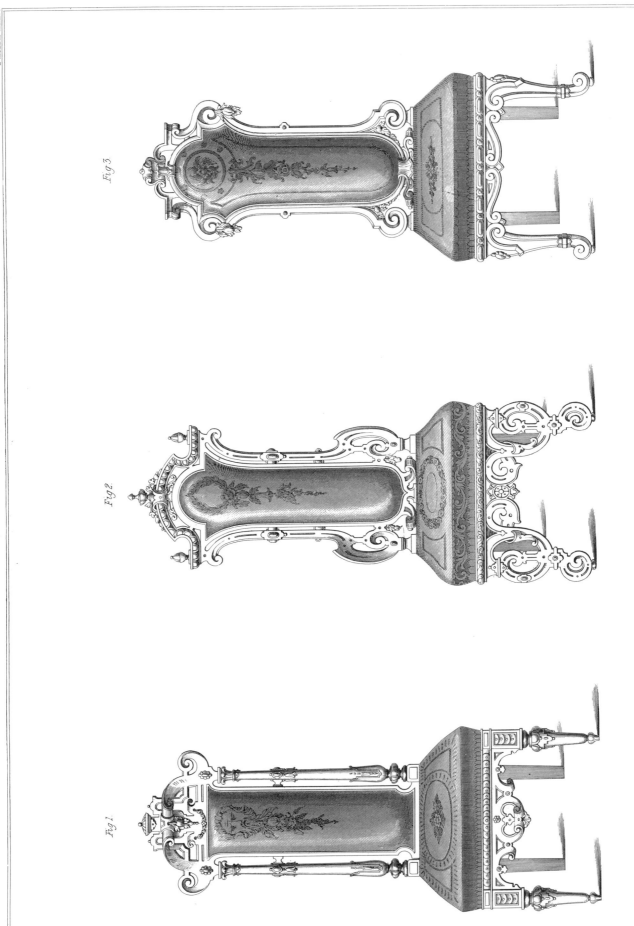

Fig.1

Fig.2.

Fig.3

Inches 12   5 Feet

F. Thomson Del.

J.H.Le Keux Sc.

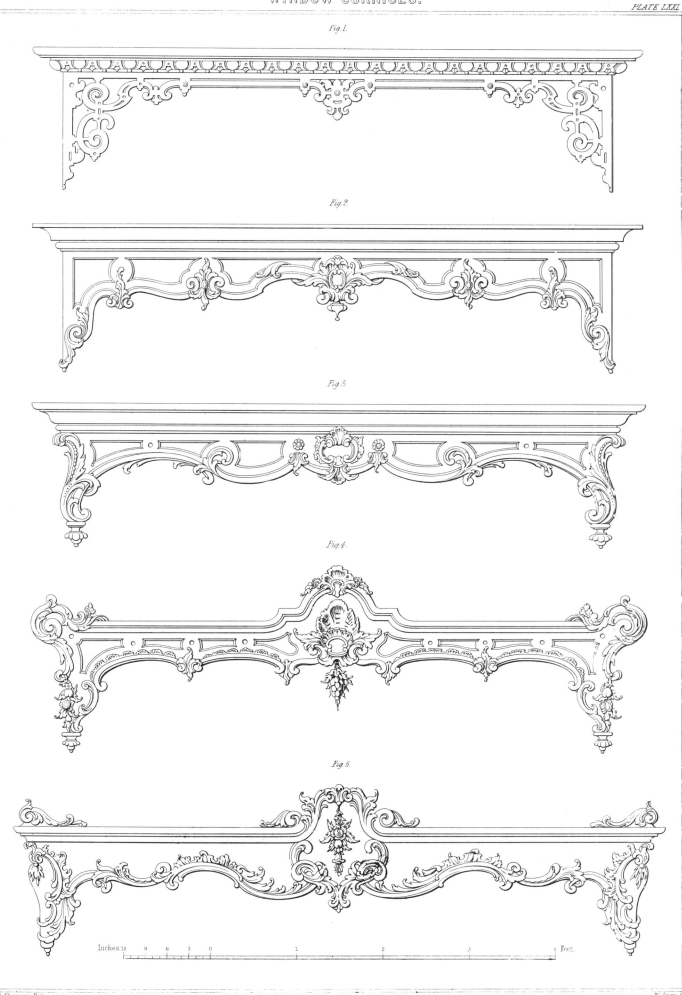

Fig. 1.

Fig. 2.

Fig. 3.

Fig. 4.

Fig. 5.

Inches 12   9   6   3   0   1   2   3   4   Feet.

Fig. 1.

Fig. 2.

Fig. 3.

Fig. 4.

Fig. 5.

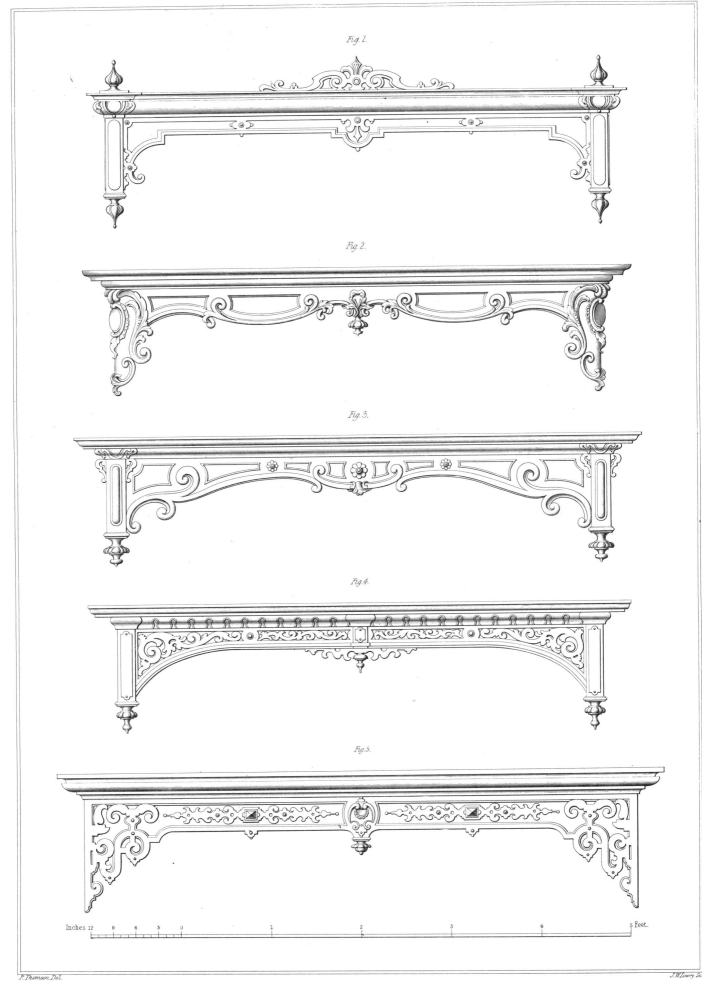

Inches 12 9 6 3 0   1   2   3   4   5 Feet.

PLATE LXXIII

WHAT-NUTS.

Fig 3.

Fig 1.

Fig 2.

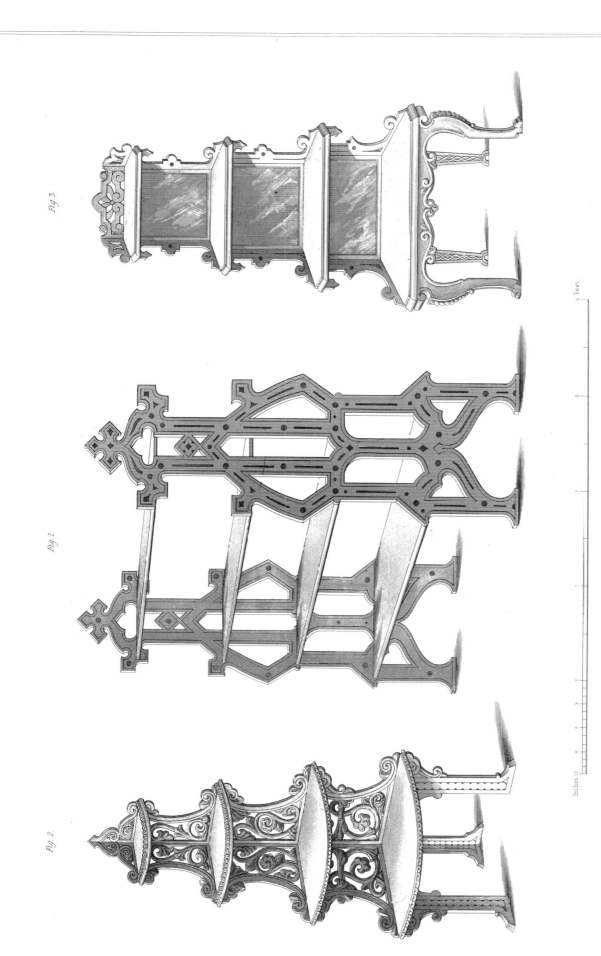

Inches 12   9   6   3   0   1   2   3   4   5 Feet.

PLATE LXXIV.

MUSIC SEATS.

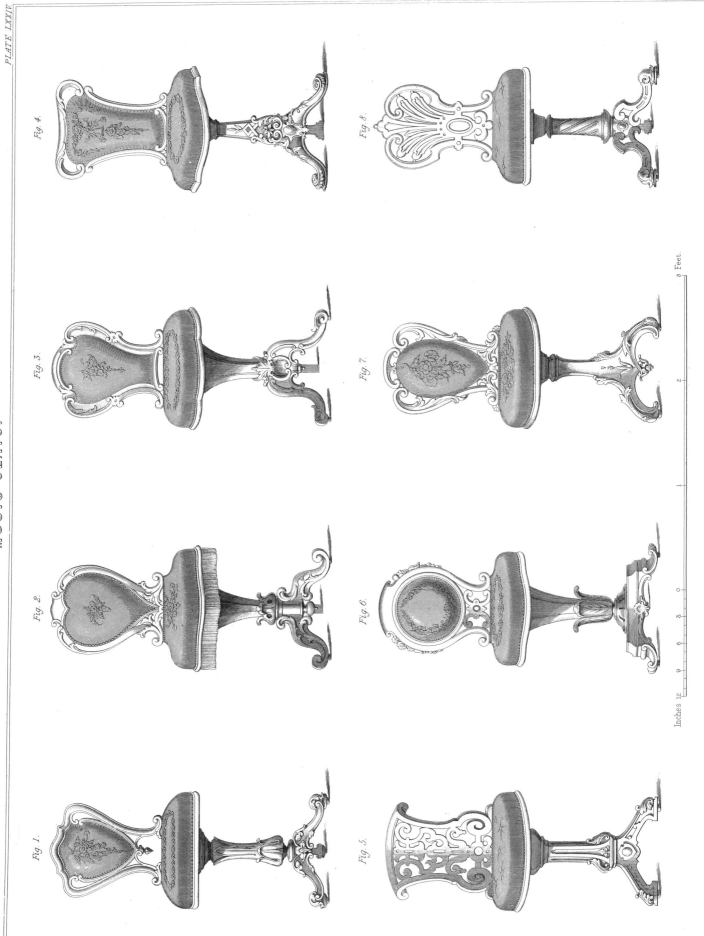

Fig. 4.

Fig. 8.

Fig. 3.

Fig. 7.

Fig. 2.

Fig. 6.

Fig. 1.

Fig. 5.

Inches 12   9   6   3   0   1   2   3 Feet.

P. Thomson, Del.

J. H. Le Keux Sc.

PLATE LXXV.

CANTERBURYS AND FIRE SCREENS.

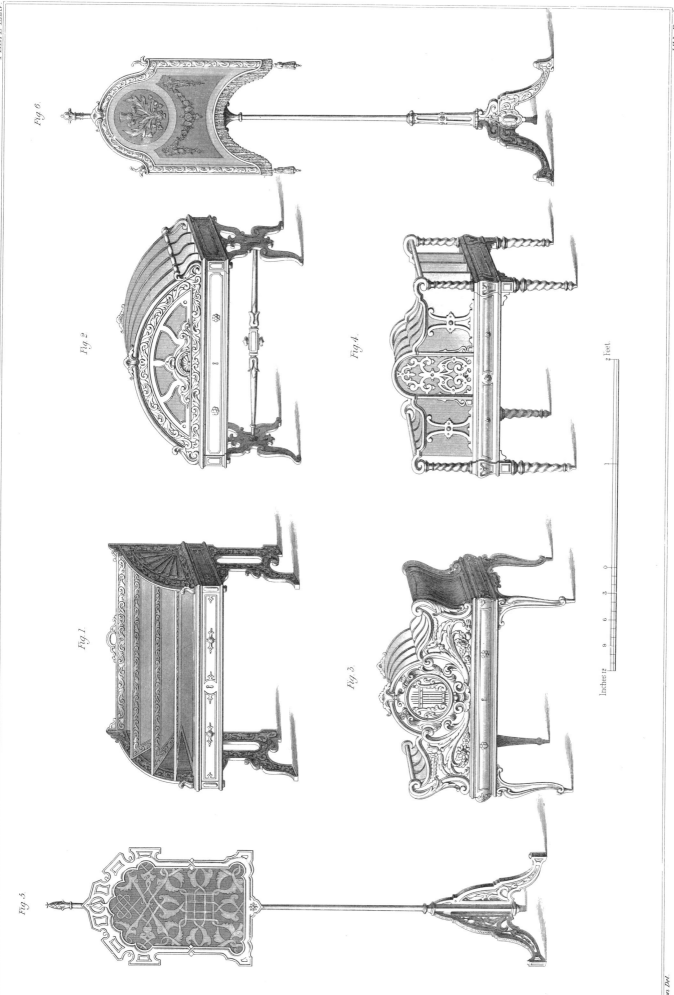

Fig. 6.

Fig. 2.

Fig. 4.

Fig. 1.

Fig. 3.

Fig. 5.

Inches 12   9   6   3   0   ½ Feet.

P. Thomson. Del.

J. H. Le Keux. Sc.

FIRE SCREENS.

PLATE LXVII.

Fig. 1.

Fig. 2.

Fig. 3.

Fig. 4.

Inches 12 9 6 3 0 1 2 3 4 5 Feet.
Scale for Figs. 1 & 2.

Inches 12 9 6 3 0 1 2 Feet.
Scale for Figs. 3 & 4.

J. Thomson Del.

J. H. Le Keux Sc.

PLATE LXVII.

FRENCH BEDSTEADS.

Fig 3

Fig 2

Fig 1

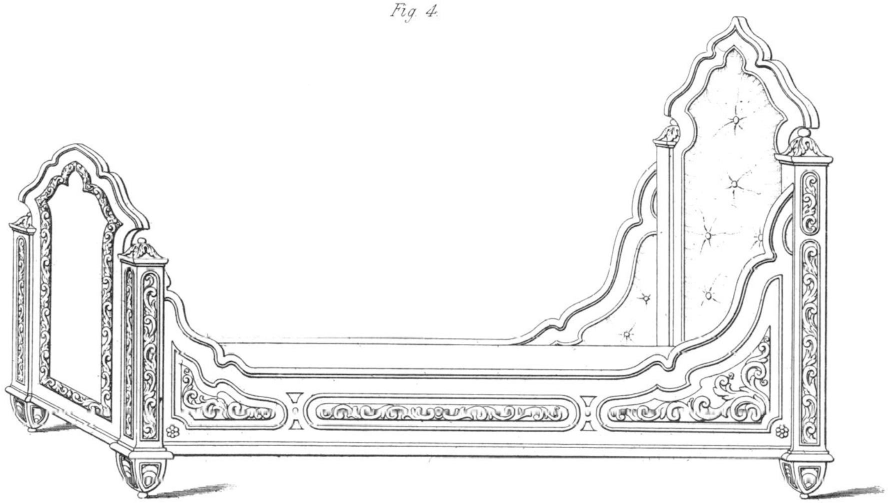

Fig 5

Fig 4

Inches 12 9 6 3 0   1   2   3   4   5   6   7   8 Feet

P. Thomson. Del.   J. H. Le Keux. Sc.

PLATE LXXVIII.

HALF TESTER BEDSTEADS.

Fig. 2.

Fig. 1.

Inches 12 9 6 3 0   1   2   3   4   5   6   7   8   9   10 Feet.

F. Thomson. Del.

J. H. Le Keux Sc.

PLATE LXXIX.

HALF TESTER BEDSTEADS.

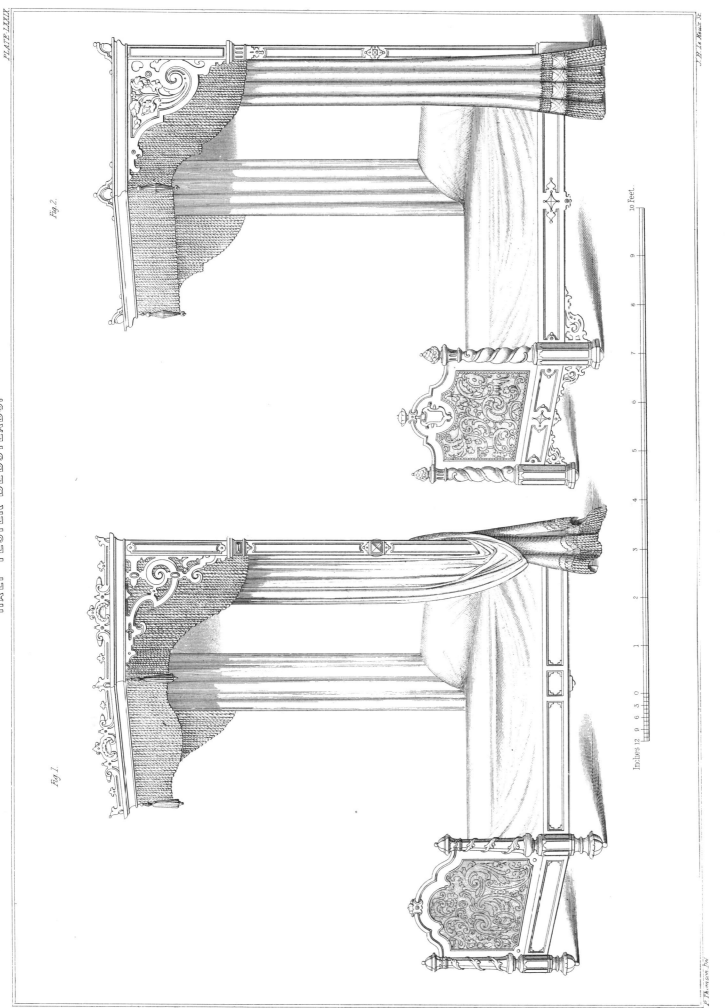

Fig. 1.

Fig. 2.

Inches 12 9 6 3 0   1   2   3   4   5   6   7   8   9   10 Feet.

P. Thomson Del.

J. R. Le Maire Sc.

PLATE LXXX

HALF TESTER BEDSTEAD.

Inches 12   9 6 3 0   1   2   3 Feet.

PLATE LXXXI.

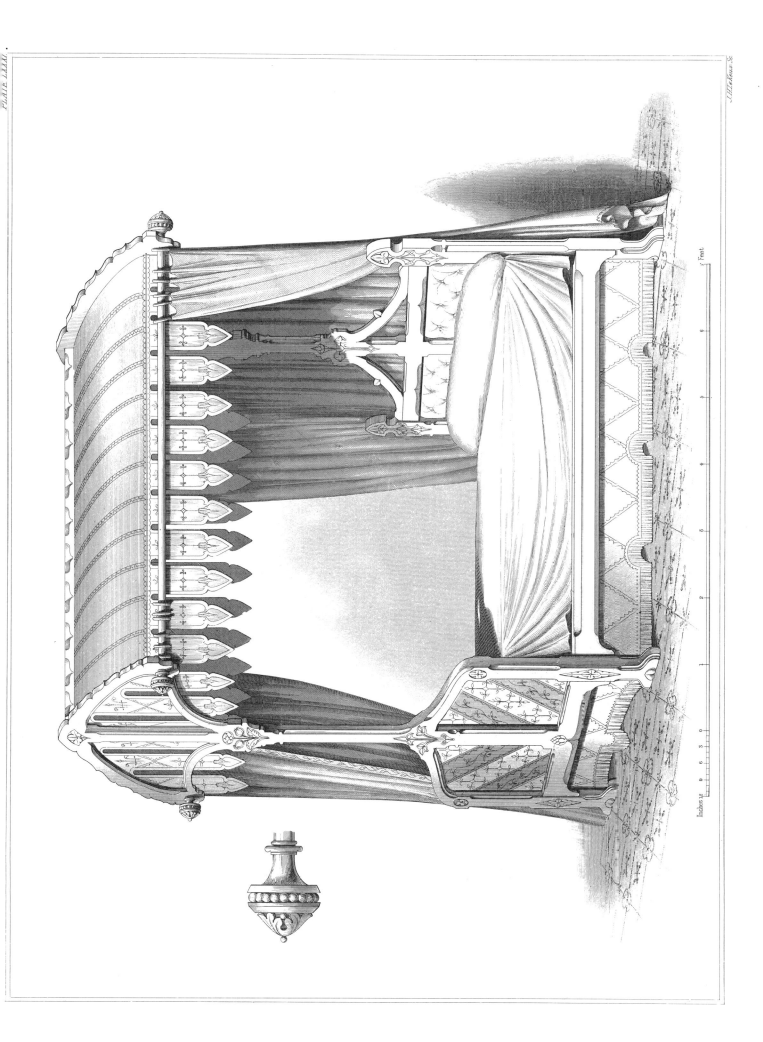

J. H. Le Keux, Sc.

Inches 12   9   6   3   0   1   2   3   4   5   6   Feet.

PLATE LXXXII.

POSTED BEDSTEADS.

P. Thomson. Del.

J. H. Le Keux Sc.

Inches 12   9   6   3   0   1   2   3   4   5   6 Feet.

[*Pl. LXXXIII is the frontispiece.*]

BED PILLARS.

PLATE LXXXIV.

Fig. 1.   Fig. 2.   Fig. 3.   Fig. 4.   Fig. 5.

Inches 12   9   6   3   0   1   2   3   4   5 Feet

P. Thomson Del.

J. West Sc.

PLATE LXXXV.

BED PILLARS.

Fig. 1.
Fig. 2.
Fig. 3.
Fig. 4.
Fig. 5.
Fig. 6.

Fig. 7.

Fig. 8.

A
B
c
d

Fig. 9.

A
B

Inches 12 9 6 3 0 1 2 3 4 Feet.

PLATE LXXXVI

COIS and CRADLES.

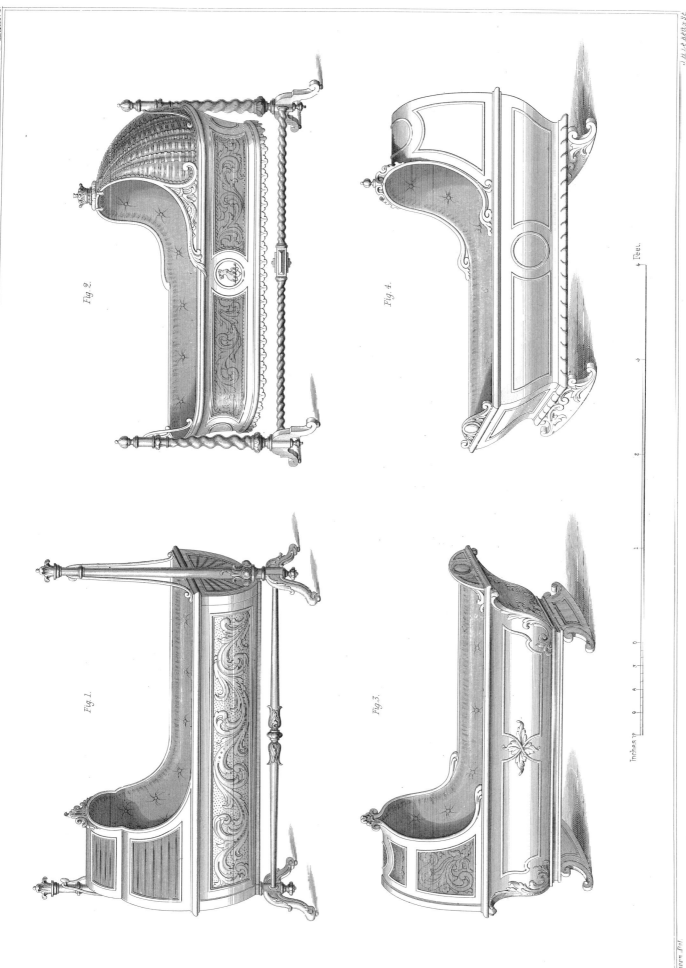

Fig 1.

Fig 2.

Fig 3.

Fig 4.

Inches

4 Feet.

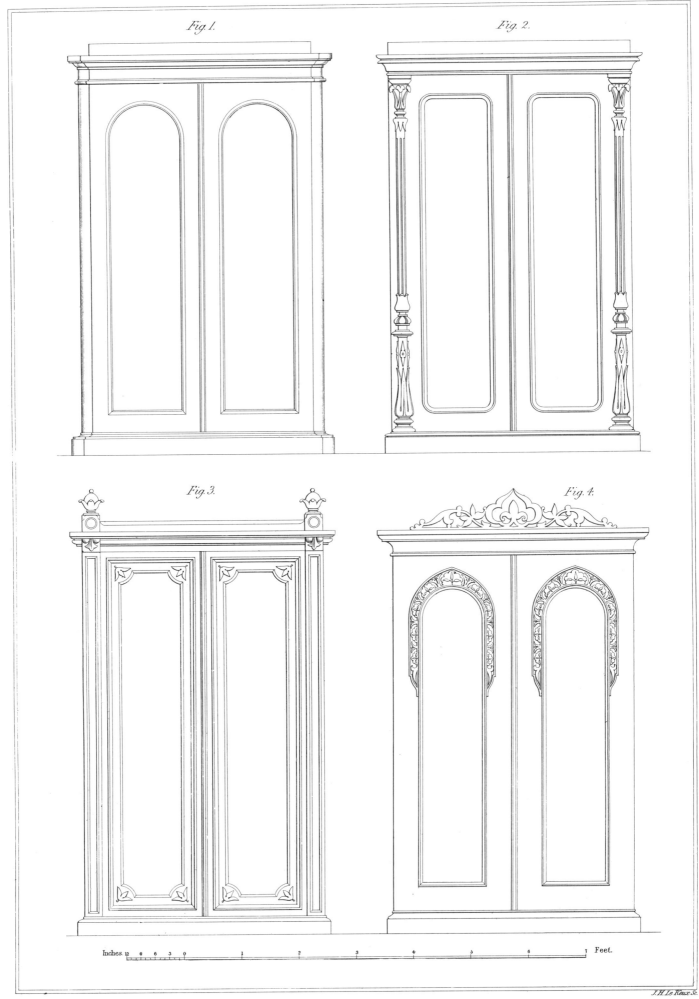

Fig. 1. Fig. 2. Fig. 3. Fig. 4.

Inches. 12 9 6 3 0 1 2 3 4 5 6 7 Feet.

J. H. Le Keux Sc.

PLATE LXXXVIII.

WARDROBES.

Fig 2

Fig 1

Inches 12 9 6 3 0   1   2   3   4   5   6   7   8 Feet.

PLATE LXXXIX

WARDROBE.

J.H. Le Keux Sc.

P. Thomson Del.

Inches 12 9 6 3 0   1   2   3   4   5   6   7 Feet.

PLATE XI

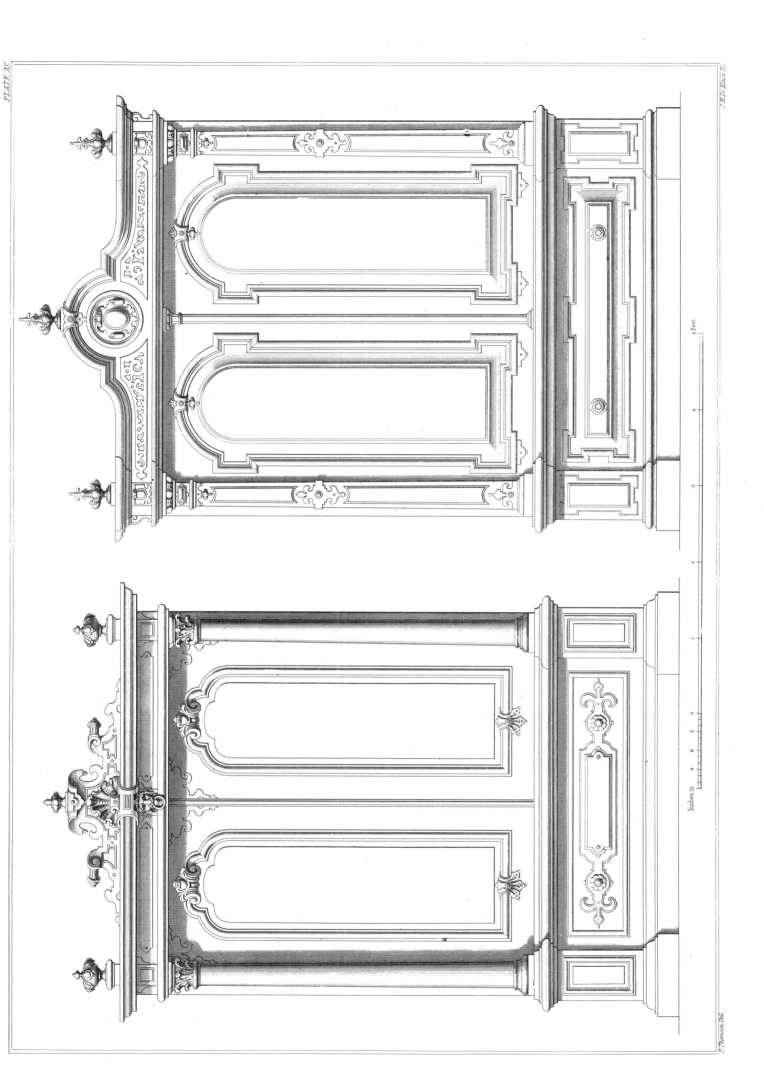

T. Thomson Del.   J.H.L. Edwr. Sc.

Inches 12   9   6   3   0   1   2   3   4   5 Feet

PLATE XCI.

PILASTERS and BRACKETS.

Fig 1.

Fig 2.

Fig 3.

Fig 4.

Fig 5.

Fig 6.

Fig 7.

Fig 8.

P. Thomson and C. Hambuch, Del.

J. H. Le Keux Sc.

PLATE XCII.

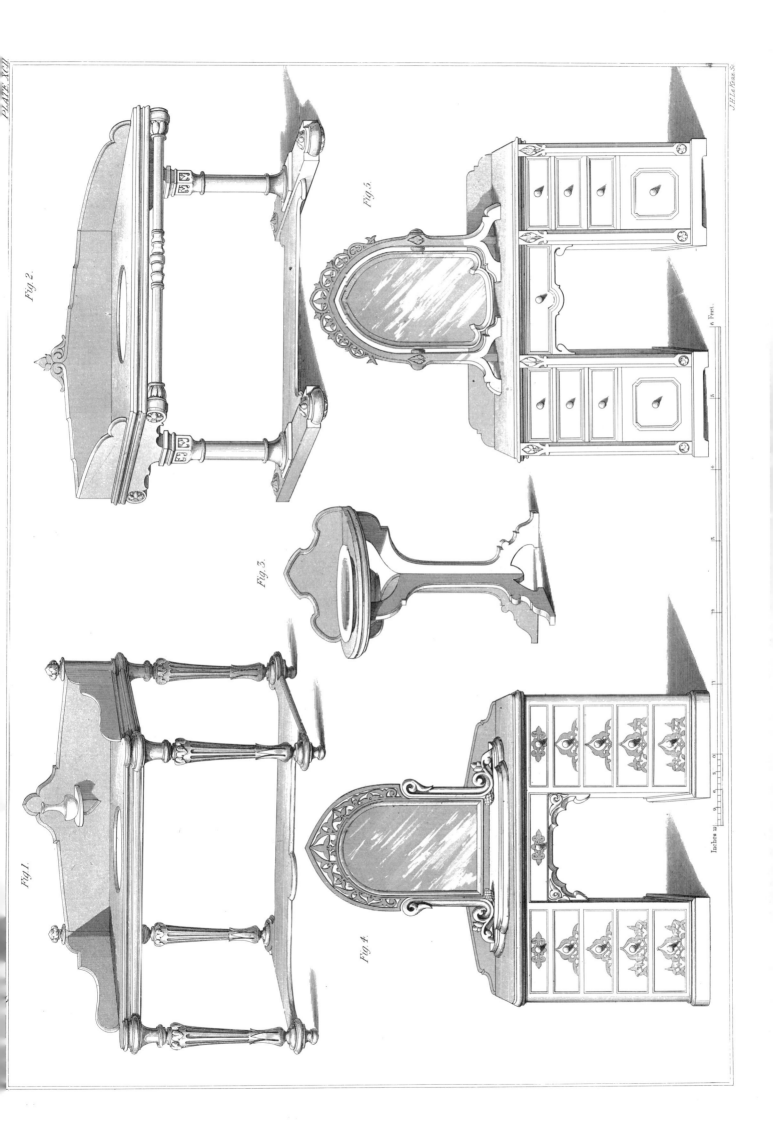

Fig. 2.

Fig. 1.

Fig. 3.

Fig. 5.

Fig. 4.

Inches

PLATE XCIII.

MOULDINGS.

CORNICE MOULDINGS AND MOULDINGS FOR PANELS.

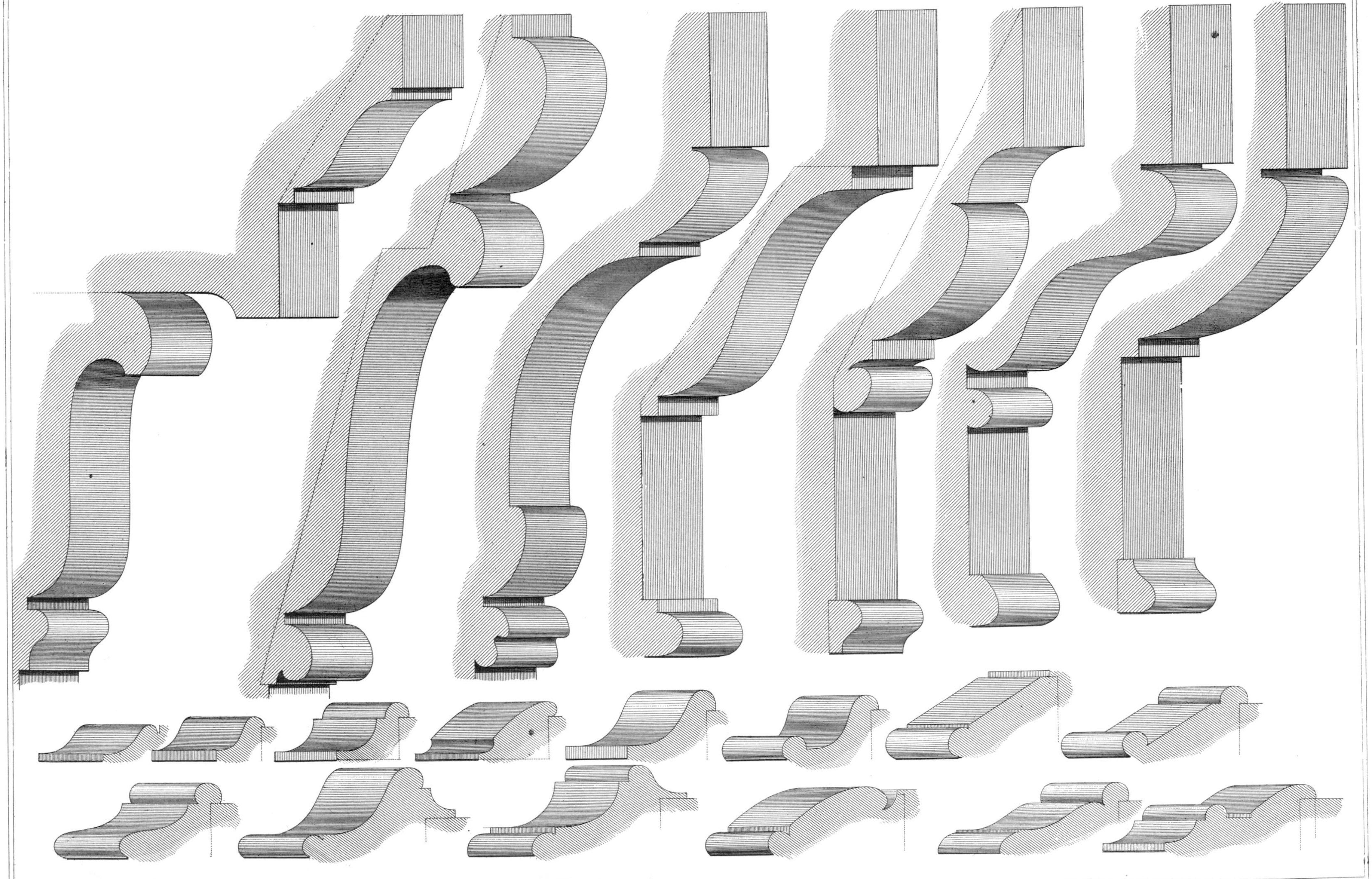

J.H.LeKeux Sc.

PLATE XVIV

MOULDINGS FOR TABLES CHIFFIONEERS &c.

PLINTH MOULDINGS.

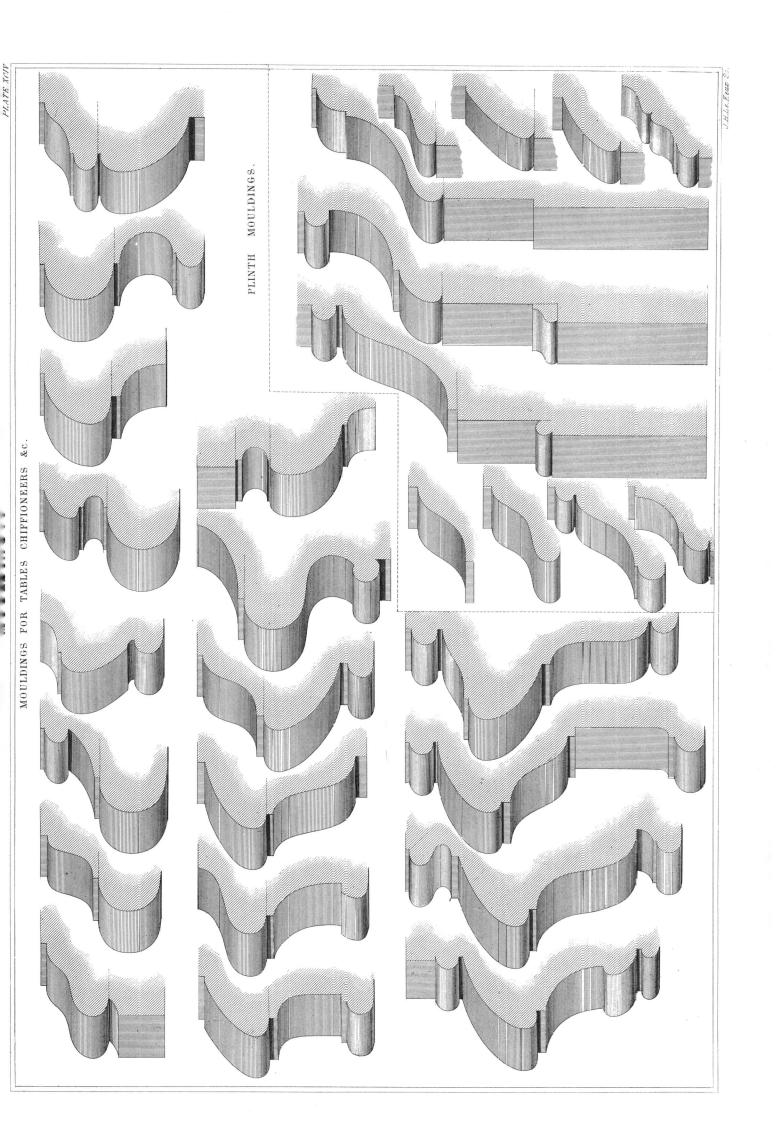

J.H.Le Keux sc.

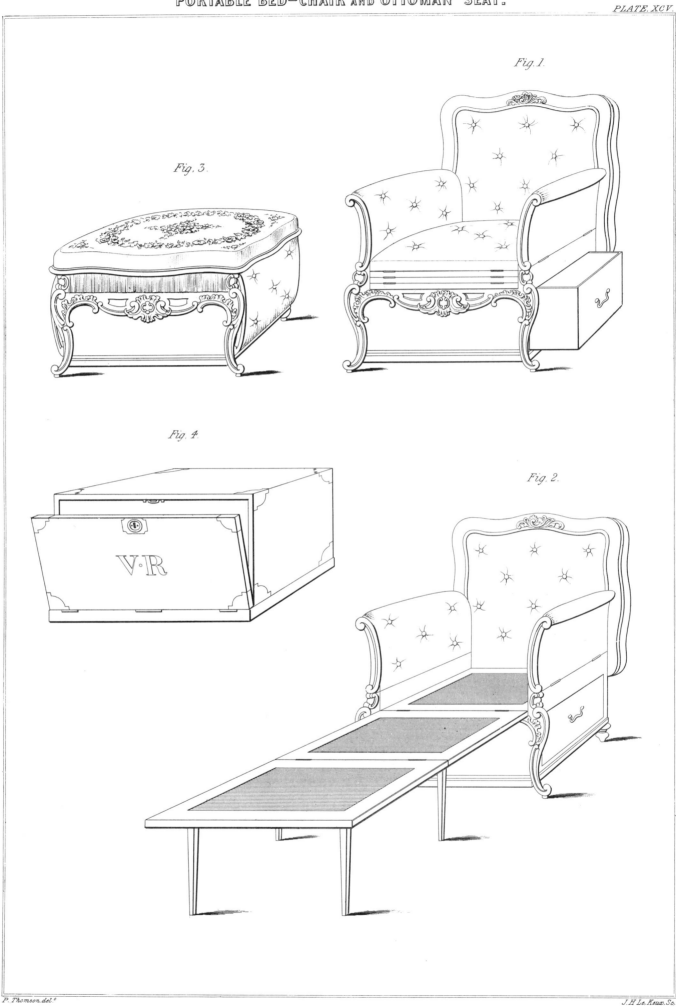

Fig. 1.

Fig. 3.

Fig. 4.

Fig. 2.

V·R

PLATE XCVI.

FRET-RAILS & CLOCK FOR STEAM-BOAT CABINS.

Fig. 1.

Fig. 2.

Fig. 3.

Inches 12

5 Feet

P. Thomson Del.

H. Adlard Sc.

PLATE XCVII

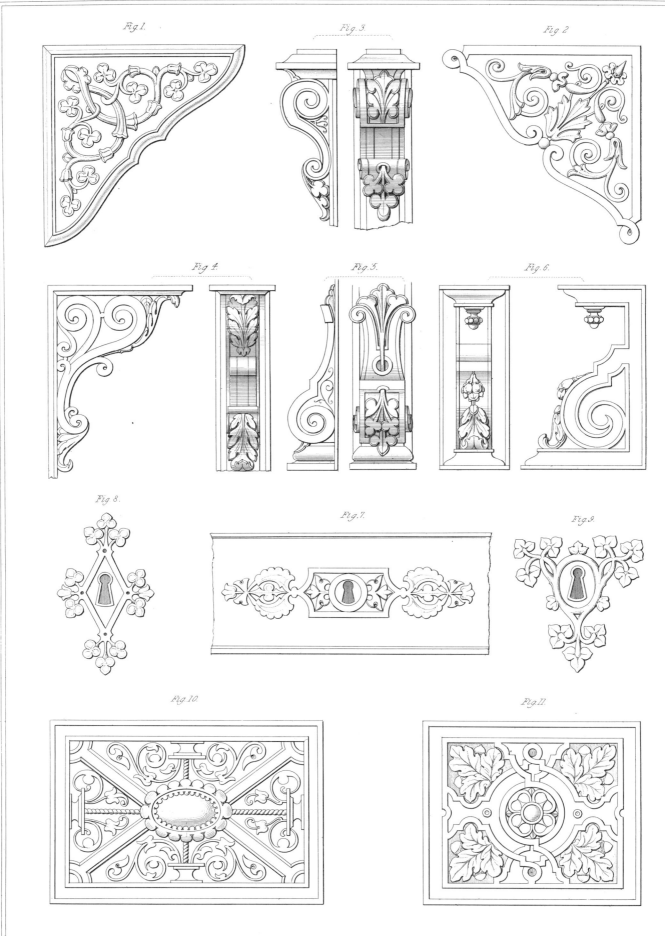

Fig. 1.

Fig. 3.

Fig. 2.

Fig. 4.

Fig. 5.

Fig. 6.

Fig. 8.

Fig. 7.

Fig. 9.

Fig. 10.

Fig. 11.

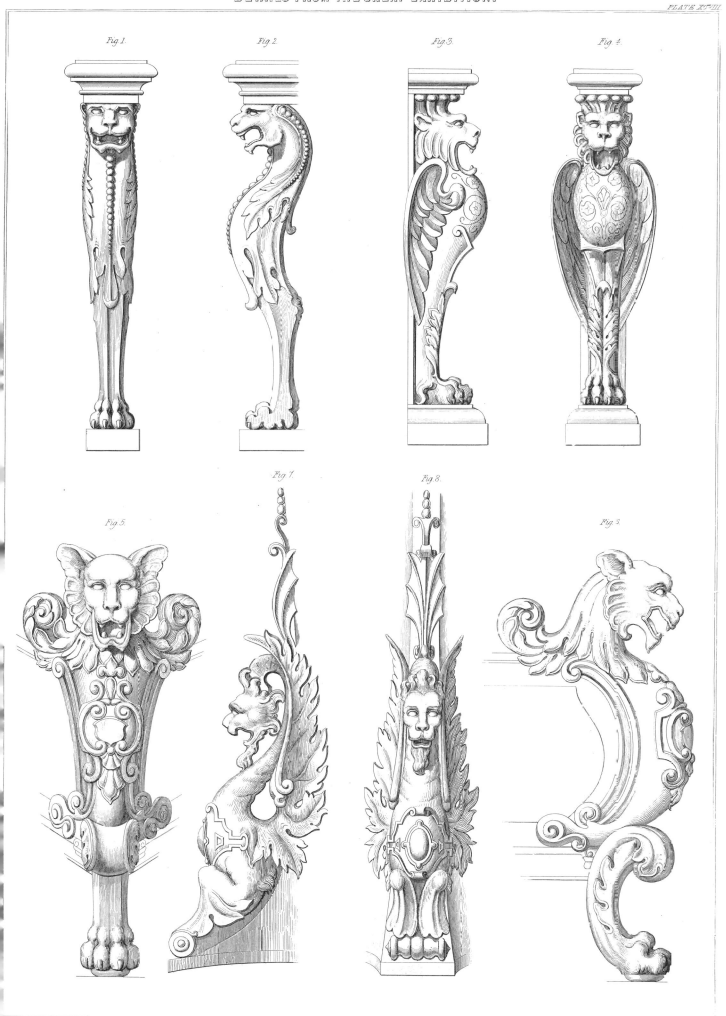

Fig. 1.   Fig. 2.   Fig. 3.   Fig. 4.

Fig. 5.   Fig. 7.   Fig. 8.   Fig. 9.

Fig 1

Fig 5

Fig. 2

Fig 6.

Fig. 3

Fig 4

1851

C. Hambuch Del.

J.H. LeKeux Sc.

Fig. 2.a.

Fig. 3.

Fig. 3.a.

J. H. Le Keux Sc.

Fig. 2.

Fig. 1.a.

Fig. 5.

Fig. 4.a.

Fig. 1.

Fig. 4.

Fig. 5.a.

PLATE. CI.

ORNAMENTS ADAPTED FROM NATURE.

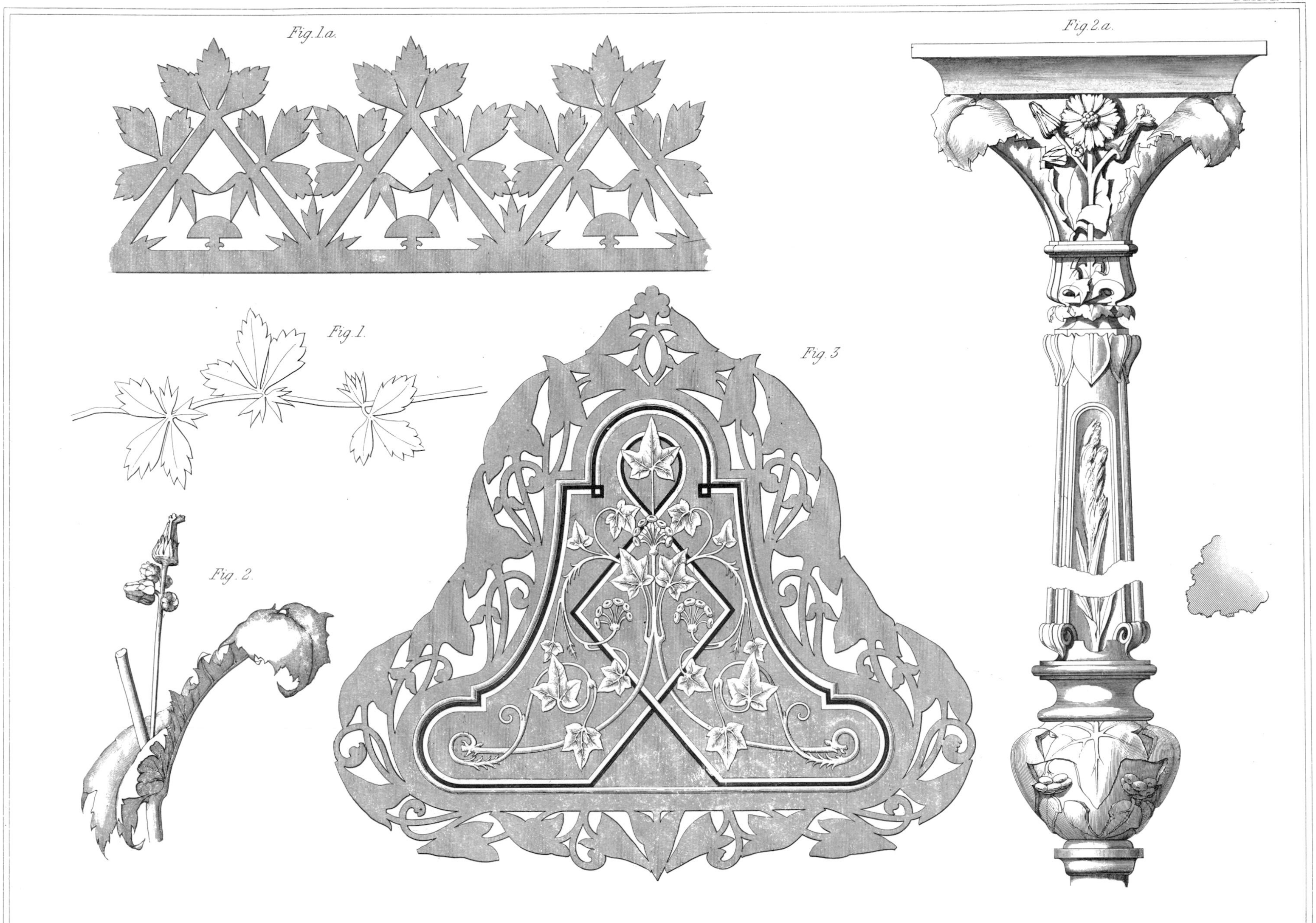

Fig. 2 a.

Fig. 1 a.

Fig. 3

Fig. 1.

Fig. 2.